1974

THE TRADITION
OF THE THEATRE

Greek Theatre at Syracuse, Sicily.
(Courtesy of Trans World Airlines)

THE TRADITION
OF THE THEATRE

Editors:

PETER BAULAND
WILLIAM INGRAM
The University of Michigan

Allyn and Bacon, Inc.
Boston

Library of Congress Catalog Card Number: 72–113264.
Printed in the United States of America.

CONTENTS

ACKNOWLEDGMENTS

THE ANTIGONE OF SOPHOCLES: an English version by Dudley Fitts and Robert Fitzgerald, Copyright 1939 by Harcourt, Brace and World, Inc.; renewed, 1967, by Dudley Fitts and Robert Fitzgerald and reprinted by permission of the publishers. *Caution:* All rights, including professional, amateur, motion picture, recitation, lecturing, public reading, radio broadcasting, and television are strictly reserved. Inquiries on all rights should be addressed to Harcourt, Brace and World, Inc., 757 Third Avenue, New York, New York 10017.

THE SECOND SHEPHERDS' PLAY: from *Representative Medieval and Tudor Plays*, translated and edited by Henry W. Wells and Roger S. Loomis, Copyright 1942 by Sheed and Ward, Inc., New York.

THE WOULD-BE GENTLEMAN: from *Eight Plays by Molière*, translated by Morris Bishop. © Copyright 1957 by Morris Bishop. Reprinted by permission of Random House, Inc.

HEDDA GABLER: from *Hedda Gabler* by Henrik Ibsen, translated by Otto Reinert, published by Chandler Publishing Company, San Francisco. © Copyright 1962 by Chandler Publishing Company. Reprinted by permission.

THE DEVIL'S DISCIPLE: reprinted by courtesy of The Public Trustee and of The Society of Authors, 34 Drayton Gardens, London SW 10.

A DREAM PLAY: translated by Elizabeth Sprigge. © Copyright 1955 by Elizabeth Sprigge. Reprinted by permission of Collins-Knowlton-Wing, Inc.

THE CHERRY ORCHARD: from *The Portable Chekhov*, edited and translated by Avrahm Yarmolinsky. © Copyright 1947 by The Viking Press, Inc. Reprinted by permission of The Viking Press, Inc.

THE CAUCASIAN CHALK CIRCLE: © Copyright 1947, 1948, 1961, 1963 by Eric Bentley: Introduction © Copyright 1965 by Eric Bentley. Originally published in the volume *Parables for the Theatre: Two Plays by Bertolt Brecht* by the University of Minnesota Press, Minneapolis. Reprinted by permission.

THE CRUCIBLE: © Copyright 1952, 1953 by Arthur Miller. Reprinted by permission of The Viking Press, Inc.

THE VISIT: © Copyright 1956 by Maurice Valency, as an unpublished work entitled "The Old Lady's Visit," adapted by Maurice Valency from *Der Besuch der Alten Dame*, by Friedrich Dürrenmatt. © Copyright 1958 by Maurice Valency. Reprinted from *Masters of Modern Drama*, edited by Haskell M. Block and Robert G. Shedd, by permission of Random House, Inc.

INTRODUCTION

The characteristics of a play may seem self-evident on first reflection, and one may feel a certain annoyance at what appears to be an elaboration of the obvious. Yet there are certain differences between plays and such literary forms as novels or poems that are worth reiterating, for otherwise these differences have a distressing tendency to be treated as minor considerations. A play is a work of literature only to a limited exent; whereas the novelist or poet hopes to confront his audience in a reading situation, and presumably a quiet and isolated one, the playwright expects his encounter to be public and to require viewing and listening. A play is not an object but an activity in which a written text furnished by the playwright is translated into theatrical terms by a separate corps of professional interpreters— actors, designers, directors. The text and the production together constitute the play in its proper sense.

This volume does not contain plays. It contains only the scripts of plays, the blueprints for the dramatic structure that is each playwright's goal. The scripts are unquestionably worth our serious consideration, even as the scores of symphonies are, but we must not, like many of our nineteenth-century predecessors, think that the script is sufficient, that the library or the study is its proper home, and that the production of plays in the theatre is somehow vulgar. Plays are more than just specialized works of literature, and they are also more than just "raw material for acting," as Harley Granville-Barker once said in desperation. But the limitations of the classroom usually restrict us to the use of printed volumes, since we cannot have theatrical companies performing for us each day. Ideally we would wish to have both.

All art is an organization of experience, and the organization of plays is both verbal and visual. A specific demand is placed on the reader, therefore, to supply with his imagination the missing ingredients. But this is not to be construed as a license for undisciplined romanticizing: one must try to overcome the normal tendency in play reading to conjure up fanciful settings for the action, as though *Macbeth* were really taking place in a drafty Scottish castle, or *Hamlet* in a royal palace or graveyard. With practice one can learn to break this habit, and instead to develop a propensity for seeing in his mind's eye a stage of definite dimensions, with a set of a certain size and shape, and specific entrances and exits. One can, in other words, encourage an awareness of the playscript as an outline for a specific form of artistic activity and not merely as a recipe for daydreaming. The famous

Russian actor Stanislavski was once heard to comment that after two decades of working in the theatre he had finally learned how to read a play properly.

From any teacher's point of view, the best anthology in print can be no better than the second best of all possible anthologies, and the ideal text is ultimately the one containing the selections each teacher would make for himself. Drama anthologies are no more than a pedagogic, spatial, and economic convenience for both teachers and students. They are not a critical judgment that proclaims, "These are the twelve (or six, or thirty-five) best plays that have been written or performed," but are rather a selection intended to demonstrate the scope and variety of the finest dramatic art from its beginnings in ancient Greece to its most important manifestations on our contemporary stage. Somebody's favorite play or playwright, form or period, is bound to be left out within the limits imposed on any collection. We regret what we must omit; we need not apologize for what we include. However, we must explain the conspicuous absence of one playwright whose art should, by all standards, be represented in any course that purports to introduce the drama: William Shakespeare. Any play by Shakespeare that we might have chosen would have been an imposition, and conveniences should not be imposed. The plays of William Shakespeare are easily available in many excellent and inexpensive texts. We encourage each teacher to invite the thirteenth guest of his choice to our banquet. The superstitious, the ambitious, and those endowed with sufficient time might wish to make room at their table for additional company.

The chronology of first performances of the twelve plays in this collection determined their sequential arrangement in the text. We are in no way proposing that such an order is the only or even the best way to approach the study of drama. There are many alternatives of organization, among them theme, convention, mode, or degree of familiarity of form. In this matter, as in all others, we believe that the responsibility for the guiding principles of a course, its work, and its enjoyment are the proper domain of teachers and students, not of editors. For that reason our introductory remarks for each play are purposely brief, and not so much definitive as suggestive. In each instance, they indicate a possible "handle" by which to grasp the text rather than a bagful of opinions about it. To further the usefulness of these notes we have cast them in a variety of forms, the result of a deliberate eclecticism on our part; for in truth—and despite our title—the "tradition" of the theatre is a many-faceted phenomenon, and our notes are attempts to suggest some of the possibilities. Selection of a viable classroom procedure from among the range of choices is the teacher's privilege; the provision of such a range is the editors' obligation. Our ultimate goal, the student's understanding of literary and theatrical relationships and critical values, requires such classroom exposure.

This book is not meant to replace the teacher or to do his work for him, but rather to free him from the tyranny of the introduction that tells his students what to think about a play even before they have read it. To that end, we have deliberately avoided the temptation to offer formulaic definitions of such pat and misused terms as "tragedy" and "comedy." Art, after all, precedes criticism: as clear distinctions, these Aristotelian terms are useless and even misleading once the art form changes with the journey beyond ancient Athens. The language of criticism, to be useful, must keep pace with the art it criticizes. Each age makes drama meaningful for itself—perhaps that is the real tradition of the theatre. Therefore, our intent has been to couch our definitions in more specific terms as they relate to the individual plays. One can, by reading inductively, form a definition of his own. The perceptive reader will accumulate a notion of the concepts of tragedy and comedy, and these will be, as they ought to be, descriptive rather than prescriptive.

Textbooks and anthologies usually require revision and improvement to help them meet the continuing and changing needs of those who use them. The editors of this collection will welcome the comments and suggestions of both teachers and students.

Peter Bauland
William Ingram
Ann Arbor, Michigan

Sophocles: ANTIGONE

The milestones of the celestial year are predictably regular, and most ancient societies knew how to calculate the dates of such events as the equinoxes, the summer and winter solstices, or the full moon. Less mathematically regular, but just as important in early agrarian societies, were the landmarks of the terrestrial year: the early spring day when frost was gone and planting could begin, the late summer harvest season, the winter wine-broaching. The yearly repetition, however erratic, of these essentially human and social events was a comforting manifestation of the continuity of life, especially if one viewed the earthly calendar as an imperfect reflection of the heavenly order itself. Seen in that light, a community's annual events might appear to have a sort of cosmic sanction, and would come in time to be the focal point for commemorative celebrations. This was the case in the city of Athens, where such celebrations provided the setting for the earliest dramas.

By the late fifth century B.C. Athens had outgrown its basically agrarian beginnings; though it was the center of an agricultural society, the city itself had become quite cosmopolitan, the hub of a culture whose sophistication is still admired. The occasions in the life of the city that called for public observance were the expected ones—spring, fall, midwinter —but they were by this time institutionalized, and their origins perhaps forgotten or unknown to the majority of citizens. One such public holiday was the Dionysia (called the City Dionysia to distinguish it from other festivals bearing the same name.) The City Dionysia was an early spring celebration, falling in what is now late March or early April. The festivities were dedicated to Dionysos, the god of fertility and wine, and were celebrated with a procession and a dramatic competition. Each year, before the festival, a number of playwrights would submit playscripts for consideration; from these a certain number were selected for performance at the festival, and on the basis of the performances in the city's public theatre the judges would select a winning playwright for the year.

The theatre at Athens, like the theatres in most Greek cities, was built into a hillside. Since Greek cities usually originated as defensive hilltop positions, the hilltop (*acropolis*) of a city (*polis*) would normally be the site of the city's most important possessions—its treasury as well as its cult temple, for example. The theatre's location in close proximity to these other structures is more than coincidental. A city's theatre was in a sense a religious structure, and the tragedies performed there at festival time were, like the festival itself, religious in a sense that we perhaps can never fully understand. Often the plays dealt with social problems; but always one senses the conviction that social problems were at root moral problems, and that moral problems invited religious solutions. It is perhaps the identity of social, moral, and religious concepts that makes the dramas of this particular society so all-encompassing.

The Greek theatre itself was a social phenomenon. To begin with, it was in the open air (it was not really a building in the conventional sense) with the seats placed into the hillside in a semicircular pattern. A cleared circular area at the bottom served as a dancing area (*orchestra*) for the chorus, and behind this was a raised platform for the actors. There were no wings or backstage area as we know them today, though there was usually a temporary structure or tent (the *skene*) at the back of the acting area into which the players might retire when they were not onstage. Except for the platform, occupied by the actors, and the orchestra in front of it, occupied by the singing and dancing chorus, the Greek theatre was curiously fluid and nonillusory. A spectator might look up from the play and observe activity in the streets beyond, or watch the mountains or the clouds. The seats, ranged around the orchestra to the extent that the topography would allow, usually formed somewhat more than a half-circle. The relationship between the seating area and the acting area was one of convenience, dictated primarily by the shape of the land.

1

This was the physical setting that the Athenian playwright had to keep in mind as he wrote his play. One problem he had to resolve was the matter of entrances and exits. He could not, like his modern counterpart, simply open the curtain and reveal fifteen members of the chorus already in place on the stage. The chorus had to be brought in, either from behind the *skene* or from somewhere outside the stage area. And he could not afford to interrupt his action while they came in; they had to be speaking as they entered, so that the pace would not slow down. The *parodos*, or song of the entering chorus, was his solution to this problem, and it is a standard feature of most Greek plays. Another aid for the playwright was the formal division of his text into choral songs and dramatic episodes; by providing a certain fluidity in the overlapping of successive portions of the drama, this structural device further helped to avoid slowing the pace for entrances or exits. Greek acting was more stylized than the taste of the present age would find satisfying, and this propensity was emphasized when actors began to wear thick-soled boots, heavy robes, and masks to afford greater visibility and audibility to the upper reaches of the audience. Such physical elements, tending toward slowness, had to be balanced by the playwright with literary features suggesting speed—by quick exchanges of dialogue (*stichomythia*), for example, or by surprising turns, reversals, and discoveries in the plot. Facility in handling these techniques was the mark of a good playwright. The importance of such skills can best be seen in Aristotle's treatise on dramatic poetry, the *Poetics*, a work written during the decline of Athenian tragedy in the fourth century B.C. Aristotle devoted a good deal of his attention to precisely these literary devices and illustrated at some length the various ways in which the earlier, greater playwrights (such as Aeschylus, Sophocles, and Euripides) had used them to best effect.

Sophocles was one of a great many Athenians who competed regularly for the annual dramatic prize at the city's spring festival. He seems to have written more than a hundred plays in his long lifetime, most of which were probably chosen for production at the City Dionysia, and the few fragments of records that survive suggest that he won the first prize about twenty times. When we consider the remains of Athenian drama as found on most school library shelves we may be lulled into thinking that there were only three men who wrote tragedies—Aeschylus, Sophocles, and Euripides—and that they wrote not quite forty plays in all. In truth there were perhaps hundreds of playwrights and certainly many hundreds of plays written and performed in this age, and much first-rate drama surely has been lost. For example, when Sophocles entered in competition his universally admired play *Oedipus the King*, he had to be content with second prize; the judges awarded the first prize that year to a playwright named Philocles for a play whose name we do not even know.

Antigone, which is reputed to be Sophocles' thirty-second play, was performed at the City Dionysia in 441 B.C. when the playwright was about sixty years old. The citizens of Athens afterwards appointed him to be one of the generals for the ensuing Samian campaign. There is an ancient story that his generalship was the result of public enthusiasm for his play, but this may be apocryphal. One may be certain, however, that Sophocles was a man of experience in public affairs, and his concerns in *Antigone* mirror this experience.

ANTIGONE

Translated by Dudley Fitts and Robert Fitzgerald

The Characters

Antigone, daughter of Oedipus, a former King of Thebes
Ismene, her younger sister
Creon, the present King of Thebes
Eurydice, his wife
Haimon, their son
Teiresias, a blind prophet
A *Sentry*
A *Messenger*
A *Chorus of Citizens*

SCENE: *Before the palace of* CREON, *King of Thebes. A central double door, and two lateral doors. A platform extends the length of the façade, and from this platform three steps lead down into the "orchestra," or chorus-ground.*
TIME: *Dawn of the day after the repulse of the Argive army from the assault on Thebes.*

Prologue

[ANTIGONE *and* ISMENE *enter from the central door of the Palace.*]

Antigone.   Ismene, dear sister,
  You would think that we had already suffered enough
  For the curse on Oedipus:
  I cannot imagine any grief
  That you and I have not gone through. And now—
  Have they told you of the new decree of our King Creon?
Ismene.   I have heard nothing: I know
  That two sisters lost two brothers, a double death
  In a single hour; and I know that the Argive army
  Fled in the night; but beyond this, nothing.
Antigone.   I thought so. And that is why I wanted you
  To come out here with me. There is something we must do.
Ismene.   Why do you speak so strangely?
Antigone.   Listen, Ismene:
  Creon buried our brother Eteocles
  With military honors, gave him a soldier's funeral,
  And it was right that he should; but Polyneices,
  Who fought as bravely and died as miserably,—
  They say that Creon has sworn
  No one shall bury him, no one mourn for him,
  But his body must lie in the fields, a sweet treasure

3

For carrion birds to find as they search for food.
That is what they say, and our good Creon is coming here
To announce it publicly; and the penalty—
Stoning to death in the public square!
                                        There it is,
And now you can prove what you are:
A true sister, or a traitor to your family.

Ismene.   Antigone, you are mad! What could I possibly do?
Antigone.   You must decide whether you will help me or not.
Ismene.   I do not understand you. Help you in what?
Antigone.   Ismene, I am going to bury him. Will you come?
Ismene.   Bury him! You have just said the new law forbids it.
Antigone.   He is my brother. And he is your brother, too.
Ismene.   But think of the danger! Think what Creon will do!
Antigone.   Creon is not strong enough to stand in my way.
Ismene.   Ah sister!
Oedipus died, everyone hating him
For what his own search brought to light, his eyes
Ripped out by his own hand; and Iocaste died,
His mother and wife at once: she twisted the cords
That strangled her life; and our two brothers died,
Each killed by the other's sword. And we are left:
But oh, Antigone,
Think how much more terrible than these
Our own death would be if we should go against Creon
And do what he has forbidden! We are only women,
We cannot fight with men, Antigone!
The law is strong, we must give in to the law
In this thing, and in worse. I beg the Dead
To forgive me, but I am helpless: I must yield
To those in authority. And I think it is dangerous business
To be always meddling.
Antigone.   If that is what you think,
I should not want you, even if you asked to come.
You have made your choice, you can be what you want to be.
But I will bury him; and if I must die,
I say that this crime is holy: I shall lie down
With him in death, and I shall be as dear
To him as he is to me.
                        It is the dead,
Not the living, who make the longest demands:
We die for ever . . .
                        You may do as you like,
Since apparently the laws of the gods mean nothing to you.
Ismene.   They mean a great deal to me; but I have no strength
To break laws that were made for the public good.
Antigone.   That must be your excuse, I suppose. But as for me,
I will bury the brother I love.

Ismene.   Antigone,
   I am so afraid for you!
Antigone.   You need not be:
   You have yourself to consider, after all.
Ismene.   But no one must hear of this, you must tell no one!
   I will keep it a secret, I promise!
Antigone.   Oh tell it! Tell everyone!
   Think how they'll hate you when it all comes out
   If they learn that you knew about it all the time!
Ismene.   So fiery! You should be cold with fear.
Antigone.   Perhaps. But I am doing only what I must.
Ismene.   But can you do it? I say that you cannot.
Antigone.   Very well: when my strength gives out, I shall do no more.
Ismene.   Impossible things should not be tried at all.
Antigone.   Go away, Ismene:
   I shall be hating you soon, and the dead will too,
   For your words are hateful. Leave me my foolish plan:
   I am not afraid of the danger; if it means death,
   It will not be the worst of deaths—death without honor.
Ismene.   Go then, if you feel that you must.
   You are unwise,
   But a loyal friend indeed to those who love you.

   [*Exit into the Palace.* ANTIGONE *goes off, L.   Enter the* CHORUS.]

Parodos

Chorus.   Now the long blade of the sun, lying   [*Strophe* 1
   Level east to west, touches with glory
   Thebes of the Seven Gates. Open, unlidded
   Eye of golden day! O marching light
   Across the eddy and rush of Dirce's stream,
   Striking the white shields of the enemy
   Thrown headlong backward from the blaze of morning!
Choragos.   Polyneices their commander
   Roused them with windy phrases,
   He the wild eagle screaming
   Insults above our land,
   His wings their shields of snow,
   His crest their marshalled helms.

Chorus.   Against our seven gates in a yawning ring   [*Antistrophe* 1
   The famished spears came onward in the night;
   But before his jaws were sated with our blood,
   Or pinefire took the garland of our towers,
   He was thrown back; and as he turned, great Thebes—
   No tender victim for his noisy power—
   Rose like a dragon behind him, shouting war.

Choragos.   For God hates utterly
    The bray of bragging tongues;
    And when he beheld their smiling,
    Their swagger of golden helms,
    The frown of his thunder blasted
    Their first man from our walls.

Chorus.   We heard his shout of triumph high in the air   [*Strophe* 2
    Turn to a scream; far out in a flaming arc
    He fell with his windy torch, and the earth struck him.
    And others storming in fury no less than his
    Found shock of death in the dusty joy of battle.
Choragos.   Seven captains at seven gates
    Yielded their clanging arms to the god
    That bends the battle-line and breaks it.
    These two only, brothers in blood,
    Face to face in matchless rage,
    Mirroring each the other's death,
    Clashed in long combat.

Chorus.   But now in the beautiful morning of victory   [*Antistrophe* 2
    Let Thebes of the many chariots sing for joy!
    With hearts for dancing we'll take leave of war:
    Our temples shall be sweet with hymns of praise,
    And the long night shall echo with our chorus.

Scene I

Choragos.   But now at last our new King is coming:
    Creon of Thebes, Menoikeus' son.
    In this auspicious dawn of his reign
    What are the new complexities
    That shifting Fate has woven for him?
    What is his counsel? Why has he summoned
    The old men to hear him?

[*Enter* CREON *from the Palace, C. He addresses the* CHORUS *from the top step.*]

Creon.   Gentlemen: I have the honor to inform you that our Ship of State, which
recent storms have threatened to destroy, has come safely to harbor at last,
guided by the merciful wisdom of Heaven. I have summoned you here this
morning because I know that I can depend upon you: your devotion to King
Laïos was absolute; you never hesitated in your duty to our late ruler Oedipus;
and when Oedipus died, your loyalty was transferred to his children. Unfortunately, as you know, his two sons, the princes Eteocles and Polyneices, have
killed each other in battle; and I, as the next in blood, have succeeded to the
full power of the throne.
    I am aware, of course, that no Ruler can expect complete loyalty from his
subjects until he has been tested in office. Nevertheless, I say to you at the very

outset that I have nothing but contempt for the kind of Governor who is afraid, for whatever reason, to follow the course that he knows is best for the State; and as for the man who sets private friendship above the public welfare,—I have no use for him, either. I call God to witness that if I saw my country headed for ruin, I should not be afraid to speak out plainly; and I need hardly remind you that I would never have any dealings with an enemy of the people. No one values friendship more highly than I; but we must remember that friends made at the risk of wrecking our Ship are not real friends at all.

These are my principles, at any rate, and that is why I have made the following decision concerning the sons of Oedipus: Eteocles, who died as a man should die, fighting for his country, is to be buried with full military honors, with all the ceremony that is usual when the greatest heroes die; but his brother Polyneices, who broke his exile to come back with fire and sword against his native city and the shrines of his fathers' gods, whose one idea was to spill the blood of his blood and sell his own people into slavery—Polyneices, I say, is to have no burial: no man is to touch him or say the least prayer for him; he shall lie on the plain, unburied; and the birds and the scavenging dogs can do with him whatever they like.

This is my command, and you can see the wisdom behind it. As long as I am King, no traitor is going to be honored with the loyal man. But whoever shows by word and deed that he is on the side of the State,—he shall have my respect while he is living, and my reverence when he is dead.

Choragos. If that is your will, Creon son of Menoikeus,
    You have the right to enforce it: we are yours.
Creon. That is my will. Take care that you do your part.
Choragos. We are old men: let the younger ones carry it out.
Creon. I do not mean that: the sentries have been appointed.
Choragos. Then what is it that you would have us do?
Creon. You will give no support to whoever breaks this law.
Choragos. Only a crazy man is in love with death!
Creon. And death it is; yet money talks, and the wisest
    Have sometimes been known to count a few coins too many.

[*Enter* SENTRY *from L.*]

Sentry. I'll not say that I'm out of breath from running, King, because every time I stopped to think about what I have to tell you, I felt like going back. And all the time a voice kept saying, "You fool, don't you know you're walking straight into trouble?"; and then another voice: "Yes, but if you let somebody else get the news to Creon first, it will be even worse than that for you!" But good sense won out, at least I hope it was good sense, and here I am with a story that makes no sense at all; but I'll tell it anyhow, because, as they say, what's going to happen's going to happen, and—
Creon. Come to the point. What have you to say?
Sentry. I did not do it. I did not see who did it. You must not punish me for what someone else has done.
Creon. A comprehensive defense! More effective, perhaps,
    If I knew its purpose. Come: what is it?
Sentry. A dreadful thing . . . I don't know how to put it—

Creon.   Out with it!
Sentry.   Well, then;
    The dead man—
                    Polyneices—

[*Pause. The* SENTRY *is overcome, fumbles for words.* CREON *waits impassively.*]

                                        out there—
                                            someone,—

    New dust on the slimy flesh!

[*Pause. No sign from* CREON.]

    Someone has given it burial that way, and
    Gone . . .

[*Long pause.* CREON *finally speaks with deadly control.*]

Creon.   And the man who dared do this?
Sentry.   I swear I
    Do not know! You must believe me!
                                        Listen:
    The ground was dry, not a sign of digging, no,
    Not a wheeltrack in the dust, no trace of anyone.
    It was when they relieved us this morning: and one of them,
    The corporal, pointed to it.
                                There it was,
    The strangest—
                Look:
    The body, just mounded over with light dust: you see?
    Not buried really, but as if they'd covered it
    Just enough for the ghost's peace. And no sign
    Of dogs or any wild animal that had been there.

    And then what a scene there was! Every man of us
    Accusing the other: we all proved the other man did it,
    We all had proof that we could not have done it,
    We were ready to take hot iron in our hands,
    Walk through fire, swear by all the gods,
    It was not I!
    I do not know who it was, but it was not I!

[CREON's *rage has been mounting steadily, but the* SENTRY *is too intent upon his story to notice it.*]

    And then, when this came to nothing, someone said
    A thing that silenced us and made us stare
    Down at the ground: you had to be told the news,
    And one of us had to do it! We threw the dice,
    And the bad luck fell to me. So here I am,
    No happier to be here than you are to have me:
    Nobody likes the man who brings bad news.

Choragos. I have been wondering, King: can it be that the gods have done this?
Creon [*furiously*]: Stop!
  Must you doddering wrecks
  Go out of your heads entirely? "The gods!"
  Intolerable!
  The gods favor this corpse? Why? How had he served them?
  Tried to loot their temples, burn their images,
  Yes, and the whole State, and its laws with it!
  Is it your senile opinion that the gods love to honor bad men?
  A pious thought!—
                          No, from the very beginning
  There have been those who have whispered together,
  Stiff-necked anarchists, putting their heads together,
  Scheming against me in alleys. These are the men,
  And they have bribed my own guard to do this thing.

  [*Sententiously.*]

  Money!
  There's nothing in the world so demoralizing as money.
  Down go your cities,
  Homes gone, men gone, honest hearts corrupted,
  Crookedness of all kinds, and all for money!
  [*To* SENTRY.]   But you—!
  I swear by God and by the throne of God,
  The man who has done this thing shall pay for it!
  Find that man, bring him here to me, or your death
  Will be the least of your problems: I'll string you up
  Alive, and there will be certain ways to make you
  Discover your employer before you die;
  And the process may teach you a lesson you seem to have missed:
  The dearest profit is sometimes all too dear:
  That depends on the source. Do you understand me?
  A fortune won is often misfortune.
Sentry. King, may I speak?
Creon.   Your very voice distresses me.
Sentry. Are you sure that it is my voice, and not your conscience?
Creon. By God, he wants to analyze me now!
Sentry. It is not what I say, but what has been done, that hurts you.
Creon. You talk too much.
Sentry.   Maybe; but I've done nothing.
Creon. Sold your soul for some silver: that's all you've done.
Sentry. How dreadful it is when the right judge judges wrong!
Creon. Your figures of speech
  May entertain you now; but unless you bring me the man,
  You will get little profit from them in the end.

  [*Exit* CREON *into the Palace.*]

Sentry.   "Bring me the man"—!
   I'd like nothing better than bringing him the man!
   But bring him or not, you have seen the last of me here.
   At any rate, I am safe!

[*Exit* SENTRY.]

Ode I

Chorus.   Numberless are the world's wonders, but none   [*Strophe* 1
   More wonderful than man; the stormgray sea
   Yields to his prows, the huge crests bear him high;
   Earth, holy and inexhaustible, is graven
   With shining furrows where his plows have gone
   Year after year, the timeless labor of stallions.

   The lightboned birds and beasts that cling to cover,   [*Antistrophe* 1
   The lithe fish lighting their reaches of dim water,
   All are taken, tamed in the net of his mind;
   The lion on the hill, the wild horse windy-maned,
   Resign to him; and his blunt yoke has broken
   The sultry shoulders of the mountain bull.

   Words also, and thought as rapid as air,   [*Strophe* 2
   He fashions to his good use; statecraft is his,
   And his the skill that deflects the arrows of snow,
   The spears of winter rain: from every wind
   He has made himself secure—from all but one:
   In the late wind of death he cannot stand.

   O clear intelligence, force beyond all measure!   [*Antistrophe* 2
   O fate of man, working both good and evil!
   When the laws are kept, how proudly his city stands!
   When the laws are broken, what of his city then?
   Never may the anárchic man find rest at my hearth,
   Never be it said that my thoughts are his thoughts.

Scene II

[*Re-enter* SENTRY *leading* ANTIGONE.]

Choragos.   What does this mean? Surely this captive woman
   Is the Princess, Antigone. Why should she be taken?
Sentry.   Here is the one who did it! We caught her
   In the very act of burying him.—Where is Creon?
Choragos.   Just coming from the house.

[*Enter* CREON, C.]

Creon.   What has happened?
    Why have you come back so soon?
Sentry   [*expansively*]:   O King,
    A man should never be too sure of anything: I would have sworn
    That you'd not see me here again: your anger
    Frightened me so, and the things you threatened me with;
    But how could I tell then
    That I'd be able to solve the case so soon?

    No dice-throwing this time: I was only too glad to come!

    Here is this woman. She is the guilty one:
    We found her trying to bury him.
    Take her, then; question her; judge her as you will.
    I am through with the whole thing now, and glád óf it.
Creon.   But this is Antigone! Why have you brought her here?
Sentry.   She was burying him, I tell you!
Creon   [*severely*]:   Is this the truth?
Sentry.   I saw her with my own eyes. Can I say more?
Creon.   The details: come, tell me quickly!
Sentry.   It was like this:
    After those terrible threats of yours, King,
    We went back and brushed the dust away from the body.
    The flesh was soft by now, and stinking,
    So we sat on a hill to windward and kept guard.
    No napping this time! We kept each other awake.
    But nothing happened until the white round sun
    Whirled in the center of the round sky over us:
    Then, suddenly,
    A storm of dust roared up from the earth, and the sky
    Went out, the plain vanished with all its trees
    In the stinging dark. We closed our eyes and endured it.
    The whirlwind lasted a long time, but it passed;
    And then we looked, and there was Antigone!
    I have seen
    A mother bird come back to a stripped nest, heard
    Her crying bitterly a broken note or two
    For the young ones stolen. Just so, when this girl
    Found the bare corpse, and all her love's work wasted,
    She wept, and cried on heaven to damn the hands
    That had done this thing.
                 And then she brought more dust
    And sprinkled wine three times for her brother's ghost.

    We ran and took her at once. She was not afraid,
    Not even when we charged her with what she had done.
    She denied nothing.
                 And this was a comfort to me,

And some uneasiness: for it is a good thing
To escape from death, but it is no great pleasure
To bring death to a friend.
                                    Yet I always say
There is nothing so comfortable as your own safe skin!
Creon   [*slowly, dangerously*]: And you, Antigone,
    You with your head hanging,—do you confess this thing?
Antigone.   I do. I deny nothing.
Creon   [*to* SENTRY]:   You may go.   [*Exit* SENTRY.]
    [*To* ANTIGONE] Tell me, tell me briefly:
    Had you heard my proclamation touching this matter?
Antigone.   It was public. Could I help hearing it?
Creon.   And yet you dared defy the law.
Antigone.   I dared.
    It was not God's proclamation. That final Justice
    That rules the world below makes no such laws.
    Your edict, King, was strong,
    But all your strength is weakness itself against
    The immortal unrecorded laws of God.
    They are not merely now: they were, and shall be,
    Operative for ever, beyond man utterly.
    I knew I must die, even without your decree:
    I am only mortal. And if I must die
    Now, before it is my time to die,
    Surely this is no hardship: can anyone
    Living, as I live, with evil all about me,
    Think Death less than a friend? This death of mine
    Is of no importance; but if I had left my brother
    Lying in death unburied, I should have suffered.
    Now I do not.
                    You smile at me. Ah Creon,
    Think me a fool, if you like; but it may well be
    That a fool convicts me of folly.
Choragos.   Like father, like daughter: both headstrong, deaf to reason!
    She has never learned to yield.
Creon.   She has much to learn.
    The inflexible heart breaks first, the toughest iron
    Cracks first, and the wildest horses bend their necks
    At the pull of the smallest curb.
                                    Pride? In a slave?
    This girl is guilty of a double insolence,
    Breaking the given laws and boasting of it.
    Who is the man here,
    She or I, if this crime goes unpunished?
    Sister's child, or more than sister's child,
    Or closer yet in blood—she and her sister
    Win bitter death for this!
    [*To* SERVANTS.]   Go, some of you,

Arrest Ismene. I accuse her equally.
Bring her: you will find her sniffling in the house there.

Her mind's a traitor: crimes kept in the dark
Cry for light, and the guardian brain shudders;
But how much worse than this
Is brazen boasting of barefaced anarchy!
Antigone.   Creon, what more do you want than my death?
Creon.   Nothing.
     That gives me everything.
Antigone.   Then I beg you: kill me.
     This talking is a great weariness: your words
     Are distasteful to me, and I am sure that mine
     Seem so to you. And yet they should not seem so:
     I should have praise and honor for what I have done.
     All these men here would praise me
     Were their lips not frozen shut with fear of you.

     [*Bitterly.*]

     Ah the good fortune of kings,
        Licensed to say and do whatever they please!
Creon.   You are alone here in that opinion.
Antigone.   No, they are with me. But they keep their tongues in leash.
Creon.   Maybe. But you are guilty, and they are not.
Antigone.   There is no guilt in reverence for the dead.
Creon.   But Eteocles—was he not your brother too?
Antigone.   My brother too.
Creon.   And you insult his memory?
Antigone   [*softly*]: The dead man would not say that I insult it.
Creon.   He would: for you honor a traitor as much as him.
Antigone.   His own brother, traitor or not, and equal in blood.
Creon.   He made war on his country. Eteocles defended it.
Antigone.   Nevertheless, there are honors due all the dead.
Creon.   But not the same for the wicked as for the just.
Antigone.   Ah Creon, Creon,
     Which of us can say what the gods hold wicked?
Creon.   An enemy is an enemy, even dead.
Antigone.   It is my nature to join in love, not hate.
Creon   [*finally losing patience*]: Go join them, then; if you must have your love,
     Find it in hell!
Choragos.   But see, Ismene comes:

     [*Enter* ISMENE, *guarded.*]

     Those tears are sisterly, the cloud
     That shadows her eyes rains down gentle sorrow.
Creon.   You too, Ismene,
     Snake in my ordered house, sucking my blood
     Stealthily—and all the time I never knew

That these two sisters were aiming at my throne!

                                    Ismene,

Do you confess your share in this crime, or deny it?

Answer me.

Ismene.   Yes, if she will let me say so. I am guilty.

Antigone   [*coldly*]: No, Ismene. You have no right to say so.

   You would not help me, and I will not have you help me.

Ismene.   But now I know what you meant; and I am here

   To join you, to take my share of punishment.

Antigone.   The dead man and the gods who rule the dead

   Know whose act this was. Words are not friends.

Ismene.   Do you refuse me, Antigone? I want to die with you:

   I too have a duty that I must discharge to the dead.

Antigone.   You shall not lessen my death by sharing it.

Ismene.   What do I care for life when you are dead?

Antigone.   Ask Creon. You're always hanging on his opinions.

Ismene.   You are laughing at me. Why, Antigone?

Antigone.   It's a joyless laughter, Ismene.

Ismene.   But can I do nothing?

Antigone.   Yes. Save yourself. I shall not envy you.

   There are those who will praise you; I shall have honor, too.

Ismene.   But we are equally guilty!

Antigone.   No more, Ismene.

   You are alive, but I belong to Death.

Creon   [*to the* CHORUS]: Gentlemen, I beg you to observe these girls:

   One has just now lost her mind; the other,

   It seems, has never had a mind at all.

Ismene.   Grief teaches the steadiest minds to waver, King.

Creon.   Yours certainly did, when you assumed guilt with the guilty!

Ismene.   But how could I go on living without her?

Creon.   You are.

   She is already dead.

Ismene.   But your own son's bride!

Creon.   There are places enough for him to push his plow.

   I want no wicked women for my sons!

Ismene.   O dearest Haimon, how your father wrongs you!

Creon.   I've had enough of your childish talk of marriage!

Choragos.   Do you really intend to steal this girl from your son?

Creon.   No; Death will do that for me.

Choragos.   Then she must die?

Creon   [*ironically*]: You dazzle me.

                         —But enough of this talk!

[*To* GUARDS.]

You, there, take them away and guard them well:

For they are but women, and even brave men run

When they see Death coming.

[*Exeunt* ISMENE, ANTIGONE, *and* GUARDS.]

Ode II

Chorus.   Fortunate is the man who has never tasted God's vengeance!
    Where once the anger of heaven has struck, that house is shaken
    For ever: damnation rises behind each child
    Like a wave cresting out of the black northeast,
    When the long darkness under sea roars up
    And bursts drumming death upon the windwhipped sand.

I have seen this gathering sorrow from time long past   [*Antistrophe* 1
    Loom upon Oedipus' children: generation from generation
    Takes the compulsive rage of the enemy god.
    So lately this last flower of Oedipus' line
    Drank the sunlight! but now a passionate word
    And a handful of dust have closed up all its beauty.

        What mortal arrogance   [*Strophe* 2
        Transcends the wrath of Zeus?
    Sleep cannot lull him, nor the effortless long months
    Of the timeless gods: but he is young for ever,
    And his house is the shining day of high Olympos.
        All that is and shall be,
        And all the past, is his.
    No pride on earth is free of the curse of heaven.

        The straying dreams of men   [*Antistrophe* 2
        May bring them ghosts of joy:
    But as they drowse, the waking embers burn them;
    Or they walk with fíxed éyes, as blind men walk.
    But the ancient wisdom speaks for our own time:
        Fate works most for woe
        With Folly's fairest show.
    Man's little pleasure is the spring of sorrow.

Scene III

Choragos.   But here is Haimon, King, the last of all your sons.
    Is it grief for Antigone that brings him here,
    And bitterness at being robbed of his bride?

    [*Enter* HAIMON.]

Creon.   We shall soon see, and no need of diviners.
                                  —Son,
    You have heard my final judgment on that girl:
    Have you come here hating me, or have you come
    With deference and with love, whatever I do?
Haimon.   I am your son, father. You are my guide.
    You make things clear for me, and I obey you.

No marriage means more to me than your continuing wisdom.
Creon.   Good. That is the way to behave: subordinate
Everything else, my son, to your father's will.
This is what a man prays for, that he may get
Sons attentive and dutiful in his house,
Each one hating his father's enemies,
Honoring his father's friends. But if his sons
Fail him, if they turn out unprofitably,
What has he fathered but trouble for himself
And amusement for the malicious?
                                    So you are right
Not to lose your head over this woman.
Your pleasure with her would soon grow cold, Haimon,
And then you'd have a hellcat in bed and elsewhere.
Let her find her husband in Hell!
Of all the people in this city, only she
Has had contempt for my law and broken it.
Do you want me to show myself weak before the people?
Or to break my sworn word? No, and I will not.
The woman dies.
I suppose she'll plead "family ties." Well, let her.
If I permit my own family to rebel,
How shall I earn the world's obedience?
Show me the man who keeps his house in hand,
He's fit for public authority.
                                    I'll have no dealings
With law-breakers, critics of the government:
Whoever is chosen to govern should be obeyed—
Must be obeyed, in all things, great and small,
Just and unjust! O Haimon,
The man who knows how to obey, and that man only,
Knows how to give commands when the time comes.
You can depend on him, no matter how fast
The spears come: he's a good soldier, he'll stick it out.
Anarchy, anarchy! Show me a greater evil!
This is why cities tumble and the great houses rain down,
This is what scatters armies!

No, no: good lives are made so by discipline.
We keep the laws then, and the lawmakers,
And no woman shall seduce us. If we must lose,
Let's lose to a man, at least! Is a woman stronger than we?
Choragos.   Unless time has rusted my wits,
What you say, King, is said with point and dignity.
Haimon [*boyishly earnest*]:   Father:
Reason is God's crowning gift to man, and you are right
To warn me against losing mine. I cannot say—

I hope that I shall never want to say!—that you
Have reasoned badly. Yet there are other men
Who can reason, too; and their opinions might be helpful.
You are not in a position to know everything
That people say or do, or what they feel:
Your temper terrifies them—everyone
Will tell you only what you like to hear.
But I, at any rate, can listen; and I have heard them
Muttering and whispering in the dark about this girl.
They say no woman has ever, so unreasonably,
Died so shameful a death for a generous act:
"She covered her brother's body. Is this indecent?
She kept him from dogs and vultures. Is this a crime?
Death?—She should have all the honor that we can give her!"

This is the way they talk out there in the city.

You must believe me:
Nothing is closer to me than your happiness.
What could be closer? Must not any son
Value his father's fortune as his father does his?
I beg you, do not be unchangeable:
Do not believe that you alone can be right.
The man who thinks that,
The man who maintains that only he has the power
To reason correctly, the gift to speak, the soul—
A man like that, when you know him, turns out empty.

It is not reason never to yield to reason!

In flood time you can see how some trees bend,
And because they bend, even their twigs are safe,
While stubborn trees are torn up, roots and all.
And the same thing happens in sailing:
Make your sheet fast, never slacken,—and over you go,
Head over heels and under: and there's your voyage.
Forget you are angry! Let yourself be moved!
I know I am young; but please let me say this:
The ideal condition
Would be, I admit, that men should be right by instinct;
But since we are all too likely to go astray,
The reasonable thing is to learn from those who can teach.
Choragos. You will do well to listen to him, King,
  If what he says is sensible. And you, Haimon,
  Must listen to your father.—Both speak well.
Creon. You consider it right for a man of my years and experience
  To go to school to a boy?

Haimon.   It is not right
  If I am wrong. But if I am young, and right,
  What does my age matter?
Creon.   You think it right to stand up for an anarchist?
Haimon.   Not at all. I pay no respect to criminals.
Creon.   Then she is not a criminal?
Haimon.   The City would deny it, to a man.
Creon.   And the City proposes to teach me how to rule?
Haimon.   Ah. Who is it that's talking like a boy now?
Creon.   My voice is the one voice giving orders in this City!
Haimon.   It is no City if it takes orders from one voice.
Creon.   The State is the King!
Haimon.   Yes, if the State is a desert.

  [*Pause.*]

Creon.   This boy, it seems, has sold out to a woman.
Haimon.   If you are a woman: my concern is only for you.
Creon.   So? Your "concern"! In a public brawl with your father!
Haimon.   How about you, in a public brawl with justice?
Creon.   With justice, when all that I do is within my rights?
Haimon.   You have no right to trample on God's right.
Creon [*completely out of control*]:   Fool, adolescent fool! Taken in by a woman!
Haimon.   You'll never see me taken in by anything vile.
Creon.   Every word you say is for her!
Haimon [*quietly, darkly*]:   And for you.
  And for me. And for the gods under the earth.
Creon.   You'll never marry her while she lives.
Haimon.   Then she must die.—But her death will cause another.
Creon.   Another?
  Have you lost your senses? Is this an open threat?
Haimon.   There is no threat in speaking to emptiness.
Creon.   I swear you'll regret this superior tone of yours!
  You are the empty one!
Haimon.   If you were not my father,
  I'd say you were perverse.
Creon.   You girlstruck fool, don't play at words with me!
Haimon.   I am sorry. You prefer silence.
Creon.   Now, by God—!
  I swear, by all the gods in heaven above us,
  You'll watch it, I swear you shall!
  [*To the* servants.]   Bring her out!
  Bring the woman out! Let her die before his eyes!
  Here, this instant, with her bridegroom beside her!
Haimon.   Not here, no; she will not die here, King.
  And you will never see my face again.
  Go on raving as long as you've a friend to endure you.

  [*Exit* haimon.]

Choragos.   Gone, gone.
   Creon, a young man in a rage is dangerous!
Creon.   Let him do, or dream to do, more than a man can.
   He shall not save these girls from death.
Choragos.   These girls?
   You have sentenced them both?
Creon.   No, you are right.
   I will not kill the one whose hands are clean.
Choragos.   But Antigone?
Creon [*somberly*]:   I will carry her far away
   Out there in the wilderness, and lock her
   Living in a vault of stone. She shall have food,
   As the custom is, to absolve the State of her death.
   And there let her pray to the gods of hell:
   They are her only gods:
   Perhaps they will show her an escape from death,
   Or she may learn,
                        though late,
   That piety shown the dead is pity in vain.

   [*Exit* CREON.]

Ode III

Chorus.   Love, unconquerable   [*Strophe*
   Waster of rich men, keeper
   Of warm lights and all-night vigil
   In the soft face of a girl:
   Sea-wanderer, forest-visitor!
   Even the pure Immortals cannot escape you,
   And mortal man, in his one day's dusk,
   Trembles before your glory.

   Surely you swerve upon ruin   [*Antistrophe*
   The just man's consenting heart,
   As here you have made bright anger
   Strike between father and son—
   And none has conquered but Love!
   A girl's glánce wórking the will of heaven:
   Pleasure to her alone who mocks us,
   Merciless Aphrodite.

Scene IV

   [*As* ANTIGONE *enters guarded.*]
Choragos.   But I can no longer stand in awe of this,
   Nor, seeing what I see, keep back my tears.

Here is Antigone, passing to that chamber
Where all find sleep at last.

Antigone.   Look upon me, friends, and pity me   [*Strophe* 1
  Turning back at the night's edge to say
  Good-by to the sun that shines for me no longer;
  Now sleepy Death
  Summons me down to Acheron, that cold shore:
  There is no bridesong there, nor any music.
Chorus.   Yet not unpraised, not without a kind of honor,
  You walk at last into the underworld;
  Untouched by sickness, broken by no sword.
  What woman has ever found your way to death?

Antigone.   How often I have heard the story of Niobe,   [*Antistrophe* 1
  Tantalos' wretched daughter, how the stone
  Clung fast about her, ivy-close: and they say
  The rain falls endlessly
  And sifting soft snow; her tears are never done.
  I feel the loneliness of her death in mine.
Chorus.   But she was born of heaven, and you
  Are woman, woman-born. If her death is yours,
  A mortal woman's, is this not for you
  Glory in our world and in the world beyond?

Antigone.   You laugh at me. Ah, friends, friends,   [*Strophe* 2
  Can you not wait until I am dead? O Thebes,
  O men many-charioted, in love with Fortune,
  Dear springs of Dirce, sacred Theban grove,
  Be witnesses for me, denied all pity,
  Unjustly judged! and think a word of love
  For her whose path turns
  Under dark earth, where there are no more tears.
Chorus.   You have passed beyond human daring and come at last
  Into a place of stone where Justice sits.
  I cannot tell
  What shape of your father's guilt appears in this.

Antigone.   You have touched it at last: that bridal bed   [*Antistrophe* 2
  Unspeakable, horror of son and mother mingling:
  Their crime, infection of all our family!
  O Oedipus, father and brother!
  Your marriage strikes from the grave to murder mine.
  I have been a stranger here in my own land:
  All my life
  The blasphemy of my birth has followed me.
Chorus.   Reverence is a virtue, but strength
  Lives in established law: that must prevail.

You have made your choice,
Your death is the doing of your conscious hand.

Antigone.   Then let me go, since all your words are bitter,   [*Epode*
And the very light of the sun is cold to me.
Lead me to my vigil, where I must have
Neither love nor lamentation; no song, but silence.

[CREON *interrupts impatiently.*]

Creon.   If dirges and planned lamentations could put off death,
Men would be singing for ever.
[*To the* SERVANTS.]   Take her, go!
You know your orders: take her to the vault
And leave her alone there. And if she lives or dies,
That's her affair, not ours: our hands are clean.
Antigone.   O tomb, vaulted bride-bed in eternal rock,
Soon I shall be with my own again
Where Persephone welcomes the thin ghosts underground:
And I shall see my father again, and you, mother,
And dearest Polyneices—
                              dearest indeed
To me, since it was my hand
That washed him clean and poured the ritual wine:
And my reward is death before my time!

And yet, as men's hearts know, I have done no wrong,
I have not sinned before God. Or if I have,
I shall know the truth in death. But if the guilt
Lies upon Creon who judged me, then, I pray,
May his punishment equal my own.
Choragos.   O passionate heart,
Unyielding, tormented still by the same winds!
Creon.   Her guards shall have good cause to regret their delaying.
Antigone.   Ah! That voice is like the voice of death!
Creon.   I can give you no reason to think you are mistaken.
Antigone.   Thebes, and you my fathers' gods,
And rulers of Thebes, you see me now, the last
Unhappy daughter of a line of kings,
Your kings, led away to death. You will remember
What things I suffer, and at what men's hands,
Because I would not transgress the laws of heaven.

[*To the* GUARDS, *simply.*]

Come: let us wait no longer.

[*Exit* ANTIGONE, L., *guarded.*]

Ode IV

Chorus.   All Danae's beauty was locked away   [*Strophe* 1
   In a brazen cell where the sunlight could not come:
   A small room, still as any grave, enclosed her.
   Yet she was a princess too,
   And Zeus in a rain of gold poured love upon her.
   O child, child,
   No power in wealth or war
   Or tough sea-blackened ships
   Can prevail against untiring Destiny!

And Dryas' son also, that furious king,   [*Antistrophe* 1
   Bore the god's prisoning anger for his pride:
   Sealed up by Dionysos in deaf stone,
   His madness died among echoes.
   So at the last he learned what dreadful power
   His tongue had mocked:
   For he had profaned the revels,
   And fired the wrath of the nine
   Implacable Sisters that love the sound of the flute.

And old men tell a half-remembered tale   [*Strophe* 2
   Of horror done where a dark ledge splits the sea
   And a double surf beats on the gráy shóres:
   How a king's new woman, sick
   With hatred for the queen he had imprisoned,
   Ripped out his two sons' eyes with her bloody hands
   While grinning Ares watched the shuttle plunge
   Four times: four blind wounds crying for revenge,

Crying, tears and blood mingled.—Piteously born,   [*Antistrophe* 2
   Those sons whose mother was of heavenly birth!
   Her father was the god of the North Wind
   And she was cradled by gales,
   She raced with young colts on the glittering hills
   And walked untrammeled in the open light:
   But in her marriage deathless Fate found means
   To build a tomb like yours for all her joy.

Scene V

[*Enter blind* TEIRESIAS, *led by a* BOY. *The opening speeches of* TEIRESIAS *should
be in singsong contrast to the realistic lines of* CREON.]

Teiresias.   This is the way the blind man comes, Princes, Princes,
   Lock-step, two heads lit by the eyes of one.

Creon. What new thing have you to tell us, old Teiresias?
Teiresias. I have much to tell you: listen to the prophet, Creon.
Creon. I am not aware that I have ever failed to listen.
Teiresias. Then you have done wisely, King, and ruled well.
Creon. I admit my debt to you. But what have you to say?
Teiresias. This, Creon: you stand once more on the edge of fate.
Creon. What do you mean? Your words are a kind of dread.
Teiresias. Listen, Creon:

I was sitting in my chair of augury, at the place
Where the birds gather about me. They were all a-chatter,
As is their habit, when suddenly I heard
A strange note in their jangling, a scream, a
Whirring fury; I knew that they were fighting,
Tearing each other, dying
In a whirlwind of wings clashing. And I was afraid.
I began the rites of burnt-offering at the altar,
But Hephaistos failed me: instead of bright flame,
There was only the sputtering slime of the fat thigh-flesh
Melting: the entrails dissolved in gray smoke,
The bare bone burst from the welter. And no blaze!

This was a sign from heaven. My boy described it,
Seeing for me as I see for others.

I tell you, Creon, you yourself have brought
This new calamity upon us. Our hearths and altars
Are stained with the corruption of dogs and carrion birds
That glut themselves on the corpse of Oedipus' son.
The gods are deaf when we pray to them, their fire
Recoils from our offering, their birds of omen
Have no cry of comfort, for they are gorged
With the thick blood of the dead.
         O my son,
These are no trifles! Think: all men make mistakes,
But a good man yields when he knows his course is wrong,
And repairs the evil. The only crime is pride.

Give in to the dead man, then: do not fight with a corpse—
What glory is it to kill a man who is dead?
Think, I beg you:
It is for your own good that I speak as I do.
You should be able to yield for your own good.

Creon. It seems that prophets have made me their especial province:
All my life long
I have been a kind of butt for the dull arrows
Of doddering fortune-tellers!
      No, Teiresias:

If your birds—if the great eagles of God himself
Should carry him stinking bit by bit to heaven
I would not yield. I am not afraid of pollution:
No man can defile the gods.
                                              Do what you will,
Go into business, make money, speculate
In India gold or that synthetic gold from Sardis,
Get rich otherwise than by my consent to bury him.
Teiresias, it is a sorry thing when a wise man
Sells his wisdom, lets out his words for hire!
Teiresias. Ah Creon! Is there no man left in the world—
Creon. To do what?—come, let's have the aphorism!
Teiresias. No man who knows that wisdom outweighs any wealth?
Creon. As surely as bribes are baser than any baseness.
Teiresias. You are sick, Creon! You are deathly sick!
Creon. As you say: it is not my place to challenge a prophet.
Teiresias. Yet you have said my prophecy is for sale.
Creon. The generation of prophets has always loved gold.
Teiresias. The generation of kings has always loved brass.
Creon. You forget yourself! You are speaking to your King.
Teiresias. I know it. You are a king because of me.
Creon. You have a certain skill; but you have sold out.
Teiresias. King, you will drive me to words that—
Creon.   Say them, say them!
   Only remember: I will not pay you for them.
Teiresias. No, you will find them too costly.
Creon.   No doubt. Speak:
   Whatever you say, you will not change my will.
Teiresias. Then take this, and take it to heart!
   The time is not far off when you shall pay back
   Corpse for corpse, flesh of your own flesh.
   You have thrust the child of this world into living night,
   You have kept from the gods below the child that is theirs:
   The one in a grave before her death, the other,
   Dead, denied the grave. This is your crime:
   And the Furies and the dark gods of Hell
   Are swift with terrible punishment for you.

   Do you want to buy me now, Creon?
                                              Not many days,
   And your house will be full of men and women weeping,
   And curses will be hurled at you from far
   Cities grieving for sons unburied, left to rot
   Before the walls of Thebes.

   These are my arrows, Creon: they are all for you.

[*To* BOY.]

But come, child: lead me home.
Let him waste his fine anger upon younger men.
Maybe he will learn at last
To control a wiser tongue in a better head.

[*Exit* TEIRESIAS.]

Choragos. The old man has gone, King, but his words
  Remain to plague us. I am old, too,
  But I cannot remember that he was ever false.
Creon. That is true. . . . It troubles me.
  Oh it is hard to give in! but it is worse
  To risk everything for stubborn pride.
Choragos. Creon: take my advice.
Creon.   What shall I do?
Choragos. Go quickly: free Antigone from her vault
  And build a tomb for the body of Polyneices.
Creon. You would have me do this?
Choragos.   Creon, yes!
  And it must be done at once: God moves
  Swiftly to cancel the folly of stubborn men.
Creon. It is hard to deny the heart! But I
  Will do it: I will not fight with destiny.
Choragos. You must go yourself, you cannot leave it to others.
Creon. I will go.
          —Bring axes, servants:
  Come with me to the tomb. I buried her, I
  Will set her free.
          Oh quickly!
  My mind misgives—
  The laws of the gods are mighty, and a man must serve them
  To the last day of his life!

[*Exit* CREON.]

Paean

Choragos. God of many names   [*Strophe* 1
Chorus.   O Iacchos
                   son
  of Kadmeian Sémele
             O born of the Thunder!
  Guardian of the West
            Regent
  of Eleusis' plain
           O Prince of maenad Thebes
  and the Dragon Field by rippling Ismenos:

Choragos.   God of many names   [*Antistrophe* 1
Chorus.   the flame of torches
  flares on our hills
          the nymphs of Iacchos
  dance at the spring of Castalia:

  from the vine-close mountain
            come ah come in ivy:
  Evohé evohé! sings through the streets of Thebes

Choragos.   God of many names   [*Strophe* 2
Chorus.   Iacchos of Thebes
  heavenly Child
        of Sémele bride of the Thunderer!
  The shadow of plague is upon us:
               come
  with clement feet
        oh come from Parnasos
  down the long slopes
        across the lamenting water

Choragos.   Io Fire! Chorister of the throbbing stars!   [*Antistrophe* 2
  O purest among the voices of the night!
  Thou son of God, blaze for us!
Chorus.   Come with choric rapture of circling Maenads
  Who cry *Io Iacche!*
        God of many names!

Exodos

  [*Enter* MESSENGER, *L.*]

Messenger.   Men of the line of Kadmos, you who live
  Near Amphion's citadel:
             I cannot say
  Of any condition of human life "This is fixed,
  This is clearly good, or bad." Fate raises up,
  And Fate casts down the happy and unhappy alike:
  No man can foretell his Fate.
             Take the case of Creon:
  Creon was happy once, as I count happiness:
  Victorious in battle, sole governor of the land,
  Fortunate father of children nobly born.
  And now it has all gone from him! Who can say
  That a man is still alive when his life's joy fails?
  He is a walking dead man. Grant him rich,
  Let him live like a king in his great house:

If his pleasure is gone, I would not give
So much as the shadow of smoke for all he owns.
Choragos. Your words hint at sorrow: what is your news for us?
Messenger. They are dead. The living are guilty of their death.
Choragos. Who is guilty? Who is dead? Speak!
Messenger.   Haimon.
   Haimon is dead; and the hand that killed him
   Is his own hand.
Choragos.   His father's? or his own?
Messenger. His own, driven mad by the murder his father had done.
Choragos. Teiresias, Teiresias, how clearly you saw it all!
Messenger. This is my news: you must draw what conclusions you can from it.
Choragos. But look: Eurydice, our Queen:
   Has she overheard us?

[*Enter* EURYDICE *from the Palace, C.*]

Eurydice. I have heard something, friends:
   As I was unlocking the gate of Pallas' shrine,
   For I needed her help today, I heard a voice
   Telling of some new sorrow. And I fainted
   There at the temple with all my maidens about me.
   But speak again: whatever it is, I can bear it:
   Grief and I are no strangers.
Messenger.   Dearest Lady,
   I will tell you plainly all that I have seen.
   I shall not try to comfort you: what is the use,
   Since comfort could lie only in what is not true?
   The truth is always best.
                              I went with Creon
   To the outer plain where Polyneices was lying,
   No friend to pity him, his body shredded by dogs.
   We made our prayers in that place to Hecate
   And Pluto, that they would be merciful. And we bathed
   The corpse with holy water, and we brought
   Fresh-broken branches to burn what was left of it,
   And upon the urn we heaped up a towering barrow
   Of the earth of his own land.
                              When we were done, we ran
   To the vault where Antigone lay on her couch of stone.
   One of the servants had gone ahead,
   And while he was yet far off he heard a voice
   Grieving within the chamber, and he came back
   And told Creon. And as the King went closer,
   The air was full of wailing, the words lost,
   And he begged us to make all haste. "Am I a prophet?"
   He said, weeping, "And must I walk this road,
   The saddest of all that I have gone before?

My son's voice calls me on. Oh quickly, quickly!
Look through the crevice there, and tell me
If it is Haimon, or some deception of the gods!"
We obeyed; and in the cavern's farthest corner
We saw her lying:
She had made a noose of her fine linen veil
And hanged herself. Haimon lay beside her,
His arms about her waist, lamenting her,
His love lost under ground, crying out
That his father had stolen her away from him.
When Creon saw him the tears rushed to his eyes
And he called to him: "What have you done, child? Speak to me.
What are you thinking that makes your eyes so strange?
O my son, my son, I come to you on my knees!"
But Haimon spat in his face. He said not a word,
Staring—
                    And suddenly drew his sword
And lunged. Creon shrank back, the blade missed; and the boy,
Desperate against himself, drove it half its length
Into his own side, and fell. And as he died
He gathered Antigone close in his arms again,
Choking, his blood bright red on her white cheek.
And now he lies dead with the dead, and she is his
At last, his bride in the houses of the dead.

[*Exit* EURYDICE *into the Palace.*]

Choragos.   She has left us without a word. What can this mean?
Messenger.   It troubles me, too; yet she knows what is best,
    Her grief is too great for public lamentation,
    And doubtless she has gone to her chamber to weep
    For her dead son, leading her maidens in his dirge.
Choragos.   It may be so: but I fear this deep silence.

    [*Pause.*]

Messenger.   I will see what she is doing. I will go in.

    [*Exit* MESSENGER *into the Palace.   Enter* CREON *with attendants, bearing* HAI-
    MON's *body.*]

Choragos.   But here is the King himself: oh look at him,
    Bearing his own damnation in his arms.
Creon.   Nothing you say can touch me any more.
    My own blind heart has brought me
    From darkness to final darkness. Here you see
    The father murdering, the murdered son—
    And all my civic wisdom!

    Haimon my son, so young, so young to die,
    I was the fool, not you; and you died for me.

Choragos.   That is the truth; but you were late in learning it.
Creon.   This truth is hard to bear. Surely a god
  Has crushed me beneath the hugest weight of heaven.
  And driven me headlong a barbaric way
  To trample out the thing I held most dear.

  The pains that men will take to come to pain!

[*Enter* MESSENGER *from the Palace.*]

Messenger.   The burden you carry in your hands is heavy,
  But it is not all: you will find more in your house.
Creon.   What burden worse than this shall I find there?
Messenger.   The Queen is dead.
Creon.   O port of death, deaf world,
  Is there no pity for me? And you, Angel of evil,
  I was dead, and your words are death again.
  Is it true, boy? Can it be true?
  Is my wife dead? Has death bred death?
Messenger.   You can see for yourself.

[*The doors are opened, and the body of* EURYDICE *is disclosed within.*]

Creon.   Oh pity!
  All true, all true, and more than I can bear!
  O my wife, my son!
Messenger.   She stood before the altar, and her heart
  Welcomed the knife her own hand guided,
  And a great cry burst from her lips for Megareus dead,
  And for Haimon dead, her sons; and her last breath
  Was a curse for their father, the murderer of her sons.
  And she fell, and the dark flowed in through her closing eyes.
Creon.   O God, I am sick with fear.
  Are there no swords here? Has no one a blow for me?
Messenger.   Her curse is upon you for the deaths of both.
Creon.   It is right that it should be. I alone am guilty.
  I know it, and I say it. Lead me in,
  Quickly, friends.
  I have neither life nor substance. Lead me in.
Choragos.   You are right, if there can be right in so much wrong.
  The briefest way is best in a world of sorrow.
Creon.   Let it come,
  Let death come quickly, and be kind to me.
  I would not ever see the sun again.
Choragos.   All that will come when it will; but we, meanwhile,
  Have much to do. Leave the future to itself.
Creon.   All my heart was in that prayer!
Choragos.   Then do not pray any more: the sky is deaf.

Creon.   Lead me away. I have been rash and foolish.
I have killed my son and my wife.
I look for comfort; my comfort lies here dead.
Whatever my hands have touched has come to nothing.
Fate has brought all my pride to a thought of dust.

[As CREON *is being led into the house, the* CHORAGOS *advances and speaks directly to the audience.*]

Choragos.   There is no happiness where there is no wisdom;
No wisdom but in submission to the gods.
Big words are always punished,
And proud men in old age learn to be wise.

THE SECOND SHEPHERDS' PLAY

The Greeks were not alone in their conviction that significant community events should be celebrated with festivals and dramas. Later societies shared their views. During the middle ages, the major festive occasions—midwinter and spring—were the feasts of Christmas and Easter. To amplify the services on these sacred occasions, some priests and bishops began to dramatize portions of the liturgy, and gradually this practice became widespread. By the late middle ages these Christmas and Easter celebrations had so increased in size and complexity that they threatened to disrupt the holy service that had produced them, and it seemed better to detach them from the Mass; better, in fact, to get them out of the church altogether and into the street, where space and decorum would no longer be problems. One by one the churches prohibited plays within their doors, and—with this formal connection severed—the dramas, though religious in origin and tone, found themselves of necessity secular in personnel and practice.

They also found themselves colder, since neither Christmas nor Easter is a particularly hospitable time of year in England for outdoor drama. The steps of the church, though spacious, were hardly the sort of stage facility one would wish; and most towns had no place else suitable for performances. As a result, Christmas plays dwindled; and in the middle of the thirteenth century, when the Pope established a major holiday, the Feast of Corpus Christi, to be celebrated in the late spring, most northern communities seized the opportunity to move their shivering Easter presentations to that new day. This holiday soon became the major occasion for dramatic performance in England, despite the handicap of inadequate facilities.

English towns, unlike Greek cities, were often built in valleys or plains. There were no hillside theatres; in fact there were no theatres at all (except for a few decaying Roman theatres), because the Church had strongly disapproved of secular drama. St. Ambrose and St. Augustine had long before set the tone in their descriptions of theatres as temples of the devil and as foul pits. The natural histrionic tendencies of western Europe were only chastened, not eliminated, by such warnings, however, and though we hear nothing of theatres or playwrights in the middle ages we ought not conclude that secular drama had disappeared. Part of the explanation for this lies in the changed social structures resulting from the collapse of the Roman empire. Theatre is the art form of a settled community, chiefly because it requires for its full fruition the kind of physical facilities that presuppose permanence. Nomadic peoples, having no such facilities, carry their art with them in the form of epic tales and romances. With the destruction of Rome and the spread of nomadic peoples over Europe, theatre as a settled art form disappeared. The barbarians were not hostile to drama; simply indifferent. But they greatly facilitated the activity of the early Church in suppressing drama, and their combined attitudes were overpowering. Theatres fell into disuse, and playwrights became a thing of the past. The craft of performing never quite died, however, though in the middle ages we find it turning to minstrelsy, tumbling, and tricks with animals. Occasionally a few performers would travel as a troupe and play from the tailgate of their wagon, and with the passage of time this practice became more and more common. Such practice served as a partial solution to the problem presented by the lack of theatre buildings; for the "stage" itself was on wheels, and could be moved from audience to audience. When the fledgling religious drama of the medieval church found itself turned out of doors, it had no better model to follow than the traveling wagons of the secular acting troupes.

The Feast of Corpus Christi was not instituted to provide an occasion for drama; it was a proper Church holiday, and many communities observed it with a procession and the appropriate ceremonies. But some of the larger towns in England expanded the celebration by including their locally conceived religious plays as a part of the procession. These plays were biblical in theme, though no longer specifically about Christmas or Easter, and had become notably more popular in tone. In time the practice of including a procession of plays in the Corpus Christi celebration became widespread. The common subject matter of these plays made possible their presentation as a sequence, or cycle, beginning with a play about the Creation and proceeding through the Fall of Man and the Redemption to the final play about Doomsday. The practice of performing these plays from wagons seemed to suit their form perfectly, for a spectator on Corpus Christi Day could seat himself on the village high street, at one of the predetermined stopping places, and one by one the actors would bring up their wagons, perform their play, and move on. The actors themselves were local people, and in fact the production of the plays was managed entirely by the various craft guilds, each guild being responsible for one play. The arrangement seems at the outset to have been a happy one; the guilds entered into enthusiastic rivalry with one another in the opulence of their costumes and the magnificence of their productions.

Not every guild could boast a playwright, however, and as a result the scripts of these early cycle plays are predictably uneven. In Wakefield, a northerly town that had grown prosperous in the wool trade, periodic attempts were made to get better scripts, even if necessary by borrowing from the cycles of other towns, like nearby York. Finally, about the middle of the fifteenth century, an unknown man of considerable dramatic talents undertook the revision of Wakefield's entire cycle of plays. Some of the scripts he merely touched up, but he rewrote others completely and added new ones of his own. It was a major task, since by this time the cycle consisted of almost thirty plays. A manuscript of the cycle, containing the revisions of this unknown "Wakefield master," was written about 1460 and still survives: included in it are two plays about the Nativity, in which the traditional appearance of the Angel to the shepherds is represented. They are alike in many ways, but the second play is generally considered better. The citizens of Wakefield, sheep-raisers themselves, must have felt a special affinity with the shepherds here portrayed.

THE SECOND SHEPHERDS' PLAY

Translated by Henry W. Wells and Roger S. Loomis

The Characters

First Shepherd (Coll)
Second Shepherd (Gib)
Third Shepherd (Daw), a youth
Mak
Jill
Angel
Mary

Scene I

[*Scene a moor. Enter* FIRST SHEPHERD, *stamping his feet and blowing on his nails.*]

First Shepherd.   Lord, but it's cold and wretchedly I'm wrapped;
My wits are frozen, so long it is I've napped;
My legs are cramped, and every finger chapped.
All goes awry; in misery I'm trapped.
By storms and gales distressed,
Now in the east, now west,
Woe's him who gets no rest!
We simple shepherds walking on the moor,
We're like, in faith, to be put out of door,
And it's no wonder if we are so poor.
Our fields they lie as fallow as a floor;
We're driven till we're bowed;
We're taxed until we're cowed
By gentry, rich and proud.
They take our rest; them may our Lady blast!
For their own lords they make our plows stick fast.
Some say it's for the best, but at the last
We know that's false. We tenants are downcast,
And always we're kept under.
If we don't thrive, no wonder
When they so rob and plunder.
A man with broidered sleeve or brooch, these days,
Can ruin anyone who him gainsays.
There's not a soul believes one word he says,
Or dares rebuke him for his bumptious ways.
He makes his pride and boast,
He gets his very post

From those who have the most.
There comes a fellow, proud as a peacock, now,
He'd carry off my wagon and my plow.
Before he'd leave, I must seem glad and bow.
A wretched life we lead, you must allow.
Whatever he has willed
Must be at once fulfilled,
Or surely I'd be killed.
It does me good, when I walk round alone,
About this world to grumble and to groan.
Now to my sheep I'll slowly walk, and moan,
And rest awhile on some old balk or stone.
Some other men I'll see;
Before it's noon I'll be
In true men's company.

[*Enter* SECOND SHEPHERD, *not noticing* FIRST SHEPHERD.]

Second Shepherd.   Good Lord, good Lord, what does this misery mean?
What ails the world? The like has seldom been.
The weather's spiteful cold and bitter keen;
My eyes they weep, such hideous frosts they've seen.
Now in the snow and sleet
My shoes freeze to my feet;
No easy life I meet.
So far as I can see, where'er I go,
The griefs of married men increase and grow.
We're always out of luck; I tell you so.
Capul, our hen, goes cackling to and fro,
But if she starts to croak,
Our cock suffers a stroke;
For him it is no joke.
These wedded men have never once their will;
When they're hard pressed, they sigh and just keep still,
Groan to themselves and take the bitter pill.
God knows they've got a nasty part to fill!
And as for me I've found—
I know the lesson's sound—
Woe to the man who's bound!
Late in my life it still amazes me,
And my heart stops such miracles to see;
But yet when destiny drives, such things can be:
Some men have two wives, some have even three!
But if his lot is sore
Who has one wife in store,
It's hell for him with more!
Young men who'd woo, before you're fairly caught,
Beware of wedding! Give the matter thought.

To moan, "Had I but known!" will help you nought.
Much misery has wedding often brought,
And many a stormy shower.
You catch in one short hour
A lifelong taste of sour.
I've one for mate, if ever I read the Epistle,
Who's rough as is a briar and sharp as thistle.
Her looks are sour; her eyebrows, like hog's bristle.
She'd sing "Our Father" if once she wet her whistle.
And like a whale she's fat,
Full of gall as a vat.
I don't know where I'm at.

First Shepherd.   Gib, look over the hedge! Are you deaf or no?
Second Shepherd.   The devil take you! Was ever man so slow?
Have you seen Daw?
First Shepherd.   Just now I heard him blow
His horn. I see him on the lea below.
Be quiet!
Second Shepherd.   Tell me why.
First Shepherd.   I think he's coming by.
Second Shepherd.   He'll trick us with some lie.

[FIRST *and* SECOND SHEPHERDS *hide.   Enter* THIRD SHEPHERD.]

Third Shepherd.   May Christ's cross help me, and St. Nicholas!
I've need of it; life's harder than it was.
Let men beware and let the false world pass.
It slips and slides, more brittle far than glass.
Never did it change so,
For now it's weal, now woe.
It's all a passing show.
Since Noah's flood, such floods were never seen,
Such dreadful winds and rains, and storms so keen.
Folk stammer or stand dumb with fear, I ween.
God turn it all to good! That's what I mean.
Just think how these floods drown
Us out in field and town;
No wonder that we're down.
We that walk at night, our herds to keep,
We see queer sights when others are asleep.

[*He spies the other shepherds.*]

My heart jumps. There I see two fellows peep,
Tall rascals both. I'll turn back to my sheep.
It was a bad mistake
This lonely path to take;
My toes I'll stub and break.

[FIRST *and* SECOND SHEPHERDS *come forward.*]

May God save you, and you, O master sweet!
I want a drink and then a bite to eat.
First Shepherd.   Christ's curse, my boy, but you're a lazy cheat!
Second Shepherd.   Does the boy rave? Let him wait for his meat!
  Bad luck now on your pate!
  The wretch, though he comes late,
  Would eat, so starved his state.
Third Shepherd.   Servants like me, who always sweat and swink,
  We eat our bread too dry, that's what I think.
  We're wet and weary while our masters blink.
  It's late before we get to eat or drink.
  Grand dame and noble sire
  Delay and dock our hire,
  Though we have run through mire.
  But hear a truth, my master, for God's sake!
  A fuss about my appetite you make!
  But never supper gave me stomach-ache.
  Henceforth I'll work as little as I take;
  Or I can run away.
  What one buys cheap, they say,
  Won't in the long run pay.
First Shepherd.   A fool you'd be if you yourself should bring
  To serve a man who'd not spend anything.
Second Shepherd.   Peace, boy! I want no more rude chattering.
  Or I will make you smart, by Heaven's King!
  Our sheep are they left lorn?
Third Shepherd.   This very day at morn
  I left them in the corn.
  They have good pasture, so they can't go wrong.
First Shepherd.   That's right. Oh, by the Rood, these nights are long!
  Before we go, I wish we'd have a song.
Second Shepherd.   I thought myself 'twould cheer us all along.
Third Shepherd.   I'm set.
First Shepherd.   Tenor I'll try.
Second Shepherd.   And I the treble high.
Third Shepherd.   Then the middle am I.

[*Then* MAK *enters with a cloak drawn over his tunic.*]

Mak.   Lord, of seven names, who made the moon that sails
  And more stars than I know, Thy good will fails.
  My brain is in a whirl; it's that which ails.
  I wish I were in heaven where no child wails.
First Shepherd.   Who is it pipes so poor?
Mak.   God knows what I endure,
  A-walking on the moor!

Second Shepherd [*stepping forward*]: Where do you come from, Mak? What
  news d'you bring?
Third Shepherd. Is he come? Keep close watch on everything!

[*He snatches the cloak from him.*]

Mak [*with a southern accent*]: I tell you I'm a yeoman of the King.
  Make way for me! Lord's messages I bring.
  Fie on you! Get ye hence!
  This is no mere pretense.
  I must have reverence!
First Shepherd. Why put on airs, Mak? It's no good to try.
Second Shepherd. Or play the actor, for I know you lie.
Third Shepherd. The scamp talks well, the Devil hang him high!
Mak. I'll make complaint; I'll make you sizzle and fry!
  I'll tell on you, in sooth.
First Shepherd. O Mak, ere you speak truth,
  Take out your Southron tooth!
Second Shepherd. The Devil's in your eye. You need a whack!

[*Strikes* MAK.]

Third Shepherd. So you don't know me? I'll teach you better, Mak!
Mak [*changing his tune*]: God keep all three! What I said I take back.
  You're all good fellows.
First Shepherd. Now you've changed your tack.
Second Shepherd. Why out so late, pray tell?
  Everyone knows right well
  You love roast-mutton smell.
Mak. I'm true as steel, as anyone will say,
  But I've a sickness takes my health away.
  My belly's in a parlous state today.
Third Shepherd. "The Devil seldom lies dead by the way."
Mak. As still as stone I'll lie.
  If this whole month have I
  Eat even a needle's eye.
First Shepherd. How is your wife? how is she? tell us true.
Mak. She's sprawling by the fire; that's nothing new.
  The house is full of brats. She drinks ale, too.
  Come good or ill, that she will always do.
  She eats fast as she can,
  And each year gives a man
  A babe or two to scan.
  Though I had much more money in my purse,
  She'd eat and drink us to the Devil, sirs.
  Just look at her near by, the ugly curse!
  Will no one rid me of her?
  I'd give all in my coffer
  Mass for her soul to offer.

Second Shepherd.   I swear there's no one so tired in this shire.
   I must get sleep though I take less for hire.
Third Shepherd.   I'm cold and nearly naked; I'd like a fire.
First Shepherd.   And I'm worn out with running in the mire.
   Keep watch.

   [*Lies down.*]

Second Shepherd.   Not so, for I
   Must sleep. I'll put me by.

   [*Lies down.*]

Third Shepherd.   Equal with you I'll lie.

   [*Lies down.*]

   Here, Mak, come here! Between us you must be.
Mak.   You're sure you don't want to talk privately?

   [*Lies down, crosses himself and prays.*]

   And now from head to toe
   Manus tuas commendo,
   Pontio Pilato.

Mak [*while the* SHEPHERDS *sleep, rises and says*] :

   Now is the time for one who's short of gold
   To enter stealthily into a fold
   And nimbly work and yet be not too bold,
   For he might rue the bargain if 'twere told.
   He must be shrewd and wise
   Who likes his victuals nice,
   Yet hasn't got the price.

   [*Pretends to be a magician.*]

   A circle round the moon I here fulfill.
   Until it's noon or I have done my will,
   You must each one lie there and be stone still.
   To make it sure some good strong words I'll spill.
   Over you my hands I lift;
   Your eyes go out and drift
   Till I make better shift.
   Lord, but they're sleeping sound! All men can hear!
   I never was a shepherd, but now I'll learn their gear,
   And though the flock be scared, I'll creep right near.
   This fat sheep with its fleece improves my cheer.
   And now goodbye to sorrow!

                                        [*Seizes sheep.*]

Though I pay not tomorrow,
I'll in the meantime borrow.

[Exit MAK.]

Scene II

[*Interior of* MAK'S *cottage.* JILL *sits spinning.*]

Mak [*outside*]:   Jill, are you in? Hello, get us some light!
Jill.   Who makes this racket at this time of night?
  I'm busy spinning; I'll not stir a mite
  To get a day's pay. Curses on you light!
  It's thus a housewife fares.
  She's always rushed with cares,
  And all for nothing bears!

Mak [*outside*]:   Open the latch, good wife! See what I bring!
Jill.   I'll let you pull.

[*Opens door.* MAK *enters.*]

Jill.   Come in, my own sweet thing!
Mak.   Not much you care how long I stand and sing!
Jill.   By your bare neck, for this you're like to swing!
Mak.   I'm good for something yet;
  For at a pinch I get
  More than the fools who sweat.
  I had a lucky lot and God's own grace.
Jill.   To hang for it would be a foul disgrace!
Mak.   I've dodged before, my Jill, as hard a case.
Jill.   Folk say that just so long a pot or vase
  To water it can come,
  Then broken it's brought home.
Mak.   On that old saw be dumb!
  I wish that he were skinned; I want to eat.
  For twelve months I've not hankered so for meat.
Jill.   Suppose they come here first and hear him bleat!
Mak.   They'd catch me then. That puts me in a heat.
  Go bolt the door at back!
  I'd get from that whole pack
  The devil of a whack!
Jill.   A good trick I have spied since you have none:
  We'll hide him in the crib till they have done.
  I'll lie and groan and say that he's my son.
  Let me alone to do what I've begun.
Mak.   And I will say, tonight
  Of this boy you are light.
Jill.   It's luck I was born bright.
  For cleverness this trick can't be surpassed.

A woman's wit helps always at the last.
Before they get suspicious, hurry fast.
Mak.   If I don't get there soon, they'll blow a blast!

[*Exit* MAK.]

Scene III

[*The moor.* SHEPHERDS *sleeping. Enter* MAK.]

Mak.   These men are still asleep.
Their company I'll keep
As if I'd stolen no sheep.

[*Lies down between them.*]
[SHEPHERDS *wake one by one, and cross themselves.*]

First Shepherd.   *Resurrex a mortruis!* Here, take my hand!
Judas carnas Dominus! I can't well stand.
My foot's asleep and I'm as dry as sand.
I dreamt we lay down near the English land!
Second Shepherd.   I slept so well, I feel
As fresh as any eel,
And light upon my heel!
Third Shepherd.   Lord bless us all! My body's all a-quake!
My heart jumps from my skin, and that's no fake.
Who's making all this din and my head ache?
I'll teach him something! hear, you fellows, wake!
Where's Mak?
First Shepherd.   I vow he's near.
He went nowhere, that's clear.
Third Shepherd.   I dreamt he was dressed up in a wolf's skin.
First Shepherd.   That's what too many rogues are wrapped up in!
Third Shepherd.   While we were snoozing, seemed he did begin
To catch a sheep, without the slightest din.
Second Shepherd.   Your dream has made you brood
On phantoms, by the Rood.
May God turn all to good!

[*Shakes* MAK.]

Rise, Mak, for shame! You're sleeping far too long.
Mak.   Now may Christ's holy name keep us from wrong!
What's this? St. James! I can hardly move along.
I'm just the same, and yet my neck's all wrong.

[SHEPHERDS *help him to his feet.*]

Thank you! It's still uneven
For I've been plagued since even
With nightmares, by St. Stephen!

I thought that Jill she groaned in travail bad;
At the first cockcrow she had borne a lad
To increase our flock. Guess whether I am glad!
That's more wool on my distaff than I had!
Woe's him who has no bread
For young ones to be fed.
The Devil crack each head!
I must go home to Jill; she's in my thought.
Just look into my sleeve that I steal nought.
I wouldn't grieve you or take from you aught.
Third Shepherd.   Go on, bad luck to you!

[*Exit* MAK.]

I think we ought
To count our sheep this morn.
First Shepherd.   I'll see if any's gone.
Third Shepherd.   We'll meet at the Crooked Thorn.

[*Exeunt* SHEPHERDS.]

Scene IV

[*Interior of* MAK's *cottage.* JILL *at work.*]

Mak [*outside*]:   Undo this door! How long shall I stand here?
Jill.   Go walk in the waning moon! Who's shouting there?
Mak [*outside*]:   It's me, your husband, Mak. Hey, Jill, what cheer?
Jill.   Now we shall see the Devil hanged, that's clear.
I seem to hear a sound
As if a rope were round
His throat, and tightly bound.
Mak [*outside*]:   Just hear the fuss she makes for an excuse;
She doesn't do a stroke but to amuse.
Jill.   Who sits up late? Who comes and goes? Who brews?
Who bakes? Whose hand knits stockings, tell me, whose?

[*Opens the door.* MAK *enters.*]

It's a pity to behold,
Whether in hot or cold,
A womanless household!
But tell me how you left the herdsmen, Mak.
Mak.   The last word that they said when I turned back
Was that they'd count the sheep, the cursed pack!
They'll not be pleased to find a sheep they lack!
And so, however it goes,
They surely will suppose
From me the trouble rose.
You'll keep your promise?

Jill.   Why, of course, I will.
   I'll put him in the cradle, and with skill
   I'll swaddle him. Trust in a pinch to Jill!

[*She wraps sheep and puts it in cradle. Goes to bed.*]

   Come tuck me up. I'll lie here very still.
   It may be a narrow squeak.
Mak.   Yes, if too close they peek,
   Or if the sheep should speak!
Jill.   Hark, when they call, for they'll be here anon.
   Let everything be ready. Sing alone
   A lullaby, for I must lie and groan
   And cry out by the wall on Mary and John.
   You sing the lullaby,
   And never doubt that I
   Will pull wool over their eye.

Scene V

[*The moor. Enter three* SHEPHERDS.]

Third Shepherd.   Good morrow, Coll. What's wrong? Why not asleep?
First Shepherd.   Alas that I was born! For this we'll keep
   A villain's name. We've lost a good fat sheep!
Second Shepherd.   God save us! Who on us such wrong would heap?
First Shepherd.   Some rascal. With my dogs
   I've searched through Horbury Shrogs,
   Found one ewe of fifteen hogs.[1]
Third Shepherd.   Trust me, by Thomas, holy saint of Kent,
   'Twas Mak or Jill who on that theft was bent.
First Shepherd.   Peace, man, be quiet. I saw when he went.
   You slander him unjustly and should repent.
Second Shepherd.   Though I may never succeed,
   I'd say it though I bleed,
   'Twas he who did the deed.
Third Shepherd.   Then let's go thither at a running trot.
   I won't eat bread till at the truth I've got.
First Shepherd.   And I won't drink until I've solved the plot.
Second Shepherd.   Until I find him, I won't rest one jot.
   I make this vow aright:
   Till I have him in sight
   I will not sleep one night
   In the same spot.

                                                      [*Exeunt.*]

---

[1]   Young sheep.

Scene VI

[MAK's *cottage. Within* MAK *sings,* JILL *groans.* SHEPHERDS *approach the door.*]

Third Shepherd.   D'you hear them sing? Mak thinks that he can croon!
First Shepherd.   I never heard a voice so out of tune!
Second Shepherd.   Hey, Mak, open your door, and do it soon.
Mak.   Who is it shouts as if it were high noon?
Third Shepherd.   Good men, if it were day—
Mak [*opening door*]:   As much as ever you may,
   Speak very soft, I pray.
   Here is a woman sick and ill at ease;
   I'd rather die than she had more misease.
Jill.   Go to some other place, I beg you, please,
   Each footfall knocks my nose and makes me sneeze.
First Shepherd.   How are you, Mak, I say?
Mak.   And how are you today,
   And what brings you this way?
   You're wet all through; you've run so in the mire.
   If you'll sit down, I'll light you here a fire.
   I've got what's coming to me. I'm no liar;
   My dream's come true; a nurse I've got to hire.
   I've more babes than you knew.
   Surely the saying's true:
   "We must drink what we brew."
   Stay eat before you go; I see you sweat.
Second Shepherd.   Nothing will cheer us, neither drink nor meat.
Mak.   What ails you, sir?
Third Shepherd.   We've had a loss that's great;
   We found a sheep was stolen, when we met.
Mak.   Alas! Had I been there,
   Someone had paid full dear.
First Shepherd.   Marry, some think you were!
Second Shepherd.   Yes, Mak, just tell us who else could it be?
Third Shepherd.   'Twas either you or else your wife, say we.
Mak.   If you suspect us, either Jill or me,
   Come rip our house apart, and then you'll see
   That here within this spot
   No sheep or cow I've got;
   And Jill's not stirred a jot.
   As I am true and leal, to God I pray,
   This is the first meal that I've had today.
First Shepherd.   Upon my soul, Mak, have a care, I say;
   He's early learned to steal who can't say nay.

[SHEPHERDS *begin to search.*]

Jill.   Out, thieves, get out from here!
Mak.   When her great groans you hear,
   Your hearts should melt for fear.
Jill.   Out, thieves; don't touch my child! Get out the door!
Mak.   Knew you her pangs, your conscience would be sore.
   You're wrong, I warn you, thus to come before
   A woman in her pain. I say no more.
Jill.   O God, who art so mild,
   If you I e'er beguiled,
   Let me eat up this child!
Mak.   Peace, woman, for God's passion, speak more low!
   You spoil your brains and terrify me so.
Second Shepherd.   I think our sheep is slain. Think you not so?
Third Shepherd.   We search here all in vain. We may well go.
   There's nothing I can find,
   No bone or scrap or rind,
   But empty plates behind.
   Here's no tame cattle, and no wild there is
   That smells like our old ram, I'll swear to this.
Jill.   You're right; and of this child God give me bliss!
First Shepherd.   I think we've failed and that we've done amiss.
Second Shepherd.   Dame, is't a boy you have?
   Him may Our Lady save!
Mak.   A son a lord might crave.
   He grabs so when he wakes, it's a joy to see.
Third Shepherd.   Luck on his buttocks! Happy may they be!
   But who god-fathered him so hurriedly?
Mak [*hesitating*]:   Blest be their lips!
First Shepherd.   A lie it's going to be!
Mak.   Gibbon Waller was one,
   And Perkin's mother's son;
   John Horn supplied the fun.
Second Shepherd.   Mak, let us all be friends again, I say.
Mak [*haughtily*]:   It's little friendship you've shown me today.
   Goodbye, I'm glad to see you go away.
Third Shepherd.   Fair words, no warmth—that's just as plain as day.

[SHEPHERDS *turn to go out.*]

First Shepherd.   Gave you the child a thing?
Second Shepherd.   Not even one farthing!
Third Shepherd.   Wait here; fast back I'll fling.

[THIRD SHEPHERD *returns.* SECOND *and* FIRST SHEPHERDS *follow.*]

Third Shepherd.   To see your baby, Mak, I ask your leave.
Mak.   No. Only insults from you I receive.

Third Shepherd.   Well, it won't make that little daystar grieve
   If you let me give sixpence, I believe.

[*Approaches cradle.*]

Mak.   Go way; I say he sleeps.
Third Shepherd.   I think instead he peeps.
Mak.   When he wakes up, he weeps.
Third Shepherd.   Just let me kiss him once and lift the clout.
   What in the devil! What a monstrous snout!
First Shepherd.   He's birth-marked maybe. Let's not wait about!
   The ill-spun cloth in truth comes foully out.
   He looks like our own sheep!
Third Shepherd.   What, Gib! give me a peep.
First Shepherd.   Where Truth can't walk 'twill creep.
Second Shepherd.   That was a clever trick, a shabby fraud!
   The bare-faced swindle should be noised abroad.
Third Shepherd.   Yes, sirs, let's bind her fast and burn the bawd.
   If she should hang, everyone would applaud.
   Tucked in a cradle so,
   I never saw, I vow,
   A boy with horns till now!
Mak.   Peace, peace I ask! You'll give the child a scare.
   For I'm his father and that's his mother there.
First Shepherd.   What devil is he named for? Look, Mak's heir!
Second Shepherd.   Let be all that! I say, God give him care!
Jill.   A pretty child is he
   To sit on woman's knee,
   And make his father glee!
Third Shepherd.   I know him by his earmark, a good token.
Mak.   I tell you, sirs, his nose in truth was broken.
   He was bewitched; so has a wise clerk spoken.
First Shepherd.   Liar! you deserve to have your noddle broken!
Jill.   An elf took him away;
   I saw him changed for aye
   At stroke of twelve today.
Second Shepherd.   You two are fit to lie in the same bed!
Third Shepherd.   Since they maintain their theft, let's leave them dead.
Mak.   If I do wrong again, cut off my head!
   I'm at your will.
Third Shepherd.   Men, take my plan instead.
   We'll neither curse nor fight,
   But here in canvas tight
   We'll toss him good and right.

[SHEPHERDS *exeunt, carrying* MAK *in a blanket.*]

Scene VII

[*Moor. Enter* SHEPHERDS.]

First Shepherd.   Lord, I'm about to burst, I am so sore!
   Until I rest, in faith I can't do more.
Second Shepherd.   He's heavy as a sheep of seven score.
   And now I'll lay me down to snooze and snore.
Third Shepherd.   Let's lie down on this green.
First Shepherd.   These thieves are rascals mean!
Third Shepherd.   We'd best forget what's been.

[SHEPHERDS *lie down.*]

[*An* ANGEL *sings "Gloria in excelsis"; then let him say:*]

Angel.   Rise, herdsmen, rise, for now the Child is born
   Who frees mankind, for Adam's sin forlorn.
   To thwart the wicked fiend this night He's born.
   High God is made your friend. This very morn,
   To Bethlehem go ye;
   The new-born Deity
   In manger laid ye'll see.

[*The* ANGEL *withdraws.*]

First Shepherd.   That was as queer a voice as ever I heard;
   Wonder enough to make a man be scared.
Second Shepherd.   To speak of God's own Son of Heaven he dared,
   And all the wood I thought with lightning glared.
Third Shepherd.   He said the Baby lay
   In Bethlehem today.
First Shepherd.   That star points out the way.

[*Points to star.*]

   Let's seek Him there!
Second Shepherd.   Did you hear how he cracked it?
   Three breves, one long.
Third Shepherd.   Yes, and he surely smacked it.
   There was no crotchet wrong, and nothing lacked it.
First Shepherd.   I'd like us three to sing, just as he knacked it.
Second Shepherd.   Let's harken how you croon.
   Can you bark at the moon?
Third Shepherd.   Shut up and hark, you loon!

[SHEPHERDS *sing off tune.*]

Second Shepherd.   To Bethlehem he ordered us to go.
   I'm much afraid that we have been too slow.
Third Shepherd.   Be merry, fellow, and don't croak like a crow.
   This news means endless joy to men below.

First Shepherd. Though we are tired and wet,
  We'll hurry now and get
  Where Mother and Child are set.

[They start to walk.]

Second Shepherd. We find by ancient prophets—stop your din!—
  David, Isaiah, others of their kin,
  That God's own Son would someday light within
  A virgin's womb, to cleanse away our sin.
  Isaiah, don't forget,
  Foretold that one day yet
  "*Virgo concipiet.*"
Third Shepherd. Right merry should we be that now's the day
  The lovely Lord is come who rules for aye.
  I'd be the happiest man if I could say
  That I had knelt before that Child to pray.
  But still the angel said
  The Babe was poorly arrayed
  And in a manger laid!
First Shepherd. Prophets and patriarchs of old were torn
  With yearning to behold this Child now born.
  Without that sight they never ceased to mourn.
  But we shall see Him, now this very morn.
  When I see Him, I'll know
  The prophets' words were so.
  No liars were they, no!
  To men as poor as we He will appear.
  We'll find Him first, His messenger said clear.
Second Shepherd. Then let us hurry, for the place is near.
Third Shepherd. Ready am I and glad; let's go with cheer.
  Lord, if Thy will it be,
  Allow poor yokels three
  This happy sight to see.

Scene VIII

[*Bethlehem, a stable. The* VIRGIN *seated, the* CHILD *on her knee. The* SHEPHERDS *enter and kneel.*]

First Shepherd. Hail, pure and sweet one; hail, thou holy Child!
  Maker of all, born of a Maiden mild.
  Thou hast o'ercome the Devil, fierce and wild.
  That wily Trickster now has been beguiled.
  Look, how He laughs, sweet thing!
  As my poor offering
  A cherry bunch I bring.
Second Shepherd. Hail, Savior King, our ransom Thou hast bought!
  Hail, mighty Babe, Thou madest all of naught.

Hail, God of mercy, Thou the Fiend has fought.
I kneel and bow before Thee. Look, I've brought
A bird, my tiny one!
Other faith we have none,
Our day-star and God's Son.
Third Shepherd.   Hail, pretty darling, Thou art God indeed.
I pray to Thee, be near when I have need.
Sweet is Thy look, although my heart does bleed
To see Thee here, and dressed in such poor weed.
Hail, Babe, on Thee I call.
I bring a tennis ball.
Take it and play withal.
Mary.   The Lord of Heaven, God omnipotent,
Who made all things aright, His Son has sent.
My name He named and blessed me ere He went.
Him I conceived through grace, as God had meant.
And now I pray Him so
To keep you from all woe!
Tell this where'er you go.
First Shepherd.   Farewell, Lady, thou fairest to behold,
With Christ-child on thy knee!
Second Shepherd.   He lies full cold,
But well it is for me that Him you hold.
Third Shepherd.   Already this does seem a thing oft told.
First Shepherd.   Let's spread the tidings round!
Second Shepherd.   Come; our salvation's found!
Third Shepherd.   To sing it we are bound!

[*Exeunt* SHEPHERDS *singing.*]
Here ends the Pageant of the SHEPHERDS.

Webster: THE DUCHESS OF MALFI

As Europe grew more settled and mercantile, and towns became more important, people (and players) gathered in greater numbers in centers of activity like innyards, where merchants could meet customers, where travelers would stop to eat and spend the night, where arriving goods were unloaded for transfer to other wagons or for sale on the spot, and where the availability of beer would assure a steady patronage. Wherever such a group of people was gathered together, an incipient audience could be found. The innyard bore little resemblance to a Greek theatre: it was small, crowded, busy with its own activities. The players who chose to play in the innyards—and this is perhaps a logical outgrowth of playing from a wagon—sought to meet these difficulties with plays that were rapid, various, and exciting. They were successful, and managed to manipulate their surroundings so well that when the first public playhouses were built in England they resembled in many ways the yard of an English inn, with a cleared space in the center open to the sky, and rows of galleries, like balconies, surrounding the cleared space in ascending tiers. The players stood in or near the center of this area, on a raised scaffold, addressing spectators on all sides. An Elizabethan spectator, looking beyond the acting area, would see not streets or mountains like his Athenian predecessor but other spectators watching the play or looking back at him. The theatre was fully enclosed and focused in on itself. This concentration was mirrored in the plays themselves, which were unashamedly theatrical. The sense of moral preoccupation, so evident in Greek tragedy, is lacking in much Elizabethan drama, replaced perhaps by the vigor and excitement of worldly affairs. And worldly affairs, to the majority of Elizabethan spectators, meant Italy.

Italy and the Italian way of life were popular topics in Elizabethan England. Florence, Venice, and Milan seemed to exercise a strong fascination on the mind of the ordinary Londoner, who was intrigued by the strange mixture of beauty and wickedness, learning and depravity, culture and diabolism, which he imagined to exist there. In London, Italian fashions were deplored yet sought out, Italian customs imitated even while scorned. The Elizabethan reading public was fond of Italian stories, and some Elizabethan writers capitalized on the demand. One such was William Painter, who wrote English versions of a number of short tales he had found in Italian books and published them as a collection under the title of *The Palace of Pleasure*. Some of the tales in this collection are pure fancy, others are based loosely on historical events, but almost all are Italianate in substance. Painter was not concerned with perceptive commentary on the world about him, but merely with the telling of stories, and consequently his tales are chiefly concerned with what happened, not why or how. Character, sentiment, and atmosphere exist only for the sake of the event.

One of his historical stories, which seems to have been originally chronicled by Bandello, is about a certain Duchess of Amalfi of the royal house of Aragon, who was widowed at the age of twenty and who subsequently contracted a secret marriage with her major-domo, one Antonio Bologna. As Painter told the story, their marriage remained unsuspected for some time, though their liaisons were recognized; but after the birth of their second child the scandal of the Duchess' behavior grew so great that Antonio was forced to flee to Ancona to avoid the understandable wrath of her brothers. The Duchess soon followed him, publicly proclaiming their marriage and renouncing her rank. After the birth of a third child her brothers managed to have the pair expelled from Ancona, and later from Siena as well. While fleeing to Venice they were beset by armed men; Antonio and the oldest child escaped, but the Duchess was taken to one of her own castles. Here the men were revealed as agents of her brothers, and she, her children, and her waiting maid were secretly murdered. The following year Antonio, ignorant of his wife's death and still hoping to appease the brothers, was stabbed to death in Milan by a hired assassin named Bozolo. The murderer escaped, and the dishonor brought upon the family name by the Duchess' incontinent behavior was at last expunged.

Told thus in summary, the story seems a bare recital of events, and hardly a character study of anyone, especially of the hired assassin. But of such scant beginnings most Elizabethan dramas were made.

Painter's *Palace of Pleasure* was published early in Queen Elizabeth's reign, when William Shakespeare was still a baby. Shakespeare's fellow playwright John Webster was not born until some fifteen years later, and the book had been in circulation for nearly half a century by the time Webster decided to dramatize this particular tale. "Italy" had by this time become a standard literary and dramatic convention—not the real Italy, but the fantasy-Italy that existed in the Londoner's mind, an Italy of lust and vice, of corrupt priests, of poisonings, stabbings—in short, of the Machiavel. Many of Shakespeare's plays were set in this hypothetical country, and the precedent was ready at hand and suitable for Webster's purpose.

Webster sold *The Duchess of Malfi* to the most prominent acting company of the day, the King's Men, and they seem to have first presented it to the public at their theatre, the Globe, in 1614. Richard Burbage, the most accomplished actor of the troupe, and the actor for whom Shakespeare had written his most famous roles, played the part of Duke Ferdinand; and John Lowin, who was the "heavy" in many of Shakespeare's plays (he may have played Iago to Burbage's Othello), was Bosola.

THE DUCHESS OF MALFI

The Characters

Ferdinand, Duke of Calabria
The Cardinal, his Brother
Antonio Bologna, Steward of the household to the Duchess
Delio, his Friend
Daniel de Bosola, Gentleman of the horse to the Duchess
Castruchio
Marquis of Pescara
Count Malateste
Silvio, a Lord, of Milan ⎰ Gentlemen attending on the
Roderigo ⎱　　　　　　Duchess
Grisolan
Doctor
Several Madmen, Pilgrims, Executioners, Officers, Attendants, &c.

Duchess of Malfi, sister of Ferdinand and the Cardinal
Cariola, her Woman
Julia, Castruchio's Wife, and the Cardinal's Mistress
Old Lady, Ladies and Children

SCENE: *Amalfi, Rome, and Milan*

Act The First

[*Amalfi. The Presence-chamber in the Duchess's Palace.*]

[*Enter* ANTONIO *and* DELIO]

Delio. You are welcome to your country, dear Antonio;
　　You have been long in France, and you return
　　A very formal Frenchman in your habit:
　　How do you like the French court?
Antonio.　　　　　　　　　I admire it:
　　In seeking to reduce both state and people
　　To a fix'd order, their judicious king
　　Begins at home; quits first his royal palace
　　Of flattering sycophants, of dissolute
　　And infamous persons,—which he sweetly terms
　　His master's masterpiece, the work of Heaven;
　　Considering duly that a prince's court
　　Is like a common fountain, whence should flow
　　Pure silver drops in general, but if't chance

51

Some curs'd example poison't near the head,
Death and diseases through the whole land spread.
And what is't makes this blessed government
But a most provident council, who dare freely
Inform him the corruption of the times?
Though some o' th' court hold it presumption
To instruct princes what they ought to do,
It is a noble duty to inform them
What they ought to foresee.—Here comes Bosola,
The only court-gall; yet I observe his railing
Is not for simple love of piety:
Indeed, he rails at those things which he wants;
Would be as lecherous, covetous, or proud,
Bloody, or envious, as any man,
If he had means to be so.—Here's the Cardinal.

[*Enter the* CARDINAL *and* BOSOLA]

Bosola. I do haunt you still.
Cardinal. So.
Bosola. I have done you better service than to be slighted thus. Miserable age,
where only the reward of doing well is the doing of it!
Cardinal. You enforce your merit too much.
Bosola. I fell into the galleys in your service; where, for two years together, I
wore two towels instead of a shirt, with a knot on the shoulder, after the fashion
of a Roman mantle. Slighted thus? I will thrive some way: blackbirds fatten
best in hard weather; why not I in these dog-days?
Cardinal. Would you could become honest!
Bosola. With all your divinity, do but direct me the way to it. I have known
many travel far for it, and yet return as arrant knaves as they went forth, because
they carried themselves always along with them. [*Exit* CARDINAL] Are you gone?
Some fellows, they say, are possessed with the devil, but this great fellow were
able to possess the greatest devil, and make him worse.
Antonio. He hath denied thee some suit?
Bosola. He and his brother are like plum-trees that grow crooked over standing-
pools; they are rich and o'er-laden with fruit, but none but crows, pies, and
caterpillars feed on them. Could I be one of their flattering panders, I would
hang on their ears like a horseleech, till I were full, and then drop off. I pray,
leave me. Who would rely upon these miserable dependencies, in expectation
to be advanc'd tomorrow? what creature ever fed worse than hoping Tantalus?
nor ever died any man more fearfully than he that hop'd for a pardon. There are
rewards for hawks and dogs when they have done us service; but for a soldier
that hazards his limbs in a battle, nothing but a kind of geometry in his last
supportation.
Delio. Geometry?
Bosola. Aye, to hang in a fair pair of slings, take his latter swing in the world
upon an honourable pair of crutches, from hospital to hospital. Fare ye well,
sir: and yet do not you scorn us; for places in the court are but like beds in the
hospital, where this man's head lies at that man's foot, and so lower and lower.
                                                                              [*Exit*]

Delio. I knew this fellow seven years in the galleys
    For a notorious murder; and 'twas thought
    The Cardinal suborn'd it: he was releas'd
    By the French general, Gaston de Foix,
    When he recover'd Naples.
Antonio.   'Tis great pity
    He should be thus neglected: I have heard
    He's very valiant. This foul melancholy
    Will poison all his goodness; for, I'll tell you,
    If too immoderate sleep be truly said
    To be an inward rust unto the soul,
    It then doth follow want of action
    Breeds all black malcontents; and their close rearing,
    Like moths in cloth, do hurt for want of wearing.
Delio. The presence 'gins to fill: you promis'd me
    To make me the partaker of the natures
    Of some of your great courtiers.
Antonio.   The lord Cardinal's,
    And other strangers' that are now in court?
    I shall.—Here comes the great Calabrian duke.

[*Enter* FERDINAND, CASTRUCHIO, SILVIO, RODERIGO, GRISOLAN, *and Attendants*]

Ferdinand. Who took the ring oftenest?
Silvio. Antonio Bologna, my lord.
Ferdinand. Our sister duchess's great-master of her household? give him the
    jewel.—When shall we leave this sportive action, and fall to action indeed?
Castruchio. Methinks, my lord, you should not desire to go to war in person.
Ferdinand. Now for some gravity:—why, my lord?
Castruchio. It is fitting a soldier arise to be a prince, but not necessary a prince
    descend to be a captain.
Ferdinand. No?
Castruchio. No, my lord; he were far better do it by a deputy.
Ferdinand. Why should he not as well sleep or eat by a deputy? this might take
    idle, offensive, and base office from him, where as the other deprives him of
    honour.
Castruchio. Believe my experience, that realm is never long in quiet where the
    ruler is a soldier.
Ferdinand. Thou told'st me thy wife could not endure fighting.
Castruchio. True, my lord.
Ferdinand. And of a jest she broke of a captain she met full of wounds: I have
    forgot it.
Castruchio. She told him, my lord, he was a pitiful fellow, to lie, like the
    children of Ismael, all in tents.[1]
Ferdinand. Why, there's a wit were able to undo all the chirurgeons o' the city;
    for although gallants should quarrel, and had drawn their weapons, and were
    ready to go to it, yet her persuasions would make them put up.

---

1 A *tent* is a roll of lint or other bandage.

Castruchio.   That she would, my lord.

Ferdinand.   How do you like my Spanish gennet?

Roderigo.   He is all fire.

Ferdinand.   I am of Pliny's opinion, I think he was begot by the wind; he runs as if he were ballass'd with quick-silver.

Silvio.   True, my lord, he reels from the tilt often.

Roderigo and Grisolan.   Ha, ha, ha!

Ferdinand.   Why do you laugh? methinks you that are courtiers should be my touchwood, take fire when I give fire; that is, laugh but when I laugh, were the subject never so witty.

Castruchio.   True, my lord: I myself have heard a very good jest, and have scorn'd to seem to have so silly a wit as to understand it.

Ferdinand.   But I can laugh at your fool, my lord.

Castruchio.   He cannot speak, you know, but he makes faces: my lady cannot abide him.

Ferdinand.   No?

Castruchio.   Nor endure to be in merry company; for she says too much laughing, and too much company, fills her too full of the wrinkle.

Ferdinand.   I would, then, have a mathematical instrument made for her face, that she might not laugh out of compass.—I shall shortly visit you at Milan, Lord Silvio.

Silvio.   Your grace shall arrive most welcome.

Ferdinand.   You are a good horseman, Antonio: you have excellent riders in France: what do you think of good horsemanship?

Antonio.   Nobly, my lord: as out of the Grecian horse issued many famous princes, so out of brave horsemanship arise the first sparks of growing resolution, that raise the mind to noble action.

Ferdinand.   You have bespoke it worthily.

Silvio.   Your brother, the lord Cardinal, and sister duchess.

[*Re-enter* CARDINAL, *with* DUCHESS, CARIOLA, *and* JULIA]

Cardinal.   Are the galleys come about?

Grisolan.   They are, my lord.

Ferdinand.   Here's the Lord Silvio is come to take his leave.

Delio [*Aside to* ANTONIO]:   Now, sir, your promise; what's that Cardinal?
   I mean his temper? they say he's a brave fellow,
   Will play his five thousand crowns at tennis, dance,
   Court ladies, and one that hath fought single combats.

Antonio.   Some such flashes superficially hang on him for form; but observe his inward character: he is a melancholy churchman; the spring in his face is nothing but the engendering of toads; where he is jealous of any man, he lays worse plots for them than ever was impos'd on Hercules, for he strews in his way flatterers, panders, intelligencers, atheists, and a thousand such political monsters. He should have been Pope; but instead of coming to it by the primitive decency of the Church, he did bestow bribes so largely and so impudently as if he would have carried it away without Heaven's knowledge. Some good he hath done——

Delio. You have given too much of him. What's his brother?
Antonio. The duke there? a most perverse and turbulent nature:
    What appears in him mirth is merely outside;
    If he laughs heartily, it is to laugh
    All honesty out of fashion.
Delio.   Twins?
Antonio.   In quality.
    He speaks with others' tongues, and hears men's suits
    With others' ears; will seem to sleep o' th' bench
    Only to entrap offenders in their answers;
    Dooms men to death by information;
    Rewards by hearsay.
Delio.   Then the law to him
    Is like a foul black cobweb to a spider,—
    He makes of it his dwelling and a prison
    To entangle those shall feed him.
Antonio.   Most true:
    He never pays debts unless they be shrewd turns,
    And those he will confess that he doth owe.
    Last, for his brother there, the Cardinal,
    They that do flatter him most say oracles
    Hang at his lips; and verily I believe them,
    For the devil speaks in them.
    But for their sister, the right noble duchess,
    You never fixed your eye on three fair medals
    Cast in one figure, of so different temper.
    For her discourse, it is so full of rapture,
    You only will begin then to be sorry
    When she doth end her speech, and wish, in wonder,
    She held it less vain-glory to talk much,
    Than your penance to hear her: whilst she speaks,
    She throws upon a man so sweet a look,
    That it were able to raise one to a galliard[1]
    That lay in a dead palsy, and to dote
    On that sweet countenance; but in that look
    There speaketh so divine a continence
    As cuts off all lascivious and vain hope.
    Her days are practis'd in such noble virtue,
    That sure her nights, nay, more, her very sleeps,
    Are more in heaven than other ladies' shrifts.
    Let all sweet ladies break their flattering glasses,
    And dress themselves in her.
Delio.   Fie, Antonio,
    You play the wire-drawer[2] with her commendations.

---

[1]   A lively dance.
[2]   You spin out at great length.

Antonio.   I'll case the picture up: only thus much;
   All her particular worth grows to this sum,—
   She stains the time past, lights the time to come.
Cariola.   You must attend my lady in the gallery,
   Some half an hour hence.
Antonio.   I shall.

                              [*Exeunt* ANTONIO *and* DELIO]

Ferdinand.   Sister, I have a suit to you.
Duchess.   To me, sir?
Ferdinand.   A gentleman here, Daniel de Bosola,
   One that was in the galleys—
Duchess.   Yes, I know him.
Ferdinand.   A worthy fellow he is; pray, let me entreat for
   The provisorship of your horse.
Duchess.   Your knowledge of him
   Commends him and prefers him.
Ferdinand.   Call him hither.

                                   [*Exit* ATTENDANT]

   We are now upon parting. Good Lord Silvio,
   Do us commend to all our noble friends
   At the leaguer.
Silvio.   Sir, I shall.
Ferdinand.   You are for Milan?
Silvio.   I am.
Duchess.   Bring the caroches.[1] We'll bring you down
   To the haven.   [*Exeunt all but* FERDINAND *and*
                                              the CARDINAL]

Cardinal.   Be sure you entertain[2] that Bosola
   For your intelligence: I would not be seen in 't;
   And therefore many times I have slighted him
   When he did court our furtherance, as this morning.
Ferdinand.   Antonio, the great-master of her household,
   Had been far fitter.
Cardinal.   You are deceiv'd in him:
   His nature is too honest for such business.—
   He comes: I'll leave you.   [*Exit*]

   [*Re-enter* BOSOLA]

Bosola.   I was lur'd to you.
Ferdinand.   My brother, here, the Cardinal could never
   Abide you.
Bosola.   Never since he was in my debt.

¹ Coaches.
² Use.

Ferdinand.   Maybe some oblique character in your face
  Made him suspect you.
Bosola.   Doth he study physiognomy?
  There's no more credit to be given to th' face
  Than to a sick man's urine, which some call
  The physician's whore because she cozens him.
  He did suspect me wrongfully.
Ferdinand.   For that
  You must give great men leave to take their times.
  Distrust doth cause us seldom be deceiv'd:
  You see the oft shaking of the cedar-tree
  Fastens it more at root.
Bosola.   Yet, take heed;
  For to suspect a friend unworthily
  Instructs him the next way to suspect you,
  And prompts him to deceive you.
Ferdinand [*Giving him money*]:   There's gold.
Bosola.   So:
  What follows? never rained such showers as these
  Without thunderbolts i' th' tail of them: whose throat must I cut?
Ferdinand.   Your inclination to shed blood rides post
  Before my occasion to use you. I give you that
  To live i' th' court here, and observe the duchess;
  To note all the particulars of her haviour,
  What suitors do solicit her for marriage,
  And whom she best affects. She's a young widow:
  I would not have her marry again.
Bosola.   No, sir?
Ferdinand.   Do not you ask the reason; but be satisfied
  I say I would not.
Bosola.   It seems you would create me
  One of your familiars.
Ferdinand.   Familiar? what's that?
Bosola.   Why, a very quaint invisible devil in flesh,
  An intelligencer.
Ferdinand.   Such a kind of thriving thing
  I would wish thee; and ere long thou may'st arrive
  At a higher place by 't.
Bosola [*returning the money*]:   Take your devils,
  Which hell calls angels; these curs'd gifts would make
  You a corrupter, me an impudent traitor;
  And should I take these, they'd take me to hell.
Ferdinand.   Sir, I'll take nothing from you that I have given:
  There is a place that I procur'd for you
  This morning, the provisorship o' th' horse;
  Have you heard on 't?
Bosola.   No.
Ferdinand.   'Tis yours: is't not worth thanks?

Bosola.   I would have you curse yourself now, that your bounty,
 Which makes men truly noble, e'er should make me
 A villain. Oh, that to avoid ingratitude
 For the good deed you have done me, I must do
 All the ill man can invent! Thus the devil
 Candies all sins o'er; and what heaven terms vile,
 That names he complimental.
Ferdinand.   Be yourself;
 Keep your old garb of melancholy; 'twill express
 You envy those that stand above your reach,
 Yet strive not to come near 'em: this will gain
 Access to private lodgings, where yourself
 May, like a politic dormouse—
Bosola.   As I have seen some
 Feed in a lord's dish, half asleep, not seeming
 To listen to any talk; and yet these rogues
 Have cut his throat in a dream. What's my place?
 The provisorship o' th' horse? say, then, my corruption
 Grew out of horse-dung: I am your creature.
Ferdinand.   Away!
Bosola.   Let good men, for good deeds, covet good fame,
 Since place and riches oft are bribes of shame:
 Sometimes the devil doth preach.   [*Exit*]

[*Enter* DUCHESS, CARDINAL, *and* CARIOLA]

Cardinal.   We are to part from you; and your own discretion
 Must now be your director.
Ferdinand.   You are a widow:
 You know already what man is; and therefore
 Let not youth, high promotion, eloquence—
Cardinal.   No,
 Nor any thing without the addition, honour,
 Sway your high blood.
Ferdinand.   Marry! they are most luxurious[1]
 Will wed twice.
Cardinal.   Oh, fie!
Ferdinand.   Their livers are more spotted
 Than Laban's sheep.
Duchess.   Diamonds are of most value,
 They say, that have passed through most jewellers' hands.
Ferdinand.   Whores by that rule are precious.
Duchess.   Will you hear me?
 I'll never marry.
Cardinal.   So most widows say;
 But commonly that motion lasts no longer

---

[1]   Lascivious.

Than the turning of an hour-glass: the funeral sermon
And it end both together.
Ferdinand.   Now hear me:
  You live in a rank pasture, here, i' th' court;
  There is a kind of honey-dew that's deadly;
  'Twill poison your fame; look to't: be not cunning;
  For they whose faces do belie their hearts
  Are witches ere they arrive at twenty years,
  Aye, and give the devil suck.
Duchess.   This is terrible good counsel.
Ferdinand. Hypocrisy is woven of a fine small thread,
  Subtler than Vulcan's engine:[1] yet, believe't,
  Your darkest actions, nay, your privat'st thoughts,
  Will come to light.
Cardinal.   You may flatter yourself,
  And take your own choice; privately be married
  Under the eaves of night—
Ferdinand.   Think'st the best voyage
  That e'er you made; like the irregular crab,
  Which, though't goes backward, thinks that it goes right
  Because it goes its own way; but observe,
  Such weddings may more properly be said
  To be executed than celebrated.
Cardinal.   The marriage night
  Is the entrance into some prison.
Ferdinand.   And those joys,
  Those lustful pleasures, are like heavy sleeps
  Which do forerun man's mischief.
Cardinal.   Fare you well.
  Wisdom begins at the end: remember it.   *[Exit.]*
Duchess. I think this speech between you both was studied,
  It came so roundly off.
Ferdinand.   You are my sister;
  This was my father's poniard, do you see?
  I'd be loth to see 't look rusty, 'cause 'twas his.
  I would have you to give o'er these chargeable revels:
  A visor and a mask are whispering-rooms
  That were never built for goodness;—fare ye well;—
  And women like that part which, like the lamprey,
  Hath never a bone in 't.
Duchess.   Fie, sir!
Ferdinand.   Nay,
  I mean the tongue; variety of courtship:
  What cannot a neat knave with a smooth tale
  Make a woman believe? Farewell, lusty widow.   *[Exit]*

---

[1] The net in which he caught Mars and Venus. ·

Duchess.   Shall this move me? If all my royal kindred
  Lay in my way unto this marriage,
  I'd make them my low footsteps: and even now,
  Even in this hate, as men in some great battles,
  By apprehending danger, have achiev'd
  Almost impossible actions (I have heard soldiers say so),
  So I through frights and threatenings will assay
  This dangerous venture. Let old wives report
  I wink'd and chose a husband.—Cariola,
  To thy known secrecy I have given up
  More than my life—my fame.
Cariola.   Both shall be safe;
  For I'll conceal this secret from the world
  As warily as those that trade in poison
  Keep poison from their children.
Duchess.   Thy protestation
  Is ingenuous and hearty: I believe it.
  Is Antonio come?
Cariola.   He attends you.
Duchess.   Good dear soul,
  Leave me; but place thyself behind the arras,
  Where thou mayst overhear us. Wish me good speed;
  For I am going into a wilderness
  Where I shall find nor path nor friendly clue
  To be my guide.   [CARIOLA *goes behind the arras.*]

[*Enter* ANTONIO.]

                         I sent for you: sit down;
  Take pen and ink, and write: are you ready?
Antonio.   Yes.
Duchess.   What did I say?
Antonio.   That I should write somewhat.
Duchess.   Oh, I remember.
  After these triumphs and this large expense,
  It's fit, like thrifty husbands, we inquire
  What's laid up for to-morrow.
Antonio.   So please your beauteous excellence.
Duchess.   Beauteous?
  Indeed, I thank you: I look young for your sake;
  You have ta'en my cares upon you.
Antonio.   I'll fetch your grace
  The particulars of your revenue and expense.
Duchess.   Oh, you are an upright treasurer: but you mistook;
  For when I said I meant to make inquiry
  What's laid up for to-morrow, I did mean
  What's laid up yonder for me.
Antonio.   Where?

Duchess.   In heaven.
  I am making my will (as 'tis fit princes should,
  In perfect memory), and, I pray, sir, tell me,
  Were not one better make it smiling, thus,
  Than in deep groans and terrible ghastly looks,
  As if the gifts we parted with procur'd
  That violent distraction?
Antonio.   Oh, much better.
Duchess.   If I had a husband now, this care were quit:
  But I intend to make you overseer.
  What good deed shall we first remember? say.
Antonio.   Begin with that first good deed began i' th' world
  After man's creation, the sacrament of marriage:
  I'd have you first provide for a good husband;
  Give him all.
Duchess.   All?
Antonio.   Yes, your excellent self.
Duchess.   In a winding-sheet?
Antonio.   In a couple.
Duchess.   Saint Winfred,
  That were a strange will!
Antonio.   'Twere stranger if there were no will in you
  To marry again.
Duchess.   What do you think of marriage?
Antonio.   I take't, as those that deny purgatory;
  It locally contains or Heaven or hell;
  There's no third place in 't.
Duchess.   How do you affect it?
Antonio.   My banishment, feeling my melancholy,
  Would often reason thus.
Duchess.   Pray, let's hear it.
Antonio.   Say a man never marry, nor have children,
  What takes that from him? only the bare name
  Of being a father, or the weak delight
  To see the little wanton ride a-cock-horse
  Upon a painted stick, or hear him chatter
  Like a taught starling.
Duchess.   Fie, fie, what's all this?
  One of your eyes is blood-shot; use my ring to 't,
  They say 'tis very sovereign: 'twas my wedding-ring,
  And I did vow never to part with it
  But to my second husband.
Antonio.   You have parted with it now.
Duchess.   Yes, to help your eyesight.
Antonio.   You have made me stark blind.
Duchess.   How?
Antonio.   There is a saucy and ambitious devil
  Is dancing in this circle.

Duchess.   Remove him.
Antonio.   How?
Duchess.   There needs small conjuration, when your finger
    May do it: thus; is it fit?

[*She puts the ring upon his finger: he kneels*]

Antonio.   What said you?
Duchess.   Sir,
    This goodly roof of yours is too low built;
    I cannot stand upright in 't nor discourse,
    Without I raise it higher: raise yourself;
    Or, if you please, my hand to help you: so.

[*Raises him*]

Antonio.   Ambition, madam, is a great man's madness,
    That is not kept in chains and close-pent rooms,
    But in fair lightsome lodgings, and is girt
    With the wild noise of prattling visitants,
    Which makes it lunatic beyond all cure.
    Conceive not I am so stupid but I aim[1]
    Whereto your favours tend: but he's a fool
    That, being a-cold, would thrust his hands i' th' fire
    To warm them.
Duchess.   So, now the ground's broke,
    You may discover what a wealthy mine
    I make you lord of.
Antonio.   O my unworthiness!
Duchess.   You were ill to sell yourself:
    This darkening of your worth is not like that
    Which tradesmen use i' th' city, their false lights
    Are to rid bad wares off: and I must tell you,
    If you will know where breathes a complete man
    (I speak it without flattery), turn your eyes,
    And progress through yourself.
Antonio.   Were there nor heaven
    Nor hell, I should be honest: I have long serv'd virtue,
    And ne'er ta'en wages of her.
Duchess.   Now she pays it.
    The misery of us that are born great!
    We are forc'd to woo, because none dare woo us;
    And as a tyrant doubles with his words,
    And fearfully equivocates, so we
    Are forc'd to express our violent passions
    In riddles and in dreams, and leave the path
    Of simple virtue, which was never made

---

1   Guess.

To seem the thing it is not. Go, go brag
You have left me heartless; mine is in your bosom:
I hope 'twill multiply love there. You do tremble:
Make not your heart so dead a piece of flesh,
To fear more than to love me. Sir, be confident:
What is 't distracts you? This is flesh and blood, sir;
'Tis not the figure cut in alabaster
Kneels at my husband's tomb. Awake, awake, man!
I do here put off all vain ceremony,
And only do appear to you a young widow
That claims you for her husband, and, like a widow,
I use but half a blush in 't.
Antonio.   Truth speak for me:
I will remain the constant sanctuary
Of your good name.
Duchess.   I thank you, gentle love:
And 'cause you shall not come to me in debt,
Being now my steward, here upon your lips
I sign your Quietus est.[1] This you should have begg'd now:
I have seen children oft eat sweetmeats thus,
As fearful to devour them too soon.
Antonio.   But for your brothers?
Duchess.   Do not think of them:
All discord without this circumference
Is only to be pitied, and not fear'd:
Yet, should they know it, time will easily
Scatter the tempest.
Antonio.   These words should be mine,
And all the parts you have spoke, if some part of it
Would not have savour'd flattery.
Duchess.   Kneel.

[CARIOLA *comes from behind the arras.*]

Antonio.   Ha!
Duchess.   Be not amazed; this woman's of my counsel:
I have heard lawyers say, a contract in a chamber
Per verba presenti is absolute marriage.

[*She and* ANTONIO *kneel.*]

Bless, heaven, this sacred gordian, which let violence
Never untwine!
Antonio.   And may our sweet affections, like the spheres,
Be still in motion!
Duchess.   Quickening, and make
The like soft music!

---

[1]   Acquittance.

Antonio.   That we may imitate the loving palms,
   Best emblem of a peaceful marriage, that ne'er
   Bore fruit, divided!
Duchess.   What can the Church force more?
Antonio.   That fortune may not know an accident,
   Either of joy or sorrow, to divide
   Our fixèd wishes!
Duchess.   How can the Church build faster?
   We now are man and wife, and 'tis the Church
   That must but echo this.—Maid, stand apart:
   I now am blind.
Antonio.   What's your conceit in this?
Duchess.   I would have you lead your fortune by the hand
   Unto your marriage bed:
   (You speak in me this, for we now are one:)
   We'll only lie, and talk together, and plot
   To appease my humorous[1] kindred; and if you please,
   Like the old tale in 'Alexander and Lodowick,'
   Lay a naked sword between us, keep us chaste.
   Oh, let me shroud my blushes in your bosom,
   Since 'tis the treasury of all my secrets!

                                [*Exeunt* DUCHESS *and* ANTONIO.]

Cariola.   Whether the spirit of greatness or of woman
   Reign most in her, I know not; but it shows
   A fearful madness: I owe her much of pity.   [*Exit.*]

Act The Second

[*A Room in the Palace of the Duchess*]

[*Enter* BOSOLA *and* CASTRUCHIO.]

Bosola.   You say you would fain be taken for an eminent courtier?
Castruchio.   'Tis the very main of my ambition.
Bosola.   Let me see: you have a reasonable good face for 't already, and your night-cap expresses your ears sufficient largely. I would have you learn to twirl the strings of your band with a good grace, and in a set speech, at th' end of every sentence, to hum three or four times, or blow your nose till it smart again, to recover your memory. When you come to be a president in criminal causes, if you smile upon a prisoner, hang him, but if you frown upon him and threaten him, let him be sure to scape the gallows.
Castruchio.   I would be a very merry president.
Bosola.   Do not sup o' night; 'twill beget you an admirable wit.

---

[1]   *I.e.*, ill-humored.

Castruchio.   Rather it would make me have a good stomach to quarrel; for they say, your roaring boys eat meat seldom, and that makes them so valiant. But how shall I know whether the people take me for an eminent fellow?

Bosola.   I will teach a trick to know it: give out you lie a-dying, and if you hear the common people curse you, be sure you are taken for one of the prime nightcaps.[1]

[*Enter an* OLD LADY.]

You come from painting[2] now.

Old Lady.   From what?

Bosola.   Why, from your scurvy face-physic. To behold thee not painted inclines somewhat near a miracle; these in thy face here were deep ruts and foul sloughs the last progress.[3] There was a lady in France that, having had the small-pox, flayed the skin off her face to make it more level; and whereas before she look'd like a nutmeg-grater, after she resembled an abortive hedgehog.

Old Lady.   Do you call this painting?

Bosola.   No, no, but you call it careening of an old morphewed[4] lady, to make her disembogue[5] again: there's rough-cast phrase to your plastic.[6]

Old Lady.   It seems you are well acquainted with my closet.

Bosola.   One would suspect it for a shop of witchcraft, to find in it the fat of serpents, spawn of snakes, Jews' spittle, and their young children's ordure; and all these for the face. I would sooner eat a dead pigeon taken from the soles of the feet of one sick of the plague than kiss one of you fasting. Here are two of you, whose sin of your youth is the very patrimony of the physician; makes him[7] renew his foot-cloth with the spring, and change his high-priced courtezan with the fall of the leaf. I do wonder you do not loathe yourselves. Observe my meditation now.

What thing is in this outward form of man
To be belov'd? We account it ominous,
If nature do produce a colt, or lamb,
A fawn, or goat, in any limb resembling
A man, and fly from 't as a prodigy:
Man stands amaz'd to see his deformity
In any other creature but himself.
But in our own flesh, though we bear diseases
Which have their true names only ta'en from beasts,
As the most ulcerous wolf and swinish measle,
Though we are eaten up of lice and worms,
And though continually we bear about us
A rotten and dead body, we delight

---

1   One of the worst of the town rowdies or rioters.
2   Making up her face.
3   At the last royal procession, *i.e.*, the last social season.
4   Leprous.
5   Discharge her bowels.
6   Plain hard language to match your finer talk; with a pun on "plastic" as a cosmetic item.
7   Enables him to.

To hide it in rich tissue: all our fear,
Nay, all our terror, is lest our physician
Should put us in the ground to be made sweet—
Your wife's gone to Rome: you two couple, and get you
To the wells at Lucca to recover your aches.
I have other work on foot.

[*Exeunt* CASTRUCHIO *and* OLD LADY.]
                              I observe our duchess
Is sick a-days, she pukes, her stomach seethes,
The fins of her eye-lids look most teeming blue,
She wanes i' th' cheek, and waxes fat i' th' flank,
And, contrary to our Italian fashion,
Wears a loose-bodied gown: there's somewhat in 't.
I have a trick may chance discover it,
A pretty one; I have brought some apricocks,
The first our spring yields.

[*Enter* ANTONIO *and* DELIO, *talking together apart.*]

Delio.   And so long since married?
   You amaze me.
Antonio.   Let me seal your lips for ever:
   For, did I think that anything but th' air
   Could carry these words from you, I should wish
   You had no breath at all.—[*He sees* BOSOLA *musing*] Now, sir, in your contem-
      plation?
   You are studying to become a great wise fellow?
Bosola.   Oh, sir, the opinion of wisdom is a foul tetter[1] that runs all over a man's
   body: if simplicity direct us to have no evil, it directs us to a happy being; for
   the subtlest folly proceeds from the subtlest wisdom: let me be simply honest.
Antonio.   I do understand your inside.
Bosola.   Do you so?
Antonio.   Because you would not seem to appear to th' world
   Puff'd up with your preferment, you continue
   This out-of-fashion melancholy: leave it, leave it.
Bosola.   Give me leave to be honest in any phrase, in any compliment whatsoever.
   Shall I confess myself to you? I look no higher than I can reach: they are the
   gods that must ride on winged horses. A lawyer's mule of a slow pace will both
   suit my disposition and business; for, mark me, when a man's mind rides faster
   than his horse can gallop, they quickly both tire.
Antonio.   You would look up to heaven, but I think
   The devil, that rules i' th' air, stands in your light.
Bosola.   Oh, sir, you are lord of the ascendant, chief man with the duchess; a
   duke was your cousin-german remov'd. Say you were lineally descended from
   King Pepin, or he himself, what of this? search the heads of the greatest rivers
   in the world, you shall find them but bubbles of water. Some would think the

---

1   Skin disease.

souls of princes were brought forth by some more weighty cause than those of meaner persons: they are deceiv'd there's the same hand to them; the like passions sway them; the same reason that makes a vicar go to law for a tithe-pig, and undo his neighbours, makes them spoil a whole province, and batter down goodly cities with the cannon.

[*Enter* DUCHESS *and Ladies.*]

Duchess.   Your arm, Antonio: do I not grow fat?
I am exceeding short-winded.—Bosola,
I would have you, sir, provide for me a litter;
Such a one as the Duchess of Florence rode in.
Bosola.   The duchess used one when she was great with child.
Duchess.   I think she did.—[*To one of her ladies*] Come hither, mend my ruff;
Here, when?[1]
Thou art such a tedious lady; and thy breath smells
Of lemon-peels; would thou hadst done! Shall I swoon
Under thy fingers! I am so troubled
With the mother![2]
Bosola [*Aside*]:   I fear too much.
Duchess.   I have heard you say
That the French courtiers wear their hats on 'fore
The king.
Antonio.   I have seen it.
Duchess.   In the presence?
Antonio.   Yes.
Duchess.   Why should not we bring up that fashion? 'Tis
Ceremony more than duty that consists
In the removing of a piece of felt:
Be you the example to the rest o' th' court;
Put on your hat first.
Antonio.   You must pardon me:
I have seen, in colder countries than in France,
Nobles stand bare to th' prince; and the distinction
Methought show'd reverently.
Bosola.   I have a present for your grace.
Duchess.   For me, sir?
Bosola.   Apricocks, madam.
Duchess.   O, sir, where are they?
I have heard of none to-year.
Bosola [*Aside*]:   Good; her colour rises.
Duchess.   Indeed, I thank you: they are wondrous fair ones.
What an unskilful fellow is our gardener!
We shall have none this month.

---

[1]   A common exclamation of impatience.

[2]   A common Elizabethan term for hysteria: here, an unconscious *double entendre* which Bosola observes in his next line.

Bosola.   Will not your grace pare them?
Duchess.   No: they taste of musk, methinks; indeed they do.
Bosola.   I know not: yet I wish your grace had pared 'em.
Duchess.   Why?
Bosola.   I forgot to tell you, the knave gardener,
    Only to raise his profit by them the sooner,
    Did ripen them in horse-dung.
Duchess.   O, you jest.—
    You shall judge: pray taste one.
Antonio.   Indeed, madam,
    I do not love the fruit.
Duchess.   Sir, you are loath
    To rob us of our dainties: 'tis a delicate fruit;
    They say they are restorative.
Bosola.   'Tis a pretty art,
    This grafting.
Duchess.   'Tis so; a bettering of nature.
Bosola.   To make a pippin grow upon a crab,
    A damson on a blackthorn.—[*Aside*] How greedily she eats them!
    A whirlwind strike off these bawd farthingales!
    For, but for that and the loose-bodied gown,
    I should have discovered apparently
    The young springal[1] cutting a caper in her belly.
Duchess.   I thank you, Bosola: they were right good ones,
    If they do not make me sick.
Antonio.   How now, madam?
Duchess.   This green fruit and my stomach are not friends:
    How they swell me!
Bosola [*Aside*]:   Nay, you are too much swelled already.
Duchess.   Oh, I am in an extreme cold sweat!
Bosola.   I am very sorry.
Duchess.   Lights to my chamber!—O good Antonio,
    I fear I am undone!
Delio.   Lights there, lights!

                        [*Exeunt* DUCHESS *and Ladies.*]

Antonio.   O my most trusty Delio, we are lost!
    I fear she's fall'n in labour; and there's left
    No time for her remove.
Delio.   Have you prepar'd
    Those ladies to attend her? and procur'd
    That politic safe conveyance for the midwife
    Your duchess plotted?
Antonio.   I have.
Delio.   Make use, then, of this forc'd occasion:
    Give out that Bosola hath poison'd her

---

[1] Stripling.

With these apricocks; that will give some colour
For her keeping close.
Antonio.   Fie, fie, the physicians
Will then flock to her.
Delio.   For that you may pretend
She'll use some prepar'd antidote of her own,
Lest the physicians should re-poison her.
Antonio.   I am lost in amazement: I know not what to think on 't.   [*Exeunt*][1]
Bosola.   So, so, there's no question but her tetchiness and most vulturous eating
of the apricocks are apparent signs of breeding.

[*Enter an* OLD LADY; BOSOLA *blocks her path.*]

Now?
Old Lady.   I am in haste, sir.
Bosola.   There was a young waiting-woman had a monstrous desire to see the
glass-house——
Old Lady.   Nay, pray let me go.
Bosola.   And it was only to know what strange instrument it was should swell up
a glass to the fashion of a woman's belly.
Old Lady.   I will hear no more of the glass-house. You are still abusing women?
Bosola.   Who, I? no; only, by the way now and then, mention your frailties. The
orange-tree bears ripe and green fruit and blossoms all together; and some of you
give entertainment for pure love, but more for more precious reward. The lusty
spring smells well; but drooping autumn tastes well. If we have the same golden
showers that rained in the time of Jupiter the thunderer, you have the same
Danaës still, to hold up their laps to receive them. Didst thou never study the
mathematics?
Old Lady.   What's that, sir?
Bosola.   Why, to know the trick how to make a many lines meet in one centre.
Go, go, give your foster-daughters good counsel: tell them, that the devil takes
delight to hang at a woman's girdle, like a false rusty watch, that she cannot
discern how the time passes.   [*Exit* OLD LADY.]

[*Enter* ANTONIO, DELIO, RODERIGO, *and* GRISOLAN.]

Antonio.   Shut up the court-gates.
Roderigo.   Why, sir? what's the danger?
Antonio.   Shut up the posterns presently, and call
All the officers o' th' court.
Grisolan.   I shall instantly.   [*Exit.*]
Antonio.   Who keeps the key o' th' park gate?
Roderigo.   Forobosco.[2]
Antonio.   Let him bring 't presently.

[*Re-enter* GRISOLAN *with* SERVANTS.]

---

[1]   In the old editions, Scene 2 begins here. The action is, however, continuous.

[2]   This character is included in the *dramatis personæ* of the first edition (1623), and
assigned to the actor Nicholas Tooley, a regular member of the company that produced
the play. He speaks no lines, but presumably had some stage business that is lost to us.

First Servant.   O, gentlemen o' the court, the foulest treason!
Bosola [*Aside*]:   If that these apricocks should be poison'd now,
   Without my knowledge!
First Servant.   There was taken even now
   A Switzer in the duchess' bed chamber—
Second Servant.   A Switzer?
First Servant.   With a pistol in his great cod-piece.
Bosola.   Ha, ha, ha!
First Servant.   The cod-piece was the case for 't.
Second Servant.   There was
   A cunning traitor: who would have search'd his cod-piece?
First Servant.   True, if he had kept out of the ladies' chambers:
   And all the moulds of his buttons were leaden bullets.
Second Servant.   O wicked cannibal!
   A fire-lock in 's cod-piece!
First Servant.   'Twas a French plot,
   Upon my life.
Second Servant.   To see what the devil can do!
Antonio.   Are all the officers here?
Servants.   We are.
Antonio.   Gentlemen,
   We have lost much plate you know; and but this evening
   Jewels, to the value of four thousand ducats,
   Are missing in the duchess' cabinet.
   Are the gates shut?
Servant.   Yes.
Antonio.   'Tis the duchess' pleasure
   Each officer be lock'd into his chamber
   Till the sun-rising; and to send the keys
   Of all their chests and of their outward doors
   Into her bed-chamber. She is very sick.
Roderigo.   At her pleasure.
Antonio.   She entreats you take 't not ill:
   The innocent shall be the more approv'd by it.
Bosola.   Gentleman o' th' wood-yard, where's your Switzer now?
First Servant.   By this hand, 'twas credibly reported by one o' th' black guard.

                  [*Exeunt all except* ANTONIO *and* DELIO.]

Delio.   How fares it with the duchess?
Antonio.   She's expos'd
   Unto the worst of torture, pain and fear.
Delio.   Speak to her all happy comfort.
Antonio.   How I do play the fool with mine own danger!
   You are this night, dear friend, to post to Rome:
   My life lies in your service.
Delio.   Do not doubt me.
Antonio.   Oh, 'tis far from me: and yet fear presents me
   Somewhat that looks like danger.

Delio.   Believe it,
    'Tis but the shadow of your fear, no more;
    How superstitiously we mind our evils!
    The throwing down salt, or crossing of a hare,
    Bleeding at nose, the stumbling of a horse,
    Or singing of a cricket, are of power
    To daunt whole man in us. Sir, fare you well:
    I wish you all the joys of a bless'd father:
    And, for my faith, lay this unto your breast,—
    Old friends, like old swords, still are trusted best.   [*Exit.*]

    [*Enter* CARIOLA.]

Cariola.   Sir, you are the happy father of a son:
    Your wife commends him to you.
Antonio.   Blessèd comfort!—
    For Heaven's sake tend her well: I'll presently[1]
    Go set a figure for 's nativity.[2]   [*Exeunt.*]

*   *   *

[*Courtyard of the same Palace*]

    [*Enter* BOSOLA, *with a dark lantern.*]

Bosola.   Sure I did hear a woman shriek: list, ha!
    And the sound came, if I receiv'd it right,
    From the duchess' lodgings. There's some stratagem
    In the confining all our courtiers
    To their several wards: I must have part of it;
    My intelligence will freeze else. List, again!
    It may be 'twas the melancholy bird,
    Best friend of silence and of solitariness,
    The owl, that scream'd so.—Ha! Antonio?

    [*Enter* ANTONIO *with a candle, his sword drawn.*]

Antonio.   I heard some noise.—Who's there? what art thou? speak.
Bosola.   Antonio? put not your face nor body
    To such a forc'd expression of fear:
    I am Bosola, your friend.
Antonio.   Bosola!—
    [*Aside*] This mole does undermine me.—Heard you not
    A noise even now?
Bosola.   From whence?
Antonio.   From the duchess' lodging
Bosola.   Not I: did you?
Antonio.   I did, or else I dream'd.

---

1   This present moment, *i.e.*, immediately.
2   Cast his horoscope.

Bosola.   Let's walk towards it.
Antonio.   No: it may be 'twas
  But the rising of the wind.
Bosola.   Very likely.
  Methinks 'tis very cold, and yet you sweat:
  You look wildly.
Antonio.   I have been setting a figure
  For the duchess' jewels.
Bosola.   Ah, and how falls your question?
  Do you find it radical?[1]
Antonio.   What's that to you?
  'Tis rather to be questioned what design,
  When all men were commanded to their lodgings,
  Makes you a night-walker.
Bosola.   In sooth, I'll tell you:
  Now all the court's asleep, I thought the devil
  Had least to do here; I came to say my prayers;
  And if it do offend you I do so,
  You are a fine courtier.
Antonio [*Aside*]:   This fellow will undo me.—
  You gave the duchess apricocks to-day:
  Pray Heaven they were not poison'd!
Bosola.   Poison'd? A Spanish fig
  For the imputation!
Antonio.   Traitors are ever confident
  Till they are discover'd. There were jewels stol'n too:
  In my conceit, none are to be suspected
  More than yourself.
Bosola.   You are a false steward.
Antonio.   Saucy slave, I'll pull thee up by the roots.
Bosola.   Maybe the ruin will crush you to pieces.
Antonio.   You are an impudent snake indeed, sir:
  Are you scarce warm, and do you show your sting?

[BOSOLA *makes an obscene gesture.*]

  You libel well, sir.
Bosola.   No, sir: copy it out,
  And I will set my hand to't.
Antonio [*Aside*]:   My nose bleeds,

[*Pulls out his handkerchief, inadvertently dropping the horoscope.*]

  One that were superstitious would count
  This ominous, when it merely comes by chance:
  Two letters, that are wrought here[2] for my name,

---

[1]   *I.e.*, capable of solution.
[2]   *I.e.*, on the handkerchief.

Are drown'd in blood!
Mere accident.—For you, sir, I'll take order
I' th' morn you shall be safe:—[*Aside*] 'tis that must colour
Her lying-in: —sir, this door you pass not:
I do not hold it fit that you come near
The duchess' lodgings, till you have quit yourself.—
[*Aside*]   The great are like the base, nay, they are the same,
When they seek shameful ways to avoid shame.   [*Exit.*]
Bosola.   Antonio hereabout did drop a paper:—
   Some of your help, false friend: [*Opening his lantern*] —Oh, here it is.
   What's here? a child's nativity calculated? [*Reads*]
      'The duchess was deliver'd of a son, 'tween the hours of twelve and one in the
   night, Anno Dom. 1504,'—that's this year—'decimo nono Decembris,'—that's
   this night,—'taken according to the meridian of Malfi,'—that's our duchess:
   happy discovery!—'The lord of the first house being combust in the ascendant,
   signifies short life; and Mars being in a human sign, join'd to the tail of the
   Dragon, in the eighth house, doth threaten a violent death. Cætera non scru-
   tantur.'
   Why, now 'tis most apparent: this precise fellow
   Is the duchess' bawd:—I have it to my wish!
   This is a parcel of intelligency
   Our courtiers were cas'd up for: it needs must follow
   That I must be committed on pretence
   Of poisoning her; which I'll endure, and laugh at.
   If one could find the father now! but that
   Time will discover. Old Castruchio
   I' th' morning posts to Rome: by him I'll send
   A letter that shall make her brothers' galls
   O'erflow their livers. This was a thrifty way.
   Though lust do mask in ne'er so strange disguise,
   She's oft found witty, but is never wise.   [*Exit.*]

*   *   *

[*A Room in the Palace of the Cardinal at Rome*]

   [*Enter* CARDINAL *and* JULIA.]

Cardinal.   Sit: thou art my best of wishes. Prithee, tell me
   What trick didst thou invent to come to Rome
   Without thy husband.
Julia.   Why, my lord, I told him
   I came to visit an old anchorite
   Here for devotion.
Cardinal.   Thou art a witty false one,—
   I mean, to him.
Julia.   You have prevailed with me
   Beyond my strongest thoughts! I would not now
   Find you inconstant.

Cardinal.   Do not put thyself
  To such a voluntary torture, which proceeds
  Out of your own guilt.
Julia.   How, my lord?
Cardinal.   You fear
  My constancy, because you have approved
  Those giddy and wild turnings in yourself.
Julia.   Did you e'er find them?
Cardinal.   Sooth, generally for women;
  A man might strive to make glass malleable,
  Ere he should make them fixed.
Julia.   So, my lord.
Cardinal.   We had need go borrow that fantastic glass
  Invented by Galileo the Florentine
  To view another spacious world i' th' moon,
  And look to find a constant woman there.
Julia.   This is very well, my lord.
Cardinal.   Why do you weep?
  Are tears your justification? the self-same tears
  Will fall into your husband's bosom, lady,
  With a loud protestation that you love him
  Above the world. Come, I'll love you wisely,
  That's jealously; since I am very certain
  You cannot make me cuckold.
Julia.   I'll go home
  To my husband.
Cardinal.   You may thank me, lady,
  I have taken you off your melancholy perch,
  Bore you upon my fist, and show'd you game,
  And let you fly at it.—I pray thee, kiss me.—
  When thou wast with thy husband, thou wast watch'd
  Like a tame elephant:—still you are to thank me:—
  Thou hadst only kisses from him and high feeding;
  But what delight was that? 'twas just like one
  That hath a little fingering on the lute,
  Yet cannot tune it:—still you are to thank me.
Julia.   You told me of a piteous wound i' th' heart
  And a sick liver, when you wooed me first,
  And spake like one in physic.
Cardinal.   Who's that?—

  [*Enter* SERVANT.]

  Rest firm, for my affection to thee,
  Lightning moves slow to 't.
Servant.   Madam, a gentleman,
  That's come post from Malfi, desires to see you.
Cardinal.   Let him enter: I'll withdraw.   [*Exit.*]

Servant. He says
  Your husband, old Castruchio, is come to Rome,
  Most pitifully tir'd with riding post. [*Exit.*]

[*Enter* DELIO.]

Julia. Signior Delio! [*Aside*] 'tis one of my old suitors.
Delio. I was bold to come and see you.
Julia. Sir, you are welcome.
Delio. Do you lie here?
Julia. Sure, your own experience
  Will satisfy you no: our Roman prelates
  Do not keep lodging for ladies.
Delio. Very well:
  I have brought you no commendations from your husband,
  For I know none by him.
Julia. I hear he's come to Rome.
Delio. I never knew man and beast, of a horse and a knight,
  So weary of each other: if he had had a good back,
  He would have undertook to have borne his horse,
  His breech was so pitifully sore.
Julia. Your laughter
  Is my pity.
Delio. Lady, I know not whether
  You want money, but I have brought you some.
Julia. From my husband?
Delio. No, from mine own allowance.
Julia. I must hear the condition, ere I be bound to take it.
Delio. Look on 't, 'tis gold: hath it not a fine colour?
Julia. I have a bird more beautiful.
Delio. Try the sound on 't.
Julia. A lute-string far exceeds it:
  It hath no smell, like cassia or civet;
  Nor is it physical, though some fond doctors
  Persuade us seethe 't in cullises.[1] I'll tell you,
  This is a creature bred by——

[*Re-enter* SERVANT.]

Servant. Your husband's come,
  Hath deliver'd a letter to the Duke of Calabria
  That, to my thinking, hath put him out of his wits. [*Exit.*]
Julia. Sir, you hear:
  Pray, let me know your business and your suit
  As briefly as can be.
Delio. With good speed: I would wish you,

---

[1] "Nor is it medicinal, though some foolish doctors persuade us to boil it in the strong broths we eat when we are sick."

At such time as you are non-resident
With your husband, my mistress.
Julia.   Sir, I'll go ask my husband if I shall,
And straight return your answer.   [*Exit.*]
Delio.   Very fine!
Is this her wit, or honesty, that speaks thus?
I heard one say the duke was highly mov'd
With a letter sent from Malfi. I do fear
Antonio is betray'd: how fearfully
Shows his ambition now! unfortunate fortune!
They pass through whirlpools, and deep woes do shun,
Who the event weigh ere the action's done.   [*Exit.*]

[*Re-enter* CARDINAL, *and* FERDINAND *with a letter*].[1]

Ferdinand.   I have this night digged up a mandrake.[2]

Cardinal.   Say you?
Ferdinand.   And I am grown mad with 't.
Cardinal.   What's the prodigy?
Ferdinand.   Read there,—a sister damn'd: she's loose i' th' hilts;
Grown a notorious strumpet.
Cardinal.   Speak lower.
Ferdinand.   Lower?
Rogues do not whisper 't now, but seek to publish 't
(As servants do the bounty of their lords)
Aloud; and with a covetous searching eye,
To mark who note them. O, confusion seize her!
She hath had most cunning bawds to serve her turn,
And more secure conveyances for lust
Than towns of garrison for service.
Cardinal.   Is 't possible?
Can this be certain?
Ferdinand.   Rhubarb, oh, for rhubarb
To purge this choler! here's the cursèd day
To prompt my memory; and here 't shall stick
Till of her bleeding heart I make a sponge
To wipe it out.
Cardinal.   Why do you make yourself
So wild a tempest?
Ferdinand.   Would I could be one,
That I might toss her palace 'bout her ears,
Root up her goodly forests, blast her meads, .

---

[1]   Scene 5 begins here in older texts.
[2]   The mandrake, when dug up, supposedly gave forth shrieks which drove the hearer mad.
Compare Shakespeare:

> "And shrieks, like mandrakes torn out of the earth,
> That living mortals hearing them run mad."

And lay her general territory as waste
As she hath done her honours.
Cardinal.   Shall our blood,
The royal blood of Aragon and Castile,
Be thus attainted?
Ferdinand.   Apply desperate physic:
We must not now use balsamum, but fire,
The smarting cupping-glass, for that 's the mean
To purge infected blood, such blood as hers.
There is a kind of pity in mine eye,—
I'll give it to my handkercher; and now 'tis here,
I'll bequeath this to her bastard.
Cardinal.   What to do?
Ferdinand.   Why, to make soft lint for his mother's wounds,
When I have hewed her to pieces.
Cardinal.   Curs'd creature!
Unequal nature, to place women's hearts
So far upon the left side!
Ferdinand.   Foolish men,
That e'er will trust their honour in a bark
Made of so slight weak bulrush as is woman,
Apt every minute to sink it!
Cardinal.   Thus ignorance, when it hath purchas'd honour,
It cannot wield it.
Ferdinand.   Methinks I see her laughing—
Excellent hyena! Talk to me somewhat, quickly,
Or my imagination will carry me
To see her in the shameful act of sin.
Cardinal.   With whom?
Ferdinand.   Haply with some strong-thigh'd bargeman,
Or one o' the woodyard that can quoit the sledge
Or toss the bar, or else some lovely squire
That carries coals up to her privy lodgings.
Cardinal.   You fly beyond your reason.
Ferdinand.   Go to, mistress!
'Tis not your whore's milk that shall quench my wild fire,
But your whore's blood.
Cardinal.   How idly shows this rage, which carries you,
As men convey'd by witches through the air,
On violent whirlwinds! this intemperate noise
Fitly resembles deaf men's shrill discourse,
Who talk aloud, thinking all other men
To have their imperfection.   ·
Ferdinand.   Have not you
My palsy?   · •
Cardinal.   Yes, I can be angry, but
Without this rupture: there is not in nature
A thing that makes man so deform'd, so beastly,

As doth intemperate anger. Chide yourself.
You have divers men who never yet express'd
Their strong desire of rest but by unrest,
By vexing of themselves. Come, put yourself
In tune.
Ferdinand. So; I will only study to seem
The thing I am not. I could kill her now,
In you, or in myself; for I do think
It is some sin in us heaven doth revenge
By her.
Cardinal. Are you stark mad?
Ferdinand.   I would have their bodies
Burnt in a coal-pit with the ventage stopp'd,
That their curs'd smoke might not ascend to heaven;
Or dip the sheets they lie in in pitch or sulphur,
Wrap them in 't, and then light them like a match;
Or else to boil their bastard to a cullis,
And give 't his lecherous father to renew
The sin of his back.
Cardinal.   I'll leave you.
Ferdinand.   Nay, I have done.
I am confident, had I been damn'd in hell,
And should have heard of this, it would have put me
Into a cold sweat. In, in; I'll go sleep.
Till I know who leaps my sister, I'll not stir:
That known, I'll find scorpions to string my whips,
And fix her in a general eclipse.   [*Exeunt.*]

Act The Third

[A *Room in the Palace of the Duchess*]

[*Enter* ANTONIO *and* DELIO.]

Antonio. Our noble friend, my most beloved Delio!
Oh, you have been a stranger long at court;
Came you along with the Lord Ferdinand?
Delio. I did, sir: and how fares your noble duchess?
Antonio. Right fortunately well: she 's an excellent
Feeder of pedigrees; since you last saw her,
She hath had two children more, a son and daughter.
Delio. Methinks 'twas yesterday: let me but wink,
And not behold your face, which to mine eye
Is somewhat leaner; verily I should dream
It were within this half-hour.
Antonio. You have not been in law, friend Delio,
Nor in prison, nor a suitor at the court,
Nor begged the reversion of some great man's place,

Nor troubled with an old wife, which doth make
Your time so insensibly hasten.
Delio.   Pray, sir, tell me,
Hath not this news arriv'd yet to the ear
Of the lord cardinal?
Antonio.   I fear it hath:,
The Lord Ferdinand, that 's newly come to court,
Doth bear himself right dangerously.
Delio.   Pray, why?
Antonio.   He is so quiet that he seems to sleep
The tempest out, as dormice do in winter:
Those houses that are haunted are most still
Till the devil be up.
Delio.   What say the common people?
Antonio.   The common rabble do directly say
She is a strumpet.
Delio.   And your graver heads
Which would be politic, what censure they?
Antonio.   They do observe I grow to infinite purchase,[1]
The left hand way, and all suppose the duchess
Would amend it, if she could; for, say they,
Great princes, though they grudge their officers
Should have such large and unconfinèd means
To get wealth under them, will not complain,
Lest thereby they should make them odious
Unto the people; for other obligation
Of love or marriage between her and me
They never dream of.

[*Enter* DUCHESS, FERDINAND, *and* BOSOLA.]

Delio.   The Lord Ferdinand
Is going to bed.
Ferdinand.   I'll instantly to bed,
For I am weary.—I am to bespeak
A husband for you.
Duchess.   For me, sir? pray, who is 't?
Ferdinand.   The great Count Malateste.
Duchess.   Fie upon him!
A count? he 's a mere stick of sugar-candy;
You may look quite thorough him. When I choose
A husband, I will marry for your honour.
Ferdinand.   You shall do well in 't.—How is 't, worthy Antonio?
Duchess.   But, sir, I am to have private conference with you
About a scandalous report is spread
Touching mine honour.

---

[1]   Acquired property, wealth.

Ferdinand.   Let me be ever deaf to 't:
  One of Pasquil's paper bullets, court-calumny,
  A pestilent air, which princes' palaces
  Are seldom purged of. Yet, say that it were true,
  I pour it in your bosom, my fix'd love
  Would strongly excuse, extenuate, nay, deny
  Faults, were they apparent in you. Go, be safe
  In your own innocency.
Duchess [*Aside*]:   O bless'd comfort!
  This deadly air is purg'd.

                              [*Exeunt* DUCHESS, ANTONIO, *and* DELIO]

Ferdinand.   Her guilt treads on
  Hot-burning coulters.—Now, Bosola,
  How thrives our intelligence?
Bosola.   Sir, uncertainly
  'Tis rumour'd she hath had three bastards, but
  By whom we may go read i' th' stars.
Ferdinand.   Why, some
  Hold opinion all things are written there.
Bosola.   Yes, if we could find spectacles to read them.
  I do suspect there hath been some sorcery
  Us'd on the duchess.
Ferdinand.   Sorcery? to what purpose?
Bosola.   To make her dote on some desertless fellow
  She shames to acknowledge.
Ferdinand.   Can your faith give way
  To think there's power in potions or in charms,
  To make us love whether we will or no?
Bosola.   Most certainly.
Ferdinand.   Away! these are mere gulleries, horrid things,
  Invented by some mountebanks
  To abuse us. Do you think that herbs or charms
  Can force the will? Some trials have been made
  In this foolish practice, but the ingredients
  Were lenitive poisons, such as are of force
  To make the patient mad; and straight the witch
  Swears by equivocation they are in love. ·
  The witchcraft lies in her rank blood. This night
  I will force confession from her. You told me
  You had got, within these two days, a false key
  Into her bed-chamber.
Bosola.   I have.
Ferdinand.   As I would wish.
Bosola.   What do you intend to do?
Ferdinand.   Can you guess?

Bosola. No.

Ferdinand. Do not ask, then:
    He that can compass me, and know my drifts,
    May say he hath put a girdle 'bout the world,
    And sounded all her quicksands.

Bosola.   .   I do not
    Think so.

Ferdinand. What do you think, then, pray?

Bosola.   That you
    Are your own chronicle too much, and grossly
    Flatter yourself.

Ferdinand. Give me thy hand; I thank thee:
    I never gave pension but to flatterers,
    Till I entertained thee. Farewell.
    That friend a great man's ruin strongly checks,
    Who rails into his belief all his defects.   [*Exeunt.*]

* * *

[*The Bedchamber of the Duchess*]

[*Enter* DUCHESS, ANTONIO, *and* CARIOLA]

Duchess. Bring me the casket hither, and the glass.—
    You get no lodging here to-night, my lord.

Antonio. Indeed, I must persuade one.

Duchess.   Very good:
    I hope in time 'twill grow into a custom,
    That noblemen shall come with cap and knee
    To purchase a night's lodging of their wives.

Antonio. I must lie here.

Duchess.   Must! you are a lord of misrule.

Antonio. Indeed, my rule is only in the night.

Duchess. To what use will you put me?

Antonio.   We'll sleep together.

Duchess. Alas,
    What pleasure can two lovers find in sleep!

Cariola. My lord, I lie with her often; and I know
    She'll much disquiet you.

Antonio.   See, you are complain'd of.

Cariola. For she's the sprawling'st bedfellow.

Antonio.   I shall like her
    The better for that.

Cariola.   Sir, shall I ask you a question?

Antonio. Oh, I pray thee, Cariola.

Cariola.   Wherefore still, when you lie
    With my lady, do you rise so early?

Antonio.   Labouring men
   Count the clock oftenest, Cariola, are glad
   When their task's ended.
Duchess.   I'll stop your mouth. [*Kisses him.*]
Antonio.   Nay, that's but one; Venus had two soft doves
   To draw her chariot; I must have another— [*She kisses him again.*]
   When wilt thou marry, Cariola?
Cariola.   Never, my lord.
Antonio.   Oh, fie upon this single life! forgo it.
   We read how Daphne, for her peevish flight,
   Became a fruitless bay-tree; Syrinx turn'd
   To the pale empty reed; Anaxarete
   Was frozen into marble: whereas those
   Which married, or prov'd kind unto their friends,
   Were by a gracious influence transhap'd
   Into the olive, pomegranate, mulberry,
   Became flowers, precious stones, or eminent stars.
Cariola.   This is a vain poetry: but I pray you tell me,
   If there were propos'd me, wisdom, riches, and beauty,
   In three several young men, which should I choose?
Antonio.   'Tis a hard question: this was Paris' case,
   And he was blind in 't, and there was great cause;
   For how was 't possible he could judge right,
   Having three amorous goddesses in view,
   And they stark naked? 'twas a motion
   Were able to benight the apprehension
   Of the severest counsellor of Europe.
   Now I look on both your faces so well form'd,
   It puts me in mind of a question I would ask.
Cariola.   What is 't?
Antonio.   I do wonder why hard-favour'd ladies,
   For the most part, keep worse-favour'd waiting-women
   To attend them, and cannot endure fair ones.
Duchess.   Oh, that's soon answer'd.
   Did you ever in your life know an ill painter
   Desire to have his dwelling next door to the shop
   Of an excellent picture-maker? 'twould disgrace
   His face-making, and undo him. I prithee,
   When were we so merry?—My hair tangles.
Antonio [*whispering.*]   Pray thee, Cariola, let's steal forth the room,
   And let her talk to herself: I have divers times
   Serv'd her the like, when she hath chaf'd extremely.
   I love to see her angry. Softly, Cariola.

                  [*Exeunt* ANTONIO *and* CARIOLA.]

Duchess.   Doth not the colour of my hair 'gin to change?
   When I wax grey, I shall have all the court

Powder their hair with arras,[1] to be like me.
You have cause to love me; I enter'd you into my heart
Before you would vouchsafe to call for the keys.

[*Enter* FERDINAND *behind, unseen.*]

We shall one day have my brothers take you napping;
Methinks his presence, being now in court,
Should make you keep your own bed; but you'll say
Love mix'd with fear is sweetest. I'll assure you,
You shall get no more children till my brothers
Consent to be your gossips. Have you lost you tongue?

[*Turning, she sees* FERDINAND *with drawn poniard.*]

'Tis welcome:
For know, whether I am doom'd to live or die,
I can do both like a prince.
Ferdinand.   Die, then, quickly!

[*Giving her the poniard.*]

Virtue, where art thou hid? what hideous thing
Is it that doth eclipse thee?
Duchess.   Pray, sir, hear me.
Ferdinand.   Or is it true thou art but a bare name,
And no essential thing?
Duchess.   Sir,—
Ferdinand.   Do not speak.
Duchess.   No, sir: I will plant my soul in mine ears, to hear you.
Ferdinand.   O most imperfect light of human reason,
That mak'st us so unhappy to foresee
What we can least prevent! Pursue thy wishes,
And glory in them: there's in shame no comfort
But to be past all bounds and sense of shame.
Duchess.   I pray, sir, hear me: I am married.
Ferdinand.   So!
Duchess.   Haply, not to your liking: but for that,
Alas, your shears do come untimely now
To clip the bird's wings that 's already flown!
Will you see my husband?
Ferdinand.   Yes, if I could change
Eyes with a basilisk.
Duchess.   Sure, you came hither
By his confederacy.
Ferdinand.   The howling of a wolf
Is music to thee, screech-owl: prithee, peace.—
Whate'er thou art that hast enjoy'd my sister,

---

[1]   Orris powder, which was the colour of flour.

For I am sure thou hear'st me, for thine own sake
Let me not know thee. I came hither prepar'd
To work thy discovery; yet am now persuaded
It would beget such violent effects
As would damn us both. I would not for ten millions
I had beheld thee: therefore use all means
I never may have knowledge of thy name;
Enjoy thy lust still, and a wretched life,
On that condition.—And for thee, vile woman,
If thou do wish thy lecher may grow old
In thy embracements, I would have thee build
Such a room for him as our anchorites
To holier use inhabit. Let not the sun
Shine on him till he's dead; let dogs and monkeys
Only converse with him, and such dumb things
To whom nature denies use to sound his name;
Do not keep a paraquito, lest she learn it;
If thou do love him, cut out thine own tongue,
Lest it bewray him.
Duchess.   Why might not I marry?
    I have not gone about in this to create
    Any new world or custom.
Ferdinand.   Thou art undone;
    And thou hast ta'en that massy sheet of lead
    That hid thy husband's bones, and folded it
    About my heart.
Duchess.   Mine bleeds for 't.
Ferdinand.   Thine? thy heart?
    What should I name 't unless a hollow bullet
    Fill'd with unquenchable wild-fire?
Duchess.   You are in this
    Too strict; and were you not my princely brother,
    I would say, too wilful: my reputation
    Is safe.
Ferdinand. Dost thou know what reputation is?
    I'll tell thee,—to small purpose, since the instruction
    Comes now too late.
    Upon a time Reputation, Love, and Death,
    Would travel o'er the world; and it was concluded
    That they should part, and take three several ways.
    Death told them, they should find him in great battles,
    Or cities plagu'd with plagues: Love gives them counsel
    To inquire for him 'mongst unambitious shepherds,
    Where dowries were not talk'd of, and sometimes
    'Mongst quiet kindred that had nothing left
    By their dead parents: 'Stay,' quoth Reputation,
    'Do not forsake me; for it is my nature,
    If once I part from any man I meet,

I am never found again.' And so for you:
You have shook hands with Reputation,
And made him invisible. So, fare you well:
I will never see you more.
Duchess.   Why should only I,
Of all the other princes of the world,
Be cas'd up, like a holy relic? I have youth
And a little beauty.
Ferdinand.   So you have some virgins
That are witches. I will never see thee more.   [*Exit.*]

[*Re-enter* ANTONIO *with a pistol, and* CARIOLA.]

Duchess.   You saw this apparition?
Antonio.   Yes: we are
Betray'd. How came he hither?—I should turn
This to thee, for that. [*Pointing the pistol at* CARIOLA.]
Cariola.   Pray, sir, do; and when
That you have cleft my heart, you shall read there
Mine innocence.
Duchess.   That gallery gave him entrance.
Antonio.   I would this terrible thing would come again,
That, standing on my guard, I might relate
My warrantable love.—[*She shows the poniard.*] Ha! what means this?
Duchess.   He left this with me.
Antonio.   And it seems did wish
You would use it on yourself.
Duchess.   His action seem'd
To intend so much.
Antonio.   This hath a handle to 't,
As well as a point: turn it towards him, and
So fasten the keen edge in his rank gall. [*Knocking within.*]
How now! who knocks? more earthquakes?
Duchess.   I stand
As if a mine beneath my feet were ready
To be blown up.
Cariola.   'Tis Bosola.
Duchess [*To Antonio.*]   Away!
O misery! methinks unjust actions
Should wear these masks and curtains, and not we.
You must instantly part hence: I have fashion'd it
Already.   [*Exit* ANTONIO.]

[*Enter* BOSOLA.]

Bosola.   The duke your brother is ta'en up in a whirlwind,
Hath took horse, and 's rid post to Rome.
Duchess.   So late?

Bosola.   He told me, as he mounted into th' saddle,
  You were undone.
Duchess.   Indeed, I am very near it.
Bosola.   What 's the matter?
Duchess.   Antonio, the master of our household,
  Hath dealt so falsely with me in 's accounts:
  My brother stood engag'd with me for money
  Ta'en up of certain Neapolitan Jews,
  And Antonio lets the bonds be forfeit.
Bosola.   Strange!—[*Aside*] This is cunning.
Duchess.   And hereupon
  My brother's bills at Naples are protested
  Against.—Call up our officers.
Bosola.   I shall.   [*Exit.*]

  [*Re-enter* ANTONIO.]

Duchess.   The place that you must fly to is Ancona:
  Hire a house there; I'll send after you
  My treasure and my jewels. Our weak safety
  Runs upon enginous wheels: short syllables
  Must stand for periods. I must now accuse you
  Of such a feignèd crime as Tasso calls
  Magnanima menzogna, a noble lie,
  'Cause it must shield our honours.—Hark! they are coming.

  [*Re-enter* BOSOLA *and Officers;* ANTONIO *and* DUCHESS *commence feigning.*]

Antonio.   Will your grace hear me?
Duchess.   I have got well by you; you have yielded me
  A million of loss: I am like to inherit
  The people's curses for your stewardship.
  You had the trick in audit-time to be sick,
  Till I had sign'd your quietus; and that cur'd you
  Without help of a doctor.—Gentlemen,
  I would have this man be an example to you all;
  So shall you hold my favour; I pray, let him;
  For h'as done that, alas, you would not think of,
  And, because I intend to be rid of him,
  I mean not to publish.—Use your fortune elsewhere.
Antonio.   I am strongly arm'd to brook my overthrow;
  As commonly men bear with a hard year,
  I will not blame the cause on 't; but do think
  The necessity of my malevolent star
  Procures this, not her humour. Oh, the inconstant
  And rotten ground of service! you may see,
  'Tis even like him, that in a winter night,
  Takes a long slumber o'er a dying fire,

A loth to part from 't; yet parts thence as cold
As when he first sat down.
Duchess.   We do confiscate,
Towards the satisfying of your accounts,
All that you have.
Antonio.   I am all yours; and 'tis very fit
All mine should be so.
Duchess.   So, sir you have your pass.
Antonio.   You may see, gentlemen, what 'tis to serve
A prince with body and soul.   [*Exit.*]
Bosola.   Here's an example for extortion: what moisture is drawn out of the sea, when foul weather comes, pours down, and runs into the sea again.
Duchess.   I would know what are your opinions of this Antonio.
Second Officer.   He could not abide to see a pig's head gaping: I thought your grace would find him a Jew.
Third Officer.   I would you had been his officer, for your own sake.
Fourth Officer.   You would have had more money.
First Officer.   He stopped his ears with black wool, and to those came to him for money said he was thick of hearing.
Second Officer.   Some said he was an hermaphrodite, for he could not abide a woman.
Fourth Officer.   How scurvy proud he would look when the treasury was full! Well, let him go!
First Officer.   Yes, and the chippings of the buttery fly after him, to scour his gold chain!
Duchess.   Leave us. [*Exeunt officers.*] What do you think of these?
Bosola.   That these are rogues that in 's prosperity, but to have waited on his fortune, could have wish'd his dirty stirrup riveted through their noses, and follow'd after 's mule, like a bear in a ring; would have prostituted their daughters to his lust; made their first-born intelligencers; thought none happy but such as were born under his blest planet, and wore his livery: and do these lice drop off now? Well, never look to have the like again: he hath left a sort of flattering rogues behind him; their doom must follow. Princes pay flatterers in their own money: flatterers dissemble their vices, and they dissemble their lies;[1] that 's justice. Alas, poor gentleman!
Duchess.   Poor? he hath amply fill'd his coffers.
Bosola.   Sure, he was too honest. Pluto,[2] the god of riches, when he's sent by Jupiter to any man, he goes limping, to signify that wealth that comes on God's name comes slowly; but when he 's sent on the devil's errand, he rides post and comes in by scuttles.[3] Let me show you what a most unvalued jewel you have in a wanton humour thrown away, to bless the man shall find him. He was an excellent courtier and most faithful; a soldier that thought it as beastly to know

---

[1] *I.e.*, Flatterers pretend that kings have no vices, and kings pretend that flatterers tell no lies.
[2] Plutus.
[3] Quick steps.

his own value too little as devilish to acknowledge it too much. Both his virtue and form deserv'd a far better fortune: his discourse rather delighted to judge itself than show itself: his breast was fill'd with all perfection, and yet it seem'd a private whispering-room, it made so little noise of 't.

Duchess. But he was basely descended.

Bosola. Will you make yourself a mercenary herald, rather to examine men's pedigrees than virtues? You shall want him: for know, an honest statesman to a prince is like a cedar planted by a spring; the spring bathes the tree's root, the grateful tree rewards it with his shadow: you have not done so. I would sooner swim to the Bermoothes[1] on two politicians' rotten bladders, tied together with an intelligencer's heart-string, than depend on so changeable a prince's favour. Fare thee well, Antonio! since the malice of the world would needs down with thee, it cannot be said yet that any ill happened unto thee, considering thy fall was accompanied with virtue.

Duchess. Oh, you render me excellent music!

Bosola.   Say you?

Duchess. This good one that you speak of is my husband.

Bosola. Do I not dream? can this ambitious age
Have so much goodness in 't as to prefer
A man merely for worth, without these shadows
Of wealth and painted honours? possible?

Duchess. I have had three children by him.

Bosola.   Fortunate lady!
For you have made your private nuptial bed
The humble and fair seminary of peace.
No question but many an unbeneficed scholar.
Shall pray for you for this deed, and rejoice
That some preferment in the world can yet
Arise from merit. The virgins of your land
That have no dowries shall hope your example
Will raise them to rich husbands. Should you want
Soldiers, 'twould make the very Turks and Moors
Turn Christians, and serve you for this act.
Last, the neglected poets of your time,
In honour of this trophy of a man,
Raised by that curious engine, your white hand,
Shall thank you, in your grave, for 't; and make that
More reverend than all the cabinets
Of living princes. For Antonio,
His fame shall likewise flow from many a pen,
When heralds shall want coats to sell to men.

Duchess. As I taste comfort in this friendly speech,
So would I find concealment.

Bosola. Oh, the secret of my prince,
Which I will wear on th' inside of my heart!

[1] To Bermuda.

Duchess.   You shall take charge of all my coin and jewels,
And follow him; for he retires himself
To Ancona.
Bosola.   So.
Duchess.   Whither, within few days,
I mean to follow thee.
Bosola.   Let me think:
I would wish your grace to feign a pilgrimage
To our Lady of Loretto, scarce seven leagues
From fair Ancona; so may you depart
Your country with more honour, and your flight
Will seem a princely progress, retaining
Your usual train about you.
Duchess.   Sir, your direction
Shall lead me by the hand.
Cariola.   In my opinion,
She were better progress to the baths at Lucca,
Or go visit the Spa in Germany;
For, if you will believe me, I do not like
This jesting with religion, this feigned
Pilgrimage.
Duchess.   Thou art a superstitious fool:
Prepare us instantly for our departure.
Past sorrows, let us moderately lament them;
For those to come, seek wisely to prevent them.

[*Exeunt* DUCHESS *and* CARIOLA.]

Bosola.   A politician is the devil's quilted[1] anvil;
He fashions all sins on him, and the blows
Are never heard: he may work in a lady's chamber,
As here for proof. What rests but I reveal
All to my lord? Oh, this base quality
Of intelligencer! why, every quality i' th' world
Prefers but gain or commendation:
Now for this act I am certain to be rais'd,
And men that paint weeds to the life are prais'd.   [*Exit.*]

*   *   *

[*A Room in the Cardinal's Palace at Rome*]

[*Enter* CARDINAL, FERDINAND, MALATESTE, PESCARA, SILVIO, *and* DELIO.]

Cardinal.   Must we turn soldier, then?
Malateste.   The emperor,
Hearing your worth that way, ere you attain'd

---

[1]   *I.e.,* muffled.

This reverend garment, joins you in commission
With the right fortunate soldier the Marquis of Pescara,
And the famous Lannoy.
Cardinal.   He that had the honour
Of taking the French king prisoner?
Malateste.   The same.
Here's a plot[1] drawn for a new fortification
At Naples.

[*They talk apart.*]

Ferdinand.   This great Count Malateste, I perceive,
Hath got employment?
Delio.   No employment, my lord;
A marginal note in the muster-book, that he is
A voluntary lord.
Ferdinand.   He 's no soldier?
Delio.   He has worn gunpowder in 's hollow tooth for the toothache.
Silvio.   He comes to the leaguer[2] with a full intent
To eat fresh beef and garlic, means to stay
Till the scent be gone, and straight return to court.
Delio.   He hath read all the late service as the city chronicle relates it; and keeps
two painters going, only to express battles in model.
Silvio.   Then he'll fight by the book.
Delio.   By the almanac, I think, to choose good days and shun the critical; that 's
his mistress's scarf.
Silvio.   Yes, he protests he would do much for that taffeta.
Delio.   I think he would run away from a battle, to save it from taking[3] prisoner.
Silvio.   He is horribly afraid gunpowder will spoil the perfume on 't.
Delio.   I saw a Dutchman break his pate once for calling him pot-gun; he made
his head have a bore in 't like a musket.
Silvio.   I would he had made a touchhole to 't. He is indeed a guarded sumpter-
cloth,[4] only for the remove of the court.

[*Enter* BOSOLA *and speaks to* FERDINAND *and the* CARDINAL.]

Pescara.   Bosola arriv'd? what should be the business?
Some falling-out amongst the cardinals.
These factions amongst great men, they are like
Foxes; when their heads are divided,
They carry fire in their tails, and all the country
About them goes to wrack for 't.
Silvio.   What's that Bosola?
Delio.   I knew him in Padua—a fantastical scholar, like such who study to
know how many knots was in Hercules' club, of what colour Achilles' beard

1   Plan.
2   Camp.
3   *I.e.*, being taken.
4   An ornamental horse-cloth.

was, or whether Hector were not troubled with the toothache. He hath studied himself half blear-ey'd to know the true symmetry of Caesar's nose by a shoeing-horn; and this he did to gain the name of a speculative man.[1]

Pescara.   Mark Prince Ferdinand:
A very salamander lives in 's eye.
To mock the eager violence of fire.

Silvio.   That Cardinal hath made more bad faces with his oppression than ever Michael Angelo made good ones: he lifts up 's nose, like a foul porpoise before a storm.

Pescara.   The Lord Ferdinand laughs.

Delio.   Like a deadly cannon that lightens
Ere it smokes.

Pescara.   These are your true pangs of death.
The pangs of life, that struggle with great statesmen.

Delio.   In such a deformed silence witches whisper
Their charms.

Cardinal.   Doth she make religion her riding-hood
To keep her from the sun and tempest?

Ferdinand.   That,
That damns her. Methinks her fault and beauty,
Blended together, show like leprosy,
The whiter, the fouler. I make it a question
Whether her beggarly brats were ever christened.

Cardinal.   I will instantly solicit the state of Ancona
To have them banish'd.

Ferdinand.   You are for Loretto?
I shall not be at your ceremony; fare you well.—
Write to the Duke of Malfi, my young nephew
She had by her first husband, and acquaint him
With 's mother's honesty.

Bosola.   I will.

Ferdinand.   Antonio!
A slave that only smell'd of ink and counters,
And never in 's life look'd like a gentleman,
But in the audit-time.—Go, go presently,
Draw me out an hundred and fifty of our horse,
And meet me at the fort-bridge.   [*Exeunt.*]

*   *   *

[*The Shrine of Our Lady of Loretto*]

[*Enter Two* PILGRIMS.]

First Pilgrim.   I have not seen a goodlier shrine than this;
Yet I have visited many.

---

[1]   *I.e.,* a student.

Second Pilgrim.   The Cardinal of Aragon
    Is this day to resign his cardinal's hat:
    His sister duchess likewise is arriv'd
    To pay her vow of pilgrimage. I expect
    A noble ceremony.
First Pilgrim.   No question.
    —They come.

[*Here the ceremony of the* CARDINAL'*s instalment, in the habit of a soldier, is
performed in delivering up his cross, hat, robes, and ring, at the shrine, and
investing him with sword, helmet, shield, and spurs; then* ANTONIO, *the* DUCHESS,
*and their children, having presented themselves at the shrine, are, by a form of
banishment in dumb-show expressed towards them by the* CARDINAL *and the
state of Ancona, banished: during all which ceremony, this ditty is sung, to very
solemn music, by divers churchmen.*

Arms and honours deck thy story,
To thy fame's eternal glory!
Adverse fortune ever fly thee;
No disastrous fate come nigh thee!

I alone will sing thy praises,
Whom to honour virtue raises;
And thy study, that divine is,
Bent to martial discipline is.
Lay aside all those robes lie by thee;
Crown thy arts with arms, they'll beautify thee.

O worthy of worthiest name, adorn'd in this manner,
Lead bravely thy forces on under war's warlike banner!
Oh, mayst thou prove fortunate in all martial courses!
Guide thou still by skill in arts and forces!
Victory attend thee nigh, whilst fame sings loud thy powers;
Triumphant conquest crown thy head, and blessings pour down showers![1]

                              [*Exeunt all except the Two* PILGRIMS.]

First Pilgrim.   Here's a strange turn of state! who would have thought
    So great a lady would have match'd herself
    Unto so mean a person? yet the Cardinal
    Bears himself much too cruel.
Second Pilgrim.   They are banish'd.
First Pilgrim.   But I would ask what power hath this state
    Of Ancona to determine of a free prince?
Second Pilgrim.   They are a free state, sir, and her brother show'd
    How that the Pope, fore-hearing of her looseness,
    Hath seiz'd into th' protection of the Church
    The dukedom which she held as dowager.

1   'The Author disclaims this Ditty to be his.'—(Note in the 1623 quarto.)

First Pilgrim.   But by what justice?
Second Pilgrim.   Sure, I think by none,
  Only her brother's instigation.
First Pilgrim.   What was it with such violence he took
  Off from her finger?
Second Pilgrim.   'Twas her wedding-ring;
  Which he vow'd shortly he would sacrifice
  To his revenge.
First Pilgrim.   Alas, Antonio!
  If that a man be thrust into a well,
  No matter who sets hands to 't, his own weight
  Will bring him sooner to th' bottom. Come, let 's hence.
  Fortune makes this conclusion general,
  All things do help th' unhappy man to fall.   [*Exeunt.*]

[*Enter* DUCHESS, ANTONIO, *Children,* CARIOLA, *and Servants.*][1]

Duchess.   Banish'd Ancona?
Antonio.   Yes, you see what power
  Lightens in great men's breath.
Duchess.   Is all our train
  Shrunk to this poor remainder?
Antonio.   These poor men,
  Which have got little in your service, vow
  To take your fortune[2]: but your wiser buntings,
  Now they are fledg'd, are gone.
Duchess.   They have done wisely.
  This puts me in mind of death: physicians thus,
  With their hands full of money, use to give o'er
  Their patients.
Antonio.   Right the fashion of the world:
  From decayed fortunes every flatterer shrinks;
  Men cease to build where the foundation sinks.
Duchess.   I had a very strange dream to-night.
Antonio.   What was 't?
Duchess.   Methought I wore my coronet of state,
  And on a sudden all the diamonds
  Were chang'd to pearls.
Antonio.   My interpretation
  Is, you'll weep shortly; for to me the pearls
  Do signify your tears.
Duchess.   The birds that live
  I' th' field on the wild benefit of nature
  Live happier than we; for they may choose their mates,
  And carol their sweet pleasures to the spring.

[*Enter* BOSOLA *with a letter.*]

---

[1] Scene 5 begins here.
[2] *I.e.,* to endure your misfortune.

Bosola.   You are happily o'erta'en.
Duchess.   From my brother?
Bosola.   Yes, from the Lord Ferdinand your brother
 All love and safety.
Duchess.   Thou dost blanch mischief,
 Wouldst make it white. See, see, like to calm weather
 At sea before a tempest, false hearts speak fair
 To those they intend most mischief. [*Reads.*]
 'Send Antonio to me; I want his head in a business.'
 A politic equivocation!
 He doth not want your counsel, but your head;
 That is, he cannot sleep till you be dead.
 And here's another pitfall that's strew'd o'er
 With roses: mark it, 'tis a cunning one: [*Reads.*]
 'I stand engaged for your husband for several debts at Naples: let not that
 trouble him; I had rather have his heart than his money:'—
 And I believe so too.
Bosola.   What do you believe?
Duchess.   That he so much distrusts my husband's love,
 He will by no means believe his heart is with him
 Until he see it: the devil is not cunning
 Enough to circumvent us in riddles.
Bosola.   Will you reject that noble and free league
 Of amity and love which I present you?
Duchess.   Their league is like that of some politic kings,
 Only to make themselves of strength and power
 To be our after-ruin: tell them so.
Bosola.   And what from you?
Antonio.   Thus tell him; I will not come.
Bosola.   And what of this? [*Pointing to the letter.*]
Antonio.   My brothers have dispers'd
 Blood-hounds abroad; which till I hear are muzzl'd,
 No truce, though hatch'd with ne'er such politic skill,
 Is safe, that hangs upon our enemies' will.
 I'll not come at them.
Bosola.   This proclaims your breeding:
 Every small thing draws a base mind to fear,
 As the adamant draws iron. Fare you well, sir;
 You shall shortly hear from 's.   [*Exit.*]
Duchess.   I suspect some ambush:
 Therefore by all my love I do conjure you
 To take your eldest son, and fly towards Milan.
 Let us not venture all this poor remainder
 In one unlucky bottom.
Antonio.   You counsel safely.
 Best of my life, farewell. Since we must part,
 Heaven hath a hand in 't; but no otherwise
 Than as some curious artist takes in sunder

A clock or watch, when it is out of frame,
To bring 't in better order.
Duchess.   I know not
Which is best, to see you dead, or part with you.
[*To her eldest son.*]—Farewell, boy:
Thou art happy that thou hast not understanding
To know thy misery; for all our wit
And reading brings us to a truer sense
Of sorrow.—In the eternal church, sir,
I do hope we shall not part thus.
Antonio.   Oh, be of comfort!
Make patience a noble fortitude,
And think not how unkindly we are used:
Man, like to cassia, is prov'd best being bruised.
Duchess.   Must I, like to a slave-born Russian,
Account it praise to suffer tyranny?
And yet, O heaven, thy heavy hand is in 't!
I have seen my little boy oft scourge his top,[1]
And compar'd myself to 't: naught made me e'er
Go right but heaven's scourge-stick.
Antonio.   Do not weep:
Heaven fashion'd us of nothing, and we strive
To bring ourselves to nothing.—Farewell, Cariola,
And thy sweet armful.—If I do never see thee more,
Be a good mother to your little ones,
And save them from the tiger: fare you well.
Duchess.   Let me look upon you once more; for that speech
Came from a dying father.—Your kiss is colder
Than that I have seen an holy anchorite
Give to a dead man's skull.
Antonio.   My heart is turn'd to a heavy lump of lead,
With which I sound my danger: fare you well.

                          [*Exeunt* ANTONIO *and his Son.*]

Duchess.   My laurel is all withered.
Cariola.   Look, madam, what a troop of armèd men
Make toward us.
Duchess.   Oh, they are very welcome:
When Fortune's wheel is over-charg'd with princes,
The weight makes it move swift: I would have my ruin
Be sudden.

[*Re-enter* BOSOLA *masked, with a Guard.*]

               I am your adventure, am I not?
Bosola.   You are: you must see your husband no more.
Duchess.   What devil art thou that counterfeits heaven's thunder?

---

[1]   *I.e.*, strike it with a stick to keep it spinning.

Bosola.   Is that terrible? I would have you tell me whether
   Is that note worse that frights the silly birds
   Out of the corn, or that which doth allure them
   To the nets? you have hearkened to the last too much.
Duchess.   Oh, misery! like to a rusty o'ercharg'd cannon,
   Shall I never fly in pieces?—Come, to what prison?
Bosola.   To none.
Duchess.   Whither, then?
Bosola.   To your palace.
Duchess.   I have heard
   That Charon's boat serves to convey all o'er
   The dismal lake, but brings none back again.
Bosola.   Your brothers mean you safety and pity.
Duchess.   Pity!
   With such a pity men preserve alive
   Pheasants and quails, when they are not fat enough
   To be eaten.
Bosola.   These are your children?
Duchess.   Yes.
Bosola.   Can they prattle?
Duchess.   No;
   But I intend, since they were born accurs'd,
   Curses shall be their language.
Bosola.   Fie, madam!
   Forget this base, low fellow,—
Duchess.   Were I a man,
   I'd beat that counterfeit face into thy other.
Bosola.   One of no birth.
Duchess.   Say that he was born mean,
   Man is most happy when 's own actions
   Be arguments and examples of his virtue.
Bosola.   A barren, beggarly virtue!
Duchess.   I prithee, who is greatest? can you tell?
   Sad tales befit my woe: I'll tell you one.
   A salmon, as she swam unto the sea,
   Met with a dog-fish, who encounters her
   With this rough language: 'Why art thou so bold
   To mix thyself with our high state of floods,
   Being no eminent courtier, but one
   That for the calmest and fresh time o' the year
   Dost live in shallow rivers, rank'st thyself
   With silly smelts and shrimps? and darest thou
   Pass by our dog-ship without reverence?'
   'Oh!' quoth the salmon, 'sister, be at peace:
   Thank Jupiter we both have pass'd the net!
   Our value never can be truly known,
   Till in the fisher's basket we be shown:
   'I th' market then my price may be the higher,

Even when I am nearest to the cook and fire.'
So to great men the moral may be stretchèd;
Men oft are valued high, when they're most wretched.—
But come, whither you please. I am arm'd 'gainst misery;
Bent to all sways of the oppressor's will:
There 's no deep valley but near some great hill.   [*Exeunt.*]

Act The Fourth

[*A Room in the Duchess's Palace at Malfi*]

[*Enter* FERDINAND *and* BOSOLA.]

Ferdinand.   How doth our sister duchess bear herself
   In her imprisonment?
Bosola.   Nobly: I'll describe her.
   She 's sad as one long used to 't, and she seems
   Rather to welcome the end of misery
   Than shun it; a behaviour so noble
   As gives a majesty to adversity:
   You may discern the shape of loveliness
   More perfect in her tears than in her smiles:
   She will muse four hours together; and her silence,
   Methinks, expresseth more than if she spake.
Ferdinand.   Her melancholy seems to be fortified
   With a strange disdain.
Bosola.   'Tis so; and this restraint,
   Like English mastiffs that grow fierce with tying,
   Makes her too passionately apprehend
   Those pleasures she 's kept from.
Ferdinand.   Curse upon her!
   I will no longer study in the book
   Of another's heart. Inform her what I told you.   [*Exit.*]

   [*Enter* DUCHESS.]

Bosola.   All comfort to your grace!
Duchess.   I will have none.
   Pray thee, why dost thou wrap thy poison'd pills
   In gold and sugar?
Bosola.   Your elder brother, the Lord Ferdinand,
   Is come to visit you, and sends you word,
   'Cause once he rashly made a solemn vow
   Never to see you more, he comes i' th' night;
   And prays you gently neither torch nor taper
   Shine in your chamber: he will kiss your hand.
   And reconcile himself; but for his vow
   He dares not see you.

Duchess.   At his pleasure.—Take hence the lights.—
    He's come.

[*Enter* FERDINAND.]

Ferdinand.   Where are you?
Duchess.   Here, sir.
Ferdinand.   This darkness suits you well.
Duchess.   I would ask you pardon.
Ferdinand.   You have it; for I account it
    The honorabl'st revenge, where I may kill,
    To pardon.—Where are your cubs?
Duchess.   Whom?
Ferdinand.   Call them your children;
    For though our national law distinguish bastards
    From true legitimate issue, compassionate nature
    Makes them all equal.
Duchess.   Do you visit me for this?
    You violate a sacrament o' th' Church
    Shall make you howl in hell for 't.
Ferdinand.   It had been well
    Could you have liv'd thus always; for indeed,
    You were too much i' th' light:—but no more;
    I come to seal my peace with you. Here 's a hand

[*Gives her a dead man's hand.*]

    To which you have vow'd much love; the ring upon 't
    You gave.
Duchess.   I affectionately kiss it.
Ferdinand.   Pray, do, and bury the print of it in your heart.
    I will leave this ring with you for a love-token;
    And the hand as sure as the ring; and do not doubt
    But you shall have the heart too: when you need a friend,
    Send it to him that owned it; you shall see
    Whether he can aid you.
Duchess.   You are very cold:
    I fear you are not well after your travel.—
    Ha! lights!——Oh, horrible!
Ferdinand.   Let her have lights enough.   [*Exit.*]
Duchess.   What witchcraft doth he practice, that he hath left
    A dead man's hand here?

[*Here is discovered, behind a traverse,*[1] *the artificial figures of* Antonio *and his* Children, *appearing as if they were dead.*]

Bosola.   Look you, here 's the piece from which 'twas ta'en.
    He doth present you this sad spectacle,

---

[1]   Curtain.

That, now you know directly they are dead,
Hereafter you may wisely cease to grieve
For that which cannot be recovered.
Duchess. There is not between heaven and earth one wish
I stay for after this: it wastes me more
Than were 't my picture, fashion'd out of wax,
Stuck with a magical needle, and then buried
In some foul dunghill; and yond 's an excellent property
For a tyrant, which I would account mercy.
Bosola.   What 's that?
Duchess. If they would bind me to that lifeless trunk,
And let me freeze to death.
Bosola.   Come, you must live.
Duchess. That 's the greatest torture souls feel in hell,
In hell, that they must live, and cannot die.
Portia, I'll new kindle thy coals again,
And revive the rare and almost dead example
Of a loving wife.
Bosola.   Oh, fie! despair? remember
You are a Christian.
Duchess.   The Church enjoins fasting:
I'll starve myself to death.
Bosola.   Leave this vain sorrow.
Things being at the worst begin to mend: the bee
When he hath shot his sting into your hand, may then
Play with your eyelid.
Duchess.   Good comfortable fellow,
Persuade a wretch that 's broke upon the wheel
To have all his bones new set; entreat him live
To be executed again. Who must dispatch me?
I account this world a tedious theatre,
For I do play a part in 't 'gainst my will.
Bosola. Come, be of comfort; I will save your life.
Duchess.   Indeed,
I have not leisure to tend so small a business.
Bosola. Now, by my life, I pity you.
Duchess.   Thou art a fool, then,
To waste thy pity on a thing so wretched
As cannot pity itself. I am full of daggers.
Puff, let me blow these vipers from me.

[*Enter a* SERVANT.]

What are you?
Servant.   One that wishes you long life.
Duchess. I would thou wert hang'd for the horrible curse
Thou hast given me: I shall shortly grow one

Of the miracles of pity. I'll go pray;—
   No, I'll go curse.
Bosola.   Oh, fie!
Duchess.   I could curse the stars—
Bosola.   Oh, fearful!
Duchess.   And those three smiling seasons of the year
   Into a Russian winter: nay, the world
   To its first chaos.
Bosola.   Look you, the stars shine still.
Duchess.   Oh, but you must
   Remember, my curse hath a great way to go.—
   Plagues, that make lanes through largest families
   Consume them!—
Bosola.   Fie, lady!
Duchess.   Let them, like tyrants,
   Never be remembered but for the ill they have done;
   Let all the zealous prayers of mortified
   Churchmen forget them!—
Bosola.   Oh, uncharitable!
Duchess.   Let Heaven a little while cease crowning martyrs
   To punish them!—
   Go, howl them this, and say, I long to bleed:
   It is some mercy when men kill with speed.

                                    [*Exeunt* DUCHESS *and* SERVANT.]

[*Re-enter* FERDINAND.]

Ferdinand.   Excellent, as I would wish; she 's plagued in art:
   These presentations are but fram'd in wax
   By the curious master in that quality,
   Vincentio Lauriola, and she takes them
   For true substantial bodies.
Bosola.   Why do you do this?
Ferdinand.   To bring her to despair.
Bosola.   'Faith, end here,
   And go no farther in your cruelty:
   Send her a penitential garment to put on
   Next to her delicate skin, and furnish her
   With beads and prayer-books.
Ferdinand.   Damn her! that body of hers,
   While that my blood ran pure in 't, was more worth
   Than that which thou wouldst comfort, called a soul.
   I will send her masks of common courtezans,
   Have her meat serv'd up by bawds and ruffians,
   And, 'cause she'll needs be mad, I am resolv'd
   To remove forth the common hospital
   All the mad-folk, and place them near her lodging;
   There let them practise together, sing and dance,

And act their gambols to the full o' th' moon:
If she can sleep the better for it, let her.
Your work is almost ended.
Bosola.   Must I see her again?
Ferdinand.   Yes.
Bosola.   Never.
Ferdinand.   You must.
Bosola.   Never in mine own shape;
   That's forfeited by my intelligence
   And this last cruel lie: when you send me next,
   The business shall be comfort.
Ferdinand.   Very likely;
   Thy pity is nothing of kin to thee. Antonio
   Lurks about Milan: thou shalt shortly thither
   To feed a fire as great as my revenge,
   Which ne'er will slack till it have spent his fuel:
   Intemperate agues make physicians cruel.   [*Exeunt.*]

[*The sound of horrid laughter and timbrels; re-enter* DUCHESS *and* CARIOLA[1].]

Duchess.   What hideous noise was that?
Cariola.   'Tis the wild consort
   Of madmen, lady, which your tyrant brother
   Hath plac'd about your lodging: this tyranny,
   I think, was never practis'd till this hour.
Duchess.   Indeed, I thank him: nothing but noise and folly
   Can keep me in my right wits; whereas reason
   And silence make me stark mad. Sit down;
   Discourse to me some dismal tragedy.
Cariola.   Oh, 'twill increase your melancholy.
Duchess.   Thou art deceived:
   To hear of greater grief would lessen mine.
   This is a prison?
Cariola.   Yes, but you shall live
   To shake this durance off.
Duchess.   Thou art a fool:
   The robin-redbreast and the nightingale
   Never live long in cages.
Cariola.   Pray, dry your eyes.
   What think you of, madam?
Duchess.   Of nothing; when I muse thus,
   I sleep.
Cariola.   Like a madman, with your eyes open?
Duchess.   Dost thou think we shall know one another in th' other world?
Cariola.   Yes, out of question.

1   Scene 2 begins here.

Duchess.   Oh, that it were possible
  We might but hold some two days' conference
  With the dead! From them I should learn somewhat, I am sure,
  I never shall know here. I'll tell thee a miracle;
  I am not mad yet, to my cause of sorrow:
  Th' heaven o'er my head seems made of molten brass,
  The earth of flaming sulphur, yet I am not mad.
  I am acquainted with sad misery
  As the tann'd galley-slave is with his oar;
  Necessity makes me suffer constantly,
  And custom makes it easy. Who do I look like now?
Cariola.   Like to your picture in the gallery,
  A deal of life in show, but none in practice;
  Or rather like some reverend monument
  Whose ruins are even pitied.
Duchess.   Very proper;
  And Fortune seems only to have her eyesight
  To behold my tragedy.—
  How now! what noise is that?

  [*Enter a* SERVANT.]

Servant.   I am come to tell you
  Your brother hath intended you some sport.
  A great physician, when the Pope was sick
  Of a deep melancholy, presented him
  With several sorts of madmen, which wild object
  Being full of change and sport, forc'd him to laugh,
  And so the imposthume broke: the self-same cure
  The duke intends on you.
Duchess.   Let them come in.
Servant.   There's a mad lawyer; and a secular priest;
  A doctor that hath forfeited his wits
  By jealousy; an astrologian
  That in his works said such a day o' th' month
  Should be the day of doom, and, failing of 't,
  Ran mad; an English tailor crazed i' th' brain
  With the study of new fashions; a gentleman-usher
  Quite beside himself with care to keep in mind
  The number of his lady's salutations
  Or 'How do you's' she employ'd him in each morning;
  A farmer, too, an excellent knave in grain,
  Mad 'cause he was hindered transportation:
  And let one broker that 's mad loose to these,
  You'd think the devil were among them.
Duchess.   Sit, Cariola.—Let them loose when you please,
  For I am chain'd to endure all your tyranny.

  [*Enter* MADMEN.]

[Here this Song is sung by a Madman to a dismal kind of music.]

> Oh, let us howl some heavy note,
>   Some deadly dogged howl,
> Sounding as from the threatening throat
>   Of beasts and fatal fowl!
> As ravens, screech-owls, bulls, and bears,
>   We'll bell,[1] and bawl our parts,
> Till irksome noise have cloy'd your ears
>   And corrosived your hearts.
> At last, whenas our quire wants breath,
>   Our bodies being blest,
> We'll sing, like swans, to welcome death,
>   And die in love and rest.

First Madman.   Doom's-day not come yet? I'll draw it nearer by a perspective, or make a glass that shall set all the world on fire upon an instant. I cannot sleep; my pillow is stuffed with a litter of porcupines.

Second Madman.   Hell is a mere glass-house, where the devils are continually blowing up women's souls on hollow irons, and the fire never goes out.

Third Madman.   I will lie with every woman in my parish the tenth night; I will tithe them over like haycocks.

Fourth Madman.   Shall my pothecary out-go me because I am a cuckold? I have found out his roguery; he makes alum of his wife's urine, and sells it to Puritans that have sore throats with overstraining.

First Madman.   I have skill in heraldry.

Second Madman.   Hast?

First Madman.   You do give for your crest a woodcock's head with the brains picked out on 't; you are a very ancient gentleman.

Third Madman.   Greek is turn'd Turk: we are only to be sav'd by the Helvetian translation.[2]

First Madman.   Come on, sir, I will lay the law to you.

Second Madman.   Oh, rather lay a corrosive: the law will eat to the bone.

Third Madman.   He that drinks but to satisfy nature is damned.

Fourth Madman.   If I had my glass here, I would show a sight should make all the women here call me mad doctor.

First Madman.   What's he? a rope-maker?

Second Madman.   No, no, no, a snuffling knave that, while he shows the tombs, will have his hand in a wench's placket.

Third Madman.   Woe to the caroche[3] that brought home my wife from the masque at three o'clock in the morning! it had a large feather-bed in it.

Fourth Madman.   I have pared the devil's nails forty times, roasted them in raven's eggs, and cur'd agues with them.

Third Madman.   Get me three hundred milchbats, to make possets to procure sleep.

---

[1]   Bellow.

[2]   The so-called Geneva Bible, made by English refugees at Geneva, published in 1560, and prohibited in England because of its Puritan tone.

[3]   Coach.

Fourth Madman. All the college may throw their caps at me: I have made a soap-boiler costive; it was my masterpiece.

[*Here the dance, consisting of Eight* MADMEN, *with music answerable thereunto; after which* BOSOLA, *like an Old Man, enters.*]

Duchess. Is he mad too?
Servant.   Pray question him. I'll leave you.
                                                      [*Exeunt* SERVANT *and* MADMEN.]
Bosola. I am come to make thy tomb.
Duchess.   Ha! my tomb?
  Thou speak'st as if I lay upon my death-bed,
  Gasping for breath: dost thou perceive me sick?
Bosola. Yes, and the more dangerously, since thy sickness
  Is insensible.
Duchess. Thou art not mad, sure: dost know me?
Bosola. Yes.
Duchess.   Who am I?
Bosola. Thou art a box of worm-seed, at best but a salvatory[1] of green mummy. What's this flesh? a little crudded[2] milk, fantastical puff-paste. Our bodies are weaker than those paper-prisons boys use to keep flies in; more contemptible, since ours is to preserve earthworms. Didst thou ever see a lark in a cage? Such is the soul in the body: this world is like her little turf of grass, and the heaven o'er our heads, like her looking-glass, only gives us a miserable knowledge of the small compass of our prison.
Duchess. Am not I thy duchess?
Bosola. Thou art some great woman, sure, for riot begins to sit on thy forehead (clad in grey hairs) twenty years sooner than on a merry milk-maid's. Thou sleep'st worse than if a mouse should be forc'd to take up her lodging in a cat's ear: a little infant that breeds its teeth, should it lie with thee, would cry out, as if thou wert the more unquiet bedfellow.
Duchess. I am Duchess of Malfi still.
Bosola. That makes thy sleeps so broken:
    Glories, like glow-worms, afar off shine bright,
    But looked to near, have neither heat nor light.
Duchess. Thou art very plain.
Bosola. My trade is to flatter the dead, not the living; I am a tomb-maker.
Duchess. And thou com'st to make my tomb?
Bosola. Yes.
Duchess. Let me be a little merry:—of what stuff wilt thou make it?
Bosola. Nay, resolve me first, of what fashion?
Duchess. Why, do we grow fantastical in our death-bed? do we affect fashion in the grave?
Bosola. Most ambitiously. Princes' images on their tombs do not lie, as they were wont, seeming to pray up to heaven; but with their hands under their cheeks, as

1   Ointment-box.
2   Curded.

if they died of the toothache: they are not carved with their eyes fix'd upon the
stars; but as their minds were wholly bent upon the world, the self-same way they
seem to turn their faces.

Duchess.   Let me know fully therefore the effect
Of this thy dismal preparation,
This talk fit for a charnel.

Bosola.   Now I shall:—

[*Enter* EXECUTIONERS, *with a coffin, cords, and a bell.*]

Here is a present from your princely brothers;
And may it arrive welcome, for it brings
Last benefit, last sorrow.

Duchess.   Let me see it:
I have so much obedience in my blood,
I wish it in their veins to do them good.

Bosola.   This is your last presence-chamber.
Cariola.   O my sweet lady!
Duchess.   Peace; it affrights not me.
Bosola.   I am the common bellman,
That usually is sent to condemn'd persons
The night before they suffer.

Duchess.   Even now
Thou said'st thou wast a tomb-maker.

Bosola.   'Twas to bring you
By degrees to mortification. Listen. [*Rings his bell.*]

> Hark, now every thing is still
> The screech-owl and the whistler shrill
> Call upon our dame aloud,
> And bid her quickly don her shroud!
> Much you had of land and rent:
> Your length in clay's now competent:[1]
> A long war disturb'd your mind;
> Here your perfect peace is sign'd.
> Of what is 't fools make such vain keeping?
> Sin their conception, their birth weeping,
> Their life a general mist of error,
> Their death a hideous storm of terror.
> Strew your hair with powders sweet,
> Don clean linen, bathe your feet,
> And (the foul fiend more to check)
> A crucifix let bless your neck:
> 'Tis now full tide 'tween night and day;
> End your groan, and come away.

Cariola.   Hence, villains, tyrants, murderers! alas!
What will you do with my lady?—Call for help.
Duchess.   To whom? to our next neighbours? they are mad-folks.

---

[1]   *I.e.,* all you require.

Bosola.   Remove that noise.
Duchess.   Farewell, Cariola.
  In my last will I have not much to give:
  A many hungry guests have fed upon me;
  Thine will be a poor reversion.
Cariola.   I will die with her.
Duchess.   I pray thee, look thou giv'st my little boy
  Some syrup for his cold, and let the girl
  Say her prayers ere she sleep.

          [CARIOLA *is forced out by the* EXECUTIONERS.]

                    Now what you please:
  What death?
Bosola.   Strangling;
  Here are your executioners.
Duchess.   I forgive them:
  The apoplexy, catarrh, or cough o' th' lungs,
  Would do as much as they do.
Bosola.   Doth not death fright you?
Duchess.   Who would be afraid on 't,
  Knowing to meet such excellent company
  In th' other world?
Bosola.   Yet, methinks,
  The manner of your death should much afflict you:
  This cord should terrify you.
Duchess.   Not a whit:
  What would it pleasure me to have my throat cut
  With diamonds? or to be smothered
  With cassia? or to be shot to death with pearls?
  I know death hath ten thousand several doors
  For men to take their exits; and 'tis found
  They go on such strange geometrical hinges,
  You may open them both ways.—Any way, for heaven sake,
  So I were out of your whispering. Tell my brothers
  That I perceive death, now I am well awake,
  Best gift is they can give or I can take.
  I would fain put off my last woman's fault,
  I'd not be tedious to you.
First Executioner.   We are ready.
Duchess.   Dispose my breath how please you; but my body
  Bestow upon my women, will you?
First Executioner.   Yes.
Duchess.   Pull, and pull strongly, for your able strength
  Must pull down heaven upon me:—
  Yet stay; heaven-gates are not so highly arch'd
  As princes' palaces; they that enter there
  Must go upon their knees [*Kneels*].—Come, violent death

Serve for mandragora to make me sleep!—
Go tell my brothers, when I am laid out,
They then may feed in quiet.

[*They strangle her.*]

Bosola.   Where's the waiting woman? Fetch her: some other
Strangle the children.

                [*Exeunt* EXECUTIONERS, *some of whom return with* CARIOLA.]

Look you, there sleeps your mistress.
Cariola.   Oh, you are damn'd
Perpetually for this! My turn is next,
Is 't not so order'd?
Bosola.   Yes, and I am glad
You are so well prepar'd for 't.
Cariola.   You are deceiv'd, sir,
I am not prepar'd for 't, I will not die;
I will first come to my answer, and know
How I have offended.
Bosola.   Come, dispatch her.—
You kept her counsel; now you shall keep ours.
Cariola.   I will not die, I must not; I am contracted
To a young gentleman.
First Executioner.   Here's your wedding-ring.
Cariola.   Let me but speak with the duke; I'll discover
Treason to his person.
Bosola.   Delays:—throttle her.
First Executioner.   She bites and scratches.
Cariola.   If you kill me now,
I am damn'd; I have not been at confession
This two years.
Bosola. [*To Executioners*].   When?[1]
Cariola.   I am quick with child.
Bosola.   Why, then,
Your credit's sav'd.

[*They strangle* CARIOLA.]

              Bear her into th' next room;
Let this lie still.

            [*Exeunt the* EXECUTIONERS *with the body of* CARIOLA.]

[*Enter* FERDINAND.]

Ferdinand.   Is she dead?

---

[1]   A common exclamation of impatience.

Bosola.   She is what
  You'd have her. But here begin your pity:

[*Shows the* CHILDREN *strangled.*]

  Alas, how have these offended?
Ferdinand.   The death
  Of young wolves is never to be pitied.
Bosola.   Fix
  Your eye here.
Ferdinand.   Constantly.
Bosola.   Do you not weep?
  Other sins only speak; murder shrieks out:
  The element of water moistens the earth,
  But blood flies upwards and bedews the heavens.
Ferdinand.   Cover her face; mine eyes dazzle: she died young.
Bosola.   I think not so; her infelicity
  Seem'd to have years too many.
Ferdinand.   She and I were twins;
  And should I die this instant, I had liv'd
  Her time to a minute.
Bosola.   It seems she was born first:
  You have bloodily approv'd the ancient truth,
  That kindred commonly do worse agree
  Than remote strangers.
Ferdinand.   Let me see her face
  Again. Why didst not thou pity her? what
  An excellent honest man mightst thou have been,
  If thou hadst borne her to some sanctuary!
  Or, bold in a good cause, oppos'd thyself,
  With thy advancèd sword above thy head,
  Between her innocence and my revenge!
  I bade thee, when I was distracted of my wits,
  Go kill my dearest friend, and thou hast done 't.
  For let me but examine well the cause:
  What was the meanness of her match to me?
  Only I must confess I had a hope,
  Had she continu'd widow, to have gain'd
  An infinite mass of treasure by her death:
  And that was the main cause; her marriage,
  That drew a stream of gall quite through my heart.
  For thee, as we observe in tragedies
  That a good actor many times is curs'd
  For playing a villain's part, I hate thee for 't,
  And, for my sake, say thou hast done much ill well.
Bosola.   Let me quicken your memory, for I perceive
  You are falling into ingratitude: I challenge
  The reward due to my service.

Ferdinand. I'll tell thee
What I'll give thee.
Bosola. Do.
Ferdinand. I'll give thee a pardon
For this murder.
Bosola. Ha!
Ferdinand. Yes, and 'tis
The largest bounty I can study to do thee.
By what authority didst thou execute
This bloody sentence?
Bosola. By yours.
Ferdinand. Mine? was I her judge?
Did any ceremonial form of law
Doom her to not-being? did a complete jury
Deliver her conviction up i' th' court?
Where shalt thou find this judgment register'd,
Unless in hell? See, like a bloody fool,
Thou'st forfeited thy life, and thou shalt die for 't.
Bosola. The office of justice is perverted quite
When one thief hangs another. Who shall dare
To reveal this?
Ferdinand. Oh, I'll tell thee;
The wolf shall find her grave, and scrape it up,
Not to devour the corpse, but to discover
The horrid murder.
Bosola. You, not I, shall quake for 't.
Ferdinand. Leave me.
Bosola. I will first receive my pension.
Ferdinand. You are a villain.
Bosola. When your ingratitude
Is judge, I am so.
Ferdinand. Oh, horror, that not the fear
Of him which binds the devils can prescribe man
Obedience!—Never look upon me more.
Bosola. Why, fare thee well.
Your brother and yourself are worthy men:
You have a pair of hearts are hollow graves,
Rotten, and rotting others; and your vengeance,
Like two chain'd bullets, still goes arm in arm:
You may be brothers; for treason, like the plague,
Doth take much in a blood. I stand like one
That long hath ta'en a sweet and golden dream:
I am angry with myself, now that I wake.
Ferdinand. Get thee into some unknown part o' th' world,
That I may never see thee.
Bosola. Let me know
Wherefore I should be thus neglected. Sir,
I serv'd your tyranny, and rather strove

    To satisfy yourself than all the world:
    And though I loath'd the evil, yet I lov'd
    You that did counsel it; and rather sought
    To appear a true servant than an honest man.
Ferdinand.   I'll go hunt the badger by owl-light:
    'Tis a deed of darkness.   *[Exit.]*
Bosola. He's much distracted. [*Removes his old man's disguise.*]
    Off, my painted honour!
    While with vain hopes our faculties we tire,
    We seem to sweat in ice and freeze in fire.
    What would I do, were this to do again?
    I would not change my peace of conscience
    For all the wealth of Europe.—She stirs; here's life:—
    Return, fair soul, from darkness, and lead mine
    Out of this sensible hell:—she's warm, she breathes:—
    Upon thy pale lips I will melt my heart,
    To store them with fresh colour.—Who's there!
    Some cordial drink!—Alas! I dare not call:
    So pity would destroy pity.—Her eye opes,
    And heaven in it seems to ope, that late was shut,
    To take me up to mercy.
Duchess.   Antonio!
Bosola.   Yes, madam, he is living;
    The dead bodies you saw were but feign'd statues:
    He's reconcil'd to your brothers: the Pope hath wrought
    The atonement.
Duchess.   Mercy!   *[Dies.]*
Bosola.   Oh, she's gone again! there the cords of life broke.
    Oh, sacred innocence, that sweetly sleeps
    On turtles'[1] feathers, whilst a guilty conscience
    Is a black register wherein is writ
    All our good deeds and bad, a perspective
    That shows us hell! That we cannot be suffer'd
    To do good when we have a mind to it!
    This is manly sorrow; these tears, I am very certain,
    Never grew in my mother's milk: my estate
    Is sunk below the degree of fear: where were
    These penitent fountains while she was living?
    Oh, they were frozen up! Here is a sight
    As direful to my soul as is the sword
    Unto a wretch hath slain his father. Come, I'll bear thee
    Hence, and execute thy last will; that's deliver
    Thy body to the reverend dispose
    Of some good women: that the cruel tyrant

---

[1] *I.e.,* turtledoves.

Shall not deny me. Then I'll post to Milan,
Where somewhat I will speedily enact
Worth my dejection.   [*Exit with the body.*]

Act The Fifth

[*A Public Place in Milan*]

[*Enter* ANTONIO *and* DELIO.]

Antonio.   What think you of my hope of reconcilement
   To the Aragonian brethren?
Delio.   I misdoubt it;
   For though they have sent their letters of safe-conduct
   For your repair to Milan, they appear
   But nets to entrap you. The Marquis of Pescara,
   Under whom you hold certain land in cheat,[1]
   Much 'gainst his noble nature hath been mov'd
   To seize those lands; and some of his dependants
   Are at this instant making it their suit
   To be invested in your revenues.
   I cannot think they mean well to your life
   That do deprive you of your means of life,
   Your living.
Antonio.   You are still an heretic
   To any safety I can shape myself.
Delio.   Here comes the marquis: I will make myself
   Petitioner for some part of your land,
   To know whither it is flying.
Antonio   I pray do. [*Withdraws to back.*]

[*Enter* PESCARA.]

Delio.   Sir, I have a suit to you.
Pescara.   To me?
Delio.   An easy one:
   There is the citadel of Saint Bennet,
   With some demesnes, of late in the possession
   Of Antonio Bologna,—please you bestow them on me.
Pescara.   You are my friend; but this is such a suit,
   Nor fit for me to give, nor you to take.
Delio.   No, sir?
Pescara.   I will give you ample reason for 't
   Soon in private:—here's the Cardinal's mistress.

[*Enter* JULIA.]

---

[1]   Escheat, subject to forfeiture on the outlawry of the tenant.

Julia.   My lord, I am grown your poor petitioner,
   And should be an ill beggar, had I not
   A great man's letter here, the Cardinal's,
   To court you in my favour. [*Gives a letter.*]
Pescara.   He entreats for you
   The citadel of Saint Bennet, that belong'd
   To the banish'd Bologna.
Julia.   Yes.
Pescara.   I could not
   Have thought of a friend I could rather pleasure with it:
   'Tis yours.
Julia.   Sir, I thank you; and he shall know
   How doubly I am engag'd both in your gift,
   And speediness of giving, which makes your grant
   The greater.   [*Exit.*]
Antonio [*Aside*].   How they fortify themselves
   With my ruin!
Delio.   Sir, I am little bound to you.
Pescara.   Why?
Delio.   Because you denied this suit to me, and gave 't
   To such a creature.
Pescara.   Do you know what it was?
   It was Antonio's land; not forfeited
   By course of law, but ravish'd from his throat
   By the Cardinal's entreaty: it were not fit
   I should bestow so main a piece of wrong
   Upon my friend; 'tis a gratification
   Only due to a strumpet, for it is injustice.
   Shall I sprinkle the pure blood of innocents
   To make those followers I call my friends
   Look ruddier upon me? I am glad
   This land, ta'en from the owner by such wrong,
   Returns again unto so foul an use
   As salary for his lust. Learn, good Delio,
   To ask noble things of me, and you shall find
   I'll be a noble giver.
Delio.   You instruct me well.
Antonio [*Aside*].   Why, here's a man who would fright impudence
   From sauciest beggars.
Pescara.   Prince Ferdinand's come to Milan,
   Sick, as they give out, of an apoplexy;
   But some say 'tis a frenzy: I am going
   To visit him.   [*Exit.*]
Antonio.   'Tis a noble old fellow.
Delio.   What course do you mean to take, Antonio?
Antonio.   This night I mean to venture all my fortune,
   Which is no more than a poor lingering life,
   To the Cardinal's worst of malice: I have got

Private access to his chamber; and intend
To visit him about the mid of night,
As once his brother did our noble duchess.
It may be that the sudden apprehension
Of danger,—for I'll go in mine own shape,—
When he shall see it fraight[1] with love and duty,
May draw the poison out of him, and work
A friendly reconcilement: if it fail,
Yet it shall rid me of this infamous calling;
For better fall once than be ever falling.
Delio.   I'll second you in all danger; and, howe'er,
   My life keeps rank with yours.
Antonio.   You are still my lov'd
   And best friend.   [*Exeunt.*]

*   *   *

[A *Gallery in the Cardinal's Palace at Milan*]

[*Enter* PESCARA *and* DOCTOR.]

Pescara.   Now, doctor, may I visit your patient?
Doctor.   If't please your lordship: but he's instantly
   To take the air here in the gallery
   By my direction.
Pescara.   Pray thee, what's his disease?
Doctor.   A very pestilent disease, my lord,
   They call lycanthropia.
Pescara.   What's that?
   I need a dictionary to 't.
Doctor.   I'll tell you.
   In those that are possess'd with 't there o'erflows
   Such melancholy humour they imagine
   Themselves to be transformed into wolves;
   Steal forth to churchyards in the dead of night,
   And dig dead bodies up: as two nights since
   One met the duke 'bout midnight in a lane
   Behind Saint Mark's Church, with the leg of a man
   Upon his shoulder; and he howl'd fearfully;
   Said he was a wolf, only the difference
   Was, a wolf's skin was hairy on the outside,
   His on the inside; bade them take their swords,
   Rip up his flesh, and try: straight I was sent for,
   And, having minister'd to him, found his grace
   Very well recovered.
Pescara.   I am glad on 't.

---

[1]   Fraught.

Doctor.   Yet not without some fear
Of a relapse. If he grow to his fit again,
I'll go a nearer way to work with him
Than ever Paracelsus dream'd of; if
They'll give me leave, I'll buffet his madness
Out of him. Stand aside; he comes.

[*Enter* FERDINAND, CARDINAL, MALATESTE, *and* BOSOLA.]

Ferdinand.   Leave me.
Malateste.   Why doth your lordship love this solitariness?
Ferdinand.   Eagles commonly fly alone: they are crows, daws, and starlings that
flock together. Look, what's that follows me?
Malateste.   Nothing, my lord.
Ferdinand.   Yes.
Malateste.   'Tis your shadow.
Ferdinand.   Stay it; let it not haunt me.
Malateste.   Impossible, if you move, and the sun shine.
Ferdinand.   I will throttle it. [*Throws himself on the ground.*]
Malateste.   O, my lord, you are angry with nothing.
Ferdinand.   You are a fool: how is 't possible I should catch my shadow, unless I
fall upon 't? When I go to hell, I mean to carry a bribe; for, look you, good gifts
evermore make way for the worst persons.
Pescara.   Rise, good my lord.
Ferdinand.   I am studying the art of patience.
Pescara.   'Tis a noble virtue.
Ferdinand.   To drive six snails before me from this town to Moscow; neither use
goad nor whip to them, but let them take their own time;—the patient'st man
i' th' world match me for an experiment;—and I'll crawl after like a sheep-biter.
Cardinal.   Force him up. [*They raise him.*]
Ferdinand.   Use me well, you were best. What I have done, I have done: I'll con-
fess nothing.
Doctor.   Now let me come to him.—Are you mad, my lord? are you out of your
princely wits?
Ferdinand.   What's he?
Pescara.   Your doctor.
Ferdinand.   Let me have his beard saw'd off, and his eyebrows fil'd more civil.
Doctor.   I must do mad tricks with him, for that's the only way on 't.—I have
brought your grace a salamander's skin to keep you from sunburning.
Ferdinand.   I have cruel sore eyes.
Doctor.   The white of a cockatrix's egg is present remedy.
Ferdinand.   Let it be a new laid one, you were best.—Hide me from him: physi-
cians are like kings,—they brook no contradiction.
Doctor.   Now he begins to fear me: now let me alone with him.
Cardinal.   How now? put off your gown?
Doctor.   Let me have some forty urinals fill'd with rosewater: he and I'll go pelt
one another with them.—Now he begins to fear me.—Can you fetch a frisk,[1]

---

[1]   Cut a caper.

sir?—Let him go, let him go, upon my peril: I find by his eye he stands in awe of me; I'll make him as tame as a dormouse.

Ferdinand. Can you fetch your frisks, sir?—I will stamp him into a cullis, flay off his skin, to cover one of the anatomies[1] this rogue hath set i' th' cold yonder in Barber-Chirurgeon's-hall.—Hence, hence! you are all of you like beasts for sacrifice: there's nothing left of you but tongue and belly, flattery and lechery. [*Exit.*]

Pescara. Doctor, he did not fear you throughly.

Doctor. True;
I was somewhat too forward.

Bosola. Mercy upon me,
What a fatal judgement hath fall'n upon this Ferdinand!

Pescara. Knows your grace what accident hath brought
Unto the prince this strange distraction?

Cardinal [*Aside*]. I must feign somewhat.—Thus they say it grew.
You have heard it rumour'd, for these many years
None of our family dies but there is seen
The shape of an old woman, which is given
By tradition to us to have been murder'd
By her nephews for her riches. Such a figure
One night, as the prince sat up late at 's book,
Appear'd to him; when crying out for help,
The gentleman of's chamber found his grace
All on a cold sweat, alter'd much in face
And language: since which apparition,
He hath grown worse and worse, and I much fear
He cannot live.

Bosola [*To the* CARDINAL]. Sir, I would speak with you.

Pescara. We'll leave your grace,
Wishing to the sick prince, our noble lord,
All health of mind and body.

Cardinal. You are most welcome.

[*Exeunt* PESCARA, MALATESTE, *and* DOCTOR.]

Are you come? so.—[*Aside*] This fellow must not know
By any means I had intelligence
In our duchess' death; for, though I counsell'd it,
The full of all th' engagement seem'd to grow
From Ferdinand.—Now, sir, how fares our sister?
I do not think but sorrow makes her look
Like to an oft-dyed garment: she shall now
Taste comfort from me. Why do you look so wildly?
Oh, the fortune of your master here the prince
Dejects you; but be you of happy comfort:
If you'll do one thing for me I'll entreat,
Though he had a cold tombstone o'er his bones,
I'd make you what you would be.

[1] Skeletons.

Bosola.   Anything;
   Give it me in a breath, and let me fly to 't:
   They that think long small expedition win,
   For musing much o' th' end cannot begin.

   [*Enter* JULIA.]

Julia.   Sir, will you come in to supper?
Cardinal.   I am busy;
   Leave me.
Julia [*Aside*].   What an excellent shape hath that fellow!   [*Exit.*]
Cardinal.   'Tis thus. Antonio lurks here in Milan:
   Inquire him out, and kill him. While he lives,
   Our sister cannot marry; and I have thought
   Of an excellent match for her. Do this, and style me
   Thy advancement.
Bosola.   But by what means shall I find him out?
Cardinal.   There is a gentleman called Delio
   Here in the camp, that hath been long approv'd
   His loyal friend. Set eye upon that fellow;
   Follow him to mass; maybe Antonio,
   Although he do account religion
   But a school-name, for fashion of the world
   May accompany him; or else go inquire out
   Delio's confessor, and see if you can bribe
   Him to reveal it. There are a thousand ways
   A man might find to trace him; as to know
   What fellows haunt the Jews for taking up
   Great sums of money, for sure he 's in want;
   Or else to go to th' picture-makers, and learn
   Who bought her picture lately: some of these
   Haply may take.
Bosola.   Well, I'll not freeze i' th' business:
   I would see that wretched thing, Antonio,
   Above all sights i' th' world.
Cardinal.   Do, and be happy.   [*Exit.*]
Bosola.   This fellow doth breed basilisks in 's eyes,
   He's nothing else but murder; yet he seems
   Not to have notice of the duchess' death.
   'Tis his cunning: I must follow his example;
   There cannot be a surer way to trace
   Than that of an old fox.

   [*Re-enter* JULIA, *with a pistol.*]

Julia.   So, sir, you are well met.
Bosola.   How now?
Julia.   Nay, the doors are fast enough: Now, sir,
   I will make you confess your treachery.

Bosola.   Treachery?
Julia.   Yes,
    Confess to me which of my women 'twas
    You hired to put love-powder into my drink?
Bosola.   Love-powder?
Julia.   Yes, when I was at Malfi.
    Why should I fall in love with such a face else?
    I have already suffer'd for thee so much pain,
    The only remedy to do me good
    Is to kill my longing.
Bosola.   Sure, your pistol holds
    Nothing but perfumes or kissing-comfits.
    Excellent lady! You have a pretty way on 't
    To discover your longing. Come, come, I'll disarm you,
    And arm you thus: yet this is wondrous strange.
Julia.   Compare thy form and my eyes together, you'll find
    My love no such great miracle. Now you'll say
    I am wanton: this nice modesty in ladies
    Is but a troublesome familiar that haunts them.
Bosola.   Know you me, I am a blunt soldier.
Julia.   The better:
    Sure, there wants fire where there are no lively sparks
    Of roughness.
Bosola.   And I want compliment.
Julia.   Why, ignorance
    In courtship cannot make you do amiss,
    If you have a heart to do well.
Bosola.   You are very fair.
Julia.   Nay, if you lay beauty to my charge,
    I must plead unguilty.
Bosola.   Your bright eyes carry
    A quiver of darts in them sharper than sunbeams.
Julia.   You will mar me with commendation,
    Put yourself to the charge of courting me,
    Whereas now I woo you.
Bosola [*Aside*].   I have it, I will work upon this creature.—
    Let us grow most amorously familiar:
    If the great Cardinal now should see me thus,
    Would he not count me a villain?
Julia.   No; he might
    Count me a wanton, not lay a scruple
    Of offence on you; for if I see and steal
    A diamond, the fault is not i' th' stone,
    But in me the thief that purloins it. I am sudden
    With you: we that are great women of pleasure
    Use to cut off these uncertain wishes
    And unquiet longings, and in an instant join
    The sweet delight and the pretty excuse together.

Had you been i' th' street, under my chamber-window,
Even there I should have courted you.
Bosola.   Oh, you are
An excellent lady!
Julia.   Bid me do somewhat for you
Presently to express I love you.
Bosola.   I will;
And if you love me, fail not to effect it.
The Cardinal is grown wondrous melancholy;
Demand the cause, let him not put you off
With feign'd excuse; discover the main ground on 't.
Julia.   Why would you know this?
Bosola.   I have depended on him,
And I hear that he is fall'n in some disgrace
With the emperor: if he be, like the mice
That forsake falling houses, I would shift
To other dependence.
Julia.   You shall not need
Follow the wars: I'll be your maintenance.
Bosola.   And I your loyal servant: but I cannot
Leave my calling.
Julia.   Not leave an ungrateful
General for the love of a sweet lady?
You are like some cannot sleep in feather-beds,
But must have blocks for their pillows.
Bosola.   Will you do this?
Julia.   Cunningly.
Bosola.   To-morrow I'll expect th' intelligence.
Julia.   To-morrow? get you into my cabinet;
You shall have it with you. Do not delay me,
No more than I do you: I am like one
That is condemn'd; I have my pardon promis'd,
But I would see it seal'd. Go, get you in:
You shall see me wind my tongue about his heart
Like a skein of silk.   [*Exit* BOSOLA.]

[*Re-enter* CARDINAL.]

Cardinal.   Where are you?

[*Enter* SERVANTS.]

Servants.   Here.
Cardinal.   Let none, upon your lives, have conference
With the Prince Ferdinand, unless I know it.—
[*Aside*] In this distraction he may reveal
The murder.   [*Exeunt* SERVANTS.]
            Yond's my lingering consumption:

  I am weary of her, and by any means
  Would be quit of.
Julia.   How now, my lord? what ails you?
Cardinal. Nothing.
Julia.   Oh, you are much alter'd: come, I must be
  Your secretary, and remove this lead
  From off your bosom: what's the matter?
Cardinal.   I may not
  Tell you.
Julia. Are you so far in love with sorrow
  You cannot part with part of it? or think you
  I cannot love your grace when you are sad
  As well as merry? or do you suspect
  I, that have been a secret to your heart
  These many winters, cannot be the same
  Unto your tongue?
Cardinal.   Satisfy thy longing,—
  The only way to make thee keep my counsel
  Is, not to tell thee.
Julia.   Tell your echo this,
  Or flatterers, that like echoes still report
  What they hear though most imperfect, and not me;
  For if that you be true unto yourself,
  I'll know.
Cardinal. Will you rack me?
Julia.   No, judgment shall
  Draw it from you: it is an equal fault,
  To tell one's secrets unto all or none.
Cardinal. The first argues folly.
Julia.   But the last tyranny.
Cardinal. Very well: why, imagine I have committed
  Some secret deed which I desire the world
  May never hear of.
Julia.   Therefore may not I know it?
  You have conceal'd for me as great a sin
  As adultery. Sir, never was occasion
  For perfect trial of my constancy
  Till now: sir, I beseech you——
Cardinal.   You'll repent it.
Julia. Never.
Cardinal. It hurries thee to ruin: I'll not tell thee.
  Be well advis'd, and think what danger 'tis
  To receive a prince's secrets: they that do,
  Had need have their breasts hoop'd with adamant
  to contain them. I pray thee, yet be satisfi'd;
  Examine thine own frailty; 'tis more easy
  To tie knots than unloose them: 'tis a secret

That, like a lingering poison, may chance lie
Spread in thy veins, and kill thee seven year hence.
Julia.   Now you dally with me.
Cardinal.   No more; thou shalt know it.
By my appointment the great Duchess of Malfi
And two of her young children, four nights since,
Were strangled.
Julia.   O Heaven! sir, what have you done!
Cardinal.   How now? how settles this? think you your bosom
Will be a grave dark and obscure enough
For such a secret?
Julia.   You have undone yourself, sir.
Cardinal.   Why?
Julia.   It lies not in me to conceal it.
Cardinal.   No?
Come, I will swear you to 't upon this book.
Julia.   Most religiously.
Cardinal.   Kiss it. [*She kisses the book.*]
        Now you shall
Never utter it; thy curiosity
Hath undone thee: thou'rt poison'd with that book;
Because I knew thou couldst not keep my counsel,
I have bound thee to 't by death.

[*Re-enter* BOSOLA.]

Bosola.   For pity sake,
    Hold!
Cardinal.   Ha! Bosola?
Julia.   I forgive you
This equal piece of justice you have done;
For I betray'd your counsel to that fellow:
He overheard it; that was the cause I said
It lay not in me to conceal it.
Bosola.   O foolish woman,
Couldst not thou have poison'd him?
Julia.   'Tis weakness,
Too much to think what should have been done. I go,
I know not whither.   [*Dies.*]
Cardinal.   Wherefore com'st thou hither?
Bosola.   That I might find a great man like yourself,
Not out of his wits as the Lord Ferdinand,
To remember my service.
Cardinal.   I'll have thee hew'd in pieces.
Bosola.   Make not yourself such a promise of that life
Which is not yours to dispose of.
Cardinal.   Who plac'd thee here?
Bosola.   Her lust, as she intended.

Cardinal.   Very well:
   Now you know me for your fellow-murderer.
Bosola.   And wherefore should you lay fair marble colours
   Upon your rotten purposes to me?
   Unless you imitate some that do plot great treasons,
   And when they have done, go hide themselves i' th' graves
   Of those were actors in 't?
Cardinal.   No more; there is
   A fortune attends thee.
Bosola.   Shall I go sue
   To Fortune any longer? 'Tis the fool's
   Pilgrimage.
Cardinal.   I have honours in store for thee.
Bosola.   There are a many ways that conduct to seeming
   Honour, and some of them very dirty ones.
Cardinal.   Throw
   To the devil thy melancholy. The fire burns well:
   What need we keep a stirring of 't, and make
   A greater smother? Thou wilt kill Antonio?
Bosola.   Yes.
Cardinal.   Take up that body.
Bosola.   I think I shall
   Shortly grow the common bearer for churchyards.
Cardinal.   I will allow thee some dozen of attendants
   To aid thee in the murder.
Bosola.   Oh, by no means. Physicians that apply horse-leeches to any rank swelling
   use to cut off their tails, that the blood may run through them the faster: let me
   have no train when I go to shed blood, lest it make me have a greater when I
   ride to the gallows.
Cardinal.   Come to me after midnight, to help to remove
   That body to her own lodging: I'll give out
   She died o' th' plague; 'twill breed the less inquiry
   After her death.
Bosola.   Where's Castruchio her husband?
Cardinal.   He's rode to Naples, to take possession
   Of Antonio's citadel.
Bosola.   Believe me, you have done
   A very happy turn.
Cardinal.   Fail not to come:
   There is the master-key of our lodgings; and by that
   You may conceive what trust I plant in you.
Bosola.   You shall find me ready.   [*Exit* CARDINAL.]
                O poor Antonio,
   Though nothing be so needful to thy estate
   As pity, yet I find nothing so dangerous;
   I must look to my footing:
   In such slippery ice-pavements men had need

To be frost-nailed well, they may break their necks else;
The precedent's here afore me. How this man
Bears up in blood! seems fearless! Why, 'tis well:
Security some men call the suburbs of hell,
Only a dead wall between. Well, good Antonio,
I'll seek thee out; and all my care shall be
To put thee into safety from the reach
Of these most cruel biters that have got
Some of thy blood already. It may be,
I'll join with thee in a most just revenge:
The weakest arm is strong enough that strikes
With the sword of justice. Still methinks the duchess
Haunts me.—There, there, 'tis nothing but my melancholy.
O Penitence, let me truly taste thy cup,
That throws men down only to raise them up!   [*Exit.*]

*   *   *

[*A Fortification at Milan*]

[*Enter* ANTONIO *and* DELIO.]

Delio.   Yond's the Cardinal's window. This fortification
    Grew from the ruins of an ancient abbey;
    And to yond side o' th' river lies a wall,
    Piece of a cloister, which in my opinion
    Gives the best echo that you ever heard,
    So hollow and so dismal, and withal
    So plain in the distinction of our words,
    That many have suppos'd it is a spirit
    That answers.
Antonio.   I do love these ancient ruins.
    We never tread upon them but we set
    Our foot upon some reverend history:
    And, questionless, here in this open court,
    Which now lies naked to the injuries
    Of stormy weather, some men lie interr'd
    Lov'd the church so well, and gave so largely to 't,
    They thought it should have canopied their bones
    Till doomsday; but all things have their end:
    Churches and cities, which have diseases
    Like to men, must have like death that we have.
Echo.   'Like death that we have.'
Delio.   Now the echo hath caught you.
Antonio.   It groaned, methought, and gave
    A very deadly accent.
Echo.   'Deadly accent.'

Delio.   I told you 'twas a pretty one: you may make it
   A huntsman, or a falconer, a musician,
   Or a thing of sorrow.
Echo.   'A thing of sorrow.'
Antonio.   Aye, sure, that suits it best.
Echo.   'That suits it best.'
Antonio.   'Tis very like my wife's voice.
Echo.   'Aye, wife's voice.'
Delio.   Come, let's walk further from 't. I would not have you
   Go to th' Cardinal's to-night: do not.
Echo.   'Do not.'
Delio.   Wisdom doth not more moderate wasting sorrow
   Than time: take time for 't; be mindful of thy safety.
Echo.   'Be mindful of thy safety.'
Antonio.   Necessity compels me:
   Make scrutiny throughout the passes of
   Your own life, you'll find it impossible
   To fly your fate.
Echo.   'Oh, fly your fate.'
Delio.   Hark!
   The dead stones seem to have pity on you, and give you
   Good counsel.
Antonio.   Echo, I will not talk with thee,
   For thou art a dead thing.
Echo.   'Thou art a dead thing.'
Antonio.   My duchess is asleep now,
   And her little ones, I hope sweetly: O Heaven,
   Shall I never see her more?
Echo.   'Never see her more.'
Antonio.   I mark'd not one repetition of the echo
   But that; and on the sudden a clear light
   Presented me a face folded in sorrow.
Delio.   Your fancy merely.
Antonio.   Come, I'll be out of this ague,
   For to live thus is not indeed to live;
   It is a mockery and abuse of life:
   I will not henceforth save myself by halves;
   Lose all, or nothing.
Delio.   Your own virtue save you!
   I'll fetch your eldest son, and second you:
   It may be that the sight of his own blood
   Spread in so sweet a figure may beget
   The more compassion. However, fare you well.
   Though in our miseries Fortune have a part,
   Yet in our noble sufferings she hath none:
   Contempt of pain, that we may call our own.   [*Exeunt.*]

*   *   *

[*A Room in the Cardinal's Palace*]

[*Enter* CARDINAL, PESCARA, MALATESTE, RODERIGO, *and* GRISOLAN.]

Cardinal.   You shall not watch to-night by the sick prince;
   His grace is very well recover'd.
Malateste.   Good my lord, suffer us.
Cardinal.   Oh, by no means;
   The noise, and change of object in his eye,
   Doth more distract him: I pray, all to bed;
   And though you hear him in his violent fit,
   Do not rise, I entreat you.
Pescara.   So, sir; we shall not.
Cardinal.   Nay, I must have you promise upon your honours,
   For I was enjoin'd to 't by himself; and he seem'd
   To urge it sensibly.
Pescara.   Let our honours bind
   This trifle.
Cardinal.   Nor any of your followers.
Malateste.   Neither.
Cardinal.   It may be, to make trial of your promise,
   When he's asleep, myself will rise and feign
   Some of his mad tricks, and cry out for help,
   And feign myself in danger.
Malateste.   If your throat were cutting,
   I'd not come at you, now I have protested against it.
Cardinal.   Why, I thank you.
Grisolan.   'Twas a foul storm to-night.
Roderigo.   The Lord Ferdinand's chamber shook like an osier.
Malateste.   'Twas nothing but pure kindness in the devil,
   To rock his own child.   [*Exeunt all except the* CARDINAL.]
Cardinal.   The reason why I would not suffer these
   About my brother, is, because at midnight
   I may with better privacy convey
   Julia's body to her own lodging. Oh, my conscience!
   I would pray now; but the devil takes away my heart
   For having any confidence in prayer.
   About this hour I appointed Bosola
   To fetch the body: when he hath serv'd my turn,
   He dies.   [*Exit.*]

[*Enter* BOSOLA.]

Bosola.   Ha! 'twas the Cardinal's voice; I heard him name
   Bosola and my death. Listen; I hear
   One's footing. [*He hides.*]

[*Enter* FERDINAND.]

Ferdinand.   Strangling is a very quiet death.

Bosola [Aside.]   Nay, then, I see I must stand upon my guard.

Ferdinand.   What say to that? whisper softly; do you agree to 't? So; it must be
done i' th' dark: the Cardinal would not for a thousand pounds the doctor
should see it.   [*Exit.*]

Bosola.   My death is plotted; here 's the consequence of murder.
We value not desert nor Christian breath,
When we know black deeds must be cur'd with death.

[*Enter* ANTONIO *and* SERVANT.]

Servant.   Here stay, sir, and be confident, I pray:
I'll fetch you a dark lantern.   [*Exit.*]

Antonio [Standing where FERDINAND *stood.]* Could I take him
At his prayers, there were hope of pardon.

Bosola.   Fall right, my sword!— [*Stabs him.*]
I'll not give thee so much leisure as to pray.

Antonio.   Oh, I am gone! Thou hast ended a long suit
In a minute.

Bosola.   What art thou?

Antonio.   A most wretched thing,
That only have thy benefit in death,
To appear myself.

[*Re-enter* SERVANT *with a lantern.*]

Servant.   Where are you, sir?

Antonio.   Very near my home.—Bosola?

Servant. Oh, misfortune!

Bosola.   Smother thy pity, thou are dead else.—Antonio?
The man I would have saved 'bove mine own life!
We are merely the stars' tennis-balls, struck and bandied
Which way please them.—O good Antonio,
I'll whisper one thing in thy dying ear
Shall make thy heart break quickly! thy fair duchess
And two sweet children——

Antonio.   Their very names
Kindle a little life in me.

Bosola.   Are murder'd.

Antonio.   Some men have wish'd to die
At the hearing of sad tidings; I am glad
That I shall do 't in sadness:[1] I would not now
Wish my wounds balm'd nor heal'd, for I have no use
To put my life to. In all our quest of greatness,
Like wanton boys, whose pastime is their care,
We follow after bubbles blown in th' air.
Pleasure of life, what is 't? only the good

---

[1]   *I.e.,* in earnest.

Hours of an ague; merely a preparative
To rest, to endure vexation. I do not ask
The process of my death; only commend me
To Delio.
Bosola.   Break, heart!
Antonio.   And let my son
Fly the courts of princes.   [*Dies.*]
Bosola.   Thou seem'st
To have lov'd Antonio?
Servant.   I brought him hither,
To have reconcil'd him to the Cardinal.
Bosola.   I do not ask thee that.
Take him up, if thou tender thine own life,
And bear him where the lady Julia
Was wont to lodge.—Oh, my fate moves swift;
I have this Cardinal in the forge already;
Now I'll bring him to th' hammer. O direful misprision![1]
I will not imitate things glorious,
No more than base; I'll be mine own example.—
[*To Servant.*] On, on, and look thou represent, for silence,
The thing thou bear'st.   [*Exeunt.*]

*   *   *

[*Another Room in the same*]

[*Enter* CARDINAL, *with a book.*]

Cardinal.   I am puzzled in a question about hell:
He says, in hell there's one material fire,
And yet it shall not burn all men alike.
Lay him by. How tedious is a guilty conscience!
When I look into the fish-ponds in my garden,
Methinks I see a thing arm'd with a rake,
That seems to strike at me.

[*Enter* BOSOLA, *and* SERVANT *bearing* ANTONIO's *body.*]

                    Now, art thou come?
Thou look'st ghastly:
There sits in thy face some great determination
Mix'd with some fear.
Bosola.   Thus it lightens into action:
I am come to kill thee.
Cardinal.   Ha!—Help! our guard!
Bosola.   Thou art deceived; They are out of thy howling.

---

1 Mistake.

Cardinal.   Hold; and I will faithfully divide
  Revenues with thee.
Bosola.   Thy prayers and proffers
  Are both unseasonable.
Cardinal.   Raise the watch!
  We are betrayed!
Bosola.   I have confin'd your flight:
  I'll suffer your retreat to Julia's chamber,
  But no further.
Cardinal.   Help! we are betrayed!

[*Enter, above,* PESCARA, MALATESTE, RODERIGO, *and* GRISOLAN.]

Malateste.   Listen.
Cardinal.   My dukedom for rescue!
Roderigo.   Fie upon
  His counterfeiting!
Malateste.   Why, 'tis not the Cardinal.
Roderigo.   Yes, yes, 'tis he: but I'll see him hang'd
  Ere I'll go down to him.
Cardinal.   Here 's a plot upon me;
  I am assaulted! I am lost, unless some rescue.
Grisolan.   He doth this pretty well; but it will not serve
  To laugh me out of mine honour.
Cardinal.   The sword 's at my throat!
Roderigo.   You would not bawl so loud then.
Malateste.   Come, come,
  Let's go to bed: he told us thus much aforehand.
Pescara.   He wish'd you should not come at him; but believe 't,
  The accent of the voice sounds not in jest:
  I'll down to him, howsoever, and with engines
  Force ope the doors.   [*Exit above.*]
Roderigo.   Let's follow him aloof,
  And note how the Cardinal will laugh at him.

[*Exeunt, above,* MALATESTE, RODERIGO, *and* GRISOLAN.]

Bosola.   There's for first, [*Kills the* SERVANT.]
  'Cause you shall not unbarricade the door
  To let in rescue.
Cardinal.   What cause hast thou to pursue my life?
Bosola.   Look there.
Cardinal.   Antonio?
Bosola.   Slain by my hand unwittingly.
  Pray, and be sudden: when thou killed'st thy sister,
  Thou took'st from Justice her most equal balance,
  And left her naught but her sword.
Cardinal.   Oh, mercy!

Bosola.   Now, it seems thy greatness was only outward;
   For thou fall'st faster of thyself than calamity
   Can drive thee. I'll not waste longer time; there! [*Stabs him.*]
Cardinal.   Thou hast hurt me.
Bosola.   Again! [*Stabs him again.*]
Cardinal.   Shall I die like a leveret,
   Without and resistance?—Help, help, help!
   I am slain!

[*Enter* FERDINAND.]

Ferdinand.   Th' alarum? give me a fresh horse;
   Rally the vaunt-guard, or the day is lost.
   Yield, yield! I give you the honour of arms,
   Shake my sword over you; will you yield?
Cardinal.   Help me;
   I am your brother!
Ferdinand.   The devil! My brother fight
   Upon the adverse party?

[*He wounds the* CARDINAL, *and, in the scuffle, gives* BOSOLA *his death-wound.*]

   There flies your ransom.
Cardinal.   O justice!
   I suffer now for what hath former been:
   Sorrow is held the eldest child of sin.
Ferdinand.   Now you're brave fellows. Caesar's fortune was harded than Pom-
   pey's; Caesar died in the arms of prosperity, Pompey at the feet of disgrace.
   You both died in the field. The pain's nothing: pain many times is taken away
   with the apprehension of greater, as the toothache with the sight of a barber
   that comes to pull it out: there's philosophy for you.
Bosola.   Now my revenge is perfect.—Sink, thou main cause [*Stabs* FERDINAND.]
   Of my undoing!—The last part of my life
   Hath done me best service.
Ferdinand.   Give me some wet hay; I am broken-winded. I do account this world
   but a dog-kennel: I will vault credit[1] and affect high pleasures beyond death.
Bosola.   He seems to come to himself, now he 's so near
   The bottom.
Ferdinand.   My sister, O my sister! there 's the cause on 't.
   Whether we fall by ambition, blood, or lust,
   Like diamonds we are cut with our own dust.   [*Dies.*]
Cardinal.   Thou hast thy payment too.
Bosola.   Yes, I hold my weary soul in my teeth.
   'Tis ready to part from me. I do glory
   That thou, which stood'st like a huge pyramid
   Begun upon a large and ample base,
   Shalt end in a little point, a kind of nothing.

---

[1]   Do incredible deeds.

[*Enter, below,* PESCARA, MALATESTE, RODERIGO, *and* GRISOLAN.]

Pescara. How now, my lord?
Malateste.   O sad disaster!
Roderigo.   How
  Comes this?
Bosola.   Revenge for the Duchess of Malfi murdered
  By th' Aragonian brethren; for Antonio
  Slain by this hand; for lustful Julia
  Poison'd by this man; and lastly for myself,
  That was an actor in the main of all,
  Much 'gainst mine own good nature, yet i' th' end
  Neglected.
Pescara. How now, my lord?
Cardinal. Look to my brother: he gave us these large wounds
  As we were struggling here i' the rushes.[1] And now,
  I pray, let me be laid by and never thought of.   [*Dies.*]
Pescara. How fatally, it seems, he did withstand
  His own rescue!
Malateste.   Thou wretched thing of blood,
  How came Antonio by his death?
Bosola.   In a mist;
  I know not how: such a mistake as I
  Have often seen in a play. Oh, I am gone!
  We are only like dead walls or vaulted graves,
  That, ruin'd, yield no echo. Fare you well.
  It may be pain, but no harm, to me to die
  In so good a quarrel. Oh, this gloomy world!
  In what a shadow, or deep pit of darkness,
  Doth womanish and fearful mankind live!
  Let worthy minds ne'er stagger in distrust
  To suffer death or shame for what is just:
  Mine is another voyage.   [*Dies.*]
Pescara. The noble Delio, as I came to the palace,
  Told me of Antonio's being here, and show'd me
  A pretty gentleman, his son and heir.

  [*Enter* DELIO *and* ANTONIO'S *Son.*]

Malateste. O sir,
  You come too late!
Delio.   I heard so, and was arm'd for 't,
  Ere I came. Let us make noble use
  Of this great ruin; and join all our force
  To establish this young hopeful gentleman
  In 's mother's right. These wretched eminent things
  Leave no more fame behind 'em, than should one

---

1 Floors were commonly strewn with rushes.

Fall in a frost, and leave his print in snow;
As soon as the sun shines, it ever melts,
Both form and matter. I have ever thought
Nature doth nothing so great for great men
As when she's pleas'd to make them lords of truth:
Integrity of life is fame's best friend,
Which nobly, beyond death, shall crown the end.   [*Exeunt.*]

Molière: THE WOULD-BE GENTLEMAN

The world, according to Horace Walpole, is a comedy to those who think, a tragedy to those who feel. Like most sweeping generalities, this statement has limited usefulness—a Greek from Sophocles' time, for example, would have found it incomprehensible—but it has value as an index of the kind of attitude held by a witty, urbane, and sophisticated society more interested in form than in content. The conviction that fundamental issues are at root amusing, and serious only to nonthinkers, or the conviction that these issues merit consideration only if the tediousness of their substance is mitigated by the style of their presentation, encourages a sort of courtly arrogance, an amused tolerance of the indecorous misfortunes of others. And if style is so important, then everyone will seek to have it, and as a result the pretensions of those without it will become fair game for ridicule. The rough, earthy humor of *The Second Shepherds' Play*, the humor of mother-in-law jokes, stolen sheep, and blanket-tossing, would seem quite vulgar and out of place in such a setting, where polish and cadence are the measure of elegance. Dress and manners require one's primary attention, even in international affairs, as the following incident illustrates.

In the winter of 1669–70 Suleiman Aga, the personal envoy of the Turkish Sultan, announced that he would come with his retinue to visit King Louis XIV at Versailles. The Turks had not always been on visiting terms with European courts; they had been a distinct menace in earlier times, known and feared as the sackers of Constantinople, the besiegers of Vienna, the indomitable fighters of the battle of Lepanto. By the mid-seventeenth century, however, Europeans' fears had largely subsided, for the Turk was seen as less of a threat, though still enough of a power to command respect. The proposed visit to Versailles could well mark the beginning of a new era, and Louis XIV was pleased at the prospect. He spared no effort to dazzle his visitors, emphasizing the opulence of his royal residence by appearing in a diamond-encrusted coat to receive them. The Turks, when they came into the royal presence, seemed to be dressed in rather ordinary clothing, which some observers suspected was not even clean. They seemed to take no notice of the splendor of Versailles or of the King's person. Nothing they saw or heard moved them to compliment or praise. The King was insulted, and exerted himself no further. To lend force to his new disdain, scorn for things Turkish became the mood of the court that season.

The King's own acting troupe was quick to sense the possibilities inherent in the situation. These actors knew that the King's fancies, whatever they might be in any given year, formed the best ground for their own activities and the surest way to continued royal approval. They had developed their skills originally as a troupe playing in the provinces, but by the time of the Turkish visit they were considerably more sophisticated: they had been a successful Paris repertory company for over a decade and officially the *Troupe du Roi* for five years. The idea of satirizing the Turks in a new comedy must have seemed obvious to them, though it may well be true that the King himself suggested the idea to the leader of the company, Jean-Baptiste Poquelin. This Poquelin was not only an actor but a playwright, who used the professional name "Molière"; he also had some musical skill, which served him in good stead, for the French court was quite fond of ballet and spectacle, and the King a devoted patron of music and dancing. The celebrated Italian musician Giovanni Battista Lulli was also at Versailles; he and Molière often collaborated on shows with acting, dancing, and music to serve the royal pleasure, and sometimes the King himself would dance in these *divertissements*. In this instance Molière and Lulli worked an extended Turkish episode into their next joint enterprise, a *comédie-ballet* or musical comedy about the upward aspirations of a merchant-class Parisian. At first glance such material might seem to be an intrusion in a story about a city businessman, but Molière managed the fusion, while Lulli wrote the music, directed the choreography, and himself played the part of the Mufti.

In October, 1670, the entire cast, dancers, musicians, costumes, and props were transported on a four day journey to the royal castle of Chambord, near Blois, where the King and his party were vacationing. The play, *Le Bourgeois Gentilhomme*, was first performed in this setting, and was subsequently offered to the public in Paris. The play, though obstensibly a mockery of middle-class values and desires, proved as popular in the commercial theatre as it had at court, an indication that its satiric sword had two edges. It remained in the repertory of Molière's company after his death, and continued to be played even after that company joined with its rivals in a merger to form the organization known as the *Comédie Française*.

THE WOULD-BE GENTLEMAN

Translated by Morris Bishop

The Characters

Monsieur Jourdain, bourgeois
Madame Jourdain, his wife
Lucile, his daughter
Cléonte, in love with Lucile
Dorimène, a marquise
Dorante, a count
Nicole, servant of Monsieur Jourdain
Covielle, manservant of Cléonte
A Music Master
The Music Master's Pupil
A Dancing Master
A Fencing Master
A Philosophy Master
A Merchant Tailor
A Journeyman Tailor
Two Lackeys, several *Singers, Instrumentalists, Dancers, Cooks, Tailor's Apprentices,* and other characters in the ballets.

The scene is in Paris, in Monsieur Jourdain's house.

Act I

[*After the overture, the curtain rises. The* MUSIC MASTER'S PUPIL *is working at a table. He may rise, strike some notes on a harpsichord, and return to his composition. He hums his tune, trying both the men's and women's parts.*]

[*Enter the* MUSIC MASTER, *three* SINGERS, *and two* VIOLINISTS.]

Music Master [*to his musicians*]. All right, come in here, and take a rest until he comes.

[*Enter from the opposite side the* DANCING MASTER *and four* DANCERS.]

Dancing Master [*to his dancers*]. Come in this way.
Music Master [*to* PUPIL]. All done?
Pupil. Yes.
Music Master. Let me see it a minute. [*Inspects composition*] That will do nicely.
Dancing Master. Is it something new?
Music Master. Yes; it's the music for a serenade I've had him working on here, while we're waiting for our man to get up.

Dancing Master.   May I take a look?

Music Master.   You will hear it, with the words, when he comes. He won't be long.

Dancing Master.   We're certainly occupied now, both of us.

Music Master.   That's right. We've both found the man we've been looking for. This Monsieur Jourdain is a very nice property, with his visions of nobility and gallantry. In the interests of your art dance and mine of music, we could well wish there were many more like him.

Dancing Master.   Well, not exactly like him. I could wish he had more appreciation of the things we do for him.

Music Master.   It's true he doesn't know much about them. But he pays well; and that's what our arts need more than anything else right now.

Dancing Master.   Well, personally, I admit I enjoy a little recognition. Applause really stimulates me. And I find it an actual torture to perform for idiots, and to bear their uncouth comments on our creations. There is genuine pleasure, confess it, in working for people who can recognize the fine points of our art, and reward us for our work with heart-warming approval. Yes, the best payment we can receive is to see our work appreciated, and welcomed with the applause which does us honor. There is no better return for all our labor and fatigue; and enlightened praise gives exquisite delight.

Music Master.   I agree; I enjoy such praise as much as you do. Certainly nothing gratifies us like that kind of applause. But you can't live on applause; praise alone won't pay the rent. We need something a bit more solid; the best hand people can give us is a hand with cash in it. True enough, our man has no cultivation; he gets everything all wrong, and he is sure to applaud the wrong thing; but his money purifies his bad taste. His fat purse is full of critical insight; his approval is convertible into cash; and this ignorant commoner is a lot more useful to us, as you are well aware, than that noble amateur of the arts who introduced us to him.

Dancing Master.   There is some truth in what you're saying. But I think you dwell on money a little too much. Material advantage is so base a thing that a man of character should never show any concern for it.

Music Master.   Still, you seem to accept the money our man hands you.

Dancing Master.   By all means; but I don't make my happiness depend upon it; and I could wish that with all his wealth he had some tincture of good taste.

Music Master.   Naturally I should like that too. That's what we're both laboring to bring about, as best we can. But at any rate, he is helping us to get a reputation; he will underwrite the things that others will applaud for him.

Dancing Master.   Here he is now.

[*Enter* MONSIEUR JOURDAIN *and two* LACKEYS. MONSIEUR JOURDAIN *wears a gorgeous striped dressing gown, lined with green and orange.*]

M. Jourdain.   Well, sirs, how's things? You're going to show me your little thingamajig?

Dancing Master.   What? What little thingamajig?

M. Jourdain.   Why, the—what d'you call it? Your prologue or dialogue of song and dance.

Dancing Master. Ha, ha!

Music Master. We are quite ready, sir.

M. Jourdain. I've held you up a little. But the fact is I'm dressing today in court style; and my tailor sent me some silk stockings I thought I'd never get on.

Music Master. We are here only to await your leisure.

M. Jourdain. I'll ask you both not to leave until they've brought my coat, so you can see it.

Dancing Master. Whatever you wish.

M. Jourdain. You'll see me turned out properly from head to foot.

Music Master. We don't doubt it.

M. Jourdain. I've just had this dressing gown made.

Dancing Master. It is very handsome.

M. Jourdain. My tailor told me that people of quality are like this in the morning.

Music Master. It looks very well on you.

M. Jourdain. Lackeys! Hey, my two lackeys!

First Lackey. What do you wish, sir?

M. Jourdain. Nothing. I just wanted to see if you hear me all right. [*To the two* MASTERS] What do you think of my servants' liveries?

Dancing Master. Magnificent.

M. Jourdain [*opens his dressing gown, displaying tight red velvet breeches and a short green velvet jacket*]. And here's a little sports costume to do my exercises in, in the morning.

Music Master. Very smart.

M. Jourdain. Lackey!

First Lackey. Yes, sir?

M. Jourdain. Other lackey!

Second Lackey. Yes, sir?

M. Jourdain. Here, hold my gown. [*He removes his gown*] How do you like me this way?

Dancing Master. Splendid. It couldn't be more perfect.

M. Jourdain. Now let's have your little business.

Music Master. First, I should like to have you hear a composition which this young man here has just done for the serenade you ordered. He is one of my pupils; he is very gifted for this sort of thing.

M. Jourdain. Yes; but you shouldn't have had it done by a pupil. You aren't too good to do the job yourself.

Music Master. Don't let the word "pupil" put you off, sir. Such pupils as this know as much as the greatest masters; and the melody is as lovely as it can be. Just listen.

M. Jourdain. Give me my dressing gown so I can listen better . . . Wait a minute, I think it will be better without the dressing gown . . . No, give it back to me. It'll be better that way.

A Woman Singer.

Ah, grievous is my woe, I languish night and day
Since thy imperious eye has brought me 'neath thy sway;
If thus thou deal'st, my fair, with one who loves thee so,
Ah, what must be the fate of one who is thy foe?

M. Jourdain.   That song seems to me rather dismal. It puts you to sleep. I wish you could brighten it up a little here and there.

Music Master.   It is necessary, sir, that the music fit the words.

M. Jourdain.   I learned a very pretty one a little while ago. Wait a minute . . . now . . . how did it go?

Dancing Master.   Really, I don't know.

M. Jourdain.   Something about a sheep.

Dancing Master.   A sheep?

M. Jourdain.   Yes. Aha! [*He sings*]

> I thought my dear Jeannette
> Was just a little lamb;
> I thought my dear Jeannette
> Was sweet as currant jam.
> Oh, dear, oh, dear, oh dear!
> I must have made a bungle!
> She's crueler, it's clear,
> Than a tiger in the jungle!

Isn't that pretty?

Music Master.   Extremely pretty.

Dancing Master.   And you sing it well.

M. Jourdain.   And I never studied music!

Music Master.   You ought to learn music, sir, as you are learning the dance. The two arts have a very close connection.

Dancing Master.   And they open a man's mind to things of beauty.

M. Jourdain.   Do people of quality study music too?

Music Master.   Oh, yes, sir.

M. Jourdain.   Well, then, I'll study it. But I don't know how I'll find the time; for not to mention the fencing master who's giving me lessons, I have hired a philosophy professor; he's to begin this morning.

Music Master.   Philosophy is very fine; but music, sir, music—

Dancing Master.   Music and the dance; music and the dance, that's all you really need.

Music Master.   There is nothing so useful in a state as music.

Dancing Master.   There is nothing so necessary to men as the dance.

Music Master.   Without music, a state can hardly persist.

Dancing Master.   Without the dance, a man is totally helpless.

Music Master.   All the disorders and wars in the world come about because men haven't learned music.

Dancing Master.   All men's misfortunes, and the appalling disasters of history, the blunders of statesmen and the errors of great generals, they have all occurred for lack of knowledge of dancing.

M. Jourdain.   How is that?

Music Master.   Doesn't war come from discords among men?

M. Jourdain.   That's true.

Music Master.   And if everybody should learn music, wouldn't that be a way to harmonize everything, and to bring universal peace to the world?

M. Jourdain.   You're right.

Dancing Master.   When a man has made some blunder, whether in his family affairs, or in government, or in generalship, don't we always say: "So-and-so has made a false step in such a matter"?

M. Jourdain.   Yes, we say that.

Dancing Master.   And taking a false step, can that result from anything else than not knowing how to dance?

M. Jourdain.   That's true. You're both right!

Dancing Master.   It's just to show you the excellence and utility of dancing and music.

M. Jourdain.   I understand that now.

Music Master.   Do you want to see our productions?

M. Jourdain.   Yes.

Music Master.   I have already told you, this is a little effort of mine to delineate the various emotions that music can express.

M. Jourdain.   Very good.

Music Master [*to the* SINGERS].   Step forward, please. [*To* MONSIEUR JOURDAIN] You must imagine that they are dressed as shepherds.

M. Jourdain.   Why are they always shepherds? All I ever see around is shepherds.

Music Master.   When one wants to make people speak in music, one must always put them in a pastoral setting. That's what we call verisimilitude. Singing has always been the specialty of shepherds and shepherdesses. It is hardly natural, in a dramatic dialogue, that princes or commoners should sing their emotions.

M. Jourdain.   All right, all right. Let's hear it.

Woman Singer.

> A heart that tyrant love's dictation captures
> Is filled with turbulence incessantly.
> They say that languishing and sighs are raptures,
> But still our dearest boon is liberty!

First Male Singer.

> Nought is so sweet as tender ardors thronging
> To make twin hearts blend in a lover's kiss.
> There is no happiness without love's longing;
> Take love from life, you cancel all its bliss.

Second Male Singer.

> It would be sweet to enter love's domain,
> If one could find in love true steadfastness;
> But oh, alas! Oh, cruelty and pain!
> How can one find a faithful shepherdess?
> The sex is fickle and inconstant; hence
> One must renounce for aye love's blandishments!

First Male Singer.

> Dear love is revealed—

Woman Singer.

> How delightful to yield—

Second Male Singer.

> But love is a cheat!

First Male Singer.

> My darling, my sweet!

Woman Singer [*to* SECOND MALE SINGER].

> Dear love, I adjure you—

Second Male Singer.

> I cannot endure you!

First Male Singer [*to* SECOND MALE SINGER].

> Ah, learn to love, forget your peevishness!

Woman Singer.

> And I shall gladly tell you where you'll see
> A faithful shepherdess!

Second Male Singer.

> Where to discover such a prodigy?

First Male Singer [*to* SECOND MALE SINGER].

> Just in defense of womankind,
> I offer here my heart to you!

Second Male Singer.

> Sweet shepherdess, and shall I find
> That it will be forever true?

Woman Singer.

> Let us essay, and make a test
> Which of us two can love the best!

Second Male Singer.

> And may the one accursèd be
> Who first shall fail in constancy!

The Three Singers.

> The power that kindles deathless fires
> Now let us all pay tribute to!
> How sweet it is when love inspires
> Two hearts that ever shall be true!

M. Jourdain.   Is that all?

Music Master.   Yes.

M. Jourdain.   A neat job. Very neat. There were some remarks in it that weren't bad.

Dancing Master.   Now, as my part of the performance, here is a little effort to display the most beautiful postures and evolutions with which a dance may be varied.

M. Jourdain.   More shepherds?

Dancing Master.   They are anything you please.

[*Four* DANCERS *execute various steps and evolutions at the* DANCING MASTER'S *order. This is the first* Interlude, *marking the division of the play into acts.*]

Act II

[*The action is continuous. After the* Interlude, *the dancers retire, leaving* MONSIEUR JOURDAIN, *the* MUSIC MASTER, *the* DANCING MASTER, *and the two* LACKEYS.]

M. Jourdain.   No nonsense about that! Those boys cut some fine capers.

Music Master.   When the dance is combined with the music, it will be much more effective. You will find very gallant the little ballet we have organized for you.

M. Jourdain.   Have it ready soon, anyhow. The person I've ordered all this for is to do me the honor of coming to dinner[1] today.

Dancing Master.   It's all ready.

Music Master.   Incidentally, sir, you should go farther. A person like you, doing things in a big way, and with a taste for the finer things of life, should have a musicale at home every Wednesday or Thursday.

M. Jourdain.   Do people of quality have that?

Music Master.   Yes, sir.

M. Jourdain.   I'll have it then. It will be nice, will it?

Music Master.   Certainly. You will need three voices: a soprano, a counter-tenor, and a basso; they will be accompanied by a bass viol, a theorbo or archlute, and a harpsichord for the sustained bass, with two violins to play the refrains.

M. Jourdain.   You ought to put in an accordion too. The accordion is an instrument I like; it's harmonious.

Music Master.   Just let us arrange things.

M. Jourdain.   Anyway, don't forget to send me some singers by and by, to sing at the dinner.

Music Master.   You will have everything you need.

M. Jourdain.   And especially, be sure the ballet is nice.

Music Master.   You will be pleased, I am sure; especially with certain minuets you will see.

M. Jourdain.   The minuet! That's my dance! You should see me dance the minuet! Come on, dancing master!

Dancing Master.   A hat for the gentleman, please! [MONSIEUR JOURDAIN *siezes a lackey's hat, claps it on over his nightcap, removing it to make the sweeping bows required by the dance; the* DANCING MASTER *sings the music, and also his instructions*] La, la, la; La, la, la, la, la, la. La, la, la, repeat. La, la, la; La, la. Keep in tune—if you please. La, la, la, la. Right leg stiff, la, la, la. Don't move shoulders—quite so much. La, la, la, la, la; La, la, la, la, la. Both your arms—are they crippled? La, la, la, la, la. Lift your head—turn toe out. La, la, la. Stand up straight.

M. Jourdain [*with an intonation between "I'm done in!" and "How's that?"*]. Uh!

Music Master.   Splendid! Splendid!

M. Jourdain.   This reminds me. Teach me how to make a bow to salute a marquise. I'm going to need it soon.

Dancing Master.   A bow to salute a marquise?

M. Jourdain.   Yes. A marquise named Dorimène.

Dancing Master.   Give me your hand.

M. Jourdain.   No, you do it alone. I'll get the idea.

Dancing Master.   If you want to make a very respectful salute, you must first make a bow stepping backward, then advance toward the lady with three forward bows, and at the last you bow down to the level of her knees.

---

1   Dinner commonly occurred about midday.

M. Jourdain.   Show me . . . Good.

[*Enter a* LACKEY.]

Lackey.   Monsieur, here is your fencing master who's come.

M. Jourdain.   Tell him to come in and give me my lesson. [*Exit* LACKEY] I want
you two to watch how I do it.

[*Enter* FENCING MASTER. *He salutes and hands* MONSIEUR JOURDAIN *a foil.*]

Fencing Master.   Now, sir; first make your bow . . . Body straight . . .
Weight a little more on the left thigh. Legs not so wide apart. Feet on the same
line. Your wrist in line with your forward hip. The point of your weapon on the
level of your shoulder. The arm not quite so straight out. The left hand at the
level of the eye. Left shoulder drawn back a little more. Head up. Put on a
confident look. . . . Advance . . . Keep the body tense. Engage my foil in
quart, and carry through . . . One, two . . . Recover . . . Thrust again,
keeping feet in same position . . . Backward jump . . . When you make your
thrust, sir, the sword should start before the foot, and you must keep your body
protected . . . One, two . . . Now, touch my sword in tierce, and carry
through . . . Advance . . . Body firm . . . Advance . . . Thrust from that
position. One, two . . . Recover . . . Thrust . . . Backward jump . . . On
guard, sir, on guard! [*Penetrating* MONSIEUR JOURDAIN's *guard, he pinks his
breast.*]

M. Jourdain.   Uh?

Music Master.   You're doing marvelously.

Fencing Master.   As I have already told you, the whole secret of swordplay
consists in two things: to give; and not to receive. And as I proved the other
day, with demonstrative logic, it is impossible for you to receive, if you know
how to divert your enemy's weapon from the line of your body; and that
depends only on a simple twist of the wrist, either inward or outward.

M. Jourdain.   So a person who may not be very brave can be sure of killing his
man, and not getting killed?

Fencing Master.   Exactly. Didn't you see the demonstration?

M. Jourdain.   Yes.

Fencing Master.   Thus we can see how highly we swordsmen should be esteemed
in a state, and how far the science of fencing is superior to the useless branches
of knowledge, like dancing, music, and—

Dancing Master.   Wait a minute, swordsman; please speak of the dance with
respect.

Music Master.   And learn, I beg of you, to treat music with proper consideration.

Fencing Master.   You're a funny pair, trying to compare your subjects with
mine!

Music Master.   Look at the great man, will you?

Dancing Master.   He's a comic sight, with his padded chest protector!

Fencing Master.   My little dancing master, I'll show you some new steps. And
you, my little musician, I'll make you sing—but small!

Dancing Master.   My good blacksmith, I'll teach you your trade!

M. Jourdain [*to the* DANCING MASTER].   Are you crazy, to pick a fight with him, who knows all about tierce and quart, and can kill a man by demonstrative logic?

Dancing Master. Little I care for his demonstrative logic, and his tierce and quart.

M. Jourdain. Take it easy, I tell you.

Fencing Master [*to* DANCING MASTER]. What, you impertinent puppy!

M. Jourdain. Now, now, fencing master.

Dancing Master. What, you big cart horse!

M. Jourdain. Now, now, dancing master.

Fencing Master. If I let myself go—

M. Jourdain. Easy, easy there!

Dancing Master. If I lay a finger on you—

M. Jourdain. Gently, gently!

Fencing Master. I'll beat you to a pulp!

M. Jourdain. Please!

Dancing Master. I'll trim you down to size!

M. Jourdain. I beg and pray you!

Music Master. We'll teach him how to talk!

M. Jourdain. Dear God! Stop, stop! [*Enter* PHILOSOPHY MASTER] Hello, Monsieur Philosopher, you arrive in the nick of time with your philosophy. Come and make peace among these people.

Philosophy Master. What is it? What is the matter, good sirs?

M. Jourdain. They have got angry about the standing of their professions, to the point of calling each other names and starting to fight.

Philosophy Master. Dear, dear! My friends, should you let yourselves get so excited? Haven't you read the learned treatise Seneca composed upon anger? Is anything more base and shameful than that passion, which turns man into a wild beast? Should not reason be the mistress of all our actions?

Dancing Master. Why, sir, he goes and insults us both, sneering at my trade, the dance; and at music, which is *his* profession!

Philosophy Master. A wise man is superior to any insult he may hear. The proper reply one should make to all affronts is moderation and patience.

Fencing Master. They have both had the audacity to compare their professions to mine.

Philosophy Master. Should such a thing move you? Men should not dispute about vainglory and precedence; what truly distinguishes men one from another is wisdom and virtue.

Dancing Master. I am simply telling him that dancing is a science which can hardly be sufficiently honored.

Music Master. And I was saying that music is a science revered throughout history.

Fencing Master. And I was pointing out that the science of arms is the most beautiful and necessary of all sciences.

Philosophy Master. And what, then, is the place of philosophy? I find all three of you very impudent, to speak before me with this arrogance, and to give brazenly the name of science to things which one should not even honor with the title of craft, and which can be grouped only under the denomination of wretched trades of gladiator, minstrel, and posturer!

Fencing Master.   Get out, you pig of a philosopher!
Music Master.   Get out, you half-wit highbrow!
Dancing Master.   Get out, you crackpot professor!
Philosophy Master.   What, you yokels!

[*He throws himself upon them; the other three unite to beat him.*]

M. Jourdain.   Philosopher, sir!
Philosophy Master.   The insolent scoundrels! The rascals!
M. Jourdain.   Philosopher, sir!
Fencing Master.   Devil take the swine!
M. Jourdain.   Dear sirs!
Philosophy Master.   Impudent rogues!
M. Jourdain.   Philosopher, sir!
Dancing Master.   To hell with the jackass!
M. Jourdain.   My friends!
Philosophy Master.   Blackguards!
M. Jourdain.   Philosopher, sir!
Music Master.   Damn him and his insolence!
M. Jourdain.   My dear sirs!
Philosophy Master.   Villains! Beggars! Traitors! Impostors!
M. Jourdain.   Philosopher, sir! Dear sirs! Philosopher, sir! My friends! Philosopher, sir! [*Exit the four* MASTERS, *fighting*] Oh, fight all you like. There's nothing I can do about it, and I won't get my dressing gown dirty trying to separate you. I'd be crazy to get into that mess; I might get a nasty bang.

[*Enter* PHILOSOPHY MASTER, tidying his clothing.]

Philosophy Master.   And now let's have our lesson.
M. Jourdain.   Ah, sir, I'm sorry for the blows you've received.
Philosophy Master.   That's nothing. A philosopher knows how to take things as they come; and I am going to compose a satire against them, in the style of Juvenal, which will settle their hash. We'll drop the matter. What do you want to learn?
M. Jourdain.   Everything I can, for I am crazy to be a scholar. It makes me furious that my father and mother didn't make me study all the branches of knowledge when I was young.
Philosophy Master.   That is a very laudable sentiment. *Nam sine doctrina vita est quasi mortis imago.* You understand that; you know Latin, of course.
M. Jourdain.   Yes; but let's pretend I don't know it. Explain to me what that means.
Philosophy Master.   That means: "Without knowledge, life is almost an image of death."
M. Jourdain.   That Latin is right.
Philosophy Master.   Don't you have some basic elements, some beginnings in the fields of study?
M. Jourdain.   Oh, yes; I know how to read and write.
Philosophy Master.   Now where would you like to begin? Would you like to have me teach you logic?
M. Jourdain.   Just what is that logic?

Philosophy Master.   Logic teaches the three operations of the mind.

M. Jourdain.   What are these three operations of the mind?

Philosophy Master.   The first, the second, and the third. The first is true conception by means of the universals. The second is true judgment by means of categories; and the third, the true drawing of logical consequences by means of the figures Barbara, Celarent, Darii, Ferio, Baralipton, and so forth.

M. Jourdain.   Those words sound kind of repulsive. I don't like that logic. Let's learn something prettier.

Philosophy Master.   Would you like to learn ethics?

M. Jourdain.   Ethics?

Philosophy Master.   Yes.

M. Jourdain.   What do they do?

Philosophy Master.   Ethics treats of the nature of happiness, teaches men to moderate their passions, and—

M. Jourdain.   No, none of that. I have a devilish excitable nature; no ethics for me. When I want to get mad, I want to get good and mad.

Philosophy Master.   Would you like to learn physics?

M. Jourdain.   Physics? Why not leave them to the doctors?

Philosophy Master.   Physics is the science which explains the principles of the natural world and the properties of matter. It treats the nature of the elements, of the metals, of minerals, stones, plants, and animals, and teaches us the causes of meteors, rainbows, shooting stars, comets, lightning, thunder and thunderbolts, rain, snow, hail, winds and whirlwinds.

M. Jourdain.   There's too much rowdydow in that; too much rumpus and ruckus.

Philosophy Master.   Well, then, what do you want me to teach you?

M. Jourdain.   Teach me spelling.

Philosophy Master.   Gladly.

M. Jourdain.   And afterwards, you can teach me the almanac, so I'll know when there's a moon and when there isn't.

Philosophy Master.   Very well. To follow your idea and to treat this subject from a philosophical point of view, one must proceed according to the natural order of things, by an exact understanding of the nature of the letters, and of the different manner of pronouncing them. I shall first inform you that the letters are divided into vowels, from the Latin meaning "vocal," so called because they express the voiced sounds; and into consonants, meaning "with-sounding," so called because they "sound with" the vowels, and merely mark the various articulations of the voiced sounds. There are five vowels, or voiced sounds: A, E, I, O, U.

M. Jourdain.   I understand all that.

Philosophy Master.   The vowel A, pronounced *ah*, is formed by opening the mouth wide: Ah.

M. Jourdain.   Ah, *ah*. Yes, yes.

Philosophy Master.   The vowel E, pronounced *euh*, is formed by bringing the lower jaw closer to the upper jaw: Euh. Ah, euh.

M. Jourdain.   Ah, *euh*; *ah, euh*. Bless my soul, yes! Oh, how beautiful that is!

Philosophy Master.   The vowel I, pronounced *Ee*, is made by bringing the jaws still closer together, and by widening the mouth, or extending its corners toward the ears: Ee. Ah, euh, ee.

M. Jourdain.   *Ah, euh, ee, ee, ee.* That's true! Hurrah for science!

Philosophy Master.   The vowel O is formed by opening the jaws again, and by bringing the corners of the mouth closer together: *Oh.*

M. Jourdain.   *Oh, oh.* Nothing could be truer! *Ah, euh, ee, oh, ee, oh.* That's wonderful! *Ee, oh, ee, oh!*[1]

Philosophy Master.   The opening of the mouth makes, as it happens, a small circle which represents an O.

M. Jourdain.   *Oh, oh, oh.* You're right: *oh.* Oh, what a fine thing it is to know something!

Philosophy Master.   The vowel U[2] is formed by bringing the teeth close together, without their quite touching, and by thrusting out the lips, thus making a small aperture: *U.*

M. Jourdain.   *U, u.* It couldn't be truer! *U!*

Philosophy Master.   The lips are extended as if you are pouting; hence it comes that if you want to make this sound at someone, expressing contempt, all you say to him is U.[3]

M. Jourdain.   *U, u.* That's right! Oh, why didn't I study sooner, to learn all that?

Philosophy Master.   Tomorrow we shall take up the other letters, the consonants.

M. Jourdain.   Are they as remarkable as these vowels?

Philosophy Master.   Certainly. The consonant D, for example, is pronounced by touching the tip of the tongue to the hard palate, just above the teeth: *Da.*

M. Jourdain.   *Da, da.* Yes. Oh, how wonderful, wonderful!

Philosophy Master.   The F is pronounced by applying the upper teeth to the lower lip: *Fa.*

M. Jourdain.   *Fa. fa.* It's the truth! Oh, Father and Mother, how I blame you!

Philosophy Master.   And the R, by placing the tip of the tongue against the upper palate, so that it is brushed by the air, forcefully expelled, and yields to it, and returns constantly to the same position, making a kind of vibration: *Rra.*

M. Jourdain.   *R, r, ra; R, rr, rrra.* That's right! Oh, what a clever man you are! And how much time I've lost! *Rrrrra.*

Philosophy Master.   I shall explain to you all these important facts in detail.

M. Jourdain.   Please do. And by the way, I must take you into my confidence. I am in love with a person of very high rank, and I should like to have your help in writing something in a little note I want to drop at her feet.

Philosophy Master.   I shall be delighted.

M. Jourdain.   It will be in the gallant style, yes?

Philosophy Master.   Certainly. Is it poetry you want to write her?

M. Jourdain.   No, no; no poetry.

Philosophy Master.   You want only prose?

M. Jourdain.   No; I don't want either poetry or prose.

Philosophy Master.   Well, it has to be either one or the other.

M. Jourdain.   Why?

Philosophy Master.   For the reason, sir, that we have no means of expression other than prose and poetry.

---

[1]   Traditionally, the actor here imitates an ass braying.

[2]   The French U, like a German ü.

[3]   The sound is used by the French for booing.

M. Jourdain. There's nothing but prose or poetry?

Philosophy Master. Quite so, sir. All that is not prose is poetry; and all that is not poetry is prose.

M. Jourdain. And when a man talks, what's that?

Philosophy Master. Prose.

M. Jourdain. What? When I say: "Nicole, bring me my slippers and give me my nightcap," that's prose?

Philosophy Master. Yes, sir.

M. Jourdain. Well, I'll be hanged! For more than forty years I've been talking prose without any idea of it; I'm very much obliged to you for telling me that. So, I'd like to put in a letter: "Beautiful Marquise, your lovely eyes make me die of love." But I'd like to have it put in the gallant style; neatly turned, you know.

Philosophy Master. Put it, then, that the rays of her eyes reduce your heart to ashes; that for her sake you suffer night and day the tortures of—

M. Jourdain. No, no, no. I don't want all that. I just want what I told you: "Beautiful Marquise, your lovely eyes make me die of love."

Philosophy Master. Well, you ought to stretch it out a little.

M. Jourdain. No, I tell you. I just want only those words in the letter; but elegantly put, properly arranged. So I'm asking you to tell me, out of curiosity, the different ways you could write them.

Philosophy Master. Well, firstly, you could put them the way you said: "Beautiful Marquise, your lovely eyes make me die of love." Or else: "Of love, beautiful Marquise, your beautiful eyes make me die." Or else: "Your eyes, lovely, of love, Marquise beautiful, make die me." Or else: "Die, beautiful Marquise, of love your lovely eyes me make." Or else: "Me your lovely eyes of love make die, beautiful Marquise."

M. Jourdain. But of all those ways, which one is the best?

Philosophy Master. The one you said: "Beautiful Marquise, your lovely eyes make me die of love."

M. Jourdain. And nevertheless I have never studied; I did that straight off! I thank you with all my heart; please come again tomorrow early.

Philosophy Master. I won't fail to.

[*Exit* PHILOSOPHY MASTER.]

M. Jourdain [*to his* LACKEYS]. Look here, hasn't my new suit come yet?

Second Lackey. No, sir.

M. Jourdain. That damned tailor makes me wait until a day when I have so much to do! He makes me furious. May the quartan fever take that hangbird tailor! To the devil with the tailor! May the galloping plague seize the tailor! If I had him here now, that infernal tailor, that dog of a tailor, that pig of a tailor, I'd . . . [*Enter* MERCHANT TAILOR *and his* APPRENTICE, *carrying* M. JOURDAIN's *suit*] Oh, here you are! I was on the point of getting angry with you.

Merchant Tailor. I couldn't come sooner; I have had twenty journeymen working on your coat.

M. Jourdain. The silk stockings you sent me were so tight that I had a terrible time getting them on, and already there are a couple of stiches broken.

Merchant Tailor. They will get looser.

M. Jourdain.   Yes, if all the stitches break. And what's more, you made me some shoes which hurt frightfully.

Merchant Tailor.   Not at all, sir.

M. Jourdain.   What do you mean, not at all?

Merchant Tailor.   They don't hurt you.

M. Jourdain.   I tell you they do hurt me!

Merchant Tailor.   You just imagine it.

M. Jourdain.   I imagine it because I feel it. What kind of talk is that?

Merchant Tailor.   Now look, here is the finest coat in all the court, the most harmoniously matched. It is a great achievement to have invented a formal coat which is not black. I defy the most eminent tailors to equal it in a dozen tries.

M. Jourdain.   What's this? You've got the flowers upside down.

Merchant Tailor.   You didn't tell me you wanted them right side up.

M. Jourdain.   Did I have to tell you that?

Merchant Tailor.   Yes, indeed. All the people of quality wear them this way.

M. Jourdain.   People of quality wear the flowers upside down?

Merchant Tailor.   Yes, sir.

M. Jourdain.   Oh, well, it's all right then.

Merchant Tailor.   If you prefer, I'll turn them right side up.

M. Jourdain.   No, no.

Merchant Tailor.   You have only to say so.

M. Jourdain.   No, I tell you. You did all right . . . Do you think the costume will look well on me?

Merchant Tailor.   What a question! I defy any artist to paint a finer ensemble. I have a workman who, for assembling a wide trouser, is the greatest genius on earth; and another who, for confecting a doublet, is the hero of our age.

M. Jourdain.   The peruke and the plumes, are they all right?

Merchant Tailor.   Perfect.

M. Jourdain [*noticing the tailor's coat*].   Ah, master tailor, there is some material from the last coat you made me! I recognize it perfectly.

Merchant Tailor.   The fact is, the material seemed to me so beautiful that I made a coat for myself from it.

M. Jourdain.   Yes, but you shouldn't have made it with my material.

Merchant Tailor.   Do you want to try on your coat?

M. Jourdain.   Yes; give it to me.

Merchant Tailor.   Wait a moment. That's not the way to do it. I have brought some men to dress you to music; that kind of costume has to be put on with ceremony. Holà! Come in, you men. [*Enter four* JOURNEYMEN TAILORS] Put this coat on the gentleman, in the way you do for persons of quality.

[*Two* TAILORS *remove* MONSIEUR JOURDAIN's *breeches, two others remove his jacket. They try on his new coat.* MONSIEUR JOURDAIN *promenades among them for their inspection. All takes place to the music of the entire orchestra.*]

A Tailor.   Gentleman, sir, will you give a little tip to the workmen?

M. Jourdain.   What did you call me?

Tailor.   Gentleman, sir.

M. Jourdain.   Gentleman, sir! That's what comes from dressing like a person of quality. If you go around always dressed as a commoner, no one will say to you: "Gentleman, sir!" Here; that's for "gentleman, sir."

Tailor. Monsignor, we are very much obliged to you.

M. Jourdain. Monsignor! Oh, oh, Monsignor! Wait a bit, my friend; "Monsignor" deserves a little something. Here; that's a present from Monsignor.

Tailor. Monsignor, we shall all drink to the health of Your Grace.

M. Jourdain. Your Grace! Oh, oh, oh! Wait; don't go away. "Your Grace"—to me! Faith, if he goes as far as Royal Highness he'll have my whole purse! . . . Here; that's for My Grace.

Tailor. Monsignor, we thank you very humbly for your generosity.

M. Jourdain. A good thing he stopped there. I was going to give him the whole business.

[*The four* JOURNEYMEN TAILORS *express their joy in a dance, which forms the second* Interlude.]

Act III

[*The* MERCHANT TAILOR *and his assistants exit, leaving* MONSIEUR JOURDAIN *and his two* LACKEYS *on the stage.*]

M. Jourdain. Follow me, while I take a little walk to show my new suit around town. And especially, both of you be sure to walk directly behind me, so that everybody can see that you belong to me.

Lackeys. Yes, sir.

M. Jourdain. Get Nicole for me. I want to give her some orders. No, don't move. Here she is now. [*Enter* NICOLE] Nicole!

Nicole. Yes, what is it?

M. Jourdain. Listen to me.

Nicole. He, he, he, he, he!

M. Jourdain. What is there to laugh at?

Nicole. He, he, he, he, he, he!

M. Jourdain. What does the rascal mean?

Nicole. He, he, he! How funny you look! He, he, he!

M. Jourdain. What's the matter?

Nicole. Oh, oh, good Lord! He, he, he, he, he!

M. Jourdain. You scamp! Are you trying to make fun of me?

Nicole. Oh, no, sir. I'd hate to do that. He, he, he, he, he, he!

M. Jourdain. I'll land one on your nose, if you laugh any more.

Nicole. Monsieur, I can't help it. He, he, he, he, he, he!

M. Jourdain. You won't stop?

Nicole. Monsieur, I beg your pardon. But you look so funny, I can't keep from laughing. He, he, he!

M. Jourdain. I never saw such impudence.

Nicole. You're so comical like that. He, he!

M. Jourdain. I'm going to—

Nicole. I beg you to excuse me. He, he, he, he!

M. Jourdain. Look here, if you laugh once more, I swear I'll apply to your cheek the biggest slap that has ever been slapped.

Nicole. It's all over, sir. I won't laugh any more.

M. Jourdain. Make sure you don't. Now, I want you to clean up, in preparation for—

Nicole. He, he!

M. Jourdain. To clean up properly—

Nicole. He, he!

M. Jourdain. I say I want you to clean up the parlor, and—

Nicole. He, he!

M. Jourdain. What, again!

Nicole. Look here, sir, I'd rather have you beat me and let me laugh myself out. That will do me more good. He, he, he, he, he!

M. Jourdain. You'll drive me crazy!

Nicole. Please, monsieur, I beg you to let me laugh. He, he, he!

M. Jourdain. If I catch you—

Nicole. Monsieu-eur, I'll blow-ow-ow up, if I don't laugh. He, he, he!

M. Jourdain. Has anyone ever seen such a hussy! She comes and laughs insolently in my face, instead of obeying my orders!

Nicole. What do you want me to do, sir?

M. Jourdain. I want you, you rogue, to see to getting the house ready for the company that is due to come soon.

Nicole. Well, my sakes, I've lost all fancy to laugh. Your company always makes such a mess around here that the mere mention of it is enough to put me out of humor.

M. Jourdain. So, for your convenience, I ought to shut my door to everybody?

Nicole. At least, you ought to shut it to certain people.

[*Enter* MADAME JOURDAIN.]

Mme Jourdain. Aha, here's something new! Tell me, my good husband, what's this getup of yours? Are you crazy, to go and rig yourself out that way? Do you want people to mock you everywhere?

M. Jourdain. My good wife, only the fools, male and female, will mock me.

Mme Jourdain. Well, they haven't waited for this occasion to start. Your behavior has been making everybody laugh for quite some time.

M. Jourdain. Everybody! What do you mean by everybody, if you please?

Mme Jourdain. I mean everybody who knows what's what, and who has got more sense than you. For my part, I am scandalized by the kind of life you are leading. I vow I don't recognize our own house. You'd say it was carnival time here every day; and to make sure of it, from early morning on there's nothing but a great row of fiddlers and singers, enough to disturb the whole neighborhood.

Nicole. Madame is quite right. I can never keep the house clean any more, with all that gang of people you bring in here. They've got big feet which go and hunt for mud in every quarter of the city, in order to bring it back here. And poor Françoise is worn almost to a shadow, scrubbing the floors that your fine folks dirty up regularly every day.

M. Jourdain. Now, now, Nicole, you've got to be quite a speech-maker for a peasant servant girl.

Mme Jourdain. Nicole is quite right; she's got more sense than you. I'd like to know what you think you're doing with a dancing teacher, at your age.

Nicole. And with a great big bully of a fighter, who stamps so he shakes the whole house, and loosens up all the tiles on the parlor floor.

M. Jourdain. Shut up, servant; and shut up, wife.

Mme Jourdain. You want to learn to dance, for when you won't be able to walk?

Nicole. You want to kill somebody?

M. Jourdain. Shut up, I tell you! You are both ignorant fools; you don't know the prerogatives of all that.

Mme Jourdain. You ought to think rather of marrying off your daughter. She's of an age to have a husband now.

M. Jourdain. I'll think of marrying my daughter when a proper match for her appears. But I also want to think of learning the finer things of life.

Nicole. I've also heard, madame, that to top it off he took on a philosophy teacher today.

M. Jourdain. Quite right. I want to sharpen my wits, and be able to discuss things among intelligent people.

Mme Jourdain. One of these days you'll be going to school to get yourself whipped, at your age.

M. Jourdain. Why not? I wish to heaven I could be whipped now, in front of everybody, if I could know what one learns in school.

Nicole. Yes, my faith! Much good that would do you!

M. Jourdain. It would indeed.

Mme Jourdain. A lot of use that would be for running your house.

M. Jourdain. You're right, it would. You both talk like simpletons, and I'm ashamed of your ignorance. [*To* MADAME JOURDAIN] For example, do you know what you're saying now?

Mme Jourdain. Yes, I know that what I am saying is very well said, and you ought to think of changing your way of life.

M. Jourdain. I'm not talking of that. I ask you, what are the words that you are saying now?

Mme Jourdain. They are very sensible words, and that's what your conduct is not.

M. Jourdain. I'm not talking of that, I tell you. I ask you; what I'm speaking to you, what I'm saying to you now, what is it?

Mme Jourdain. Stuff and nonsense.

M. Jourdain. No, no, not at all. What we are both saying, the language we are talking now?

Mme Jourdain. Well?

M. Jourdain. What is that called?

Mme Jourdain. That is called whatever you've a mind to call it.

M. Jourdain. It is called prose, ignorant woman!

Mme Jourdain. Prose?

M. Jourdain. Yes, prose. Everything which is prose is not poetry; and everything which is not poetry is not prose. Ha, that's what comes of studying! [*To* NICOLE] And you, do you know what you have to do to make an U?

Nicole. How's that?

M. Jourdain. Yes. What do you do when you make an U?

Nicole.   What?

M. Jourdain.   Just say U, for example.

Nicole.   All right, U.

M. Jourdain.   Now what are you doing?

Nicole.   I'm saying U.

M. Jourdain.   Yes, but when you say U, what are you doing?

Nicole.   I'm doing what you tell me.

M. Jourdain.   Oh, what a dreadful thing it is to have to deal with idiots! You thrust your lips outward, and you bring the upper jaw down close to the lower jaw: U. You see, U. I pout: U.

Nicole.   Yes, that's right pretty.

Mme Jourdain.   Wonderful!

M. Jourdain.   It's quite different, if you'd seen O, and Da, da, and Fa, fa.

Mme Jourdain.   What's all this rubbish?

Nicole.   What does all that cure you of?

M. Jourdain.   It makes me sick to see such ignorant women.

Mme Jourdain.   You ought to kick all those fellows out, with their moonshine.

Nicole.   And especially that big gawk of a fencing master, who fills the whole house with dust.

M. Jourdain.   Yes, that fencing master worries you a lot. I'll show you how stupid you are, right away. [*He has a lackey bring him the foils, takes one, and hands one to* NICOLE] Take this. Logical demonstration, the line of the body. When you thrust in quart, this is all you have to do. And when you thrust in tierce, that's what you do. In this way, you can never get killed. Isn't it fine, to be assured of the result, when you're fighting with someone? There now, just make a thrust, to try it out.

Nicole.   All right. [*She makes several lunges, pricking* MONSIEUR JOURDAIN.]

M. Jourdain.   Hold on! Hey, easy there! The devil take the wench!

Nicole.   You told me to thrust.

M. Jourdain.   Yes, but you thrust in tierce before thrusting in quart; and you wouldn't wait for me to parry.

Mme Jourdain.   You're crazy, my poor husband, with your fancy ideas. It's all happened since you took it into your head to hang around with the nobility.

M. Jourdain.   When I hang around with the nobility, I show my good judgment. It's a lot finer thing than to hang around with your bourgeoisie.

Mme Jourdain.   Really now! There's a lot to be gained by associating with your nobles! You've done some nice business with that Monsieur le Comte you're so fascinated with.

M. Jourdain.   Quiet! Think what you're saying. Are you aware, wife, that when you mention him, you don't know who he really is? He is a person of greater importance than you think, a lord who is highly considered at court. He speaks to the King just the way I am speaking to you. Isn't it a very honorable thing for people to see a person of such quality come to my house so often, calling me his dear friend, and treating me as if I were his equal? He has done me some kindnesses you would never guess; and in front of everybody he shows me such special regards that I am embarrassed myself.

Mme Jourdain.   Yes, he does you kindnesses, and he shows you special regards; but he borrows your money.

M. Jourdain. Well, isn't it an honor for me to lend money to a man of that rank? And can I do any less for a lord who calls me his dear friend?

Mme Jourdain. And this lord, what does he do for you?

M. Jourdain. He does things that would astonish people, if they were known.

Mme Jourdain. What things, for instance?

M. Jourdain. Enough; I won't explain. Let it suffice that if I have lent him money, he will repay me well, and that soon.

Mme Jourdain. Yes; you can expect it any minute.

M. Jourdain. Certainly; didn't he tell me so?

Mme Jourdain. Yes, yes; he won't fail to do nothing of the sort.

M. Jourdain. He gave me his word as a gentleman.

Mme Jourdain. Nonsense!

M. Jourdain. You are very obstinate, wife. I tell you he'll keep his word. I'm sure of it.

Mme Jourdain. And I tell you he won't; and all the attentions he shows you are just to take you in.

M. Jourdain. Shut up; here he is.

Mme Jourdain. That's the last straw. Perhaps he's coming to get another loan from you. The sight of him takes away my appetite.

M. Jourdain. Shut up, I tell you.

[*Enter* DORANTE.]

Dorante. My dear friend Monsieur Jourdain, and how are you?

M. Jourdain. Very well, sir, at your humble service.

Dorante. And Madame Jourdain here, how is she doing?

Mme Jourdain. Madame Jourdain is doing the best she can.

Dorante. Well, well, Monsieur Jourdain! How elegantly you're gotten up!

M. Jourdain. Well, you see.

Dorante. You look very brave in that suit; we have no young sprigs at court better turned out than you are.

M. Jourdain. He, he!

Mme Jourdain [*aside*]. He scratches him where he itches.

Dorante. Turn around. It's really stylish.

Mme Jourdain [*aside*]. Yes; as silly behind as in front.

Dorante. 'Pon my word, Monsieur Jourdain, I have been extraordinarily anxious to see you. I have a higher opinion of you than of absolutely anyone else. I was talking about you this very morning in the King's bedchamber.

M. Jourdain. You do me too much honor, sir. [*To* MADAME JOURDAIN] In the King's bedchamber!

Dorante. Come, come; put on your hat.

M. Jourdain. Monsieur, I know the respect I owe you.

Dorante. Good Lord, put it on! Let's have no ceremony between us, please.

M. Jourdain. Monsieur . . .

Dorante. Cover, I tell you, Monsieur Jourdain; you are my friend.

M. Jourdain. Monsieur, I am your humble servant.

Dorante. I won't cover, if you don't.

M. Jourdain [*covering*]. I'd rather be unmannerly than troublesome.

Dorante. I am your debtor, as you know.

Mme Jourdain [*aside*].   Yes, we know it only too well.

Dorante.   You have generously lent me money on several occasions, and you have obliged me with the best grace in the world, most assuredly.

M. Jourdain.   You're joking, sir.

Dorante.   But I make a point of repaying all loans, and recognizing the kindnesses that are done me.

M. Jourdain.   I don't doubt it, sir.

Dorante.   I want to clean matters up between us. I've come so we can go over our accounts together.

M. Jourdain [*to* MADAME JOURDAIN].   See how unjust you were!

Dorante.   I am the kind of fellow who likes to pay off his debts as soon as possible.

M. Jourdain [*to* MADAME JOURDAIN].   I told you so!

Dorante.   Let's see now how much I owe you.

M. Jourdain [*to* MADAME JOURDAIN].   You and your ridiculous suspicions!

Dorante.   Do you remember exactly how much you lent me?

M. Jourdain.   I think so. I made a little memorandum. Here it is. On one occasion, given to you, two hundred louis.

Dorante.   That's right.

M. Jourdain.   Another time, one hundred twenty.

Dorante.   Yes.

M. Jourdain.   And another time, a hundred and forty.

Dorante.   You're right.

M. Jourdain.   These three items add up to four hundred and sixty louis, which makes five thousand and sixty francs.

Dorante.   The accounting is excellent. Five thousand and sixty francs.

M. Jourdain.   One thousand eight hundred and thirty-two francs to your feather supplier.

Dorante.   Exactly.

M. Jourdain.   Two thousand seven hundred and eighty francs to your tailor.

Dorante.   True enough.

M. Jourdain.   Four thousand three hundred seventy-nine francs twelve sous and eight farthings to your haberdasher.

Dorante.   Excellent. Twelve sous eight farthings. Very exact accounting.

M. Jourdain.   And one thousand seven hundred forty-eight francs seven sous and four farthings to your saddler.

Dorante.   That's all correct. How much does it come to?

M. Jourdain.   Sum total, fifteen thousand eight hundred francs.

Dorante.   The sum total is quite correct: fifteen thousand eight hundred francs. Now add two hundred pistoles you can give me now; that will make exactly eighteen thousand francs, which I will pay you at the earliest possible moment.

Mme Jourdain [*to* MONSIEUR JOURDAIN].   Well, didn't I guess it?

M. Jourdain [*to* MADAME JOURDAIN].   Silence!

Dorante.   Would it be inconvenient for you to give me that amount?

M. Jourdain.   No, no.

Mme Jourdain [*to* MONSIEUR JOURDAIN].   That fellow is milking you like a cow.

M. Jourdain [*to* MADAME JOURDAIN].   Shut up!

Dorante. If it's inconvenient, I can get it somewhere else.

M. Jourdain. No, indeed.

Mme Jourdain [*to* MONSIEUR JOURDAIN]. He won't be satisfied until he's ruined you.

M. Jourdain [*to* MADAME JOURDAIN]. Shut up, I tell you!

Dorante. If it embarrasses you, you have only to say so.

M. Jourdain. Not at all, sir.

Mme Jourdain [*to* MONSIEUR JOURDAIN]. He's nothing but a crook.

M. Jourdain [*to* MADAME JOURDAIN]. Will you shut up?

Mme Jourdain [*to* MONSIEUR JOURDAIN]. He'll suck you dry, down to your last penny.

M. Jourdain [*to* MADAME JOURDAIN]. I tell you to shut your mouth!

Dorante. There are plenty of people who would be delighted to lend it to me; but since you're my best friend, I thought I would be doing you an injury if I asked anyone else.

M. Jourdain. You do me too much honor, my dear sir. I'll go and fetch what you want.

Mme Jourdain [*to* MONSIEUR JOURDAIN]. What! You're going to give it to him?

M. Jourdain [*to* MADAME JOURDAIN]. What can I do? Do you expect me to refuse a man of such rank, who talked of me this very morning in the King's bedchamber?

Mme Jourdain [*to* MONSIEUR JOURDAIN]. Go on, you're just an easy mark!

[*Exit* MONSIEUR JOURDAIN.]

Dorante. You seem cast down about something. What is the matter, Madame Jourdain?

Mme Jourdain. I've cut my eyeteeth; I wasn't born yesterday.

Dorante. And your charming daughter, I don't see her. Where is she?

Mme Jourdain. My charming daughter is all right where she is.

Dorante. How is she getting along?

Mme Jourdain. She is getting along on her two legs.

Dorante. Wouldn't you like to bring her some day to see the command performance of the ballet and comedy before the King?

Mme Jourdain. Oh, yes, we certainly need a good laugh; a good laugh is certainly what we need.

Dorante. I think, Madame Jourdain, you must have had many admirers in your youth; you must have been so pretty and of such a charming humor.

Mme Jourdain. Good land, sir, is Madame Jourdain doddering already? She's got one foot in the grave, maybe?

Dorante. 'Pon my soul, Madame Jourdain, I ask your pardon. I didn't realize you're still young; I'm so unobservant. I beg you to excuse my impoliteness.

[*Enter* MONSIEUR JOURDAIN.]

M. Jourdain. Here are two hundred louis exactly.

Dorante. I assure you, Monsieur Jourdain, that I am very much at your service; I am most eager to do you some good turn at court.

M. Jourdain. I am very deeply obliged to you.

Dorante.   If Madame Jourdain wants to see the performance before His Majesty, I shall get the best seats in the house for her.

Mme Jourdain.   Madame Jourdain kisses your hands with gratitude.

Dorante [*aside to* MONSIEUR JOURDAIN].   As I told you in my note, our lovely Marquise will come here soon for the ballet and the refreshments. I have finally persuaded her to accept the party you want to give her.

M. Jourdain [*aside to* DORANTE].   Let's move farther off, for good reason.

Dorante.   I haven't seen you for a week, and I haven't given you any news of the diamond ring you asked me to present to her in your name. But the fact is I had all sorts of trouble in overcoming her scruples, and it's only today she made up her mind to accept it.

M. Jourdain.   How did she find it?

Dorante.   Marvelous! And unless I'm much mistaken, the beauty of the diamond will work wonders for you.

M. Jourdain.   Would to God it were so!

Mme Jourdain [*to* NICOLE].   When he once gets with that Count, he can't leave him.

Dorante [*to* MONSIEUR JOURDAIN].   I played up to her properly the value of the present and the greatness of your love.

M. Jourdain.   Your kindness overwhelms me, sir. I am embarrassed beyond words to see a person of your rank lower himself to do what you are doing for me.

Dorante.   Are you joking? Between friends, does one worry about scruples of that sort? Wouldn't you do the same thing for me, if the occasion should arise?

M. Jourdain.   Oh, assuredly; with the utmost willingness.

Mme Jourdain [*to* NICOLE].   I can't abide seeing that fellow around.

Dorante.   Personally, I stick at nothing when it's a question of serving a friend. And when you confided to me your passion for my friend, the charming Marquise, you saw that I immediately offered to aid your love.

M. Jourdain.   That's true. I am confounded by your kindnesses.

Mme Jourdain [*to* NICOLE].   Won't he ever go away?

Nicole.   They just like each other's company.

Dorante.   You have taken the right course to touch her heart. Women love above all things to have people spend money on them; and your frequent serenades, and the continual offerings of flowers, and the superb fireworks on the lake, and the diamond ring she received in your name, and the party you are preparing for her—that sort of thing speaks far better in favor of your love than all the words you might utter to her in person.

M. Jourdain.   There are no expenditures I wouldn't make, if they would help me find the way to touch her heart. A lady of quality has ravishing charms for me; I would pay any price for the honor of her love.

Mme Jourdain [*to* NICOLE].   What can they be argufying so much about? Sneak over and see if you can't pick up something.

Dorante.   Very soon you will enjoy at your ease the pleasure of seeing her; and your eyes will have plenty of time to satisfy their longing.

M. Jourdain.   To get free, I have arranged that my wife shall go and dine with her sister, and she'll spend the whole afternoon there.

Dorante.   That's very prudent. Your wife might have made trouble. I have given all the directions to the caterer, in your name; and I've done everything necessary for the ballet. I worked out the scheme for it myself; if the execution comes up to my idea, I am sure it will be found—

M. Jourdain [*perceiving that* NICOLE *is listening, gives her a box on the ear*]. What's this, saucebox! [*To* DORANTE] Please, let's get out of here.

[*Exit* MONSIEUR JOURDAIN *and* DORANTE.]

Nicole. My stars, madame, curiosity cost me something. But I think there's more here than meets the eye. They're talking about some affair they don't want you to know about.

Mme Jourdain. Well, Nicole, this isn't the first time I've had some suspicions about my husband. Unless I am very much mistaken, he's setting his cap at someone, and I'm trying to find out who it is. But let's think about my daughter a moment. You know how Cléonte loves her. He's a man I like, and I want to help his suit, and give Lucile to him, if I can.

Nicole. Really, madame, I am just delighted to know you feel that way; for if you like the master, I like the manservant just as much, and it would make me very happy if our marriage could take place in the shadow of theirs.

Mme Jourdain. Go and give him a message from me. Tell him to come and see me soon, and we'll go together to my husband and ask my daughter's hand.

Nicole. I'll do so right away, madame, and very gladly. I couldn't do a pleasanter errand. [*Exit* MADAME JOURDAIN] I think I'm going to make some people very happy. [*Enter* CLÉONTE *and* COVIELLE] Ah, here you are, by a lucky chance! I bring you good news. I've come—

Cléonte. Withdraw, perfidious creature! Don't try to distract me with your treacherous words!

Nicole. So that's the way you take—

Cléonte. Withdraw, I tell you! And go straightway and tell your faithless mistress that she will never befool the too confiding Cléonte!

Nicole. What kind of a fit is this? My dear Covielle, do tell me what this means.

Covielle. Your dear Covielle! You scoundrel! Quick, out of my sight, villain! Leave me in peace!

Nicole. What! You too—

Covielle. Out of my sight, I tell you! Never speak to me again!

Nicole [*aside*]. Ouch! What's biting them both? I'd better go right away and tell my mistress of this fine to-do.

[*Exit* NICOLE.]

Cléonte. What! To treat in such a way a lover, the most faithful and ardent of all lovers!

Covielle. It's appalling, how they treat us both.

Cléonte. I display for a certain person all the ardor and affection conceivable. I love only her in all the world; I have her alone in my thought; she has all my devotion, all my desires, all my joy; I speak only of her, I think only of her, I dream only of her, I breathe only for her, my heart exists only for her; and here is the fit reward for so much love! I pass two days without seeing her, which are to me two frightful centuries; I meet her by chance; and at the sight my heart is utterly transported, my joy manifests itself upon my countenance. Ravished with delight, I fly to her; and the faithless one turns her face from me, and passes grimly by, as if she had never seen me in her life!

Covielle.   I say—exactly the same thing.

Cléonte.   Has anything, Covielle, ever matched the perfidy of the ingrate Lucile?

Covielle.   Or that, sir, of the hussy Nicole?

Cléonte.   After so many devout sacrifices, sighs, and vows that I have offered to her charms!

Covielle.   After so many attentions, services, and helping hands I have extended to her in her kitchen!

Cléonte.   So many tears I have shed at her knees!

Covielle.   So many buckets of water I have pulled up out of the well for her!

Cléonte.   So much ardor I have evidenced, in cherishing her more than my own self!

Covielle.   So much heat I have endured in turning the spit for her!

Cléonte.   She flees me with contempt!

Covielle.   She turns her back on me with an uppity air!

Cléonte.   It is perfidy deserving the utmost chastisement.

Covielle.   It is treason deserving a thousand slaps in the face.

Cléonte.   Never, I beg you, take it into your head to speak in her defense.

Covielle.   I, sir? Heaven forbid!

Cléonte.   Don't try to excuse the action of the faithless one.

Covielle.   Don't be afraid, I won't.

Cléonte.   No. For you see, all your efforts to defend her will avail nothing.

Covielle.   Defend her? Who could have that idea?

Cléonte.   I want to keep my resentment fresh, and break off all relations with her.

Covielle.   I give my consent.

Cléonte.   That Monsieur le Comte who goes to her house dazzles her perhaps; and I can see that she may let herself be allured by rank and quality. But, for my own honor, I must forestall the public revelation of her inconstancy. I can see her moving in the direction of a change of heart, and I want to keep step with her, and not let her have all the credit for quitting me.

Covielle.   That's very well said. I share in all your feelings.

Cléonte.   Come to the aid of my rancor, and support my resolution against any lingering remains of love that might speak in her favor. Tell me, please, all the evil you can about her; paint me a portrait of her person which will make her despicable to me; and to complete my disillusionment, point out all the defects you can see in her.

Covielle.   What, in her, sir? She's a fine poser, an affected show-off, for you to fall in love with! She seems very ordinary to me; you could find a hundred girls worthier of you. In the first place, her eyes are too small.[1]

Cléonte.   That's true; her eyes are small. But they are full of fire, very brilliant and sparkling, and unusually touching.

Covielle.   She has a big mouth.

Cléonte.   Perhaps. But one sees in it graces that are not in ordinary mouths. That

---

[1] According to tradition the description is of Molière's wife, who played Lucile.

mouth, when one looks at it, inspires desires. It is the most attractive and amorous mouth on earth.

Covielle.   For her figure, it isn't a tall one.

Cléonte.   No; but it's dainty and flexible.

Covielle.   She affects a kind of carefree speech and behavior.

Cléonte.   True; but she does so gracefully, and her manners are engaging; she has a certain charm which insinuates itself into the heart.

Covielle.   As for wit—

Cléonte.   Ah, that she has, Covielle, the keenest and most delicate.

Covielle.   Her conversation—

Cléonte.   Her conversation is delightful.

Covielle.   She is always serious.

Cléonte.   Well, do you want broad gaiety, everlasting outbursts of glee? Is there anything more tiresome than those women who are always laughing at everything?

Covielle.   But finally, she's as capricious as anybody alive.

Cléonte.   Yes, she's capricious, I agree. But that suits a beauty. We can bear anything from a beauty.

Covielle.   Since that's the way of it, I can see that you want to love her forever.

Cléonte.   I? I'd rather die. I am going to hate her as much as I have loved her.

Covielle.   And how will you do that, if you find her so perfect?

Cléonte.   That is exactly how my revenge is going to be so sensational, and how I'm going to show so clearly the resolution of my heart, in hating and leaving her, beautiful, attractive, and lovable as she is . . . But here she is.

[*Enter* LUCILE *and* NICOLE.]

Nicole [*to* LUCILE].   As for me, I was quite scandalized.

Lucile.   The only explanation, Nicole, is what I was telling you . . . But there he is.

Cléonte [*to* COVIELLE].   I won't even speak to her.

Covielle.   I'll do just like you.

Lucile.   What is it, Cléonte? What is the matter?

Nicole.   What's got into you, Covielle?

Lucile.   Why this distress of mind?

Nicole.   Why are you so sulky?

Lucile.   Are you dumb, Cléonte?

Nicole.   Has the cat got your tongue, Covielle?

Cléonte [*to* COVIELLE].   What an outrageous way to act!

Covielle.   Just a couple of Judases!

Lucile [*to* CLÉONTE].   I see that our recent encounter has troubled you.

Cléonte [*to* COVIELLE].   Aha! She realizes what she has done.

Nicole [*to* COVIELLE].   Our greeting this morning has got your goat.

Covielle [*to* CLÉONTE].   They've guessed where the shoe pinches.

Lucile.   Isn't it true, Cléonte, that that is the cause of your ill humor?

Cléonte.   Yes, perfidious one, it is, since I must speak. And I have this information for you: that you won't laugh off your infidelity as you expect, that I intend to be the first to break with you, and that you won't have the satisfaction of dismissing me. No doubt I shall have trouble in conquering my love for you.

That will cause me some pain; I shall suffer for a time. But I shall overmaster it, and I'll sooner pierce my own heart than be so weak as to return to you.

Covielle. With me, ditto.

Lucile. That's a lot of fuss about nothing, Cléonte. I want to tell you why I avoided your greeting this morning.

Cléonte [*turning his back*]. No, I don't want to hear a word.

Nicole [*to* COVIELLE, *who turns his back*]. I want to tell you the reason we went by so quick.

Covielle. I won't listen.

Lucile. Know, then, that this morning—

Cléonte. No, I tell you.

Nicole. Here are the facts—

Covielle. No, traitor.

Lucile. Listen—

Cléonte. There's no use talking.

Nicole. Let me tell you—

Covielle. I'm deaf.

Lucile. Cléonte!

Cléonte. No.

Lucile. Covielle!

Covielle. I won't!

Lucile. But stop—

Cléonte. Rubbish!

Nicole. Listen to me!

Covielle. Fiddlededee!

Lucile. Just a moment!

Cléonte. Not at all!

Nicole. Be patient.

Covielle. Applesauce!

Lucile. Just two words—

Cléonte. No, it's all over.

Nicole. Just one word—

Covielle. I'll have no truck with you.

Lucile. Well, since you won't listen to me, think what you please, and do what you please.

[LUCILE *and* NICOLE, *who have been following* CLÉONTE *and* COVIELLE *about the stage, cease their pursuit. The business is reversed, the men interceding with the girls.*]

Nicole. Since that's the way you behave, take it any way you like.

Cléonte [*to* LUCILE]. You might as well tell me why you greeted me so coldly.

Lucile. I don't feel like telling you now.

Covielle. Go on, tell us the story.

Nicole. I don't want to any more.

Cléonte. Tell me—

Lucile. No, I won't say a thing.

Covielle. Go ahead; speak up.

Nicole. Not a word.

Cléonte. Please!

Lucile. No, I tell you.

Covielle. Oh, be nice—

Nicole. Nothing doing.

Cléonte. I beg you—

Lucile. Let me alone.

Covielle. I beseech you—

Nicole. Get out!

Cléonte. Lucile!

Lucile. No.

Covielle. Nicole!

Nicole. Not on your life.

Cléonte. In heaven's name!

Lucile. I don't want to.

Covielle. Speak to me!

Nicole. I won't.

Cléonte. Explain my doubts away!

Lucile. I'll do nothing of the sort.

Covielle. Cure my ailing mind!

Nicole. I don't feel like it.

Cléonte. Well, since you care so little about relieving my suffering and justifying yourself for the unworthy way you have treated my devotion, you see me, ingrate, for the last time. I am going far away to die of grief and love.

Covielle. And I'll be right behind you.

[COVIELLE *and* CLÉONTE *start for the exit.*]

Lucile. Cléonte!

Nicole. Covielle!

Cléonte. Eh?

Covielle. What is it?

Lucile. Where are you going?

Cléonte. Where I told you.

Covielle. We're going to die!

Lucile. You are going to die, Cléonte?

Cléonte. Yes, cruel beauty, since that is what you wish.

Lucile. You mean I wish you to die?

Cléonte. Yes, you wish it.

Lucile. Who told you so?

Cléonte. Don't you wish my death, if you refuse to clear up my suspicions?

Lucile. Is that my fault? If you had been willing to listen to me, wouldn't I have told you that the occurrence this morning, which you're complaining about, was caused by the presence of my old aunt, who is convinced that the mere approach of a man dishonors a girl? She lectures us perpetually on this theme, and she pictures all men to us as devils we must flee from.

Nicole. That's the secret of the whole business.

Cléonte. You aren't deceiving me, Lucile?

Covielle. You aren't trying to bamboozle me?

Lucile. It's absolutely true.

Nicole.   That's just the way things happened.

Covielle [*to* CLÉONTE].   Do we surrender to that?

Cléonte.   Ah, Lucile, how a word from your lips can appease my heart's tumult! How readily one lets oneself be convinced by a loved one!

Covielle.   How easily a man is hooked by those confounded creatures!

[*Enter* MADAME JOURDAIN.]

Mme Jourdain.   I am very glad to see you, Cléonte; you are here at just the right moment. My husband is coming; so take this chance to ask him for Lucile's hand.

Cléonte.   Ah, madame, how sweet are these words! How they flatter my desires! Could I receive a more delightful order? A more precious favor? [*Enter* MONSIEUR JOURDAIN] Sir, I did not wish to get any intermediary to make to you a request I have been long meditating. This request touches me so closely that I have chosen to undertake it myself. Without further preamble, I shall tell you that the honor of being your son-in-law would be a glorious favor which I beg you to bestow upon me.

M. Jourdain.   Before giving you an answer, sir, I ask you to tell me if you are a gentleman.

Cléonte.   Sir, most people do not hesitate long at such a question. The word is easily spoken. People assume the appellation without scruple, and common usage today seems to authorize its theft. But as for me, I freely grant, I have somewhat more delicate feelings on the subject. I think that any imposture is unworthy of a decent man, and I think it is mean and base to conceal the state to which it has pleased God to call us, and to adorn oneself in the world's eye with a stolen title, and to try to pass oneself off for what one is not. Certainly, I am the son of a line which has held honorable offices. In the army I acquired the merit of six years of service; and I am possessed of sufficient wealth to sustain a very respectable position in society. But with all that, I am unwilling to give myself a name which others, in my place, would feel justified in assuming; and I will tell you frankly that I am not a gentleman.

M. Jourdain.   Shake hands, sir; my daughter is not for you.

Cléonte.   What?

M. Jourdain.   You are not a gentleman; you won't have my daughter.

Mme Jourdain [*to* MONSIEUR JOURDAIN].   What do you mean, with this gentleman business? Are we descended from the rib of Saint Louis?

M. Jourdain.   Shut up, wife. I see what you're driving at.

Mme Jourdain.   Were our ancestors anything but good bourgeois?

M. Jourdain.   Slander!

Mme Jourdain.   And wasn't your father a merchant, just like mine?

M. Jourdain.   Drat the woman! She never misses a chance! If your father was a merchant, so much the worse for him; but as for my father, it's only the ignorant who say so. All I have to tell you is that I want a son-in-law who's a gentleman.

Mme Jourdain.   What your daughter needs is a husband who suits her, and she'd much better have an honorable man who is rich and handsome than some ugly gentleman without a penny.

Nicole. That's right. There's the son of the gentleman in our village, he's the biggest booby and ninny ever seen.

M. Jourdain. Shut up, saucebox. You're always sticking your oar in the conversation. I have enough property for my daughter; all I need is honor; and I want to make her a marquise.

Mme Jourdain. Marquise?

M. Jourdain. Yes, marquise.

Mme Jourdain. Alas, God forbid!

M. Jourdain. It's something I've made up my mind to.

Mme Jourdain. As for me, it's something I'll never consent to. Alliances with people above our own rank are always likely to have very unpleasant results. I don't want to have my son-in-law able to reproach my daughter for her parents, and I don't want her children to be ashamed to call me their grandma. If she should happen to come and visit me in her grand lady's carriage, and if by mistake she should fail to salute some one of the neighbors, you can imagine how they'd talk. "Take a look at that fine Madame la Marquise showing off," they'd say. "She's the daughter of Monsieur Jourdain, and when she was little, she was only too glad to play at being a fine lady. She wasn't always so high and mighty as she is now, and both her grandfathers sold dry goods besides the Porte Saint Innocent. They both piled up money for their children, and now perhaps they're paying dear for it in the next world; you don't get so rich by being honest." Well, I don't want that kind of talk to go on; and in short, I want a man who will feel under obligation to my daughter, and I want to be able to say to him: "Sit down there, my boy, and eat dinner with us."

M. Jourdain. Those views reveal a mean and petty mind, that wants to remain forever in its base condition. Don't answer back to me again. My daughter will be a marquise in spite of everyone; and if you get me angry, I'll make her a duchess.

[*Exit* MONSIEUR JOURDAIN.]

Mme Jourdain. Cléonte, don't lose courage yet. Lucile, come with me; and tell your father straight out that if you can't have him, you won't marry anybody.

[*Exit* MADAME JOURDAIN, LUCILE, *and* NICOLE.]

Covielle. You've got yourself into a nice mess with your high principles.

Cléonte. Well, what can I do? I have serious scruples on that point, that can't be overcome by the example others set us.

Covielle. It's foolish to take your scruples seriously with a man like that. Don't you see he's crazy? Would it have cost you anything to fall in with his fancies?

Cléonte. No doubt you're right. But I didn't think one had to give proofs of nobility to be the son-in-law of Monsieur Jourdain.

Covielle. Ha, ha, ha!

Cléonte. What are you laughing at?

Covielle. At an idea I had to take the fellow in, and get you what you want.

Cléonte. How's that?

Covielle. It's rather funny.

Cléonte. What is it, then?

Covielle. There's been a comic performance recently which would fit in perfectly here. I could work the troupe into a practical joke we could play on our joker. It would be rather on the burlesque side, perhaps; but with him you can go to any lengths; you don't have to be too fussy. He could act his own part in it perfectly; he'd play up to all the farce. I can get the actors, and they have the costumes all ready. Just let me manage it.

Cléonte. But tell me—

Covielle. I'll tell you everything. But he's coming back; let's get out.

[*Exit* COVIELLE *and* CLÉONTE. *Enter* MONSIEUR JOURDAIN.]

M. Jourdain. What the devil! The only thing they have to reproach me for is my noble friends; and as for me, I think there's nothing so splendid as to associate with noble lords. They have the monopoly of honor and civility. I'd gladly give two fingers off my hand, to have been born a count or a marquis.

[*Enter a* LACKEY.]

Lackey. Monsieur, here is Monsieur le Comte, and a lady on his arm.

M. Jourdain. Oh, good God! I have some orders to give. Tell them I'll be here right away.

[*Exit* MONSIEUR JOURDAIN. *Enter* DORANTE *and* DORIMÈNE.]

Lackey. The master has just gone and said he'd be here right away.

Dorante. Very well.

[*Exit* LACKEY.]

Dorimène. I don't know, Dorante; it seems to me rather peculiar, to let you bring me into a house where I don't know anyone.

Dorante. Well, my dear lady, what place can my love find to entertain you properly, since, to avoid gossip, you won't let me use either your house or mine?

Dorimène. Yes, but you don't say that I am becoming involved every day, by accepting such excessive evidences of your devotion. I do my best to refuse, but you wear down my resistance; and you show a polite obstinacy which makes me yield gently to anything you like. The frequent visits began it; and then the impassioned declarations; and they brought along the serenades and the parties; and then came the presents. I made opposition to everything; but you don't let yourself be discouraged, and step by step you are breaking down my resolutions. Really, I can no longer be quite sure of myself; and I think that in the end you will drag me into marriage, in spite of my reluctance.

Dorante. My word, madame, you ought to be already in that happy state. You are a widow; you have no obligations to anyone but yourself. I am independent; and I love you more than my life. What obstacle is there to your making me immediately the happiest of men?

Dorimène. Good heavens, Dorante, for a happy married life many qualities are necessary in both parties; and the most reasonable pair of people alive often have much trouble in forming a quite satisfactory union.

Dorante. You are absurd, my dear, in imagining so many difficulties. From one unfortunate experience you should not draw conclusions about all the others.

Dorimène. Anyway, I keep coming back to the same point. I am disturbed by the expenditures I see you making for me, and for two reasons: one, that they obligate me more than I like; and two, that I am sure—if you will forgive me—that you aren't making them without embarrassment; and I don't want that.

Dorante. Ah, madame, they are mere trifles! It is not by such means—

Dorimène. I know what I am saying. Among other things, the diamond you forced me to accept is of such value—

Dorante. Oh, madame, please! Don't rate so highly something my love regards as all unworthy of you! And permit— But here comes the master of the house.

[*Enter* MONSIEUR JOURDAIN. *He makes two sweeping bows, stepping forward. He finds himself close to* DORIMÈNE.]

M. Jourdain. Stand back a little, madame.

Dorimène. What?

M. Jourdain. One step back, please.

Dorimène. What for?

M. Jourdain. Back up a little, for the third.

Dorante. Madame, Monsieur Jourdain knows his etiquette.

M. Jourdain. Madame, it is a very great distinction to me to find myself so fortunate as to be so happy as to have the happiness that you have had the kindness to grant me the grace of doing me the honor of honoring me with the favor of your presence; and if I had also the merit of meriting a merit like yours, and if heaven . . . envious of my bliss . . . had granted me . . . the privilege of finding myself worthy . . . of the . . .

Dorante. Monsieur Jourdain, that is enough. Madame does not care for high compliments, and she knows that you are an intelligent man. [*Aside to* DORIMÈNE] He is a good bourgeois, and rather ridiculous in his behavior, as you see.

Dorimène [*aside to* DORANTE]. That's not hard to recognize.

Dorante. Madame, this is the best of my friends.

M. Jourdain. You do me too much honor.

Dorante. A man of the world, absolutely.

Dorimène. I have much esteem for him.

M. Jourdain. I have done nothing as yet, madame, to deserve such kindness.

Dorante [*aside to* MONSIEUR JOURDAIN]. Be sure, anyway, you don't mention the diamond ring you've given her.

M. Jourdain [*aside to* DORANTE]. Couldn't I even ask her how she likes it?

Dorante [*aside to* MONSIEUR JOURDAIN]. Not by any means. That would be horribly vulgar. As a man of the world, you must act as if you hadn't made the present at all. [*To* DORIMÈNE] Madame, Monsieur Jourdain says he is overjoyed to see you in his house.

Dorimène. He honors me deeply.

M. Jourdain [*aside to* DORANTE]. How much obliged I am to you for speaking to her in such a way!

Dorante [*aside to* MONSIEUR JOURDAIN]. I had a dreadful time getting her to come here.

M. Jourdain [*aside to* DORANTE]. I don't know how to thank you.

Dorante. He says, madame, that he thinks you are the most beautiful person on earth.

Dorimène. It is very kind of him.

M. Jourdain. Madame, the kindness is all on your side, and . . .

[*Enter a* LACKEY.]

Dorante. Let's think about dinner.

Lackey. Everything is ready, sir.

Dorante. Then let's sit down; and send in the musicians.

[*Six* COOKS *enter dancing. They bring in a table covered with various dishes. This makes the third* Interlude.]

Act IV

[*After the* Interlude, DORIMÈNE, DORANTE, MONSIEUR JOURDAIN, *two* MALE SINGERS, *a* WOMAN SINGER, *and several* LACKEYS *remain on the stage.*]

Dorimène. Why, Dorante! What a magnificent repast!

M. Jourdain. You are joking, Madame. I wish it were more worthy of being offered to you.

[DORIMÈNE, DORANTE, MONSIEUR JOURDAIN *and the* SINGERS *sit at table.*]

Dorante. Monsieur Jourdain is quite right, madame, in speaking in that way, and he puts me under a deep obligation by doing so well the honors of his house. I agree with him that the repast is unworthy of you. As it was I who ordered it, and as I have not the finesse of some of our friends on this subject, you will not find here a culinary symphony, and you will perhaps notice some gastronomic incongruities, some solecisms of good taste. If Damis had had a hand in it, the rules would be strictly observed; you would recognize a mingling of elegance and erudition. He would not fail to call your attention to the dishes he would serve; he would make you applaud his high capacity in the science of cookery. He would mention the rolls, cooked golden-brown on the hearth's edge with a uniform crust, crumbling delicately under the tooth; the wine with a velvet bouquet, somewhat young and saucy, but not to the point of impudence; a breast of lamb pinked with parsley; a loin of riverside veal from Normandy, no longer than that, white, dainty, like almond paste on the tongue; partridges prepared with a special spice and mushroom sauce; and for his crowning triumph, a young fat turkey flanked by squabs, crested with white onions blended with chicory, swimming in a pearl bouillon. But for my part, I must admit my ignorance; and as Monsieur Jourdain has very well said, I could wish that the repast was more worthy of being offered you.

Dorimène. I reply to this compliment by devouring the dinner as I do.

M. Jourdain. Oh, what beautiful hands!

Dorimène. The hands are ordinary hands, Monsieur Jourdain; but you notice the diamond, which is indeed beautiful.

M. Jourdain. I, Madame? God forbid that I should mention it. That would not be the action of a man of the world. The diamond is nothing much.

Dorimène. You are hard to please.

M. Jourdain. You are too kind—

Dorante [*with a cautionary gesture to* MONSIEUR JOURDAIN]. Come, some wine for Monsieur Jourdain, and for our musical guests, who will give us the pleasure of singing us a drinking song.

Dorimène. There's no better seasoning for good cheer than to combine it with music. I am being magnificently regaled here.

M. Jourdain. Madame, it is not—

Dorante. Monsieur Jourdain, let us lend an ear to the musicians; their songs will express our feelings better than we could in words.

[*The* SINGERS *take glasses in hand, and sing two drinking songs, accompanied by the orchestra.*]

Duet

Phyllis, a drop of wine, to make the moment pass!
How daintily your hand holds the delightful glass!
Ah, Phyllis, you and wine, you lend each other arms,
For wine and love together increase each other's charms.
So you and wine and I, come let us vow to be
    A constant trinity.
The wine that wets your lip itself doth beautify;
And yet your lovely lip is lovelier thereby.
The lips, they bid me drink; the wine, it bids me kiss!
Ah, what intoxication can ever equal this!
So you and wine and I, come let us vow to be
    A constant trinity.

Duet

Drink, my comrades, drink;
    The hour's propitious.
Let your glasses clink;
    The wine's delicious.
Too swift our steps we bend
    To the dark shore,
Where love is at an end,
    And we drink no more.
The scholars can't agree
    Where lives the soul;
By our philosophy
    It's in the bowl.
Not glory, wealth, nor wit
    Chase care away;
But wine doth still permit
    Man to be gay.

Chorus

> Come, wine for all, my lads; and never cease to pour,
> And pour and pour again, while men can ask for more!

Dorimène. That couldn't be better sung; it's really lovely.

M. Jourdain. I can see something even lovelier around here.

Dorimène. Oho! Monsieur Jourdain is more gallant than I thought.

Dorante. Why, madame, what do you take Monsieur Jourdain for?

M. Jourdain. I wish she would take me for something I could suggest.

Dorimène. You're still at it?

Dorante [*to* DORIMÈNE]. You don't know him.

M. Jourdain. She can know me better whenever she likes.

Dorimène. Oh, I give up!

Dorante. He always has an answer ready. But you haven't noticed, madame, that Monsieur Jourdain eats all the bits that your spoon has touched in the serving dish.

Dorimène. Monsieur Jourdain is a man who ravishes me.

M. Jourdain. If I could ravish your heart, I would be—

[*Enter* MADAME JOURDAIN.]

Mme Jourdain. Aha! I find some fine company here, and I can see that I wasn't expected. So, it's for this pretty business, my good husband, that you were so anxious to send me off to dine with my sister? I've just seen a kind of a theatre downstairs; and here I see a kind of a wedding feast. So that's how you spend your money? And that's the way you put on a big party for ladies in my absence, and you give them music and a play, while you send me to Jericho?

Dorante. What do you mean, Madame Jourdain? You must have hallucinations, to get it into your head that your husband is spending his own money, and that he's the one who is giving the party for Madame. Let me inform you that I'm footing the bill. He is merely lending me his house; you ought to be more careful about what you say.

M. Jourdain. Yes, insolence! It's Monsieur le Comte who is giving all this to Madame, who is a lady of quality. He does me the honor to borrow my house, and to ask me to join him.

Mme Jourdain. Stuff and nonsense! I know what I know.

Dorante. Madame Jourdain, you need some new spectacles.

Mme Jourdain. I don't need any spectacles at all, monsieur; I can see all right without them. I've known what's up for quite some time now; I'm not such a fool. It's a very cheap business for you, a great lord, to encourage my husband's follies the way you're doing. And you, madame, for a great lady, it's neither pretty nor decent for you to bring trouble into a family, and to allow my husband to be in love with you.

Dorimène. What is the meaning of all this? Dorante, you're unpardonable, to expose me to the delusions of this fantastic creature. [*She starts to leave.*]

Dorante [*following* DORIMÈNE]. Madame, look here! Madame, where are you running off to?

[*Exit* DORIMÈNE.]

M. Jourdain. Madame! . . . Monsieur le Comte, make my apologies to her, and try to bring her back. [*Exit* DORANTE. To MADAME JOURDAIN] Impudence! These are nice tricks of yours! You come and insult me before everybody, and you drive people of quality out of the house!

Mme Jourdain. I don't care a straw for their quality.

M. Jourdain. You cursèd troublemaker, I don't know why I don't crack your skull with the leftovers of the dinner you ruined!

[*The* LACKEYS *carry out the table and dishes.*]

Mme Jourdain. I don't care a pin. I'm defending my rights; and every woman will be on my side. [*She starts for the door.*]

M. Jourdain. You do well to escape my anger. [*Exit* MADAME JOURDAIN] What a time she picked to interrupt! I was just in the mood to say some very neat things. I never felt myself so bubbling over with inspiration . . . But what's all this?

[*Enter* COVIELLE, *wearing an Oriental costume and a long beard.*]

Covielle. Monsieur, I don't know if I have the honor of being known to you.

M. Jourdain. No, sir.

Covielle. I last saw you when you weren't any bigger than that. [*Holds his hand a foot from the floor.*]

M. Jourdain. Me?

Covielle. Yes, you were the prettiest child ever seen, and all the ladies would take you in their arms to kiss you.

M. Jourdain. To kiss me!

Covielle. Yes. I was a great friend of your late honorable father.

M. Jourdain. My late honorable father?

Covielle. Yes. He was a very worthy gentleman.

M. Jourdain. What did you say?

Covielle. I said he was a very worthy gentleman.

M. Jourdain. My father?

Covielle. Yes.

M. Jourdain. You knew him well?

Covielle. Certainly.

M. Jourdain. And you knew him to be a gentleman?

Covielle. Of course.

M. Jourdain. The world is certainly a funny place!

Covielle. How is that?

M. Jourdain. There are some stupid people who try to tell me he was a merchant.

Covielle. He, a merchant? It's pure slander; he never was anything of the sort. The fact is, he was very obliging, very helpful by nature. And as he was a remarkable judge of woolens, he used to go here and there and pick them out, and have them brought to his house; and then he would give them to his friends—for money.

M. Jourdain. I am delighted to know you, and to have your testimony that my father was a gentleman.

Covielle. I will testify to the fact before everyone.

M. Jourdain. That's very kind. And what brings you here?

Covielle. Since the time when I knew your late honorable father, that worthy gentleman, I have been roving the wide world.

M. Jourdain. The wide world!

Covielle. Yes.

M. Jourdain. That must be quite a trip.

Covielle. It is, certainly. I returned from my far journeys only four days ago; and because of my interest in everything that concerns you, I have come to announce to you some excellent news.

M. Jourdain. What's that?

Covielle. You know that the son of the Grand Turk is here?

M. Jourdain. Me? No.

Covielle. Really! He has come with a magnificent retinue. Everyone goes to see him; and he was received in this country as a noble lord of great importance.

M. Jourdain. Bless me! I didn't know that.

Covielle. And what concerns you, to your great advantage, is that he has fallen in love with your daughter.

M. Jourdain. The son of the Grand Turk?

Covielle. Yes. And he wants to be your son-in-law.

M. Jourdain. My son-in-law? The son of the Grand Turk?

Covielle. The son of the Grand Turk wants to be your son-in-law. I went to call on him; and as I understand his language perfectly, he said to me, after discussing various matters: "Acciam croc soler ouch alla moustaph gidelum amanahem varahini oussere carbulath."[1] That is, "Have you by chance seen a beautiful girl, the daughter of Monsieur Jourdain, a Parisian gentleman?"

M. Jourdain. The son of the Grand Turk said that about me?

Covielle. Yes. When I replied that I had a particular acquaintance with you, and that I had chanced to see your daughter, he said: "Ah! marababa sahem!" That means: "Oh, how much I love her!"

M. Jourdain. "Marababa sahem" means "Oh, how much I love her?"

Covielle. Yes.

M. Jourdain. Bless my soul, I'm glad you told me, for personally I would never have imagined that "marababa sahem" could mean "Oh, how much I love her." Turkish is certainly a wonderful language.

Covielle. More wonderful than you would think. Do you know what "cacaracamouchen" means?

M. Jourdain. "Cacaracamouchen?" No.

Covielle. That means "my darling."

M. Jourdain. "Cacaracamouchen" means "my darling"?

Covielle. Yes.

M. Jourdain. That's really marvelous. "Cacaracamouchen; my darling." Can you imagine? You amaze me.

Covielle. In short, to fulfill the purpose of my embassy, he wants to ask the hand of your daughter in marriage. And to have a father-in-law of a rank suitable for him, he wants to make you a mamamouchi, which is a certain high dignity of his own country.

M. Jourdain. A mamamouchi?

---

[1] Molière's Turkish is a mingling of genuine Turkish, Arabic, and Hebrew with mere gibberish.

Covielle. Yes, a mamamouchi. That is to say, in our language, a paladin. The paladins, they were those old-time—well, in short, paladins. There is nothing nobler than that anywhere. You will be the equal of the greatest lords on earth.

M. Jourdain. The son of the Grand Turk honors me very profoundly. I beg you to take me to his presence so that I can express my thanks.

Covielle. It's unnecessary. He is coming here.

M. Jourdain. He's coming here?

Covielle. Yes. And he's bringing everything needful for the ceremony of your ennoblement.

M. Jourdain. He certainly works fast.

Covielle. His love is such that he can bear no delay.

M. Jourdain. There's just one awkward thing. My daughter is very stubborn, and she's gone and set her mind on a certain Cléonte, and she swears she won't marry anyone else but him.

Covielle. She will change her views when she sees the son of the Grand Turk. And also—a very remarkable fact—the son of the Grand Turk has a striking resemblance to Cléonte. I've just seen this Cléonte; I had him pointed out to me. Her love for the one may easily shift to the other; and . . . But I think I hear him coming. Indeed, here he is.

[*Enter* CLÉONTE *in Turkish costume, with three* PAGES *carrying his train.*]

Cléonte. Ambousahim oqui boraf, Jordina salamalequi!

Covielle [*to* MONSIEUR JOURDAIN]. That is, "Monsieur Jourdain, may your heart be all year long like a rosebush in bloom!" That is a courteous expression in those countries.

M. Jourdain. I am the very humble servant of his Turkish Highness.

Covielle. Carigar camboto oustin moraf.

Cléonte. Oustin yoc catamalequi basum base alla moran!

Covielle. He says: "May Heaven give you the strength of lions and the prudence of serpents!"

M. Jourdain. His Turkish Highness does me too much honor, and I wish him every kind of prosperity.

Covielle. Ossa binamen sadoc babally oracaf ouram.

Cléonte. Bel-men.

Covielle. He says you must go with him right away to make preparations for the ceremony, and afterwards you'll see your daughter and conclude the marriage.

M. Jourdain. All that in two words?

Covielle. Yes, the Turkish language is like that. It says a great deal in very few words. You go where he wants you to, quickly.

[*Exit* MONSIEUR JOURDAIN, CLÉONTE, *and* PAGES.]

Covielle. Ha, ha, ha! That was a good one! What a dupe he is! He couldn't play his part better if he'd learned it by heart! Ha, ha, ha! [*Enter* DORANTE] I beg you, sir, to help us out in a little performance we're staging.

Dorante. Ha, ha! Covielle, I would never have recognized you! What kind of getup is this?

Covielle. Well, take a look. Ha, ha!

Dorante.   What are you laughing at?
Covielle. At something, sir, which deserves a laugh.
Dorante.   How's that?
Covielle. You'd never guess, sir, the trick we're playing on Monsieur Jourdain, to induce him to give his daughter to my master.
Dorante.   I can't guess the trick, but I can guess that it is pretty sure to work, since you are organizing it.
Covielle. Evidently, sir, you are a judge of character.
Dorante.   Tell me the story.
Covielle. Be so kind as to come to one side, and give room to what I see coming in. You will see a part of the story, and I will tell you the rest.

[*The Turkish ceremony of the ennobling of* MONSIEUR JOURDAIN, *performed with music and dance, forms the fourth* Interlude.

Six DANCING TURKS *enter gravely, two by two, to the full orchestra. They carry three long carpets, with which they make various evolutions, and finally raise them high. The* TURKISH MUSICIANS *and other instrumentalists pass beneath. Four* DERVISHES, *accompanying the* MUFTI, *or legal-religious dignitary, close the procession.*

The TURKS *spread the carpets on the ground and kneel upon them. The* MUFTI, *standing in the middle, makes an invocation with contortions and grimaces, turning up his face, and wiggling his hands outward from his head, like wings. The* TURKS *bow forward, touching their foreheads to the floor, singing "Ali"; they resume the kneeling position, singing "Allah." They continue thus to the end of the invocation; then they all stand, singing "Allah akbar."*

Then the DERVISHES *bring before the* MUFTI MONSIEUR JOURDAIN, *dressed in Turkish costume, clean-shaven, without turban or sword. The* MUFTI *sings in solemn tones.*]

Mufti.

> Se ti sabir,
> Ti respondir;
> Se non sabir,
> Tazir, tazir.
>
> Mi star muphty;
> To qui star ti?
> Non intendir:
> Tazir, tazir.[1]

---

[1] "If you know, answer; if you don't know, keep still, keep still. I am a mufti; you, who are you? You don't understand; keep still, keep still." Most of the language of the Turkish ceremony is *lingua franca*, once used for commercial and diplomatic purposes around the Mediterranean, still known to sailors and harbor men. It is a blend mostly of French, Spanish, Italian, and Arabic. All grammatical forms are simplified; verbs have only the infinitive form. (A sort of Basic Romance.) Any Frenchman, or Spaniard or Italian, could understand the Mufti well enough.

[*Two* DERVISHES *lead out* MONSIEUR JOURDAIN. *The* MUFTI *questions the* TURKS *as to the candidate's religion.*]

Mufti.
Dice, Turque, qui star quista?
Anabatista, anabatista?[1]
Turks.
Ioc.[2]
Mufti.
Zwinglista?[3]
Turks.
Ioc.
Mufti.
Coffita?[4]
Turks.
Ioc.
Mufti.
Hussita? Morista? Fronista?[5]
Turks.
Ioc. Ioc. Ioc.
Mufti.
Ioc, Ioc, Ioc!
Star pagana?
Turks.
Ioc.
Mufti.
Luterana?
Turks.
Ioc.
Mufti.
Puritana?
Turks.
Ioc.
Mufti.
Bramina? Moffina? Zurina?[6]
Turks.
Ioc. Ioc. Ioc.
Mufti.
Ioc. Ioc. Ioc.
Mahametana? Mahametana?

1 "Tell me, Turks, what is this man? An Anabaptist?"
2 "No." An authentic Turkish word.
3 Follower of Zwingli, Protestant reformer.
4 Member of the Coptic Church.
5 A Hussite, follower of Bohemian reformer John Huss. The meaning of the other two words is obscure.
6 Brahmin; "Moffina" and "Zurina" are apparently invented words.

Turks.
  Hey valla! Hey valla![1]
Mufti.
  Como chamara? Como chamara?[2]
Turks.
  Giourdina, Giourdina.
Mufti.
  Giourdina!

[*He leaps high, and peers in all directions.*]

  Giourdina? Giourdina? Giourdina?
Turks.
  Giourdina! Giourdina! Giourdina!
Mufti.
  Mahameta per Giourdina
  Mi pregar sera e matina;
  Voler far un paladina
  De Giourdina, de Giourdina.
  Dar turbanta e dar scarcina
  Con galera e brigantina
  Per deffender Palestina.
  Mahameta per Giourdina
  Mi pregar sera e mattina.[3]

[*Questioning the* TURKS]

  Star bon Turca Giourdina?
  Star bon Turca Giourdina?
Turks.
  Hey valla, hey valla!
  Hey valla, hey valla!
Mufti [*dancing*].
  Hu la ba ba la chou ba la ba ba la da!

[*The* MUFTI *exits; the* TURKS *dance and sing.*]

Turks.
  Hu la ba ba la chou ba la ba ba la da!

[*The* MUFTI *returns, wearing an enormous ceremonial turban, adorned with four or five rows of blazing candles. Two* DERVISHES *accompany him, wearing pointed hats, also adorned with lighted candles. They solemnly bear the Koran. The two other* DERVISHES *conduct* MONSIEUR JOURDAIN, *who is terrified by the ceremony. They make him kneel down with his back to the* MUFTI: *then they make him bend forward till his hands rest on the floor. They put the Koran on*

---

1 "Yes, by Allah!" (Arabic.)
2 "What is his name?"
3 "I pray to Mahomet for Jourdain night and morning. I want to make a paladin of Jourdain, of Jourdain. Give a turban and a scimitar, with a galley and a brigantine, to defend Palestine. I pray to Mahomet for Jourdain night and morning."

his back, which serves as a reading desk for the MUFTI. *The* MUFTI *makes a burlesque invocation, scowling and opening and shutting his mouth without uttering a word. Then he speaks vehemently, now muttering, now shouting with terrifying passion, slapping his sides as if to force out his words, occasionally striking the Koran, turning its leaves briskly. He finally raises his hands and exclaims loudly: "Hou!"*[1] *During this invocation, the* TURKS *sing, "Hou, hou, hou!" bending forward three times, then straightening up, singing, "Hou, hou, hou!" They continue doing so throughout the* MUFTI's *invocation. After the invocation, the* DERVISHES *remove the Koran from* MONSIEUR JOURDAIN's *back. He exclaims, "Ouf!" with relief. The* DERVISHES *raise him to his feet.*]

Mufti [*to* MONSIEUR JOURDAIN].
  Ti non star furba?[2]
Turks.
  No, no, no.
Mufti.
  Non star forfanta?[3]
Turks.
  No, no, no.
Mufti [*to the* TURKS].
  Donar turbanta, donar turbanta.[4]

[*Exit the* MUFTI. *The* TURKS *repeat the* MUFTI's *words, and with song and dance present the turban to* MONSIEUR JOURDAIN. *The* MUFTI *re-enters with a scimitar, which he presents to* MONSIEUR JOURDAIN.]

Mufti.
  Ti star nobile, non star fabola.
  Pigliar schiabola.[5]

[*Exit the* MUFTI. *The* TURKS *draw their scimitars and repeat the* MUFTI's *words. Six of them dance around* MONSIEUR JOURDAIN, *feigning to strike him with their weapons. The* MUFTI *returns.*]

Mufti.
  Dara, dara bastonara, bastonara, bastonara.[6]

[*Exit the* MUFTI. *The* TURKS *repeat his words, beating* MONSIEUR JOURDAIN *to music. Re-enter the* MUFTI.]

Mufti.
  Non tener honta;
  Questa star l'ultima affronta.[7]

----

1 *He*, or *God*, in Arabic.
2 "You aren't an evildoer?"
3 "You aren't a rascal?"
4 "Give the turban."
5 "You're a noble, it's no lie. Take this sword."
6 "Give him a beating."
7 "Feel no shame; this is the last affront."

[*The* TURKS *repeat the* MUFTI's *words. The* MUFTI, *leaning on the* DERVISHES, *makes another invocation, to the full orchestra. Evidently fatigued by the ceremony, he is respectfully supported by the* DERVISHES. *The* TURKS, *leaping, dancing, and singing around the* MUFTI, *conduct him off-stage to the sound of Turkish musical instruments.*]

Act V

[*After the* Interlude, *all retire except* MONSIEUR JOURDAIN. *Enter* MADAME JOURDAIN.]

Mme Jourdain. Lord have mercy on us! What's all this? What a figure of fun! You're dressing up for Hallowe'en at this time of year? Tell me, what's going on? Who rigged you up that way?

M. Jourdain. Insolent creature, to talk that way to a mamamouchi!

Mme Jourdain. How's that?

M. Jourdain. Yes, now you've got to show me some respect. I've just been made a mamamouchi.

Mme Jourdain. What do you mean with your mamamouchi?

M. Jourdain. Mamamouchi, I tell you! I'm a mamamouchi!

Mme Jourdain. What kind of a creature is that?

M. Jourdain. Mamamouchi! That is, in our language, a paladin.

Mme Jourdain. Aballadin'!¹ You're going to go around aballadin', at your age?

M. Jourdain. Such ignorance! I said a paladin. That's a dignity that just has been conferred upon me, with due ceremony.

Mme Jourdain. What kind of ceremony?

M. Jourdain. Mahameta per Giourdina!

Mme Jourdain. What does that mean?

M. Jourdain. Giourdina, that is, Jourdain.

Mme Jourdain. Well, what of it, Jourdain?

M. Jourdain. Voler far un paladina de Giourdina.

Mme Jourdain. What?

M. Jourdain. Dar turbanta con galera.

Mme Jourdain. What sense is there in that?

M. Jourdain. Per deffender palestina.

Mme Jourdain. What are you trying to say?

M. Jourdain. Dara dara bastonara.

Mme Jourdain. What's all that gibberish?

M. Jourdain. Non tener honta; questa star l'ultima affronta.

Mme Jourdain. What's the idea, anyway?

M. Jourdain [*singing and dancing*]. Hou la ba ba la chou ba la ba ba la da.

Mme Jourdain. Alas, dear God! My husband has gone crazy!

M. Jourdain. Silence, insolent woman! Show proper respect to a noble mamamouchi.

[*Exit* MONSIEUR JOURDAIN.]

¹ The pun is better in French.

Mme Jourdain. How has he gone and lost his wits? I must keep him from going out. Oh, dear, oh, dear, this is the last straw! There's nothing but trouble everywhere!

[*Exit* MADAME JOURDAIN. *After a moment, enter* DORANTE *and* DORIMÈNE.]

Dorante. Yes, madame, you will see a very amusing sight. I don't think you will ever find a crazier man than he is. And besides, madame, we must try to aid Cléonte's love affair, and fall in with his masquerade. He's a very decent fellow, who deserves our interest and help.

Dorimène. I think very highly of him; he merits good fortune in his enterprise.

Dorante. Besides, we have a ballet due us. We shouldn't let it be wasted. And I want to see if my scheme for the performance works out well.

Dorimène. I've just seen some of the preparations; they are magnificent. And I must tell you, Dorante, that I simply cannot allow this sort of thing. I must put a stop to your lavishness; and to check your mad spending of money on me, I have decided to marry you very soon. That's the best solution; with marriage, all the extravagances stop.

Dorante. Ah, madame, is it possible that you have made so welcome a resolution in my favor?

Dorimène. It's only to prevent you from ruining yourself. Otherwise, I can see that soon you wouldn't have a penny.

Dorante. What an obligation I have, my dear, to your concern for preserving my property! It is all yours, and my heart is too; you can do with them what you will.

Dorimène. I shall take proper care of both of them . . . But here is our good man; he certainly looks extraordinary.

[*Enter* MONSIEUR JOURDAIN.]

Dorante. Sir, madame and I have come to render homage to your new dignity, and to felicitate you on the proposed marriage of your daughter to the son of the Grand Turk.

M. Jourdain [*after making obeisances in the Turkish style*]. Sir, I wish you the strength of serpents and the wisdom of lions.

Dorimène. I am happy to be one of the first, Monsieur, to congratulate you upon the high degree of glory you have attained.

M. Jourdain. Madame, I wish your rosebush may be in bloom all year long. I am infinitely obliged to you for your sympathetic interest in the honors which have come to me, and I take great joy in seeing you here again, so that I may make my very humble apologies for my wife's excesses.

Dorimène. It was nothing at all; I can readily excuse her impulse. Your heart is no doubt precious to her; it is not strange that the possession of a man like you may expose her to some alarms.

M. Jourdain. The possession of my heart is entirely yours to dispose of.

Dorante. You see, madame, that Monsieur Jourdain is not one of those people who are dazzled by prosperity. Even in his glory, he does not forget his old friends.

Dorimène. That is the character of a really noble soul.

Dorante.   But where is His Turkish Highness? As your friends, we should like to pay him our respects.

M. Jourdain.   There he is, coming now. I have sent for my daughter, in order to give him her hand.

[*Enter* CLÉONTE, *in Turkish costume.*]

Dorante [*to* CLÉONTE].   Sir, as friends of your honorable father-in-law, we have come to make obeisance to Your Highness, and to respectfully assure Your Highness of our humble service.

M. Jourdain.   Where is the interpreter, to tell him who you are, and make him understand what you are saying? You'll see that he'll answer you; he speaks Turkish wonderfully. Hello, hello! Where the deuce did he go to? [*To* CLÉ-ONTE] Strouf, strif, strof, straf. This gentleman is a *grande segnore, grande segnore, grande segnore;* and Madame is a *granda dama, granda dama.* [*Recognizing that he fails to make himself understood*] Oh, dear! Sir, him French mamamouchi; Madame here, French female mamamouchi. I can't make it any clearer . . . Good! Here's the interpreter! [*Enter* COVIELLE] Where did you get off to? We can't say a thing without you. Just tell him that the gentleman and lady are persons of high rank, who have come to salute him, as my friends, and to assure him of their regards. [*To* DORIMÈNE *and* DORANTE] You'll see how he'll answer you.

Covielle.   Alabala crociam acci boram alabamen.

Clèonte.   Catalequi tubal ourin soter amalouchan.

M. Jourdain.   You see?

Covielle.   He says: "May the rain of prosperity forever sprinkle the garden of your family."

M. Jourdain.   Didn't I tell you he spoke Turkish?

Dorante.   It's certainly amazing.

[*Enter* LUCILE.]

M. Jourdain.   Come here, daughter, come here. Come and give your hand to the gentleman, who does you the honor of asking to marry you.

Lucile.   Father! How you're gotten up! Are you acting in a play?

M. Jourdain.   No, no; it isn't a play. It's a very serious matter, and one that does you the greatest honor you could conceive. Here is the husband I'm giving you.

Lucile.   Husband—to me, Father?

M. Jourdain.   Yes, to you. Go on, shake hands with him, and thank heaven for your good fortune.

Lucile.   I don't want to get married.

M. Jourdain.   Well, I want you to, and I'm your father.

Lucile.   Well, I won't.

M. Jourdain.   Oh, talk, talk! Come on, I tell you. Here, give me your hand.

Lucile.   No, Father, I have told you, no power on earth can force me to take any other husband than Cléonte; and I'll go to any lengths, rather than—[*She recognizes* CLÉONTE] It is true that you are my father, and I owe you entire obedience, and it is your right to dispose of me according to your decision.

M. Jourdain. Ah, I'm delighted to see you recognize your duty so quickly. It's always a pleasure to have an obedient daughter.

[*Enter* MADAME JOURDAIN.]

Mme Jourdain. What's this? What in the world is up? They say you're trying to marry your daughter to a circus clown!

M. Jourdain. Will you shut up, impertinence? You always come sticking your oar into everything, and there's no way to teach you to be reasonable.

Mme Jourdain. You're the one there's no getting any sense into; you go from one crazy fool trick to another. What's your idea? And what are you trying to do with this tomfool marriage?

M. Jourdain. I want to marry our daughter to the son of the Grand Turk.

Mme Jourdain. The son of the Grand Turk!

M. Jourdain. Yes. You can have the interpreter there pay him your compliments for you.

Mme Jourdain. I don't care a hoot for any interpreter, and I'll tell him myself to his face that he won't have my daughter.

M. Jourdain. Once more, will you shut up?

Dorante. What, Madame Jourdain, you are opposing such a happy opportunity as this? You refuse His Turkish Highness for a son-in-law?

Mme Jourdain. My good sir, mind your own business.

Dorimène. It's a glorious honor, hardly to be turned down.

Mme Jourdain. Madame, I shall beg you also not to interfere in matters with which you have no concern.

Dorante. It is our friendly feeling for you which makes us take an interest in your welfare.

Mme Jourdain. I don't need any of your friendly feelings.

Dorante. But your daughter has yielded to her father's wishes.

Mme Jourdain. My daughter consents to marry a Turk?

Dorante. Certainly.

Mme Jourdain. She can forget Cléonte?

Dorante. Ah, well, what won't a girl do to be a great lady?

Mme Jourdain. I would strangle her with my own hands, if she ever did a trick like that.

M. Jourdain. Talk, talk, talk! I tell you that this marriage will take place.

Mme Jourdain. And I tell you it won't.

M. Jourdain. Gabble, gabble, gabble!

Lucile. Mother!

Mme Jourdain. You're a nasty girl!

M. Jourdain [*to* MADAME JOURDAIN]. You're scolding her because she obeys me?

Mme Jourdain. Yes; she belongs to me as well as to you.

Covielle [*to* MADAME JOURDAIN]. Madame!

Mme Jourdain. What are you trying to tell me, you?

Covielle. Just a word—

Mme Jourdain. I don't want to hear any "just a word" out of you.

Covielle [*to* MONSIEUR JOURDAIN]. Sir, if she will listen to me a moment in private, I promise you I'll make her consent to your desires.

Mme Jourdain. I won't consent.

Covielle. But just listen to me!

Mme Jourdain. I won't.

M. Jourdain. Listen to him!

Mme Jourdain. I don't want to listen to him.

M. Jourdain. He will tell you—

Mme Jourdain. I don't want him to tell me anything.

M. Jourdain. How obstinate women are! Will it do you any harm to hear what he says?

Covielle [*to* MADAME JOURDAIN]. Just listen to me; and afterwards you can do whatever you please.

Mme Jourdain. Well, all right. What?

Covielle [*to* MADAME JOURDAIN]. We've been trying to signal to you for the last half-hour. Don't you see that we're doing all this just to fall in with your husband's mania, and we're fooling him under this disguise, and it's Cléonte himself who is the son of the Grand Turk?

Mme Jourdain. Aha!

Covielle. And I'm Covielle!

Mme Jourdain [*aside to* COVIELLE]. Oh, well, in that case, I surrender.

Covielle. Don't give anything away.

Mme Jourdain [*to* MONSIEUR JOURDAIN]. Well, all right. I consent to the marriage.

M. Jourdain. Ah, now everybody's reasonable at last. You wouldn't listen to me. But I knew very well he would explain to you what it means to be the son of the Grand Turk.

Mme Jourdain. He's explained it to me very nicely, and I'm satisfied. Let's send out for a notary.

Dorante. That's very well said. And Madame Jourdain, in order that you may have your mind entirely at ease, and dismiss any suspicion you may have conceived about your husband, Madame Dorimène and I shall make use of the same notary for our own marriage contract.

Mme Jourdain. I consent to that too.

M. Jourdain [*aside to* DORANTE]. That's just to throw dust in her eyes, I suppose?

Dorante [*aside to* MONSIEUR JOURDAIN]. It's a good thing to play her along with this pretense.

M. Jourdain [*aside*]. Good, good. [*Aloud*] Have the notary sent for, right away.

Dorante. While we're waiting for him to come and draft the contracts, let's have a look at our ballet. It will be a nice entertainment for His Turkish Highness.

M. Jourdain. A very good idea. Let's take our seats.

Mme Jourdain. How about Nicole?

M. Jourdain. I'll give her to the interpreter; and my wife to anyone that wants her.

Covielle. Sir, I thank you. [*Aside*] If anyone can find a madder madman, I'll go to Rome and tell it to the world.

[*The play concludes with the Ballet of the Nations. As this has nothing to do with the previous action and characters, it is here omitted.*]

Wycherley: THE COUNTRY WIFE

The Puritans had been the enemies of the theatre in England since they first began to be a powerful sect early in Queen Elizabeth's reign. Their opposition was based on the belief that theatres were the playground of the devil and the fount of immorality and heresy; they were able to support these claims by citing the Bible, ancient philosophers, and Church Fathers like Jerome and Augustine. It was only natural, then, when the Puritans and their sympathizers finally gained control of Parliament in the middle of the seventeenth century, that they should suppress stage plays. The prohibition was intended to rid the new Puritan Commonwealth of this evil, but it served only to drive the drama underground. The restraint lasted for nearly twenty years, however, and in that time the traditional accoutrements of the theatre were effectively destroyed. The organization of the acting companies was shattered; actors were fewer, and no young men had been trained as apprentices; most costumes and props had long since deteriorated, and the playhouses themselves had been put to other uses. When, after a long period of Puritan rule under the Protectorate of Oliver Cromwell, the royalist and libertarian sentiments of the English people at last reasserted themselves, the English found their theatrical traditions in sad disarray.

The Puritan rule in England affected far more than the theatre; it resulted in a civil war, during which the King was taken prisoner and ultimately executed. His young son Charles had fled for safety to France in the early days of the conflict, and grew to manhood there during the many years before the Puritan Protectorate collapsed and the English people invited him to come home and reclaim the empty throne. He returned to England in 1660 as King Charles II. Safety restored as monarch, Charles turned out to be a licentious and fun-loving King whose tastes had been fairly well shaped by his long French sojourn. He liked the theatre, but preferred the drama of the French to the ranting Elizabethan kind where the sentiments were not elegant, the humor not salacious, and the women's roles were played by boys. The French theatre had actresses—the King had even brought a few back with him—and he saw no reason why the English stage should not profit by their example. The collapse of the apprentice system had in fact made some such move necessary, and the King's wishes made it proper as well.

Fashionable society also required fashionable theatres, more elegant than the imitation innyards of earlier days. Indoor theatres had been known in England before: converted from dining halls or other large rooms, they usually had a raised platform at one end that could be concealed by drawing a curtain over it. These early theatres provided the basis for the London theatres of Charles' reign, with their picture-frame stage, comfortable chairs, and fitful illumination from banks of guttering tallow candles whose smell was one of the hazards of playgoing. These theatres offered new possibilities for flexibility in the changing of scenes and for the use of machinery backstage, but were not an unqualified improvement over the older type; changing tastes in theatre fashion prompted their adoption as much as their own inherent virtues. These indoor theatres were the direct ancestors of our own modern theatres, but one must bear in mind that they were for the most part quite small, encouraging the development of a coterie and making quite plausible the intimate drawing-room scenes in many of the plays.

The period of the Restoration (so called after the restoration of the monarchy in 1660) is often characterized as one of crude vulgarity, with London society taking its cue from the predilections of the "merry monarch" with his mistresses and his bawdy festivities. Fundamentally, though, the age was perhaps no different from any other, and it may well be that the perennial sins of hypocrisy and greed were more in need of purging than the momentary excess of libertinism. William Wycherley seems to have felt that way. Charles had been back on the throne for some ten years when Wycherley decided to write plays in earnest; over the next five years he wrote four, all of which were produced with indifferent success, and then he lost interest and wrote no more. He wanted to say something about the society in which he lived, and explained the unpopularity of one of his dramas as follows: " 'Tis the plaindealing of the play, not the obscenity; 'tis taking off the ladies' masks, not offering at their petticoats, which offends 'em." *The Country Wife*, the third of his four plays, was produced in 1675.

THE COUNTRY WIFE

The Characters

Mr. Horner
Mr. Harcourt
Mr. Dorilant
Mr. Pinchwife
Mr. Sparkish
Sir Jasper Fidget
A Boy
A Quack
Waiters, Servants, and Attendants
Mrs. Margery Pinchwife
Alithea, sister of Pinchwife
Lady Fidget
Mrs. Dainty Fidget, sister of Sir Jasper
Mrs. Squeamish
Old Lady Squeamish
Lucy, Alithea's maid

SCENE—*London*

Prologue

[*spoken in the first production by Mr. Charles Hart, the actor who played* HORNER.]

Poets, like cudgelled bullies, never do
At first or second blow submit to you;
But will provoke you still, and ne'er have done,
Till you are weary first with laying on.
The late so baffled scribbler of this day,[1]
Though he stands trembling, bids me boldly say,
What we before most plays are used to do,
For poets out of fear first draw on you;
In a fierce prologue the still pit defy,
And, ere you speak, like Castril[2] give the lie.
But though our Bayes's[3] battles oft I've fought,
And with bruised knuckles their dear conquests bought;
Nay, never yet feared odds upon the stage,

---

[1] *I.e.*, Wycherley himself, whose last play had been a failure.
[2] An angry boy from Ben Jonson's *The Alchemist* who, without even hearing another's story, would shout "you lie."
[3] A generic name for an inept poet, and a pun on the bay wreath or laurel wreath traditionally worn by poets laureate. Here Wycherley seems to mean himself.

In prologue dare not hector with the age;
But would take quarter from your saving hands,
Though Bayes within all yielding countermands,
Says, you confederate wits no quarter give,
Therefore his play shan't ask your leave to live.
Well, let the vain rash fop, by huffing so,
Think to obtain the better terms of you;
But we, the actors, humbly will submit,
Now, and at any time, to a full pit;
Nay, often we anticipate your rage,
And murder poets for you on our stage:
We set no guards upon our tiring-room,
But when with flying colours there you come,
We patiently, you see, give up to you
Our poets, virgins, nay, our matrons too.

Act I

[HORNER's *Lodging.*]

[*Enter* HORNER, *and* QUACK *following him at a distance.*]

Horner [*aside*].   A quack is as fit for a pimp, as a midwife for a bawd; they are
still but in their way, both helpers of nature.—[*aloud*] Well, my dear doctor,
hast thou done what I desired?

Quack.   I have undone you for ever with the women, and reported you throughout the whole town as bad as an eunuch, with as much trouble as if I had made
you one in earnest.

Horner.   But have you told all the midwives you know, the orange wenches at the
playhouses, the city husbands, and old fumbling keepers of this end of the
town? for they'll be the readiest to report it.

Quack.   I have told all the chambermaids, waiting-women, tire-women, and old
women of my acquaintance; nay, and whispered it as a secret to 'em, and to the
whisperers of Whitehall; so that you need not doubt 'twill spread, and you will
be as odious to the handsome young women, as—

Horner.   As the small-pox. Well—

Quack.   And to the married women of this end of the town, as—

Horner.   As the great one; nay, as their own husbands.

Quack.   And to the city dames, as aniseed Robin, of filthy and contemptible
memory; and they will frighten their children with your name, especially their
females.

Horner.   And cry, Horner's coming to carry you away. I am only afraid 'twill not
be believed. You told 'em it was by an English-French disaster, and an English-
French chirurgeon, who has given me at once not only a cure, but an antidote
for the future against that damned malady, and that worse distemper, love, and
all other women's evils?

Quack.   Your late journey into France has made it the more credible, and your
being here a fortnight before you appeared in public, looks as if you appre-

liended the shame, which I wonder you do not. Well, I have been hired by young gallants to belie 'em t'other way; but you are the first would be thought a man unfit for women.

Horner. Dear Mr. Doctor, let vain rogues be contented only to be thought abler men than they are, generally 'tis all the pleasure they have; but mine lies another way.

Quack. You take, methinks, a very preposterous way to it, and as ridiculous as if we operators in physic should put forth bills to disparage our medicaments, with hopes to gain customers.

Horner. Doctor, there are quacks in love as well as physic, who get but the fewer and worse patients for their boasting; a good name is seldom got by giving it one's self; and women, no more than honour, are compassed by bragging. Come, come, Doctor, the wisest lawyer never discovers the merits of his cause till the trial; the wealthiest man conceals his riches, and the cunning gamester his play. Shy husbands and keepers, like old rooks, are not to be cheated but by a new unpractised trick: false friendship will pass now no more than false dice upon 'em; no, not in the city.

[*Enter* BOY.]

Boy. There are two ladies and a gentleman coming up. [*Exit.*]

Horner. A pox! some unbelieving sisters of my former acquaintance, who, I am afraid, expect their sense should be satisfied of the falsity of the report. No— This formal fool and women!

[*Enter* SIR JASPER FIDGET, LADY FIDGET, *and* MRS. DAINTY FIDGET.]

Quack. His wife and sister.

Sir Jasper. My coach breaking just now before your door, sir, I look upon as an occasional reprimand to me, sir, for not kissing your hands, sir, since your coming out of France, sir; and so my disaster, sir, has been my good fortune, sir; and this is my wife and sister, sir.

Horner. What then, sir?

Sir Jasper. My lady, and sister, sir.—Wife, this is Master Horner.

Lady Fidget. Master Horner, husband!

Sir Jasper. My lady, my Lady Fidget, sir.

Horner. So, sir.

Sir Jasper. Won't you be acquainted with her, sir?—[*aside*] So, the report is true, I find, by his coldness or aversion to the sex; but I'll play the wag with him.—[*aloud*] Pray salute my wife, my lady, sir.

Horner. I will kiss no man's wife, sir, for him, sir; I have taken my eternal leave, sir, of the sex already, sir.

Sir Jasper [*aside*]. Ha! ha! ha! I'll plague him yet.—[*aloud*] Not know my wife, sir?

Horner. I do know your wife, sir; she's a woman, sir, and consequently a monster, sir, a greater monster than a husband, sir.

Sir Jasper. A husband! how, sir?

Horner. So sir; [*makes horns*][1] but I make no more cuckolds, sir.

---

[1] Horns were the sign of the cuckold.

Sir Jasper. Ha! ha! ha! Mercury! Mercury![1]

Lady Fidget.   Pray, Sir Jasper, let us be gone from this rude fellow.

Mrs. Dainty Fidget.   Who, by his breeding, would think he had ever been in France?

Lady Fidget.   Foh! he's but too much a French fellow, such as hate women of quality and virtue for their love to their husbands. Sir Jasper, a woman is hated by 'em as much for loving her husband as for loving their money. But pray let's be gone.

Horner.   You do well, madam; for I have nothing that you came for. I have brought over not so much as a bawdy picture, no new postures, nor the second part of the *Ecole des Filles*; nor—

Quack.   Hold, for shame, sir! what d'ye mean? you'll ruin yourself for ever for the sex—[*apart to* HORNER]

Sir Jasper.   Ha! ha! ha! he hates women perfectly, I find.

Mrs. Dainty Fidget.   What pity 'tis he should!

Lady Fidget.   Ay, he's a base fellow for't. But affectation makes not a woman more odious to them than virtue.

Horner.   Because your virtue is your greatest affectation, madam.

Lady Fidget.   How, you saucy fellow! would you wrong my honour?

Horner.   If I could.

Lady Fidget.   How d'ye mean, sir?

Sir Jasper.   Ha! ha! ha! no, he can't wrong your ladyship's honour, upon my honour. He, poor man—hark you in your ear—a mere eunuch. [*whispers*]

Lady Fidget.   O filthy French beast! foh! foh! why do we stay? let's be gone: I can't endure the sight of him.

Sir Jasper.   Stay but till the chairs come; they'll be here presently.

Lady Fidget.   No.

Sir Jasper.   Nor can I stay longer. 'Tis, let me see, a quarter and half quarter of a minute past eleven. The council will be sat; I must away. Business must be preferred always before love and ceremony with the wise, Mr. Horner.

Horner.   And the impotent, Sir Jasper.

Sir Jasper.   Ay, ay, the impotent, Master Horner; hah! hah! hah!

Lady Fidget.   What, leave us with a filthy man alone in his lodgings?

Sir Jasper.   He's an innocent man now, you know. Pray stay, I'll hasten the chairs to you.—Mr. Horner, your servant; I should be glad to see you at my house. Pray come and dine with me, and play at cards with my wife after dinner; you are fit for women at that game yet, ha! ha!—[*aside*] 'Tis as much a husband's prudence to provide innocent diversion for a wife as to hinder her unlawful pleasures; and he had better employ her than let her employ herself.—[*aloud*] Farewell.

Horner.   Your servant, Sir Jasper.

[*Exit* SIR JASPER.]

Lady Fidget.   I will not stay with him, foh!—

Horner.   Nay, madam, I beseech you stay, if it be but to see I can be as civil to ladies yet as they would desire.

---

1   Mercury was commonly used as a treatment for venereal disease.

Lady Fidget. No, no, foh! you cannot be civil to ladies.
Mrs. Dainty Fidget. You as civil as ladies would desire?
Lady Fidget. No, no, no, foh! foh! foh!

[*Exeunt* LADY FIDGET *and* MRS. DAINTY FIDGET.]

Quack. Now, I think, I, or you yourself, rather, have done your business with the women.
Horner. Thou art an ass. Don't you see already, upon the report, and my carriage, this grave man of business leaves his wife in my lodgings, invites me to his house and wife, who before would not be acquainted with me out of jealousy?
Quack. Nay, by this means you may be the more acquainted with the husbands, but the less with the wives.
Horner. Let me alone; if I can but abuse the husbands, I'll soon disabuse the wives. Stay—I'll reckon you up the advantages I am like to have by my stratagem. First, I shall be rid of all my old acquaintances, the most insatiable sort of duns, that invade our lodgings in a morning; and next to the pleasure of making a new mistress is that of being rid of an old one, and of all old debts. Love, when it comes to be so, is paid the most unwillingly.
Quack. Well, you may be so rid of your old acquaintances; but how will you get any new ones?
Horner. Doctor, thou wilt never make a good chemist, thou art so incredulous and impatient. Ask but all the young fellows of the town if they do not lose more time, like huntsmen, in starting the game, than in running it down. One knows not where to find 'em; who will or will not. Women of quality are so civil, you can hardly distinguish love from good breeding, and a man is often mistaken: but now I can be sure she that shows an aversion to me loves the sport, as those women that are gone, whom I warrant to be right. And then the next thing is, your women of honour, as you call 'em, are only chary of their reputations, not their persons; and 'tis scandal they would avoid, not men. Now may I have, by the reputation of an eunuch, the privileges of one, and be seen in a lady's chamber in a morning as early as her husband; kiss virgins before their parents or lovers; and may be, in short, the *passe-partout* of the town. Now, doctor.
Quack. Nay, now you shall be the doctor; and your process is so new that we do not know but it may succeed.
Horner. Not so new neither; *probatum est*, doctor.
Quack. Well, I wish you luck, and many patients, whilst I go to mine. [*Exit.*]

[*Enter* HARCOURT *and* DORILANT.]

Harcourt. Come, your appearance at the play yesterday, has, I hope, hardened you for the future against the women's contempt, and the men's raillery; and now you'll abroad as you were wont.
Horner. Did I not bear it bravely?
Dorilant. With a most theatrical impudence, nay, more than the orange-wenches show there, or a drunken vizard-mask,[1] or a great-bellied actress; nay, or the

---

[1] Prostitute.

most impudent of creatures, an ill poet; or what is yet more impudent, a second-hand critic.

Horner.   But what say the ladies? have they no pity?

Harcourt.   What ladies? The vizard-masks, you know, never pity a man when all's gone, though in their service.

Dorilant.   And for the women in the boxes, you'd never pity them when 'twas in your power.

Harcourt.   They say 'tis pity but all that deal with common women should be served so.

Dorilant.   Nay, I dare swear they won't admit you to play at cards with them, go to plays with 'em, or do the little duties which other shadows of men are wont to do for 'em.

Horner.   What do you call shadows of men?

Dorilant.   Half-men.

Horner.   What, boys?

Dorilant.   Ay, your old boys, old *beaux garçons*, who, like superannuated stallions, are suffered to run, feed, and whinny with the mares as long as they live, though they can do nothing else.

Horner.   Well, a pox on love and wenching! Women serve but to keep a man from better company. Though I can't enjoy them, I shall you the more. Good fellowship and friendship are lasting, rational, and manly pleasures.

Harcourt.   For all that, give me some of those pleasures you call effeminate too; they help to relish one another.

Horner.   They disturb one another.

Harcourt.   No, mistresses are like books. If you pore upon them too much, they doze you, and make you unfit for company; but if used discreetly, you are the fitter for conversation by 'em.

Dorilant.   A mistress should be like a little country retreat near the town; not to dwell in constantly, but only for a night and away, to taste the town the better when a man returns.

Horner.   I tell you, 'tis as hard to be a good fellow, a good friend, and a lover of women, as 'tis to be a good fellow, a good friend, and a lover of money. You cannot follow both, then choose your side. Wine gives you liberty, love takes it away.

Dorilant.   Gad, he's in the right on't.

Horner.   Wine gives you joy; love, grief and tortures, besides surgeons.[1] Wine makes us witty; love, only sots. Wine makes us sleep; love breaks it.

Dorilant.   By the world he has reason, Harcourt.

Horner.   Wine makes—

Dorilant.   Ay, wine makes us—makes us princes; love makes us beggars, poor rogues, egad—and wine—

Horner.   So, there's one converted.—No, no, love and wine, oil and vinegar.

Harcourt.   I grant it; love will still be uppermost.

Horner.   Come, for my part, I will have only those glorious manly pleasures of being very drunk and very slovenly.

---

[1]   *I.e.*, the tortures of love and also the painful medication afterward.

[*Enter* BOY.]

Boy.   Mr. Sparkish is below, sir. [*Exit.*]

Harcourt.   What, my dear friend! a rogue that is fond of me only, I think, for abusing him.

Dorilant.   No, he can no more think the men laugh at him than that women jilt him; his opinion of himself is so good.

Horner.   Well, there's another pleasure by drinking I thought not of,—I shall lose his acquaintance, because he cannot drink: and you know 'tis a very hard thing to be rid of him; for he's one of those nauseous offerers at wit, who, like the worst fiddlers, run themselves into all companies.

Harcourt.   One that, by being in the company of men of sense, would pass for one.

Horner.   And may so to the short-sighted world; as a false jewel amongst true ones is not discerned at a distance. His company is as troublesome to us as a cuckold's when you have a mind to his wife's.

Harcourt.   No, the rogue will not let us enjoy one another, but ravishes our conversation; though he signifies no more to't than Sir Martin Mar-all's gaping, and awkward thrumming upon the lute, does to his man's voice and music.

Dorilant.   And to pass for a wit in town shows himself a fool every night to us, that are guilty of the plot.

Horner.   Such wits as he are, to a company of reasonable men, like rooks to the gamesters; who only fill a room at the table, but are so far from contributing to the play, that they only serve to spoil the fancy of those that do.

Dorilant.   Nay, they are used like rooks too, snubbed, checked, and abused; yet the rogues will hang on.

Horner.   A pox on 'em, and all that force nature, and would be still what she forbids 'em! Affectation is her greatest monster.

Harcourt.   Most men are the contraries to that they would seem. Your bully, you see, is a coward with a long sword; the little humbly fawning physician, with his ebony cane, is he that destroys men.

Dorilant.   The usurer, a poor rogue, possessed of mouldy bonds and mortgages; and we they call spendthrifts, are only wealthy, who lay out his money upon daily new purchases of pleasure.

Horner.   Ay, your arrantest cheat is your trustee or executor; your jealous man, the greatest cuckold; your churchman the greatest atheist; and your noisy pert rogue of a wit, the greatest fop, dullest ass, and worst company, as you shall see; for here he comes.

[*Enter* SPARKISH.]

Sparkish.   How is't, sparks? how is't? Well, faith, Harry, I must rally thee a little, ha! ha! ha! upon the report in town of thee, ha! ha! ha! I can't hold i'faith; shall I speak?

Horner.   Yes; but you'll be so bitter then.

Sparkish.   Honest Dick and Frank here shall answer for me; I will not be extreme bitter, by the universe.

Harcourt.   We will be bound in a ten thousand pound bond, he shall not be bitter at all.

Dorilant. Nor sharp, nor sweet.

Horner. What, not downright insipid?

Sparkish. Nay then, since you are so brisk, and provoke me, take what follows. You must know, I was discoursing and rallying with some ladies yesterday, and they happened to talk of the fine new signs in town—

Horner. Very fine ladies, I believe.

Sparkish. Said I, I know where the best new sign is.—Where? says one of the ladies.—In Covent-Garden, I replied.—Said another, In what street?—In Russel-street, answered I.—Lord, says another, I'm sure there was never a fine new sign there yesterday.—Yes, but there was, said I again; and it came out of France, and has been there a fortnight.

Dorilant. A pox! I can hear no more, prithee.

Horner. No, hear him out; let him tune his crowd a while.

Harcourt. The worst music, the greatest preparation.

Sparkish. Nay, faith, I'll make you laugh.—It cannot be, says a third lady.—Yes, yes, quoth I again.—Says a fourth lady—

Horner. Look to't, we'll have no more ladies.

Sparkish. No—then mark, mark, now. Said I to the fourth, Did you never see Mr. Horner? he lodges in Russel-street, and he's a sign of a man, you know, since he came out of France; ha! ha! ha!

Horner. But the devil take me if thine be the sign of a jest.

Sparkish. With that they all fell a-laughing, till they bepissed themselves. What, but it does not move you, methinks? Well, I see one had as good go to law without a witness, as break a jest without a laugher on one's side.—Come, come, sparks, but where do we dine? I have left at Whitehall an earl, to dine with you.

Dorilant. Why, I thought thou hadst loved a man with a title, better than a suit with a French trimming to't.

Harcourt. Go to him again.

Sparkish. No, sir, a wit to me is the greatest title in the world.

Horner. But go dine with your earl, sir; he may be exceptious. We are your friends, and will not take it ill to be left, I do assure you.

Harcourt. Nay, faith, he shall go to him.

Sparkish. Nay, pray, gentlemen.

Dorilant. We'll thrust you out, if you won't; what, disappoint anybody for us?

Sparkish. Nay, dear gentlemen, hear me.

Horner. No, no, sir, by no means; pray go, sir.

Sparkish. Why, dear rogues—

Dorilant. No, no.

[*They all thrust him out of the room.*]

All. Ha! ha! ha!

[*Re-enter* SPARKISH.]

Sparkish. But, sparks, pray hear me. What, d'ye think I'll eat then with gay shallow fops and silent coxcombs? I think wit as necessary at dinner, as a glass of good wine; and that's the reason I never have any stomach when I eat alone.—Come, but where do we dine?

Horner. Even where you will.

Sparkish. At Chateline's?

Dorilant. Yes, if you will.

Sparkish. Or at the Cock?

Dorilant. Yes, if you please.

Sparkish. Or at the Dog and Partridge?

Horner. Ay, if you have a mind to't; for we shall dine at neither.

Sparkish. Pshaw! with your fooling we shall lose the new play; and I would no more miss seeing a new play the first day, than I would miss sitting in the wit's row. Therefore I'll go fetch my mistress, and away. [*Exit.*]

[*Enter* PINCHWIFE.]

Horner. Who have we here? Pinchwife?

Pinchwife. Gentlemen, your humble servant.

Horner. Well, Jack, by thy long absence from the town, the grumness of thy countenance, and the slovenliness of thy habit, I should give thee joy, should I not, of marriage?

Pinchwife [*aside*]. Death! does he know I'm married too? I thought to have concealed it from him at least.—[*aloud*] My long stay in the country will excuse my dress; and I have a suit of law that brings me up to town, that puts me out of humour. Besides, I must give Sparkish to-morrow five thousand pounds to lie with my sister.

Horner. Nay, you country gentlemen, rather than not purchase, will buy anything; and he is a cracked title, if we may quibble. Well, but am I to give thee joy? I heard thou wert married.

Pinchwife. What then?

Horner. Why, the next thing that is to be heard, is, thou'rt a cuckold.

Pinchwife. Insupportable name! [*aside*]

Horner. But I did not expect marriage from such a whoremaster as you; one that knew the town so much, and women so well.

Pinchwife. Why, I have married no London wife.

Horner. Pshaw! that's all one. That grave circumspection in marrying a country wife, is like refusing a deceitful pampered Smithfield jade, to go and be cheated by a friend in the country.

Pinchwife [*aside*]. A pox on him and his simile!—[*aloud*] At least we are a little surer of the breed there, know what her keeping has been, whether foiled or unsound.

Horner. Come, come, I have known a clap gotten in Wales; and there are cousins, justices' clerks, and chaplains in the country, I won't say coachmen. But she's handsome and young?

Pinchwife [*aside*]. I'll answer as I should do.—[*aloud*] No, no; she has no beauty but her youth, no attraction but her modesty: wholesome, homely, and huswifely; that's all.

Dorilant. He talks as like a grazier as he looks.

Pinchwife. She's too awkward, ill-favoured, and silly to bring to town.

Harcourt. Then methinks you should bring her to be taught breeding.

Pinchwife. To be taught! no, sir, I thank you. Good wives and private soldiers should be ignorant—I'll keep her from your instructions, I warrant you.

Harcourt. The rogue is as jealous as if his wife were not ignorant. [*aside*]

Horner. Why, if she be ill-favoured, there will be less danger here for you than by leaving her in the country. We have such variety of dainties that we are seldom hungry.

Dorilant. But they have always coarse, constant, swingeing stomachs in the country.

Harcourt. Foul feeders indeed!

Dorilant. And your hospitality is great there.

Harcourt. Open house; every man's welcome.

Pinchwife. So, so, gentlemen.

Horner. But prithee, why shouldst thou marry her? If she be ugly, ill-bred, and silly, she must be rich then.

Pinchwife. As rich as if she brought me twenty thousand pound out of this town; for she'll be as sure not to spend her moderate portion, as a London baggage would be to spend hers, let it be what it would: so 'tis all one. Then, because she's ugly, she's the likelier to be my own; and being ill-bred, she'll hate conversation; and since silly and innocent, will not know the difference betwixt a man of one-and-twenty and one of forty.

Horner. Nine—to my knowledge. But if she be silly, she'll expect as much from a man of forty-nine, as from him of one-and-twenty. But methinks wit is more necessary than beauty; and I think no young woman ugly that has it, and no handsome woman agreeable without it.

Pinchwife. 'Tis my maxim, he's a fool that marries; but he's a greater that does not marry a fool. What is wit in a wife good for, but to make a man a cuckold?

Horner. Yes, to keep it from his knowledge.

Pinchwife. A fool cannot contrive to make her husband a cuckold.

Horner. No; but she'll club with a man that can: and what is worse, if she cannot make her husband a cuckold, she'll make him jealous, and pass for one: and then 'tis all one.

Pinchwife. Well, well, I'll take care for one. My wife shall make me no cuckold, though she had your help, Mr. Horner. I understand the town, sir.

Dorilant. His help! [*aside*]

Harcourt. He's come newly to town, it seems, and has not heard how things are with him. [*aside*]

Horner. But tell me, has marriage cured thee of whoring, which it seldom does?

Harcourt. 'Tis more than age can do.

Horner. No, the word is, I'll marry and live honest: but a marriage vow is like a penitent gamester's oath, and entering into bonds and penalties to stint himself to such a particular small sum at play for the future, which makes him but the more eager; and not being able to hold out, loses his money again, and his forfeit to boot.

Dorilant. Ay, ay, a gamester will be a gamester whilst his money lasts, and a whoremaster whilst his vigour.

Harcourt. Nay, I have known 'em, when they are broke, and can lose no more, keep a fumbling with the box in their hands to fool with only, and hinder other gamesters.

Dorilant. That had wherewithal to make lusty stakes.

Pinchwife. Well, gentlemen, you may laugh at me; but you shall never lie with my wife: I know the town.

Horner. But prithee, was not the way you were in better? is not keeping better than marriage?

Pinchwife. A pox on't! the jades would jilt me, I could never keep a whore to myself.

Horner. So, then you only married to keep a whore to yourself. Well, but let me tell you, women, as you say, are like soldiers, made constant and loyal by good pay, rather than by oaths and covenants. Therefore I'd advise my friends to keep rather than marry, since too I find, by your example, it does not serve one's turn; for I saw you yesterday in the eighteenpenny place[1] with a pretty country-wench.

Pinchwife. How the devil! did he see my wife then? I sat there that she might not be seen. But she shall never go to a play again. [*aside*]

Horner. What! dost thou blush, at nine-and-forty, for having been seen with a wench?

Dorilant. No, faith, I warrant 'twas his wife, which he seated there out of sight; for he's a cunning rogue, and understands the town.

Harcourt. He blushes. Then 'twas his wife; for men are now more ashamed to be seen with them in public than with a wench.

Pinchwife. Hell and damnation! I'm undone, since Horner has seen her, and they know 'twas she. [*aside*]

Horner. But prithee, was it thy wife? She was exceeding pretty: I was in love with her at that distance.

Pinchwife. You are like never to be nearer to her. Your servant, gentlemen. [*offers to go*]

Horner. Nay, prithee stay.

Pinchwife. I cannot; I will not.

Horner. Come, you shall dine with us.

Pinchwife. I have dined already.

Horner. Come, I know thou hast not: I'll treat thee, dear rogue; thou sha't spend none of thy Hampshire money to-day.

Pinchwife. Treat me! So, he uses me already like his cuckold. [*aside*]

Horner. Nay, you shall not go.

Pinchwife. I must; I have business at home. [*Exit.*]

Harcourt. To beat his wife. He's as jealous of her, as a Cheapside husband of a Covent-garden wife.[2]

Horner. Why, 'tis as hard to find an old whoremaster without jealousy and the gout, as a young one without fear, or the pox:—

> As gout in age from pox in youth proceeds,
> So wenching past, then jealousy succeeds;
> The worst disease that love and wenching breeds.

[*Exeunt.*]

---

1 In a theater, the middle gallery. Fashionable patrons would have been below, in the pit and boxes, and therefore more conspicuous.

2 As a shopkeeper is of an aristocratic wife.

Act II

[*A room in* PINCHWIFE'S *House.*]

[MRS. MARGERY PINCHWIFE *and* ALITHEA. PINCHWIFE *peeping behind at the door.*]

Mrs. Pinchwife. Pray, sister, where are the best fields and woods to walk in, in London?

Alithea [*aside*]. A pretty question!—[*aloud*] Why, sister, Mulberrygarden and St. James's-park; and, for close walks, the New Exchange.

Mrs. Pinchwife. Pray, sister, tell me why my husband looks so grum here in town, and keeps me up so close, and will not let me go a-walking, nor let me wear my best gown yesterday.

Alithea. O, he's jealous, sister.

Mrs. Pinchwife. Jealous! what's that?

Alithea. He's afraid you should love another man.

Mrs. Pinchwife. How should he be afraid of my loving another man, when he will not let me see any but himself?

Alithea. Did he not carry you yesterday to a play?

Mrs. Pinchwife. Ay; but we sat amongst ugly people. He would not let me come near the gentry, who sat under us, so that I could not see 'em. He told me, none but naughty women sat there, whom they toused and moused. But I would have ventured, for all that.

Alithea. But how did you like the play?

Mrs. Pinchwife. Indeed I was weary of the play; but I liked hugeously the actors. They are the goodliest, properest men, sister!

Alithea. O, but you must not like the actors, sister.

Mrs. Pinchwife. Ay, how should I help it, sister? Pray, sister, when my husband comes in, will you ask leave for me to go a-walking?

Alithea. A-walking! ha! ha! Lord, a country-gentle-woman's pleasure is the drudgery of a footpost; and she requires as much airing as her husband's horses. —[*aside*] But here comes your husband: I'll ask, though I'm sure he'll not grant it.

Mrs. Pinchwife. He says he won't let me go abroad for fear of catching the pox.

Alithea. Fy! the small-pox you should say.

[*Enter* PINCHWIFE.]

Mrs. Pinchwife. O my dear, dear bud, welcome home! Why dost thou look so fropish? who has nangered thee?

Pinchwife. You're a fool.

[MRS. PINCHWIFE *goes aside, and cries.*]

Alithea. Faith, so she is, for crying for no fault, poor tender creature!

Pinchwife. What, you would have her as impudent as yourself, as arrant a jilflirt, a gadder, a magpie; and to say all, a mere notorious town-woman?

Alithea. Brother, you are my only censurer; and the honour of your family will sooner suffer in your wife there than in me, though I take the innocent liberty of the town.

Pinchwife. Hark you, mistress, do not talk so before my wife.—The innocent liberty of the town!

Alithea. Why, pray, who boasts of any intrigue with me? what lampoon has made my name notorious? what ill women frequent my lodgings? I keep no company with any women of scandalous reputations.

Pinchwife. No, you keep the men of scandalous reputations company.

Alithea. Where? would you not have me civil? answer 'em in a box at the plays, in the drawing-room at Whitehall, in St. James'-park, Mulberry-garden, or—

Pinchwife. Hold, hold! Do not teach my wife where the men are to be found: I believe she's the worse for your town-documents already. I bid you keep her in ignorance, as I do.

Mrs. Pinchwife. Indeed, be not angry with her, bud, she will tell me nothing of the town, though I ask her a thousand times a day.

Pinchwife. Then you are very inquisitive to know, I find?

Mrs. Pinchwife. Not I indeed, dear; I hate London. Our placehouse in the country is worth a thousand of't: would I were there again!

Pinchwife. So you shall, I warrant. But were you not talking of plays and players when I came in?—[*to* ALITHEA] You are her encourager in such discourses.

Mrs. Pinchwife. No, indeed, dear; she chid me just now for liking the playermen.

Pinchwife [*aside*]. Nay, if she be so innocent as to own to me her liking them, there is no hurt in't.—[*aloud*] Come, my poor rogue, but thou likest none better than me?

Mrs. Pinchwife. Yes, indeed, but I do. The playermen are finer folks.

Pinchwife. But you love none better than me?

Mrs. Pinchwife. You are my own dear bud, and I know you. I hate a stranger.

Pinchwife. Ay, my dear, you must love me only; and not be like the naughty town-women, who only hate their husbands, and love every man else; love plays, visits, fine coaches, fine clothes, fiddles, balls, treats, and so lead a wicked town-life.

Mrs. Pinchwife. Nay, if to enjoy all these things to be a town-life, London is not so bad a place, dear.

Pinchwife. How! if you love me, you must hate London.

Alithea. The fool has forbid me discovering to her the pleasures of the town, and he is now setting her agog upon them himself. [*aside*]

Mrs. Pinchwife. But, husband, do the town-women love the playermen too?

Pinchwife. Yes, I warrant you.

Mrs. Pinchwife. Ay, I warrant you.

Pinchwife. Why, you do not, I hope?

Mrs. Pinchwife. No, no, bud. But why have we no playermen in the country?

Pinchwife. Ha!—Mrs. Minx, ask me no more to go to a play.

Mrs. Pinchwife. Nay, why, love? I did not care for going: but when you forbid me, you make me, as 'twere, desire it.

Alithea. So 'twill be in other things, I warrant. [*aside*]

Mrs. Pinchwife. Pray let me go to a play, dear.

Pinchwife. Hold your peace, I wo' not.

Mrs. Pinchwife.   Why, love?

Pinchwife.   Why, I'll tell you.

Alithea.   Nay, if he tell her, she'll give him more cause to forbid her that place. [*aside*]

Mrs. Pinchwife.   Pray why, dear?

Pinchwife.   First, you like the actors; and the gallants may like you.

Mrs. Pinchwife.   What, a homely country girl! No, bud, nobody will like me.

Pinchwife.   I tell you yes, they may.

Mrs. Pinchwife.   No, no, you jest—I won't believe you: I will go.

Pinchwife.   I tell you then, that one of the lewdest fellows in town, who saw you there, told me he was in love with you.

Mrs. Pinchwife.   Indeed! who, who, pray who was't?

Pinchwife.   I've gone too far, and slipped before I was aware; how overjoyed she is! [*aside*]

Mrs. Pinchwife.   Was it any Hampshire gallant, any of our neighbours? I promise you, I am beholden to him.

Pinchwife.   I promise you, you lie; for he would but ruin you, as he has done hundreds. He has no other love for women but that; such as he look upon women, like basilisks, but to destroy 'em.

Mrs. Pinchwife.   Ay, but if he loves me, why should he ruin me? answer me to that. Methinks he should not, I would do him no harm.

Alithea.   Ha! ha! ha!

Pinchwife.   'Tis very well; but I'll keep him from doing you any harm, or me either. But here comes company; get you in, get you in.

Mrs. Pinchwife.   But pray, husband, is he a pretty gentleman that loves me?

Pinchwife.   In, baggage, in. [*thrusts her in, and shuts the door*]

[*Enter* SPARKISH *and* HARCOURT.]

What, all the lewd libertines of the town brought to my lodging by this easy coxcomb! 'sdeath, I'll not suffer it.

Sparkish.   Here, Harcourt, do you approve my choice?— [*to* ALITHEA] Dear little rogue, I told you I'd bring you acquainted with all my friends, the wits and—

[HARCOURT *salutes her.*]

Pinchwife.   Ay, they shall know her, as well as you yourself will, I warrant you.

Sparkish.   This is one of those, my pretty rogue, that are to dance at your wedding to-morrow; and him you must bid welcome ever, to what you and I have.

Pinchwife.   Monstrous! [*aside*]

Sparkish.   Harcourt, how dost thou like her, faith? Nay, dear, do not look down; I should hate to have a wife of mine out of countenance at anything.

Pinchwife.   Wonderful! [*aside*]

Sparkish.   Tell me, I say, Harcourt, how dost thou like her? Thou hast stared upon her enough, to resolve me.

Harcourt.   So infinitely well, that I could wish I had a mistress too, that might differ from her in nothing but her love and engagement to you.

Alithea.   Sir, Master Sparkish has often told me that his acquaintance were all wits and railleurs, and now I find it.

Sparkish. No, by the universe, madam, he does not rally now; you may believe him. I do assure you, he is the honestest, worthiest, true-hearted gentleman—a man of such perfect honour, he would say nothing to a lady he does not mean.

Pinchwife. Praising another man to his mistress! [*aside*]

Harcourt. Sir, you are so beyond expectation obliging, that—

Sparkish. Nay, egad, I am sure you do admire her extremely; I see't in your eyes.—He does admire you, madam.—By the world, don't you?

Harcourt. Yes, above the world, or the most glorious part of it, her whole sex: and till now I never thought I should have envied you, or any man about to marry, but you have the best excuse for marriage I ever knew.

Alithea. Nay, now, sir, I'm satisfied you are of the society of the wits and railleurs, since you cannot spare your friend, even when he is but too civil to you; but the surest sign is, since you are an enemy to marriage,—for that I hear you hate as much as business or bad wine.

Harcourt. Truly, madam, I was never an enemy to marriage till now, because marriage was never an enemy to me before.

Alithea. But why, sir, is marriage an enemy to you now? because it robs you of your friend here? for you look upon a friend married, as one gone into a monastery, that is, dead to the world.

Harcourt. 'Tis indeed, because you marry him; I see, madam, you can guess my meaning. I do confess heartily and openly, I wish it were in my power to break the match; by Heavens I would.

Sparkish. Poor Frank!

Alithea. Would you be so unkind to me?

Harcourt. No, no, 'tis not because I would be unkind to you.

Sparkish. Poor Frank! no gad, 'tis only his kindness to me.

Pinchwife. Great kindness to you indeed! Insensible fop, let a man make love to his wife to his face! [*aside*]

Sparkish. Come, dear Frank, for all my wife there, that shall be, thou shalt enjoy me sometimes, dear rogue. By my honour, we men of wit condole for our deceased brother in marriage, as much as for one dead in earnest: I think that was prettily said of me, ha, Harcourt?—But come, Frank, be not melancholy for me.

Harcourt. No, I assure you, I am not melancholy for you.

Sparkish. Prithee, Frank, dost think my wife that shall be there, a fine person?

Harcourt. I could gaze upon her till I became as blind as you are.

Sparkish. How as I am? how?

Harcourt. Because you are a lover, and true lovers are blind, stock blind.

Sparkish. True, true; but by the world she has wit too, as well as beauty: go, go with her into a corner, and try if she has wit; talk to her anything, she's bashful before me.

Harcourt. Indeed if a woman wants wit in a corner, she has it nowhere.

Alithea. Sir, you dispose of me a little before your time—[*aside to* SPARKISH]

Sparkish. Nay, nay, madam, let me have an earnest of your obedience, or—go, go, madam—

[HARCOURT *courts* ALITHEA *aside.*]

Pinchwife. How, sir! if you are not concerned for the honour of a wife, I am for that of a sister; he shall not debauch her. Be a pander to your own wife! bring men to her! let 'em make love before your face! thrust 'em into a corner together, then leave 'em in private! is this your town wit and conduct?

Sparkish. Ha! ha! ha! a silly wise rogue would make one laugh more than a stark fool, ha! ha! I shall burst. Nay, you shall not disturb 'em; I'll vex thee, by the world. [*struggles with* PINCHWIFE *to keep him from* HARCOURT *and* ALITHEA]

Alithea. The writings are drawn, sir, settlements made; 'tis too late, sir, and past all revocation.

Harcourt. Then so is my death.

Alithea. I would not be unjust to him.

Harcourt. Then why to me so?

Alithea. I have no obligation to you.

Harcourt. My love.

Alithea. I had his before.

Harcourt. You never had it; he wants, you see, jealousy, the only infallible sign of it.

Alithea. Love proceeds from esteem; he cannot distrust my virtue: besides, he loves me, or he would not marry me.

Harcourt. Marrying you is no more sign of his love than bribing your woman, that he may marry you, is a sign of his generosity. Marriage is rather a sign of interest than love; and he that marries a fortune covets a mistress, not loves her. But if you take marriage for a sign of love, take it from me immediately.

Alithea. No, now you have put a scruple in my head; but in short, sir, to end our dispute, I must marry him, my reputation would suffer in the world else.

Harcourt. No; if you do marry him, with your pardon, madam, your reputation suffers in the world, and you would be thought in necessity for a cloak.

Alithea. Nay, now you are rude, sir.—Mr. Sparkish, pray come hither, your friend here is very troublesome, and very loving.

Harcourt. Hold! hold!—[*aside to* ALITHEA]

Pinchwife. D'ye hear that?

Sparkish. Why, d'ye think I'll seem to be jealous, like a country bumpkin?

Pinchwife. No, rather be a cuckold, like a credulous cit.

Harcourt. Madam, you would not have been so little generous as to have told him.

Alithea. Yes, since you could be so little generous as to wrong him.

Harcourt. Wrong him! no man can do't, he's beneath an injury: a bubble, a coward, a senseless idiot, a wretch so contemptible to all the world but you, that—

Alithea. Hold, do not rail at him, for since he is like to be my husband, I am resolved to like him: nay, I think I am obliged to tell him you are not his friend.—Master Sparkish, Master Sparkish!

Sparkish. What, what?—[*to* HARCOURT] Now, dear rogue, has not she wit?

Harcourt. Not so much as I thought, and hoped she had. [*speaks surlily*]

Alithea. Mr. Sparkish, do you bring people to rail at you?

Harcourt. Madam—

Sparkish. How! no; but if he does rail at me, 'tis but in jest, I warrant: what we wits do for one another, and never take any notice of it.

Alithea. He spoke so scurrilously of you, I had no patience to hear him; besides, he has been making love to me.

Harcourt. True, damned tell-tale woman! [*aside*]

Sparkish. Pshaw! to show his parts—we wits rail and make love often, but to show our parts: as we have no affections, so we have no malice, we—

Alithea. He said you were a wretch below an injury—

Sparkish. Pshaw!

Harcourt. Damned, senseless, impudent, virtuous jade! Well, since she won't let me have her, she'll do as good, she'll make me hate her. [*aside*]

Alithea. A common bubble—

Sparkish. Pshaw!

Alithea. A coward—

Sparkish. Pshaw, pshaw!

Alithea. A senseless, drivelling idiot—

Sparkish. How! did he disparage my parts? Nay, then, my honour's concerned, I can't put up that, sir, by the world—brother, help me to kill him—[*aside*] I may draw now, since we have the odds of him:—'tis a good occasion, too, before my mistress—[*offers to draw*]

Alithea. Hold, hold!

Sparkish. What, what?

Alithea [*aside*]. I must not let 'em kill the gentleman neither, for his kindness to me: I am so far from hating him, that I wish my gallant had his person and understanding. Nay, if my honour—

Sparkish. I'll be thy death.

Alithea. Hold, hold! Indeed, to tell the truth, the gentleman said after all, that what he spoke was but out of friendship to you.

Sparkish. How! say, I am, I am a fool, that is, no wit, out of friendship to me?

Alithea. Yes, to try whether I was concerned enough for you; and made love to me only to be satisfied of my virtue, for your sake.

Harcourt. Kind, however. [*aside*]

Sparkish. Nay, if it were so, my dear rogue, I ask thee pardon; but why would not you tell me so, faith?

Harcourt. Because I did not think on't, faith.

Sparkish. Come, Horner does not come; Harcourt, let's be gone to the new play.—Come, madam.

Alithea. I will not go, if you intend to leave me alone in the box, and run into the pit, as you use to do.

Sparkish. Pshaw! I'll leave Harcourt with you in the box to entertain you, and that's as good; if I sat in the box, I should be thought no judge but of trimmings.—Come away, Harcourt, lead her down.

[*Exeunt* SPARKISH, HARCOURT, *and* ALITHEA.]

Pinchwife. Well, go thy ways, for the flower of the true town fops, such as spend their estates before they come to 'em, and are cuckolds before they're married. But let me go look to my own freehold.—How!

[*Enter* LADY FIDGET, MRS. DAINTY FIDGET, *and* MRS. SQUEAMISH.]

Lady Fidget. Your servant, sir: where is your lady? We are come to wait upon her to the new play.

Pinchwife.   New play!

Lady Fidget.   And my husband will wait upon you presently.

Pinchwife [*aside*].   Damn your civility.—[*aloud*] Madam, by no means; I will not see Sir Jasper here, till I have waited upon him at home; nor shall my wife see you till she has waited upon your ladyship at your lodgings.

Lady Fidget.   Now we are here, sir?

Pinchwife.   No, Madam.

Mrs. Dainty Fidget.   Pray, let us see her.

Mrs. Squeamish.   We will not stir till we see her.

Pinchwife [*aside*].   A pox on you all!—[*goes to the door, and returns*] She has locked the door, and is gone abroad.

Lady Fidget.   No, you have locked the door, and she's within.

Mrs. Dainty Fidget.   They told us below she was here.

Pinchwife [*aside*].   Will nothing do?—[*aloud*] Well, it must out then. To tell you the truth, ladies, which I was afraid to let you know before, lest it might endanger your lives, my wife has just now the small-pox come out upon her; do not be frightened; but pray be gone, ladies; you shall not stay here in danger of your lives; pray get you gone, ladies.

Lady Fidget.   No, no, we have all had 'em.

Mrs. Squeamish.   Alack, alack!

Mrs. Dainty Fidget.   Come, come, we must see how it goes with her; I understand the disease.

Lady Fidget.   Come!

Pinchwife [*aside*].   Well, there is no being too hard for women at their own weapon, lying, therefore I'll quit the field. [*Exit.*]

Mrs. Squeamish.   Here's an example of jealousy!

Lady Fidget.   Indeed, as the world goes, I wonder there are no more jealous, since wives are so neglected.

Mrs. Dainty Fidget.   Pshaw! as the world goes, to what end should they be jealous?

Lady Fidget.   Foh! 'tis a nasty world.

Mrs. Squeamish.   That men of parts, great acquaintance, and quality, should take up with and spend themselves and fortunes in keeping little playhouse creatures, foh!

Lady Fidget.   Nay, that women of understanding, great acquaintance, and good quality, should fall a-keeping too of little creatures, foh!

Mrs. Squeamish.   Why, 'tis the men of quality's fault; they never visit women of honour and reputation as they used to do; and have not so much as common civility for ladies of our rank, but use us with the same indifferency and ill-breeding as if we were all married to 'em.

Lady Fidget.   She says true; 'tis an arrant shame women of quality should be so slighted; methinks birth—birth should go for something; I have known men admired, courted, and followed for their titles only.

Mrs. Squeamish.   Ay, one would think men of honour should not love, no more than marry, out of their own rank.

Mrs. Dainty Fidget.   Fy, fy, upon 'em! they are come to think cross breeding for themselves best, as well as for their dogs and horses.

Lady Fidget.   They are dogs and horses for't.

Mrs. Squeamish. One would think, if not for love, for vanity a little.

Mrs. Dainty Fidget. Nay, they do satisfy their vanity upon us sometimes; and are kind to us in their report, tell all the world they lie with us.

Lady Fidget. Damned rascals, that we should be only wronged by 'em! To report a man has had a person, when he has not had a person, is the greatest wrong in the whole world that can be done to a person.

Mrs. Squeamish. Well, 'tis an arrant shame noble persons should be so wronged and neglected.

Lady Fidget. But still 'tis an arranter shame for a noble person to neglect her own honour, and defame her own noble person with little inconsiderable fellows, foh!

Mrs. Dainty Fidget. I suppose the crime against our honour is the same with a man of quality as with another.

Lady Fidget. How! no sure, the man of quality is likest one's husband, and therefore the fault should be the less.

Mrs. Dainty Fidget. But then the pleasure should be the less.

Lady Fidget. Fy, fy, fy, for shame, sister! whither shall we ramble? Be continent in your discourse, or I shall hate you.

Mrs. Dainty Fidget. Besides, an intrigue is so much the more notorious for the man's quality.

Mrs. Squeamish. 'Tis true that nobody takes notice of a private man, and therefore with him 'tis more secret; and the crime's the less when 'tis not known.

Lady Fidget. You say true; i'faith, I think you are in the right on't: 'tis not an injury to a husband, till it be an injury to our honours; so that a woman of honour loses no honour with a private person; and to say truth—

Mrs. Dainty Fidget. So, the little fellow is grown a private person—with her— [*apart to* MRS. SQUEAMISH]

Lady Fidget. But still my dear, dear honour—

[*Enter* SIR JASPER FIDGET, HORNER, *and* DORILANT.]

Sir Jasper. Ay, my dear, dear of honour, thou hast still so much honour in thy mouth—

Horner. That she has none elsewhere. [*aside*]

Lady Fidget. Oh, what d'ye mean to bring in these upon us?

Mrs. Dainty Fidget. Foh! these are as bad as wits.

Mrs. Squeamish. Foh!

Lady Fidget. Let us leave the room.

Sir Jasper. Stay, stay; faith, to tell you the naked truth—

Lady Fidget. Fy, Sir Jasper! do not use that word naked.

Sir Jasper. Well, well, in short I have business at Whitehall, and cannot go to the play with you, therefore would have you go—

Lady Fidget. With those two to a play?

Sir Jasper. No, not with t'other, but with Mr. Horner; there can be no more scandal to go with him than with Mr. Tattle, or Master Limberham.

Lady Fidget. With that nasty fellow! no—no.

Sir Jasper. Nay, prithee, dear, hear me. [*whispers to* LADY FIDGET]

Horner. Ladies—

[HORNER *and* DORILANT *draw near* MRS. SQUEAMISH *and* MRS. DAINTY FIDGET.]

Mrs. Dainty Fidget.   Stand off.

Mrs. Squeamish.   Do not approach us.

Mrs. Dainty Fidget.   You herd with the wits, you are obscenity all over.

Mrs. Squeamish.   And I would as soon look upon a picture of Adam and Eve, without fig-leaves, as any of you, if I could help it; therefore keep off, and do not make us sick.

Dorilant.   What a devil are these?

Horner.   Why, these are pretenders to honour, as critics to wit, only by censuring others; and as every raw, peevish, out-of-humoured, affected, dull, tea-drinking, arithmetical fop, sets up for a wit by railing at men of sense, so these for honour, by railing at the court, and ladies of as great honour as quality.

Sir Jasper.   Come, Mr. Horner, I must desire you to go with these ladies to the play, sir.

Horner.   I, sir?

Sir Jasper.   Ay, ay, come, sir.

Horner.   I must beg your pardon, sir, and theirs; I will not be seen in women's company in public again for the world.

Sir Jasper.   Ha, ha, strange aversion!

Mrs. Squeamish.   No, he's for women's company in private.

Sir Jasper.   He—poor man—he—ha! ha! ha!

Mrs. Dainty Fidget.   'Tis a greater shame amongst lewd fellows to be seen in virtuous women's company, than for the women to be seen with them.

Horner.   Indeed, madam, the time was I only hated virtuous women, but now I hate the other too; I beg your pardon, ladies.

Lady Fidget.   You are very obliging, sir, because we would not be troubled with you.

Sir Jasper.   In sober sadness, he shall go.

Dorilant.   Nay, if he wo' not, I am ready to wait upon the ladies, and I think I am the fitter man.

Sir Jasper.   You sir! no, I thank you for that. Master Horner is a privileged man amongst the virtuous ladies, 'twill be a great while before you are so; he! he! he! he's my wife's gallant; he! he! he! No, pray withdraw, sir, for as I take it, the virtuous ladies have no business with you.

Dorilant.   And I am sure he can have none with them. 'Tis strange a man can't come amongst virtuous women now, but upon the same terms as men are admitted into the Great Turk's seraglio. But heavens keep me from being an ombre player with 'em!—But where is Pinchwife? [*Exit.*]

Sir Jasper.   Come, come, man; what, avoid the sweet society of womankind? that sweet, soft, gentle, tame, noble creature, woman, made for man's companion—

Horner.   So is that soft, gentle, tame, and more noble creature a spaniel, and has all their tricks; can fawn, lie down, suffer beating, and fawn the more; barks at your friends when they come to see you, makes your bed hard, gives you fleas, and the mange sometimes. And all the difference is, the spaniel's the more faithful animal, and fawns but upon one master.

Sir Jasper.   He! he! he!

Mrs. Squeamish.   O the rude beast!

Mrs. Dainty Fidget.   Insolent brute!

Lady Fidget.   Brute! stinking, mortified, rotten French wether, to dare—

Sir Jasper.   Hold, an't please your ladyship.—For shame, Master Horner! your mother was a woman—[*aside*] Now shall I never reconcile 'em.—[*aside to* LADY FIDGET] Hark you, madam, take my advice in your anger. You know you often want one to make up your drolling pack of ombre players, and you may cheat him easily; for he's an ill gamester, and consequently loves play. Besides, you know you have but two old civil gentlemen (with stinking breaths too) to wait upon you abroad; take in the third into your service. The other are but crazy; and a lady should have a supernumerary gentleman-usher as a supernumerary coach-horse, lest sometimes you should be forced to stay at home.

Lady Fidget.   But are you sure he loves play, and has money?

Sir Jasper.   He loves play as much as you, and has money as much as I.

Lady Fidget.   Then I am contented to make him pay for his scurrility. Money makes up in a measure all other wants in men.—Those whom we cannot make hold for gallants, we make fine. [*aside*]

Sir Jasper.   [*aside*] So, so; now to mollify, wheedle him.—[*aside to* HORNER] Master Horner, will you never keep civil company? methinks 'tis time now, since you are only fit for them. Come, come, man, you must e'en fall to visiting our wives, eating at our tables, drinking tea with our virtuous relations after dinner, dealing cards to 'em, reading plays and gazettes to 'em, picking fleas out of their smocks for 'em, collecting receipts, new songs, women, pages, and footmen for 'em.

Horner.   I hope they'll afford me better employment, sir.

Sir Jasper.   He! he! he! 'tis fit you know your work before you come into your place. And since you are unprovided of a lady to flatter, and a good house to eat at, pray frequent mine, and call my wife mistress, and she shall call you gallant, according to the custom.

Horner.   Who, I?

Sir Jasper.   Faith, thou sha't for my sake; come, for my sake only.

Horner.   For your sake—

Sir Jasper.   Come, come, here's a gamester for you; let him be a little familiar sometimes; nay, what if a little rude? Gamesters may be rude with ladies, you know.

Lady Fidget.   Yes; losing gamesters have a privilege with women.

Horner.   I always thought the contrary, that the winning gamester had most privilege with women; for when you have lost your money to a man, you'll lose anything you have, all you have, they say, and he may use you as he pleases.

Sir Jasper.   He! he! he! well, win or lose, you shall have your liberty with her.

Lady Fidget.   As he behaves himself; and for your sake I'll give him admittance and freedom.

Horner.   All sorts of freedom, madam?

Sir Jasper.   Ay, ay, ay, all sorts of freedom thou canst take. And so go to her, begin thy new employment; wheedle her, jest with her, and be better acquainted one with another.

Horner [*aside*].   I think I know her already; therefore may venture with her my secret for hers.

[HORNER *and* LADY FIDGET *whisper.*]

Sir Jasper. Sister cuz, I have provided an innocent playfellow for you there.

Mrs. Dainty Fidget. Who, he?

Mrs. Squeamish. There's a playfellow, indeed!

Sir Jasper. Yes sure.—What, he is good enough to play at cards, blindman's-buff, or the fool with, sometimes!

Mrs. Squeamish. Foh! we'll have no such playfellows.

Mrs. Dainty Fidget. No, sir; you shan't choose playfellows for us, we thank you.

Sir Jasper. Nay, pray hear me. [*whispering to them*]

Lady Fidget. But, poor gentleman, could you be so generous, so truly a man of honour, as for the sakes of us women of honour, to cause yourself to be reported no man? No man! and to suffer yourself the greatest shame that could fall upon a man, that none might fall upon us women by your conversation? but, indeed, sir, as perfectly, perfectly the same man as before your going into France, sir? as perfectly, perfectly, sir?

Horner. As perfectly, perfectly, madam. Nay, I scorn you should take my word; I desire to be tried only, madam.

Lady Fidget. Well, that's spoken again like a man of honour: all men of honour desire to come to the test. But, indeed, generally you men report such things of yourselves, one does not know how or whom to believe; and it is come to that pass, we dare not take your words no more than your tailor's, without some staid servant of yours be bound with you. But I have so strong a faith in your honour, dear, dear, noble sir, that I'd forfeit mine for yours, at any time, dear sir.

Horner. No, madam, you should not need to forfeit it for me; I have given you security already to save you harmless, my late reputation being so well known in the world, madam.

Lady Fidget. But if upon any future falling-out, or upon a suspicion of my taking the trust out of your hands, to employ some other, you yourself should betray your trust, dear sir? I mean, if you'll give me leave to speak obscenely, you might tell, dear sir.

Horner. If I did, nobody would believe me. The reputation of impotency is as hardly recovered again in the world as that of cowardice, dear madam.

Lady Fidget. Nay, then, as one may say, you may do your worst, dear, dear sir.

Sir Jasper. Come, is your ladyship reconciled to him yet? have you agreed on matters? for I must be gone to Whitehall.

Lady Fidget. Why, indeed, Sir Jasper, Master Horner is a thousand, thousand times a better man than I thought him. Cousin Squeamish, sister Dainty, I can name him now. Truly, not long ago, you know, I thought his very name obscenity; and I would as soon have lain with him as have named him.

Sir Jasper. Very likely, poor madam.

Mrs. Dainty. I believe it.

Mrs. Squeamish. No doubt on't.

Sir Jasper. Well, well—that your ladyship is as virtuous as any she, I know, and him all the town knows—he! he! he! therefore now you like him, get you gone to your business together, go, go to your business, I say, pleasure, whilst I go to my pleasure, business.

Lady Fidget.   Come, then, dear gallant.
Horner.   Come away, my dearest mistress.
Sir Jasper.   So, so; why, 'tis as I'd have it. [*Exit.*]
Horner.   And as I'd have it.
Lady Fidget.   Who for his business from his wife will run,
            Takes the best care to have her business done.

[*Exeunt.*]

Act III

SCENE I—*A Room in* PINCHWIFE'S *House.*

[*Enter* ALITHEA *and* MRS. PINCHWIFE.]

Alithea.   Sister, what ails you? you are grown melancholy.
Mrs. Pinchwife.   Would it not make any one melancholy to see you go every day fluttering about abroad, whilst I must stay at home like a poor lonely sullen bird in a cage?
Alithea.   Ay, sister; but you came young, and just from the nest to your cage: so that I thought you liked it, and could be as cheerful in't as others that took their flight themselves early, and are hopping abroad in the open air.
Mrs. Pinchwife.   Nay, I confess I was quiet enough till my husband told me what pure lives the London ladies live abroad, with their dancing, meetings, and junketings, and dressed every day in their best gowns; and I warrant you, play at nine-pins every day of the week, so they do.

[*Enter* PINCHWIFE.]

Pinchwife.   Come, what's here to do? you are putting the town-pleasures in her head, and setting her a-longing.
Alithea.   Yes, after nine-pins. You suffer none to give her those longings you mean but yourself.
Pinchwife.   I tell her of the vanities of the town like a confessor.
Alithea.   A confessor! just such a confessor as he that, by forbidding a silly ostler to grease the horse's teeth, taught him to do't.
Pinchwife.   Come, Mrs. Flippant, good precepts are lost when bad examples are still before us: the liberty you take abroad makes her hanker after it, and out of humour at home. Poor wretch! she desired not to come to London; I would bring her.
Alithea.   Very well.
Pinchwife.   She has been this week in town, and never desired till this afternoon to go abroad.
Alithea.   Was she not at a play yesterday?
Pinchwife.   Yes; but she ne'er asked me; I was myself the cause of her going.
Alithea.   Then if she ask you again, you are the cause of her asking, and not my example.
Pinchwife.   Well, to-morrow night I shall be rid of you; and the next day, before 'tis light, she and I'll be rid of the town, and my dreadful apprehensions.—

Come, be not melancholy; for thou sha't go into the country after to-morrow, dearest.

Alithea.   Great comfort!

Mrs. Pinchwife.   Pish! what d'ye tell me of the country for?

Pinchwife.   How's this! what, pish at the country?

Mrs. Pinchwife.   Let me alone; I am not well.

Pinchwife.   Oh, if that be all—what ails my dearest?

Mrs. Pinchwife.   Truly, I don't know: but I have not been well since you told me there was a gallant at the play in love with me.

Pinchwife.   Ha!—

Alithea.   That's by my example too!

Pinchwife.   Nay, if you are not well, but are so concerned, because a lewd fellow chanced to lie, and say he liked you, you'll make me sick too.

Mrs. Pinchwife.   Of what sickness?

Pinchwife.   O, of that which is worse than the plague, jealousy.

Mrs. Pinchwife.   Pish, you jeer! I'm sure there's no such disease in our receipt-book at home.

Pinchwife.   No, thou never met'st with it, poor innocent.—Well, if thou cuckold me, 'twill be my own fault—for cuckolds and bastards are generally makers of their own fortune. [*aside*]

Mrs. Pinchwife.   Well, but pray, bud, let's go to a play tonight.

Pinchwife.   'Tis just done, she comes from it. But why are you so eager to see a play?

Mrs. Pinchwife.   Faith, dear, not that I care one pin for their talk there; but I like to look upon the player-men, and would see, if I could, the gallant you say loves me: that's all, dear bud.

Pinchwife.   Is that all, dear bud?

Alithea.   This proceeds from my example!

Mrs. Pinchwife.   But if the play be done, let's go abroad, however, dear bud.

Pinchwife.   Come have a little patience and thou shalt go into the country on Friday.

Mrs. Pinchwife.   Therefore I would see first some sights to tell my neighbours of. Nay, I will go abroad, that's once.

Alithea.   I'm the cause of this desire too!

Pinchwife.   But now I think on't, who, who was the cause of Horner's coming to my lodgings to-day? That was you.

Alithea.   No, you, because you would not let him see your handsome wife out of your lodging.

Mrs. Pinchwife.   Why, O Lord! did the gentleman come hither to see me indeed?

Pinchwife.   No, no.—You are not the cause of that damned question too, Mistress Alithea?—[*aside*] Well, she's in the right of it. He is in love with my wife—and comes after her—'tis so—but I'll nip his love in the bud; lest he should follow us into the country, and break his chariot-wheel near our house, on purpose for an excuse to come to't. But I think I know the town.

Mrs. Pinchwife.   Come, pray, bud, let's go abroad before 'tis late; for I will go, that's flat and plain.

Pinchwife [*aside*].   So! the obstinacy already of the town-wife; and I must, whilst she's here, humour her like one.—[*aloud*] Sister, how shall we do, that she may not be seen, or known?

Alithea. Let her put on her mask.

Pinchwife. Pshaw! a mask makes people but the more inquisitive, and is as ridiculous a disguise as a stage-beard: her shape, stature, habit will be known. And if we should meet with Horner, he would be sure to take acquaintance with us, must wish her joy, kiss her, talk to her, leer upon her, and the devil and all. No, I'll not use her to a mask, 'tis dangerous; for masks have made more cuckolds than the best faces that ever were known.

Alithea. How will you do then?

Mrs. Pinchwife. Nay, shall we go? The Exchange will be shut, and I have a mind to see that.

Pinchwife. So—I have it—I'll dress her up in the suit we are to carry down to her brother, little Sir James; nay, I understand the town-tricks. Come, let's go dress her. A mask! no—a woman masked, like a covered dish, gives a man curiosity and appetite; when, it may be, uncovered, 'twould turn his stomach: no, no.

Alithea. Indeed your comparison is something a greasy one: but I had a gentle gallant used to say, A beauty masked, like the sun in eclipse, gathers together more gazers than if it shined out.

[*Exeunt.*]

SCENE II—*The New Exchange.*

[*Enter* HORNER, HARCOURT, *and* DORILANT.]

Dorilant. Engaged to women, and not sup with us!

Horner. Ay, a pox on 'em all!

Harcourt. You were much a more reasonable man in the morning, and had as noble resolutions against 'em, as a widower of a week's liberty.

Dorilant. Did I ever think to see you keep company with women in vain?

Horner. In vain: no—'tis since I can't love 'em, to be revenged on 'em.

Harcourt. Now your sting is gone, you looked in the box amongst all those women like a drone in the hive; all upon you, shoved and ill-used by 'em all, and thrust from one side to t'other.

Dorilant. Yet he must be buzzing amongst 'em still, like other beetle-headed liquorish drones. Avoid 'em and hate 'em, as they hate you.

Horner. Because I do hate 'em, and would hate 'em yet more, I'll frequent 'em. You may see by marriage, nothing makes a man hate a woman more than her constant conversation. In short, I converse with 'em, as you do with rich fools, to laugh at 'em and use 'em ill.

Dorilant. But I would no more sup with women, unless I could lie with 'em, than sup with a rich coxcomb, unless I could cheat him.

Horner. Yes, I have known thee sup with a fool for his drinking; if he could set out your hand that way only, you were satisfied, and if he were a wine-swallowing mouth, 'twas enough.

Harcourt. Yes, a man drinks often with a fool, as he tosses with a marker, only to keep his hand in use. But do the ladies drink?

Horner. Yes, sir; and I shall have the pleasure at least of laying 'em flat with a bottle, and bring as much scandal that way upon 'em as formerly t'other.

Harcourt. Perhaps you may prove as weak a brother among 'em that way as t'other.

Dorilant. Foh! drinking with women is as unnatural as scolding with 'em. But 'tis a pleasure of decayed fornicators, and the basest way of quenching love.

Harcourt. Nay, 'tis drowning love, instead of quenching it. But leave us for civil women too!

Dorilant. Ay, when he can't be the better for 'em. We hardly pardon a man that leaves his friend for a wench, and that's a pretty lawful call.

Horner. Faith, I would not leave you for 'em, if they would not drink.

Dorilant. Who would disappoint his company at Lewis's for a gossiping?

Harcourt. Foh! Wine and women, good apart, together are as nauseous as sack and sugar. But hark you, sir, before you go, a little of your advice; an old maimed general, when unfit for action, is fittest for counsel. I have other designs upon women than eating and drinking with them; I am in love with Sparkish's mistress, whom he is to marry to-morrow: now how shall I get her?

[*Enter* SPARKISH, *looking about.*]

Horner. Why, here comes one will help you to her.

Harcourt. He! he, I tell you, is my rival, and will hinder my love.

Horner. No; a foolish rival and a jealous husband assist their rival's designs; for they are sure to make their women hate them, which is the first step to their love for another man.

Harcourt. But I cannot come near his mistress but in his company.

Horner. Still the better for you; for fools are most easily cheated when they themselves are accessories: and he is to be bubbled of his mistress as of his money, the common mistress, by keeping him company.

Sparkish. Who is that that is to be bubbled? Faith, let me snack; I han't met with a bubble since Christmas. 'Gad, I think bubbles are like their brother woodcocks, go out with the cold weather.

Harcourt. A pox! he did not hear all, I hope. [*apart to* HORNER]

Sparkish. Come, you bubbling rogues you, where do we sup?—Oh, Harcourt, my mistress tells me you have been making fierce love to her all the play long: ha! ha!—But I—

Harcourt. I make love to her!

Sparkish. Nay, I forgive thee, for I think I know thee, and I know her; but I am sure I know myself.

Harcourt. Did she tell you so? I see all women are like these of the Exchange; who, to enhance the prize of their commodities, report to their fond customers offers which were never made 'em.

Horner. Ay, women are apt to tell before the intrigue, as men after it, and so show themselves the vainer sex. But hast thou a mistress, Sparkish? 'Tis as hard for me to believe it, as that thou ever hadst a bubble, as you bragged just now.

Sparkish. O, your servant, sir: are you at your raillery, sir? But we are some of us beforehand with you to-day at the play. The wits were something bold with you, sir; did you not hear us laugh?

Horner. Yes; but I thought you had gone to plays, to laugh at the poet's wit, not at your own.

Sparkish.   Your servant, sir: no, I thank you. 'Gad I go to a play as to a country treat; I carry my own wine to one, and my own wit to t'other, or else I'm sure I should not be merry at either. And the reason why we are so often louder than the players, is, because we think we speak more wit, and so become the poet's rivals in his audience: for to tell you the truth, we hate the silly rogues; nay, so much, that we find fault even with their bawdy upon the stage, whilst we talk nothing else in the pit as loud.

Horner.   But why shouldst thou hate the silly poets? Thou hast too much wit to be one; and they, like whores, are only hated by each other: and thou dost scorn writing, I'm sure.

Sparkish.   Yes; I'd have you to know I scorn writing: but women, women, that make men do all foolish things, make 'em write songs too. Everybody does it. 'Tis even as common with lovers, as playing with fans; and you can no more help rhyming to your Phillis, than drinking to your Phillis.

Harcourt.   Nay, poetry in love is no more to be avoided than jealousy.

Dorilant.   But the poets damned your songs, did they?

Sparkish.   Damn the poets! they have turned 'em into burlesque, as they call it. That burlesque is a hocus-pocus trick they have got, which, by the virtue of *Hictius doctius topsy turvy,* they make a wise and witty man in the world, a fool upon the stage you know not how: and 'tis therefore I hate 'em too, for I know not but it may be my own case; for they'll put a man into a play for looking asquint. Their predecessors were contented to make serving-men only their stage-fools: but these rogues must have gentlemen, with a pox to 'em, nay, knights; and, indeed, you shall hardly see a fool upon the stage but he's a knight. And to tell you the truth, they have kept me these six years from being a knight in earnest, for fear of being knighted in a play, and dubbed a fool.

Dorilant.   Blame 'em not, they must follow their copy, the age.

Harcourt.   But why shouldst thou be afraid of being in a play, who expose yourself every day in the play-houses, and at public places?

Horner.   'Tis but being on the stage, instead of standing on a bench in the pit.

Dorilant.   Don't you give money to painters to draw you like? and are you afriad of your pictures at length in a playhouse, where all your mistresses may see you?

Sparkish.   A pox! painters don't draw the small-pox or pimples in one's face. Come, damn all your silly authors whatever, all books and booksellers, by the world; and all readers, courteous or uncourteous!

Harcourt.   But who comes here, Sparkish?

[*Enter* PINCHWIFE *and* MRS. PINCHWIFE *in man's clothes,* ALITHEA, *and* LUCY.]

Sparkish.   Oh, hide me! There's my mistress too.

[SPARKISH *hides himself behind* HARCOURT.]

Harcourt.   She sees you.

Sparkish.   But I will not see her. 'Tis time to go to Whitehall, and I must not fail the drawing-room.

Harcourt.   Pray, first carry me, and reconcile me to her.

Sparkish.   Another time. Faith, the king will have supped.

Harcourt.   Not with the worse stomach for thy absence. Thou art one of those fools that think their attendance at the king's meals as necessary as his physicians, when you are more troublesome to him than his doctors or his dogs.

Sparkish.   Pshaw! I know my interest, sir. Prithee hide me.

Horner.   Your servant, Pinchwife.—What, he knows us not!

Pinchwife.   Come along. [*to his wife aside*]

Mrs. Pinchwife.   Pray, have you any ballads? give me sixpenny worth.

Bookseller.   We have no ballads.

Mrs. Pinchwife.   Then give me "Covent Garden Drollery," and a play or two— Oh, here's "Tarugo's Wiles," and "The Slighted Maiden"; I'll have them.

Pinchwife.   No; plays are not for your reading. Come along; will you discover yourself? [*apart to her*]

Horner.   Who is that pretty youth with him, Sparkish?

Sparkish.   I believe his wife's brother, because he's something like her: but I never saw her but once.

Horner.   Extremely handsome; I have seen a face like it too. Let us follow 'em.

[*Exeunt* PINCHWIFE, MRS. PINCHWIFE, ALITHEA, *and* LUCY; HORNER *and* DORILANT *following them.*]

Harcourt.   Come, Sparkish, your mistress saw you, and will be angry you go not to her. Besides, I would fain be reconciled to her, which none but you can do, dear friend.

Sparkish.   Well, that's a better reason, dear friend. I would not go near her now for her's or my own sake; but I can deny you nothing: for though I have known thee a great while, never go, if I do not love thee as well as a new acquaintance.

Harcourt.   I am obliged to you indeed, dear friend. I would be well with her, only to be well with thee still; for these ties to wives usually dissolve all ties to friends. I would be contented she should enjoy you a-nights, but I would have you to myself a-days as I have had, dear friend.

Sparkish.   And thou shalt enjoy me a-days, dear, dear friend, never stir: and I'll be divorced from her, sooner than from thee. Come along.

Harcourt [*aside*].   So, we are hard put to't, when we make our rival our procurer; but neither she nor her brother would let me come near her now. When all's done, a rival is the best cloak to steal to a mistress under, without suspicion; and when we have once got to her as we desire, we throw him off like other cloaks.

[*Exit* SPARKISH, HARCOURT *following him. Re-enter* PINCHWIFE *and* MRS. PINCHWIFE.]

Pinchwife [*to* ALITHEA].   Sister, if you will not go, we must leave you.—[*aside*] The fool her gallant and she will muster up all the young saunterers of this place, and they will leave their dear sempstresses to follow us. What a swarm of cuckolds and cuckold-makers are here!—Come, let's be gone, Mistress Margery.

Mrs. Pinchwife.   Don't you believe that; I han't half my bellyfull of sights yet.

Pinchwife.   Then walk this way.

Mrs. Pinchwife.   Lord, what a power of brave signs are here! stay—the Bull's-Head, the Ram's-Head, and the Stag's-Head, dear—

Pinchwife.   Nay, if every husband's proper sign here were visible, they would be all alike.

Mrs. Pinchwife.   What d'ye mean by that, bud?

Pinchwife.   'Tis no matter—no matter, bud.

Mrs. Pinchwife.   Pray tell me: nay, I will know.

Pinchwife.   They would be all Bulls, Stags, and Ramsheads.

[*Exeunt* PINCHWIFE *and* MRS. PINCHWIFE. *Re-enter* SPARKISH, HARCOURT, ALITHEA, *and* LUCY, *at the other side.*]

Sparkish.   Come, dear madam, for my sake you shall be reconciled to him.

Alithea.   For your sake I hate him.

Harcourt.   That's something too cruel, madam, to hate me for his sake.

Sparkish.   Ay indeed, madam, too, too cruel to me, to hate my friend for my sake.

Alithea.   I hate him because he is your enemy; and you ought to hate him too, for making love to me, if you love me.

Sparkish.   That's a good one! I hate a man for loving you! If he did love you, 'tis but what he can't help; and 'tis your fault, not his, if he admires you. I hate a man for being of my opinion! I'll n'er do't, by the world.

Alithea.   Is it for your honour, or mine, to suffer a man to make love to me, who am to marry you to-morrow?

Sparkish.   Is it for your honour, or mine, to have me jealous? That he makes love to you, is a sign you are handsome; and that I am not jealous, is a sign you are virtuous. That I think is for your honour.

Alithea.   But 'tis your honour too I am concerned for.

Harcourt.   But why, dearest madam, will you be more concerned for his honour than he is himself? Let his honour alone, for my sake and his. He! he has no honour—

Sparkish.   How's that?

Harcourt.   But what my dear friend can guard himself.

Sparkish.   O ho—that's right again.

Harcourt.   Your care of his honour argues his neglect of it, which is no honour to my dear friend here. Therefore once more, let his honour go which way it will, dear madam.

Sparkish.   Ay, ay; were it for my honour to marry a woman whose virtue I suspected, and could not trust her in a friend's hands?

Alithea.   Are you not afraid to lose me?

Harcourt.   He afraid to lose you, madam! No, no—you may see how the most estimable and most glorious creature in the world is valued by him. Will you not see it?

Sparkish.   Right, honest Frank, I have that noble value for her that I cannot be jealous of her.

Alithea.   You mistake him. He means, you care not for me, nor who has me.

Sparkish.   Lord, madam, I see you are jealous! Will you wrest a poor man's meaning from his words?

Alithea.   You astonish me, sir, with your want of jealousy.

Sparkish.   And you make me giddy, madam, with your jealousy and fears, and virtue and honour. 'Gad, I see virtue makes a woman as troublesome as a little reading or learning.

Alithea.   Monstrous!

Lucy. Well, to see what easy husbands these women of quality can meet with! a poor chambermaid can never have such ladylike luck. Besides, he's thrown away upon her. She'll make no use of her fortune, her blessing, none to a gentleman, for a pure cuckold; for it requires good breeding to be a cuckold. [*aside*]

Alithea. I tell you then plainly, he pursues me to marry me.

Sparkish. Pshaw!

Harcourt. Come, madam, you see you strive in vain to make him jealous of me. My dear friend is the kindest creature in the world to me.

Sparkish. Poor fellow!

Harcourt. But his kindness only is not enough for me, without your favour, your good opinion, dear madam: 'tis that must perfect my happiness. Good gentleman, he believes all I say: would you would do so! Jealous of me! I would not wrong him nor you for the world.

Sparkish. Look you there. Hear him, hear him, and do not walk away so.

[ALITHEA *walks carelessly to and fro.*]

Harcourt. I love you, madam, so—

Sparkish. How's that? Nay, now you begin to go too far indeed.

Harcourt. So much, I confess, I say, I love you, that I would not have you miserable, and cast yourself away upon so unworthy and inconsiderable a thing as what you see here. [*clapping his hand on his breast, points at* SPARKISH]

Sparkish. No, faith, I believe thou wouldst not: now his meaning is plain; but I knew before thou wouldst not wrong me, nor her.

Harcourt. No, no, Heavens forbid the glory of her sex should fall so low, as into the embraces of such a contemptible wretch, the least of mankind—my friend here—I injure him! [*embracing* SPARKISH]

Alithea. Very well.

Sparkish. No, no, dear friend, I knew it.—Madam, you see he will rather wrong himself than me, in giving himself such names.

Alithea. Do not you understand him yet?

Sparkish. Yes: how modestly he speaks of himself, poor fellow!

Alithea. Methinks he speaks impudently of yourself, since—before yourself too; insomuch that I can no longer suffer his scurrilous abusiveness to you, no more than his love to me. [*offers to go*]

Sparkish. Nay, nay, madam, pray stay—his love to you! Lord madam, has he not spoke yet plain enough?

Alithea. Yes, indeed, I should think so.

Sparkish. Well then, by the world, a man can't speak civilly to a woman now, but presently she says, he makes love to her. Nay, madam, you shall stay, with your pardon, since you have not yet understood him, till he has made an eclaircissement of his love to you, that is, what kind of love it is. Answer to thy catechism, friend; do you love my mistress here?

Harcourt. Yes, I wish she would not doubt it.

Sparkish. But how do you love her?

Harcourt. With all my soul.

Alithea. I thank him, methinks he speaks plain enough now.

Sparkish [*to* ALITHEA]. You are out still.—But with what kind of love, Harcourt?

Harcourt. With the best and the truest love in the world.

Sparkish. Look you there then, that is with no matrimonial love, I'm sure.

Alithea. How's that? do you say matrimonial love is not best?

Sparkish. 'Gad, I went too far ere I was aware. But speak for thyself, Harcourt, you said you would not wrong me nor her.

Harcourt. No, no, madam, e'en take him for Heaven's sake.

Sparkish. Look you there, madam.

Harcourt. Who should in all justice be yours, he that loves you most. [*claps his hand on his breast*]

Alithea. Look you there, Mr. Sparkish, who's that?

Sparkish. Who should it be?—Go on, Harcourt.

Harcourt. Who loves you more than women, titles, or fortune fools. [*points at* SPARKISH]

Sparkish. Look you there, he means me still, for he points at me.

Alithea. Ridiculous!

Harcourt. Who can only match your faith and constancy in love.

Sparkish. Ay.

Harcourt. Who knows, if it be possible, how to value so much beauty and virtue.

Sparkish. Ay.

Harcourt. Whose love can no more be equalled in the world, than that heavenly form of yours.

Sparkish. No.

Harcourt. Who could no more suffer a rival, than your absence, and yet could no more suspect your virtue, than his own constancy in his love to you.

Sparkish. No.

Harcourt. Who, in fine, loves you better than his eyes, that first made him love you.

Sparkish. Ay—Nay, madam, faith, you shan't go till—

Alithea. Have a care, lest you make me stay too long.

Sparkish. But till he has saluted you; that I may be assured you are friends, after his honest advice and declaration. Come, pray, madam, be friends with him.

[*Re-enter* PINCHWIFE *and* MRS. PINCHWIFE.]

Alithea. You must pardon me, sir, that I am not yet so obedient to you.

Pinchwife. What, invite your wife to kiss men? Monstrous! are you not ashamed? I will never forgive you.

Sparkish. Are you not ashamed, that I should have more confidence in the chastity of your family than you have? You must not teach me, I am a man of honour, sir, though I am frank and free; I am frank, sir—

Pinchwife. Very frank, sir, to share your wife with your friends.

Sparkish. He is an humble, menial friend, such as reconciles the differences of the marriage bed; you know man and wife do not always agree; I design him for that use, therefore would have him well with my wife.

Pinchwife. A menial friend!—you will get a great many menial friends, by showing your wife as you do.

Sparkish. What then? It may be I have a pleasure in't, as I have to show fine clothes at a play-house, the first day, and count money before poor rogues.

Pinchwife. He that shows his wife or money, will be in danger of having them borrowed sometimes.

Sparkish. I love to be envied, and would not marry a wife that I alone could love; loving alone is as dull as eating alone. Is it not a frank age? and I am a frank person; and to tell you the truth, it may be, I love to have rivals in a wife, they make her seem to a man still but as a kept mistress; and so good night, for I must to Whitehall.—Madam, I hope you are now reconciled to my friend; and so I wish you a good night, madam, and sleep if you can: for to-morrow you know I must visit you early with a canonical gentleman. Good night, dear Harcourt. [*Exit.*]

Harcourt. Madam, I hope you will not refuse my visit tomorrow, if it should be earlier with a canonical gentleman than Mr. Sparkish's.

Pinchwife. This gentlewoman is yet under my care, therefore you must yet forbear your freedom with her, sir. [*coming between* ALITHEA *and* HARCOURT]

Harcourt. Must, sir?

Pinchwife. Yes, sir, she is my sister.

Harcourt. 'Tis well she is, sir—for I must be her servant, sir.—Madam—

Pinchwife. Come away, sister, we had been gone, if it had not been for you, and so avoided these lewd rake-hells, who seem to haunt us.

[*Re-enter* HORNER *and* DORILANT.]

Horner. How now, Pinchwife!

Pinchwife. Your servant.

Horner. What! I see a little time in the country makes a man turn wild and unsociable, and only fit to converse with his horses, dogs, and his herds.

Pinchwife. I have business, sir, and must mind it; your business is pleasure, therefore you and I must go different ways.

Horner. Well, you may go on, but this pretty young gentleman—[*takes hold of* MRS. PINCHWIFE]

Harcourt. The lady—

Dorilant. And the maid—

Horner. Shall stay with us; for I suppose their business is the same with ours, pleasure.

Pinchwife. 'Sdeath, he knows her, she carries it so sillily! yet if he does not, I should be more silly to discover it first. [*aside*]

Alithea. Pray, let us go, sir.

Pinchwife. Come, come—

Horner [*to* MRS. PINCHWIFE]. Had you not rather stay with us?—Prithee, Pinchwife, who is this pretty young gentleman?

Pinchwife. One to whom I'm a guardian.—[*aside*] I wish I could keep her out of your hands.

Horner. Who is he? I never saw anything so pretty in all my life.

Pinchwife. Pshaw! do not look upon him so much, he's a poor bashful youth, you'll put him out of countenance.—Come away, brother. [*offers to take her away*]

Horner. O, your brother!

Pinchwife. Yes, my wife's brother.—Come, come, she'll stay supper for us.

Horner.   I thought so, for he is very like her I saw you at the play with, whom I told you I was in love with.

Mrs. Pinchwife [aside].   O jeminy! is that he that was in love with me? I am glad on't, I vow, for he's a curious fine gentleman, and I love him already, too.—[*to* PINCHWIFE] Is this he, bud?

Pinchwife.   Come away, come away. [*to his wife*]

Horner.   Why, what haste are you in? Why won't you let me talk with him?

Pinchwife.   Because you'll debauch him; he's yet young and innocent, and I would not have him debauched for anything in the world.—[*aside*] How she gazes on him! the devil!

Horner.   Harcourt, Dorilant, look you here, this is the likeness of that dowdy he told us of, his wife; did you ever see a lovelier creature? The rogue has reason to be jealous of his wife, since she is like him, for she would make all that see her in love with her.

Harcourt.   And, as I remember now, she is as like him here as can be.

Dorilant.   She is indeed very pretty, if she be like him.

Horner.   Very pretty? a very pretty commendation!—she is a glorious creature, beautiful beyond all things I ever beheld.

Pinchwife.   So, so.

Harcourt.   More beautiful than a poet's first mistress of imagination.

Horner. Or another man's last mistress of flesh and blood.

Mrs. Pinchwife.   Nay, now you jeer, sir; pray don't jeer me.

Pinchwife.   Come, come.—[*aside*] By Heavens, she'll discover herself!

Horner.   I speak of your sister, sir.

Pinchwife.   Ay, but saying she was handsome, if like him, made him blush.—[*aside*] I am upon a rack!

Horner.   Methinks he is so handsome he should not be a man.

Pinchwife [aside].   O, there 'tis out! he has discovered her! I am not able to suffer any longer.—[*to his wife*] Come, come away, I say.

Horner.   Nay, by your leave, sir, he shall not go yet.—[*aside to them*] Harcourt, Dorilant, let us torment this jealous rogue a little.

Harcourt, Dorilant.   How?

Horner.   I'll show you.

Pinchwife.   Come, pray let him go, I cannot stay fooling any longer; I tell you his sister stays supper for us.

Horner.   Does she? Come then, we'll all go to sup with her and thee.

Pinchwife.   No, now I think on't, having stayed so long for us, I warrant she's gone to bed.—[*aside*] I wish she and I were well out of their hands.—[*to his wife*] Come, I must rise early tomorrow, come.

Horner.   Well then, if she be gone to bed, I wish her and you a good night. But pray, young gentleman, present my humble service to her.

Mrs. Pinchwife.   Thank you heartily, sir.

Pinchwife [aside].   'Sdeath, she will discover herself yet in spite of me.—[*aloud*] He is something more civil to you, for your kindness to his sister, than I am, it seems.

Horner.   Tell her, dear sweet little gentleman, for all your brother there, that you have revived the love I had for her at first sight in the playhouse.

Mrs. Pinchwife.   But did you love her indeed, and indeed?

Pinchwife [*aside*].   So, so.—[*aloud*] Away, I say.

Horner.   Nay, stay.—Yes, indeed, and indeed, pray do you tell her so, and give her this kiss from me. [*kisses her*]

Pinchwife [*aside*].   O Heavens! what do I suffer? Now 'tis too plain he knows her, and yet—

Horner.   And this, and this—[*kisses her again*]

Mrs. Pinchwife.   What do you kiss me for? I am no woman.

Pinchwife [*aside*].   So, there, 'tis out.—[*aloud*] Come, I cannot, nor will stay any longer.

Horner.   Nay, they shall send your lady a kiss too. Here, Harcourt, Dorilant, will you not? [*They kiss her.*]

Pinchwife [*aside*].   How! do I suffer this? Was I not accusing another just now for this rascally patience, in permitting his wife to be kissed before his face? Ten thousand ulcers gnaw away their lips.—[*aloud*] Come, come.

Horner.   Good night, dear little gentleman; madam, good night; farewell, Pinchwife.—[*apart to* HARCOURT *and* DORILANT] Did not I tell you I would raise his jealous gall?

[*Exeunt* HORNER, HARCOURT, *and* DORILANT.]

Pinchwife.   So, they are gone at last; stay, let me see first if the coach be at this door. [*Exit.*]

[*Re-enter* HORNER, HARCOURT, *and* DORILANT.]

Horner.   What, not gone yet? Will you be sure to do as I desired you, sweet sir?

Mrs. Pinchwife.   Sweet sir, but what will you give me then?

Horner.   Anything. Come away into the next walk. [*exit, haling away* MRS. PINCHWIFE]

Alithea.   Hold! hold! what d'ye do?

Lucy.   Stay, stay, hold—

Harcourt.   Hold, madam, hold, let him present him—he'll come presently; nay, I will never let you go till you answer my question.

Lucy.   For God's sake, sir, I must follow 'em.

[ALITHEA *and* LUCY, *struggling with* HARCOURT *and* DORILANT.]

Dorilant.   No, I have something to present you with too, you shan't follow them.

[*Re-enter* PINCHWIFE.]

Pinchwife.   Where?—how—what's become of?—gone!—whither?

Lucy.   He's only gone with the gentleman, who will give him something, an't please your worship.

Pinchwife.   Something!—give him something, with a pox!—where are they?

Alithea.   In the next walk only, brother.

Pinchwife.   Only, only! where, where? [*Exit and returns presently, then goes out again.*]

Harcourt. What's the matter with him? why so much concerned? But, dearest madam—

Alithea. Pray let me go, sir; I have said and suffered enough already.

Harcourt. Then you will not look upon, nor pity, my sufferings?

Alithea. To look upon 'em, when I cannot help 'em, were cruelty, not pity; therefore, I will never see you more.

Harcourt. Let me then, madam, have my privilege of a banished lover, complaining or railing, and giving you but a farewell reason why, if you cannot condescend to marry me, you should not take that wretch, my rival.

Alithea. He only, not you, since my honour is engaged so far to him, can give me a reason why I should not marry him; but if he be true, and what I think him to me, I must be so to him. Your servant, sir.

Harcourt. Have women only constancy when 'tis a vice, and are, like Fortune, only true to fools?

Dorilant. Thou sha't not stir, thou robust creature; you see I can deal with you, therefore you should stay the rather, and be kind. [*to* LUCY, *who struggles to get from him*]

[*Re-enter* PINCHWIFE.]

Pinchwife. Gone, gone, not to be found! quite gone! ten thousand plagues go with 'em! Which way went they?

Alithea. But into t'other walk, brother.

Lucy. Their business will be done presently sure, an't please your worship; it can't be long in doing, I'm sure on't.

Alithea. Are they not there?

Pinchwife. No, you know where they are, you infamous wretch, eternal shame of your family, which you do not dishonour enough yourself you think, but you must help her to do it too, thou legion of bawds!

Alithea. Good brother—

Pinchwife. Damned, damned sister!

Alithea. Look you here, she's coming.

[*Re-enter* MRS. PINCHWIFE *running, with her hat full of oranges and dried fruit under her arm,* HORNER *following.*]

Mrs. Pinchwife. O dear bud, look you here what I have got, see!

Pinchwife. And what I have got here too, which you can't see. [*aside, rubbing his forehead*][1]

Mrs. Pinchwife. The fine gentleman has given me better things yet.

Pinchwife. Has he so?—[*aside*] Out of breath and coloured!—I must hold yet.

Horner. I have only given your little brother an orange, sir.

Pinchwife [*to* HORNER]. Thank you, sir.—[*aside*] You have only squeezed my orange, I suppose, and given it me again; yet I must have a city patience.—[*to his wife*] Come, come away.

Mrs. Pinchwife. Stay, till I have put up my fine things, bud.

[*Enter* SIR JASPER FIDGET.]

---

[1] Where he feels his cuckold's horns sprouting.

Sir Jasper.   O, Master Horner, come, come, the ladies stay for you; your mistress, my wife, wonders you make not more haste to her.

Horner.   I have stayed this half hour for you here, and 'tis your fault I am not now with your wife.

Sir Jasper.   But, pray, don't let her know so much; the truth on't is, I was advancing a certain project to his majesty about—I'll tell you.

Horner.   No, let's go, and hear it at your house. Good night, sweet little gentle-man; one kiss more, you'll remember me now, I hope. [*kisses her*]

Dorilant.   What, Sir Jasper, will you separate friends? He promised to sup with us, and if you take him to your house, you'll be in danger of our company too.

Sir Jasper.   Alas! gentlemen, my house is not fit for you; there are none but civil women there, which are not for your turn. He, you know, can bear with the society of civil women now, ha! ha! ha! besides, he's one of my family—he's—he! he! he!

Dorilant.   What is he?

Sir Jasper.   Faith, my eunuch, since you'll have it; he! he! he!

[*Exeunt* SIR JASPER FIDGET *and* HORNER.]

Dorilant.   I rather wish thou wert his or my cuckold. Harcourt, what a good cuckold is lost there for want of a man to make him one? Thee and I cannot have Horner's privilege, who can make use of it.

Harcourt.   Ay, to poor Horner 'tis like coming to an estate at threescore, when a man can't be the better for't.

Pinchwife.   Come.

Mrs. Pinchwife.   Presently, bud.

Dorilant.   Come, let us go too.—[*to* ALITHEA] Madam, your servant.—[*to* LUCY] Good night, strapper.

Harcourt.   Madam, though you will not let me have a good day or night, I wish you one; but dare not name the other half of my wish.

Alithea.   Good night, sir, for ever.

Mrs. Pinchwife.   I don't know where to put this here, dead bud, you shall eat it; nay, you shall have part of the fine gentleman's good things, or treat, as you call it, when we come home.

Pinchwife.   Indeed, I deserve it, since I furnished the best part of it. [*strikes away the orange*]

> The gallant treats presents, and gives the ball;
> But 'tis the absent cuckold pays for all.

[*Exeunt.*]

Act IV

SCENE I—PINCHWIFE'S *House in the morning.*

[*Enter* ALITHEA *dressed in new clothes, and* LUCY.]

Lucy. Well—madam, now have I dressed you, and set you out with so many ornaments, and spent upon you ounces of essence and pulvillio; and all this for no other purpose but as people adorn and perfume a corpse for a stinking second-hand grave: such, or as bad, I think Master Sparkish's bed.

Alithea. Hold your peace.

Lucy. Nay, madam, I will ask you the reason why you would banish poor Master Harcourt for ever from your sight; how could you be so hard-hearted?

Alithea. 'Twas because I was not hard-hearted.

Lucy. No, no; 'twas stark love and kindness, I warrant.

Alithea. It was so; I would see him no more because I love him.

Lucy. Hey day, a very pretty reason!

Alithea. You do not understand me.

Lucy. I wish you may yourself.

Alithea. I was engaged to marry, you see, another man, whom my justice will not suffer me to deceive or injure.

Lucy. Can there be a greater cheat or wrong done to a man than to give him your person without your heart? I should make a conscience of it.

Alithea. I'll retrieve it for him after I am married a while.

Lucy. The woman that marries to love better, will be as much mistaken as the wencher that marries to live better. No, madam, marrying to increase love is like gaming to become rich; alas! you only lose what little stock you had before.

Alithea. I find by your rhetoric you have been bribed to betray me.

Lucy. Only by his merit, that has bribed your heart, you see, against your word and rigid honour. But what a devil is this honour! 'tis sure a disease in the head, like the megrim or falling-sickness, that always hurries people away to do themselves mischief. Men lose their lives by it; women, what's dearer to 'em, their love, the life of life.

Alithea. Come, pray talk you no more of honour, nor Master Harcourt; I wish the other would come to secure my fidelity to him and his right in me.

Lucy. You will marry him then?

Alithea. Certainly, I have given him already my word, and will my hand too, to make it good, when he comes.

Lucy. Well, I wish I may never stick pin more, if he be not an arrant natural, to t'other fine gentleman.

Alithea. I own he wants the wit of Harcourt, which I will dispense withal for another want he has, which is want of jealousy, which men of wit seldom want.

Lucy. Lord, madam, what should you do with a fool to your husband? You intend to be honest, don't you? then that husbandly virtue, credulity, is thrown away upon you.

Alithea. He only that could suspect my virtue should have cause to do it; 'tis Sparkish's confidence in my truth that obliges me to be so faithful to him.

Lucy. You are not sure his opinion may last.

Alithea. I am satisfied, 'tis impossible for him to be jealous after the proofs I have had of him. Jealousy in a husband—Heaven defend me from it! it begets a thousand plagues to a poor woman, the loss of her honour, her quiet, and her—

Lucy. And her pleasure.

Alithea. What d'ye mean, impertinent?

Lucy. Liberty is a great pleasure, madam.

Alithea. I say, loss of her honour, her quiet, nay, her life sometimes; and what's as bad almost, the loss of this town; that is, she is sent into the country, which is the last ill-usage of a husband to a wife, I think.

Lucy [aside]. O, does the wind lie there?—[*aloud*] Then of necessity, madam, you think a man must carry his wife into the country, if he be wise. The country is as terrible, I find, to our young English ladies, as a monastery to those abroad; and on my virginity, I think they would rather marry a London jailer, than a high sheriff of a county, since neither can stir from his employment. Formerly women of wit married fools for a great estate, a fine seat, or the like; but now 'tis for a pretty seat only in Lincoln's-Inn-Fields, St. James's-Fields, or the Pall-Mall.

[*Enter* SPARKISH, *and* HARCOURT, *dressed like a parson.*]

Sparkish. Madam, your humble servant, a happy day to you, and to us all.

Harcourt. Amen.

Alithea. Who have we here?

Sparkish. My chaplain, faith—O madam, poor Harcourt remembers his humble service to you; and, in obedience to your last commands, refrains coming into your sight.

Alithea. Is not that he?

Sparkish. No, fy, no; but to show that he ne'er intended to hinder our match, has sent his brother here to join our hands. When I get me a wife, I must get her a chaplain, according to the custom; that is his brother, and my chaplain.

Alithea. His brother!

Lucy. And your chaplain, to preach in your pulpit then—[*aside*]

Alithea. His brother!

Sparkish. Nay, I knew you would not believe it.—I told you, sir, she would take you for your brother Frank.

Alithea. Believe it!

Lucy. His brother! ha! ha! he! he has a trick left still, it seems. [*aside*]

Sparkish. Come, my dearest, pray let us go to church before the canonical hour is past.

Alithea. For shame, you are abused still.

Sparkish. By the world, 'tis strange now you are so incredulous.

Alithea. 'Tis strange you are so credulous.

Sparkish. Dearest of my life, hear me. I tell you this is Ned Harcourt of Cambridge, by the world; you see he has a sneaking college look. 'Tis true he's something like his brother Frank; and they differ from each other no more than in their age, for they were twins.

Lucy. Ha! ha! ha!

Alithea. Your servant, sir; I cannot be so deceived, though you are. But come, let's hear, how do you know what you affirm so confidently?

Sparkish. Why, I'll tell you all. Frank Harcourt coming to me this morning to wish me joy, and present his service to you, I asked him if he could help me to a parson. Whereupon he told me, he had a brother in town who was in orders; and he went straight away, and sent him, you see there, to me.

Alithea. Yes, Frank goes and puts on a black coat, then tells you he is Ned; that's all you have for't.

Sparkish. Pshaw! pshaw! I tell you, by the same token, the midwife put her garter about Frank's neck, to know 'em asunder, they were so like.

Alithea. Frank tells you this too?

Sparkish. Ay, and Ned there too: nay, they are both in a story.

Alithea. So, so; very foolish.

Sparkish. Lord, if you won't believe one, you had best try him by your chambermaid there; for chambermaids must needs know chaplains from other men, they are so used to 'em.

Lucy. Let's see: nay, I'll be sworn he has the canonical smirk, and the filthy clammy palm of a chaplain.

Alithea. Well, most reverend doctor, pray let us make an end of this fooling.

Harcourt. With all my soul, divine heavenly creature, when you please.

Alithea. He speaks like a chaplain indeed.

Sparkish. Why, was there not soul, divine, heavenly, in what he said?

Alithea. Once more, most impertinent black coat, cease your persecution, and let us have a conclusion of this ridiculous love.

Harcourt. I had forgot, I must suit my style to my coat, or I wear it in vain. [*aside*]

Alithea. I have no more patience left; let us make once an end of this troublesome love, I say.

Harcourt. So be it, seraphic lady, when your honour shall think it meet and convenient so to do.

Sparkish. 'Gad I'm sure none but a chaplain could speak so, I think.

Alithea. Let me tell you, sir, this dull trick will not serve your turn; though you delay our marriage, you shall not hinder it.

Harcourt. Far be it from me, munificent patroness, to delay your marriage; I desire nothing more than to marry you presently, which I might do, if you yourself would; for my noble, goodnatured, and thrice generous patron here would not hinder it.

Sparkish. No, poor man, not I, faith.

Harcourt. And now, madam, let me tell you plainly nobody else shall marry you; by Heavens! I'll die first, for I'm sure I should die after it.

Lucy. How his love has made him forget his function, as I have seen it in real parsons!

Alithea. That was spoken like a chaplain too? now you understand him, I hope.

Sparkish. Poor man, he takes it heinously to be refused; I can't blame him, 'tis putting an indignity upon him, not to be suffered; but you'll pardon me, madam, it shan't be; he shall marry us; come away, pray madam.

Lucy. Ha! ha! he! more ado! 'tis late.

Alithea. Invincible stupidity! I tell you, he would marry me as your rival, not as your chaplain.

Sparkish. Come, come, madam. [*pulling her away*]

Lucy. I pray, madam, do not refuse this reverend divine the honour and satisfaction of marrying you; for I dare say, he has set his heart upon't, good doctor.

Alithea. What can you hope or design by this?

Harcourt. I could answer her, a reprieve for a day only, often revokes a hasty doom. At worst, if she will not take mercy on me, and let me marry her, I have at least the lover's second pleasure, hindering my rival's enjoyment, though but for a time. [*aside*]

Sparkish. Come, madam, 'tis e'en twelve o'clock, and my mother charged me never to be married out of the canonical hours. Come, come; Lord, here's such a deal of modesty, I warrant, the first day.

Lucy. Yes, an't please your worship, married women show all their modesty the first day, because married men show all their love the first day.

[*Exeunt.*]

SCENE II—A *Bedchamber in* PINCHWIFE's *House.*

[PINCHWIFE *and* MRS. PINCHWIFE *discovered.*]

Pinchwife. Come, tell me, I say.

Mrs. Pinchwife. Lord! han't I told it a hundred times over?

Pinchwife [*aside*]. I would try, if in the repetition of the ungrateful tale, I could find her altering it in the least circumstance; for if her story be false, she is so too.—[*aloud*] Come, how was't, baggage?

Mrs. Pinchwife. Lord, what pleasure you take to hear it sure!

Pinchwife. No, you take more in telling it I find; but speak, how was't?

Mrs. Pinchwife. He carried me up into the house next to the Exchange.

Pinchwife. So, and you two were only in the room!

Mrs. Pinchwife. Yes, for he sent away a youth that was there, for some dried fruit, and China oranges.

Pinchwife. Did he so? Damn him for it—and for—

Mrs. Pinchwife. But presently came up the gentlewoman of the house.

Pinchwife. O, 'twas well she did; but what did he do whilst the fruit came?

Mrs. Pinchwife. He kissed me a hundred times, and told me he fancied he kissed my fine sister, meaning me, you know, whom he said he loved with all his soul, and bid me be sure to tell her so, and to desire her to be at her window, by eleven of the clock this morning, and he would walk under it at that time.

Pinchwife. And he was as good as his word, very punctual; a pox reward him for't. [*aside*]

Mrs. Pinchwife. Well, and he said if you were not within, he would come up to her, meaning me, you know, bud, still.

Pinchwife [*aside*]. So—he knew her certainly; but for this confession, I am obliged to her simplicity.—[*aloud*] But what, you stood very still when he kissed you?

Mrs. Pinchwife. Yes, I warrant you; would you have had me discover myself?

Pinchwife. But you told me he did some beastliness to you, as you call it; what was't?

Mrs. Pinchwife. Why, he put—

Pinchwife. What?

Mrs. Pinchwife. Why, he put the tip of his tongue between my lips, and so mousled me—and I said, I'd bite it.

Pinchwife. An eternal canker seize it, for a dog!

Mrs. Pinchwife. Nay, you need not be so angry with him neither, for to say truth, he has the sweetest breath I ever knew.

Pinchwife. The devil! you were satisfied with it then, and would do it again?

Mrs. Pinchwife. Not unless he should force me.

Pinchwife. Force you, changeling! I tell you, no woman can be forced.

Mrs. Pinchwife. Yes, but she may sure, by such a one as he, for he's a proper, goodly, strong man; 'tis hard, let me tell you, to resist him.

Pinchwife [*aside*]. So, 'tis plain she loves him, yet she has not love enough to make her conceal it from me; but the sight of him will increase her aversion for me and love for him; and that love instruct her how to deceive me and satisfy him, all idiot as she is. Love! 'twas he gave women first their craft, their art of deluding. Out of Nature's hands they came plain, open, silly, and fit for slaves, as she and Heaven intended 'em; but damned Love—well—I must strangle that little monster whilst I can deal with him.—[*aloud*] Go fetch pen, ink, and paper out of the next room.

Mrs. Pinchwife. Yes, bud. [*Exit.*]

Pinchwife. Why should women have more invention in love than men? It can only be, because they have more desires, more soliciting passions, more lust, and more of the devil. [*re-enter* MRS. PINCHWIFE] Come, minx, sit down and write.

Mrs. Pinchwife. Ay, dear bud, but I can't do't very well.

Pinchwife. I wish you could not at all.

Mrs. Pinchwife. But what should I write for?

Pinchwife. I'll have you write a letter to your lover.

Mrs. Pinchwife. O Lord, to the fine gentleman a letter!

Pinchwife. Yes, to the fine gentleman.

Mrs. Pinchwife. Lord, you do but jeer: sure you jest.

Pinchwife. I am not so merry: come, write as I bid you.

Mrs. Pinchwife. What, do you think I am a fool?

Pinchwife [*aside*]. She's afraid I would not dictate any love to him, therefore she's unwilling.—[*aloud*] But you had best begin.

Mrs. Pinchwife. Indeed, and indeed, but I won't, so I won't.

Pinchwife. Why?

Mrs. Pinchwife. Because he's in town; you may send for him if you will.

Pinchwife. Very well, you would have him brought to you; is it come to this? I say, take the pen and write, or you'll provoke me.

Mrs. Pinchwife. Lord, what d'ye make a fool of me for? Don't I know that letters are never writ but from the country to London, and from London into the country? Now he's in town, and I am in town too; therefore I can't write to him, you know.

Pinchwife [*aside*]. So, I am glad it is no worse; she is innocent enough yet.— [*aloud*] Yes, you may, when your husband bids you, write letters to people that are in town.

Mrs. Pinchwife. O, may I so? then I'm satisfied.

Pinchwife. Come, begin:—"Sir"—[*dictates*]

Mrs. Pinchwife. Shan't I say, "Dear Sir?"—You know one says always something more than bare "sir."

Pinchwife. Write as I bid you, or I will write whore with this penknife in your face.

Mrs. Pinchwife.   Nay, good bud—"Sir"—[*writes*]

Pinchwife.   "Though I suffered last night your nauseous, loathed kisses and embraces"—Write!

Mrs. Pinchwife.   Nay, why should I say so? You know I told you he had a sweet breath.

Pinchwife.   Write!

Mrs. Pinchwife.   Let me but put out "loathed."

Pinchwife.   Write, I say!

Mrs. Pinchwife.   Well then. [*writes*]

Pinchwife.   Let's see, what have you writ?—[*takes the paper and reads*] "Though I suffered last night your kisses and embraces"—Thou impudent creature! where is "nauseous" and "loathed?"

Mrs. Pinchwife.   I can't abide to write such filthy words.

Pinchwife.   Once more write as I'd have you, and question it not, or I will spoil thy writing with this. I will stab out those eyes that cause my mischief. [*holds up the penknife*]

Mrs. Pinchwife.   O Lord! I will.

Pinchwife.   So—so—let's see now.—[*reads*] "Though I suffered last night your nauseous, loathed kisses and embraces"—go on—"yet I would not have you presume that you shall ever repeat them"—so—[*She writes.*]

Mrs. Pinchwife.   I have writ it.

Pinchwife.   On, then—"I then concealed myself from your knowledge, to avoid your insolencies."—[*She writes.*]

Mrs. Pinchwife.   So—

Pinchwife.   "The same reason, now I am out of your hands—" [*She writes.*]

Mrs. Pinchwife.   So—

Pinchwife.   "Makes me own to you my unfortunate, though innocent frolic, of being in man's clothes"—[*She writes.*]

Mrs. Pinchwife.   So—

Pinchwife.   "That you may for evermore cease to pursue her, who hates and detests you"—[*She writes on.*]

Mrs. Pinchwife.   So—heigh! [*sighs*]

Pinchwife.   What, do you sigh?—"detests you—as much as she loves her husband and her honour—"

Mrs. Pinchwife.   I vow, husband, he'll ne'er believe I should write such a letter.

Pinchwife.   What, he'd expect a kinder from you? Come, now your name only.

Mrs. Pinchwife.   What, shan't I say "Your most faithful humble servant till death?"

Pinchwife.   No, tormenting fiend!—[*aside*] Her style, I find, would be very soft.—[*aloud*] Come, wrap it up now, whilst I go fetch wax and a candle; and write on the backside, "For Mr. Horner." [*Exit.*]

Mrs. Pinchwife.   "For Mr. Horner."—So, I am glad he has told me his name. Dear Mr. Horner! but why should I send thee such a letter that will vex thee, and make thee angry with me?—Well, I will not send it.—Ay, but then my husband will kill me—for I see plainly he won't let me love Mr. Horner—but what care I for my husband?—I won't, so I won't, send poor Mr. Horner such a letter—But then my husband—but oh, what if I writ at bottom my husband made me write it?—Ay, but then my husband would see't—Can one have no shift? ah, a London woman would have had a hundred presently. Stay—what if I should write a letter, and wrap it up like this, and write upon't too? Ay, but then my husband would see't—I don't know what to do.—But yet evads I'll try, so I will—for I will not send this letter to poor Mr. Horner, come what will on't.

"Dear, sweet Mr. Horner"—[*writes and repeats what she writes*]—so—"my husband would have me send you a base, rude, unmannerly letter; but I won't"—so—"and would have me forbid you loving me; but I won't"—so— "and would have me say to you, I hate you, poor Mr. Horner; but I won't tell a lie for him"—there—"for I'm sure if you and I were in the country at cards together"—so—"I could not help treading on your toe under the table"—so— "or rubbing knees with you, and staring in your face, till you saw me"—very well—"and then looking down, and blushing for an hour together"—so—"but I must make haste before my husband comes: and now he has taught me to write letters, you shall have longer ones from me, who am, dear, dear, poor, dear Mr. Horner, your most humble friend, and servant to command till death,— Margery Pinchwife."

Stay, I must give him a hint at bottom—so—now wrap it up just like t'other—so—now write "For Mr. Horner"—But oh now, what shall I do with it? for here comes my husband.

[*Re-enter* PINCHWIFE.]

Pinchwife [*aside*].   I have been detained by a sparkish coxcomb, who pretended a visit to me; but I fear 'twas to my wife—[*aloud*] What, have you done?
Mrs. Pinchwife.   Ay, ay, bud, just now.
Pinchwife.   Let's see't: what d'ye tremble for? what, you would not have it go?
Mrs. Pinchwife.   Here—[*aside*] No, I must not give him that: so I had been served if I had given him this.

[*He opens and reads the first letter.*]

Pinchwife.   Come, where's the wax and seal?
Mrs. Pinchwife [*aside*].   Lord, what shall I do now? Nay, then I have it—[*aloud*] Pray let me see't. Lord, you think me so arrant a fool, I cannot seal a letter; I will do't, so I will. [*snatches the letter from him, changes it for the other, seals it, and delivers it to him*]
Pinchwife.   Nay, I believe you will learn that, and other things too, which I would not have you.
Mrs. Pinchwife.   So, han't I done it curiously?—[*aside*] I think I have; there's my letter going to Mr. Horner, since he'll needs have me send letters to folks.
Pinchwife.   'Tis very well; but I warrant, you would not have it go now?
Mrs. Pinchwife.   Yes, indeed, but I would, bud, now.
Pinchwife.   Well, you are a good girl then. Come, let me lock you up in your chamber, till I come back; and be sure you come not within three strides of the window when I am gone, for I have a spy in the street.—[*Exit* MRS. PINCHWIFE, PINCHWIFE *locks the door.*] At least, 'tis fit she think so. If we do not cheat women, they'll cheat us, and fraud may be justly used with secret enemies, of which a wife is the most dangerous; and he that has a handsome one to keep, and a frontier town, must provide against treachery, rather than open force.

Now I have secured all within, I'll deal with the foe without, with false intelligence. [*Holds up the letter. Exit.*]

[*Enter* HORNER *and* QUACK.]

Quack.   Well, sir, how fadges the new design? have you not the luck of all your brother projectors, to deceive only yourself at last?

Horner.   No, good domine doctor, I deceive you, it seems, and others too; for the grave matrons, and old, rigid husbands think me as unfit for love, as they are; but their wives, sisters, and daughters know, some of 'em, better things already.

Quack.   Already!

Horner.   Already, I say. Last night I was drunk with half-a-dozen of your civil persons, as you call 'em, and people of honour, and so was made free of their society and dressing-rooms for ever hereafter; and am already come to the privileges of sleeping upon their pallets, warming smocks, tying shoes and garters, and the like, doctor, already, already, doctor.

Quack.   You have made good use of your time, sir.

Horner.   I tell thee, I am now no more interruption to 'em, when they sing, or talk bawdy, than a little squab French page who speaks no English.

Quack.   But do civil persons and women of honour drink, and sing bawdy songs?

Horner.   O, amongst friends, amongst friends. For your bigots in honour are just like those in religion; they fear the eye of the world more than the eye of Heaven; and think there is no virtue, but railing at vice, and no sin, but giving scandal. They rail at a poor, little, kept player, and keep themselves some young, modest pulpit comedian to be privy to their sins in their closets, not to tell 'em of them in their chapels.

Quack.   Nay, the truth on't is, priests, amongst the women now, have quite got the better of us lay-confessors, physicians.

Horner.   And they are rather their patients; but—

[*Enter* LADY FIDGET, *looking about her.*]

Now we talk of women of honour, here comes one. Step behind the screen there, and but observe, if I have not particular privileges with the women of reputation already, doctor, already.

[QUACK *retires.*]

Lady Fidget.   Well, Horner, am not I a woman of honour? you see, I'm as good as my word.

Horner.   And you shall see, madam, I'll not be behindhand with you in honour; and I'll be as good as my word too, if you please but to withdraw into the next room.

Lady Fidget.   But first, my dear sir, you must promise to have a care of my dear honour.

Horner.   If you talk a word more of your honour, you'll make me incapable to wrong it. To talk of honour in the mysteries of love, is like talking of Heaven or the Deity, in an operation of witchcraft, just when you are employing the devil: it makes the charm impotent.

Lady Fidget. Nay, fy! let us not be smutty. But you talk of mysteries and bewitching to me; I don't understand you.

Horner. I tell you, madam, the word money is a mistress's mouth, at such a nick of time, is not a more disheartening sound to a younger brother, than that of honour to an eager lover like myself.

Lady Fidget. But you can't blame a lady of my reputation to be chary.

Horner. Chary! I have been chary of it already, by the report I have caused of myself.

Lady Fidget. Ay, but if you should ever let other women know that dear secret, it would come out. Nay, you must have a great care of your conduct; for my acquaintance are so censorious, (oh, 'tis a wicked, censorious world, Mr. Horner!) I say, are so censorious, and detracting, that perhaps they'll talk to the prejudice of my honour, though you should not let them know the dear secret.

Horner. Nay, madam, rather than they shall prejudice your honour, I'll prejudice theirs; and, to serve you, I'll lie with 'em all, make the secret their own, and then they'll keep it. I am a Machiavel in love, madam.

Lady Fidget. O, no sir, not that way.

Horner. Nay, the devil take me, if censorious women are to be silenced any other way.

Lady Fidget. A secret is better kept, I hope, by a single person than a multitude; therefore pray do not trust anybody else with it, dear, dear Mr. Horner. [*embracing him*]

[*Enter* SIR JASPER FIDGET.]

Sir Jasper. How now!

Lady Fidget [*aside*]. O my husband!—prevented—and what's almost as bad, found with my arms about another man—that will appear too much—what shall I say?—[*aloud*] Sir Jasper, come hither: I am trying if Mr. Horner were ticklish, and he's as ticklish as can be. I love to torment the confounded toad; let you and I tickle him.

Sir Jasper. No, your ladyship will tickle him better without me, I suppose. But is this your buying china? I thought you had been at the china-house.

Horner [*aside*]. China-house! that's my cue, I must take it.—[*aloud*] A pox! can't you keep your impertinent wives at home? Some men are troubled with the husbands, but I with the wives; but I'd have you to know, since I cannot be your journeyman by night, I will not be your drudge by day, to squire your wife about, and be your man of straw, or scarecrow only to pies and jays, that would be nibbling at your forbidden fruit; I shall be shortly the hackney gentleman-usher of the town.

Sir Jasper [*aside*]. He! he! he! poor fellow, he's in the right on't, faith. To squire women about for other folks is as ungrateful an employment, as to tell money for other folks.—[*aloud*] He! he! he! be'n't angry, Horner.

Lady Fidget. No, 'tis I have more reason to be angry, who am left by you, to go abroad indecently alone; or, what is more indecent, to pin myself upon such ill-bred people of your acquaintance as this is.

Sir Jasper. Nay, prithee, what has he done?

Lady Fidget. Nay, he has done nothing.

Sir Jasper. But what d'ye take ill, if he has done nothing?

Lady Fidget. Ha! ha! ha! faith, I can't but laugh however; why, d'ye think the unmannerly toad would come down to me to the coach? I was fain to come up to fetch him, or go without him, which I was resolved not to do; for he knows china very well, and has himself very good, but will not let me see it, lest I should beg some; but I will find it out, and have what I came for yet.

Horner [*apart to* LADY FIDGET, *as he follows her to the door*] Lock the door, madam.—[*Exit* LADY FIDGET, *and locks the door.*]—[*aloud*] So, she has got into my chamber and locked me out. Oh the impertinency of woman-kind! Well, Sir Jasper, plain-dealing is a jewel; if ever you suffer your wife to trouble me again here, she shall carry you home a pair of horns; by my lord mayor she shall; though I cannot furnish you myself, you are sure, yet I'll find a way.

Sir Jasper. Ha! ha! he!—[*aside*] At my first coming in, and finding her arms about him, tickling him it seems, I was half jealous, but now I see my folly.— [*aloud*] He! he! he! poor Horner.

Horner. Nay, though you laugh now, 'twill be my turn ere long. Oh women, more impertinent, more cunning, and more mischievous than their monkeys, and to me almost as ugly!—Now is she throwing my things about and rifling all I have; but I'll get into her the back way, and so rifle her for it.

Sir Jasper. Ha! ha! ha! poor angry Horner.

Horner. Stay here a little, I'll ferret her out to you presently, I warrant. [*Exit at the other door.*]

[SIR JASPER *talks through the door to his wife, she answers from within.*]

Sir Jasper. Wife! my Lady Fidget! wife! he is coming in to you the back way.

Lady Fidget. Let him come, and welcome, which way he will.

Sir Jasper. He'll catch you, and use you roughly, and be too strong for you.

Lady Fidget. Don't you trouble yourself, let him if he can.

Quack [*aside*]. This indeed I could not have believed from him, nor any but my own eyes.

[*Enter* MRS. SQUEAMISH.]

Mrs. Squeamish. Where's this woman-hater, this toad, this ugly, greasy, dirty sloven?

Sir Jasper [*aside*]. So, the women all have him ugly: methinks he is a comely person, but his wants make his form contemptible to 'em; and 'tis e'en as my wife said yesterday, talking of him, that a proper handsome eunuch was as ridiculous a thing as a gigantic coward.

Mrs. Squeamish. Sir Jasper, your servant: where is the odious beast?

Sir Jasper. He's within in his chamber, with my wife; she's playing the wag with him.

Mrs. Squeamish. Is she so? and he's a clownish beast, he'll give her no quarter, he'll play the wag with her again, let me tell you: come, let's go help her—What, the door's locked?

Sir Jasper. Ay, my wife locked it.

Mrs. Squeamish. Did she so? let's break it open then.

Sir Jasper. No, no, he'll do her no hurt.

Mrs. Squeamish [*aside*]. But is there no other way to get in to 'em? whither goes this? I will disturb 'em. [*Exit at another door.*]

[*Enter* OLD LADY SQUEAMISH.]

Lady Squeamish. Where is this harlotry, this impudent baggage, this rambling tomrigg?[1] O Sir Jasper, I'm glad to see you here; did you not see my vile grandchild come in hither just now?

Sir Jasper. Yes.

Lady Squeamish. Ay, but where is she then? where is she? Lord, Sir Jasper, I have e'en rattled myself to pieces in pursuit of her: but can you tell what she makes here? they say below, no woman lodges here.

Sir Jasper. No.

Lady Squeamish. No! what does she here then? say, if it be not a woman's lodging, what makes she here? But are you sure no woman lodges here?

Sir Jasper. No, nor no man neither, this is Mr. Horner's lodging.

Lady Squeamish. Is it so, are you sure?

Sir Jasper. Yes, yes.

Lady Squeamish. So; then there's no hurt in't, I hope. But where is he?

Sir Jasper. He's in the next room with my wife.

Lady Squeamish. Nay, if you trust him with your wife, I may with my Biddy. They say, he's a merry harmless man now, e'en as harmless a man as ever came out of Italy with a good voice[2] and as pretty, harmless company for a lady, as a snake without his teeth.

Sir Jasper. Ay, ay, poor man.

[*Re-enter* MRS. SQUEAMISH.]

Mrs. Squeamish. I can't find 'em.—Oh, are you here, grandmother? I followed, you must know, my Lady Fidget hither; 'tis the prettiest lodging, and I have been staring on the prettiest pictures—

[*Re-enter* LADY FIDGET *with a piece of china in her hand, and* HORNER *following.*]

Lady Fidget. And I have been toiling and moiling for the prettiest piece of china, my dear.

Horner. Nay, she has been too hard for me, do what I could.

Mrs. Squeamish. Oh, Lord, I'll have some china too. Good Mr. Horner, don't think to give other people china and me none; come in with me too.

Horner. Upon my honour, I have none left now.

Mrs. Squeamish. Nay, nay, I have known you deny your china before now, but you shan't put me off so. Come.

Horner. This lady had the last there.

Lady Fidget. Yes indeed, madam, to my certain knowledge, he has no more left.

Mrs. Squeamish. O, but it may be he may have some you could not find.

---

1 Tomboy.
2 *I.e.,* a eunuch.

Lady Fidget.   What, d'ye think if he had had any left, I would not have had it too? for we women of quality never think we have china enough.

Horner.   Do not take it ill, I cannot make china for you all, but I will have a roll-waggon for you too, another time.

Mrs. Squeamish.   Thank you, dear toad.

Lady Fidget.   What do you mean by that promise? [*aside to* HORNER]

Horner.   Alas, she has an innocent, literal understanding. [*aside to* LADY FIDGET]

Lady Squeamish.   Poor Mr. Horner! he has enough to do to please you all, I see.

Horner.   Ay, madam, you see how they use me.

Lady Squeamish.   Poor gentleman, I pity you.

Horner.   I thank you, madam: I could never find pity, but from such reverend ladies as you are; the young ones will never spare a man.

Mrs. Squeamish.   Come, come, beast, and go dine with us; for we shall want a man at ombre after dinner.

Horner.   That's all their use of me, madam, you see.

Mrs. Squeamish.   Come, sloven, I'll lead you, to be sure of you. [*pulls him by the cravat*]

Lady Squeamish.   Alas, poor man, how she tugs him! Kiss, kiss her; that's the way to make such nice women quiet.

Horner.   No, madam, that remedy is worse than the torment; they know I dare suffer anything rather than do it.

Lady Squeamish.   Prithee kiss her, and I'll give you her picture in little, that you admired so last night; prithee do.

Horner.   Well, nothing but that could bribe me: I love a woman only in effigy, and good painting as much as I hate them.—I'll do't, for I could adore the devil well painted. [*kisses* MRS. SQUEAMISH]

Mrs. Squeamish.   Foh, you filthy toad! nay, now I've done jesting.

Lady Squeamish.   Ha! ha! ha! I told you so.

Mrs. Squeamish.   Foh! a kiss of his—

Sir Jasper.   Has no more hurt in't than one of my spaniel's.

Mrs. Squeamish.   Nor no more good neither.

Quack.   I will now believe anything he tells me. [*aside*]

[*Enter* PINCHWIFE.]

Lady Fidget.   O lord, here's a man! Sir Jasper, my mask, my mask! I would not be seen here for the world.

Sir Jasper.   What, not when I am with you?

Lady Fidget.   No, no, my honour—let's be gone.

Mrs. Squeamish.   Oh grandmother, let's be gone; make haste, make haste, I know not how he may censure us.

Lady Fidget.   Be found in the lodging of anything like a man!—Away.

[*Exeunt* SIR JASPER FIDGET, LADY FIDGET, OLD LADY SQUEAMISH, *and* MRS. SQUEAMISH.]

Quack.   What's here? another cuckold? he looks like one, and none else sure have any business with him. [*aside*]

Horner. Well, what brings my dear friend hither?

Pinchwife. Your impertinency.

Horner. My impertinency!—why, you gentlemen that have got handsome wives, think you have a privilege of saying anything to your friends, and are as brutish as if you were our creditors.

Pinchwife. No, sir, I'll ne'er trust you any way.

Horner. But why not, dear Jack? why diffide[1] in me thou know'st so well?

Pinchwife. Because I do know you so well.

Horner. Han't I been always thy friend, honest Jack, always ready to serve thee, in love or battle, before thou wert married, and am so still?

Pinchwife. I believe so, you would be my second now, indeed.

Horner. Well then, dear Jack, why so unkind, so grum, so strange to me? Come, prithee kiss me, dear rogue: gad I was always, I say, and am still as much thy servant as—

Pinchwife. As I am yours, sir. What, you would send a kiss to my wife, is that it?

Horner. So, there 'tis—a man can't show his friendship to a married man, but presently he talks of his wife to you. Prithee, let thy wife alone, and let thee and I be all one, as we were wont. What, thou art as shy of my kindness, as a Lombard-street alderman of a courtier's civility at Locket's!

Pinchwife. But you are over-kind to me, as kind as if I were your cuckold already; yet I must confess you ought to be kind and civil to me, since I am so kind, so civil to you, as to bring you this: look you there, sir. [*delivers him a letter*]

Horner. What is't?

Pinchwife. Only a love-letter, sir.

Horner. From whom?—how! this is from your wife—hum—and hum—[*reads*]

Pinchwife. Even from my wife, sir: am I not wondrous kind and civil to you now too?—[*aside*] But you'll not think her so.

Horner. Ha! is this a trick of his or hers? [*aside*]

Pinchwife. The gentleman's surprised I find.—What, you expected a kinder letter?

Horner. No faith, not I, how could I?

Pinchwife. Yes, yes, I'm sure you did. A man so well made as you are, must needs be disappointed, if the women declare not their passion at first sight or opportunity.

Horner [*aside*]. But what should this mean? Stay, the postscript—[*reads aside*] "Be sure you love me, whatsoever my husband says to the contrary, and let him not see this, lest he should come home and pinch me, or kill my squirrel."—It seems he knows not what the letter contains.

Pinchwife. Come, ne'er wonder at it so much.

Horner. Faith, I can't help it.

Pinchwife. Now, I think I have deserved your infinite friendship and kindness, and have showed myself sufficiently an obliging kind friend and husband; am I not so, to bring a letter from my wife to her gallant?

Horner. Ay, the devil take me, art thou, the most obliging, kind friend and husband in the world, ha! ha!

---

[1] Distrust.

Pinchwife. Well, you may be merry, sir; but in short I must tell you, sir, my honour will suffer no jesting.

Horner. What dost thou mean?

Pinchwife. Does the letter want a comment? Then, know, sir, though I have been so civil a husband, as to bring you a letter from my wife, to let you kiss and court her to my face, I will not be a cuckold, sir, I will not.

Horner. Thou art mad with jealousy. I never saw thy wife in my life but at the play yesterday, and I know not if it were she or no. I court her, kiss her!

Pinchwife. I will not be a cuckold, I say; there will be danger in making me a cuckold.

Horner. Why, wert thou not well cured of thy last clap?

Pinchwife. I wear a sword.

Horner. It should be taken from thee, lest thou shouldst do thyself a mischief with it; thou art mad, man.

Pinchwife. As mad as I am, and as merry as you are, I must have more reason from you ere we part. I say again, though you kissed and courted last night my wife in man's clothes, as she confesses in her letter—

Horner. Ha! [*aside*]

Pinchwife. Both she and I say, you must not design it again, for you have mistaken your woman, as you have done your man.

Horner [*aside*]. O—I understand something now—[*aloud*] Was that thy wife! Why wouldst thou not tell me 'twas she? Faith, my freedom with her was your fault, not mine.

Pinchwife. Faith, so 'twas. [*aside*]

Horner. Fy! I'd never do't to a woman before her husband's face, sure.

Pinchwife. But I had rather you should do't to my wife before my face, than behind my back; and that you shall never do.

Horner. No—you will hinder me.

Pinchwife. If I would not hinder you, you see by her letter she would.

Horner. Well, I must e'en acquiesce then, and be contented with what she writes.

Pinchwife. I'll assure you 'twas voluntarily writ; I had no hand in't you may believe me.

Horner. I do believe thee, faith.

Pinchwife. And believe her too, for she's an innocent creature, has no dissembling in her: and so fare you well, sir.

Horner. Pray, however, present my humble service to her, and tell her, I will obey her letter to a tittle, and fulfil her desires, be what they will, or with what difficulty soever I do't; and you shall be no more jealous of me, I warrant her, and you.

Pinchwife. Well then, fare you well; and play with any man's honour but mine, kiss any man's wife but mine, and welcome. [*Exit.*]

Horner. Ha! ha! ha! doctor.

Quack. It seems, he has not heard the report of you, or does not believe it.

Horner. Ha! ha!—now, doctor, what think you?

Quack. Pray let's see the letter—hum—"for—dear—love you—" [*reads the letter*]

Horner. I wonder how she could contrive it! What say'st thou to't? 'tis an original.

Quack. So are your cuckolds too originals: for they are like no other common cuckolds, and I will henceforth believe it not impossible for you to cuckold the Grand Signior amidst his guards of eunuchs, that I say.

Horner. And I say for the letter, 'tis the first love-letter that ever was without flames, darts, fates, destinies, lying and dissembling in't.

[*Enter* SPARKISH *pulling in* PINCHWIFE.]

Sparkish. Come back, you are a pretty brother-in-law, neither go to church nor to dinner with your sister bride!

Pinchwife. My sister denies her marriage, and you see is gone away from you dissatisfied.

Sparkish. Pshaw! upon a foolish scruple, that our parson was not in lawful orders, and did not say all the common-prayer; but 'tis her modesty only I believe. But let all women be never so modest the first day, they'll be sure to come to themselves by night, and I shall have enough of her then. In the mean time, Harry Horner, you must dine with me: I keep my wedding at my aunt's in the Piazza.

Horner. Thy wedding! what stale maid has lived to despair of a husband, or what young one of a gallant?

Sparkish. O, your servant, sir—this gentleman's sister then,—no stale maid.

Horner. I'm sorry for't.

Pinchwife. How comes he so concerned for her? [*aside*]

Sparkish. You sorry for't? why, do you know any ill by her?

Horner. No, I know none but by thee; 'tis for her sake, not yours, and another man's sake that might have hoped, I thought.

Sparkish. Another man! another man! what is his name?

Horner. Nay, since 'tis past, he shall be nameless.—[*aside*] Poor Harcourt! I am sorry thou hast missed her.

Pinchwife. He seems to be much troubled at the match. [*aside*]

Sparkish. Prithee, tell me—Nay, you shan't go, brother.

Pinchwife. I must of necessity, but I'll come to you to dinner. [*Exit.*]

Sparkish. But, Harry, what, have I a rival in my wife already? But with all my heart, for he may be of use to me hereafter; for though my hunger is now my sauce, and I can fall on heartily without, the time will come, when a rival will be as good sauce for a married man to a wife, as an orange to veal.

Horner. O thou damned rogue! thou hast set my teeth on edge with thy orange.

Sparkish. Then let's to dinner—there I was with you again. Come.

Horner. But who dines with thee?

Sparkish. My friends and relations, my brother Pinchwife, you see, of your acquaintance.

Horner. And his wife?

Sparkish. No, 'gad, he'll ne'er let her come amongst us good fellows; your stingy country coxcomb keeps his wife from his friends, as he does his little firkin of ale, for his own drinking, and a gentleman can't get a smack on't; but his servants, when his back is turned, broach it at their pleasures, and dust it away, ha! ha! ha!—'Gad, I am witty, I think, considering I was married to-day, by the world; but come—

Horner. No, I will not dine with you, unless you can fetch her too.

Sparkish. Pshaw! what pleasure canst thou have with women now, Harry?

Horner.   My eyes are not gone; I love a good prospect yet, and will not dine with you unless she does too; go fetch her, therefore, but do not tell her husband 'tis for my sake.

Sparkish.   Well, I'll go try what I can do; in the meantime, come away to my aunt's lodging, 'tis in the way to Pinchwife's.

Horner.   The poor woman has called for aid, and stretched forth her hand, doctor; I cannot but help her over the pale out of the briars.

[*Exeunt.*]

SCENE IV—A *Room in* PINCHWIFE'S *House.*

[MRS. PINCHWIFE *alone, leaning on her elbow.—A table, pen, ink and paper.*]

Mrs. Pinchwife.   Well, 'tis e'en so, I have got the London disease they call love; I am sick of my husband, and for my gallant. I have heard this distemper called a fever, but methinks 'tis like an ague; for when I think of my husband, I tremble, and am in a cold sweat, and have inclinations to vomit; but when I think of my gallant, dear Mr. Horner, my hot fit comes, and I am all in a fever indeed; and, as in other fevers, my own chamber is tedious to me, and I would fain be removed to his, and then methinks I should be well. Ah, poor Mr. Horner! Well, I cannot, will not stay here; therefore I'll make an end of my letter to him, which shall be a finer letter than my last, because I have studied it like anything. Oh sick, sick! [*takes the pen and writes*]

[*Enter* PINCHWIFE, *who seeing her writing, steals softly behind her and looking over her shoulder, snatches the paper from her.*]

Pinchwife.   What, writing more letters?
Mrs. Pinchwife.   O Lord, bud, why d'ye fright me so?

[*She offers to run out; he stops her, and reads.*]

Pinchwife.   How's this? nay, you shall not stir, madam:—"Dear, dear, dear Mr. Horner"—very well—I have taught you to write letters to good purpose—but let us see't. "First, I am to beg your pardon for my boldness in writing to you, which I'd have you to know I would not have done, had not you said first you loved me so extremely, which if you do, you will never suffer me to lie in the arms of another man whom I loathe, nauseate, and detest."—Now you can write these filthy words. But what follows?—"Therefore, I hope you will speedily find some way to free me from this unfortunate match, which was never, I assure you, of my choice, but I'm afraid 'tis already too far gone; however, if you love me, as I do you, you will try what you can do; but you must help me away before to-morrow, or else, alas! I shall be for ever out of your reach, for I can defer no longer our—our—" what is to follow "our"?—speak, what—our journey into the country I suppose—Oh woman, damned woman! and Love, damned Love, their old tempter! for this is one of his miracles; in a moment he can make those blind that could see, and those see that were blind, those dumb that could speak, and those prattle who were dumb before; nay, what is more than all, make these dough-baked, senseless, indocile animals, women, too hard

tor us their politic lords and rulers, in a moment. But make an end of your
letter, and then I'll make an end of you thus, and all my plagues together.
[*draws his sword*]

Mrs. Pinchwife.   O Lord, O Lord, you are such a passionate man, bud!

[*Enter* SPARKISH.]

Sparkish.   How now, what's here to do?

Pinchwife.   This fool here now!

Sparkish.   What! drawn upon your wife? You should never do that, but at night
in the dark, when you can't hurt her. This is my sister-in-law, is it not? ay, faith,
e'en our country Margery; [*pulls aside her handkerchief*] one may know her.
Come, she and you must go dine with me; dinner's ready, come. But where's my
wife? is she not come home yet? where is she?

Pinchwife.   Making you a cuckold; 'tis that they all do, as soon as they can.

Sparkish.   What, the wedding-day? no, a wife that designs to make a cully of her
husband will be sure to let him win the first stake of love, by the world. But
come, they stay dinner for us: come, I'll lead down our Margery.

Pinchwife.   No—sir, go, we'll follow you.

Sparkish.   I will not wag without you.

Pinchwife.   This coxcomb is a sensible torment to me amidst the greatest in the
world. [*aside*]

Sparkish.   Come, come, Madam Margery.

Pinchwife.   No; I'll lead her my way: what, would you treat your friends with
mine, for want of your own wife?—[*leads her to the other door, and locks her
in and returns*] I am contented my rage should take breath—[*aside*]

Sparkish.   I told Horner this.

Pinchwife.   Come now.

Sparkish.   Lord, how shy you are of your wife! but let me tell you, brother, we
men of wit have amongst us a saying, that cuckolding, like the small-pox, comes
with a fear; and you may keep your wife as much as you will out of danger of
infection, but if her constitution incline her to't, she'll have it sooner or later, by
the world, say they.

Pinchwife [*aside*].   What a thing is a cuckold, that every fool can make him
ridiculous!—[*aloud*] Well, sir—but let me advise you, now you are come to be
concerned, because you suspect the danger, not to neglect the means to prevent
it, especially when the greatest share of the malady will light upon your own
head, for

　　Hows'e'er the kind wife's belly comes to swell,
　　The husband breeds for her, and first is ill.

[*Exeunt.*]

Act V

SCENE I—PINCHWIFE'S *House.*

[*Enter* PINCHWIFE *and* MRS. PINCHWIFE. *A table and candle.*]

Pinchwife. Come, take the pen and make an end of the letter, just as you intended; if you are false in a tittle, I shall soon perceive it, and punish you as you deserve.—[*lays his hand on his sword*] Write what was to follow—let's see—"You must make haste, and help me away before to-morrow, or else I shall be for ever out of your reach, for I can defer no longer our"—What follows "our"?

Mrs. Pinchwife. Must all out, then, bud?—Look you there, then.

[MRS. PINCHWIFE *takes the pen and writes.*]

Pinchwife. Let's see—"For I can defer no longer our—wedding—Your slighted Alithea."—What's the meaning of this? my sister's name to't? speak, unriddle.

Mrs. Pinchwife. Yes, indeed, bud.

Pinchwife. But why her name to't? speak—speak, I say.

Mrs. Pinchwife. Ay, but you'll tell her then again. If you would not tell her again—

Pinchwife. I will not:—I am stunned, my head turns round. Speak.

Mrs. Pinchwife. Won't— you tell her, indeed, and indeed?

Pinchwife. No; speak, I say.

Mrs. Pinchwife. She'll be angry with me; but I had rather she should be angry with me than you, bud; And, to tell you the truth, 'twas she made me write the letter, and taught me what I should write.

Pinchwife [*aside*]. Ha!—I thought the style was somewhat better than her own.—[*aloud*] Could she come to you to teach you, since I had locked you up alone?

Mrs. Pinchwife. O, through the key-hole, bud.

Pinchwife. But why should she make you write a letter for her to him, since she can write herself?

Mrs. Pinchwife. Why, she said because—for I was unwilling to do it—

Pinchwife. Because what—because?

Mrs. Pinchwife. Because, lest Mr. Horner should be cruel, and refuse her; or be vain afterwards, and show the letter, she might disown it, the hand not being hers.

Pinchwife [*aside*]. How's this? Ha!—then I think I shall come to myself again.—This changeling could not invent this lie: but if she could, why should she? she might think I should soon discover it.—Stay—now I think on't too, Horner said he was sorry she had married Sparkish; and her disowning her marriage to me makes me think she has evaded it for Horner's sake: yet why should she take this course? But men in love are fools; women may well be so—[*aloud*] But hark you, madam, your sister went out in the morning, and I have not seen her within since.

Mrs. Pinchwife. Alack-a-day, she has been crying all day above, it seems, in a corner.

Pinchwife. Where is she? let me speak with her.

Mrs. Pinchwife [*aside*]. O Lord, then she'll discover all!—[*aloud*] Pray hold, bud; what, d'ye mean to discover me? she'll know I have told you then. Pray, bud, let me talk with her first.

Pinchwife. I must speak with her, to know whether Horner ever made her any promise, and whether she be married to Sparkish or no.

Mrs. Pinchwife. Pray, dear bud, don't, till I have spoken with her, and told her that I have told you all; for she'll kill me else.

Pinchwife. Go then, and bid her come out to me.

Mrs. Pinchwife. Yes, yes, bud.

Pinchwife. Let me see—[*pausing*]

Mrs. Pinchwife [*aside*]. I'll go, but she is not within to come to him: I have just got time to know of Lucy her maid, who first set me on work, what lie I shall tell next; for I am e'en at my wit 's end. [*Exit.*]

Pinchwife. Well, I resolve it, Horner shall have her: I'd rather give him my sister than lend him my wife; and such an alliance will prevent his pretensions to my wife, sure. I'll make him of kin to her, and then he won't care for her.

[*Re-enter* MRS. PINCHWIFE.]

Mrs. Pinchwife. O Lord, bud! I told you what anger you would make me with my sister.

Pinchwife. Won't she come hither?

Mrs. Pinchwife. No, no. Lack-a-day, she's ashamed to look you in the face: and she says, if you go in to her, she'll run away down stairs, and shamefully go herself to Mr. Horner, who has promised her marriage, she says; and she will have no other, so she won't.

Pinchwife. Did he so?—promise her marriage!—then she shall have no other. Go tell her so; and if she will come and discourse with me a little concerning the means, I will about it immediately. Go.—[*Exit* MRS. PINCHWIFE.] His estate is equal to Sparkish's, and his extraction as much better than his, as his parts are; but my chief reason is, I'd rather be akin to him by the name of brother-in-law than that of cuckold. [*Re-enter* MRS. PINCHWIFE.] Well, what says she now?

Mrs. Pinchwife. Why, she says, she would only have you lead her to Horner's lodging; with whom she first will discourse the matter before she talks with you, which yet she cannot do; for alack, poor creature, she says she can't so much as look you in the face, therefore she'll come to you in a mask. And you must excuse her, if she make you no answer to any question of yours, till you have brought her to Mr. Horner; and if you will not chide her, nor question her, she'll come out to you immediately.

Pinchwife. Let her come: I will not speak a word to her, nor require a word from her.

Mrs. Pinchwife. Oh, I forgot: besides she says, she cannot look you in the face, though through a mask; therefore would desire you to put out the candle.

Pinchwife. I agree to all. Let her make haste.—There, 'tis out—[*Puts out the candle. Exit* MRS. PINCHWIFE.] My case is something better: I'd rather fight with Horner for not lying with my sister, than for lying with my wife; and of the two, I had rather find my sister too forward than my wife. I expected no other from her free education, as she calls it, and her passion for the town. Well, wife and sister are names which make us expect love and duty, pleasure and comfort; but we find 'em plagues and torments, and are equally, though differently, troublesome to their keeper; for we have as much ado to get people to lie with our sisters as to keep 'em from lying with our wives.

[*Re-enter* MRS. PINCHWIFE *masked, and in hoods and scarfs, and a dressing-gown and petticoat of* ALITHEA's.]

What, are you come, sister? let us go then—But first, let me lock up my wife.
Mrs. Margery, where are you?

Mrs. Pinchwife.   Here, bud.

Pinchwife.   Come hither, that I may lock you up: get you in.—[*locks the door*]
Come, sister, where are you now?

[MRS. PINCHWIFE *gives him her hand; but when he lets her go, she steals softly
on to the other side of him, and is led away by him for his sister,* ALITHEA.]

SCENE II—HORNER'S *Lodging.*

[HORNER *and* QUACK.]

Quack.   What, all alone? not so much as one of your cuckolds here, nor one of
their wives! They use to take their turn with you, as if they were to watch you.

Horner.   Yes, it often happens that a cuckold is but his wife's spy, and is more
upon family duty when he is with her gallant abroad, hindering his pleasure,
than when he is at home with her playing the gallant. But the hardest duty a
married woman imposes upon a lover is keeping her husband company always.

Quack.   And his fondness wearies you almost as soon as hers.

Horner.   A pox! keeping a cuckold company, after you have had his wife, is as
tiresome as the company of a country squire to a witty fellow of the town, when
he has got all his money.

Quack.   And as at first a man makes a friend of the husband to get the wife, so at
last you are fain to fall out with the wife to be rid of the husband.

Horner.   Ay, most cuckold-makers are true courtiers; when once a poor man has
cracked his credit for 'em, they can't abide to come near him.

Quack.   But at first, to draw him in, are so sweet, so kind, so dear! just as you are
to Pinchwife. But what becomes of that intrigue with his wife?

Horner.   A pox! he's as surly as an alderman that has been bit; and since he's so
coy, his wife's kindness is in vain, for she's a silly innocent.

Quack.   Did she not send you a letter by him?

Horner.   Yes; but that's a riddle I have not yet solved. Allow the poor creature to
be willing, she is silly too, and he keeps her up so close—

Quack.   Yes, so close, that he makes her but the more willing, and adds but
revenge to her love; which two, when met, seldom fail of satisfying each other
one way or other.

Horner.   What! here's the man we are talking of, I think.

[*Enter* PINCHWIFE, *leading in his wife masked, muffled, and in her sister's
gown.*]

Pshaw!

Quack.   Bringing his wife to you is the next thing to bringing a loveletter from
her.

Horner.   What means this?

Pinchwife.   The last time, you know, sir, I brought you a loveletter; now, you see,
a mistress; I think you'll say I am a civil man to you.

Horner.   Ay, the devil take me, will I say thou art the civilest man I ever met with; and I have known some. I fancy I understand thee now better than I did the letter. But, hark thee, in they ear—

Pinchwife. What?

Horner. Nothing but the usual question, man: is she sound, on thy word?

Pinchwife. What, you take her for a wench, and me for a pimp?

Horner. Pshaw! wench and pimp, paw[1] words; I know thou art an honest fellow, and hast a great acquaintance among the ladies, and perhaps hast made love for me, rather than let me make love to thy wife.

Pinchwife. Come, sir, in short, I am for no fooling.

Horner. Nor I neither: therefore prithee, let's see her face presently. Make her show, man: art thou sure I don't know her?

Pinchwife. I am sure you do know her.

Horner. A pox! why dost thou bring her to me then?

Pinchwife. Because she's a relation of mine—

Horner. Is she, faith, man? then thou art still more civil and obliging, dear rogue.

Pinchwife. Who desired me to bring her to you.

Horner. Then she is obliging, dear rogue.

Pinchwife. You'll make her welcome for my sake, I hope.

Horner. I hope she is handsome enough to make herself welcome. Prithee let her unmask.

Pinchwife. Do you speak to her; she would never be ruled by me.

Horner. Madam—[MRS. PINCHWIFE *whispers to* HORNER.] She says she must speak with me in private. Withdraw, prithee.

Pinchwife [*aside*]. She's unwilling, it seems, I should know all her indecent conduct in this business—[*aloud*] Well then, I'll leave you together, and hope When I am gone, you'll agree; if not, you and I shan't agree, sir.

Horner. What means the fool? if she and I agree 'tis no matter what you and I do. [*whispers to* MRS. PINCHWIFE, *who makes signs with her hand for him to be gone*]

Pinchwife. In the mean time I'll fetch a parson, and find out Sparkish, and disabuse him. You would have me fetch a parson, would you not? Well then— now I think I am rid of her, and shall have no more trouble with her—our sisters and daughters, like usurers' money, are safest when put out; but our wives, like their writings, never safe, but in our closets under lock and key. [*Exit.*]

[*Enter* BOY.]

Boy. Sir Jasper Fidget, sir, is coming up. [*Exit.*]

Horner. Here's the trouble of a cuckold now we are talking of. A pox on him! has he not enough to do to hinder his wife's sport, but he must other women's too?—Step in here, madam.

[*Exit* MRS. PINCHWIFE. *Enter* SIR JASPER FIDGET.]

Sir Jasper. My best and dearest friend.

Horner [*aside to* QUACK]. The old style, doctor.—[*aloud*] Well, be short, for I am busy. What would your impertinent wife have now?

---

[1] Naughty.

Sir Jasper.   Well guessed, i'faith; for I do come from her.

Horner.   To invite me to supper! Tell her, I can't come: go.

Sir Jasper.   Nay, now you are out, faith; for my lady, and the whole knot of the virtuous gang, as they call themselves, are resolved upon a frolic of coming to you to-night in masquerade, and are all dressed already.

Horner.   I shan't be at home.

Sir Jasper [*aside*].   Lord, how churlish he is to women!—[*aloud*] Nay, prithee don't disappoint 'em; they'll think 'tis my fault: prithee don't. I'll send in the banquet and the fiddles. But make no noise on't; for the poor virtuous rogues would not have it known, for the world, that they go a-masquerading; and they would come to no man's ball but yours.

Horner.   Well, well—get you gone; and tell 'em, if they come, t'will be at the peril of their honour and yours.

Sir Jasper.   He! he! he!—we'll trust you for that: farewell. [*Exit.*]

Horner.   Doctor, anon you too shall be my guest,
　　　　But now I'm going to a private feast.

[*Exeunt.*]

SCENE III—*The Piazza of Covent Garden.*

[*Enter* SPARKISH *with a letter in his hand,* PINCHWIFE *following.*]

Sparkish.   But who would have thought a woman could have been false to me? By the world, I could not have thought it.

Pinchwife.   You were for giving and taking liberty: she has taken it only, sir, now you find in that letter. You are a frank person, and so is she, you see there.

Sparkish.   Nay, if this be her hand—for I never saw it.

Pinchwife.   'Tis no matter whether that be her hand or no; I am sure this hand, at her desire, led her to Mr. Horner, with whom I left her just now, to go fetch a parson to 'em at their desire too, to deprive you of her for ever; for it seems yours was but a mock marriage.

Sparkish.   Indeed, she would needs have it that 'twas Harcourt himself, in a parson's habit, that married us; but I'm sure he told me 'twas his brother Ned.

Pinchwife.   O, there 'tis out; and you were deceived, not she: for you are such a frank person. But I must be gone.—You'll find her at Mr. Horner's. Go, and believe your eyes. [*Exit.*]

Sparkish.   Nay, I'll to her, and call her as many crocodiles, sirens, harpies, and other heathenish names, as a poet would do a mistress who had refused to hear his suit, nay more, his verses on her.—But stay, is not that she following a torch at t'other end of the Piazza? and from Horner's certainly—'tis so.

[*Enter* ALITHEA *following a torch, and* LUCY *behind.*]

You are well met, madam, though you don't think so. What, you have made a short visit to Mr. Horner? but I suppose you'll return to him presently, by that time the parson can be with him.

Alithea. Mr. Horner and the parson, sir!

Sparkish. Come, madam, no more dissembling, no more jilting; for I am no more a frank person.

Alithea. How's this?

Lucy. So, 'twill work, I see. [*aside*]

Sparkish. Could you find out no easy country fool to abuse? none but me, a gentleman of wit and pleasure about the town? But it was your pride to be too hard for a man of parts, unworthy false woman! false as a friend that lends a man money to lose; false as dice, who undo those that trust all they have to 'em.

Lucy. He has been a great bubble, by his similes, as they say. [*aside*]

Alithea. You have been too merry, sir, at your wedding-dinner, sure.

Sparkish. What, d'ye mock me too?

Alithea. Or you have been deluded.

Sparkish. By you.

Alithea. Let me understand you.

Sparkish. Have you the confidence, (I should call it something else, since you know your guilt,) to stand my just reproaches? you did not write an impudent letter to Mr. Horner? who I find now has clubbed with you in deluding me with his aversion for women, that I might no, forsooth, suspect him for my rival.

Lucy. D'ye think the gentleman can be jealous now, madam? [*aside*]

Alithea. I write a letter to Mr. Horner!

Sparkish. Nay, madam, do not deny it. Your brother showed it me just now; and told me likewise, he left you at Horner's lodging to fetch a parson to marry you to him: and I wish you joy, madam, joy, joy; and to him too, much joy; and to myself more joy, for not marrying you.

Alithea [*aside*]. So, I find my brother would break off the match; and I can consent to't, since I see this gentleman can be made jealous.—[*aloud*] O Lucy, by his rude usage and jealousy, he makes me almost afraid I am married to him. Art thou sure 'twas Harcourt himself, and no parson, that married us?

Sparkish. No, madam, I thank you. I suppose, that was a contrivance too of Mr. Horner's and yours, to make Harcourt play the parson; but I would as little as you have him one now, no, not for the world. For, shall I tell you another truth? I never had any passion for you till now, for now I hate you. 'Tis true, I might have married your portion, as other men of parts of the town do sometimes; and so, your servant. And to show my unconcernedness, I'll come to your wedding, and resign you with as much joy, as I would a stale wench to a new cully; nay, with as much joy as I would after the first night, if I had been married to you. There's for you; and so your servant, servant. [*Exit.*]

Alithea. How was I deceived in a man!

Lucy. You'll believe then a fool may be made jealous now? for that easiness in him that suffers him to be led by a wife, will likewise permit him to be persuaded against her by others.

Alithea. But marry Mr. Horner! my brother does not intend it, sure: if I thought he did, I would take thy advice, and Mr. Harcourt for my husband. And now I wish, that if there be any overwise woman of the town, who, like me, would marry a fool for fortune, liberty, or title, first, that her husband may love play, and be a cully to all the town but her, and suffer none but Fortune to be mistress of his purse; then, if for liberty, that he may send her into the country, under the conduct of some huswifely mother-in-law; and if for title, may the world give 'em none but that of cuckold.

Lucy. And for her greater curse, madam, may he not deserve it.

Alithea. Away, impertinent! Is not this my old Lady Lanterlu's?

Lucy. Yes, madam.—[*aside*] And here I hope we shall find Mr. Harcourt.

[*Exeunt.*]

SCENE IV—HORNER's *Lodging. A table, banquet, and bottles.*

[*Enter* HORNER, LADY FIDGET, MRS. DAINTY FIDGET, *and* MRS. SQUEAMISH.]

Horner. A pox! they are come too soon—before I have sent back my new mistress. All that I have now to do is to lock her in, that they may not see her. [*aside*]

Lady Fidget. That we may be sure of our welcome, we have brought our entertainment with us, and are resolved to treat thee, dear toad.

Mrs. Dainty Fidget. And that we may be merry to purpose, have left Sir Jasper and my old Lady Squeamish, quarrelling at home at backgammon.

Mrs. Squeamish. Therefore let us make use of our time, lest they should chance to interrupt us.

Lady Fidget. Let us sit then.

Horner. First, that you may be private, let me lock this door and that, and I'll wait upon you presently.

Lady Fidget. No, sir, shut 'em only, and your lips for ever; for we must trust you as much as our women.

Horner. You know all vanity's killed in me; I have no occasion for talking.

Lady Fidget. Now, ladies, supposing we had drank each of us our two bottles, let us speak the truth of our hearts.

Mrs. Dainty Fidget and Mrs. Squeamish. Agreed.

Lady Fidget. By this brimmer, for truth is nowhere else to be found—[*aside to* HORNER] not in thy heart, false man!

Horner. You have found me a true man, I'm sure. [*aside to* LADY FIDGET]

Lady Fidget [*aside to* HORNER]. Not every way.—But let us sit and be merry. [*sings*]

> Why should our damned tyrants oblige us to live
> On the pittance of pleasure which they only give?
> We must not rejoice
> With wine and with noise:
> In vain we must wake in a dull bed alone,
> Whilst to our warm rival the bottle they're gone.
> Then lay aside charms,
> And take up these arms.
>
> 'Tis wine only gives 'em their courage and wit:
> Because we live sober, to men we submit.
> If for beauties you'd pass,
> Take a lick of the glass,
> 'Twill mend your complexions, and when they are gone,

> The best red we have is the red of the grape:
> Then, sisters, lay't on,
> And damn a good shape.

Mrs. Dainty Fidget. Dear brimmer! Well, in token of our openness and plain-dealing, let us throw our masks over our heads.

Horner. So, 'twill come to the glasses anon. [*aside*]

Mrs. Squeamish. Lovely brimmer! let me enjoy him first.

Lady Fidget. No, I never part with a gallant till I've tried him. Dear brimmer! that makest our husbands short-sighted.

Mrs. Dainty Fidget. And our bashful gallants bold.

Mrs. Squeamish. And, for want of a gallant, the butler lovely in our eyes.—Drink, eunuch.

Lady Fidget. Drink, thou representative of a husband.—Damn a husband!

Mrs. Dainty Fidget. And, as it were a husband, an old keeper.

Mrs. Squeamish. And an old grandmother.

Horner. And an English bawd, and a French surgeon.

Lady Fidget. Ay, we have all reason to curse 'em.

Horner. For my sake, ladies?

Lady Fidget. No, for our own; for the first spoils all young gallants' industry.

Mrs. Dainty Fidget. And the other's art makes 'em bold only with common women.

Mrs. Squeamish. And rather run the hazard of the vile distemper amongst them, than of a denial amongst us.

Mrs. Dainty Fidget. The filthy toads choose mistresses now as they do stuffs, for having been fancied and worn by others.

Mrs. Squeamish. For being common and cheap.

Lady Fidget. Whilst women of quality, like the richest stuffs, lie untumbled, and unasked for.

Horner. Ay, neat, and cheap, and new, often they think best.

Mrs. Dainty Fidget. No, sir, the beasts will be known by a mistress longer than by a suit.

Mrs. Squeamish. And 'tis not for cheapness neither.

Lady Fidget. No; for the vain fops will take up druggets, and embroider 'em. But I wonder at the depraved appetites of witty men; they use to be out of the common road, and hate imitation. Pray tell me, beast, when you were a man, why you rather chose to club with a multitude in a common house for an entertainment, than to be the only guest at a good table.

Horner. Why, faith, ceremony and expectation are unsufferable to those that are sharp bent. People always eat with the best stomach at an ordinary, where every man is snatching for the best bit.

Lady Fidget. Though he get a cut over the fingers.—But I have heard, that people eat most heartily of another man's meat, that is, what they do not pay for.

Horner. When they are sure of their welcome and freedom; for ceremony in love and eating is as ridiculous as in fighting: falling on briskly is all should be done on those occasions.

Lady Fidget. Well then, let me tell you, sir, there is no where more freedom than in our houses; and we take freedom from a young person as a sign of good breeding; and a person may be as free as he pleases with us, as frolic, as gamesome, as wild as he will.

Horner.   Han't I heard you all declaim against wild men?

Lady Fidget.   Yes; but for all that, we think wildness in a man as desirable a quality as in a duck or rabbit: a tame man! foh!

Horner.   I know not, but your reputations frightened me as much as your faces invited me.

Lady Fidget.   Our reputation! Lord, why should you not think that we women make use of our reputation, as you men of yours, only to deceive the world with less suspicion? Our virtue is like the statesman's religion, the quaker's word, the gamester's oath, and the great man's honour; but to cheat those that trust us.

Mrs. Squeamish.   And that demureness, coyness, and modesty, that you see in our faces in the boxes at plays, is as much a sign of a kind woman, as a vizard-mask in the pit.

Mrs. Dainty Fidget.   For, I assure you, women are least masked when they have the velvet vizard on.

Lady Fidget.   You would have found us modest women in our denials only.

Mrs. Squeamish.   Our bashfulness is only the reflection of the men's.

Mrs. Dainty Fidget.   We blush when they are shamefaced.

Horner.   I beg your pardon, ladies, I was deceived in you devilishly. But why that mighty pretence to honour?

Lady Fidget.   We have told you; but sometimes 'twas for the same reason you men pretend business often, to avoid ill company, to enjoy the better and more privately those you love.

Horner.   But why would you ne'er give a friend a wink then?

Lady Fidget.   Faith, your reputation frightened us, as much as ours did you, you were so notoriously lewd.

Horner.   And you so seemingly honest.

Lady Fidget.   Was that all that deterred you?

Horner.   And so expensive—you allow freedom, you say.

Lady Fidget.   Ay. ay.

Horner.   That I was afraid of losing my little money, as well as my little time, both which my other pleasures required.

Lady Fidget.   Money! foh! you talk like a little fellow now: do such as we expect money?

Horner.   I beg your pardon, madam, I must confess, I have heard that great ladies, like great merchants, set but the higher prices upon what they have, because they are not in necessity of taking the first offer.

Mrs. Dainty Fidget.   Such as we make sale of our hearts?

Mrs. Squeamish.   We bribed for our love? foh!

Horner.   With your pardon ladies, I know, like great men in offices, you seem to exact flattery and attendance only from your followers; but you have receivers about you, and such fees to pay, a man is afraid to pass your grants. Besides, we must let you win at cards, or we lose your hearts; and if you make an assignation, 'tis at a goldsmith's, jeweller's, or china-house; where for your honour you deposit to him, he must pawn his to the punctual cit, and so paying for what you take up, pays for what he takes up.

Mrs. Dainty Fidget.   Would you not have us assured of our gallants' love?

Mrs. Squeamish. For love is better known by liberality than by jealousy.

Lady Fidget. For one may be dissembled, the other not.—[*aside*] But my jealousy can be no longer dissembled, and they are telling ripe.—[*aloud*]— Come, here's to our gallants in waiting, whom we must name, and I'll begin. This is my false rogue.[*claps him on the back*]

Mrs. Squeamish. How!

Horner. So, all will out now. [*aside*]

Mrs. Squeamish. Did you not tell me, 'twas for my sake only you reported yourself no man? [*aside to* HORNER]

Mrs. Dainty Fidget. Oh, wretch! did you not swear to me, 'twas for my love and honour you passed for that thing you do? [*aside to* HORNER]

Horner. So, so.

Lady Fidget. Come, speak, ladies: this is my false villain.

Mrs. Squeamish. And mine too.

Mrs. Dainty Fidget. And mine.

Horner. Well then, you are all three my false rogues too, and there's an end on't.

Lady Fidget. Well then, there's no remedy; sister sharers, let us not fall out, but have a care of our honour. Though we get no presents, no jewels of him, we are savers of our honour, the jewel of most value and use, which shines yet to the world unsuspected, though it be counterfeit.

Horner. Nay, and is e'en as good as if it were true, provided the world think so; for honour, like beauty now, only depends on the opinion of others.

Lady Fidget. Well, Harry Common, I hope you can be true to three. Swear; but 'tis to no purpose to require your oath, for you are as often forsworn as you swear to new women.

Horner. Come, faith, madam, let us e'en pardon one another; for all the difference I find betwixt we men and you women, we forswear ourselves at the beginning of an amour, you as long as it lasts.

[*Enter* SIR JASPER FIDGET, *and* OLD LADY SQUEAMISH.]

Sir Jasper. Oh, my Lady Fidget, was this your cunning, to come to Mr. Horner without me? but you have been nowhere else, I hope.

Lady Fidget. No, Sir Jasper.

Lady Squeamish. And you came straight hither, Biddy?

Mrs. Squeamish. Yes, indeed, lady grandmother.

Sir Jasper. 'Tis well, 'tis well; I knew when once they were thoroughly acquainted with poor Horner, they'd ne'er be from him: you may let her masquerade it with my wife and Horner, and I warrant her reputation safe.

[*Enter* BOY.]

Boy. O, sir, here's the gentleman come, whom you bid me not suffer to come up, without giving you notice, with a lady too, and other gentlemen.

Horner. Do you all go in there, whilst I send 'em away; and, boy, do you desire 'em to stay below till I come, which shall be immediately.

[*Exeunt* SIR JASPER FIDGET, LADY FIDGET, OLD LADY SQUEAMISH, MRS. SQUEAM- ISH, *and* MRS. DAINTY FIDGET.]

Boy.   Yes, sir. [*Exit.*]

[*Exit* HORNER *at the other door, and returns with* MRS. PINCHWIFE.]

Horner.   You would not take my advice, to be gone home before your husband came back, he'll now discover all; yet pray, my dearest, be persuaded to go home, and leave the rest to my management; I'll let you down the back way.

Mrs. Pinchwife.   I don't know the way home, so I don't.

Horner.   My man shall wait upon you.

Mrs. Pinchwife.   No, don't you believe that I'll go at all; what, are you weary of me already?

Horner.   No, my life, 'tis that I may love you long, 'tis to secure my love, and your reputation with your husband; he'll never receive you again else.

Mrs. Pinchwife.   What care I? d'ye think to frighten me with that? I don't intend to go to him again; you shall be my husband now.

Horner.   I cannot be your husband, dearest, since you are married to him.

Mrs. Pinchwife.   O, would you make me believe that? Don't I see every day at London here, women leave their first husbands, and go and live with other men as their wives? pish, pshaw! you'd make me angry, but that I love you so mainly.

Horner.   So, they are coming up—In again, in, I hear 'em.—[*exit* MRS. PINCHWIFE] Well, a silly mistress is like a weak place, soon got, soon lost, a man has scarce time for plunder; she betrays her husband first to her gallant, and then her gallant to her husband.

[*Enter* PINCHWIFE, ALITHEA, HARCOURT, SPARKISH, LUCY, *and a* PARSON.]

Pinchwife.   Come, madam, 'tis not the sudden change of your dress, the confidence of you asseverations, and your false witness there, shall persuade me I did not bring you hither just now; here's my witness, who cannot deny it, since you must be confronted.—Mr. Horner, did not I bring this lady to you just now?

Horner.   Now must I wrong one woman for another's sake,—but that's no new thing with me, for in these cases I am still on the criminal's side against the innocent. [*aside*]

Alithea.   Pray speak, sir.

Horner.   It must be so. I must be impudent, and try my luck; impudence uses to be too hard for truth. [*aside*]

Pinchwife.   What, you are studying an evasion or excuse for her! Speak, sir.

Horner.   No, faith, I am something backward only to speak in women's affairs or disputes.

Pinchwife.   She bids you speak.

Alithea.   Ay, pray, sir, do, pray satisfy him.

Horner.   Then truly, you did bring that lady to me just now.

Pinchwife.   O ho!

Alithea.   How, sir?

Harcourt.   How, Horner?

Alithea.   What mean you, sir? I always took you for a man of honour.

Horner.   Ay, so much a man of honour, that I must save my mistress, I thank you, come what will on't. [*aside*]

Sparkish. So, if I had had her, she'd have made me believe the moon had been made of a Christmas pie.

Lucy. Now could I speak, if I durst, and solve the riddle, who am the author of it. [*aside*]

Alithea. O unfortunate woman! A combination against my honour! which most concerns me now, because you share in my disgrace, sir, and it is your censure, which I must now suffer, that troubles me, not theirs.

Harcourt. Madam, then have no trouble, you shall now see 'tis possible for me to love too, without being jealous; I will not only believe your innocence myself, but make all the world believe it.—[*aside to* HORNER] Horner, I must now be concerned for this lady's honour.

Horner. And I must be concerned for a lady's honour too.

Harcourt. This lady has her honour, and I will protect it.

Horner. My lady has not her honour, but has given it me to keep, and I will preserve it.

Harcourt. I understand you not.

Horner. I would not have you.

Mrs. Pinchwife. What's the matter with 'em all? [*peeping in behind*]

Pinchwife. Come, come, Mr. Horner, no more disputing; here's the parson, I brought him not in vain.

Harcourt. No, sir, I'll employ him, if this lady please.

Pinchwife. How! what d'ye mean?

Sparkish. Ay, what does he mean?

Horner. Why, I have resigned your sister to him, he has my consent.

Pinchwife. But he has not mine, sir; a woman's injured honour, no more than a man's, can be repaired or satisfied by any but him that first wronged it; and you shall marry her presently, or—[*lays his hand on his sword*]

[*Re-enter* MRS. PINCHWIFE.]

Mrs. Pinchwife. O Lord, they'll kill poor Mr. Horner! besides, he shan't marry her wilst I stand by, and look on; I'll not lose my second husband so.

Pinchwife. What do I see?

Alithea. My sister in my clothes!

Sparkish. Ha!

Mrs. Pinchwife. Nay, pray now don't quarrel about finding work for the parson, he shall marry me to Mr. Horner; or now, I believe, you have enough of me. [*to* PINCHWIFE]

Horner. Damned, damned loving changeling! [*aside*]

Mrs. Pinchwife. Pray, sister, pardon me for telling so many lies of you.

Horner. I suppose the riddle is plain now.

Lucy. No, that must be my work.—Good sir, hear me. [*kneels to* PINCHWIFE, *who stands doggedly with his hat over his eyes*]

Pinchwife. I will never hear woman again, but make 'em all silent thus—[*offers to draw upon his wife*]

Horner. No, that must not be.

Pinchwife. You then shall go first, 'tis all one to me. [*offers to draw on* HORNER, *but is stopped by* HARCOURT]

Harcourt. Hold!

[*Re-enter* SIR JASPER FIDGET, LADY FIDGET, OLD LADY SQUEAMISH, MRS. DAINTY FIDGET, *and* MRS. SQUEAMISH.]

Sir Jasper. What's the matter? what's the matter? pray, what's the matter, sir? I beseech you communicate, sir.

Pinchwife. Why, my wife has communicated, sir, as your wife may have done too, sir, if she knows him, sir.

Sir Jasper. Pshaw, with him! ha! ha! he!

Pinchwife. D'ye mock me, sir? a cuckold is a kind of a wild beast; have a care, sir.

Sir Jasper. No, sure, you mock me, sir. He cuckold you! it can't be, ha! ha! he! why, I'll tell you, sir—[*offers to whisper*]

Pinchwife. I tell you again, he has whored my wife, and yours too, if he knows her, and all the women he comes near; 'tis not his dissembling, his hypocrisy, can wheedle me.

Sir Jasper. How! does he dissemble? is he a hypocrite? Nay, then—how—wife—sister, is he a hypocrite?

Lady Squeamish. A hypocrite! a dissembler! Speak, young harlotry, speak, how?

Sir Jasper. Nay, then—O my head too!—O thou libidinous lady!

Lady Squeamish. O thou harloting harlotry! hast thou done't then?

Sir Jasper. Speak, good Horner, art thou a dissembler, a rogue? hast thou—

Horner. So!

Lucy. I'll fetch you off, and her too, if she will but hold her tongue. [*apart to* HORNER]

Horner. Canst thou? I'll give thee—[*apart to* LUCY]

Lucy [*to* PINCHWIFE]. Pray have but patience to hear me, sir, who am the unfortunate cause of all this confusion. Your wife is innocent, I only culpable; for I put her upon telling you all these lies concerning my mistress, in order to the breaking off the match between Mr. Sparkish and her, to make way for Mr. Harcourt.

Sparkish. Did you so, eternal rotten tooth? Then, it seems, my mistress was not false to me, I was only deceived by you. Brother, that should have been, now man of conduct, who is a frank person now, to bring your wife to her lover, ha?

Lucy. I assure you, sir, she came not to Mr. Horner out of love, for she loves him no more—

Mrs. Pinchwife. Hold, I told lies for you, but you shall tell none for me, for I do love Mr. Horner with all my soul, and nobody shall say me nay; pray, don't you go to make poor Mr. Horner believe to the contrary; 'tis spitefully done of you, I'm sure.

Horner. Peace dear idiot. [*aside to* MRS. PINCHWIFE]

Mrs. Pinchwife. Nay, I will not peace.

Pinchwife. Not till I make you.

[*Enter* DORILANT *and* QUACK.]

Dorilant. Horner, your servant; I am the doctor's guest, he must excuse our intrusion.

Quack. But what's the matter, gentlemen? for Heaven's sake, what's the matter?

Horner. Oh, 'tis well you are come. 'Tis a censorious world we live in; you may have brought me a reprieve, or else I had died for a crime I never committed, and these innocent ladies had suffered with me; therefore, pray satisfy these worthy, honourable, jealous gentlemen—that—[*whispers*]

Quack.   O, I understand you, is that all?—Sir Jasper, by Heavens, and upon the word of a physician, sir—[*whispers to* SIR JASPER]

Sir Jasper.   Nay, I do believe you truly.—Pardon me, my virtuous lady, and dear of honour.

Lady Squeamish.   What, then all's right again?

Sir Jasper.   Ay, ay, and now let us satisfy him too.

[*They whisper with* PINCHWIFE.]

Pinchwife.   An eunuch! Pray, no fooling with me.

Quack.   I'll bring half the chirurgeons in town to swear it.

Pinchwife.   They!—they'll swear a man that bled to death through his wounds, died of an apoplexy.

Quack.   Pray, hear me, sir—why, all the town has heard the report of him.

Pinchwife.   But does all the town believe it?

Quack.   Pray, inquire a little, and first of all these.

Pinchwife.   I'm sure when I left the town, he was the lewdest fellow in't.

Quack.   I tell you, sir, he has been in France since; pray, ask but these ladies and gentlemen, your friend Mr. Dorilant. Gentlemen and ladies, han't you all heard the late sad report of poor Mr. Horner?

All the Ladies.   Ay, ay, ay.

Dorilant.   Why, thou jealous fool, dost thou doubt it? he's an arrant French capon.

Mrs. Pinchwife.   'Tis false, sir, you shall not disparage poor Mr. Horner, for to my certain knowledge—

Lucy.   O, hold!

Mrs. Squeamish.   Stop her mouth! [*aside to* LUCY]

Lady Fidget.   Upon my honour, sir, 'tis as true—[*to* PINCHWIFE]

Mrs. Dainty Fidget.   D'ye think we would have been seen in his company?

Mrs. Squeamish.   Trust our unspotted reputations with him?

Lady Fidget.   This you get, and we too, by trusting your secret to a fool. [*aside to* HORNER]

Horner.   Peace, madam.—[*aside to* QUACK] Well, doctor, is not this a good design, that carries a man on unsuspected, and brings him off safe?

Pinchwife.   Well, if this were true—but my wife—[*aside*]

[DORILANT *whispers with* MRS. PINCHWIFE.]

Alithea.   Come, brother, your wife is yet innocent, you see; but have a care of too strong an imagination, lest, like an over-concerned timorous gamester, by fancying an unlucky cast, it should come. Women and fortune are truest still to those that trust 'em.

Lucy.   And any wild thing grows but the more fierce and hungry for being kept up, and more dangerous to the keeper.

Alithea.   There's doctrine for all husbands, Mr. Harcourt.

Harcourt.   I edify, madam, so much, that I am impatient till I am one.

Dorilant.   And I edify so much by example, I will never be one.

Sparkish.   And because I will not disparage my parts, I'll ne'er be one.

Horner.   And I, alas! can't be one.

Pinchwife.   But I must be one—against my will to a country wife, with a country murrain to me!

Mrs. Pinchwife.   And I must be a country wife still too, I find; for I can't, like a city one, be rid of my musty husband, and do what I list. [*aside*]

Horner.   Now, sir, I must pronounce your wife innocent, though I blush whilst I do it; and I am the only man by her now exposed to shame, which I will straight drown in wine, as you shall your suspicion; and the ladies' troubles we'll divert with a ballad.—Doctor, where are your maskers?

Lucy.   Indeed, she's innocent, sir, I am her witness; and her end of coming out was but to see her sister's wedding; and what she has said to your face of her love to Mr. Horner, was but the usual innocent revenge on a husband's jealousy;—was it not, madam, speak?

Mrs. Pinchwife [*aside to* LUCY *and* HORNER].   Since you'll have me tell more lies—[*aloud*] Yes, indeed, bud.

Pinchwife.   For my own sake fain I would all believe;
Cuckolds, like lovers, should themselves deceive.
But—[*sighs*]
His honour is least safe (too late I find)
Who trusts it with a foolish wife or friend.

[A *Dance of Cuckolds.*]

Horner.   Vain fops but court and dress, and keep a pother,
To pass for women's men with one another;
But he who aims by women to be prized,
First by the men, you see, must be despised.

[*Exeunt.*]

Epilogue

[*Spoken by the actress who played Lady Fidget*]

> Now you the vigorous, who daily here
> O'er vizard-mask in public domineer,
> And what you'd do to her, if in place where;
> Nay, have the confidence to cry, "Come out!"
> Yet when she says, "Lead on!" you are not stout;
> But to your well-dressed brother straight turn round,
> And cry "Pox on her, Ned, she can't be sound!"
> Then slink away, a fresh one to engage,
> With so much seeming heat and loving rage,
> You'd frighten listening actress on the stage;
> Till she at last has seen you huffing come,
> And talk of keeping in the tiring-room,
> Yet cannot be provoked to lead her home.
> Next, you Falstaffs of fifty, who beset
> Your buckram maidenheads, which your friends get;

And whilst to them you of achievements boast,
They share the booty, and laugh at your cost.
In fine, you essenced boys, both old and young,
Who would be thought so eager, brisk, and strong,
Yet do the ladies, not their husbands wrong;
Whose purses for your manhood make excuse,
And keep your Flanders mares for show not use;
Encouraged by our woman's man to-day,
A Horner's part may vainly think to play;
And may intrigues so bashfully disown,
That they may doubted be by few or none;
May kiss the cards at picquet, ombre, loo,
And so be taught to kiss the lady too;
But, gallants, have a care, faith, what you do.
The world, which to no man his due will give,
You by experience know you can deceive,
And men may still believe you vigorous,
But then we women—there's no cozening us.

Ibsen: HEDDA GABLER

In the latter half of the eighteenth century, the dominant mode of dramatic expression was sentimentalism, a cloyingly moral approach in which one would regularly find virtue rewarded, vice punished, and true love triumphant. This ethical bias, coupled with the general revival of interest in the principles and forms of the classical period, the so-called "rules" of the drama, resulted in plays of persistent decorum and propriety that bore increasing resemblances to one another, until in time the whole craft of playwriting became simply a matter of reiterating the same tired clichés in new dress. This tendency reached its height in the mid-nineteenth century with the "well-made plays" of Eugène Scribe and Victorien Sardou in France.

True, the turn of the nineteenth century was also the age of Goethe and Schiller; but it was, in the main, an era when most of Europe's major literary figures were not drawn to the theatre as their medium of expression. The drama fell from favor among serious artists at the same time that the ever more prosperous audience decided that popular playgoing was essentially a social event and for which it demanded drama that was a genteel, innocuous, and mindless diversion. There were some plays and playwrights able to transcend their time, but on the whole the century following the end of Restoration drama in England was the most barren age of the European theatre since its return to respectability in the later middle ages.

With distressing frequency, Henrik Ibsen (1828–1906) has been called "the father of modern drama." He is really a co-defendant in a multiple paternity suit and must stand in the dock alongside at least Strindberg and Chekhov, but it was unquestionably this dour Norwegian who first made a sharp break with the trite and formulaic dramaturgy prevalent in the third quarter of the nineteenth century. In form, Ibsen's best known plays were not a radical departure from those well-made trifles. Their settings were the conventional interiors, scrupulously detailed to create the illusion that the stage was not a stage at all, but a real living room on whose inhabitants the audience was allowed to eavesdrop. Nevertheless, Ibsen turned the confines of the box set with its imaginary fourth wall into an arena for his art. His predecessors, and many of his imitators, used those trappings of reality to house preposterous and vacant contrivances for a theatregoing public that demanded only the patina of verisimilitude. The walls, the furniture, and the props were familiar; it was in subject matter, themes, social views, and character development that Ibsen made his unmannerly intrusion on the complacent gentility of his affluent, burgherly audiences.

To tack the label of "realism" onto Ibsen's plays today is a misleading oversimplification. Ibsen asks an audience nurtured on a popular drama far more compulsive in its attention to realistic detail and credible action to overtax its willingness to suspend disbelief. His plays abound with symmetrical constructions, convenient coincidences, concentrated crises, careful climaxes, and tidy denouements. The realism inheres in the toughness, honesty, courage, insight, and vision of a man capable of making the theatre a place where real people come to serious grips with real and cogent problems presented in all their real complexities and frustrating ambiguities.

"Naturalism," a concept often linked with "realism," is also a term too readily used to categorize Ibsen. Naturalism is a view of the human condition that essentially follows the teachings of late nineteenth century ·science and the dicta that Zola and his disciples derived from them. The naturalist believes that man has little control over his own destiny, and that his fate is not determined by his moral choices nor even by the meeting of volition and circumstance. It is the product of natural and social forces, which, in a capricious universe, pay no heed to the individual spirit that declaims, "I exist." Ibsen was no determinist in the narrow sense, for surely he insisted on the necessity for moral responsibility in man. Although his plays delineate the multitudinous pressures exerted by heredity and environment that help to mold our destinies without ever asking for our concurrence, Ibsen's characters are not mere puppets. They demand that we understand them as total human beings. They compel us to ask probing questions rather than to grasp at pat answers.

In a letter written to a friend in 1890, the year in which *Hedda Gabler* had its premiere, Ibsen said that his dramatic purpose was "to depict human beings, human emotions, and human destinies upon a groundwork of certain of the social conditions and principles of the present day." Seriousness of purpose marked his plays; he refused to cater to the middle-class taste for frivolous entertainment while he refuted the equation of morality with social respectability. Most of Ibsen's "problem plays" outraged the public in his homeland and throughout Europe. Those who today find it difficult to understand why Ibsen's work offended so many must refer to the dramatists against whom he rebelled— Scribe and Sardou, purveyors of the pap and goo that Bernard Shaw later dubbed "Sardoodledom."

Ibsen is commonly known today for his social "problem plays," most of them written during his middle years of productivity. To overlook his poetic, philosophical, symbolic, and mystical dramas is to ignore the full range of his artistry. The plays that are steeped in an intense social consciousness are but one of Henrik Ibsen's dramatic achievements. Even if he had written only these, their craft, their vision, and their thematic revolution would have assured him a permanent place among the titans of the theatre.

HEDDA GABLER

Translated by Otto Reinert

The Characters

Jørgen Tesman, University Research Fellow in the History of Civilization
Hedda, his wife
Miss Juliane Tesman, his aunt
Mrs. Elvsted
Judge Brack
Eilert Løvborg
Berte, the Tesmans' maid

SCENE: *The Tesmans' villa in a fashionable residential section of the town.*

A note on pronunciation

The approximate Norwegian pronunciation of names likely to be difficult to a
speaker of English is suggested below (the syllable in capitals is accented; the
unaccented *e* is close to English *e* in *quiet*).

Jørgen   YUR-gen (*g* as in bargain)
Julle   YOOL-le (short *oo*)
Eilert Løvborg   AY-lert LUV-borg
Berte   BAIR-te

Act I

[*A spacious, handsome, tastefully furnished room. Dark décor. In the rear, a
wide doorway with open portieres. Beyond is a smaller room, furnished in the
same style as the front room. A door, right, leads to the front hall. Left, French
doors, with portieres drawn aside, through which can be seen a part of a roofed
verandah and trees with autumn foliage. Front center, an oval table covered
with a cloth. Chairs around it. Front right, a wide, dark, porcelain stove, a high-
backed easy chair, a footstool with a pillow, and two ottomans. In the corner far
right, a sofa and a small, round table. Front left, a sofa, set out from the wall.
Far left, beyond the French doors, an upright piano. On both sides of the
doorway, rear center, whatnots with knickknacks. Against the rear wall of the
inner room, a sofa, and in front of it a table and two chairs. Above the sofa, a
portrait of a handsome, elderly man in general's uniform. Over the table hangs a
lamp with milky, white glass. There are several bouquets of flowers, in vases and
glasses, in various places in the front room. Others are lying on the tables. Thick
carpets on the floors of both rooms. The morning sun is shining through the
French doors.*

[MISS JULIANE TESMAN, *with hat and parasol, enters right, followed by* BERTE,
who carries a bouquet of flowers wrapped in paper. MISS TESMAN *is a nice-*

252

looking woman of 65, of pleasant mien, neatly but not expensively dressed in a gray suit. BERTE *is a middle-aged servant girl, of rather plain and countrified appearance.*]

Miss Tesman [*stops inside the door, listens, says in a low voice*].　On my word—I don't think they are even up yet!

Berte [*also softly*].　That's what I told you, miss. When you think how late the steamer got in last night. And afterwards—! Goodness!—all the stuff she wanted unpacked before she turned in.

Miss Tesman.　Well—just let them sleep. But fresh morning air—*that* we can give them when they come in here. [*Goes and opens the French doors wide.*]

Berte [*by the table, lost, still holding the flowers*].　Please, miss—I just don't see a bit of space anywhere! I think I'd better put these over here. [*Puts the flowers down on the piano.*]

Miss Tesman.　Well, well, my dear Berte. So you've got yourself a new mistress now. The good Lord knows it was hard for me to let you go.

Berte [*near tears*].　What about me, then, miss! What shall *I* say? I who have served you and Miss Rina all these blessed years.

Miss Tesman.　We shall just have to make the best of it, Berte. That's all. Jørgen can't do without you, you know. He just can't. You've looked after him ever since he was a little boy.

Berte.　Yes, but miss—I'm ever so worried about leaving Miss Rina. The poor dear lying there all helpless. With that new girl and all! She'll never learn how to make things nice and comfortable for an invalid.

Miss Tesman.　Oh yes, you'll see. I'll teach her. And of course, you know, I'll do most of it myself. So don't you worry yourself about my poor sister, Berte.

Berte.　Yes, but there's another thing, too, miss. I'm scared I won't be able to suit young Mrs. Tesman.

Miss Tesman.　Oh, well. Good heavens. So there is a thing or two—Right at first—

Berte.　For I believe she's ever so particular.

Miss Tesman.　Can you wonder? General Gabler's daughter? Just think of the kind of life she was used to when the General was alive. Do you remember when she rode by with her father? That long black riding habit she wore? And the feather in her hat?

Berte.　Oh, I remember, all right. But I'll be blessed if I ever thought she and the young master would make a pair of it.

Miss Tesman.　Nor did I. By the way, while I think of it, Berte. Jørgen has a new title now. From now on you should call him "the Doctor."

Berte.　Yes, the young mistress said something about that, too, last night. Soon as they were inside the door. Then it's really so, miss?

Miss Tesman.　It certainly is. Just think, Berte—they have made him a doctor abroad. During the trip, you know. I hadn't heard a thing about it till last night on the pier.

Berte.　Well, I daresay he could be anything he put his mind to, *he* could—smart as *he* is. But I must say I'd never thought he'd turn to doctoring people, too.

Miss Tesman.　Oh, that's not the kind of doctor he is. [*Nods significantly.*] And as far as that is concerned, there is no telling but pretty soon you may have to call him something grander yet.

Berte. You don't say! What might that be, miss?

Miss Tesman [*smiles*].   Wouldn't you like to know! [*Moved.*] Ah yes, indeed—!
If only dear Jochum could see from his grave what has become of his little boy!
[*Looking around.*] But look, Berte—what's this for? Why have you taken off
all the slip covers?

Berte. She told me to. Said she can't stand slip covers on chairs.

Miss Tesman.   Do you think they mean to make this their everyday living room,
then?

Berte. It sure sounded that way. Mrs. Tesman did, I mean. For he—the
doctor—he didn't say anything.

[JØRGEN TESMAN *enters from the right side of the inner room. He is humming
to himself. He carries an open, empty suitcase. He is of medium height, youth-
ful-looking, thirty-three years old; somewhat stoutish. Round, open, cheerful
face. Blond hair and beard. He wears glasses and is dressed in a comfortable,
rather casual suit.*]

Miss Tesman.   Good morning, good morning, Jørgen!

Tesman [*in the doorway*].   Auntie! Dearest Aunt Julle! [*Comes forward and
shakes her hand.*] All the way out here—as early as this! Hm?

Miss Tesman.   Well—I just had to drop in for a moment. To see how you are
getting along, you know.

Tesman.   Even though you haven't had a good night's sleep.

Miss Tesman.   Oh, that doesn't matter at all.

Tesman.   But you did get home from the pier all right, I hope. Hm?

Miss Tesman.   Oh yes, I certainly did, thank you. The Judge was kind enough to
see me all the way to my door.

Tesman.   We were so sorry we couldn't give you a ride in our carriage. But you
saw for yourself—all the boxes Hedda had.

Miss Tesman.   Yes, she certainly brought quite a collection.

Berte [*to* TESMAN].   Should I go and ask Mrs. Tesman if there's anything I can
help her with?

Tesman.   No, thank you, Berte—you'd better not. She said she'll ring if she
wants you.

Berte [*going right*].   Well, all right.

Tesman.   But, look—you might take this suitcase with you.

Berte [*takes it*].   I'll put it in the attic. [*Exits right.*]

Tesman.   Just think, Auntie—that whole suitcase was brimful of copies of old
documents. You wouldn't believe me if I told you all the things I have collected
from libraries and archives all over. Quaint old items nobody has known anything about.

Miss Tesman.   Well, no, Jørgen. I'm sure you haven't wasted your time on your
honeymoon.

Tesman.   No, I think I may say I have not. But take your hat off, Auntie—for
goodness' sake. Here! Let me untie the ribbon for you. Hm?

Miss Tesman [*while he does so*].   Ah, God forgive me, if this isn't just as if you
were still at home with us!

Tesman [*inspecting the hat*].   My, what a fine-looking hat you've got yourself!

Miss Tesman.   I bought it for Hedda's sake.

Tesman. For Hedda's sake? Hm?

Miss Tesman. So she won't need to feel ashamed of me if we ever go out together.

Tesman [*patting her cheek*]. If you don't think of everything, Auntie! [*Puts the hat down on a chair by the table.*] And now—over here to the sofa—we'll just sit and chat for a while till Hedda comes.

[*They seat themselves. She places her parasol in the corner by the sofa.*]

Miss Tesman [*takes both his hands in hers and gazes at him*]. What a blessing it is to have you back again, Jørgen, big as life! You—Jochum's little boy!

Tesman. For me, too, Aunt Julle. Seeing you again. For you have been both father and mother to me.

Miss Tesman. Ah, yes—don't you think I know you'll always keep a spot in your heart for these two old aunts of yours!

Tesman. So Aunt Rina isn't any better, hm?

Miss Tesman. Oh no. We mustn't look for improvement in her case, poor dear. She is lying there just as she has been all these years. Just the same, may the good Lord keep her for me a long time yet! For else I just wouldn't know what to do with myself, Jørgen. Especially now, when I don't have you to look after any more.

Tesman [*pats her back*]. There, there, now!

Miss Tesman [*changing tone*]. And to think that you are a married man, Jørgen! And that you were the one to walk off with Hedda Gabler. The lovely Hedda Gabler. Just think! As many admirers as she had!

Tesman [*hums a little, smiles complacently*]. Yes, I daresay I have quite a few good friends here in town who'd gladly be in my shoes, hm?

Miss Tesman. And such a long and lovely honeymoon you had! More than five—almost six months!

Tesman. Well, you know—for me it has been a kind of study tour as well. All the collections I had to go through. And the books I had to read!

Miss Tesman. Yes, I suppose. [*More confidentially, her voice lowered a little.*] But listen, Jørgen—haven't you got something—something special to tell me?

Tesman. About the trip?

Miss Tesman. Yes.

Tesman. No—I don't know of anything besides what I wrote in my letters. They gave me a doctor's degree down there—but I told you that last night; I'm sure I did.

Miss Tesman. Well, yes, sort of thing—What I mean is—don't you have certain—certain—expectations?

Tesman. Expectations?

Miss Tesman. Ah for goodness' sake, Jørgen! I am your old Auntie, after all!

Tesman. Certainly I have expectations.

Miss Tesman. Well!!

Tesman. I fully expect to be made a professor one of these days.

Miss Tesman. Professor—oh yes—

Tesman. I may even say I am quite certain of it. But dear Aunt Julle—you know this just as well as I do!

Miss Tesman [*laughing a little*]. Of course I do. You're quite right. [*Changing topic*]. But about the trip. It must have cost a great deal of money—hm, Jørgen?

Tesman. Well, now; you know that large stipend went quite a long way.

Miss Tesman. I just don't see how you made it do for both of you, though.

Tesman. No, I suppose that's not so easy to understand, hm?

Miss Tesman. Particularly with a lady along. For I have always heard that is ever so much more expensive.

Tesman. Well, yes, naturally. That *is* rather more expensive. But Hedda had to have this trip, Auntie! She really had to. Nothing less would do.

Miss Tesman. No, I daresay. For a wedding journey is quite the thing these days. But now tell me—have you had a chance to look around here yet?

Tesman. I certainly have. I have been up and about ever since dawn.

Miss Tesman. And what do you think of it all?

Tesman. Delightful! Perfectly delightful! The only thing is I don't see what we are going to do with the two empty rooms between the second sitting room in there and Hedda's bedroom.

Miss Tesman [*with a chuckle*]. Oh my dear Jørgen—you may find them useful enough—when the time comes!

Tesman. Of course, you're right, Auntie! As my library expands, hm?

Miss Tesman. Quite so, my dear boy. It was your library I was thinking of.

Tesman. But I'm really most happy on Hedda's behalf. For you know, before we were engaged she used to say she wouldn't care to live anywhere but in Secretary Falk's house.

Miss Tesman. Yes, just think—wasn't that a lucky coincidence, that it was up for sale right after you had left?

Tesman. Yes, Aunt Julle. We've certainly been lucky. Hm?

Miss Tesman. But it will be expensive, my dear Jørgen. Terribly expensive—all this.

Tesman [*looks at her, a bit crestfallen*]. Yes, I daresay it will, Auntie.

Miss Tesman. Heavens, yes!

Tesman. How much, do you think? Roughly. Hm?

Miss Tesman. No, I couldn't possibly say till all the bills arrive.

Tesman. Well, anyway, Judge Brack managed to get very reasonable terms for us. He said so himself in a letter to Hedda.

Miss Tesman. Yes, and I won't have you uneasy on that account, Jørgen. Besides, I have given security for the furniture and the carpets.

Tesman. Security? You? But dear Aunt Julle—what kind of security could you give?

Miss Tesman. The annuity.

Tesman [*jumps up*]. What! Your and Aunt Rina's annuity?

Miss Tesman. Yes. I didn't know what else to do, you see.

Tesman [*standing before her*]. But are you clear out of your mind, Auntie! That annuity—that's all the two of you have to live on!

Miss Tesman. Oh well, there's nothing to get so excited about, I'm sure. It's all just a matter of form, you know. That's what the Judge said, too. For he was kind enough to arrange the whole thing for me. Just a matter of form—those were his words.

Tesman.   That's all very well. Still—

Miss Tesman.   For now you'll have your own salary, you know. And, goodness— what if we do have a few expenses— Help out a bit right at first—? That would only be a joy for us—

Tesman.   Oh, Auntie! When will you ever stop making sacrifices for my sake!

Miss Tesman [gets up, puts her hands on his shoulders].   But what other happiness do I have in this world than being able to smooth your way a little, my own dear boy? Orphan as you were, with no one to lean on but us? And now the goal is in sight, Jørgen. Things may have looked black at times. But heaven be praised; now you've arrived!

Tesman.   Yes, it's really quite remarkable the way things have worked out.

Miss Tesman.   Yes—and those who were against you—who tried to block your way—now they are tasting defeat. They are down, Jørgen! He, the most danger- ous of them all, his fall was the greatest! He made his bed, and now he is lying in it—poor, lost wretch that he is!

Tesman.   Have you had any news about Eilert? Since I went away, I mean?

Miss Tesman.   Just that he is supposed to have published a new book.

Tesman.   What? Eilert Løvborg? Recently? Hm?

Miss Tesman.   That's what they say. But I wonder if there can be much to it. What do you think? Ah—but when *your* new book comes, that will be some- thing quite different, Jørgen! What is it going to be about?

Tesman.   It deals with the domestic industries of Brabant during the Middle Ages.

Miss Tesman.   Just think—being able to write about something like that!

Tesman.   But as far as that is concerned, it may be quite some time before it is ready. I have all these collections to put in order first, you see.

Miss Tesman.   Yes, collecting and putting things in order—you certainly know how to do that. In that you are your father's own son.

Tesman.   Well, I must say I am looking forward to getting started. Particularly now, that I've got my own delightful home to work in.

Miss Tesman.   And most of all now that you have the one your heart desired, dear Jørgen.

Tesman [embracing her].   Oh yes, yes, Aunt Julle! Hedda—she is the most wonderful part of it all! [*Looks toward the doorway.*] There—I think she is coming now, hm?

[HEDDA *enters from the left side of the inner room. She is twenty-nine years old. Both features and figure are noble and elegant. Pale, ivory complexion. Steel- gray eyes, expressive of cold, clear calm. Beautiful brown hair, though not particularly ample. She is dressed in a tasteful, rather loose-fitting morning costume.*]

Miss Tesman [going toward her].   Good morning, my dear Hedda! A very happy morning to you!

Hedda [giving her hand].   Good morning, dear Miss Tesman! So early a call? That is most kind.

Miss Tesman [seems slightly embarrassed].   And—has the little lady of the house slept well the first night in her new home?

Hedda. Passably, thank you.

Tesman [*laughs*]. Passably! You are a good one, Hedda! You were sleeping like a log when I got up.

Hedda. Fortunately. And then, of course, Miss Tesman, it always takes time to get used to new surroundings. That has to come gradually. [*Looks left.*] Oh dear. The maid has left the verandah doors wide open. There's a veritable flood of sunlight in here.

Miss Tesman [*toward the doors*]. Well, then, we'll just close them.

Hedda. No, no, not that. Tesman, dear, please pull the curtains. That will give a softer light.

Tesman [*over by the French doors*]. Yes, dear. There, now! Now you have both shade and fresh air, Hedda.

Hedda. We certainly can use some air in here. Such loads of flowers—But, Miss Tesman, please—won't you be seated?

Miss Tesman. No thanks. I just wanted to see if everything was all right—and so it is, thank goodness. I had better get back to Rina. I know she is waiting for me, poor thing.

Tesman. Be sure to give her my love, Auntie. And tell her I'll be around to see her later today.

Miss Tesman. I'll certainly do that!—Oh my! I almost forgot! [*Searches the pocket of her dress.*] I have something for you, Jørgen. Here.

Tesman. What's that, Auntie? Hm?

Miss Tesman [*pulls out a flat parcel wrapped in newspaper and gives it to him*]. Here you are, dear.

Tesman [*opens the parcel*]. Well, well, well! So you took care of them for me, Aunt Julle! Hedda! Now, isn't that sweet, hm?

Hedda [*by the whatnot, right*]. If you'd tell me what it is—

Tesman. My old slippers! *You* know!

Hedda. Oh really? I remember you often talked about them on the trip.

Tesman. Yes, for I missed them so. [*Walks over to her.*] Here—now you can see what they're like, Hedda.

Hedda [*crosses toward stove*]. Thanks. I don't know that I really care.

Tesman [*following*]. Just think—Aunt Rina embroidered these slippers for me. Ill as she was. You can't imagine how many memories they hold for me!

Hedda [*by the table*]. Hardly for me.

Miss Tesman. That's true, you know, Jørgen.

Tesman. Yes, but—I just thought that now that she's one of the family—

Hedda [*interrupting*]. I don't think we'll get on with that maid, Tesman.

Miss Tesman. Not get on with Berte?

Tesman. Whatever makes you say that, dear? Hm?

Hedda [*points*]. Look—she has left her old hat on the chair over there.

Tesman [*appalled, drops the slippers*]. But Hedda—!

Hedda. What if somebody were to come and see it!

Tesman. No, no, Hedda—that's Aunt Julle's hat!

Hedda. Oh?

Miss Tesman [*picking up the hat*]. Yes, indeed it is. And it isn't old either, my dear young lady.

Hedda. I really didn't look that closely—

Miss Tesman [*tying the ribbons*]. I want you to know that this is the first time I have had it on my head. On my word it is!

Tesman. And very handsome it is, too. Really a splendid-looking hat!

Miss Tesman. Oh, I don't know that it is anything so special, Jørgen. [*Looks around.*] My parasol—? Ah, here it is. [*Picks it up.*] For that is mine, too. [*Mutters.*] Not Berte's.

Tesman. New hat and new parasol! What do you think of that, Hedda!

Hedda. Very nice indeed.

Tesman. Yes, don't you think so? Hm? But, Auntie, take a good look at Hedda before you leave. See how pretty and blooming she looks.

Miss Tesman. Dear me, Jørgen; that's nothing new. Hedda has been lovely all her days. [*She nods and walks right.*]

Tesman [*following*]. Yes, but have you noticed how full-figured and healthy she looks after the trip? How she has filled out?

Hedda [*crossing*]. Oh—stop it!

Miss Tesman [*halts, turns around*]. Filled out?

Tesman. Yes, Aunt Julle. You can't see it so well now when she wears that dress. But I, who have the opportunity—

Hedda [*by the French doors, impatiently*]. Oh, you haven't any opportunities at all!

Tesman. It must be the mountain air in Tyrol.

Hedda [*curtly interrupting*]. I am just as I was when I left.

Tesman. Yes, so you say. I just don't think you're right. What do you think, Auntie?

Miss Tesman [*has folded her hands, gazes at* HEDDA]. Lovely—lovely—lovely; that is what Hedda is. [*Goes over to her, inclines her head forward with both her hands, and kisses her hair.*] God bless and keep Hedda Tesman. For Jørgen's sake.

Hedda [*gently freeing herself*]. There, there, Now let me go.

Miss Tesman [*in quiet emotion*]. Every single day I'll be over and see you two.

Tesman. Yes, please do, Auntie. Hm?

Miss Tesman. Goodbye, goodbye!

[*She leaves through door, right.* TESMAN *see her out. The door remains ajar.* TESMAN *is heard repeating his greetings for* AUNT RINA *and his thanks for the slippers. In the meantime,* HEDDA *paces up and down, raises her arms, clenching her fists, as in quiet rage. Opens the curtains by the French doors and stands looking out. In a few moments,* TESMAN *re-enters and closes the door behind him.*]

Tesman [*picking up the slippers*]. What are you looking at, Hedda?

Hedda [*once again calm and controlled*]. Just the leaves. They are so yellow. And withered.

Tesman [*wrapping the slippers in their paper, putting the parcel down on the table*]. Well, you know—we're in September now.

Hedda [*again restless*]. Yes—just think. It's already—September.

Tesman. Don't you think Aunt Julle acted strange, Hedda? Almost solemn. I wonder why. Hm?

Hedda. I hardly know her, you see. Isn't she often like that?

Tesman. Not the way she was today.

Hedda [*turning away from the French doors*]. Do you think she minded that business with the hat?

Tesman. Oh, I don't think so. Not much. Perhaps a little bit right at the moment—

Hedda. Well, I'm sorry, but I must say it strikes me as very odd—putting her hat down here in the living room. One just doesn't do that.

Tesman. Well, you may be sure Aunt Julle won't ever do it again.

Hedda. Anyway, I'll make it up to her, somehow.

Tesman. Oh yes, Hedda; if only you would!

Hedda. When you go over there today, why don't you ask her over for tonight?

Tesman. I'll certainly do that. And then there is one other thing you could do that she'd appreciate ever so much.

Hedda. What?

Tesman. If you could just bring yourself to call her Auntie. For my sake, Hedda, hm?

Hedda. No, Tesman, no. You really mustn't ask me to do that. I have already told you I can't. I'll try to call her Aunt Juliane. That will have to do.

Tesman. All right, if you say so. I just thought that now that you're in the family—

Hedda. Hmmm—I don't know about that—[*She walks toward the doorway.*]

Tesman [*after a brief pause*]. Anything the matter, Hedda? Hm?

Hedda. I'm just looking at my old piano. It doesn't quite go with the other furniture in here.

Tesman. As soon as I get my first pay check we'll have it traded in.

Hedda. No—I don't want to do that. I want to keep it. But let's put it in this inner room and get another one for out here. Whenever it's convenient, I mean.

Tesman [*a little taken back*]. Well—yes—we could do that—

Hedda [*picks up the bouquet from the piano*]. These flowers weren't here last night.

Tesman. I suppose Aunt Julle brought them for you.

Hedda [*looking at the flowers*]. There's a card here. [*Takes it out and reads.*] "Will be back later." Can you guess who it's from?

Tesman. No. Who? Hm?

Hedda. Thea Elvsted.

Tesman. No, really? Mrs. Elvsted! Miss Rysing that was.

Hedda. That's right. The one with that irritating head of hair she used to show off with. An old flame of yours, I understand.

Tesman [*laughs*]. Well, now—that didn't last long! Anyway, that was before I knew you, Hedda. Just think—her being in town.

Hedda. Strange, that she'd call on us. I have hardly seen her since we went to school together.

Tesman. As far as that goes, I haven't seen her either for—God knows how long. I don't see how she can stand living in that out-of-the-way place. Hm?

Hedda [*suddenly struck by a thought*].   Listen, Tesman—isn't it some place near there that he lives—what's his name—Eilert Løvborg?

Tesman.   Yes, that's right. He is up there, too.

[BERTE *enters right.*]

Berte.   Ma'am, she's here again, that lady who brought those flowers a while back. [*Pointing.*] The flowers you're holding in your hand, ma'am.

Hedda.   Ah, she is? Well, show her in, please.

[BERTE *opens the door for* MRS. ELVSTED *and exits.* MRS. ELVSTED *is of slight build, with a pretty, soft face. Her eyes are light blue, large, round, rather prominent, of a timid and querying expression. Her hair is strikingly light in color, almost whitish, and unusually rich and wavy. She is a couple of years younger than* HEDDA. *She is dressed in a dark visiting dress, tasteful, but not quite in the most recent fashion.*]

Hedda [*walks toward her. Friendly*].   Good morning, my dear Mrs. Elvsted. How very nice to see you again.

Mrs. Elvsted [*nervous, trying not to show it*].   Well, yes, it is quite some time since we met.

Tesman [*shaking hands*].   And we, too. Hm?

Hedda.   Thank you for your lovely flowers—

Mrs. Elvsted.   Please, don't—I would have come here yesterday afternoon. But I was told you were still traveling—

Tesman.   You've just arrived in town, hm?

Mrs. Elvsted.   I got here yesterday, at noon. Oh, I was quite desperate when I learned you weren't home.

Hedda.   Desperate? But why?

Tesman.   But my dear Mrs. Rysing—I mean Mrs. Elvsted—

Hedda.   There is nothing wrong, I hope?

Mrs. Elvsted.   Yes there is. And I don't know a single soul other than you that I can turn to here.

Hedda [*putting the flowers down on the table*].   Come—let's sit down here on the sofa.

Mrs. Elvsted.   Oh, I'm in no mood to sit!

Hedda.   Of course you are. Come on. [*She pulls* MRS. ELVSTED *over to the sofa and sits down next to her.*]

Tesman.   Well, now, Mrs.—? Exactly what—?

Hedda.   Has something—special happened at home?

Mrs. Elvsted.   Well, yes—and no. Oh, but I am so afraid you won't understand!

Hedda.   In that case, it seems to me you ought to tell us exactly what has happened, Mrs. Elvsted.

Tesman.   After all, that's why you are here. Hm?

Mrs. Elvsted.   Yes, yes, of course. Well, then, maybe you already know—Eilert Løvborg is in town.

Hedda.   Is Løvborg—!

Tesman.   No! You don't say! Just think, Hedda—Løvborg's back!

Hedda.   All right. I can hear.

Mrs. Elvsted. He has been here a week already. Imagine—a whole week! In this dangerous place. Alone! With all that bad company around.

Hedda. But my dear Mrs. Elvsted—why is he a concern of yours?

Mrs. Elvsted [*with an apprehensive look at her, says quickly*]. He tutored the children.

Hedda. Your children?

Mrs. Elvsted. My husband's. I don't have any.

Hedda. In other words, your stepchildren.

Mrs. Elvsted. Yes.

Tesman [*with some hesitation*]. But was he—I don't quite know how to put this—was he sufficiently—regular—in his way of life to be thus employed? Hm?

Mrs. Elvsted. For the last two years, there hasn't been a thing to object to in his conduct.

Tesman. No, really? Just think, Hedda!

Hedda. I hear.

Mrs. Elvsted. Not the least little bit, I assure you! Not in any respect. And yet—knowing he's here—in the big city—And with all that money, too! I'm scared to death!

Tesman. But in that case, why didn't he remain with you and your husband? Hm?

Mrs. Elvsted. After his book came out, he was too restless to stay.

Tesman. Ah yes, that's right. Aunt Julle said he has published a new book.

Mrs. Elvsted. Yes, a big new book, about the course of civilization in general. It came out about two weeks ago. And since it has had such big sales and been discussed so much and made such a big splash—

Tesman. It has, has it? I suppose this is something he has had lying around from better days?

Mrs. Elvsted. You mean from earlier?

Tesman. Yes.

Mrs. Elvsted. No; it's all been written since he came to stay with us. During this last year.

Tesman. Well, now! That's very good news, Hedda! Just think!

Mrs. Elvsted. Yes, if it only would last!

Hedda. Have you seen him since you came to town?

Mrs. Elvsted. No, not yet. I had a great deal of trouble finding his address. But this morning I finally tracked him down.

Hedda [*looks searchingly at her*]. Isn't it rather odd that your husband—hm—

Mrs. Elvsted [*with a nervous start*]. My husband! What about him?

Hedda. That he sends you to town on such an errand? That he doesn't go and look after his friend himself?

Mrs. Elvsted. Oh, no, no—my husband doesn't have time for things like that. Besides, I have some—some shopping to do, anyway.

Hedda [*with a slight smile*]. Well, in that case, of course—

Mrs. Elvsted [*getting up, restlessly*]. And now I beg of you, Mr. Tesman— won't you please receive Eilert Løvborg nicely if he calls on you? And I am sure he will. After all—Such good friends as you two used to be. And then you both do the same kind of work—the same field of study, as far as I know.

Tesman. We used to, at any rate.

Mrs. Elvsted. Yes. And that's why I implore you to please, please, try to keep an eye on him—you too. You'll do that, Mr. Tesman, won't you? Promise?

Tesman. With the greatest pleasure, Mrs. Rysing.

Hedda. Elvsted.

Tesman. I'll gladly do as much for Eilert as I possibly can. You may certainly count on that.

Mrs. Elvsted. Oh, how good and kind you are! [*Clasps his hands.*] Thank you, thank you, thank you! [*Nervously.*] You see, my husband is so very fond of him.

Hedda [*getting up*]. You ought to write him a note, Tesman. Maybe he won't come without an invitation.

Tesman. Yes, I suppose that would be the right thing to do, Hedda. Hm?

Hedda. The sooner the better. Right away, I think.

Mrs. Elvsted [*pleadingly*]. If only you would!

Tesman. I'll write this minute. Do you have his address, Mrs.—Mrs. Elvsted?

Mrs. Elvsted. Yes. [*Pulls a slip of paper from her bag and gives it to him.*] Here it is.

Tesman. Very good. Well, then, if you'll excuse me—[*Looks around.*] By the way—the slippers? Ah, here we are. [*Leaving with the parcel.*]

Hedda. Be sure you write a nice, warm, friendly letter, Tesman. And a long one, too.

Tesman. Certainly, certainly.

Mrs. Elvsted. But not a word that it is I who—!

Tesman. No, that goes without saying, I should think. Hm? [*Goes out right through inner room.*]

Hedda [*goes over to* MRS. ELVSTED, *smiles, says in a low voice*]. There! We just killed two birds with one stone.

Mrs. Elvsted. What do you mean?

Hedda. Didn't you see I wanted him out of the room?

Mrs. Elvsted. Yes, to write that letter—

Hedda. And to speak to you alone.

Mrs. Elvsted [*flustered*]. About this same thing?

Hedda. Exactly.

Mrs. Elvsted [*anxious*]. But there *is* nothing more, Mrs. Tesman! Really, there isn't!

Hedda. Oh yes, there is. There is considerably more. I can see that much. Over here—We are going to have a real, nice, confidential talk, you and I. [*She forces* MRS. ELVSTED *down in the easy chair and seats herself on one of the ottomans.*]

Mrs. Elvsted [*worried, looks at her watch*]. But my dear Mrs. Tesman—I had really thought I would be on my way now.

Hedda. Oh I am sure there is no rush. Now, then. Tell me about yourself. How are things at home?

Mrs. Elvsted. That is just what I don't want to talk about.

Hedda. But to me—! After all, we are old schoolmates.

Mrs. Elvsted. But you were a year ahead of me. And I used to be so scared of you!

Hedda. Scared of me?

Mrs. Elvsted. Terribly. For when we met on the stairs, you always ruffled my hair.

Hedda. Did I really?

Mrs. Elvsted. Yes. And once you said you were going to burn it off.

Hedda. Oh, but you know—I wasn't serious!

Mrs. Elvsted. No, but I was such a silly, then. Anyway, afterwards we drifted far apart. Our circles are so very different, you know.

Hedda. All the more reason for getting close again. Listen. In school we called each other by our first names.

Mrs. Elvsted. Oh I'm sure you're wrong

Hedda. I'm sure I'm not! I remember it quite clearly. And now we want to be open with one another, just the way we used to. [*Moves the ottoman closer.*] There, now! [*Kisses her cheek.*] You call me Hedda.

Mrs. Elvsted [*seizes her hands*]. Oh, you are so good and kind! I'm not used to that.

Hedda. There, there! And I'll call you my dear Thora, just as in the old days.

Mrs. Elvsted. My name is Thea.

Hedda. So it is. Of course. I meant Thea. [*Looks at her with compassion.*] So you're not much used to goodness and kindness, Thea? Not in your own home?

Mrs. Elvsted. If I even had a home! But I don't. I never have had one.

Hedda [*looks at her for a moment*]. I thought there might be something like this.

Mrs. Elvsted [*helplessly, looking straight ahead*]. Yes—yes—yes—

Hedda. I am not sure if I quite remember—Didn't you first come to your husband as his housekeeper?

Mrs. Elvsted. I was really hired as governess. But his wife—his first wife—was ailing already then and practically bedridden. So I had to take charge of the household as well.

Hedda. But in the end you became his wife.

Mrs. Elvsted [*dully*]. So I did.

Hedda. Let's see. How long ago is that?

Mrs. Elvsted. Since my marriage?

Hedda. Yes.

Mrs. Elvsted. About five years.

Hedda. Right. It must be that long.

Mrs. Elvsted. Oh, those five years! Or mostly the last two or three! Oh, Mrs. Tesman—if you could just imagine!

Hedda [*slaps her hand lightly*]. Mrs. Tesman? Shame on you!

Mrs. Elvsted. Oh yes; all right, I'll try. Yes—if you could just—conceive—understand—

Hedda [*casually*]. And Eilert Løvborg has been living near you for some three years or so, hasn't he?

Mrs. Elvsted [*looks at her uncertainly*]. Eilert Løvborg? Yes—he has.

Hedda. Did you know him before? Here in town?

Mrs. Elvsted. Hardly at all. That is, of course I did in a way. I mean, I knew *of* him.

Hedda. But up there—You saw a good deal of him; did you?

Mrs. Elvsted. Yes, he came over to us every day. He was supposed to tutor the children, you see. For I just couldn't do it all by myself.

Hedda. Of course not. And your husband—? I suppose he travels quite a bit.

Mrs. Elvsted. Well, yes, Mrs. Tes—Hedda—as a public magistrate, you know, he very often has to travel all over his district.

Hedda [*leaning against the armrest on the easy chair*]. Thea—poor, sweet Thea—now you have to tell me everything—just as it is.

Mrs. Elvsted. You'd better ask me, then.

Hedda. How *is* your husband, Thea? I mean—you know—*really?* To be with. What kind of person is he? Is he good to you?

Mrs. Elvsted [*evasively*]. I believe he thinks he does everything for the best.

Hedda. But isn't he altogether too old for you? He is more than twenty years older, isn't he?

Mrs. Elvsted [*with irritation*]. Yes, there is that, too. But there isn't just one thing. Every single little thing about him repels me! We don't have a thought in common, he and I. Not a thing in the world!

Hedda. But isn't he fond of you all the same? I mean in his own way?

Mrs. Elvsted. I don't know. I think I am just useful to him. And I don't use much money. I am inexpensive.

Hedda. That is foolish of you.

Mrs. Elvsted [*shakes her head*]. Can't be changed. Not with him. I don't think he cares for anybody much except himself. Perhaps the children a little.

Hedda. And Eilert Løvborg, Thea.

Mrs. Elvsted [*looks at her*]. Eilert Løvborg? What makes you think that?

Hedda. Well, it seems to me that when he sends you all the way to town to look after him—[*With an almost imperceptible smile.*] Besides, you said so yourself. To Tesman.

Mrs. Elvsted [*with a nervous twitch*]. Did I? I suppose I did. [*With a muted outburst.*] No! I might as well tell you now as later. For it's bound to come out, anyway.

Hedda. But my dear Thea—?

Mrs. Elvsted. All right. My husband doesn't know I've gone!

Hedda. What! He doesn't know?

Mrs. Elvsted. He wasn't even home. He's away again. Oh, I just couldn't take it any longer, Hedda! It had become utterly impossible. All alone as I was.

Hedda. So what did you do?

Mrs. Elvsted. I packed some of my things. Just the most necessary. Without telling anybody. And left.

Hedda. Just like that?

Mrs. Elvsted. Yes. And took the next train to town.

Hedda. But dearest Thea—how did you dare to do a thing like that!

Mrs. Elvsted [*rises, walks*]. What else could I do?

Hedda. But what do you think your husband will say when you go back?

Mrs. Elvsted [*by the table; looks at her*]. Go back to him?

Hedda. Yes!

Mrs. Elvsted. I'll never go back.

Hedda [*rises, approaches her slowly*]. So you have really, seriously—left every-thing?

Mrs. Elvsted.   Yes. It seemed to me there was nothing else I could do.

Hedda.   And quite openly, too.

Mrs. Elvsted.   You can't keep a thing like that secret, anyway.

Hedda.   But what do you think people will say, Thea?

Mrs. Elvsted.   In God's name, let them say whatever they like. [*Sits down on the sofa, dully, tired.*] For I have only done what I had to do.

Hedda [*after a brief silence*].   And what do you plan to do with yourself? What sort of work will you do?

Mrs. Elvsted.   I don't know yet. I only know I have to live where Eilert Løvborg is. If I am to live at all.

Hedda [*moves a chair from the table closer to* MRS. ELVSTED, *sits down, strokes her hands*].   Thea—tell me. How did this—this friendship between you and Eilert Løvborg—how did it begin?

Mrs. Elvsted.   Oh, it grew little by little. I got some sort of power over him.

Hedda.   Oh?

Mrs. Elvsted.   He dropped his old ways. Not because I asked him to. I never dared to do that. But I think he must have noticed how I felt about that kind of life. So he changed.

Hedda [*quickly suppresses a cynical smile*].   So you have—rehabilitated him, as they say. Haven't you, Thea?

Mrs. Elvsted.   At least, that's what *he* says. On the other hand, he has turned me into a real human being. Taught me to think—and understand—all sorts of things.

Hedda.   Maybe he tutored you, too?

Mrs. Elvsted.   No, not tutored exactly. But he talked to me. About so many, many things. And then came that lovely, lovely time when I could share his work with him. He let me help him!

Hedda.   He did?

Mrs. Elvsted.   Yes! Whatever he wrote, he wanted us to be together about it.

Hedda.   Just like two good comrades.

Mrs. Elvsted [*with animation*].   Comrades!—that's it! Imagine, Hedda—that's just what he called it, too. Oh, I really ought to feel so happy. But I can't. For you see, I don't know if it will last.

Hedda.   You don't trust him any more than that?

Mrs. Elvsted [*heavily*].   The shadow of a woman stands between Eilert Løvborg and me.

Hedda [*tensely, looks at her*].   Who?

Mrs. Elvsted.   I don't know. Somebody or other from—his past. I don't think he has ever really forgotten her.

Hedda.   What has he told you about it?

Mrs. Elvsted.   He has mentioned it only once—just casually.

Hedda.   And what did he say?

Mrs. Elvsted.   He said that when they parted she was going to kill him with a gun.

Hedda [*cold, controlled*].   Oh, nonsense. People don't do that sort of thing here.

Mrs. Elvsted.   No, I know. And that is why I think it must be that red-headed singer he used to—

Hedda.   Yes, I suppose so.

Mrs. Elvsted. For I remember people said she carried a loaded gun.

Hedda. Well, then I'm sure it's she.

Mrs. Elvsted [*wringing her hands*]. Yes, but just think, Hedda—now I hear that she—that singer—that she's here in town again, too! Oh, I'm just desperate—!

Hedda [*with a glance toward the inner room*]. Shhh! Here's Tesman. [*Rises and whispers.*] Not a word about all this to anybody, Thea!

Mrs. Elvsted [*jumps up*]. No, no. For God's sake!

[TESMAN, *carrying a letter, enters from the right side of the inner room.*]

Tesman. There, now—here's the missive, all ready to go!

Hedda. Good. But I believe Mrs. Elvsted wants to be on her way. Wait a moment. I'll see you to the garden gate.

Tesman. Say, Hedda—do you think Berte could take care of this?

Hedda [*takes the letter*]. I'll tell her.

[BERTE *enters right.*]

Berte. Judge Brack is here and wants to know if you're receiving.

Hedda. Yes, ask the Judge please to come in. And—here—drop this in a mailbox, will you?

Berte [*takes the letter*]. Yes, ma'am.

[*She opens the door for* JUDGE BRACK *and exits. The* JUDGE *is forty-five years of age. Rather thickset, but well-built and with brisk, athletic movements. Roundish face, aristocratic profile. His hair is short, still almost completely black, very neatly dressed. Lively, sparkling eyes. Thick eyebrows and mustache with cut-off points. He is dressed in an elegant suit, a trifle youthful for his age. He wears pince-nez glasses, attached to a string, and lets them drop from time to time.*]

Judge Brack [*hat in hand, salutes*]. May one pay one's respects as early as this?

Hedda. One certainly may.

Tesman [*shaking his hand*]. You are always welcome. [*Introducing.*] Judge Brack—Miss Rysing—

[HEDDA *groans.*]

Brack [*bowing*]. Delighted!

Hedda [*looks at him, laughs*]. How nice it is to see you in daylight, Judge!

Brack. You find me changed, perhaps?

Hedda. A bit younger, I think.

Brack. Much obliged.

Tesman. But what do you think of Hedda? Hm? Did you ever see her in such bloom? She positively—

Hedda. Will you please leave me out of this? You had better thank the Judge for all the trouble he has taken.

Brack. Oh, nonsense. It's been a pleasure.

Hedda. Yes, you are indeed a faithful soul. But my friend here is dying to be off. Don't leave, Judge. I'll be back in a minute.

[*Mutual goodbyes.* MRS. ELVSTED *and* HEDDA *exit, right.*]

Brack.   Well, now—your wife—is she tolerably satisfied?

Tesman.   Yes, indeed, and we really can't thank you enough. That is, I understand there will have to be some slight changes made here and there. And there are still a few things—just a few trifles—we'll have to get.

Brack.   Oh? Really?

Tesman.   But we certainly don't want to bother you with that. Hedda said she's going to take care of it herself. But do sit down, hm?

Brack.   Thanks. Maybe just for a moment—[*Sits down by the table.*] There's one thing I'd like to talk to you about, my dear Tesman.

Tesman.   Oh? Ah, I see! [*Sits down.*] I suppose it's the serious part of the festivities that's beginning now. Hm?

Brack.   Oh—there's no great rush as far as the money is concerned. Though I must say I wish we could have established ourselves a trifle more economically.

Tesman.   Out of the question, my dear fellow! Remember, it's all for Hedda! You, who know her so well—! After all, I couldn't put her up like any little middle-class housewife—

Brack.   No, I suppose—That's just it.

Tesman.   Besides—fortunately—it can't be long now before I receive my appointment.

Brack.   Well, you know—things like that have a way of hanging fire.

Tesman.   Perhaps you have heard something? Something definite? Hm?

Brack.   No, nothing certain—[*Interrupting himself.*] But that reminds me. I have some news for you.

Tesman.   Oh?

Brack.   Your old friend Eilert Løvborg is back in town.

Tesman.   I know that already.

Brack.   So? Who told you?

Tesman.   The lady who just left.

Brack.   I see. What did you say her name was again? I didn't quite catch—

Tesman.   Mrs. Elvsted.

Brack.   Ah yes—the Commissioner's wife. Yes, it's up in her part of the country that Løvborg has been staying, too.

Tesman.   And just think. I am so glad to hear it. He is quite respectable again.

Brack.   Yes, so they say.

Tesman.   And he has published a new book, hm?

Brack.   Oh yes.

Tesman.   Which is making quite a stir.

Brack.   Quite an unusual stir.

Tesman.   Just think! Isn't that just wonderful! He—with his remarkable gifts. And I was so sure he'd gone under for good.

Brack.   That seems to have been the general opinion.

Tesman.   What I don't understand, though, is what he is going to do with himself. What sort of living can he make? Hm?

[*During the last remark* HEDDA *re-enters, right.*]

Hedda [*to* BRACK, *with a scornful little laugh*].   Tesman is forever worrying about how people are going to make a living.

Tesman.   Well, you see, we are talking about poor Eilert Løvborg, Hedda.

Hedda [*with a quick look at him*]. You are? [*Sits down in the easy chair by the stove and asks casually.*] What is the matter with him?

Tesman. Well, you see, I believe he's run through his inheritance a long time ago. And I don't suppose he can write a new book every year. Hm? So I really must ask how he is going to make out.

Brack. Maybe I could help you answer that.

Tesman. Yes?

Brack. Remember, he has relatives with considerable influence.

Tesman. Ah—unfortunately, those relatives have washed their hands of him long ago.

Brack. Just the same, they used to call him the hope of the family.

Tesman. Yes, before! But he has ruined all that.

Hedda. Who knows? [*With a little smile.*] I hear the Elvsteds have rehabilitated him.

Brack. And then this book—

Tesman. Well, I certainly hope they will help him to find something or other. I just wrote him a letter. Hedda, dear, I asked him to come out here tonight.

Brack. Oh dear, I am sorry. Don't you remember—you're supposed to come to my little stag dinner tonight? You accepted last night on the pier, you know.

Hedda. Had you forgotten, Tesman?

Tesman. So I had.

Brack. Oh well. I'm sure he won't come, so it doesn't really make any difference.

Tesman. Why is that? Hm?

Brack [*gets up somewhat hesitantly, rests his hands on the back of the chair*]. Dear Tesman—and you, too, Mrs. Tesman—I cannot in good conscience let you remain in ignorance of something, which—which—

Tesman. Something to do with Eilert?

Brack. With both you and him.

Tesman. But my dear Judge, do speak!

Brack. You must be prepared to find that your appointment will not come through as soon as you hope and expect.

Tesman [*jumps up, nervously*]. Something's happened? Hm?

Brack. It may conceivably be made contingent upon the result of a competition.

Tesman. Competition! Just think, Hedda!

Hedda [*leaning farther back in her chair*]. Ah—I see, I see—!

Tesman. But with whom? Don't tell me with—?

Brack. Precisely. With Eilert Løvborg.

Tesman [*claps his hands together*]. No, no! This can't be! It is unthinkable! Quite impossible! Hm?

Brack. All the same, that's the way it may turn out.

Tesman. No, but Judge, this would amount to the most incredible callousness toward me! [*Waving his arms.*] For just think—I'm a married man! We married on the strength of these prospects, Hedda and I. Got ourselves deep in debt. Borrowed money from Aunt Julle, too. After all, I had practically been promised the post, you know. Hm?

Brack. Well, well. I daresay you'll get it in the end. If only after a competition.

Hedda [*motionless in her chair*]. Just think, Tesman. It will be like a kind of contest.

Tesman. But dearest Hedda, how can you be so unconcerned!

Hedda [*still without moving*].   I'm not at all unconcerned. I'm dying to see who wins.

Brack. In any case, Mrs. Tesman, I'm glad you know the situation as it is. I mean—before you proceed to make the little additional purchases I understand you threaten us with.

Hedda. This makes no difference as far as that is concerned.

Brack. Really? Well, in that case, of course—Goodbye! [*To* TESMAN.] I'll pick you up on my afternoon walk.

Tesman. What? Oh yes, yes, of course. I'm sorry; I'm just all flustered.

Hedda [*without getting up, gives her hand*]. Goodbye, Judge. Come back soon.

Brack. Thanks. Goodbye, goodbye.

Tesman [*sees him to the door*]. Goodbye, my dear Judge. You really must excuse me—

[JUDGE BRACK *exits, right.*]

Tesman [*pacing the floor*]. Oh, Hedda, Hedda! One should never venture into fairyland. Hm?

Hedda [*looks at him, smiles*]. Do *you* do that?

Tesman. Well, yes—it can't be denied—it was most venturesome of me to rush into marriage and set up a home on the strength of mere prospects.

Hedda. Well, maybe you're right.

Tesman. Anyway—we do have our own nice, comfortable home, now. Just think, Hedda—the very home both of us dreamed about. Set our hearts on, I may almost say. Hm?

Hedda [*rises, slowly, tired*]. The agreement was that we were to maintain a certain position—entertain—

Tesman. Don't I know it! Dearest Hedda—I have been so looking forward to seeing you as hostess in a select circle! Hm? Well, well, well! In the meantime, we'll just have to be content with one another. See Aunt Julle once in a while. Nothing more. And you were meant for such a different kind of life, altogether!

Hedda. I suppose a footman is completely out of the question.

Tesman. I'm afraid so. Under the circumstances, you see—we couldn't possibly—

Hedda. And as for getting my own riding horse—

Tesman [*aghast*]. Riding horse!

Hedda. I suppose I mustn't even think of that.

Tesman. Good heavens, no! That goes without saying, I hope!

Hedda [*walking*]. Well—at least I have one thing to amuse myself with in the meantime.

Tesman [*overjoyed*]. Oh thank goodness for that! And what *is* that, Hedda, hm?

Hedda [*in the doorway, looks at him with suppressed scorn*]. My guns—Jørgen!

Tesman [*in fear*]. Your guns!

Hedda [*with cold eyes*]. General Gabler's guns. [*She exits left, through the inner room.*]

Tesman [*runs up to the doorway, calls after her*]. But Hedda! Good gracious! Hedda, dear! Please don't touch those dangerous things! For my sake, Hedda! Hm?

Act II

[*The same room at the* TESMANS'. *The piano has been moved out and replaced
by an elegant little writing desk. A small table has been placed near the sofa,
left. Most of the flowers have been removed.* MRS. ELVSTED'S *bouquet is on the
big table front center. Afternoon.*]

[HEDDA, *dressed to receive callers, is alone. She is standing near the open French
doors, loading a revolver. Its mate is lying in an open case on the desk.*]

Hedda [*looking down into the garden, calls*].   Hello there, Judge! Welcome
    back!
Judge Brack [*off stage*].   Thanks, Mrs. Tesman!
Hedda [*raises the gun, sights*].   I am going to shoot you, Judge Brack!
Brack [*calls off stage*].   No—no—no! Don't point the gun at me like that!
Hedda.   That's what you get for sneaking in the back door! [*Fires.*]
Brack [*closer*].   Are you out of your mind—!
Hedda.   Oh dear—did I hit you?
Brack [*still off stage*].   Stop that nonsense!
Hedda.   Come on in, then.

[JUDGE BRACK, *dressed for dinner, enters, left. He carries a light overcoat over
his arm.*]

Brack.   Dammit! Do you still fool around with that thing? What are you
    shooting at, anyway?
Hedda.   Oh—just firing off into blue air.
Brack [*gently but firmly taking the gun away from her*].   With your permission,
    Mrs. Tesman. [*Looks at it.*] Ah yes, I remember this gun very well. [*Looks
    around.*] Where is the case? Ah, here we are. [*Puts the gun in the case and
    closes it.*] That's enough of that silliness for today.
Hedda.   But in the name of heaven, what do you expect me to do with myself?
Brack.   No callers?
Hedda [*closing the French doors*].   Not a soul. All my close friends are still out
    of town, it seems.
Brack.   And Tesman is out, too, perhaps?
Hedda [*by the desk, puts the gun case in a drawer*].   Yes. He took off for the
    aunts' right after lunch. He didn't expect you so early.
Brack.   I should have thought of that. That was stupid of me.
Hedda [*turns her head, looks at him*].   Why stupid?
Brack.   I would have come a little—sooner.
Hedda [*crossing*].   If you had, you wouldn't have found anybody home. For I
    have been in my room ever since lunch, changing my clothes.
Brack.   And isn't there the tiniest little opening in the door for negotiations?
Hedda.   You forgot to provide one.
Brack.   Another stupidity.
Hedda.   So we'll have to stay in here. And wait. For I don't think Tesman will be
    back for some time.
Brack.   By all means. I'll be very patient.

[HEDDA *sits on the sofa in the corner.* BRACK *puts his overcoat over the back of the nearest chair and sits down, keeping his hat in his hand. Brief silence. They look at one another.*]

Hedda. Well?
Brack [*in the same tone*]. Well?
Hedda. I said it first.
Brack [*leans forward a little*]. All right. Let's have a nice little chat, Mrs. Tesman.
Hedda [*leans back*]. Don't you think it's an eternity since last time we talked! I don't count last night and this morning. That was nothing.
Brack. You mean—just the two of us?
Hedda. Mmm. If you like.
Brack. There hasn't been a day I haven't wished you were back again.
Hedda. My feelings, exactly.
Brack. Yours? Really, Mrs. Tesman? And I have been assuming you were having such a wonderful time.
Hedda. I'd say!
Brack. All Tesman's letters said so.
Hedda. Oh yes, he! He's happy just poking through old collections of books. And copying old parchments—or whatever they are.
Brack [*with a touch of malice*]. Well, that's his calling, you know. Partly, anyway.
Hedda. Yes, so it is. And in that case I suppose—But I! Oh, Judge! You've no idea how bored I've been.
Brack [*with sympathy*]. Really? You're serious?
Hedda. Surely you can understand that? For a whole half year never to see anyone who knows even a little bit about our circle? And talks our language?
Brack. Yes, I think I would find that trying, too.
Hedda. And then the most unbearable thing of all—
Brack. Well?
Hedda. —everlastingly to be in the company of the same person—
Brack [*nods in agreement*]. Both early and late—yes. I can imagine—at all possible times—
Hedda. I said everlastingly.
Brack. All right. Still, it seems to me that with as excellent a person as our Tesman, it ought to be possible—
Hedda. My dear Judge—Tesman is a specialist.
Brack. Granted.
Hedda. And specialists are not at all entertaining travel companions. Not in the long run, at any rate.
Brack. Not even—the specialist—one happens to love?
Hedda. Bah! That nauseating word!
Brack [*puzzled*]. Really, now, Mrs. Tesman—?
Hedda [*half laughing, half annoyed*]. You ought to try it some time! Listening to talk about the history of civilization, early and late—
Brack. Everlastingly—
Hedda. All right. And then this business about the domestic industry in the Middle Ages—! That's the ghastliest part of it all!

Brack [*looking searchingly at her*]. But in that case—tell me—how am I to explain—?

Hedda. That Jørgen Tesman and I made a pair of it, you mean?

Brack. If you want to put it that way—yes.

Hedda. Come now. Do you really find that so strange?

Brack. Both yes and no—Mrs. Tesman.

Hedda. I had danced myself tired, my dear Judge. My season was over—[*Gives a slight start.*] No, no—I don't really mean that. Won't think it, either!

Brack. Nor do you have the slightest reason to, I am sure.

Hedda. Oh—as far as reasons are concerned—[*Looks at him as if trying to read his mind.*] And, after all, Jørgen Tesman must be said to be a most proper young man in all respects.

Brack. Both proper and substantial. Most certainly.

Hedda. And one can't say there is anything exactly comical about him. Do you think there is?

Brack. Comical? No—o. I wouldn't say that—

Hedda. All right, then. And he is a most assiduous collector. Nobody can deny that. I think it is perfectly possible he may go quite far, after all.

Brack [*looks at her rather uncertainly*]. I assumed that you, like everybody else, thought he'll in time become an exceptionally eminent man?

Hedda [*with a weary expression*]. Yes, I did. And then, you see—there he was, wanting so desperately to be allowed to provide for me—I don't know why I shouldn't have accepted?

Brack. No, certainly. From that point of view—

Hedda. For you know, Judge, that was considerably more than my other admirers were willing to do.

Brack [*laughs*]. Well! Of course I can't answer for all the others. But as far as I am concerned, I have always had a certain degree of—respect for the bonds of matrimony. You know—as a general proposition, Mrs. Tesman.

Hedda [*lightly*]. Well, I never really counted very heavily on *you*—

Brack. All I want is a nice, confidential circle, in which I can be of service, both in deed and in counsel. Be allowed to come and go like a true and trusted friend—

Hedda. You mean, of the master of the house—?

Brack [*with a slight bow*]. To be perfectly frank—rather of the mistress. But by all means—the master, too, of course. Do you know, that kind of—shall I say, triangular?—relationship can really be a great comfort to all parties involved.

Hedda. Yes, many were the times I missed a second travel companion. To be twosome in the compartment—brrr!

Brack. Fortunately, the wedding trip is over.

Hedda [*shakes her head*]. There's a long journey ahead. I've just arrived at a station on the way.

Brack. Well, at the station one gets out and moves around a bit, Mrs. Tesman.

Hedda. I never get out.

Brack. Really?

Hedda. No. For there's always someone around, who—

Brack [*laughs*]. —looks at one's legs; is that it?

Hedda. Exactly.

Brack. Oh well, really, now—

Hedda [*with a silencing gesture*].   I won't have it! Rather stay in my seat—once I'm seated. Twosome and all.

Brack.   I see. But what if a third party were to join the couple?

Hedda.   Well, now—*that* would be something altogether different!

Brack.   A proven, understanding friend—

Hedda.   —entertaining in all sorts of lively ways—

Brack.   —and not at all a specialist!

Hedda [*with audible breath*].   Yes, that would indeed be a comfort.

Brack [*hearing the front door open, looking at her*].   The triangle is complete.

Hedda [*half aloud*].   And the train goes on.

[TESMAN, *in gray walking suit and soft hat, enters, right. He carries a pile of paperbound books under his arm. Others are stuffed in his pockets.*]

Tesman [*as he walks up to the table in front of the corner sofa*].   Puuhh—! Quite some load to carry, all this—and in this heat, too. [*Puts the books down.*] I am positively perspiring, Hedda. Well, well. So you're here already, my dear Judge. Hm? And Berte didn't tell me.

Brack [*rises*].   I came through the garden.

Hedda.   What are all those books?

Tesman [*leafing through some of them*].   Just some new publications in my special field.

Hedda.   Special field, hm?

Brack.   Ah yes—professional publications, Mrs. Tesman.

[BRACK *and* HEDDA *exchange knowing smiles.*]

Hedda.   Do you still need more books?

Tesman.   Yes, my dear. There is no such thing as having too many books in one's special field. One has to keep up with what is being written and published, you know.

Hedda.   I suppose.

Tesman [*searching among the books*].   And look. Here is Eilert Løvborg's new book, too. [*Offers it to her.*] Want to take a look at it, Hedda? Hm?

Hedda.   No—thanks just the same. Or perhaps later.

Tesman.   I glanced at it on my way home.

Brack.   And what do you think of it? As a specialist yourself?

Tesman.   It is remarkable for its sobriety. He never wrote like that before. [*Gathers up all the books.*] I just want to take these into my study. I am so much looking forward to cutting them open! And then I'll change. [*To* BRACK.] I assume there's no rush to be off, is there?

Brack.   Not at all. We have plenty of time.

Tesman.   In that case, I think I'll indulge myself a little. [*On his way out with the books he halts in the doorway and turns.*] By the way, Hedda—Aunt Julle won't be out to see you tonight, after all.

Hedda.   No? Is it that business with the hat, do you think?

Tesman.   Oh, no—not at all. How can you believe a thing like that about Aunt Julle! Just think! No, it's Aunt Rina. She's feeling very poorly.

Hedda.   Isn't she always?

Tesman.   Yes, but it's especially bad today, poor thing.

Hedda. Well in that case I suppose she ought to stay home. I shall have to put up with it; that's all.

Tesman. And you have no idea how perfectly delighted Aunt Julle was, even so. Because of how splendid you look after the trip, Hedda!

Hedda [*half aloud, rising*]. Oh, these everlasting aunts!

Tesman. Hm?

Hedda [*walks over to the French doors*]. Nothing.

Tesman. No? All right. Well, excuse me. [*Exits right, through inner room.*]

Brack. What is this about a hat?

Hedda. Oh, something with Miss Tesman this morning. She had put her hat down on the chair over there. [*Looks at him, smiles.*] So I pretended to think it was the maid's.

Brack [*shakes his head*]. But my dear Mrs. Tesman—how could you do a thing like that! And to that excellent old lady, too!

Hedda [*nervously pacing the floor*]. Well, you see—something just takes hold of me at times. And then I can't help myself—[*Throws herself down in the easy chair near the stove.*] Oh I can't explain it even to myself.

Brack [*behind her chair*]. You aren't really happy—that's the trouble.

Hedda [*staring into space*]. I don't know any reason why I should be. Do you?

Brack. Well, yes—partly because you've got the home you've always wanted.

Hedda [*looks up at him and laughs*]. So you too believe that story about my great wish?

Brack. You mean, there is nothing to it?

Hedda. Well, yes; there is *something* to it.

Brack. Well?

Hedda. There is this much to it, that last summer I used Tesman to see me home from evening parties.

Brack. Unfortunately—my route was in quite a different direction.

Hedda. True. You walked on other roads last summer.

Brack [*laughs*]. Shame on you, Mrs. Tesman! So, all right—you and Tesman—?

Hedda. One evening we passed by here. And Tesman, poor thing, was practically turning himself into knots trying to find something to talk about. So I felt sorry for all that erudition—

Brack [*with a doubting smile*]. You did? Hm—

Hedda. I really did. So, just to help him out of his misery, I happened to say that I'd like to live in this house.

Brack. Just that?

Hedda. That was all—*that* evening.

Brack. But afterwards—?

Hedda. Yes, my frivolity had consequences, Judge.

Brack. Unfortunately—that's often the way with frivolities. It happens to all of us, Mrs. Tesman.

Hedda. Thanks! So in our common enthusiasm for Mr. Secretary Falk's villa Tesman and I found each other, you see! The result was engagement and wedding and honeymoon abroad and all the rest of it. Well, yes, my dear Judge—I've made my bed—I almost said.

Brack. But this is priceless! And you didn't really care for the house at all?

Hedda. Certainly not.

Brack. Not even now? After all, we've set up quite a comfortable home for you here, haven't we?

Hedda. Oh—it seems to me I smell lavender and rose sachets in all the rooms. But maybe that's a smell Aunt Julle brought with her.

Brack [*laughs*]. My guess is rather the late lamented Secretary's wife.

Hedda. It smells of mortality, whoever it is. Like corsages—the next day. [*Clasps her hands behind her neck, leans back, looks at him.*] Judge, you have no idea how dreadfully bored I'll be—out here.

Brack. But don't you think life may hold some task for you, too, Mrs. Tesman?

Hedda. A task? With any kind of appeal?

Brack. Preferably that, of course.

Hedda. Heaven knows what kind of task that might be. There are times when I wonder if—[*Interrupts herself.*] No; I'm sure that wouldn't work, either.

Brack. Who knows? Tell me.

Hedda. It has occurred to me that maybe I could get Tesman to enter politics.

Brack [*laughs*]. Tesman! No, really—I must confess that—politics doesn't strike me as being exactly Tesman's line.

Hedda. I agree. But suppose I were to prevail on him, all the same?

Brack. What satisfaction could you possibly find in that? If he can't succeed— why do you want him even to try?

Hedda. Because I am bored, I tell you! [*After a brief pause.*] So you think it's quite out of the question that Tesman could ever become prime minister?

Brack. Well, you see, Mrs. Tesman—to do that he'd first of all have to be a fairly wealthy man.

Hedda [*getting up, impatiently*]. Yes! There we are! These shabby circumstances I've married into! [*Crosses the floor.*] That's what makes life so mean. So—so—ridiculous! For that's what it is, you know.

Brack. Personally I believe something else is to blame.

Hedda. What?

Brack. You've never been through anything that's really stirred you.

Hedda. Something serious, you mean?

Brack. If you like. But maybe it's coming now.

Hedda [*with a toss of her head*]. You are thinking of that silly old professorship! That's Tesman's business. I refuse to give it a thought.

Brack. As you wish. But now—to put it in the grand style—now when a solemn challenge of responsibility is being posed? Demands made on you? [*Smiles.*] New demands, Mrs. Tesman.

Hedda [*angry*]. Quiet! You'll never see anything of the kind.

Brack [*cautiously*]. We'll talk about this a year from now—on the outside.

Hedda [*curtly*]. I'm not made for that sort of thing, Judge! No demands for me!

Brack. But surely you, like most women, are made for a duty, which—

Hedda [*over by the French doors*]. Oh, do be quiet! Often it seems to me there's only one thing in the world that I am made for.

Brack [*coming close*]. And may I ask what that is?

Hedda [*looking out*]. To be bored to death. Now you know. [*Turns, looks toward the inner room, laughs.*] Just as I thought. Here comes the professor.

Brack [*warningly, in a low voice*]. Steady, now, Mrs. Tesman!

[TESMAN, *dressed for a party, carrying his hat and gloves, enters from the right side of the inner room.*]

Tesman. Hedda, any word yet from Eilert Løvborg that he isn't coming, hm?

Hedda. No.

Tesman. In that case, I wouldn't be a bit surprised if we have him here in a few minutes.

Brack. You really think he'll come?

Tesman. I am almost certain he will. For I'm sure it's only idle gossip that you told me this morning.

Brack. Oh?

Tesman. Anyway, that's what Aunt Julle said. She doesn't for a moment believe he'll stand in my way. Just think!

Brack. I'm very glad to hear that.

Tesman [*puts his hat and his gloves down on a chair, right*]. But you must let me wait for him as long as possible.

Brack. By all means. We have plenty of time. Nobody will arrive at my place before seven—seven-thirty, or so.

Tesman. And in the meantime we can keep Hedda company. Take our time. Hm?

Hedda [*carrying* BRACK'S *hat and coat over to the sofa in the corner*]. And if worst comes to worst, Mr. Løvborg can stay here with me.

Brack [*trying to take the things away from her*]. Let me, Mrs. Tesman—What do you mean—"if worst comes to worst?"

Hedda. If he doesn't want to go with you and Tesman.

Tesman [*looks dubiously at her*]. But, dearest Hedda—do you think that will quite do? He staying here with you? Hmm? Remember, Aunt Julle won't be here.

Hedda. No, but Mrs. Elvsted will. The three of us will have a cup of tea together.

Tesman. Oh yes; *that* will be perfectly all right!

Brack [*with a smile*]. And perhaps the wiser course of action for him.

Hedda. What do you mean?

Brack. Begging your pardon, Mrs. Tesman—you've often enough looked askance at my little stag dinners. It's been your opinion that only men of the firmest principles ought to attend.

Hedda. I should think Mr. Løvborg is firm-principled enough now. A reformed sinner—

[BERTE *appears in door, right.*]

Berte. Ma'am—there's a gentleman here who asks if—

Hedda. Show him in, please.

Tesman [*softly*]. I'm sure it's he! Just think!

[EILERT LØVBORG *enters, right. He is slim, gaunt. Of* TESMAN'S *age, but he looks older and somewhat dissipated. Brown hair and beard. Pale, longish face, reddish spots on the cheekbones. Dressed for visiting in elegant, black, brand-new suit. He carries a silk hat and dark gloves in his hand. He remains near the door, makes a quick bow. He appears a little embarrassed.*]

Tesman [*goes over to him, shakes his hand*]. My dear Eilert—at last we meet again!

Eilert Løvborg [*subdued voice*]. Thanks for your note, Jørgen! [*Approaching* HEDDA.] Am I allowed to shake your hand, too, Mrs. Tesman?

Hedda [*accepting his proffered hand*]. I am very glad to see you, Mr. Løvborg. [*With a gesture.*] I don't know if you two gentlemen—

Løvborg [*with a slight bow*]. Judge Brack, I believe.

Brack [*also bowing lightly*]. Certainly. Some years ago—

Tesman [*to* LØVBORG, *both hands on his shoulders*]. And now I want you to feel quite at home here, Eilert! Isn't that right, Hedda? For you plan to stay here in town, I understand. Hm?

Løvborg. Yes, I do.

Tesman. Perfectly reasonable. Listen—I just got hold of your new book, but I haven't had a chance to read it yet.

Løvborg. You may save yourself the trouble.

Tesman. Why do you say that?

Løvborg. There's not much to it.

Tesman. Just think—you saying that!

Brack. Nevertheless, people seem to have very good things to say about it.

Løvborg. That's exactly why I wrote it—so everybody would like it.

Brack. Very wise of you.

Tesman. Yes, but Eilert—!

Løvborg. For I am trying to rebuild my position. Start all over again.

Tesman [*with some embarrassment*]. Yes, I suppose you are, aren't you? Hm?

Løvborg [*smiles, puts his hat down, pulls a parcel out of his pocket*]. When *this* appears—Jørgen Tesman—this you must read. For this is the real thing. This is me.

Tesman. Oh really? And what is it?

Løvborg. The continuation.

Tesman. Continuation? Of what?

Løvborg. Of the book.

Tesman. Of the new book?

Løvborg. Of course.

Tesman. But Eilert—you've carried the story all the way up to the present!

Løvborg. So I have. And this is about the future.

Tesman. The future! But, heavens—we don't know a thing about the future!

Løvborg. No, we don't. But there are a couple of things to be said about it all the same. [*Unwraps the parcel.*] Here, let me show you—

Tesman. But that's not your handwriting.

Løvborg. I have dictated it. [*Leafs through portions of the manuscript.*] It's in two parts. The first is about the forces that will shape the civilization of the future. And the second [*riffling through more pages*]—about the course which that future civilization will take.

Tesman. How remarkable! It would never occur to me to write anything like that.

Hedda [*over by the French doors, her fingers drumming the pane*]. Hmm—I dare say—

Løvborg [*replacing the manuscript in its wrappings and putting it down on the table*]. I brought it along, for I thought maybe I'd read parts of it aloud to you this evening.

Tesman. That's very good of you, Eilert. But this evening—? [*Looks at* BRACK.] I'm not quite sure how to arrange that—

Løvborg. Some other time, then. There's no hurry.

Brack. You see, Mr. Løvborg, there's a little get-together over at my house tonight. Mainly for Tesman, you know—

Løvborg [*looking for his hat*]. In that case, I certainly won't—

Brack. No, listen. Won't you do me the pleasure to join us?

Løvborg [*firmly*]. No, I won't. But thanks all the same.

Brack. Oh come on! Why don't you do that? We'll be a small, select circle. And I think I can promise you a fairly lively evening, as Hed—as Mrs. Tesman would say.

Løvborg. I don't doubt that. Nevertheless—

Brack. And you may bring your manuscript along and read aloud to Tesman over at my house. I have plenty of room.

Tesman. Just think, Eilert! Wouldn't that be nice, hm?

Hedda [*intervening*]. But can't you see that Mr. Løvborg doesn't want to? I'm sure he would rather stay here and have supper with me.

Løvborg [*looks at her*]. With you, Mrs. Tesman?

Hedda. And with Mrs. Elvsted.

Løvborg. Ah—! [*Casually.*] I ran into her at noon today.

Hedda. Oh? Well, she'll be here tonight. So you see your presence is really required, Mr. Løvborg. Otherwise she won't have anybody to see her home.

Løvborg. True. All right, then, Mrs. Tesman—I'll stay, thank you.

Hedda. Good. I'll just tell the maid. [*She rings for* BERTE *over by the door, right.*]

[BERTE *appears just off stage.* HEDDA *talks with her in a low voice, points toward the inner room.* BERTE *nods and exits.*]

Tesman [*while* HEDDA *and* BERTE *are talking, to* LØVBORG]. Tell me, Eilert—is it this new subject—about the future—is that what you plan to lecture on?

Løvborg. Yes.

Tesman. For the bookseller told me you have announced a lecture series for this fall.

Løvborg. Yes, I have. I hope you won't mind too much.

Tesman. Of course not! But—

Løvborg. For of course I realize it is rather awkward for you.

Tesman [*unhappily*]. Oh well—I certainly can't expect—that just for my sake—

Løvborg. But I will wait till you receive your appointment.

Tesman. Wait? But—but—but—you mean you aren't going to compete with me? Hm?

Løvborg. No. Just triumph over you. In people's opinion.

Tesman. Oh, for goodness' sake! Then Aunt Julle was right, after all! I knew it all the time. Hedda! Do you hear that! Just think—Eilert Løvborg isn't going to stand in our way after all.

Hedda [*tersely*]. Our? I have nothing to do with this.

[HEDDA *walks into the inner room, where* BERTE *is bringing in a tray with decanters and glasses.* HEDDA *nods her approval and comes forward again.*]

Tesman [*during the foregoing business*].   How about that, Judge? What do you say to this? Hm?

Brack.   I say that moral victory and all that—hm—may be glorious enough and beautiful enough—

Tesman.   Oh, I agree. All the same—

Hedda [*looks at* TESMAN *with a cold smile*].   You look thunderstruck.

Tesman.   Well, I am—pretty much—I really believe—

Brack.   After all, Mrs. Tesman, that was quite a thunderstorm that just passed over.

Hedda [*points to the inner room*].   How about a glass of cold punch, gentlemen?

Brack [*looks at his watch*].   A stirrup cup. Not a bad idea.

Tesman.   Splendid, Hedda. Perfectly splendid. In such a lighthearted mood as I am now—

Hedda.   Please. You, too, Mr. Løvborg.

Løvborg [*with a gesture of refusal*].   No, thanks. Really. Nothing for me.

Brack.   Good heavens, man! Cold punch isn't poison, you know!

Løvborg.   Perhaps not for everybody.

Hedda.   I'll keep Mr. Løvborg company in the meantime.

Tesman.   All right, Hedda. You do that.

[*He and* BRACK *go into the inner room, sit down, drink punch, smoke cigarettes, and engage in lively conversation during the next scene.* EILERT LØVBORG *remains standing near the stove.* HEDDA *walks over to the desk.*]

Hedda [*her voice a little louder than usual*].   I'll show you some pictures, if you like. You see—Tesman and I, we took a trip through Tyrol on our way back.

[*She brings an album over to the table by the sofa. She sits down in the far corner of the sofa.* LØVBORG *approaches, stops, looks at her. He takes a chair and sits down at her left, his back toward the inner room.*]

Hedda [*opens the album*].   Do you see these mountains, Mr. Løvborg? They are the Ortler group. Tesman has written their name below. Here it is: "The Ortler group near Meran."

Løvborg [*has looked steadily at her all this time. Says slowly*].   Hedda—Gabler!

Hedda [*with a quick glance sideways*].   Not that! Shhh!

Løvborg [*again*].   Hedda Gabler!

Hedda [*looking at the album*].   Yes, that used to be my name. When—when we two knew each other.

Løvborg.   And so from now on—for the whole rest of my life—I must get used to never again saying Hedda Gabler.

Hedda [*still occupied with the album*].   Yes, you must. And you might as well start right now. The sooner the better, I think.

Løvborg [*with indignation*].   Hedda Gabler married? And married to—Jørgen Tesman!

Hedda.   Yes—that's the way it goes.

Løvborg.   Oh, Hedda, Hedda—how could you throw yourself away like that!

Hedda [*with a fierce glance at him*].   What's this? I won't have any of that!
Løvborg.   What do you mean?

[TESMAN *enters from the inner room.*]

Hedda [*hears him coming and remarks casually*].   And this here, Mr. Løvborg, this is from somewhere in the Ampezzo valley. Just look at those peaks over there. [*With a kindly look at* TESMAN.] What did you say those peaks were called, dear?
Tesman.   Let me see. Oh, they—they are the Dolomites.
Hedda.   Right. Those are the Dolomites, Mr. Løvborg.
Tesman.   Hedda, I thought I'd just ask you if you don't want me to bring you some punch, after all? For you, anyway? Hm?
Hedda.   Well, yes; thanks. And a couple of cookies, maybe.
Tesman.   No cigarettes?
Hedda.   No.
Tesman.   All right.

[*He returns to the inner room, then turns right.* BRACK *is in there, keeping an eye on* HEDDA *and* LØVBORG *from time to time.*]

Løvborg [*still in a low voice*].   Answer me, Hedda. How could you do a thing like that?
Hedda [*apparently engrossed in the album*].   If you keep on using my first name I won't talk to you.
Løvborg.   Not even when we're alone?
Hedda.   No. You may think it, but you must not say it.
Løvborg.   I see. It offends your love for—Jørgen Tesman.
Hedda [*glances at him, smiles*].   Love? That's a good one!
Løvborg.   Not love, then.
Hedda.   But no infidelities, either! I won't have it.
Løvborg.   Hedda—answer me just this one thing—
Hedda.   Shhh!

[TESMAN *enters with a tray from the inner room.*]

Tesman.   Here! Here are the goodies. [*Puts the tray down.*]
Hedda.   Why don't you get Berte to do it?
Tesman [*pouring punch*].   Because I think it's so much fun waiting on you, Hedda.
Hedda.   But you've filled both glasses. And Mr. Løvborg didn't want any—
Tesman.   I know, but Mrs. Elvsted will soon be here, won't she?
Hedda.   That's right. So she will.
Tesman.   Had you forgotten about her? Hm?
Hedda.   We've been so busy looking at this. [*Shows him a picture.*] Remember that little village?
Tesman.   That's the one just below the Brenner Pass, isn't it? We spent the night there—
Hedda.   —and ran into that lively crowd of summer guests.
Tesman.   Right! Just think—if we only could have had you with us, Eilert! Oh well.

[*Returns to the inner room, sits down, and resumes his conversation with* BRACK.]

Løvborg. Just tell me this, Hedda—

Hedda. What?

Løvborg. Wasn't there love in your feelings for me, either? Not a touch—not a shimmer of love? Wasn't there?

Hedda. I wonder. To me, we seemed to be simply two good comrades. Two close friends. [*Smiles.*] You, particularly, were very frank.

Løvborg. You wanted it that way.

Hedda. And yet—when I look back upon it now, there was something beautiful, something thrilling, something brave, I think, about the secret frankness—that comradeship that not a single soul so much as suspected.

Løvborg. Yes, wasn't there, Hedda? Wasn't there? When I called on your father in the afternoons—And the General sat by the window with his newspapers— his back turned—

Hedda. And we two in the sofa in the corner—

Løvborg. —always with the same illustrated magazine—

Hedda. ——for want of an album, yes—

Løvborg. Yes, Hedda—and then when I confessed to you—! Told you all about myself, things the others didn't know. Sat and told you about my orgies by day and night. Dissipation day in and day out! Oh, Hedda—what sort of power in you was it that forced me to tell you things like that?

Hedda. You think there was some power in me?

Løvborg. How else can I explain it? And all those veiled questions you asked—

Hedda. ——which you understood so perfectly well—

Løvborg. That you could ask such questions! With such complete frankness!

Hedda. *Veiled*, if you please.

Løvborg. But frankly all the same. All about—that!

Hedda. And to think that you answered, Mr. Løvborg!

Løvborg. Yes, that's just what I can't understand—now, afterwards. But tell me, Hedda; wasn't love at the bottom of our whole relationship? Didn't you feel some kind of urge to—purify me—when I came to you in confession? Wasn't that it?

Hedda. No, not quite.

Løvborg. Then what made you do it?

Hedda. Do you find it so very strange that a young girl—when she can do so, without anyone knowing—

Løvborg. Yes—?

Hedda. that she wants to take a peek into a world which—

Løvborg. —which—?

Hedda. —she is not supposed to know anything about?

Løvborg. So that was it!

Hedda. That, too. That, too—I think—

Løvborg. Companionship in the lust for life. But why couldn't *that* at least have continued?

Hedda. That was your own fault.

Løvborg. You were the one who broke off.

Hedda. Yes, when reality threatened to enter our relationship. Shame on you, Eilert Løvborg! How could you want to do a thing like that to your frank and trusting comrade!

Løvborg [*clenching his hands*]. Oh, why didn't you do it! Why didn't you shoot me down, as you said you would!

Hedda. Because I'm scared of scandal.

Løvborg. Yes, Hedda. You are really a coward.

Hedda. A terrible coward. [*Changing her tone.*] But that was your good luck, wasn't it? And now the Elvsteds have healed your broken heart very nicely.

Løvborg. I know what Thea has told you.

Hedda. Perhaps you have told her about us?

Løvborg. Not a word. She is too stupid to understand.

Hedda. Stupid?

Løvborg. In things like that.

Hedda. And I'm a coward. [*Leans forward, without looking in his eyes, whispers.*] But now *I* am going to confess something to *you.*

Løvborg [*tense*]. What?

Hedda. That I didn't dare to shoot—

Løvborg. Yes?

Hedda. —that was not the worst of my cowardice that night.

Løvborg [*looks at her a moment, understands, whispers passionately*]. Oh, Hedda! Hedda Gabler! Now I begin to see what was behind the companionship! You and I! So it *was* your lust for life—!

Hedda [*in a low voice, with an angry glance*]. Take care! Don't you believe it!

[*Darkness is falling. The door, right, is opened, and* BERTE *enters.*]

Hedda [*closing the album, calls out, smiling*]. At last! So there you are, dearest Thea! Come in!

[MRS. ELVSTED *enters. She is dressed for a party.* BERTE *exits, closing the door behind her.*]

Hedda [*on the sofa, reaching out for* MRS. ELVSTED]. Sweetest Thea, you have no idea how I've waited for you.

[*In passing,* MRS. ELVSTED *exchanges quick greetings with* TESMAN *and* BRACK *in the inner room. She walks up to the table and shakes* HEDDA'*s hand.* EILERT LØVBORG *rises. He and* MRS. ELVSTED *greet one another with a silent nod.*]

Mrs. Elvsted. Shouldn't I go in and say hello to your husband?

Hedda. No, never mind that. Leave them alone. They're soon leaving, anyway.

Mrs. Elvsted. Leaving?

Hedda. They're going out to drink.

Mrs. Elvsted [*quickly, to* LØVBORG]. Not you?

Løvborg. No.

Hedda. Mr. Løvborg stays here with us.

Mrs. Elvsted [*pulls up a chair, is about to sit down next to* LØVBORG]. Oh, how wonderful it is to be here!

Hedda. Oh no, little Thea. Not that. Not there. Over here by me, please. I want to be in the middle.

Mrs. Elvsted. Just as you like. [*She walks in front of the table and seats herself on the sofa, on* HEDDA's *right.* LØVBORG *sits down again on his chair.*]

Løvborg [*after a brief pause, to* HEDDA]. Isn't she lovely to look at?

Hedda [*gently stroking her hair*]. Just to look at?

Løvborg. Yes. For you see—she and I—we are real comrades. We have absolute faith in one another. And we can talk together in full freedom.

Hedda. Unveiled, Mr. Løvborg?

Løvborg. Well—

Mrs. Elvsted [*in a low voice, clinging to* HEDDA]. Oh, I am so happy, Hedda! For just think—he also says I have inspired him!

Hedda [*looks at her with a smile*]. No, really! He says that?

Løvborg. And she has such courage, Mrs. Tesman! Such courage of action.

Mrs. Elvsted. Oh, my God—courage—! I!

Løvborg. Infinite courage—when it concerns the comrade.

Hedda. Yes, courage—if one only had that.

Løvborg. What then?

Hedda. Then maybe life would be tolerable, after all. [*Changing her tone.*] But now, dearest Thea, you want a glass of nice, cold punch.

Mrs. Elvsted. No, thanks. I never drink things like that.

Hedda. Then what about you, Mr. Løvborg?

Løvborg. Thanks. Nothing for me, either.

Mrs. Elvsted. No, nothing for him, either.

Hedda [*looks firmly at him*]. If I say so?

Løvborg. Makes no difference.

Hedda [*laughs*]. Oh dear! So I have no power over you at all. Is that it?

Løvborg. Not in that respect.

Hedda. Seriously, though; I really think you should. For your own sake.

Mrs. Elvsted. No, but Hedda—!

Løvborg. Why so?

Hedda. Or rather for people's sake.

Løvborg. Oh?

Hedda. For else they might think you don't really trust yourself—That you lack self-confidence—

Mrs. Elvsted [*softly*]. Don't, Hedda!

Løvborg. People may think whatever they like for all I care—for the time being.

Mrs. Elvsted [*happy*]. Exactly!

Hedda. I could easily tell from watching Judge Brack just now.

Løvborg. Tell what?

Hedda. He smiled so contemptuously when you didn't dare to join them in there.

Løvborg. Didn't I dare to! It's just that I'd much rather stay here and talk with you!

Mrs. Elvsted. But that's only natural, Hedda.

Hedda. The Judge had no way of knowing that. And I also noticed he smiled and looked at Tesman when you didn't dare to go to his silly old party.

Løvborg. Didn't dare! Are you saying I didn't dare?

Hedda. I am not. But that's how Judge Brack understood it.

Løvborg. Let him.

Hedda. So you're not going?

Løvborg. I'm staying here with you and Thea.

Mrs. Elvsted. Of course, he is, Hedda!

Hedda [*smiles, nods approvingly*]. That's what I call firm foundations. Principled forever; that's the way a man ought to be! [*Turning to* MRS. ELVSTED, *stroking her cheek.*] What did I tell you this morning—when you came here, quite beside yourself—?

Løvborg [*puzzled*]. Beside herself?

Mrs. Elvsted [*in terror*]. Hedda—Hedda—don't!

Hedda. Now do you see? There was no need at all for that mortal fear of yours—[*Interrupting herself.*] There, now! Now we can all three relax and enjoy ourselves.

Løvborg [*startled*]. What's all this, Mrs. Tesman?

Mrs. Elvsted. Oh, God, Hedda—what are you saying? What are you doing?

Hedda. Please be quiet. That horrible Judge is looking at you.

Løvborg. In mortal fear? So that's it. For my sake.

Mrs. Elvsted [*softly, wailing*]. Oh, Hedda—if you only knew how utterly miserable you have made me!

Løvborg [*stares at her for a moment. His face is distorted*]. So that was the comrade's happy confidence in me!

Mrs. Elvsted. Oh, my dearest friend—listen to me first—!

Løvborg [*picks up one of the glasses of punch, raises it, says hoarsely*]. Here's to you, Thea! [*Empties the glass, puts it down, picks up the other one.*]

Mrs. Elvsted [*softly*]. Hedda, Hedda—why did you want to do this?

Hedda. Want to! I! Are you mad?

Løvborg. And here's to you, too, Mrs. Tesman! Thanks for telling me the truth. Long live the truth! (*He drains the glass and is about to fill it again.*]

Hedda [*restrains him*]. That's enough for now. Remember you are going to a party.

Mrs. Elvsted. No, no, no!

Hedda. Shhh! They are looking at you.

Løvborg [*puts his glass down*]. Listen, Thea—tell me the truth—

Mrs. Elvsted. I will, I will!

Løvborg. Did your husband know you were coming after me?

Mrs. Elvsted [*wringing her hands*]. Oh, Hedda—do you hear what he's asking?

Løvborg. Did the two of you agree that you were to come here and look after me? Maybe it was his idea, even? Did he send you? Ah, I know what it was—he missed me in the office, didn't he? Or was it at the card table?

Mrs. Elvsted [*softly, in agony*]. Oh, Løvborg, Løvborg!

Løvborg [*grabs a glass and is about to fill it*]. Here's to the old Commissioner, too!

Hedda [*stops him*]. No more now. You're supposed to read aloud for Tesman tonight—remember?

Løvborg [*calm again, puts the glass down*]. This was silly of me, Thea. I'm sorry. Taking it this way. Please, don't be angry with me. You'll see—both you and all those others—that even if I have been down—! With your help, Thea— dear comrade.

Mrs. Elvsted [*beaming*]. Oh, thank God—!

[*In the meantime,* BRACK *has looked at his watch. He and* TESMAN *get up and come forward.*]

Brack [*picking up his coat and hat*].   Well, Mrs. Tesman; our time is up.
Hedda.   I suppose it is.
Løvborg [*rising*].   Mine, too, Judge.
Mrs. Elvsted [*softly, pleadingly*].   Oh, Løvborg—don't do it!
Hedda [*pinches her arm*].   They can hear you!
Mrs. Elvsted [*with a soft exclamation*].   Ouch!
Løvborg [*to* BRACK].   You were good enough to ask me—
Brack.   So you're coming, after all?
Løvborg.   If I may.
Brack.   I'm delighted.
Løvborg [*picks up his manuscript and says to* TESMAN].   For there are a couple of things here I'd like to show you before I send it off.
Tesman.   Just think! Isn't that nice! But—dearest Hedda—? In that case, how are you going to get Mrs. Elvsted home? Hm?
Hedda.   We'll manage somehow.
Løvborg [*looking at the two women*].   Mrs. Elvsted? I'll be back to pick her up, of course. [*Coming closer.*] About ten o'clock, Mrs. Tesman? Is that convenient?
Hedda.   Certainly. That will be fine.
Tesman.   Then everything is nice and settled. But don't expect me that early, Hedda.
Hedda.   You just stay as long as—as long as you want to, dear.
Mrs. Elvsted [*in secret fear*].   I'll be waiting for you here, then, Mr. Løvborg.
Løvborg [*hat in hand*].   Of course, Mrs. Elvsted.
Brack.   All aboard the pleasure train, gentlemen! I hope we'll have a lively evening—as a certain fair lady would say.
Hedda.   Ah—if only the fair lady could be present. Invisibly.
Brack.   Why invisibly?
Hedda.   To listen to some of your unadulterated liveliness, Judge.
Brack [*laughs*].   I shouldn't advise the fair lady to do that!
Tesman [*also laughing*].   You're a good one, Hedda! Just think!
Brack.   Well—good night, ladies!
Løvborg [*with a bow*].   Till about ten, then.

[BRACK, LØVBORG, *and* TESMAN *go out, right. At the same time* BERTE *enters from the inner room with a lighted lamp, which she places on the table, front center. She goes out the same way.*]

Mrs. Elvsted [*has risen and paces restlessly up and down*].   Hedda, Hedda—how do you think all this will end?
Hedda.   At ten o'clock he'll be here. I see him already. With vine leaves in his hair. Flushed and confident.
Mrs. Elvsted.   I only hope you're right.
Hedda.   For then, you see, he'll have mastered himself. And be a free man for all the days of his life.

. *Mrs. Elvsted.* Dear God—how I hope you are right! That he'll come back like that.

Hedda. That is the way he will come. No other way. [*She rises and goes closer to* MRS. ELVSTED.] You may doubt as long as you like. I believe in him. And now we'll see—

Mrs. Elvsted. There is something behind all this, Hedda. Some hidden purpose.

Hedda. Yes, there is! For once in my life I want to have power over a human destiny.

Mrs. Elvsted. But don't you already?

Hedda. I don't and I never have.

Mrs. Elvsted. But your husband—?

Hedda. You think that's worth the trouble? Oh, if you knew how poor I am! And you got to be so rich! [*Embraces her passionately.*] I think I'll have to burn your hair off, after all!

Mrs. Elvsted. Let me go! Let me go! You scare me, Hedda!

Berte [*in the doorway*]. Supper is served, ma'am.

Hedda. Good. We're coming.

Mrs. Elvsted. No, no, no! I'd rather go home by myself! Right now!

Hedda. Nonsense! You'll have your cup of tea first, you little silly. And then—at ten o'clock—Eilert Løvborg comes—with vine leaves in his hair! [*She almost pulls* MRS. ELVSTED *toward the doorway.*]

Act III

[*The same room at the* TESMANS'. *The doorway and the French windows both have their portieres closed. The lamp, turned half down, is still on the table. The stove is open. Some dying embers can be seen.*]

[MRS. ELVSTED, *wrapped in a big shawl, is in the easy chair near the stove, her feet on a footstool.* HEDDA, *also dressed, is lying on the sofa, covered by a blanket.*]

Mrs. Elvsted [*after a while suddenly sits up, listens anxiously; then she wearily sinks back in her chair, whimpers softly*]. Oh my God, my God—not yet!

[BERTE *enters cautiously, right, carrying a letter.*]

Mrs. Elvsted [*turns and whispers tensely*]. Well—has anybody been here?

Berte [*in a low voice*]. Yes. Just now there was a girl with this letter.

Mrs. Elvsted [*quickly, reaches for it*]. A letter! Give it to me.

Berte. No, ma'am. It's for the Doctor.

Mrs. Elvsted. I see.

Berte. Miss Tesman's maid brought it. I'll leave it here on the table.

Mrs. Elvsted. All right.

Berte [*puts the letter down*]. I'd better put out the lamp. It just reeks.

Mrs. Elvsted. Yes, do that. It must be daylight soon, anyway.

Berte [*putting out the lamp*]. It's light already, ma'am.

Mrs. Elvsted. Light already! And still not back!

Berte. No, so help us. Not that I didn't expect as much—

Mrs. Elvsted. You did?

Berte. Yes, when I saw a certain character was back in town. Taking them off with him. We sure heard enough about him in the old days!

Mrs. Elvsted. Not so loud. You are waking up Mrs. Tesman.

Berte [*looks toward the sofa, sighs*]. God forbid—! Let her sleep, poor thing. Do you want me to get the fire going again?

Mrs. Elvsted. Not on my account, thank you.

Berte. All right. [*Exits quietly, right.*]

Hedda [*awakened by the closing door*]. What's that?

Mrs. Elvsted. Just the maid.

Hedda [*looks around*]. Why in here—? Oh, I remember! [*Sits up, rubs her eyes, stretches.*] What time is it, Thea?

Mrs. Elvsted [*looks at her watch*]. Past seven.

Hedda. When did Tesman get home?

Mrs. Elvsted. He didn't.

Hedda. Not home yet!

Mrs. Elvsted [*getting up*]. Nobody's come.

Hedda. And we waited till four!

Mrs. Elvsted [*wringing her hands*]. And *how* we waited!

Hedda [*her hand covering a yawn*]. We—ll. We could have saved ourselves that trouble.

Mrs. Elvsted. Did you get any sleep at all?

Hedda. Yes, I slept pretty well, I think. Didn't you?

Mrs. Elvsted. Not a wink. I just couldn't, Hedda! It was just impossible.

Hedda [*rises, walks over to her*]. Well, now! There's nothing to worry about, for heaven's sake. I know exactly what's happened.

Mrs. Elvsted. Then tell me please. Where do you think they are?

Hedda. Well, first of all, I'm sure they were terribly late leaving the Judge's—

Mrs. Elvsted. Dear, yes. I'm sure you're right. Still—

Hedda. —and so Tesman didn't want to wake us up in the middle of the night. [*Laughs.*] Maybe he didn't want us to see him, either—after a party like that.

Mrs. Elvsted. But where do you think he has gone?

Hedda. To the aunts', of course. His old room is still there, all ready for him.

Mrs. Elvsted. No, he can't be there. Just a few minutes ago there came a letter for him from Miss Tesman. It's over there.

Hedda. Oh? [*looks at the envelope.*] So it is—Auntie Julle herself. In that case, I suppose he's still at Brack's. And there's Eilert Løvborg, too—reading aloud, with vine leaves in his hair.

Mrs. Elvsted. Oh Hedda—you're only saying things you don't believe yourself.

Hedda. My, what a little imbecile you really are, Thea!

Mrs. Elvsted. Yes, I suppose I am.

Hedda. And you look dead tired, too.

Mrs. Elvsted. I *am* dead tired.

Hedda. Why don't you do as I say. Go into my room and lie down.

Mrs. Elvsted. No, no—I wouldn't be able to go to sleep, anyway.

Hedda. Of course, you would.

Mrs. Elvsted. And your husband is bound to be home any minute now. And I have to know right away.

Hedda. I'll let you know as soon as he gets here.

Mrs. Elvsted. You promise me that, Hedda?

Hedda. I do. You just go to sleep.

Mrs. Elvsted. Thanks. At least I'll try. [*Exits through inner room.*]

[HEDDA *goes to the French doors, opens the portieres. The room is now in full daylight. She picks up a little hand mirror from the desk, looks at herself, smooths her hair. Walks over to door, right, rings the bell for the maid.* BERTE *presently appears.*]

Berte. You want something, ma'am?

Hedda. Yes. You'll have to start the fire again. I'm cold.

Berte. Yes, ma'am! I'll get it warm in no time. [*Rakes the embers together and puts in another piece of wood. Then she suddenly listens.*] There's the doorbell, ma'am.

Hedda. All right. See who it is. I'll take care of the stove myself.

Berte. You'll have a nice blaze going in a minute. [*Exits right.*]

[HEDDA *kneels on the footstool and puts in more pieces of wood. Presently* TESMAN *enters, right. He looks tired and somber. He tiptoes toward the doorway and is about to disappear between the portieres.*]

Hedda [*by the stove, without looking up*]. Good morning.

Tesman [*turning*]. Hedda! [*Comes closer.*] For heaven's sake—you up already! Hm?

Hedda. Yes, I got up very early this morning.

Tesman. And I was sure you'd still be sound asleep! Just think!

Hedda. Not so loud. Mrs. Elvsted is asleep in my room.

Tesman. Mrs. Elvsted stayed here all night?

Hedda. Yes. Nobody came for her, you know.

Tesman. No, I suppose—

Hedda [*closes the stove, rises*]. Well, did you have a good time at the Judge's?

Tesman. Were you worried about me? Hm?

Hedda. I'd never dream of worrying about you. I asked if you had a good time.

Tesman. Yes, indeed, Nice for a change, anyway. But I think I liked it best early in the evening. For then Eilert read to me. Just think—we were more than an hour early! And Brack, of course, had things to see to. So Eilert read.

Hedda [*sits down at the right side of the table*]. So? Tell me about it.

Tesman [*sits down on an ottoman near the stove*]. Oh Hedda, you'll never believe what a book that will be! It must be just the most remarkable thing ever written! Just think!

Hedda. Yes, but I don't really care about that—

Tesman. I must tell you, Hedda—I have a confession to make. As he was reading—something ugly came over me——

Hedda. Ugly?

Tesman. I sat there envying Eilert for being able to write like that! Just think, Hedda!

Hedda. All right. I'm thinking!

Tesman. And yet, with all his gifts—he's incorrigible, after all.

Hedda. I suppose you mean he has more courage for life than the rest of you?

Tesman. No, no—I don't mean that. I mean that he's incapable of exercising moderation in his pleasures.

Hedda. What happened—in the end?

Tesman. Well—I would call it a bacchanal, Hedda.

Hedda. Did he have vine leaves in his hair?

Tesman. Vine leaves? No, I didn't notice any vine leaves. But he gave a long, muddled speech in honor of the woman who had inspired him in his work. Those were his words.

Hedda. Did he mention her name?

Tesman. No, he didn't. But I'm sure it must be Mrs. Elvsted. You just wait and see if I'm not right!

Hedda. And where did you and he part company?

Tesman. On the way back to town. We left—the last of us did—at the same time. And Brack came along, too, to get some fresh air. Then we decided we'd better see Eilert home. You see, he had had altogether too much to drink!

Hedda. I can imagine.

Tesman. But then the strangest thing of all happened, Hedda! Or maybe I should say the saddest. I'm almost ashamed—on Eilert's behalf—even talking about it.

Hedda. Well—?

Tesman. You see, on the way back I happened to be behind the others a little. Just for a minute or two—you know—

Hedda. All right, all right—!

Tesman. And when I hurried to catch up with them, can you guess what I found by the roadside? Hm?

Hedda. How can I possibly—?

Tesman. You mustn't tell this to a living soul, Hedda! Do you hear! Promise me that, for Eilert's sake. [*Pulls a parcel out of his coat pocket.*] Just think—I found this!

Hedda. Isn't that what he had with him here yesterday?

Tesman. Yes! It's his whole, precious, irreplaceable manuscript! And he had dropped it—just like that! Without even noticing! Just think, Hedda! Isn't that awfully sad?

Hedda. But why didn't you give it back to him?

Tesman. In the condition he was in! Dear—I just didn't dare to.

Hedda. And you didn't tell any of the others that you had found it, either?

Tesman. Of course not. I didn't want to, for Eilert's sake—don't you see?

Hedda. So nobody knows that you have Eilert Løvborg's papers?

Tesman. Nobody. And nobody must know, either.

Hedda. And what did you and he talk about afterwards?

Tesman. I didn't have a chance to talk to him at all after that. For when we came into town, he and a couple of the others simply vanished. Just think!

Hedda. Oh? I expect they took him home.

Tesman. I suppose that must be it. And Brack took off on his own, too.

Hedda. And what have you been doing with yourself since then?

Tesman. Well, you see, I and some of the others went home with one of the younger fellows and had a cup of early morning coffee. Or night coffee maybe, rather. Hm? And now, after I've rested a bit and poor Eilert's had some sleep, I'll take this back to him.

Hedda [*reaches for the parcel*]. No—don't do that! Not right away, I mean. Let me look at it first.

Tesman. Dearest Hedda—honestly, I just don't dare to.

Hedda. Don't you dare to?

Tesman. No, for I'm sure you realize how utterly desperate he'll be when he wakes up and finds that the manuscript is gone. For he hasn't a copy, you know. He said so himself.

Hedda [*looks searchingly at him*]. But can't a thing like that be written over again?

Tesman. Hardly. I really don't think so. For, you see—the inspiration—

Hedda. Yes, I daresay that's the main thing. [*Casually.*] By the way, here's a letter for you.

Tesman. Imagine!

Hedda [*gives it to him*]. It came early this morning.

Tesman. It's from Aunt Julle, Hedda! I wonder what it can be. [*Puts the manuscript down on the other ottoman, opens the letter, skims the content, jumps up.*] Oh Hedda! She says here that poor Aunt Rina is dying!

Hedda. You know we had to expect that.

Tesman. And if I want to see her again I had better hurry. I'll rush over right away.

Hedda [*suppressing a smile*]. You'll rush?

Tesman. Dearest Hedda of mine—if only you could bring yourself to come along! Hm?

Hedda [*rises, weary, with an air of refusal*]. No, no. You mustn't ask me that. I don't want to look at death and disease. I don't want anything to do with ugliness.

Tesman. Well, all right—[*Rushing around.*] My hat? My coat? Oh—out here in the hall. I just hope I won't be too late, Hedda. Hm?

Hedda. Oh I'm sure that if you rush—

[BERTE *appears in the door, right.*]

Berte. Judge Brack is here and wants to know if he may see you.

Tesman. At this hour! No, no. I can't possibly see him now!

Hedda. But *I* can. [*To* BERTE.] Tell the Judge please to come in.

[BERTE *exits.*]

Hedda [*with a quick whisper*]. Tesman! The package! [*She grabs it from the ottoman.*]

Tesman. Yes! Give it to me!

Hedda. No, no. I'll hide it for you till later.

[*She walks over to the desk and sticks the parcel in among the books on the shelf. In his hurry* TESMAN *is having difficulties getting his gloves on.* JUDGE BRACK *enters, right.*]

Hedda [*nods to him*].   If *you* aren't an early bird—

Brack.   Yes, don't you think so? [*To* TESMAN.] You're going out, too?

Tesman.   Yes, I must go and see the aunts. Just think, the invalid—she's dying!

Brack.   Oh, I'm terribly sorry! In that case, don't let me keep you. At such a moment—

Tesman.   Yes, I really must run. Goodbye, goodbye! [*Hurries out, right.*]

Hedda [*approaching* BRACK].   It appears that things were quite lively last night over at your house.

Brack.   Indeed, Mrs. Tesman—I didn't get to bed at all.

Hedda.   You didn't either?

Brack.   As you see. But tell me—what has Tesman told you about the night's adventures?

Hedda.   Just some tiresome story about having coffee with somebody someplace—

Brack.   I believe I know all about that coffee. Eilert Løvborg wasn't one of them, was he?

Hedda.   No, they had taken him home first.

Brack.   Tesman, too?

Hedda.   No. Some of the others, he said.

Brack [*smiles*].   Jørgen Tesman is really an ingenuous soul, you know.

Hedda.   He certainly is. But why do you say that? Is there something more to all this?

Brack.   Yes, there is.

Hedda.   Well! In that case, why don't we make ourselves comfortable, Judge. You'll tell your story better, too.

[*She sits down at the left side of the table,* BRACK *near her at the adjacent side.*]

Hedda.   All right?

Brack.   For reasons of my own I wanted to keep track of my guests' movements last night. Or, rather—some of my guests.

Hedda.   Eilert Løvborg was one of them, perhaps?

Brack.   As a matter of fact—he was.

Hedda.   Now you are really making me curious.

Brack.   Do you know where he and a couple of the others spent the rest of the night, Mrs. Tesman?

Hedda.   No—tell me. If it can be told.

Brack.   Oh, certainly. They turned up at an exceptionally gay early morning gathering.

Hedda.   Of the lively kind?

Brack.   Of the liveliest.

Hedda.   A little more about this, Judge.

Brack.   Løvborg had been invited beforehand. I knew about that. But he had declined. He is a reformed character, you know.

Hedda.   As of his stay with the Elvsteds—yes. But he went after all?

Brack.   Well, yes, you see, Mrs. Tesman—unfortunately, the spirit moved him over at my house last evening.

Hedda.   Yes, I understand he became inspired.

Brack. Quite violently inspired. And that, I gather, must have changed his mind. You know, we men don't always have as much integrity as we ought to have.

Hedda. Oh, I'm sure you're an exception, Judge Brack. But about Løvborg—?

Brack. To make a long story short—he ended up at Miss Diana's establishment.

Hedda. Miss Diana's?

Brack. She was the hostess at this gathering—a select circle of intimate friends, male and female.

Hedda. Is she a redhead, by any chance?

Brack. That's correct.

Hedda. And a singer—of sorts?

Brack. Yes—that, too. And a mighty huntress—of men, Mrs. Tesman. You seem to have heard of her. Eilert Løvborg used to be one of her most devoted protectors in his more affluent days.

Hedda. And how did it all end?

Brack. Not in a very friendly fashion, apparently. It seems that after the tenderest reception Miss Diana resorted to brute force—

Hedda. Against Løvborg?

Brack. Yes. He accused her or her women friends of having stolen something of his. Said his wallet was gone. And other things, too. In brief, he's supposed to have started a pretty wicked row.

Hedda. And—?

Brack. Well—there was a general free-for-all—men and women both. Fortunately, the police stepped in—

Hedda. The police—!

Brack. Yes. But I'm afraid this will be an expensive escapade for Eilert Løvborg, crazy fool that he is.

Hedda. Well!

Brack. It appears that he made quite violent objection—struck an officer in the ear and tore his coat. So they had to take him along.

Hedda. How do you know all this?

Brack. From the police.

Hedda [*staring straight ahead*]. So that's how it was. No vine leaves in his hair.

Brack. Vine leaves, Mrs. Tesman?

Hedda [*changing her tone*]. But tell me, Judge Brack—why did you keep such a close watch on Eilert Løvborg?

Brack. Well—for one thing, it is obviously of some concern to me if he testifies that he came straight from my party.

Hedda. So you think there will be an investigation?

Brack. Naturally. But I suppose that doesn't really matter too much. However, as a friend of the house I considered it my duty to give you and Tesman a full account of his night-time exploits.

Hedda. Yes, but why?

Brack. Because I very strongly suspect that he intends to use you as a kind of screen.

Hedda. Really! Why do you think that?

Brack. Oh, come now, Mrs. Tesman! We can use our eyes, can't we? This Mrs. Elvsted—she isn't leaving town right away, you know.

Hedda. Well, even if there should be something going on between those two, I'd think there would be plenty of other places they could meet.

Brack. But no home. After last night, every respectable house will once again be closed to Eilert Løvborg.

Hedda. And so should mine, you mean?

Brack. Yes. I admit I would find it more than embarrassing if the gentleman were to become a daily guest here, Mrs. Tesman. If he, as an outsider—a highly dispensable outside—if he were to intrude himself—

Hedda. —into the triangle?

Brack. Precisely. It would amount to homelessness for me.

Hedda [*smiling*]. Sole cock-o'-the-walk—so, that's your goal, is it, Judge?

Brack [*nods slowly, lowers his voice*]. Yes. That is my goal. And for that I will fight with every means at my disposal.

Hedda [*her smile fading*]. You're really a dangerous person, you know—when you come right down to it.

Brack. You think so?

Hedda. Yes. I am beginning to think so now. And I must say I am exceedingly glad you don't have any kind of hold on me.

Brack [*with a noncommittal laugh*]. Well, well, Mrs. Tesman! Maybe there is something to what you are saying, at that. Who knows what I might do if I did.

Hedda. Really, now, Judge Brack! Are you threatening me?

Brack [*rising*]. —Nonsense! For the triangle, you see—is best maintained on a voluntary basis.

Hedda. My sentiments, exactly.

Brack. Well, I have said what I came to say. And now I should get back to town. Goodbye, Mrs. Tesman! [*Walks toward the French doors.*]

Hedda [*rises*]. You're going through the garden?

Brack. Yes. For me that's a short cut.

Hedda. Yes, and then it's a back way.

Brack. Quite true. I have nothing against back ways. There are times when they are most intriguing.

Hedda. You mean when real ammunition is used?

Brack [*in the doorway, laughs back at her*]. Oh good heavens! I don't suppose one shoots one's tame roosters!

Hedda [*laughs also*]. No—not if one has only one—!

[*They nod to each other, both still laughing. He leaves. She closes the door behind him. For a few moments she remains by the door, quite serious now, looking into the garden. Then she walks over to the doorway and opens the portieres wide enough to look into the inner room. Goes to the desk, pulls* LØVBORG'S *manuscript from the bookshelf and is about to read in it when* BERTE'S *voice, very loud, is heard from the hall, right.* HEDDA *turns around, listens. She hurriedly puts the manuscript into the drawer of the desk and puts the key down on its top.* EILERT LØVBORG, *wearing his coat and with his hat in his hand, flings open the door, right. He looks somewhat confused and excited.*]

Løvborg [*turned toward the invisible* BERTE *in the hall*]. —And I say I must! You can't stop me! [*He closes the door, turns, sees* HEDDA, *immediately controls himself, greets her.*]

Hedda [*by the desk*].   Well, well, Mr. Løvborg—aren't you a trifle late coming for Thea?

Løvborg.   Or a trifle early for calling on you. I apologize.

Hedda.   How do you know she is still here?

Løvborg.   The people she is staying with told me she's been gone all night.

Hedda [*walks over to the table*].   Did they seem—strange—when they said it?

Løvborg [*puzzled*].   Strange?

Hedda.   I mean, did they seem to find it a little—unusual?

Løvborg [*suddenly understands*].   Ah, I see what you mean! Of course! I'm dragging her down with me. No, as a matter of fact, I didn't notice anything. I suppose Tesman isn't up yet?

Hedda.   I—I don't think so—

Løvborg.   When did he get home?

Hedda.   Very late.

Løvborg.   Did he tell you anything?

Hedda.   Yes, he said you'd all had quite a time over at Brack's.

Løvborg.   Just that?

Hedda.   I think so. But I was so awfully sleepy—

[MRS. ELVSTED *enters through portieres in the rear.*]

Mrs. Elvsted [*toward him*].   Oh, Løvborg. At last!

Løvborg.   Yes, at last. And too late.

Mrs. Elvsted [*in fear*].   What is too late?

Løvborg.   Everything is too late now. It's all over with me.

Mrs. Elvsted.   Oh no, no! Don't say things like that!

Løvborg.   You'll say the same yourself when you hear—

Mrs. Elvsted.   I don't want to hear—!

Hedda.   Maybe you'd rather talk with her alone? I'll leave.

Løvborg.   No, stay—you, too. I beg you to.

Mrs. Elvsted.   But I don't want to listen, do you hear?

Løvborg.   It isn't last night I want to talk about.

Mrs. Elvsted.   What about, then?

Løvborg.   We'll have to part, Thea.

Mrs. Elvsted.   Part!

Hedda [*involuntarily*].   I knew it!

Løvborg.   For I don't need you any more.

Mrs. Elvsted.   And you can stand there and tell me a thing like that! Don't need me! Why can't I help you the way I did before? Aren't we going to keep on working together?

Løvborg.   I don't intend to work any more.

Mrs. Elvsted [*desperately*].   What am I going to do with my life, then?

Løvborg.   You'll have to try to live your life as if you'd never known me.

Mrs. Elvsted.   But I can't do that!

Løvborg.   Try, Thea. Go back home.

Mrs. Elvsted [*agitated*].   Never again! Where you are I want to be! And you can't chase me away just like that. I want to stay right here! Be with you when the book appears.

Hedda [*in a tense whisper*].   Ah—yes—the book!

Løvborg [*looks at her*].   My book—and Thea's. For that's what it is.

Mrs. Elvsted. That's what I feel, too. And that's why I have the right to be with you when it comes out. I want to see all the honor and all the fame you'll get. And the joy—I want to share the joy, too.

Løvborg. Thea, our book is never going to come out.

Hedda. Ah!

Mrs. Elvsted. It won't!

Løvborg. Can't ever appear.

Mrs. Elvsted [*with fearful suspicion*]. Løvborg, what have you done with the manuscript?

Hedda [*watching him tensely*]. Yes—what about the manuscript?

Mrs. Elvsted. Where is it?

Løvborg. Oh Thea—please, don't ask me about that!

Mrs. Elvsted. Yes, yes—I want to be told! I have the right to know—right now!

Løvborg. All right. I've torn it to pieces.

Mrs. Elvsted [*screams*]. Oh, no! No!

Hedda [*involuntarily*]. But that's not—!

Løvborg [*looks at her*]. Not true, you think?

Hedda [*composing herself*]. Well, of course, if you say so. You should know. It just sounds so—so unbelievable.

Løvborg. All the same, it's true.

Mrs. Elvsted [*hands clenched*]. Oh God—oh God, Hedda. He has torn his own work to pieces!

Løvborg. I have torn my whole life to pieces, so why not my life's work as well?

Mrs. Elvsted. And that's what you did last night?

Løvborg. Yes, I tell you! In a thousand pieces. And scattered them in the fjord. Far out—where the water is clean and salty. Let them drift there, with wind and current. Then they'll sink. Deep, deep down. Like me, Thea.

Mrs. Elvsted. Do you know, Løvborg—this thing you've done to the book—all the rest of my life I'll think of it as killing a little child.

Løvborg. You are right. It is like murdering a child.

Mrs. Elvsted. But then, how could you? For the child was mine, too!

Hedda [*almost soundlessly*]. The child—

Mrs. Elvsted [*with a deep sigh*]. So it's all over. I'll go now, Hedda.

Hedda. But you aren't leaving town?

Mrs. Elvsted. Oh, I don't know myself what I'll do. There's only darkness before me. [*Exits, right.*]

Hedda [*waits for a moment*]. Aren't you going to see her home, Mr. Løvborg?

Løvborg. I? Through the streets? Letting people see her with me?

Hedda. Of course, I don't know what else may have happened last night. But is it really so absolutely irreparable—?

Løvborg. Last night is not the end of it. That I know. And yet, I don't really care for that kind of life any more. Not again. She has broken all the courage for life and all the defiance that was in me.

Hedda [*staring ahead*]. So that sweet little goose has had her hand in a human destiny. [*Looks at him.*] But that you could be so heartless, even so!

Løvborg. Don't tell me I was heartless!

Hedda. To ruin everything that's filled her soul for a such a long time! You don't call that heartless!

Løvborg. Hedda—to you I can tell the truth.

Hedda. The truth?

Løvborg. But first promise me—give me your word you'll never let Thea know what I'm going to tell you now.

Hedda. You have it.

Løvborg. All right. It isn't true, what I just told her.

Hedda. About the manuscript?

Løvborg. Yes. I have not torn it up. Not thrown it in the sea, either.

Hedda. But then—where is it?

Løvborg. I've destroyed it just the same. Really, I have, Hedda!

Hedda. I don't understand.

Løvborg. Thea said that what I had done seemed to her like murdering a child.

Hedda. Yes—she did.

Løvborg. But killing a child, that's not the worst thing a father can do to it.

Hedda. No?

Løvborg. No. And the worst is what I don't want Thea to know.

Hedda. What *is* the worst?

Løvborg. Hedda—suppose a man, say, early in the morning, after a stupid, drunken night—suppose he comes home to his child's mother and says: Listen, I've been in such and such a place. I've been here—and I've been there. And I had our child with me. In all those places. And the child is lost. Gone. Vanished. I'll be damned if I know where it is. Who's got hold of it—

Hedda. Yes—but when all is said and done—it is only a book, you know.

Løvborg. Thea's pure soul was in that book.

Hedda. I realize that.

Løvborg. Then you surely also realize that she and I can have no future together.

Hedda. Where do you go from here?

Løvborg. Nowhere. Just finish everything off. The sooner the better.

Hedda [*a step closer*]. Listen—Eilert Løvborg—Couldn't you make sure it's done beautifully?

Løvborg. Beautifully? [*Smiles.*] With vine leaves in the hair, as you used to say.

Hedda. Oh no. I don't believe in vine leaves any more. But still beautifully! For once. Goodbye. Go now. And don't come back.

Løvborg. Goodbye, Mrs. Tesman. Give my regards to Jørgen Tesman. [*He is about to leave.*]

Hedda. Wait! I want to give you something—a remembrance. [*Goes to the desk, opens the drawer, takes out the gun case. Returns to* LØVBORG *with one of the revolvers.*]

Løvborg. The gun? That's the remembrance?

Hedda [*nods slowly*]. Do you recognize it? It was pointed at you once.

Løvborg. You should have used it then.

Hedda. Take it! *You* use it.

Løvborg [*pockets the gun*]. Thanks!

Hedda. And beautifully, Eilert Løvborg! That's all I ask!

Løvborg. Goodbye, Hedda Gabler. [*Exits, right.*]

[HEDDA *listens by the door for a moment. Then she crosses to the desk, takes out the manuscript, glances inside the cover, pulls some of the pages halfway out and looks at them. Carries the whole manuscript over to the chair by the stove. She sits down with the parcel in her lap. After a moment she opens the stove and then the manuscript.*]

Hedda [*throws a bundle of sheets into the fire, whispers*].   Now I'm burning your child, Thea. You—curlyhead! [*Throws more sheets in.*] Your and Eilert Løvborg's child. [*Throws all the rest of the manuscript into the stove.*] I am burning—I am burning your child.

Act IV

[*The same rooms at the* TESMANS'. *Evening. The front room is dark. The inner room is lighted by the ceiling lamp over the table. Portieres cover the French doors.*]

[HEDDA, *in black, is walking up and down in the dark of the front room. She goes into the inner room, turning left in the doorway. She is heard playing a few bars on the piano. She reappears and comes forward again.* BERTE *enters from the right side of the inner room. She carries a lighted lamp, which she puts down on the table in front of the corner sofa. Her eyes show signs of weeping; she wears black ribbons on her uniform. She exits quietly, right.* HEDDA *goes over to the French windows, looks between the portieres into the dark. Presently* MISS TESMAN, *in mourning, with hat and veil, enters, right.* HEDDA *walks over to meet her, gives her her hand.*]

Miss Tesman.   Yes, my dearest Hedda—here you see me in my garb of grief. For now at last my poor sister has fought her fight to the end.
Hedda.   I already know—as you see, Tesman sent word.
Miss Tesman.   Yes, he promised he'd do that. But I thought that to you, Hedda—here in the house of life—I really ought to bring you the tidings of death myself.
Hedda.   That is very kind of you.
Miss Tesman.   Ah, but Rina shouldn't have died just now. There should be no mourning in Hedda's house at this time.
Hedda [*changing the topic*].   I understand she had a very quiet end.
Miss Tesman.   Oh so beautiful, so peaceful! She left us so quietly! And then the unspeakable happiness of seeing Jørgen one more time! To say goodbye to him to her heart's content! Isn't he back yet?
Hedda.   No. He wrote I mustn't expect him back very soon. But do sit down.
Miss Tesman.   No—no, thanks, my dear, blessed Hedda. Not that I wouldn't like to. But I don't have much time. I must go back and prepare her as best I can. I want her to look right pretty when she goes into her grave.
Hedda.   Is there anything I can help you with?
Miss Tesman.   I won't have you as much as think of it! That's not for Hedda Tesman to lend a hand to. Or lend thoughts to, either. Not now, of all times!
Hedda.   Oh—thoughts! We can't always control our thoughts—

Miss Tesman [*still preoccupied*]. Ah yes—such is life. At home we're making a shroud for Rina. And here, too, there'll be sewing to do soon, I expect. But of quite a different kind, thank God!

[TESMAN *enters, right.*]

Hedda. Finally!

Tesman. You here, Aunt Julle? With Hedda? Just think!

Miss Tesman. I am just about to leave, Jørgen dear. Well—did you do all the things you promised me you'd do?

Tesman. No, I'm afraid I forgot half of them, Auntie. I'd better run in again tomorrow. I'm all confused today. I can't seem to keep my thoughts together.

Miss Tesman. But dearest Jørgen—you mustn't take it this way!

Tesman. Oh, I mustn't? How do you mean?

Miss Tesman. You ought to be joyful in the midst of your sorrow. Glad for what's happened. The way I am.

Tesman. Oh yes, of course. You're thinking of Aunt Rina.

Hedda. You're going to feel lonely now, Miss Tesman.

Miss Tesman. The first few days, yes. But I hope that won't last long. Dear Rina's little parlor won't be empty for long, if I can help it!

Tesman. Oh? And who do you want to move in there. Hm?

Miss Tesman. Ah—it's not very hard to find some poor soul who needs nursing and comfort.

Hedda. And you really want to take on such a burden all over again?

Miss Tesman. Heavens! God forgive you, child—burden? It has not been a burden to me.

Hedda. Still—a stranger, who—

Miss Tesman. Oh, it's easy to make friends with sick people. And I need somebody to live for, too. Well, the Lord be praised, maybe soon there'll be a thing or two an old aunt can turn her hand to here.

Hedda. Oh, never mind us—

Tesman. Yes, just think—how lovely it would be for the three of us, if only—

Hedda. If only—?

Tesman [*uneasy*]. Oh, nothing. I daresay it will all work out. Let's hope it will, hm?

Miss Tesman. Well, well. I can see that you two have something to talk about. [*With a smile.*] And perhaps Hedda has something to tell *you*, Jørgen! Goodbye! I'm going home to Rina, now. [*Turns around in the door.*] Dear, dear—how strange to think—Now Rina is both with me and with Jochum!

Tesman. Yes, just think, Aunt Julle! Hm?

[MISS TESMAN *exits, right.*]

Hedda [*coldly scrutinizing* TESMAN]. I wouldn't be at all surprised if you aren't more affected by this death than she is.

Tesman. Oh, it isn't just Aunt Rina's death, Hedda. It's Eilert I worry about.

Hedda [*quickly*]. Any news about him?

Tesman. I went over to his room this afternoon to tell him the manuscript is safe.

Hedda. Well? And didn't you see him?

Tesman. No. He wasn't home. But I ran into Mrs. Elvsted and she told me he'd been here early this morning.

Hedda. Yes, right after you'd left.

Tesman. And he said he'd torn up the manuscript? Did he really say that?

Hedda. Yes. So he claimed.

Tesman. But dear God—in that case he really must have been out of his mind! So I assume you didn't give it to him either, hm, Hedda?

Hedda. No. He didn't get it.

Tesman. But you told him we had it, of course?

Hedda. No. [*Quickly.*] Did you tell Mrs. Elvsted?

Tesman. No, I didn't want to. But you ought to have told him, Hedda. Just think—what if he does something rash—something to hurt himself! Give me the manuscript, Hedda! I want to rush down to him with it right this minute. Where is it?

Hedda [*cold, motionless, one arm resting on the chair*]. I haven't got it any more.

Tesman. You haven't got it! What do you mean by that?

Hedda. I burned it—the whole thing.

Tesman [*jumps up*]. Burned it! Burned Eilert's book!

Hedda. Don't shout. The maid might hear you.

Tesman. Burned it? But good God—no, no, no—! This can't be—!

Hedda. It is, all the same.

Tesman. But do you realize what you've done, Hedda? It's illegal! Willful destruction of lost property! You just ask Judge Brack! He'll tell you!

Hedda. You'd better not talk about this to anyone—the Judge or anybody else.

Tesman. But how could you do a thing like that! I never heard anything like it! What came over you? What can possibly have been going on in your head? Answer me! Hm?

Hedda [*suppresses an almost imperceptible smile*]. I did it for your sake, Jørgen.

Tesman. For my sake!

Hedda. When you came back this morning and told me he had read aloud to you—

Tesman. Yes, yes! What then?

Hedda. You admitted you were jealous of him for having written such a book.

Tesman. But good gracious—! I didn't mean it as seriously as all that!

Hedda. All the same. I couldn't stand the thought that somebody else was to overshadow you.

Tesman [*in an outburst of mingled doubt and joy*]. Hedda—oh Hedda! Is it true what you're saying! But—but—but—I never knew you loved me like that! Just think!

Hedda. In that case, I might as well tell you—that—just at this time— [*Breaks off, vehemently.*] No, no! You can ask Aunt Julle. She'll tell you.

Tesman. I almost think I know what you mean, Hedda! [*Claps his hands.*] For goodness sake! Can that really be so! Hm?

Hedda. Don't shout so! The maid can hear you.

Tesman [*laughing with exuberant joy*]. The maid! Well, if you don't take the prize, Hedda! The maid—but that's Berte! I'm going to tell Berte myself this very minute!

Hedda [*her hands clenched in despair*].   Oh I'll die—I'll die, in all this!

Tesman.   In what, Hedda? Hm?

Hedda [*cold and composed*].   In all this—ludicrousness, Jørgen.

Tesman.   Ludicrous? That I'm so happy? Still—maybe I oughtn't to tell Berte, after all.

Hedda.   Oh, go ahead. What difference does it make?

Tesman.   No, not yet. But on my word—Aunt Julle must be told. And that you've started to call me "Jørgen," too! Just think! She'll be ever so happy— Aunt Julle will!

Hedda.   Even when you tell her that I have burned Eilert Løvborg's papers?

Tesman.   No, oh, no! That's true! That about the manuscript—nobody must know about that. But to think that you'd burn for me, Hedda—I certainly want to tell *that* to Aunt Julle! I wonder now—is that sort of thing usual with young wives, hm?

Hedda.   Why don't you ask Aunt Julle about that, too?

Tesman.   I shall—I certainly shall, when I get the chance. [*Looks uneasy and disturbed again.*] But the manuscript! Good God—I don't dare to think what this is going to do to poor Eilert!

[MRS. ELVSTED, *dressed as on her first visit, wearing hat and coat, enters, right.*]

Mrs. Elvsted [*gives a hurried greeting, is obviously upset*].   Oh Hedda, you must forgive me for coming here again!

Hedda.   What has happened, Thea?

Tesman.   Something to do with Eilert Løvborg again? Hm?

Mrs. Elvsted.   Yes, yes—I'm so terribly afriad something's happened to him.

Hedda [*seizing her arm*].   Ah—you think so?

Tesman.   Oh dear—why do you think that, Mrs. Elvsted?

Mrs. Elvsted.   I heard them talking about him in the boarding house, just as I came in. And people are saying the most incredbile things about him today.

Tesman.   Yes, imagine! I heard that, too! And I can testify that he went straight home to bed! Just think!

Hedda.   And what did they say in the boarding house?

Mrs. Elvsted.   Oh, I didn't find out anything. Either they didn't know any details or—They all became silent when they saw me. And I didn't dare to ask.

Tesman [*pacing the floor uneasily*].   We'll just have to hope—to hope that you heard wrong, Mrs. Elvsted!

Mrs. Elvsted.   No, no. I'm sure it was he they were talking about. And somebody said something about the hospital or—

Tesman.   The hospital—!

Hedda.   Surely, that can't be so!

Mrs. Elvsted.   I got so terribly frightened! So I went up to his room and asked for him there.

Hedda.   Could you bring yourself to do that, Thea?

Mrs. Elvsted.   What else could I do? For I felt I just couldn't stand the uncertainty any longer.

Tesman.   But I suppose you didn't find him in, either, did you? Hm?

Mrs. Elvsted.   No. And the people there didn't know anything about him. He hadn't been home since yesterday afternoon, they said.

Tesman.   Yesterday! Just think! How could they say that!

Mrs. Elvsted.   I don't know what else *to* think—something bad must have happened to him!

Tesman.   Hedda, dear—? What if I were to walk downtown and ask around for him—?

Hedda.   No, no—don't you go and get mixed up in all this.

[JUDGE BRACK, *hat in hand, enters through the door, right, which* BERTE *opens and closes for him. He looks serious and greets the others in silence.*]

Tesman.   So here you are, Judge, hm?

Brack.   Yes. I had to see you this evening.

Tesman.   I can see you have got Aunt Julle's message.

Brack.   That, too—yes.

Tesman.   Isn't it sad, though?

Brack.   Well, my dear Tesman—that depends on how you look at it.

Tesman [*looks at him uncertainly*].   Has something else happened?

Brack.   Yes.

Hedda [*tense*].   Something sad, Judge Brack?

Brack.   That, too, depends on how you look at it, Mrs. Tesman.

Mrs. Elvsted [*bursting out*].   Oh, I'm sure it has something to do with Eilert Løvborg!

Brack [*looks at her for a moment*].   Why do you think that, Mrs. Elvsted? Maybe you already know something—?

Mrs. Elvsted [*confused*].   No, no; not at all. It's just—

Tesman.   For heaven's sake, Brack, out with it!

Brack [*shrugging his shoulders*].   Well—unfortunately, Eilert Løvborg's in the hospital. Dying.

Mrs. Elvsted [*screams*].   Oh God, oh God!

Tesman.   In the hospital! And dying!

Hedda [*without thinking*].   So soon—!

Mrs. Elvsted [*wailing*].   And we didn't even part as friends, Hedda!

Hedda [*whispers*].   Thea, Thea—for heaven's sake—!

Mrs. Elvsted [*paying no attention to her*].   I want to see him! I want to see him alive!

Brack.   Won't do you any good, Mrs. Elvsted. Nobody can see him.

Mrs. Elvsted.   Then tell me what's happened to him! What?

Tesman.   For, surely, he hasn't himself—!

Hedda.   I'm sure he has.

Tesman.   Hedda! How can you—!

Brack [*observing her all this time*].   I am sorry to say that your guess is absolutely correct, Mrs. Tesman.

Mrs. Elvsted.   Oh, how awful!

Tesman.   Did it himself! Just think!

Hedda.   Shot himself!

Brack.   Right again, Mrs. Tesman.

Mrs. Elvsted [*trying to pull herself together*].   When did this happen, Judge?

Brack.   This afternoon. Between three and four.

Tesman. But dear me—where can he have done a thing like that? Hm?

Brack [*a little uncertain*]. Where? Well—I suppose in his room. I don't really know—

Mrs. Elvsted. No, it can't have been there. For I was up there sometime between six and seven.

Brack. Well, then, some other place. I really can't say. All I know is that he was found. He had shot himself—in the chest.

Mrs. Elvsted. Oh, how horrible to think! That he was to end like that!

Hedda [*to* BRACK]. In the chest?

Brack. Yes—as I just told you.

Hedda. Not the temple?

Brack. In the chest, Mrs. Tesman.

Hedda. Well, well—the chest is a good place, too.

Brack. How is that, Mrs. Tesman?

Hedda [*turning him aside*]. Oh—nothing.

Tesman. And you say the wound is fatal? Hm?

Brack. No doubt about it—absolutely fatal. He's probably dead already.

Mrs. Elvsted. Yes, yes! I feel you're right! It's over! Oh, Hedda!

Tesman. But tell me—how do *you* know all this?

Brack [*tersely*]. A man on the force told me. One I had some business with.

Hedda [*loudly*]. At last a deed!

Tesman [*appalled*]. Oh dear—what are you saying, Hedda!

Hedda. I am saying there is beauty in this.

Brack. Well, now—Mrs. Tesman—

Tesman. Beauty—! Just think!

Mrs. Elvsted. Oh, Hedda—how can you talk about beauty in a thing like this!

Hedda. Eilert Løvborg has settled his account with himself. He has had the courage to do—what had to be done.

Mrs. Elvsted. But you mustn't believe it happened that way! He did it when he was not himself!

Tesman. In despair! That's how!

Hedda. He did not. I am certain of that.

Mrs. Elvsted. Yes he did! He was not himself! That's the way he tore up the book, too!

Brack [*puzzled*]. The book? You mean the manuscript? Has he torn it up?

Mrs. Elvsted. Yes, last night.

Tesman [*whispers*]. Oh, Hedda—we'll never get clear of all this!

Brack. That is strange.

Tesman [*walking the floor*]. To think that this was to be the end of Eilert! Not to leave behind him anything that would have preserved his name—

Mrs. Elvsted. Oh, if only it could be put together again!

Tesman. Yes, if only it could. I don't know what I wouldn't give—

Mrs. Elvsted. Maybe it can, Mr. Tesman.

Tesman. What do you mean?

Mrs. Elvsted [*searching her dress pocket*]. Look. I have kept these little slips he dictated from.

Hedda [*a step closer*]. Ah—!

Tesman. You've kept them, Mrs. Elvsted? Hm?

Mrs. Elvsted.   Yes. Here they are. I took them with me when I left. And I've had them in my pocket ever since—

Tesman.   Please, let me see—

Mrs. Elvsted [*gives him a pile of small paper slips*].   But it's such a mess. Without any kind of system or order—!

Tesman.   But just think if we could make sense out of them, all the same! Perhaps if we helped each other—

Mrs. Elvsted.   Oh yes! Let's try, anyway!

Tesman.   It will work! It *has* to work! I'll stake my whole life on this!

Hedda.   You, Jørgen? Your life?

Tesman.   Yes, or at any rate all the time I can set aside. My own collections can wait. Hedda, you understand—don't you? Hm? This is something I owe Eilert's memory.

Hedda.   Maybe so.

Tesman.   And now, my dear Mrs. Elvsted, we want to get to work. Good heavens, there's no point brooding over what's happened. Hm? We'll just have to acquire sufficient peace of mind to—

Mrs. Elvsted.   All right, Mr. Tesman. I'll try to do my best.

Tesman.   Very well, then. Come over here. Let's look at these slips right away. Where can we sit? Here? No, it's better in the other room. If you'll excuse us, Judge! Come along, Mrs. Elvsted.

Mrs. Elvsted.   Oh dear God—if only it were possible—!

[TESMAN *and* MRS. ELVSTED *go into the inner room. She takes off her hat and coat. Both sit down at the table under the hanging lamp and absorb themselves in the slips.* HEDDA *walks over toward the stove and sits down in the easy chair. After a while,* BRACK *walks over to her.*]

Hedda [*in a low voice*].   Ah, Judge—what a liberation there is in this thing with Eilert Løvborg!

Brack.   Liberation, Mrs. Tesman? Well, yes, for him perhaps one may say there was liberation of a kind—

Hedda.   I mean for me. There is liberation in knowing that there is such a thing in the world as an act of free courage. Something which becomes beautiful by its very nature.

Brack [*smiles*].   Well—dear Mrs. Tesman—

Hedda.   Oh I know what you're going to say! For you see—you really are a kind of specialist, too!

Brack [*looks at her fixedly*].   Eilert Løvborg has meant more to you than perhaps you're willing to admit, even to yourself. Or am I wrong?

Hedda.   I won't answer such questions. All I know is that Eilert Løvborg had the courage to live his own life. And then now—this—magnificence! The beauty of it! Having the strength and the will to get up and leave life's feast—so early—

Brack.   Believe me, Mrs. Tesman, this pains me, but I see it is necessary that I destroy a pretty illusion—

Hedda.   An illusion?

Brack.   Which could not have been maintained for very long, anyway.

Hedda. And what is that?

Brack. He didn't shoot himself—of his own free will.

Hedda. Not of his own—!

Brack. No. To tell the truth, the circumstances of Eilert Løvborg's death aren't exactly what I said they were.

Hedda [*tense*]. You've held something back? What?

Brack. For the sake of poor Mrs. Elvsted I used a few euphemisms.

Hedda. What?

Brack. First—he is already dead.

Hedda. In the hospital.

Brack. Yes. And without regaining consciousness.

Hedda. What else haven't you told?

Brack. That fact that it didn't happen in his room.

Hedda. Well, does that really make much difference?

Brack. Some. You see—Eilbert Løvborg was found shot in Miss Diana's bedroom.

Hedda [*is about to jump up, but sinks back*]. That's impossible, Judge Brack! He can't have been there again today!

Brack. He was there this afternoon. He came to claim something he said they had taken from him. Spoke some gibberish about a lost child—

Hedda. So that's why—!

Brack. I thought maybe he meant his manuscript. But now I hear he has destroyed that himself. So I suppose it must have been something else.

Hedda. I suppose. So it was there—so they found him there?

Brack. Yes. With a fired gun in his pocket. Mortally wounded.

Hedda. Yes—in the chest.

Brack. No—in the guts.

Hedda [*looks at him with an expression of disgust*]. That, too! What is this curse that turns everything I touch into something ludicrous and low!

Brack. There is something else, Mrs. Tesman. Something I'd call—nasty.

Hedda. And what is that?

Brack. The gun they found—

Hedda [*breathless*]. What about it?

Brack. He must have stolen it.

Hedda [*jumps up*]. Stolen! That's not true! He didn't!

Brack. Anything else is impossible. He *must* have stolen it.—Shhh!

[TESMAN *and* MRS. ELVSTED *have risen from the table and come forward into the front room.*]

Tesman [*with papers in both hands*]. D'you know, Hedda—you can hardly see in there with that lamp! Just think!

Hedda. I am thinking.

Tesman. I wonder if you'd let us use your desk, hm?

Hedda. Certainly, if you like. [*Adds quickly.*] Wait a minute, though! Let me clear it off a bit first.

Tesman. Ah, there's no need for that, Hedda. There's plenty of room.

Hedda. No, no. I want to straighten it up. I'll carry all this in here. I'll put it on top of the piano for the time being.

[*She has pulled an object, covered by note paper, out of the bookcase. She puts several other sheets of paper on top of it and carries the whole pile into the left part of the inner room.* TESMAN *puts the papers down on the desk and moves the lamp from the corner table over to the desk. He and* MRS. ELVSTED *sit down and resume their work.* HEDDA *returns.*]

Hedda [*behind* MRS. ELVSTED's *chair, softly ruffling her hair*].   Well, little Thea—how is Eilert Løvborg's memorial coming along?

Mrs. Elvsted [*looks up at her, discouraged*].   Oh God—I'm sure it's going to be terribly hard to make anything out of all this.

Tesman.   But we have to. We just don't have a choice. And putting other people's papers in order—that's just the thing for me.

[HEDDA *walks over to the stove and sits down on one of the ottomans.* BRACK *stands over her, leaning on the easy chair.*]

Hedda [*whispers*].   What were you saying about the gun?

Brack [*also softly*].   That he must have stolen it.

Hedda.   Why, necessarily?

Brack.   Because any other explanation ought to be out of the question, Mrs. Tesman.

Hedda.   Oh?

Brack [*looks at her for a moment*].   Eilert Løvborg was here this morning, of course. Isn't that so?

Hedda.   Yes.

Brack.   Were you alone with him?

Hedda.   Yes, for a while.

Brack.   You didn't leave the room while he was here?

Hedda.   No.

Brack.   Think. Not at all? Not even for a moment?

Hedda.   Well—maybe just for a moment—out in the hall.

Brack.   And where was the gun case?

Hedda.   In the—

Brack.   Mrs. Tesman?

Hedda.   On the desk.

Brack.   Have you looked to see if both guns are still there?

Hedda.   No.

Brack.   You needn't bother. I saw the gun they found on Løvborg, and I knew it immediately. From yesterday—and from earlier occasions, too.

Hedda.   Perhaps you have it?

Brack.   No, the police do.

Hedda.   What are the police going to do with it?

Brack.   Try to find the owner.

Hedda.   Do you think they will?

Brack [*leans over her, whispers*].   No, Hedda Gabler—not as long as I keep quiet.

Hedda [*with a hunted look*].   And if you don't?

Brack [*shrugs his shoulders*].   Of course, there's always the chance that the gun was stolen.

Hedda [*firmly*]. Rather die!

Brack [*smiles*]. People *say* things like that. They don't *do* them.

Hedda [*without answering*]. And if the gun was not stolen—and if they find the owner—then what happens?

Brack. Well, Hedda—then comes the scandal!

Hedda. The scandal!

Brack. Yes—the scandal. That you are so afraid of. You will of course be required to testify. Both you and Miss Diana. Obviously, she'll have to explain how the whole thing happened. Whether it was accident or homicide. Did he try to pull the gun out of his pocket to threaten her? And did it fire accidentally? Or did she grab the gun away from him, shoot him, and put it back in his pocket? She might just possibly have done that. She's a pretty tough girl—Miss Diana.

Hedda. But this whole disgusting mess has nothing to do with me.

Brack. Quite so. But you'll have to answer the question: Why did you give Eilert Løvborg the gun? And what inferences will be drawn from the fact that you did?

Hedda [*lowers her head*]. That's true. I hadn't thought of that.

Brack. Well—luckily, there's nothing to worry about as long as I don't say anything.

Hedda [*looks up at him*]. So then I'm in your power, Judge. From now on you can do anything you like with me.

Brack [*in an even softer whisper*]. Dearest Hedda—believe me, I'll not misuse my position.

Hedda. In your power, all the same. Dependent on your will. Servant to your demands. Not free. Not free! [*Rises suddenly.*] No—I can't stand that thought! Never!

Brack [*looks at her, half mockingly*]. Most people submit to the inevitable.

Hedda [*returning his glance*]. Perhaps. [*Walks over to the desk. Suppresses a smile and mimics* TESMAN's *way of speaking.*] Well? Do you think you can do it, Jørgen? Hm?

Tesman. Lord knows, Hedda. Anyway, I can already see it will take months.

Hedda [*still mimicking*]. Just think! [*Runs her hands lightly through* MRS. ELVSTED's *hair.*] Doesn't this seem strange to you, Thea? Sitting here with Tesman—just the way you used to with Eilert Løvborg?

Mrs. Elvsted. Oh dear—if only I could inspire your husband, too!

Hedda. Oh, I'm sure that will come—in time.

Tesman. Well, yes—do you know, Hedda? I really think I begin to feel something of the kind. But why don't you go and talk to the Judge again.

Hedda. Isn't there anything you two can use me for?

Tesman. No, not a thing, dear. [*Turns around.*] From now on, you must be good enough to keep Hedda company, my dear Judge!

Brack [*glancing at* HEDDA]. I'll be only too delighted.

Hedda. Thank you. But I'm tired tonight. I think I'll go and lie down for a while.

Tesman. Yes, you do that, dear; why don't you? Hm?

[HEDDA *goes into the inner room, closes the portieres behind her. Brief pause. Suddenly, she is heard playing a frenzied dance tune on the piano.*]

Mrs. Elvsted [*jumps up*].   Oh God! What's that!

Tesman [*running to the doorway*].   But dearest Hedda—you mustn't play dance music tonight, for goodness' sake! Think of Aunt Rina! And Eilert, too!

Hedda [*peeks in from between the portieres*].   And Aunt Julle. And everybody. I'll be quiet. [*She pulls the portieres shut again.*]

Tesman [*back at the desk*].   I don't think it's good for her to see us at such a melancholy task. I'll tell you what, Mrs. Elvsted. You move in with Aunt Julle, and then I'll come over in the evenings. Then we can sit and work over there. Hm?

Mrs. Elvsted.   Maybe that would be better—

Hedda [*from the inner room*].   I hear every word you're saying, Tesman. And how am I going to spend my evenings?

Tesman [*busy with the papers*].   Oh, I'm sure Judge Brack will be good enough to come out and see you, anyway.

Brack [*in the easy chair, calls out gaily*].   Every single night, as far as I'm concerned, Mrs. Tesman! I'm sure we're going to have a lovely time, you and I!

Hedda [*loud and clear*].   Yes, don't you think that would be nice, Judge Brack? You—sole cock-o'-the walk—

[*A shot is heard from the inner room.* TESMAN, MRS. ELVSTED, *and* JUDGE BRACK *all jump up.*]

Tesman.   There she is, fooling with those guns again.

[*He pulls the portieres apart and runs inside.* MRS. ELVSTED *also.* HEDDA, *lifeless, is lying on the sofa. Cries and confusion.* BERTE, *flustered, enters, right.*]

Tesman [*shouts to* BRACK].   She's shot herself! In the temple! Just think!

Brack [*half stunned in the easy chair*].   But, merciful God—! One just doesn't *do* that!

Shaw: THE DEVIL'S DISCIPLE

Bernard Shaw (1856–1950) once said that the task he set for himself was to "sweep the world clean of lies." His verbal broom assaulted the dust in many of the world's most sacred corners.

After coming to London from his native Dublin, Shaw became an active member of the Fabian Society, socialists who rejected Marxist notions of revolution but were dedicated rather to a philosophy of social evolution through education of the masses. Shaw attained notoriety as a fiery lecturer, debater, propagandist, and pamphleteer, a role he never relinquished even as he became a novelist, a critic of art, music, and drama, and eventually a playwright. He remained forever a reformer, employing both stage and page as his pulpit and lectern. Art was the weapon with which he chose to fight for the liberation of society; irreverence was the tone he assumed for expounding his passionate beliefs.

The proper Victorians had inherited and perpetuated the belief of their Puritan ancestors that the theatre was a satanic institution. What passed for drama in the London play-houses as Shaw discovered them was at best very flimsy fare, so he decided that if the English were going to meet their devil on the stage, he should at the very least be an articulate, prodding, intelligent, and serious devil. Bernard Shaw undertook to puncture the orthodoxies and explode the myths held dear, though unexamined, by the sanctimonious among his countrymen. "It isn't only good for people to be shocked occasionally," he said in *The Quintessence of Ibsenism*, "but absolutely necessary to the progress of society that they should be shocked pretty often." Shaw left no stone unthrown in his onslaught against the hypocrisies and lies that were posing as the ideals and ethics of an age. Although he believed art to be only a social utility, Bernard Shaw had a talent for putting English words back to back that has yielded what may be the most accomplished prose ever to grace a stage. Even those who question the significance of what he had to say rarely deny the genius with which he said it.

In construction, Shaw's plays (the early ones in particular) are remarkably similar to the conventional melodramas he scorned, but his comic twists and verbal pyrotechnics served to undermine the larger structure so that it made itself look ridiculous. Shaw questioned the basic assumptions of both the society and the theatre with which he chose to do battle. A play by Shaw may be well-made, but it is turned inside out. His heroes may be manifestly unheroic, while his villains may be infuriatingly reasonable. After all, standard heroes and villains are archaisms, said Bernard Shaw. Boy may get girl at the final curtain (although in Shaw's customary anti-romantic dramaturgy, girl usually gets boy), but he will shake her hand. Hero may extol the virtues of compassion while throwing his widowed mother out of her house. Social progress may not only be preached but even achieved by a munitions manufacturer. An external Calvinist may turn out to be an internal hedonist, and a renegade teacher of humanitarian morality may end up being taught by a civilized general. In his plays, as in his world view, Bernard Shaw never lets his audience forget that things may not be as they first seem.

The social preachment in Shaw reflects Ibsen, the Webbs, and Henry George, but the sparkling talk of what he himself called "the drama of discussion" is more in the vein of the comedy of manners and the comic operas of the composer he adored, Mozart. Many a Shavian speech is not a speech at all; it is a verbal aria. And more often than not, Shaw himself is singing. One of the dramatist's detractors once said that the trouble with Shaw's characters is that they don't behave like people, but like characters in a play by Bernard Shaw. That is precisely correct, and therein lies their distinction.

The Devil's Disciple, like so many of Bernard Shaw's plays, was first performed in the United States. After a brief tryout in Albany, it opened in New York on October 4, 1897. Its financial success impelled Shaw to risk marriage. If there is a heaven for Shavian characters, their laughter must have rocked the firmament.

THE DEVIL'S DISCIPLE

The Characters

Richard Dudgeon, the Devil's Disciple
Christopher Dudgeon, Richard's brother
Rev. Anthony Anderson, the Presbyterian minister in Websterbridge
General Burgoyne, a British general
Major Swindon, the commander of British troops in Websterbridge
The Sergeant, one of Burgoyne's army
Lawyer Hawkins
William Dudgeon, Richard's uncle
Titus Dudgeon, Richard's uncle
Mr. Brudenell, the British chaplain
The Executioner
Mrs. Dudgeon, Richard's mother
Judith Anderson, Rev. Anderson's wife
Mrs. William Dudgeon, Richard's aunt
Mrs. Titus Dudgeon, Richard's aunt
Essie, illegitimate daughter of Peter Dudgeon

Act I

At the most wretched hour between a black night and a wintry morning in the year 1777, MRS. DUDGEON, *of New Hampshire, is sitting up in the kitchen and general dwelling room of her farm house on the outskirts of the town of Websterbridge. She is not a prepossessing woman. No woman looks her best after sitting up all night; and* MRS. DUDGEON'S *face, even at its best, is grimly trenched by the channels into which the barren forms and observances of a dead Puritanism can pen a bitter temper and a fierce pride. She is an elderly matron who has worked hard and got nothing by it except dominion and detestation in her sordid home, and an unquestioned reputation for piety and respectability among her neighbors, to whom drink and debauchery are still so much more tempting than religion and rectitude, that they conceive goodness simply as self-denial. This conception is easily extended to others-denial, and finally generalized as covering anything disagreeable. So* MRS. DUDGEON, *being exceedingly disagreeable, is held to be exceedingly good. Short of flat felony, she enjoys complete license except for amiable weaknesses of any sort, and is consequently, without knowing it, the most licentious woman in the parish on the strength of never having broken the seventh commandment or missed a Sunday at the Presbyterian church.*

The year 1777 is the one in which the passions roused by the breaking-off of the American colonies from England, more by their own weight than by their own will, boiled up to shooting point, the shooting being idealized to the English mind as suppression of rebellion and maintenance of British dominion, and to the American as defense of liberty, resistance to tyranny, and self-sacrifice on the altar of the Rights of Man. Into the merits of these idealizations it is not here necessary to inquire: suffice it to say, without prejudice, that they have convinced both Americans and English that the most high-minded course for them to pursue is to kill as many of one another as possible, and that military operations to that end are in full swing, morally supported by confident requests from the clergy of both sides for the blessing of God on their arms.

Under such circumstances many other women besides this disagreeable MRS. DUDGEON *find themselves sitting up all night waiting for news. Like her, too, they fall asleep towards morning at the risk of nodding themselves into the kitchen fire.* MRS. DUDGEON *sleeps with a shawl over her head, and her feet on a broad fender of iron laths, the step of the domestic altar of the fireplace, with its huge hobs[1] and boiler, and its hinged arm above the smoky mantelshelf for roasting. The plain kitchen table is opposite the fire, at her elbow, with a candle on it in a tin sconce. Her chair, like all the others in the room, is uncushioned and unpainted; but as it has a round railed back and a seat conventionally moulded to the sitter's curves, it is comparatively a chair of state. The room has three doors, one on the same side as the fireplace, near the corner, leading to the best bedroom; one, at the opposite end of the opposite wall, leading to the scullery and washhouse; and the housedoor, with its latch, heavy lock, and clumsy wooden bar, in the front wall, between the window in its middle and the corner next the bedroom door. Between the door and the window a rack of pegs suggests to the deductive observer that the men of the house are all away, as there are no hats or coats on them. On the other side of the window the clock hangs on a nail, with its white wooden dial, black iron weights, and brass pendulum. Between the clock and the corner, a big cupboard, locked, stands on a dwarf dresser full of common crockery.*

On the side opposite the fireplace, between the door and the corner, a shamelessly ugly black horsehair sofa stands against the wall. An inspection of its stridulous surface shows that MRS. DUDGEON *is not alone. A girl of sixteen or seventeen has fallen asleep on it. She is a wild, timid-looking creature with black hair and tanned skin. Her frock, a scanty garment, is rent, weather-stained, berry-stained, and by no means scrupulously clean. It hangs on her with a freedom which, taken with her brown legs and bare feet, suggests no great stock of underclothing.*

Suddenly there comes a tapping at the door, not loud enough to wake the sleepers. Then knocking, which disturbs MRS. DUDGEON *a little. Finally the latch is tried, whereupon she springs up at once.*

Mrs. Dudgeon [*threateningly*]. Well, why don't you open the door? [*She sees that the girl is asleep, and immediately raises a clamor of heartfelt vexation*] Well, dear, dear me! Now this is— [*shaking her*] wake up, wake up; do you hear?

The Girl [*sitting up*]. What is it?

Mrs. Dudgeon. Wake up; and be ashamed of yourself, you unfeeling, sinful girl, falling asleep like that, and your father hardly cold in his grave.

The Girl [*half asleep still*]. I didn't mean to. I dropped off—

---

1 Shelves at the back or sides of a fireplace's interior on which things may be kept warm but off the flame.

Mrs. Dudgeon [*cutting her short*].   Oh yes, you've plenty of excuses, I daresay.
Dropped off! [*Fiercely, as the knocking recommences*] Why don't you get up
and let your uncle in? After me waiting up all night for him! [*She pushes her
rudely off the sofa*] There; I'll open the door; much good you are to wait up. Go
and mend that fire a bit. [*The girl, cowed and wretched, goes to the fire and
puts a log on.* MRS. DUDGEON *unbars the door and opens it, letting into the
stuffy kitchen a little of the freshness and a great deal of the chill of the dawn,
also her second son* CHRISTY, *a fattish, stupid, fair-haired, roundfaced man of
about 22, muffled in a plaid shawl and grey overcoat. He hurries, shivering, to
the fire, leaving* MRS. DUDGEON *to shut the door.*]

Christy [*at the fire*].   F-f-f but it is cold. [*Seeing the girl and staring lumpishly
at her*] Why, who are you?

The Girl [*shyly*].   Essie.

Mrs. Dudgeon.   Oh, you may well ask. [*To* ESSIE] Go to your room, child, and
lie down, since you haven't feeling enough to keep you awake. Your history isn't
fit for your own ears to hear.

Essie.   I—

Mrs. Dudgeon [*peremptorily*].   Don't answer me, Miss; but show your obedience
by doing what I tell you. [ESSIE, *almost in tears, crosses the room to the door
near the sofa*] And don't forget your prayers. [ESSIE *goes out*] She'd have gone
to bed last night just as if nothing had happened if I'd let her.

Christy [*phlegmatically*].   Well, she can't be expected to feel Uncle Peter's
death like one of the family.

Mrs. Dudgeon.   What are you talking about, child? Isn't she his daughter—the
punishment of his wickedness and shame? [*She assaults her chair by sitting
down.*]

Christy [*staring*].   Uncle Peter's daughter!

Mrs. Dudgeon.   Why else should she be here? D'ye think I've not had enough
trouble and care put upon me bringing up my own girls, let alone you and your
good-for-nothing brother, without having your uncle's bastards—

Christy [*interrupting her with an apprehensive glance at the door by which* ESSIE
went out].   Sh! She may hear you.

Mrs. Dudgeon [*raising her voice*].   Let her hear me. People who fear God don't
fear to give the devil's work its right name. [CHRISTY, *soullessly indifferent to
the strife of Good and Evil, stares at the fire, warming himself*] Well, how long
are you going to stare there like a stuck pig? What news have you for me?

Christy [*taking off his hat and shawl and going to the rack to hang them up*].
The minister is to break the news to you. He'll be here presently.

Mrs. Dudgeon.   Break what news?

Christy [*standing on tiptoe, from boyish habit, to hang his hat up, though he is
quite tall enough to reach the peg, and speaking with callous placidity, considering the nature of the announcement*].   Father's dead too.

Mrs. Dudgeon [*stupent*].   Your father!

Christy [*sulkily, coming back to the fire and warming himself again, attending
much more to the fire than to his mother*].   Well, it's not my fault. When we
got to Nevinstown, we found him ill in bed. He didn't know us at first. The
minister sat up with him and sent me away. He died in the night.

Mrs. Dudgeon [*bursting into dry, angry tears*].   Well, I do think this is hard on me—very hard on me. His brother, that was a disgrace to us all his life, gets hanged on the public gallows as a rebel; and your father, instead of staying at home where his duty was, with his own family, goes after him and dies, leaving everything on my shoulders. After sending this girl to me to take care of, too! [*She plucks her shawl vexedly over her ears*] It's sinful, so it is; downright sinful.

Christy [*with a slow, bovine cheerfulness, after a pause*]. I think it's going to be a fine morning, after all.

Mrs. Dudgeon [*railing at him*]. A fine morning! And your father newly dead! Where's your feelings, child?

Christy [*obstinately*]. Well, I didn't mean any harm. I suppose a man may make a remark about the weather even if his father's dead.

Mrs. Dudgeon [*bitterly*]. A nice comfort my children are to me! One son a fool, and the other a lost sinner that's left his home to live with smugglers and gypsies and villains, the scum of the earth!

[*Someone knocks.*]

Christy [*without moving*]. That's the minister.

Mrs. Dudgeon [*sharply*]. Well, aren't you going to let Mr. Anderson in? [CHRISTY *goes sheepishly to the door.* MRS. DUDGEON *buries her face in her hands, as it is her duty as a widow to be overcome with grief.* CHRISTY *opens the door and admits the minister,* ANTHONY ANDERSON, *a shrewd, genial, ready Presbyterian divine of about fifty, with something of the authority of his profession in his bearing. But it is an altogether secular authority, sweetened by a conciliatory, sensible manner not at all suggestive of a quite thorough-going other-worldliness. He is a strong, healthy man too, with a thick sanguine neck; and his keen, cheerful mouth cuts into somewhat fleshy corners. No doubt an excellent parson, but still a man capable of making the most of this world, and perhaps a little apologetically conscious of getting on better with it than a sound Presbyterian ought.*]

Anderson [*to* CHRISTY, *at the door, looking at* MRS. DUDGEON *whilst he takes off his cloak*]. Have you told her?

Christy. She made me. [*He shuts the door; yawns; and loafs across to the sofa, where he sits down and presently drops off to sleep.*]

[ANDERSON *looks compassionately at* MRS. DUDGEON. *Then he hangs his cloak and hat on the rack.* MRS. DUDGEON *dries her eyes and looks up at him.*]

Anderson. Sister, the Lord has laid His hand very heavily upon you.

Mrs. Dudgeon [*with intensely recalcitrant resignation*]. It's His will, I suppose; and I must bow to it. But I do think it hard. What call had Timothy to go to Springtown and remind everybody that he belonged to a man that was being hanged?—and [*spitefully*] that deserved it, if ever a man did.

Anderson [*gently*]. They were brothers, Mrs. Dudgeon.

Mrs. Dudgeon. Timothy never acknowledged him as his brother after we were married; he had too much respect for me to insult me with such a brother. Would such a selfish wretch as Peter have come thirty miles to see Timothy hanged, do you think? Not thirty yards, not he. However, I must bear my cross as best I may; least said is soonest mended.

Anderson [*very grave, coming down to the fire to stand with his back to it*]. Your eldest son was present at the execution, Mrs. Dudgeon.

Mrs. Dudgeon [*disagreeably surprised*]. Richard?

Anderson [*nodding*]. Yes.

Mrs. Dudgeon [*vindictively*]. Let it be a warning to him. He may end that way himself, the wicked, dissolute, godless—[*She suddenly stops; her voice fails; and she asks, with evident dread*] Did Timothy see him?

Anderson. Yes.

Mrs. Dudgeon [*holding her breath*]. Well?

Anderson. He only saw him in the crowd; they did not speak. [MRS. DUDGEON, *greatly relieved, exhales the pent up breath and sits at her ease again*] Your husband was greatly touched and impressed by his brother's awful death. [MRS. DUDGEON *sneers.* ANDERSON *breaks off to demand with some indignation*] Well, wasn't it only natural, Mrs. Dudgeon? He softened towards his prodigal son in that moment. He sent for him to come to see him.

Mrs. Dudgeon [*her alarm renewed*]. Sent for Richard!

Anderson. Yes; but Richard would not come. He sent his father a message; but I'm sorry to say it was a wicked message—an awful message.

Mrs. Dudgeon. What was it?

Anderson. That he would stand by his wicked uncle and stand against his good parents, in this world and the next.

Mrs. Dudgeon [*implacably*]. He will be punished for it. He will be punished for it—in both worlds.

Anderson. That is not in our hands, Mrs. Dudgeon.

Mrs. Dudgeon. Did I say it was, Mr. Anderson? We are told that the wicked shall be punished. Why should we do our duty and keep God's law if there is to be no difference made between us and those who follow their own likings and dislikings, and make a jest of us and of their Maker's word?

Anderson. Well, Richard's earthly father has been merciful to him; and his heavenly judge is the father of us all.

Mrs. Dudgeon [*forgetting herself*]. Richard's earthly father was a soft-headed—

Anderson [*shocked*]. Oh!

Mrs. Dudgeon [*with a touch of shame*]. Well, I am Richard's mother. If I am against him who has any right to be for him? [*Trying to conciliate him*] Won't you sit down, Mr. Anderson? I should have asked you before; but I'm so troubled.

Anderson. Thank you. [*He takes a chair from beside the fireplace, and turns it so that he can sit comfortably at the fire. When he is seated he adds, in the tone of a man who knows that he is opening a difficult subject*] Has Christy told you about the new will?

Mrs. Dudgeon [*all her fears returning*]. The new will! Did Timothy—? [*She breaks off, gasping, unable to complete the question.*]

Anderson. Yes. In his last hours he changed his mind.

Mrs. Dudgeon [*white with intense rage*]. And you let him rob me?

Anderson. I had no power to prevent him giving what was his to his own son.

Mrs. Dudgeon. He had nothing of his own. His money was the money I brought him as my marriage portion. It was for him to deal with my own money and my own son. He dare not have done it if I had been with him; and well he knew it.

That was why he stole away like a thief to take advantage of the law to rob me by making a new will behind my back. The more shame on you, Mr. Anderson,—you, a minister of the gospel—to act as his accomplice in such a crime.

Anderson [*rising*]. I will take no offense at what you say in the first bitterness of your grief.

Mrs. Dudgeon [*contemptuously*]. Grief!

Anderson. Well, of your disappointment, if you can find it in your heart to think that the better word.

Mrs. Dudgeon. My heart! My heart! And since when, pray, have you begun to hold up our hearts as trustworthy guides for us?

Anderson [*rather guiltily*]. I-er-

Mrs. Dudgeon [*vehemently*]. Don't lie, Mr. Anderson. We are told that the heart of man is deceitful above all things and desperately wicked. My heart belonged, not to Timothy, but to that poor, wretched brother of his that has just ended his days with a rope round his neck—aye, to Peter Dudgeon. You know it; old Eli Hawkins, the man to whose pulpit you succeeded, though you are not worthy to loose his shoe latchet,[1] told it you when he gave over our souls into your charge. He warned me and strengthened me against my heart, and made me marry a God-fearing man—as he thought. What else but that discipline has made me the woman I am? And you, you, who followed your heart in your marriage, you talk to me of what I find in my heart. Go home to your pretty wife, man; and leave me to my prayers. [*She turns from him and leans with her elbows on the table, brooding over her wrongs and taking no further notice of him.*]

Anderson [*willing enough to escape*]. The Lord forbid that I should come between you and the source of all comfort! [*He goes to the rack for his coat and hat.*]

Mrs. Dudgeon [*without looking at him*]. The Lord will know what to forbid and what to allow without your help.

Anderson. And whom to forgive, I hope—Eli Hawkins and myself, if we have ever set up our preaching against His law. [*He fastens his cloak, and is now ready to go*] Just one word—on necessary business, Mrs. Dudgeon. There is the reading of the will to be gone through; and Richard has a right to be present. He is in the town; but he has the grace to say that he does not want to force himself in here.

Mrs. Dudgeon. He shall come here. Does he expect us to leave his father's house for his convenience? Let them all come, and come quickly, and go quickly. They shall not make the will an excuse to shirk half their day's work. I shall be ready, never fear.

Anderson [*coming back a step or two*]. Mrs. Dudgeon, I used to have some little influence with you. When did I lose it?

Mrs. Dudgeon [*still without turning to him*]. When you married for love. Now you're answered.

Anderson. Yes, I am answered. [*He goes out, musing.*]

Mrs. Dudgeon [*to herself, thinking of her husband*]. Thief! Thief! [*She shakes herself angrily out of her chair; throws back the shawl from her head; and sets

---

[1] lace.

to work to prepare the room for the reading of the will, beginning by replacing ANDERSON's *chair against the wall and pushing back her own to the window. Then she calls, in her hard, driving, wrathful way*] Christy. [*No answer; he is fast asleep*] Christy. [*She shakes him roughly*] Get up out of that; and be ashamed of yourself—sleeping, and your father dead! [*She returns to the table; puts the candle on the mantelshelf; and takes from the table drawer a red table cloth which she spreads.*]

Christy [*rising reluctantly*].   Well, do you suppose we are never going to sleep until we are out of mourning?

Mrs. Dudgeon.   I want none of your sulks. Here: help me to set this table. [*They place the table in the middle of the room, with* CHRISTY's *end towards the fireplace and* MRS. DUDGEON's *towards the sofa.* CHRISTY *drops the table as soon as possible, and goes to the fire, leaving his mother to make the final adjustment of its position*] We shall have the minister back here with the lawyer and all the family to read the will before you have done toasting yourself. Go and wake that girl; and then light the stove in the shed: you can't have your breakfast here. And mind you wash yourself and make yourself fit to receive the company. [*She punctuates these orders by going to the cupboard; unlocking it; and producing a decanter of wine, which has no doubt stood there untouched since the last state occasion in the family, and some glasses, which she sets on the table. Also two green ware plates, on one of which she puts a barn-brack¹ with a knife beside it. On the other she shakes some biscuits out of a tin, putting back one or two, and counting the rest*] Now mind: there are ten biscuits there; let there be ten there when I come back after dressing myself. And keep your fingers off the raisins in that cake. And tell Essie the same. I suppose I can trust you to bring in the case of stuffed birds without breaking the glass? [*She replaces the tin in the cupboard, which she locks, pocketing the key carefully.*]

Christy [*lingering at the fire*].   You'd better put the inkstand instead, for the lawyer.

Mrs. Dudgeon.   That's no answer to make to me, sir. Go and do as you're told. [CHRISTY *turns sullenly to obey*] Stop; take down that shutter before you go, and let the daylight in; you can't expect me to do all the heavy work of the house with a great lout like you idling about.

[CHRISTY *takes the window bar out of its clamps and puts it aside; then opens the shutter, showing the grey morning.* MRS. DUDGEON *takes the sconce from the mantelshelf; blows out the candle; extinguishes the snuff by pinching it with her fingers, first licking them for the purpose; and replaces the sconce on the shelf.*]

Christy [*looking through the window*].   Here's the minister's wife.

Mrs. Dudgeon [*displeased*].   What! Is she coming here?

Christy.   Yes.

Mrs. Dudgeon.   What does she want troubling me at this hour, before I am properly dressed to receive people?

Christy.   You'd better ask her.

Mrs. Dudgeon [*threateningly*].   You'd better keep a civil tongue in your head.

¹   A type of bun made with currants.

[*He goes sulkily towards the door. She comes after him, plying him with instructions*] Tell that girl to come to me as soon as she's had her breakfast. And tell her to make herself fit to be seen before the people. [CHRISTY *goes out and slams the door in her face*] Nice manners, that! [*Someone knocks at the house door; she turns and cries inhospitably*] Come in. [JUDITH ANDERSON, *the minister's wife, comes in.* JUDITH *is more than twenty years younger than her husband, though she will never be as young as he in vitality. She is pretty and proper and ladylike, and has been admired and petted into an opinion of herself sufficiently favorable to give her a self-assurance which serves her instead of strength. She has a pretty taste in dress, and in her face the pretty lines of a sentimental character formed by dreams. Even her little self-complacency is pretty, like a child's vanity. Rather a pathetic creature to any sympathetic observer who knows how rough a place the world is. One feels, on the whole, that* ANDERSON *might have chosen worse, and that she, needing protection, could not have chosen better*] Oh, it's you, is it, Mrs. Anderson?

Judith [*very politely—almost patronizingly*]. Yes. Can I do anything for you, Mrs. Dudgeon? Can I help to get the place ready before they come to read the will?

Mrs. Dudgeon [*stiffly*]. Thank you, Mrs. Anderson; my house is always ready for anyone to come into.

Mrs. Anderson [*with complacent amiability*]. Yes, indeed it is. Perhaps you had rather I did not intrude on you just now.

Mrs. Dudgeon. Oh, one more or less will make no difference this morning, Mrs. Anderson. Now that you're here you'd better stay. If you wouldn't mind shutting the door! [JUDITH *smiles, implying* "How stupid of me!" *and shuts it with an exasperating air of doing something pretty and becoming*] That's better. I must go and tidy myself a bit. I suppose you don't mind stopping here to receive anyone that comes until I'm ready.

Judith [*graciously giving her leave*]. Oh yes, certainly. Leave that to me, Mrs. Dudgeon; and take your time. [*She hangs her cloak and bonnet on the rack.*]

Mrs. Dudgeon [*half sneering*]. I thought that would be more in your way than getting the house ready. [ESSIE *comes back*] Oh, here you are! [*Severely*] Come here; let me see you. [ESSIE *timidly goes to her.* MRS. DUDGEON *takes her roughly by the arm and pulls her round to inspect the results of her attempt to clean and tidy herself—results which show little practice and less conviction*] Mm! That's what you call doing your hair properly, I suppose. It's easy to see what you are and how you were brought up. [*She throws her arm away and goes on, peremptorily*] Now you listen to me and do as you're told. You sit down in the corner by the fire; and when the company comes, don't dare to speak until you're spoken to. [ESSIE *creeps away to the fireplace*] Your father's people had better see you and know you're there; they're as much bound to keep you from starvation as I am. At any rate they might help. But let me have no chattering and making free with them, as if you were their equal. Do you hear?

Essie. Yes.

Mrs. Dudgeon. Well, then go and do as you're told. [ESSIE *sits down miserably on the corner of the fender furthest from the door*] Never mind her, Mrs. Anderson; you know who she is and what she is. If she gives you any trouble, just tell me; and I'll settle accounts with her. [MRS. DUDGEON *goes into the*

*bedroom, shutting the door sharply behind her as if even it had to be made do
its duty with a ruthless hand.*]

Judith [*patronizing* ESSIE *and arranging the cake and wine on the table more
becomingly*]. You must not mind if your aunt is strict with you. She is a very
good woman and desires your good too.

Essie [*in listless misery*]. Yes.

Judith [*annoyed with* ESSIE *for her failure to be consoled and edified, and to
appreciate the kindly condescension of the remark*]. You are not going to be
sullen, I hope, Essie.

Essie. No.

Judith. That's a good girl! [*She places a couple of chairs at the table with their
backs to the window, with a pleasant sense of being a more thoughtful housekeeper than* MRS. DUDGEON] Do you know any of your father's relatives?

Essie. No. They wouldn't have anything to do with him; they were too religious.
Father used to talk about Dick Dudgeon; but I never saw him.

Judith [*ostentatiously shocked*]. Dick Dudgeon! Essie, do you wish to be a really
respectable and grateful girl, and to make a place for yourself here by steady
good conduct?

Essie [*very half-heartedly*]. Yes.

Judith. Then you must never mention the name of Richard Dudgeon—never
even think about him. He is a bad man.

Essie. What has he done?

Judith. You must not ask questions about him, Essie. You are too young to know
what it is to be a bad man. But he is a smuggler; and he lives with gypsies; and
he has no love for his mother and his family; and he wrestles and plays games on
Sunday instead of going to church. Never let him into your presence, if you can
help it, Essie; and try to keep yourself and all womanhood unspotted by contact
with such men.

Essie. Yes.

Judith [*again displeased*]. I am afraid you say Yes and No without thinking very
deeply.

Essie. Yes. At least I mean—

Judith [*severely*]. What do you mean?

Essie [*almost crying*]. Only—my father was a smuggler; and— [*Someone
knocks.*]

Judith. They are beginning to come. Now remember your aunt's directions,
Essie; and be a good girl. [CHRISTY *comes back with the stand of stuffed birds
under a glass case, and an inkstand, which he places on the table*] Good
morning, Mr. Dudgeon. Will you open the door, please; the people have come.

Christy. Good morning. [*He opens the house door.*]

[*The morning is now fairly bright and warm; and* ANDERSON, *who is the first to
enter, has left his cloak at home. He is accompanied by* LAWYER HAWKINS, *a
brisk, middleaged man in brown riding gaiters and yellow breeches, looking as
much squire as solicitor. He and* ANDERSON *are allowed precedence as representing the learned professions. After them comes the family, headed by the senior
uncle,* WILLIAM DUDGEON, *a large, shapeless man, bottle-nosed and evidently no
ascetic at table. His clothes are not the clothes, nor his anxious wife the wife, of*

a prosperous man. The junior uncle, TITUS DUDGEON, *is a wiry little terrier of a man, with an immense and visibly purse-proud wife, both free from the cares of the William household.*

HAWKINS *at once goes briskly to the table and takes the chair nearest the sofa,* CHRISTY *having left the inkstand there. He puts his hat on the floor beside him and produces the will.* UNCLE WILLIAM *comes to the fire and stands on the hearth warming his coat tails, leaving* MRS. WILLIAM *derelict near the door.* UNCLE TITUS, *who is the lady's man of the family, rescues her by giving her his disengaged arm and bringing her to the sofa, where he sits down warmly between his own lady and his brother's.* ANDERSON *hangs up his hat and waits for a word with* JUDITH.]

Judith. She will be here in a moment. Ask them to wait. [*She taps at the bedroom door. Receiving an answer from within, she opens it and passes through.*]
Anderson [*taking his place at the table at the opposite end to* HAWKINS]. Our poor afflicted sister will be with us in a moment. Are we all here?
Christy [*at the house door, which he has just shut*]. All except Dick.

[*The callousness with which* CHRISTY *names the reprobate jars on the moral sense of the family.* UNCLE WILLIAM *shakes his head slowly and repeatedly.* MRS. TITUS *catches her breath convulsively through her nose. Her husband speaks.*]

Uncle Titus. Well, I hope he will have the grace not to come. I hope so.

[*The* DUDGEONS *all murmur assent, except* CHRISTY, *who goes to the window and posts himself there, looking out.* HAWKINS *smiles secretively as if he knew something that would change their tune if they knew it.* ANDERSON *is uneasy; the love of solemn family councils, especially funeral ones, is not in his nature.* JUDITH *appears at the bedroom door.*]

Judith [*with gentle impressiveness*]. Friends, Mrs. Dudgeon. [*She takes the chair from beside the fireplace, and places it for* MRS. DUDGEON, *who comes from the bedroom in black, with a clean handkerchief to her eyes. All rise, except* ESSIE. MRS. TITUS *and* MRS. WILLIAM *produce equally clean handkerchiefs and weep. It is an affecting moment.*]
Uncle William. Would it comfort you, sister, if we were to offer up a prayer?
Uncle Titus. Or sing a hymn?
Anderson [*rather hastily*]. I have been with our sister this morning already, friends. In our hearts we ask a blessing.
All [*except* ESSIE]. Amen.

[*They all sit down, except* JUDITH, *who stands behind* MRS. DUDGEON's *chair.*]

Judith [*to* ESSIE]. Essie, did you say Amen?
Essie [*scaredly*]. No.
Judith. Then say it, like a good girl.
Essie. Amen.
Uncle William [*encouragingly*]. That's right; that's right. We know who you are; but we are willing to be kind to you if you are a good girl and deserve it. We are all equal before the Throne.

[*This republican sentiment does not please the women, who are convinced that
the Throne is precisely the place where their superiority, often questioned in
this world, will be recognized and rewarded.*]

Christy [*at the window*].   Here's Dick.

[ANDERSON *and* HAWKINS *look round sociably.* ESSIE, *with a gleam of interest
breaking through her misery, looks up.* CHRISTY *grins and gapes expectantly at
the door. The rest are petrified with the intensity of their sense of Virtue
menaced with outrage by the approach of flaunting Vice. The reprobate appears
in the doorway, graced beyond his alleged merits by the morning sunlight. He is
certainly the best looking member of the family; but his expression is reckless
and sardonic, his manner defiant and satirical, his dress picturesquely careless.
Only, his forehead and mouth betray an extraordinary steadfastness; and his
eyes are the eyes of a fanatic.*]

Richard [*on the threshold, taking off his hat*].   Ladies and gentlemen: your
servant, your very humble servant. [*With this comprehensive insult, he throws
his hat to* CHRISTY *with a suddenness that makes him jump like a negligent
wicket keeper,*[1] *and comes into the middle of the room, where he turns and
deliberately surveys the company*] How happy you all look! how glad to see me!
[*He turns towards* MRS. DUDGEON's *chair; and his lip rolls up horribly from his
dog tooth as he meets her look of undisguised hatred*] Well, mother: keeping
up appearances as usual? that's right, that's right. [JUDITH *pointedly moves
away from his neighborhood to the other side of the kitchen, holding her skirt
instinctively as if to save it from contamination.* UNCLE TITUS *promptly marks
his approval of her action by rising from the sofa and placing a chair for her to
sit down upon*] What! Uncle William! I haven't seen you since you gave up
drinking. [*Poor* UNCLE WILLIAM, *shamed, would protest; but* RICHARD *claps him
heartily on his shoulder, adding*] You have given it up, haven't you? [*Releasing
him with a playful push*] Of course you have; quite right too; you overdid it.
[*He turns away from* UNCLE WILLIAM *and makes for the sofa*] And now, where
is that upright horse-dealer Uncle Titus? Uncle Titus, come forth. [*He comes
upon him holding the chair as* JUDITH *sits down*] As usual, looking after the
ladies!

Uncle Titus [*indignantly*].   Be ashamed of yourself, sir—

Richard [*interrupting him and shaking his hand in spite of him*].   I am, I am;
but I am proud of my uncle—proud of all my relatives—[*Again surveying
them*] Who could look at them and not be proud and joyful? [UNCLE TITUS,
overborne, resumes his seat on the sofa. RICHARD *turns to the table*] Ah, Mr.
Anderson, still at the good work, still shepherding them. Keep them up to the
mark, minister, keep them up to the mark. Come! [*With a spring he seats
himself on the table and takes up the decanter*] Clink a glass with me, Pastor,
for the sake of old times.

Anderson.   You know, I think, Mr. Dudgeon, that I do not drink before dinner.

Richard.   You will, some day, Pastor; Uncle William used to drink before breakfast. Come, it will give your sermons unction. [*He smells the wine and makes a*

---

[1] A cricket player in a fielding position whose responsibility it is to stop balls that pass
the wicket.

wry face] But do not begin on my mother's company sherry. I stole some when I was six years old; and I have been a temperate man ever since. [*He puts the decanter down and changes the subject*] So I hear you are married, Pastor, and that your wife has a most ungodly allowance of good looks.

Anderson [*quietly indicating* JUDITH]. Sir, you are in the presence of my wife. [JUDITH *rises and stands with stony propriety.*]

Richard [*quickly slipping down from the table with instinctive good manners*]. Your servant, madam; no offense. [*He looks at her earnestly*] You deserve your reputation; but I'm sorry to see by your expression that you're a good woman. [*She looks shocked and sits down amid a murmur of indignant sympathy from his relatives.* ANDERSON, *sensible enough to know that these demonstrations can only gratify and encourage a man who is deliberately trying to provoke them, remains perfectly good-humored*] All the same, Pastor, I respect you more than I did before. By the way, did I hear, or did I not, that our late lamented Uncle Peter, though unmarried, was a father?

Uncle Titus. He had only one irregular child, sir.

Richard. Only one! He thinks one a mere trifle! I blush for you, Uncle Titus.

Anderson. Mr. Dudgeon, you are in the presence of your mother and her grief.

Richard. It touches me profoundly, Pastor. By the way, what has become of the irregular child?

Anderson [*pointing to* ESSIE]. There, sir, listening to you.

Richard [*shocked into sincerity*]. What! Why the devil didn't you tell me that before? Children suffer enough in this house without—[*He hurries remorsefully to* ESSIE] Come, little cousin! never mind me; it was not meant to hurt you. [*She looks up gratefully at him. Her tear-stained face affects him violently; and he bursts out, in a transport of wrath*] Who has been making her cry? Who has been ill-treating her? By God—

Mrs. Dudgeon [*rising and confronting him*]. Silence your blasphemous tongue. I will bear no more of this. Leave my house.

Richard. How do you know it's your house until the will is read? [*They look at one another for a moment with intense hatred; and then she sinks, checkmated, into her chair.* RICHARD *goes boldly up past* ANDERSON *to the window, where he takes the railed chair in his hand*] Ladies and gentlemen, as the eldest son of my late father and the unworthy head of this household, I bid you welcome. By your leave, Minister Anderson: by your leave, Lawyer Hawkins. The head of the table for the head of the family. [*He places the chair at the table between the minister and the attorney; sits down between them; and addresses the assembly with a presidential air*] We meet on a melancholy occasion: a father dead! an uncle actually hanged, and probably damned. [*He shakes his head deploringly. The relatives freeze with horror*] That's right: pull your longest faces [*His voice suddenly sweetens gravely as his glance lights on* ESSIE] provided only there is hope in the eyes of the child. [*Briskly*] Now then, Lawyer Hawkins: business, business. Get on with the will, man.

Titus. Do not let yourself be ordered or hurried, Mr. Hawkins.

Hawkins [*very politely and willingly*]. Mr. Dudgeon means no offense, I feel sure. I will not keep you one second, Mr. Dudgeon. Just while I get my glasses—[*He fumbles for them. The* DUDGEONS *look at one another with misgiving.*]

Richard. Aha! They notice your civility, Mr. Hawkins. They are prepared for the worst. A glass of wine to clear your voice before you begin. [*He pours out one for him and hands it; then pours one for himself.*]

Hawkins. Thank you, Mr. Dudgeon. Your good health, sir.

Richard. Yours, sir. [*With the glass half way to his lips, he checks himself, giving a dubious glance at the wine, and adds, with quaint intensity*] Will anyone oblige me with a glass of water?

[ESSIE, *who has been hanging on his every word and movement, rises stealthily and slips out behind* MRS. DUDGEON *through the bedroom door, returning presently with a jug and going out of the house as quietly as possible.*]

Hawkins. The will is not exactly in proper legal phraseology.

Richard. No, my father died without the consolations of the law.

Hawkins. Good again, Mr. Dudgeon, good again. [*Preparing to read*] Are you ready, sir?

Richard. Ready, aye ready. For what we are about to receive, may the Lord make us truly thankful. Go ahead.

Hawkins [*reading*]. "This is the last will and testament of me Timothy Dudgeon on my deathbed at Nevinstown on the road from Springtown to Websterbridge on this twenty-fourth day of September, one thousand seven hundred and seventy seven. I hereby revoke all former wills made by me and declare that I am of sound mind and know well what I am doing and that this is my real will according to my own wish and affections."

Richard [*glancing at his mother*]. Aha!

Hawkins [*shaking his head*]. Bad phraseology, sir, wrong phraseology. "I give and bequeath a hundred pounds to my younger son Christopher Dudgeon, fifty pounds to be paid to him on the day of his marriage to Sarah Wilkins if she will have him, and ten pounds on the birth of each of his children up to the number of five."

Richard. How if she won't have him?

Christy. She will if I have fifty pounds.

Richard. Good, my brother. Proceed.

Hawkins. "I give and bequeath to my wife Annie Dudgeon, born Annie Primrose"—you see he did not know the law, Mr. Dudgeon: your mother was not born Annie: she was christened so—"an annuity of fifty-two pounds a year for life [MRS. DUDGEON, *with all eyes on her, holds herself convulsively rigid*] to be paid out of the interest on her own money"—there's a way to put it, Mr. Dudgeon! Her own money!

Mrs. Dudgeon. A very good way to put God's truth. It was every penny my own. Fifty-two pounds a year!

Hawkins. "And I recommend her for her goodness and piety to the forgiving care of her children, having stood between them and her as far as I could to the best of my ability."

Mrs. Dudgeon. And this is my reward! [*Raging inwardly*] You know what I think, Mr. Anderson; you know the word I gave to it.

Anderson. It cannot be helped, Mrs. Dudgeon. We must take what comes to us. [*To* HAWKINS] Go on, sir.

Hawkins. "I give and bequeath my house at Websterbridge with the land belonging to it and all the rest of my property soever to my eldest son and heir, Richard Dudgeon."

Richard. Oho! The fatted calf, Minister, the fatted calf.

Hawkins. "On these conditions—"

Richard. The devil! Are there conditions?

Hawkins. "To wit: first, that he shall not let my brother Peter's natural child starve or be driven by want to an evil life."

Richard [*emphatically, striking his fist on the table*]. Agreed.

[MRS. DUDGEON, *turning to look malignantly at* ESSIE, *misses her and looks quickly round to see where she has moved to; then, seeing that she has left the room without leave, closes her lips vengefully.*]

Hawkins. "Second, that he shall be a good friend to my old horse Jim"—[*again shaking his head*] he should have written James, sir.

Richard. James shall live in clover. Go on.

Hawkins. —"and keep my deaf farm labourer Prodger Feston in his service."

Richard. Prodger Feston shall get drunk every Saturday.

Hawkins. "Third, that he make Christy a present on his marriage out of the ornaments in the best room."

Richard [*holding up the stuffed birds*]. Here you are, Christy.

Christy [*disappointed*]. I'd rather have the china peacocks.

Richard. You shall have both. [CHRISTY *is greatly pleased*] Go on.

Hawkins. "Fourthly and lastly, that he try to live at peace with his mother as far as she will consent to it."

Richard [*dubiously*]. Hm! Anything more, Mr. Hawkins?

Hawkins [*solemnly*]. "Finally I give and bequeath my soul into my Maker's hands, humbly asking forgiveness for all my sins and mistakes, and hoping that He will so guide my son that it may not be said that I have done wrong in trusting to him rather than to others in the perplexity of my last hour in this strange place."

Anderson. Amen.

The Uncles and Aunts. Amen.

Richard. My mother does not say Amen.

Mrs. Dudgeon [*rising, unable to give up her property without a struggle*]. Mr. Hawkins, is that a proper will? Remember, I have his rightful, legal will, drawn up by yourself, leaving all to me.

Hawkins. This is a very wrongly and irregularly worded will, Mrs. Dudgeon: though [*turning politely to* RICHARD] it contains in my judgment an excellent disposal of his property.

Anderson [*interposing before* MRS. DUDGEON *can retort*]. That is not what you are asked, Mr. Hawkins. Is it a legal will?

Hawkins. The courts will sustain it against the other.

Anderson. But why, if the other is more lawfully worded?

Hawkins. Because, sir, the courts sustain the claim of a man—and that man the eldest son—against any woman, if they can. I warned you, Mrs. Dudgeon, when you got me to draw that other will, that it was not a wise will, and that though you might make him sign it, he would never be easy until he revoked it. But you wouldn't take advice; and now Mr. Richard is cock of the walk. [*He takes his hat from the floor; rises; and begins pocketing his papers and spectacles.*]

[*This is the signal for the breaking-up of the party.* ANDERSON *takes his hat from the rack and joins* UNCLE WILLIAM *at the fire.* TITUS *fetches* JUDITH *her things from the rack. The three on the sofa rise and chat with* HAWKINS. MRS. DUDGEON, *now an intruder in her own house, stands inert, crushed by the weight of the law on women, accepting it, as she has been trained to accept all monstrous calamities, as proofs of the greatness of the power that inflicts them, and of her own wormlike insignificance. For at this time, remember, Mary Wollstonecraft is as yet only a girl of eighteen, and her Vindication of the Rights of Women[1] is still fourteen years off.* MRS. DUDGEON *is rescued from her apathy by* ESSIE, *who comes back with the jug full of water. She is taking it to* RICHARD *when* MRS. DUDGEON *stops her.*]

Mrs. Dudgeon [*threatening her*]. Where have you been? [ESSIE, *appalled, tries to answer, but cannot*] How dare you go out by yourself after the orders I gave you?

Essie. He asked for a drink—[*She stops, her tongue cleaving to her palate with terror.*]

Judith [*with gentler severity*]. Who asked for a drink? [ESSIE, *speechless, points to* RICHARD.]

Richard. What! I!

Judith [*shocked*]. Oh Essie, Essie!

Richard. I believe I did. [*He takes a glass and holds it to* ESSIE *to be filled. Her hand shakes*] What! afraid of me?

Essie [*quickly*]. No. I—[*She pours out the water.*]

Richard [*tasting it*]. Ah, you've been up the street to the market gate spring to get that. [*He takes a draught*] Delicious! Thank you. [*Unfortunately, at this moment he chances to catch sight of* JUDITH's *face, which expresses the most prudish disapproval of his evident attraction for* ESSIE, *who is devouring him with her grateful eyes. His mocking expression returns instantly. He puts down the glass; deliberately winds his arm round* ESSIE's *shoulders; and brings her into the middle of the company.* MRS. DUDGEON *being in* ESSIE's *way as they come past the table, he says*] By your leave, mother [*and compels her to make way for them*]. What do they call you? Bessie?

Essie. Essie.

Richard. Essie, to be sure. Are you a good gir, Essie?

Essie [*greatly disappointed that he, of all people, should begin at her in this way*]. Yes. [*She looks doubtfully at* JUDITH] I think so. I mean I—I hope so.

Richard. Essie, did you ever hear of a person called the devil?

Anderson [*revolted*]. Shame on you, sir, with a mere child—

Richard. By your leave, Minister; I do not interfere with your sermons; do not you interrupt mine. [*To* ESSIE] Do you know what they call me, Essie?

Essie. Dick.

Richard [*amused; patting her on the shoulder*]. Yes, Dick; but something else too. They call me the Devil's Disciple.

---

[1] A tract published in 1792 that vigorously denounced attitudes toward women in the 18th century.

Essie. Why do you let them?

Richard [*seriously*]. Because it's true. I was brought up in the other service; but I knew from the first that the Devil was my natural master and captain and friend. I saw that he was in the right and that the world cringed to his conqueror only through fear. I prayed secretly to him; and he comforted me, and saved me from having my spirit broken in this house of children's tears. I promised him my soul and swore an oath that I would stand up for him in this world and stand by him in the next. [*Solemnly*] That promise and that oath made a man of me. From this day this house is his home; and no child shall cry in it: this hearth is his altar; and no soul shall ever cower over it in the dark evenings and be afraid. Now [*turning forcibly on the rest*] which of you good men will take this child and rescue her from the house of the devil?

Judith [*coming to* ESSIE *and throwing a protecting arm about her*]. I will. You should be burnt alive.

Essie. But I don't want to. [*She shrinks back, leaving* RICHARD *and* JUDITH *face to face.*]

Richard [*to* JUDITH]. Actually doesn't want to, most virtuous lady!

Uncle Titus. Have a care, Richard Dudgeon. The law—

Richard [*turning threateningly on him*]. Have a care, you. In an hour from this there will be no law here but martial law. I passed the soldiers within six miles on my way here; before noon Major Swindon's gallows for rebels will be up in the market place.

Anderson [*calmly*]. What have we to fear from that, sir?

Richard. More than you think. He hanged the wrong man at Springtown: he thought Uncle Peter was respectable, because the Dudgeons had a good name. But his next example will be the best man in the town to whom he can bring home a rebellious word. Well, we're all rebels; and you know it.

All the Men [*except* ANDERSON]. No, no, no!

Richard. Yes, you are. You haven't damned King George up hill and down dale as I have; but you've prayed for his defeat; and you, Anthony Anderson, have conducted the service and sold your family bible to buy a pair of pistols. They mayn't hang me, perhaps; because the moral effect of the Devil's Disciple dancing on nothing wouldn't help them. But a minister! [JUDITH, *dismayed, clings to* ANDERSON] or a lawyer! [HAWKINS *smiles like a man able to take care of himself*] or an upright horsedealer! [UNCLE TITUS *snarls at him in rage and terror*] or a reformed drunkard! [UNCLE WILLIAM, *utterly unnerved, moans and wobbles with fear*] eh? Would that show that King George meant business—ha?

Anderson [*perfectly self-possessed*]. Come, my dear; he is only trying to frighten you. There is no danger. [*He takes her out of the house. The rest crowd to the door to follow him, except* ESSIE, *who remains near* RICHARD.]

Richard [*boisterously derisive*]. Now then: how many of you will stay with me; run up the American flag on the devil's house; and make a fight for freedom? [*They scramble out,* CHRISTY *among them, hustling one another in their haste*] Ha ha! Long live the devil! [*To* MRS. DUDGEON, *who is following them*] What, mother! Are you off too?

Mrs. Dudgeon [*deadly pale, with her hand on her heart as if she had received a deathblow*]. My curse on you! My dying curse! [*She goes out.*]

Richard [*calling after her*]. It will bring me luck. Ha ha ha!

Essie [*anxiously*].   Mayn't I stay?

Richard [*turning to her*].   What! Have they forgotten to save your soul in their anxiety about their own bodies? Oh yes, you may stay. [*He turns excitedly away again and shakes his fist after them. His left fist, also clenched, hangs down.* ESSIE *seizes it and kisses it, her tears falling on it. He starts and looks at it*] Tears! The devil's baptism! [*She falls on her knees, sobbing. He stoops good-naturedly to raise her, saying*] Oh yes, you may cry that way, Essie, if you like.

[*The Curtain Falls.*]

Act II

[MINISTER ANDERSON'S *house is in the main street of Websterbridge, not far from the town hall. To the eye of the eighteenth-century New Englander, it is much grander than the plain farmhouse of the* DUDGEONS; *but it is so plain itself that a modern house agent would let both at about the same rent. The chief dwelling room has the same sort of kitchen fireplace, with boiler, toaster hanging on the bars, movable iron griddle socketed to the hob, hook above for roasting, and broad fender, on which stand a kettle and a plate of buttered toast. The door, between the fireplace and the corner, has neither panels, fingerplates nor handles: it is made of plain boards, and fastens with a latch. The table is a kitchen table, with a treacle¹-colored cover of American cloth,² chapped at the corners by draping. The tea service on it consists of two thick cups and saucers of the plainest ware, with milk jug and bowl to match, each large enough to contain nearly a quart, on a black japanned³ tray, and, in the middle of the table, a wooden trencher⁴ with a big loaf upon it, and a square half-pound block of butter in a crock. The big oak press⁵ facing the fire from the opposite side of the room, is for use and storage, not for ornament; and the minister's house coat hangs on a peg from its door, showing that he is out; for when he is in, it is his best coat that hangs there. His big riding boots stand beside the press, evidently in their usual place, and rather proud of themselves. In fact, the evolution of the minister's kitchen, dining room and drawing room into three separate apartments has not yet taken place; and so, from the point of view of our pampered period, he is no better off than the* DUDGEONS.*

But there is a difference, for all that. To begin with,* MRS. ANDERSON *is a pleasanter person to live with than* MRS. DUDGEON. *To which* MRS. DUDGEON *would at once reply, with reason, that* MRS. ANDERSON *has no children to look after; no poultry, pigs nor cattle; a steady and sufficient income not directly dependent on harvests and prices at fairs; an affectionate husband who is a tower of strength to her: in short, that life is as easy at the minister's house as it*

---

¹   molasses.
²   oilcloth.
³   lacquered.
⁴   platter.
⁵   cupboard.

*is hard at the farm. This is true; but to explain a fact is not to alter it; and
however little credit* MRS. ANDERSON *may deserve for making her home happier,
she has certainly succeeded in doing it. The outward and visible signs of her
superior social pretensions are a drugget[1] on the floor, a plaster ceiling between
the timbers, and chairs which, though not upholstered, are stained and polished.
The fine arts are represented by a mezzotint portrait of some Presbyterian
divine, a copperplate of Raphael's St. Paul preaching at Athens, a rococo presentation clock on the mantelshelf, flanked by a couple of miniatures, a pair of
crockery dogs with baskets in their mouths, and, at the corners, two large cowrie[2]
shells. A pretty feature of the room is the low wide latticed window, nearly its
whole width, with little red curtains running on a rod half way up it to serve as
a blind. There is no sofa; but one of the seats, standing near the press, has a
railed back and is long enough to accommodate two people easily. On the
whole, it is rather the sort of room that the nineteenth century has ended in
struggling to get back to under the leadership of Mr. Philip Webb[3] and his
disciples in domestic architecture, though no genteel clergyman would have
tolerated it fifty years ago.*

*The evening has closed in; and the room is dark except for the cosy firelight
and the dim oil lamps seen through the window in the wet street, where there is
a quiet, steady, warm, windless downpour of rain. As the town clock strikes the
quarter,* JUDITH *comes in with a couple of candles in earthenware candlesticks,
and sets them on the table. Her self-conscious airs of the morning are gone: she
is anxious and frightened. She goes to the window and peers into the street. The
first thing she sees there is her husband, hurrying home through the rain. She
gives a little gasp of relief, not very far removed from a sob, and turns to the
door.* ANDERSON *comes in, wrapped in a very wet cloak.*]

Judith [*running to him*]. 'Oh, here you are at last, at last! [*She attempts to
embrace him.*]

Anderson [*keeping her off*]. Take care, my love; I'm wet. Wait till I get my
cloak off. [*He places a chair with its back to the fire; hangs his cloak on it to
dry; shakes the rain from his hat and puts it on the fender; and at last turns
with his hands outstretched to* JUDITH] Now! [*She flies ino his arms*] I am
not late, am I? The town clock struck the quarter as I came in at the front door.
And the town clock is always fast.

Judith. I'm sure it's slow this evening. I'm so glad you're back.

Anderson [*taking her more closely in his arms*]. Anxious, my dear?

Judith. A little.

Anderson. Why, you've been crying.

Judith. Only a little. Never mind; it's all over now. [*A bugle call is heard in the
distance. She starts in terror and retreats to the long seat, listening*] What's
that?

Anderson [*following her tenderly to the seat and making her sit down with him*].
Only King George, my dear. He's returning to barracks, or having his roll

---

[1] A coarse rug.

[2] A mollusk.

[3] English architect (1831–1915) who tried to change Victorian taste in interior deco-
rating.

called, or getting ready for tea, or booting or saddling or something. Soldiers don't ring the bell or call over the banisters when they want anything: they send a boy out with a bugle to disturb the whole town.

Judith. Do you think there is really any danger?

Anderson. Not the least in the world.

Judith. You say that to comfort me, not because you believe it.

Anderson. My dear, in this world there is always danger for those who are afraid of it. There's a danger that the house will catch fire in the night; but we shan't sleep any the less soundly for that.

Judith. Yes, I know what you always say; and you're quite right. Oh, quite right: I know it. But—I suppose I'm not brave: that's all. My heart shrinks every time I think of the soldiers.

Anderson. Never mind that, dear; bravery is none the worse for costing a little pain.

Judith. Yes, I suppose so. [*Embracing him again*] Oh how brave you are, my dear! [*With tears in her eyes*] Well, I'll be brave too: you shan't be ashamed of your wife.

Anderson. That's right. Now you make me happy. Well, well! [*He rises and goes cheerily to the fire to dry his shoes*] I called on Richard Dudgeon on my way back; but he wasn't in.

Judith [*rising in consternation*].   You called on that man!

Anderson [*reassuring her*].   Oh, nothing happened, dearie. He was out.

Judith [*almost in tears, as if the visit were a personal humiliation to her*].   But why did you go there?

Anderson [*gravely*].   Well, it is all the talk that Major Swindon is going to do what he did in Springtown—make an example of some notorious rebel, as he calls us. He pounced on Peter Dudgeon as the worst character there; and it is the general belief that he will pounce on Richard as the worst here.

Judith. But Richard said—

Anderson [*goodhumoredly cutting her short*].   Pooh! Richard said! He said what he thought would frighten you and frighten me, my dear. He said what perhaps (God forgive him!) he would like to believe. It's a terrible thing to think of what death must mean for a man like that. I felt that I must warn him. I left a message for him.

Judith [*querulously*].   What message?

Anderson. Only that I should be glad to see him for a moment on a matter of importance to himself, and that if he would look in here when he was passing he would be welcome.

Judith [*aghast*].   You asked that man to come here!

Anderson. I did.

Judith [*sinking on the seat and clasping her hands*].   I hope he won't come! Oh, I pray that he may not come!

Anderson. Why? Don't you want him to be warned?

Judith. He must know his danger. Oh, Tony, is it wrong to hate a blasphemer and a villain? I do hate him. I can't get him out of my mind; I know he will bring harm with him. He insulted you; he insulted me; he insulted his mother.

Anderson [*quaintly*].   Well, dear, let's forgive him; and then it won't matter.

Judith. Oh, I know it's wrong to hate anybody; but—

Anderson [*going over to her with humorous tenderness*]. Come, dear, you're not so wicked as you think. The worst sin towards our fellow creatures is not to hate them, but to be indifferent to them; that's the essence of inhumanity. After all, my dear, if you watch people carefully, you'll be surprised to find how like hate is to love. [*She starts, strangely touched—even appalled. He is amused at her*] Yes, I'm quite in earnest. Think of how some of our married friends worry one another, tax one another, are jealous of one another, can't bear to let one another out of sight for a day, are more like jailers and slave-owners than lovers. Think of those very same people with their enemies, scrupulous, lofty, self-respecting, determined to be independent of one another, careful of how they speak of one another—pooh! haven't you often thought that if they only knew it, they were better friends to their enemies than to their own husbands and wives? Come: depend on it, my dear, you are really fonder of Richard than you are of me, if you only knew it. Eh!

Judith. Oh, don't say that; don't say that, Tony, even in jest. You don't know what a horrible feeling it gives me.

Anderson [*laughing*]. Well, well: never mind, pet. He's a bad man, and you hate him as he deserves. And you're going to make the tea, aren't you?

Judith [*remorsefully*]. Oh yes, I forgot. I've been keeping you waiting all this time. [*She goes to the fire and puts on the kettle.*]

Anderson [*going to the press and taking his coat off*]. Have you stitched up the shoulder of my old coat?

Judith. Yes, dear. [*She goes to the table and sets about putting the tea into the teapot from the caddy.*]

Anderson [*as he changes his coat for the older one hanging on the press and replaces it by the one he has just taken off*]. Did anyone call when I was out?

Judith. No, only— [*Someone knocks at the door. With a start which betrays her intense nervousness, she retreats to the further end of the table with the tea caddy and spoon in her hands, exclaiming*] Who's that?

Anderson [*going to her and patting her encouragingly on the shoulder*]. All right, pet, all right. He won't eat you, whoever he is. [*She tries to smile and nearly makes herself cry. He goes to the door and opens it.* RICHARD *is there, without overcoat or cloak*] You might have raised the latch and come in, Mr. Dudgeon. Nobody stands on much ceremony with us. [*Hospitably*] Come in. [RICHARD *comes in carelessly and stands at the table, looking round the room with a slight pucker of his nose at the mezzotinted divine on the wall.* JUDITH *keeps her eyes on the tea caddy*] Is it still raining? [*He shuts the door.*]

Richard. Raining like the very [*his eye catches* JUDITH's *as she looks quickly and haughtily up*]—I beg your pardon; but [*showing that his coat is wet*] you see—!

Anderson. Take it off, sir; and let it hang before the fire a while; my wife will excuse your shirtsleeves. Judith, put in another spoonful of tea for Mr. Dudgeon.

Richard [*eyeing him cynically*]. The magic of property, Pastor! Are even you civil to me now that I have succeeded to my father's estate? [JUDITH *throws down the spoon indignantly.*]

Anderson [*quite unruffled and helping* RICHARD *off with his coat*]. I think, sir, that since you accept my hospitality, you cannot have so bad an opinion of it. Sit down. [*With the coat in his hand, he points to the railed seat.* RICHARD, *in his shirtsleeves, looks at him half quarrelsomely for a moment; then, with a nod, acknowledges that the minister has got the better of him, and sits down on the seat.* ANDERSON *pushes his cloak into a heap on the seat of the chair at the fire and hangs* RICHARD'S *coat on the back in its place.*]

Richard.   I come, sir, on your own invitation. You left word you had something important to tell me

Anderson.   I have a warning which it is my duty to give you.

Richard [*quickly rising*].   You want to preach to me. Excuse me; I prefer a walk in the rain. [*He makes for his coat.*]

Anderson [*stopping him*].   Don't be alarmed, sir; I am no great preacher. You are quite safe. [RICHARD *smiles in spite of himself. His glance softens; he even makes a gesture of excuse.* ANDERSON, *seeing that he has tamed him, now addresses him earnestly*] Mr. Dudgeon, you are in danger in this town.

Richard.   What danger?

Anderson.   Your uncle's danger. Major Swindon's gallows.

Richard.   It is you who are in danger. I warned you—

Anderson [*interrupting him good-humoredly but authoritatively*].   Yes, yes, Mr. Dudgeon, but they do not think so in the town. And even if I were in danger, I have duties here which I must not forsake. But you are a free man. Why should you run any risk?

Richard.   Do you think I should be any great loss, Minister?

Anderson.   I think that a man's life is worth saving, whoever it belongs to. [RICH-ARD *makes him an ironical bow.* ANDERSON *returns the bow humorously*] Come, you'll have a cup of tea, to prevent you catching cold?

Richard.   I observe that Mrs. Anderson is not quite so pressing as you are, Pastor.

Judith [*almost stifled with resentment, which she has been expecting her husband to share and express for her at every insult of* RICHARD'S].   You are welcome for my husband's sake. [*She brings the teapot to the fireplace and sets it on the hob.*]

Richard.   I know I am not welcome for my own, madam. [*He rises*] But I think I will not break bread here, Minister.

Anderson [*cheerily*].   Give me a good reason for that.

Richard.   Because there is something in you that I respect, and that makes me desire to have you for my enemy.

Anderson.   That's well said. On those terms, sir, I will accept your enmity or any man's. Judith, Mr. Dudgeon will stay to tea. Sit down; it will take a few minutes to draw by the fire. [RICHARD *glances at him with a troubled face, then sits down with his head bent, to hide a convulsive swelling of his throat*] I was just saying to my wife, Mr. Dudgeon, that enmity— [*She grasps his hand and looks imploringly at him, doing both with an intensity that checks him at once*] Well, well, I mustn't tell you, I see; but it was nothing that need leave us worse friend—enemies, I mean. Judith is a great enemy of yours.

Richard.   If all my enemies were like Mrs. Anderson, I should be the best Christian in America.

Anderson [*gratified, patting her hand*].   You hear that, Judith? Mr. Dudgeon knows how to turn a compliment.

[*The latch is lifted from without.*]

Judith [*starting*].   Who is that?

[CHRISTY *comes in.*]

Christy [*stopping and staring at* RICHARD].   Oh, are you here?

Richard.   Yes. Begone, you fool; Mrs. Anderson doesn't want the whole family to tea at once.

Christy [*coming further in*].   Mother's very ill.

Richard.   Well, does she want to see me?

Christy.   No.

Richard.   I thought not.

Christy.   She wants to see the minister—at once.

Judith [*to* ANDERSON].   Oh, not before you've had some tea.

Anderson.   I shall enjoy it more when I come back, dear. [*He is about to take up his cloak.*]

Christy.   The rain's over.

Anderson [*dropping the cloak and picking up his hat from the fender*].   Where is your mother, Christy?

Christy.   At Uncle Titus's.

Anderson.   Have you fetched the doctor?

Christy.   No: she didn't tell me to.

Anderson.   Go on there at once; I'll overtake you on his doorstep. [CHRISTY *turns to go*] Wait a moment. Your bother must be anxious to know the particulars.

Richard.   Psha! not I; he doesn't know, and I don't care. [*Violently*] Be off, you oaf. [CHRISTY *runs out.* RICHARD *adds, a little shamefacedly*] We shall know soon enough.

Anderson.   Well, perhaps you will let me bring you the news myself. Judith, will you give Mr. Dudgeon his tea and keep him here until I return.

Judith [*white and trembling*].   Must I—

Anderson [*taking her hands and interrupting her to cover her agitation*].   My dear, I can depend on you?

Judith [*with a piteous effort to be worthy of his trust*].   Yes.

Anderson [*pressing her hand against his cheek*].   You will not mind two old people like us, Mr. Dudgeon. [*Going*] I shall not say good evening; you will be here when I come back. [*He goes out.*]

[*They watch him pass the window and then look at each other dumbly, quite disconcerted.* RICHARD, *noting the quiver of her lips, is the first to pull himself together.*]

Richard.   Mrs. Anderson, I am perfectly aware of the nature of your sentiments towards me. I shall not intrude on you. Good evening. [*Again he starts for the fireplace to get his coat.*]

Judith [*getting between him and the coat*].   No, no. Don't go; please don't go.

Richard [*roughly*].   Why? You don't want me here.

Judith.   Yes, I— [*Wringing her hands in despair*]. Oh, if I tell you the truth, you will use it to torment me.

Richard [*indignantly*].   Torment! What right have you to say that? Do you expect me to stay after that?

Judith. I want you to stay; but [*suddenly raging at him like an angry child*] it is not because I like you.

Richard. Indeed!

Judith. Yes, I had rather you did go than mistake me about that. I hate and dread you; and my husband knows it. If you are not here when he comes back, he will believe that I disobeyed him and drove you away.

Richard [*ironically*]. Whereas, of course, you have really been so kind and hospitable and charming to me that I only want to go away out of mere contrariness, eh?

[JUDITH, *unable to bear it, sinks on the chair and bursts into tears.*]

Richard. Stop, stop, stop, I tell you. Don't do that. [*Putting his hand to his breast as if to a wound*] He wrung my heart by being a man. Need you tear it by being a woman? Has he not raised you above my insults, like himself? [*She stops crying and recovers herself somewhat, looking at him with a scared curiosity*] There, that's right. [*Sympathetically*] You're better now, aren't you? [*He puts his hand encouragingly on her shoulder. She instantly rises haughtily and stares at him defiantly. He at once drops into his usual sardonic tone*] Ah, that's better. You are yourself again; so is Richard. Well, shall we go to tea like a quiet respectable couple and wait for your husband's return?

Judith [*rather ashamed of herself*]. If you please. I—I am sorry to have been so foolish. [*She stoops to take up the plate of toast from the fender.*]

Richard. I am sorry, for your sake, that I am—what I am. Allow me. [*He takes the plate from her and goes with it to the table.*]

Judith [*following with the teapot*]. Will you sit down? [*He sits down at the end of the table nearest the press. There is a plate and knife laid there. The other plate is laid near it; but* JUDITH *stays at the opposite end of the table, next the fire, and takes her place there, drawing the tray towards her*] Do you take sugar?

Richard. No, but plenty of milk. Let me give you some toast. [*He puts some on the second plate and hands it to her, with the knife. The action shows quickly how well he knows that she has avoided her usual place so as to be as far from him as possible.*]

Judith [*consciously*]. Thanks. [*She gives him his tea*] Won't you help yourself?

Richard. Thanks. [*He puts a piece of toast on his own plate, and she pours out tea for herself.*]

Judith [*observing that he tastes nothing*]. Don't you like it? You are not eating anything.

Richard. Neither are you.

Judith [*nervously*]. I never care much for my tea. Please don't mind me.

Richard [*looking dreamily round*]. I am thinking. It is all so strange to me. I can see the beauty and peace of this home; I think I have never been more at rest in my life than at this moment; and yet I know quite well I could never live here. It's not in my nature, I suppose, to be domesticated. But it's very beautiful; it's almost holy. [*He muses a moment and then laughs softly.*]

Judith [*quickly*]. Why do you laugh?

Richard. I was thinking that if any stranger came in here now, he would take us for man and wife.

Judith [*taking offense*]. You mean, I suppose, that you are more my age than he is.

Richard [*staring at this unexpected turn*]. I never thought of such a thing. [*Sardonic again*] I see there is another side to domestic joy.

Judith [*angrily*]. I would rather have a husband whom everybody respects than—than—

Richard. Than the devil's disciple. You are right; but I daresay your love helps him to be a good man, just as your hate helps me to be a bad one.

Judith. My husband has been very good to you. He has forgiven you for insulting him and is trying to save you. Can you not forgive him for being so much better than you are? How dare you belittle him by putting yourself in his place?

Richard. Did I?

Judith. Yes, you did. You said that if anybody came in they would take us for man and— [*She stops, terror-stricken, as a squad of soldiers tramps past the window*] The English soldiers! Oh, what do they—

Richard [*listening*]. Sh!

A Voice [*outside*]. Halt! Four outside: two in with me. [JUDITH *half rises, listening and looking with dilated eyes at* RICHARD, *who takes up his cup prosaically and is drinking his tea when the latch goes up with a sharp click, and an English* SERGEANT *walks into the room with two privates, who post themselves at the door. He comes promptly to the table between them.*]

The Sergeant. Sorry to disturb you, mum. Duty! Anthony Anderson: I arrest you in King George's name as a rebel.

Judith [*pointing at* RICHARD]. But that is not— [*He looks up quickly at her, with a face of iron. She stops her mouth hastily with the hand she has raised to indicate him, and stands staring affrightedly.*]

The Sergeant. Come, parson; put your coat on and come along.

Richard. Yes, I'll come. [*He rises and takes a step towards his own coat; then recollects himself, and, with his back to the* SERGEANT, *moves his gaze slowly round the room without turning his head until he sees* ANDERSON's *black coat hanging up on the press. He goes composedly to it, takes it down, and puts it on. The idea of himself as a parson tickles him; he looks down at the black sleeve on his arm and then smiles slyly at* JUDITH, *whose white face shows him that what she is painfully struggling to grasp is not the humor of the situation but its horror. He turns to the* SERGEANT, *who is approaching him with a pair of handcuffs hidden behind him, and says lightly*] Did you ever arrest a man of my cloth before, Sergeant?

The Sergeant [*instinctively respectful, half to the black coat and to* RICHARD's *good breeding*]. Well, no sir. At least, only an army chaplain. [*Showing the handcuffs*] I'm sorry sir; but duty—

Richard. Just so, Sergeant. Well, I'm not ashamed of them; thank you kindly for the apology. [*He holds out his hands.*]

Sergeant [*not availing himself of the offer*]. One gentleman to another, sir. Wouldn't you like to say a word to your missis, sir, before you go?

Richard [*smiling*]. Oh, we shall meet again before—eh? [*Meaning "before you hang me".*]

Sergeant [*loudly, with ostentatious cheerfulness*]. Oh, of course, of course. No call for the lady to distress herself. Still— [*in a lower voice, intended for* RICHARD *alone*] your last chance, sir.

[*They look at one another significantly for a moment. Then* RICHARD *exhales a deep breath and turns towards* JUDITH.]

Richard [*very distinctly*]. My love. [*She looks at him, pitiably pale, and tries to answer, but cannot—tries also to come to him, but cannot trust herself to stand without the support of the table*] This gallant gentleman is good enough to allow us a moment of leavetaking. [*The* SERGEANT *retires delicately and joins his men near the door*] He is trying to spare you the truth; but you had better know it. Are you listening to me? [*She signifies assent*] Do you understand that I am going to my death? [*She signifies that she understands*] Remember, you must find our friend who was with us just now. Do you understand? [*She signifies yes*] See that you get him safely out of harm's way. Don't for your life let him know of my danger; but if he finds it out, tell him that he cannot save me: they would hang him; and they would not spare me. And tell him that I am steadfast in my religion as he is in his and that he may depend on me to the death. [*He turns to go and meets the eyes of the* SERGEANT, *who looks a little suspicious. He considers a moment and then, turning roguishly to* JUDITH *with something of a smile breaking through his earnestness, says*] And now, my dear, I am afraid the sergeant will not believe that you love me like a wife unless you give one kiss before I go. [*He approaches her and holds out his arms. She quits the table and almost falls into them.*]

Judith [*the words choking her*]. I ought to—it's murder—
Richard. No; only a kiss [*softly to her*] for his sake.
Judith. I can't. You must—
Richard [*folding her in his arms with an impulse of compassion for her distress*]. My poor girl!

[JUDITH, *with a sudden effort, throws her arms round him; kisses him; and swoons away, dropping from his arms to the ground as if the kiss had killed her.*]

Richard [*going quickly to the* SERGEANT]. Now, Sergeant; quick, before she comes to. The handcuffs. [*He puts out his hands.*]
Sergeant [*pocketing them*]. Never mind, sir; I'll trust you. You're a game one. You ought to a bin a soldier, sir. Between them two, please. [*The soldiers place themslves one before* RICHARD *and one behind him. The* SERGEANT *opens the door.*]
Richard [*taking a last look round him*]. Goodbye, wife; goodbye, home. Muffle the drums and quick march!

[*The* SERGEANT *signs to the leading soldier to march. They file out quickly.*

When ANDERSON *returns from* MRS. DUDGEON'S, *he is astonished to find the room apparently empty and almost in darkness except for the glow from the fire; for one of the candles has burnt out, and the other is at its last flicker.*]

Anderson. Why, what on earth—? [*Calling*] Judith, Judith! [*He listens; there is no answer*] Hm! [*He goes to the cupboard; takes a candle from the drawer; lights it at the flicker of the expiring one on the table; and looks wonderingly at the untasted meal by its light. Then he sticks it in the candlestick; takes off his hat; and scratches his head, much puzzled. This action causes him to look at the floor for the first time, and there he sees* JUDITH *lying motionless with her eyes closed. He runs to her and stoops beside her, lifting her head*] Judith.

Judith [*waking; for her swoon has passed into the sleep of exhaustion after suffering*]. Yes. Did you call? What's the matter?

Anderson. I've just come in and found you lying here with the candles burnt out and the tea poured out and cold. What has happened?

Judith [*still astray*]. I don't know. Have I been asleep? I suppose— [*She stops blankly*] I don't know.

Anderson [*groaning*]. Heaven forgive me, I left you alone with that scoundrel. [JUDITH *remembers. With an agonized cry, she clutches his shoulders and drags herself to her feet as he rises with her. He clasps her tenderly in his arms*] My poor pet!

JUDITH [*frantically clinging to him*]. What shall I do? Oh my God, what shall I do?

Anderson. Never mind, never mind, my dearest dear: it was my fault. Come, you're safe now; and you're not hurt, are you? [*He takes his arms from her to see whether she can stand*] There, that's right, that's right. If only you are not hurt, nothing else matters.

Judith. No, no, no, I'm not hurt.

Anderson. Thank Heaven for that! Come now: [*leading her to the railed seat and making her sit down beside him*] sit down and rest; you can tell me about it tomorrow. Or [*misunderstanding her distress*] you shall not tell me at all if it worries you. There, there! [*Cheerfully*] I'll make you some fresh tea; that will set you up again. [*He goes to the table and empties the teapot into the slop bowl.*]

Judith [*in a strained tone*]. Tony.

Anderson. Yes, dear?

Judith. Do you think we are only in a dream now?

Anderson [*glancing round at her for a moment with a pang of anxiety, though he goes on steadily and cheerfully putting fresh tea into the pot*]. Perhaps so, pet. But you may as well dream a cup of tea when you're about it.

Judith. Oh stop, stop. You don't know— [*Distracted, she buries her face in her knotted hands.*]

Anderson [*breaking down and coming to her*]. My dear, what is it? I can't bear it any longer; you must tell me. It was all my fault; I was mad to trust him.

Judith, No, don't say that. You mustn't say that. He—oh no, no: I can't. Tony, don't speak to me. Take my hands—both my hands. [*He takes them, wondering*] Make me think of you, not of him. There's danger, frightful danger; but it is your danger; and I can't keep thinking of it; I can't, I can't; my mind goes back to his danger. He must be saved—no, you must be saved: you, you, you. [*She springs up as if to do something or go somewhere, exclaiming*] Oh, Heaven help me!

Anderson [*keeping his seat and holding her hands with resolute composure*]. Calmly, calmly, my pet. You're quite distracted.

Judith. I may well be. I don't know what to do. I don't know what to do. [*Tearing her hands away*] I must save him. [ANDERSON *rises in alarm as she runs wildly to the door. It is opened in her face by* ESSIE, *who hurries in full of anxiety. The surprise is so disagreeable to* JUDITH *that it brings her to her senses. Her tone is sharp and angry as she demands*] What do you want?

Essie.   I was to come to you.

Anderson.   Who told you to?

Essie [*staring at him, as if his presence astonished her*].   Are you here?

Judith.   Of course. Don't be foolish, child.

Anderson.   Gently, dearest; you'll frighten her. [*Going between them*] Come here, Essie. [*She comes to him*] Who sent you?

Essie.   Dick. He sent me word by a soldier. I was to come here at once and do whatever Mrs. Anderson told me.

Anderson [*enlightened*].   A soldier! Ah, I see it all now! They have arrested Richard. [JUDITH *makes a gesture of despair*.]

Essie.   No. I asked the soldier. Dick's safe. But the soldier said you had been taken.

Anderson.   I! [*Bewildered, he turns to* JUDITH *for an explanation*.]

Judith [*coaxingly*].   All right, dear: I understand. [*To* ESSIE] Thank you, Essie, for coming; but I don't need you now. You may go home.

Essie [*suspicious*].   Are you sure Dick has not been touched? Perhaps he told the soldier to say it was the minister. [*Anxiously*] Mrs. Anderson, do you think it can have been that?

Anderson.   Tell her the truth if it is so, Judith. She will learn it from the first neighbor she meets in the street. [JUDITH *turns away and covers her eyes with her hands*.]

Essie [*wailing*].   But what will they do to him? Oh, what will they do to him? Will they hang him? [JUDITH *shudders convulsively and throws herself into the chair in which* RICHARD *sat at the tea table*.]

Anderson [*patting* ESSIE'S *shoulder and trying to comfort her*].   I hope not. I hope not. Perhaps if you're very quiet and patient, we may be able to help him in some way.

Essie.   Yes—help him—yes, yes, yes. I'll be good.

Anderson.   I must go to him at once, Judith.

Judith [*springing up*].   Oh no. You must go away—far away, to some place of safety.

Anderson.   Pooh!

Judith [*passionately*].   Do you want to kill me? Do you think I can bear to live for days and days with every knock at the door—every footstep—giving me a spasm of terror? to lie awake for nights and nights in an agony of dread, listening for them to come and arrest you?

Anderson.   Do you think it would be better to know that I had run away from my post at the first sign of danger?

Judith [*bitterly*].   Oh, you won't go. I know it. You'll stay; and I shall go mad.

Anderson.   My dear, your duty—

Judith [*fiercely*].   What do I care about my duty?

Anderson [*shocked*].   Judith!

Judith.   I am doing my duty. I am clinging to my duty. My duty is to get you away, to save you, to leave him to his fate. [ESSIE *utters a cry of distress and sinks on the chair at the fire, sobbing silently*] My instinct is the same as hers—to save him above all things, though it would be so much better for him to die! so much greater! But I know you will take your own way as he took it. I have no power. [*She sits down sullenly on the railed seat*] I'm only a woman; I can do nothing but sit here and suffer. Only, tell him I tried to save you—that I did my best to save you.

Anderson. My dear, I am afraid he will be thinking more of his own danger than of mine.

Judith. Stop; or I shall hate you.

Anderson [*remonstrating*]. Come, come, come! How am I to leave you if you talk like this? You are quite out of your senses. [*He turns to* ESSIE] Essie.

Essie [*eagerly rising and drying her eyes*]. Yes?

Anderson. Just wait outside a moment, like a good girl; Mrs. Anderson is not well. [ESSIE *looks doubtful*] Never fear; I'll come to you presently; and I'll go to Dick.

Essie. You are sure you will go to him? [*Whispering*] You won't let her prevent you?

Anderson [*smiling*]. No, no: it's all right. All right. [*She goes*] That's a good girl. [*He closes the door and returns to* JUDITH.]

Judith [*seated—rigid*]. You are going to your death.

Anderson [*quaintly*]. Then I shall go in my best coat, dear. [*He turns to the press, beginning to take off his coat*] Where—? [*He stares at the empty nail for a moment; then looks quickly round to the fire; strides across to it; and lifts* RICHARD's *coat*] Why, my dear, it seems that he has gone in my best coat.

Judith [*still motionless*]. Yes.

Anderson. Did the soldiers make a mistake?

Judith. Yes, they made a mistake.

Anderson. He might have told them. Poor fellow, he was too upset, I suppose.

Judith. Yes, he might have told them. So might I.

Anderson. Well, it's all very puzzling—almost funny. It's curious how these little things strike us even in the most— [*He breaks off and begins putting on* RICHARD's *coat*] I'd better take him his own coat. I know what he'll say—[*imitating* RICHARD's *sardonic manner*] "Anxious about my soul, Pastor, and also about your best coat." Eh?

Judith. Yes, that is just what he will say to you. [*Vacantly*] It doesn't matter; I shall never see either of you again.

Anderson [*rallying her*]. Oh pooh, pooh, pooh! [*He sits down beside her*] Is this how to keep your promise that I shan't be ashamed of my brave wife?

Judith. No, this is how I break it. I cannot keep my promises to him; why should I keep my promises to you?

Anderson. Don't speak so strangely, my love. It sounds insincere to me. [*She looks unutterable reproach at him*] Yes, dear, nonsense is always insincere; and my dearest is talking nonsense. Just nonsense. [*Her face darkens into dumb obstinacy. She stares straight before her and does not look at him again, absorbed in* RICHARD's *fate. He scans her face; sees that his rallying has produced no effect; and gives it up, making no further effort to conceal his anxiety*] I wish I knew what has frightened you so. Was there a struggle? Did he fight?

Judith. No. He smiled.

Anderson. Did he realize his danger, do you think?

Judith. He realized yours.

Anderson. Mine!

Judith [*monotonously*]. He said "See that you get him safely out of harm's way." I promised: I can't keep my promise. He said, "Don't for your life let him know of my danger." I've told you of it. He said that if you found it out, you could not save him—that they will hang him and not spare you.

Anderson [*rising in generous indignation*]. And you think that I will let a man with that much good in him die like a dog, when a few words might make him die like a Christian. I'm ashamed of you, Judith.

Judith. He will be steadfast in his religion as you are in yours; and you may depend on him to the death. He said so.

Anderson. God forgive him! What else did he say?

Judith. He said goodbye.

Anderson [*fidgeting nervously to and fro in great concern*]. Poor fellow, poor fellow! You said goodbye to him in all kindness and charity, Judith, I hope.

Judith. I kissed him.

Anderson. What! Judith!

Judith. Are you angry?

Anderson. No, no. You were right; you were right. Poor fellow, poor fellow! [*Greatly distressed*] To be hanged like that at his age! And then did they take him away?

Judith [*wearily*]. Then you were here; that's the next thing I remember. I suppose I fainted. Now bid me goodbye, Tony. Perhaps I shall faint again. I wish I could die.

Anderson. No, no, my dear, you must pull yourself together and be sensible. I am in no danger—not the least in the world.

Judith [*solemnly*]. You are going to your death, Tony—your sure death, if God will let innocent men be murdered. They will not let you see him; they will arrest you the moment you give your name. It was for you the soldiers came.

Anderson [*thunderstruck*]. For me!!! [*His fists clinch; his neck thickens; his face reddens; the fleshy purses under his eyes become injected with hot blood; the man of peace vanishes, transfigured into a choleric and formidable man of war. Still, she does not come out of her absorption to look at him; her eyes are steadfast with a mechanical reflection of* RICHARD'*s steadfastness.*]

Judith. He took your place; he is dying to save you. That is why he went in your coat. That is why I kissed him.

Anderson [*exploding*]. Blood an' owns![1] [*His voice is rough and dominant, his gesture full of brute energy*] Here! Essie, Essie!

Essie [*running in*]. Yes.

Anderson [*impetuously*]. Off with you as hard as you can run, to the inn. Tell them to saddle the fastest and strongest horse they have [JUDITH *rises breathless and stares at him incredulously*]—the chestnut mare, if she's fresh—without a moment's delay. Go into the stable yard and tell the black man there that I'll give him a silver dollar if the horse is waiting for me when I come, and that I am close on your heels. Away with you. [*His energy sends* ESSIE *flying from the room. He pounces on his riding boots; rushes with them to the chair at the fire; and begins pulling them on.*]

---

[1] "By God's blood and wounds," considered .exceedingly blasphemous by proper Englishmen.

Judith [*unable to believe such a thing of him*].   You are not going to him!

Anderson [*busy with the boots*].   Going to him! What good would that do? [*Growling to himself as he gets the first boot on with a wrench*] I'll go to them, so I will. [*To* JUDITH *peremptorily*] Get me the pistols; I want them. And money, money: I want money—all the money in the house. [*He stoops over the other boot, grumbling*] A great satisfaction it would be to him to have my company on the gallows. [*He pulls on the boot.*]

Judith.   You are deserting him, then?

Anderson.   Hold your tongue, woman; and get me the pistols. [*She goes to the press and takes from it a leather belt with two pistols, a powder horn, and a bag of bullets attached to it. She throws it on the table. Then she unlocks a drawer in the press and takes out a purse.* ANDERSON *grabs the belt and buckles it on, saying*] If they took him for me in my coat, perhaps they'll take me for him in his. [*Hitching the belt into its place*] Do I look like him?

Judith [*turning with the purse in her hand*].   Horribly unlike him.

Anderson [*snatching the purse from her and emptying it on the table*].   Hm! We shall see.

Judith [*sitting down helplessly*].   Is it of any use to pray, do you think, Tony?

Anderson [*counting the money*].   Pray! Can we pray Swindon's rope off Richard's neck?

Judith.   God may soften Major Swindon's heart.

Anderson [*contemptuously—pocketing a handful of money*].   Let him, then. I am not God; and I must go to work another way. [JUDITH *gasps at the blasphemy. He throws the purse on the table*] Keep that. I've taken 25 dollars.

Judith.   Have you forgotten even that you are a minister?

Anderson.   Minister be—faugh! My hat: where's my hat? [*He snatches up hat and cloak and puts both on in hot haste*] Now listen, you. If you can get a word with him by pretending you're his wife, tell him to hold his tongue until morning; that will give me all the start I need.

Judith [*solemnly*].   You may depend on him to the death.

Anderson.   You're a fool, a fool, Judith. [*For a moment checking the torrent of his haste and speaking with something of his old quiet and impressive conviction*] You don't know the man you're married to. [ESSIE *returns. He swoops at her at once*] Well, is the horse ready?

Essie [*breathless*].   It will be ready when you come.

Anderson.   Good. [*He makes for the door.*]

Judith [*rising and stretching out her arms after him involuntarily*].   Won't you say goodbye?

Anderson.   And waste another half minute! Psha! [*He rushes out like an avalanche.*]

Essie [*hurrying to* JUDITH].   He has gone to save Richard, hasn't he?

Judith.   To save Richard! No: Richard has saved him. He has gone to save himself. Richard must die.

[ESSIE *screams with terror and falls on her knees, hiding her face.* JUDITH, *without heeding her, looks rigidly straight in front of her, at the vision of* RICHARD, *dying.*]

[*The Curtain Falls.*]

Act III

Scene I

[*Early next morning the* SERGEANT, *at the British headquarters in the Town Hall, unlocks the door of a little empty panelled waiting room and invites* JUDITH *to enter. She has had a bad night, probably a rather delirious one; for even in the reality of the raw morning, her fixed gaze comes back at moments when her attention is not strongly held.*

The SERGEANT *considers that her feelings do her credit and is sympathetic in an encouraging military way. Being a fine figure of a man, vain of his uniform and of his rank, he feels specially qualified, in a respectful way, to console her.*]

Sergeant.   You can have a quiet word with him here, mum.

Judith.   Shall I have long to wait?

Sergeant.   No, mum, not a minute. We kep' him in the Bridewell[1] for the night; and he's just been brought over here for the court martial. Don't fret, mum; he slep' like a child, and has made a rare good breakfast.

Judith [*incredulously*].   He is in good spirits!

Sergeant.   Tip top, mum. The chaplain looked in to see him last night; and he won seventeen shillings off him at spoil five.[2] He spent it among us like the gentleman he is. Duty's duty, mum, of course; but you're among friends here. [*The tramp of a couple of soldiers is heard approaching*] There: I think he's coming. [RICHARD *comes in, without a sign of care or captivity in his bearing. The* SERGEANT *nods to the two soldiers and shows them the key of the room in his hand. They withdraw*] Your good lady, sir.

Richard [*going to her*].   What! My wife. My adored one. [*He takes her hand and kisses it with a perverse, raffish gallantry*] How long do you allow a broken-hearted husband for leave-taking, Sergeant?

Sergeant.   As long as we can, sir. We shall not disturb you till the court sits.

Richard.   But it has struck the hour.

Sergeant.   So it has, sir; but there's a delay. General Burgoyne's just arrived— Gentlemanly Johnny we call him, sir—and he won't have done finding fault with everything this side of half past. I know him, sir; I served with him in Portugal. You may count on twenty minutes, sir; and by your leave I won't waste any more of them. [*He goes out, locking the door.* RICHARD *immediately drops his raffish manner and turns to* JUDITH *with considerate sincerity.*]

Richard.   Mrs. Anderson, this visit is very kind of you. And how are you after last night? I had to leave you before you recovered; but I sent word to Essie to go and look after you. Did she understand the message?

Judith [*breathless and urgent*].   Oh, don't think of me; I haven't come here to talk about myself. Are they going to—to—[*meaning "to hang you"*]?

Richard [*whimsically*].   At noon, punctually. At least, that was when they disposed of Uncle Peter. [*She shudders*] Is your husband safe? Is he on the wing?

---

1   A prison.

2   A game of cards.

Judith. He is no longer my husband.

Richard [*opening his eyes wide*]. Eh?

Judith. I disobeyed you. I told him everything. I expected him to come here and save you. I wanted him to come here and save you. He ran away instead.

Richard. Well, that's what I meant him to do. What good would his staying have done? They'd only have hanged us both.

Judith [*with reproachful earnestness*]. Richard Dudgeon, on your honor, what would you have done in his place?

Richard. Exactly what he has done, of course.

Judith. Oh, why will you not be simple with me—honest and straightforward? If you are so selfish as that, why did you let them take you last night?

Richard [*gaily*]. Upon my life, Mrs. Anderson, I don't know. I've been asking myself that question ever since; and I can find no manner of reason for acting as I did.

Judith. You know you did it for his sake, believing he was a more worthy man than yourself.

Richard [*laughing*]. Oho! No, that's a very pretty reason, I must say; but I'm not so modest as that. No, it wasn't for his sake.

Judith [*after a pause, during which she looks shamefacedly at him, blushing painfully*]. Was it for my sake?

Richard [*gallantly*]. Well, you had a hand in it. It must have been a little for your sake. You let them take me, at all events.

Judith. Oh, do you think I have not been telling myself that all night? Your death will be at my door. [*Impulsively, she gives him her hand and adds, with intense earnestness*] If I could save you as you saved him, I would do it, no matter how cruel the death was.

Richard [*holding her hand and smiling, but keeping her almost at arms length*]. I am very sure I shouldn't let you.

Judith. Don't you see that I can save you?

Richard. How? by changing clothes with me, eh?

Judith [*disengaging her hand to touch his lips with it*]. Don't [*meaning "Don't jest"*]. No, by telling the Court who you really are.

Richard [*frowning*]. No use: they wouldn't spare me; and it would spoil half his chance of escaping. They are determined to cow us by making an example of somebody on that gallows today. Well, let us cow them by showing that we can stand by one another to the death. That is the only force that can send Burgoyne back across the Atlantic and make America a nation.

Judith [*impatiently*]. Oh, what does all that matter?

Richard [*laughing*]. True, what does it matter? What does anything matter? You see, men have these strange notions, Mrs. Anderson; and women see the folly of them.

Judith. Women have to lose those they love through them.

Richard. They can easily get fresh lovers.

Judith [*revolted*]. Oh! [*Vehemently*] Do you realize that you are going to kill yourself?

Richard. The only man I have any right to kill, Mrs. Anderson. Don't be concerned; no woman will lose her lover through my death. [*Smiling*] Bless you, nobody cares for me. Have you heard that my mother is dead?

Judith.   Dead!

Richard.   Of heart disease—in the night. Her last word to me was her curse; I don't think I could have borne her blessing. My other relatives will not grieve much on my account. Essie will cry for a day or two; but I have provided for her; I made my own will last night.

Judith [stonily, after a moment's silence].   And I!

Richard [surprised].   You?

Judith.   Yes, I. Am I not to care at all?

Richard [gaily and bluntly].   Not a scrap. Oh, you expressed your feelings towards me very frankly yesterday. What happened may have softened you for the moment; but believe me, Mrs. Anderson, you don't like a bone in my skin or a hair on my head. I shall be as good a riddance at 12 today as I should have been at 12 yesterday.

Judith [her voice trembling].   What can I do to show you that you are mistaken?

Richard.   Don't trouble. I'll give you credit for liking me a little better than you did. All I say is that my death will not break your heart.

Judith [almost in a whisper].   How do you know? [*She puts her hands on his shoulders and looks intently at him.*]

Richard [amazed—divining the truth].   Mrs. Anderson! [*The bell of the town clock strikes the quarter. He collects himself and removes her hands, saying rather coldly*] Excuse me: they will be here for me presently. It is too late.

Judith.   It is not too late. Call me as witness; they will never kill you when they know how heroically you have acted.

Richard [with some scorn].   Indeed! But if I don't go through with it, where will the heroism be? I shall simply have tricked them; and they'll hang me for that like a dog. Serve me right too!

Judith [wildly].   Oh, I believe you want to die.

Richard [obstinately].   No I don't.

Judith.   Then why not try to save yourself? I implore you—listen. You said just now that you saved him for my sake—yes [*clutching him as he recoils with a gesture of denial*] a little for my sake. Well, save yourself for my sake. And I will go with you to the end of the world.

Richard [taking her by the wrists and holding her a little way from him, looking steadily at her].   Judith.

Judith [breathless—delighted at the name].   Yes.

Richard.   If I said—to please you—that I did what I did ever so little for your sake, I lied as men always lie to women. You know how much I have lived with worthless men—aye, and worthless women too. Well, they could all rise to some sort of goodness and kindness when they were in love. [*The word "love" comes from him with true Puritan scorn*] That has taught me to set very little store by the goodness that only comes out red hot. What I did last night, I did in cold blood, caring not half so much for your husband, or [*ruthlessly*] for you [*she droops, stricken*] as I do for myself. I had no motive and no interest; all I can tell you is that when it came to the point whether I would take my neck out of the noose and put another man's into it, I could not do it. I don't know why not; I see myself as a fool for my pains; but I could not and I cannot. I have been brought up standing by the law of my own nature; and I may not go against it, gallows or no gallows. [*She has slowly raised her head and is now looking full at him*] I should have done the same for any other man in the town, or any other man's wife. [*Releasing her*] Do you understand that?

Judith.   Yes, you mean that you do not love me.

Richard [*revolted—with fierce contempt*].   Is that all it means to you?

Judith.   What more—what worse—can it mean to me? [*The* SERGEANT *knocks. The blow on the door jars on her heart*] Oh, one moment more. [*She throws herself on her knees*] I pray to you—

Richard.   Hush! [*Calling*] Come in. [*The* SERGEANT *unlocks the door and opens it. The guard is with him.*]

Sergeant [*coming in*].   Time's up, sir.

Richard.   Quite ready, Sergeant. Now, my dear. [*He attempts to raise her.*]

Judith [*clinging to him*].   Only one thing more—I entreat, I implore you. Let me be present in the court. I have seen Major Swindon; he said I should be allowed if you asked it. You will ask it. It is my last request; I shall never ask you anything again. [*She clasps his knee*] I beg and pray it of you.

Richard.   If I do, will you be silent?

Judith.   Yes.

Richard.   You will keep faith?

Judith.   I will keep—[*She breaks down, sobbing.*]

Richard [*taking her arm to lift her*].   Just—her other arm, Sergeant.

[*They go out, she sobbing convulsively, supported by the two men.*]

Scene II

[*Meanwhile, the Council Chamber is ready for the court martial. It is a large, lofty room, with a chair of state in the middle under a tall canopy with a gilt crown, and maroon curtains with the royal monogram G.R. In front of the chair is a table, also draped in maroon, with a bell, a heavy inkstand, and writing materials on it. Several chairs are set at the table. The door is at the right hand of the occupant of the chair of state when it has an occupant: at present it is empty.* MAJOR SWINDON, *a pale, sandy-haired, very conscientious looking man of about 45, sits at the end of the table with his back to the door, writing. He is alone until the* SERGEANT *announces the* GENERAL *in a subdued manner which suggests that Gentlemanly Johnny has been making his presence felt rather heavily.*]

Sergeant.   The General, sir.

[SWINDON *rises hastily. The* GENERAL *comes in; the* SERGEANT *goes out.* GENERAL BURGOYNE *is 55 and very well preserved. He is a man of fashion, gallant enough to have made a distinguished marriage by an elopement, witty enough to write successful comedies, aristocratically-connected enough to have had opportunities of high military distinction. His eyes, large, brilliant, apprehensive, and intelligent, are his most remarkable feature: without them his fine nose and small mouth would suggest rather more fastidiousness and less force than go to the making of a first-rate general. Just now the eyes are angry and tragic, and the mouth and nostrils tense.*]

Burgoyne.   Major Swindon, I presume.

Swindon.   Yes. General Burgoyne, if I mistake not. [*They bow to one another ceremoniously*] I am glad to have the support of your presence this morning. It is not particularly lively business, hanging this poor devil of a minister.

Burgoyne [*throwing himself into* SWINDON's *chair*].   No, sir, it is not. It is making too much of the fellow to execute him; what more could you have done if he had been a member of the Church of England? Martyrdom, sir, is what these people like: it is the only way in which a man can become famous without ability. However, you have committed us to hanging him; and the sooner he is hanged the better.

Swindon.   We have arranged it for 12 o'clock. Nothing remains to be done except to try him.

Burgoyne [*looking at him with suppressed anger*].   Nothing—except to save your own necks, perhaps. Have you heard the news from Springtown?

Swindon.   Nothing special. The latest reports are satisfactory.

Burgoyne [*rising in amazement*].   Satisfactory, sir! Satisfactory!! [*He stares at him for a moment and then adds, with grim intensity*] I am glad you take that view of them.

Swindon [*puzzled*].   Do I understand that in your opinion—

Burgoyne.   I do not express my opinion. I never stoop to that habit of profane language which unfortunately coarsens our profession. If I did, sir, perhaps I should be able to express my opinion of the news from Springtown—the news which you [*severely*] have apparently not heard. How soon do you get news from your supports here?—in the course of a month, eh?

Swindon [*turning sulkily*].   I suppose the reports have been taken to you, sir, instead of to me. Is there anything serious?

Burgoyne [*taking a report from his pocket and holding it up*].   Springtown's in the hands of the rebels. [*He throws the report on the table.*]

Swindon [*aghast*].   Since yesterday!

Burgoyne.   Since two o'clock this morning. Perhaps we shall be in their hands before two o'clock tomorrow morning. Have you thought of that?

Swindon [*confidently*].   As to that, General, the British soldier will give a good account of himself.

Burgoyne [*bitterly*].   And therefore, I suppose, sir, the British officer need not know his business; the British soldier will get him out of all his blunders with the bayonet. In future, sir, I must ask you to be a little less generous with the blood of your men and a little more generous with your own brains.

Swindon.   I am sorry I cannot pretend to your intellectual eminence, sir. I can only do my best and rely on the devotion of my countrymen.

Burgoyne [*suddenly becoming suavely sarcastic*].   May I ask are you writing a melodrama, Major Swindon?

Swindon [*flushing*].   No, sir.

Burgoyne.   What a pity! What a pity! [*Dropping his sarcastic tone and facing him suddenly and seriously*] Do you at all realize, sir, that we have nothing standing between us and destruction but our own bluff and the sheepishness of these colonists? They are men of the same English stock as ourselves: six to one of us [*repeating it emphatically*] six to one, sir; and nearly half our troops are Hessians, Brunswickers, German dragoons, and Indians with scalping knives.

These are the countrymen on whose devotion you rely! Suppose the colonists find a leader! Suppose the news from Springtown should turn out to mean that they have already found a leader! What shall we do then? Eh?

Swindon [*sullenly*]. Our duty, sir, I presume.

Burgoyne [*again sarcastic—giving him up as a fool*]. Quite so, quite so. Thank you, Major Swindon, thank you. Now you've settled the question, sir—thrown a flood of light on the situation. What a comfort to me to feel that I have at my side so devoted and able an officer to support me in this emergency! I think, sir, it will probably relieve both our feelings if we proceed to hang this dissenter without further delay [*he strikes the bell*] especially as I am debarred by my principles from the customary military vent for my feelings. [*The* SERGEANT *appears*] Bring your man in.

Sergeant. Yes, sir.

Burgoyne. And mention to any officer you may meet that the court cannot wait any longer for him.

Swindon [*keeping his temper with difficulty*]. The staff is perfectly ready, sir. They have been waiting your convenience for fully half an hour. Perfectly ready, sir.

Burgoyne [*blandly*]. So am I. [*Several officers come in and take their seats. One of them sits at the end of the table furthest from the door and acts throughout as clerk of the court, making notes of the proceedings. The uniforms are those of the 9th, 20th, 21st, 24th, 47th, 53rd, and 62nd British Infantry. One officer is a Major General of the Royal Artillery. There are also German officers of the Hessian Rifles, and of German dragoon and Brunswicker regiments*] Oh, good morning, gentlemen. Sorry to disturb you, I am sure. Very good of you to spare us a few moments.

Swindon. Will you preside, sir?

Burgoyne [*becoming additionally polished, lofty, sarcastic, and urbane now that he is in public*]. No, sir; I feel my own deficiencies too keenly to presume so far. If you will kindly allow me, I will sit at the feet of Gamaliel.[1] [*He takes the chair at the end of the table next the door and motions* SWINDON *to the chair of state, waiting for him to be seated before sitting down himself.*]

Swindon [*greatly annoyed*]. As you please, sir, I am only trying to do my duty under excessively trying circumstances. [*He takes his place in the chair of state.*]

[BURGOYNE, *relaxing his studied demeanor for the moment, sits down and begins to read the report with knitted brows and careworn looks, reflecting on his desperate situation and* SWINDON's *uselessness.* RICHARD *is brought in.* JUDITH *walks beside him. Two soldiers precede and two follow him, with the* SERGEANT *in command. They cross the room to the wall opposite the door; but when* RICHARD *has just passed before the chair of state the* SERGEANT *stops him with a touch on the arm and posts himself behind him, at his elbow.* JUDITH *stands timidly at the wall. The four soldiers place themselves in a squad near her.*]

Burgoyne [*looking up and seeing* JUDITH]. Who is that woman?

Sergeant. Prisoner's wife, sir.

---

[1]   The doctor of law who taught St. Paul.

Swindon [*nervously*].   She begged me to allow her to be present; and I thought—

Burgoyne [*completing the sentence for him ironically*].   You thought it would be a pleasure for her. Quite so, quite so. [*Blandly*] Give the lady a chair; and make her thoroughly comfortable.

[*The* SERGEANT *fetches a chair and places it near* RICHARD.]

Judith.   Thank you, sir. [*She sits down after an awestricken curtsy to* BURGOYNE, *which he acknowledges by a dignified bend of his head.*]

Swindon [*to* RICHARD, *sharply*].   Your name, sir?

Richard [*affable, but obstinate*].   Come, you don't mean to say that you've brought me here without knowing who I am?

Swindon.   As a matter of form, sir, give your name.

Richard.   As a matter of form then, my name is Anthony Anderson, Presbyterian minister in this town.

Burgoyne [*interested*].   Indeed! Pray, Mr. Anderson, what do you gentlemen believe?

Richard.   I shall be happy to explain if time is allowed me. I cannot undertake to complete your conversion in less than a fortnight.

Swindon [*snubbing him*].   We are not here to discuss your views.

Burgoyne [*with an elaborate bow to the unfortunate* SWINDON].   I stand rebuked.

Swindon [*embarrassed*].   Oh, not you, I as—

Burgoyne.   Don't mention it. [*To* RICHARD, *very politely*] Any political views, Mr. Anderson?

Richard.   I understand that that is just what we are here to find out.

Swindon [*severely*].   Do you mean to deny that you are a rebel?

Richard.   I am an American, sir.

Swindon.   What do you expect me to think of that speech, Mr. Anderson?

Richard.   I never expect a soldier to think, sir.

[BURGOYNE *is boundlessly delighted by this retort, which almost reconciles him to the loss of America.*]

Swindon [*whitening with anger*].   I advise you not to be insolent, prisoner.

Richard.   You can't help yourself, General. When you make up your mind to hang a man, you put yourself at a disadvantage with him. Why should I be civil to you? I may as well be hanged for a sheep as a lamb.

Swindon.   You have no right to assume that the court has made up its mind without a fair trial. And you will please not address me as General. I am Major Swindon.

Richard.   A thousand pardons. I thought I had the honor of addressing Gentlemanly Johnny.

[*Sensation among the officers. The* SERGEANT *has a narrow escape from a guffaw.*]

Burgoyne [*with extreme suavity*].   I believe I am Gentlemanly Johnny, sir, at your service. My more intimate friends call me General Burgoyne. [RICHARD *bows with perfect politeness*] You will understand, sir, I hope, since you seem to be a gentleman and a man of some spirit in spite of your calling, that if we should have the misfortune to hang you, we shall do so as a mere matter of political necessity and military duty, without any personal ill-feeling.

Richard. Oh, quite so. That makes all the difference in the world, of course.

[*They all smile in spite of themselves, and some of the younger officers burst out laughing.*]

Judith [*her dread and horror deepening at every one of these jests and compliments*]. How can you?

Richard. You promised to be silent.

Burgoyne [*to* JUDITH, *with studied courtesy*]. Believe me, madam, your husband is placing us under the greatest obligation by taking this very disagreeable business so thoroughly in the spirit of a gentleman. Sergeant, give Mr. Anderson a chair. [*The* SERGEANT *does so.* RICHARD *sits down*] Now, Major Swindon, we are waiting for you.

Swindon. You are aware, I presume, Mr. Anderson, of your obligations as a subject of His Majesty King George the Third.

Richard. I am aware, sir, that His Majesty King George the Third is about to hang me because I object to Lord North's[1] robbing me.

Swindon. That is a treasonable speech, sir.

Richard [*briefly*]. Yes. I meant it to be.

Burgoyne [*strongly deprecating this line of defense, but still polite*]. Don't you think, Mr. Anderson, that this is rather—if you will excuse the word—a vulgar line to take? Why should you cry out robbery because of a stamp duty and a tea duty and so forth? After all, it is the essence of your position as a gentleman that you pay with a good grace.

Richard. It is not the money, General. But to be swindled by a pig-headed lunatic like King George—

Swindon [*scandalized*]. Chut, sir—silence!

Sergeant [*in stentorian tones, greatly shocked*]. Silence!

Burgoyne [*unruffled*]. Ah, that is another point of view. My position does not allow of my going into that, except in private. But [*shrugging his shoulders*] of course, Mr. Anderson, if you are determined to be hanged [JUDITH *flinches*] there's nothing more to be said. An unusual taste! however [*with a final shrug*]—!

Swindon [To BURGOYNE]. Shall we call witnesses?

Richard. What need is there of witnesses? If the townspeople here had listened to me, you would have found the streets barricaded, the houses loopholed, and the people in arms to hold the town against you to the last man. But you arrived, unfortunately, before we had got out of the talking stage; and then it was too late.

Swindon [*severely*]. Well, sir, we shall teach you and your townspeople a lesson they will not forget. Have you anything more to say?

Richard. I think you might have the decency to treat me as a prisoner of war and shoot me like a man instead of hanging me like a dog.

Burgoyne [*sympathetically*]. Now there, Mr. Anderson, you talk like a civilian, if you will excuse my saying so. Have you any idea of the average marksmanship

---

[1] British prime minister during the Revolutionary War.

of the army of His Majesty King George the Third? If we make you up a firing party, what will happen? Half of them will miss you; the rest will make a mess of the business and leave you to the provo-marshal's pistol. Whereas we can hang you in a perfectly workmanlike and agreeable way. [*Kindly*] Let me persuade you to be hanged, Mr. Anderson?

Judith [*sick with horror*]. My God!

Richard [*To* JUDITH]. Your promise! [*To* BURGOYNE] Thank you, General; that view of the case did not occur to me before. To oblige you, I withdraw my objection to the rope. Hang me, by all means.

Burgoyne [*smoothly*]. Will 12 o'clock suit you, Mr. Anderson?

Richard. I shall be at your disposal then, General.

Burgoyne [*rising*]. Nothing more to be said, gentlemen. [*They all rise.*]

Judith [*rushing to the table*]. Oh, you are not going to murder a man like that, without a proper trial—without thinking of what you are doing—without— [*she cannot find words*].

Richard. Is this how you keep your promise?

Judith. If I am not to speak, you must. Defend yourself; save yourself; tell them the truth.

Richard [*worriedly*]. I have told them truth enough to hang me ten times over. If you say another word you will risk other lives; but you will not save mine.

Burgoyne. My good lady, our only desire is to save unpleasantness. What satisfaction would it give you to have a solemn fuss made, with my friend Swindon in a black cap and so forth? I am sure we are greatly indebted to the admirable tact and gentlemanly feeling shown by your husband.

Judith [*throwing the words in his face*]. Oh, you are mad. Is it nothing to you what wicked thing you do if only you do it like a gentleman? Is it nothing to you whether you are a murderer or not, if only you murder in a red coat? [*Desperately*] You shall not hang him; that man is not my husband.

[*The officers look at one another, and whisper; some of the Germans asking their neighbors to explain what the woman had said.* BURGOYNE, *who has been visibly shaken by* JUDITH'S *reproach, recovers himself promptly at this new development.* RICHARD *meanwhile raises his voice above the buzz.*]

Richard. I appeal to you, gentlemen, to put an end to this. She will not believe that she cannot save me. Break up the court.

Burgoyne [*in a voice so quiet and firm that it restores silence at once*]. One moment, Mr. Anderson. One moment, gentlemen. [*He resumes his seat.* SWINDON *and the officers follow his example*] Let me understand you clearly, madam. Do you mean that this gentleman is not your husband, or merely—I wish to put this with all delicacy—that you are not his wife?

Judith. I don't know what you mean. I say that he is not my husband—that my husband has escaped. This man took his place to save him. Ask anyone in the town—send out into the street for the first person you find there, and bring him in as a witness. He will tell you that the prisoner is not Anthony Anderson.

Burgoyne [*quietly, as before*]. Sergeant.

Sergeant. Yes, sir.

Burgoyne. Go out into the street and bring in the first townsman you see there.

Sergeant [*making for the door*]. Yes, sir.

Burgoyne [*as the* SERGEANT *passes*]. The first clean, sober townsman you see.
Sergeant. Yes, sir. [*He goes out.*]
Burgoyne. Sit down, Mr. Anderson—if I may call you so for the present. [RICHARD *sits down*] Sit down, madam, whilst we wait. Give the lady a newspaper.
Richard [*indignantly*]. Shame!
Burgoyne [*keenly, with a half smile*]. If you are not her husband, sir, the case is not a serious one—for her. [RICHARD *bites his lip, silenced.*]
Judith [*to* RICHARD, *as she returns to her seat*]. I couldn't help it. [*He shakes his head. She sits down.*]
Burgoyne. You will understand, of course, Mr. Anderson, that you must not build on this little incident. We are bound to make an example of somebody.
Richard. I quite understand. I suppose there's no use in my explaining.
Burgoyne. I think we should prefer independent testimony, if you don't mind.

[*The* SERGEANT, *with a packet of papers in his hand, returns conducting* CHRISTY, *who is much scared.*]

Sergeant [*giving* BURGOYNE *the packet*]. Dispatches, sir. Delivered by a corporal of the 33rd. Dead beat with hard riding, sir.

[BURGOYNE *opens the dispatches and presently becomes absorbed in them. They are so serious as to take his attention completely from the court martial.*]

Sergeant [*to* CHRISTY]. Now then. Attention; and take your hat off. [*He posts himself in charge of* CHRISTY, *who stands on* BURGOYNE's *side of the court.*]
Richard [*in his usual bullying tone to* CHRISTY]. Don't be frightened, you fool: you're only wanted as a witness. They're not going to hang you.
Swindon. What's your name?
Christy. Christy.
Richard [*impatiently*]. Christopher Dudgeon, you blatant idiot. Give your full name.
Swindon. Be silent, prisoner. You must not prompt the witness.
Richard. Very well. But I warn you you'll get nothing out of him unless you shake it out of him. He has been too well brought up by a pious mother to have any sense or manhood left in him.
Burgoyne [*springing up and speaking to the* SERGEANT *in a startling voice*]. Where is the man who brought these?
Sergeant. In the guard-room, sir.

[BURGOYNE *goes out with a haste that sets the officers exchanging looks.*]

Swindon [*to* CHRISTY]. Do you know Anthony Anderson, the Presbyterian minister?
Christy. Of course I do [*implying that* SWINDON *must be an ass not to know it*].
Swindon. Is he here?
Christy [*staring round*]. I don't know.
Swindon. Do you see him?
Christy. No.
Swindon. You seem to know the prisoner?
Christy. Do you mean Dick?

Swindon.   Which is Dick?

Christy [pointing to RICHARD]*.*   Him.

Swindon.   What is his name?

Christy.   Dick.

Richard.   Answer properly, you jumping jackass. What do they know about Dick?

Christy.   Well, you are Dick, ain't you? What am I to say?

Swindon.   Address me, sir; and do you, prisoner, be silent. Tell us who the prisoner is.

Christy.   He's my brother Dick—Richard—Richard Dudgeon.

Swindon.   Your brother!

Christy.   Yes.

Swindon.   You are sure he is not Anderson.

Christy.   Who?

Richard [exasperatedly].   Me, me, me, you—

Swindon.   Silence, sir.

Sergeant [shouting].   Silence.

Richard [impatiently].   Yah! [*To* CHRISTY] He wants to know am I Minister Anderson. Tell him and stop grinning like a zany.

Christy [grinning more than ever].   *You* Pastor Anderson! [*To* SWINDON] Why, Mr. Anderson's a minister—a very good man, and Dick's a bad character; the respectable people won't speak to him. He's the bad brother; I'm the good one.

[*The officers laugh outright. The soldiers grin.*]

Swindon.   Who arrested this man?

Sergeant.   I did, sir. I found him in the minister's house, sitting at tea with the lady with his coat off, quite at home. If he isn't married to her, he ought to be.

Swindon.   Did he answer to the minister's name?

Sergeant.   Yes, sir, but not to a minister's nature. You ask the chaplain, sir.

Swindon [to RICHARD, *threateningly].*   So, sir, you have attempted to cheat us. And your name is Richard Dudgeon?

Richard.   You've found it out at last, have you?

Swindon.   Dudgeon is a name well known to us, eh?

Richard.   Yes, Peter Dudgeon, whom you murdered, was my uncle.

Swindon.   Hm! [*He compresses his lips and looks at* RICHARD *with vindictive gravity.*]

Christy.   Are they going to hang you, Dick?

Richard.   Yes. Get out; they've done with you.

Christy.   And I may keep the china peacocks?

Richard [jumping up].   Get out. Get out, you blithering baboon, you.

[CHRISTY *flies, panicstricken.*]

Swindon [rising—all rise].   Since you have taken the minister's place, Richard Dudgeon, you shall go through with it. The execution will take place at 12 o'clock as arranged; and unless Anderson surrenders before then, you shall take his place on the gallows. Sergeant, take your man out.

Judith [distracted].   No, no—

Swindon [fiercely dreading a renewal of her entreaties].   Take that woman away.

Richard [*springing across the table with a tiger-like bound, and seizing* SWINDON *by the throat*]. You infernal scoundrel—

[*The* SERGEANT *rushes to the rescue from one side, the soldiers from the other. They seize* RICHARD *and drag him back to his place.* SWINDON, *who has been thrown supine on the table, rises, arranging his stock.*[1] *He is about to speak, when he is anticipated by* BURGOYNE, *who has just appeared at the door with two papers in his hand: a white letter and a blue dispatch.*]

Burgoyne [*advancing to the table, elaborately cool*]. What is this? What's happening? Mr. Anderson, I'm astonished at you.

Richard. I am sorry I disturbed you, General. I merely wanted to strangle your understrapper there. [*Breaking out violently at* SWINDON] Why do you raise the devil in me by bullying the woman like that? You oatmeal faced dog, I'd twist your cursed head off with the greatest satisfaction. [*He puts out his hands to the* SERGEANT] Here: handcuff me, will you; or I'll not undertake to keep my fingers off him.

[*The* SERGEANT *takes out a pair of handcuffs and looks to* BURGOYNE *for instructions.*]

Burgoyne. Have you addressed profane language to the lady, Major Swindon?

Swindon [*very angry*]. No, sir, certainly not. That question should not have been put to me. I ordered the woman to be removed, as she was disorderly; and the fellow sprang at me. Put away those handcuffs. I am perfectly able to take care of myself.

Richard. Now you talk like a man; I have no quarrel with you.

Burgoyne. Mr. Anderson—

Swindon. His name is Dudgeon, sir, Richard Dudgeon. He is an impostor.

Burgoyne [*brusquely*]. Nonsense, sir; you hanged Dudgeon at Springtown.

Richard. It was my uncle, General.

Burgoyne. Oh, your uncle. [*To* SWINDON, *handsomely*] I beg your pardon, Major Swindon. [SWINDON *acknowledges the apology stiffly.* BURGOYNE *turns to* RICHARD] We are somewhat unfortunate in our relations with your family. Well, Mr. Dudgeon, what I wanted to ask you is this. Who is [*reading the name from the letter*] William Maindeck Parshotter?

Richard. He is the Mayor of Springtown.

Burgoyne. Is William—Maindeck and so on—a man of his word?

Richard. Is he selling you anything?

Burgoyne. No.

Richard. Then you may depend on him.

Burgoyne. Thank you, Mr.—'m Dudgeon. By the way, since you are not Mr. Anderson, do we still—eh, Major Swindon? [*meaning "do we still hang him?"*]

Richard. The arrangements are unaltered, General.

Burgoyne. Ah, indeed. I am sorry. Good morning, Mr. Dudgeon. Good morning, madam.

Richard [*interrupting* JUDITH *almost fiercely as she is about to make some wild appeal, and taking her arm resolutely*]. Not one word more. Come. [*She looks*

---

[1] A broad neckband, somewhat resembling a cravat.

imploringly at him but is overborne by his determination. They are marched out by the four soldiers; the SERGEANT *very sulky, walking between* SWINDON *and* RICHARD, *whom he watches as if he were a dangerous animal.*]

Burgoyne. Gentlemen, we need not detain you. Major Swindon, a word with you. [*The officers go out.* BURGOYNE *waits with unruffled serenity until the last of them disappears. Then he becomes very grave and addresses* SWINDON *for the first time without his title*] Swindon, do you know what this is [*showing him the letter*]?

Swindon. What?

Burgoyne. A demand for a safe-conduct for an officer of their militia to come here and arrange terms with us.

Swindon. Oh, they are giving in.

Burgoyne. They add that they are sending the man who raised Springtown last night and drove us out; so that we may know that we are dealing with an officer of importance.

Swindon. Pooh!

Burgoyne. He will be fully empowered to arrange the terms of—guess what.

Swindon. Their surrender, I hope.

Burgoyne. No, our evacuation of the town. They offer us just six hours to clear out.

Swindon. What monstrous impudence!

Burgoyne. What shall we do, eh?

Swindon. March on Springtown and strike a decisive blow at once.

Burgoyne [*quietly*]. Hm! [*Turning to the door*] Come to the adjutant's office.

Swindon. What for?

Burgoyne. To write out that safe-conduct. [*He puts his hand to the door knob to open it.*]

Swindon [*who has not budged*]. General Burgoyne.

Burgoyne [*returning*]. Sir?

Swindon. It is my duty to tell you, sir, that I do not consider the threats of a mob of rebellious tradesmen a sufficient reason for our giving way.

Burgoyne [*imperturbable*]. Suppose I resign my command to you, what will you do?

Swindon. I will undertake to do what we have marched south from Quebec to do and what General Howe has marched north from New York to do: effect a junction at Albany and wipe out the rebel army with our united forces.

Burgoyne [*enigmatically*]. And will you wipe out our enemies in London, too?

Swindon. In London! What enemies?

Burgoyne [*forcibly*]. Jobbery and snobbery, incompetence and Red Tape. [*He holds up the dispatch and adds, with despair in his face and voice*] I have just learnt, sir, that General Howe is still in New York.

Swindon [*thunderstruck*]. Good God! He has disobeyed orders!

Burgoyne [*with sardonic calm*]. He has received no orders, sir. Some gentleman in London forgot to dispatch them; he was leaving town for his holiday, I believe. To avoid upsetting his arrangements, England will lose her American colonies; and in a few days you and I will be at Saratoga with 5,000 men to face 18,000 rebels in an impregnable position.

Swindon [*appalled*]. Impossible!

Burgoyne [*coldly*]. I beg your pardon?

Swindon. I can't believe it! What will History say?

Burgoyne. History, sir, will tell lies, as usual. Come, we must send the safe-conduct. [*He goes out.*]

Swindon [*following distractedly*]. My God, my God! We shall be wiped out.

Scene III

> *As noon approaches, there is excitement in the market place. The gallows which hangs there permanently for the terror of evildoers, with such minor advertisers and examples of crime as the pillory, the whipping post, and the stocks, has a new rope attached, with the noose hitched up to one of the uprights, out of reach of the boys. Its ladder, too, has been brought out and placed in position by the town beadle, who stands by to guard it from unauthorized climbing. The Websterbridge townsfolk are present in force, and in high spirits; for the news has spread that it is the devil's disciple and not the minister that King George and his terrible general are about to hang: consequently the execution can be enjoyed without any misgiving as to its righteousness, or to the cowardice of allowing it to take place without a struggle. There is even some fear of a disappointment as midday approaches and the arrival of the beadle with the ladder remains the only sign of preparation. But at last reassuring shouts of "Here they come: Here they are" are heard; and a company of soldiers with fixed bayonets, half British infantry, half Hessians, tramp quickly into the middle of the market place, driving the crowd to the sides.*

Sergeant. Halt. Front. Dress. [*The soldiers change their column into a square enclosing the gallows, their petty officers, energetically led by the* SERGEANT, *hustling the persons who find themselves inside the square out at the corners*] Now then! Out of it with you; out of it. Some o' you'll get strung up yourselves presently. Form that square there, will you, you damned Hoosians. No use talkin' German to them; talk to their toes with the butt ends of your muskets; they'll understand that! Get out of it, will you. [*He comes upon* JUDITH, *standing near the gallows*] Now then, you've no call here.

Judith. May I not stay? What harm am I doing?

Sergeant. I want none of your argufying. You ought to be ashamed of yourself, running to see a man hanged that's not your husband. And he's no better than yourself. I told my major he was a gentleman; and then he goes and tries to strangle him, and calls his blessed Majesty a lunatic. So out of it with you, double quick.

Judith. Will you take these two silver dollars and let me stay?

> [*The* SERGEANT, *without an instant's hesitation, looks quickly and furtively round as he shoots the money dexterously into his pocket. Then he raises his voice in virtuous indignation.*]

Sergeant. Me take money in the execution of my duty! Certainly not. Now I'll tell you what I'll do, to teach you to corrupt the King's officer. I'll put you under arrest until the execution's over. You just stand there; and don't let me see you as much as move from that spot until you're let. [*With a swift wink at her he points to the corner of the square behind the gallows on his right and turns noisily away, shouting*] Now then, dress up and keep 'em back, will you.

[*Cries of "Hush" and "Silence" are heard among the townsfolk; and the sound of a military band, playing the Dead March from Saul, is heard. The crowd becomes quiet at once; and the* SERGEANT *and petty officers, hurrying to the back of the square, with a few whispered orders and some stealthy hustling cause it to open and admit the funeral procession, which is protected from the crowd by a double file of soldiers. First come* BURGOYNE *and* SWINDON, *who, on entering the square, glance with distaste at the gallows, and avoid passing under it by wheeling a little to the right and stationing themselves on that side. Then* MR. BRUDENELL, *the chaplain, in his surplice, with his prayer book open in his hand, walking beside* RICHARD, *who is moody and disorderly. He walks doggedly through the gallows framework and posts himself a little in front of it. Behind him comes the executioner, a stalwart soldier in his shirtsleeves. Following him, two soldiers haul a light military wagon. Finally comes the band, which posts itself at the back of the square and finishes the Dead March.* JUDITH, *watching* RICHARD *painfully, steals down to the gallows and stands leaning against its right post. During the conversation which follows, the two soldiers place the cart under the gallows and stand by the shafts, which point backwards. The executioner takes a set of steps from the cart and places it ready for the prisoner to mount. Then he climbs the tall ladder which stands against the gallows, and cuts the string by which the rope is hitched up; so that the noose drops dangling over the cart, into which he steps as he descends.*]

Richard [*with suppressed impatience, to* BRUDENELL].   Look here, sir: this is no place for a man of your profession. Hadn't you better go away?

Swindon.   I appeal to you, prisoner, if you have any sense of decency left, to listen to the ministrations of the chaplain, and pay due heed to the solemnity of the occasion.

Chaplain [*gently reproving* RICHARD].   Try to control yourself and submit to the divine will. [*He lifts his book to proceed with the service.*]

Richard.   Answer for your own will, sir, and those of your accomplices here [*indicating* BURGOYNE *and* SWINDON]; I see little divinity about them or you. You talk to me of Christianity when you are in the act of hanging your enemies. Was there ever such blasphemous nonsense! [*To* SWINDON, *more rudely*] You've got up the solemnity of the occasion, as you call it, to impress the people with your own dignity—Handel's music and a clergyman to make murder look like piety! Do you suppose *I* am going to help you? You've asked me to choose the rope because you don't know your own trade well enough to shoot me properly. Well, hang away and have done with it.

Swindon [*to the* CHAPLAIN].   Can you do nothing with him, Mr. Brudenell?

Chaplain.   I will try, sir. [*Beginning to read*] Man that is born of woman hath—

Richard [*fixing his eyes on him*].   "Thou shalt not kill." [*The book drops in* BRUDENELL's *hands.*]

Chaplain [*confessing his embarrassment*].   What am I to say, Mr. Dudgeon?

Richard.   Let me alone, man, can't you?

Burgoyne [*with extreme urbanity*].   I think, Mr. Brudenell, that as the usual professional observations seem to strike Mr. Dudgeon as incongruous under the circumstances, you had better omit them until—er—until Mr. Dudgeon can no longer be inconvenienced by them. [BRUDENELL, *with a shrug, shuts his book and retires behind the gallows*] You seem in a hurry, Mr. Dudgeon.

Richard [*with the horror of death upon him*].   Do you think this is a pleasant sort of thing to be kept waiting for? You've made up your mind to commit murder; well, do it and have done with it.

Burgoyne.   Mr. Dudgeon, we are only doing this—

Richard.   Because you're paid to do it.

Swindon.   You insolent— [*He swallows his rage.*]

Burgoyne [*with much charm of manner*].   Ah, I am really sorry that you should think that, Mr. Dudgeon. If you knew what my commission cost me and what my pay is, you would think better of me. I should be glad to part from you on friendly terms.

Richard.   Hark ye, General Burgoyne. If you think that I like being hanged, you're mistaken. I don't like it; and I don't mean to pretend that I do. And if you think I'm obliged to you for hanging me in a gentlemanly way, you're wrong there too. I take the whole business in devilish bad part; and the only satisfaction I have in it is that you'll feel a good deal meaner than I'll look when it's over. [*He turns away and is striding to the cart when* JUDITH *advances and interposes with her arms stretched out to him.* RICHARD, *feeling that a very little will upset his self-possession, shrinks from her, crying*] What are you doing here? This is no place for you. [*She makes a gesture as if to touch him. He recoils impatiently*] No, go away, go away; you'll unnerve me. Take her away, will you.

Judith.   Won't you bid me goodbye?

Richard [*allowing her to take his hand*].   Oh goodbye, goodbye. Now go—go— quickly. [*She clings to his hand—will not be put off with so cold a last fare-well—at last, as he tries to disengage himself, throws herself on his breast in agony.*]

Swindon [*angrily to the* SERGEANT, *who, alarmed at* JUDITH'S *movement, has come from the back of the square to pull her back and stopped irresolutely on finding that he is too late*].   How is this? Why is she inside the lines?

Sergeant [*guiltily*].   I dunno, sir. She's that artful—can't keep her away.

Burgoyne.   You were bribed.

Sergeant [*protesting*].   No, sir—

Swindon [*severely*].   Fall back. [*He obeys.*]

Richard [*imploringly to those around him and finally to* BURGOYNE, *as the least stolid of them*].   Take her away. Do you think I want a woman near me now?

Burgoyne [*going to* JUDITH *and taking her hand*].   Here, madam: you had better keep inside the lines; but stand here behind us; and don't look. [RICHARD, *with a great sobbing sigh of relief as she releases him and turns to* BURGOYNE, *flies for refuge to the cart and mounts into it. The executioner takes off his coat and pinions him.*]

Judith [*resisting* BURGOYNE *quietly and drawing her hand away*].   No, I must stay. I won't look. [*She goes to the right of the gallows. She tries to look at* RICHARD *but turns away with a frightful shudder and falls on her knees in prayer.* BRUDENELL *comes towards her from the back of the square.*]

Burgoyne [*nodding approvingly as she kneels*].   Ah, quite so. Do not disturb her, Mr. Brudenell; that will do very nicely. [BRUDENELL *nods also and withdraws a little, watching her sympathetically.* BURGOYNE *resumes his former position and takes out a handsome gold chronometer*] Now then, are those preparations made? We must not detain Mr. Dudgeon.

[*By this time* RICHARD'S *hands are bound behind him, and the noose is round his neck. The two soldiers take the shafts of the wagon, ready to pull it away. The executioner, standing in the cart behind* RICHARD, *makes a sign to the* SERGEANT.]

Sergeant [*to* BURGOYNE].   Ready, sir.
Burgoyne.   Have you anything more to say, Mr. Dudgeon? It wants two minutes of twelve still.
Richard [*in the strong voice of a man who has conquered the bitterness of death*]. Your watch is two minutes slow by the town clock, which I can see from here, General. [*The town clock strikes the first stroke of twelve. Involuntarily the people flinch at the sound, and a subdued groan breaks from them*] Amen! my life for the world's future!
Anderson [*shouting as he rushes into the market place*].   Amen; and stop the execution. [*He bursts through the line of soldiers opposite* BURGOYNE *and rushes, panting, to the gallows*] I am Anthony Anderson, the man you want.

[*The crowd, intensely excited, listens with all its ears.* JUDITH, *half rising, stares at him, then lifts her hands like one whose dearest prayer has been granted.*]

Swindon.   Indeed. Then you are just in time to take your place on the gallows. Arrest him.

[*At a sign from the* SERGEANT, *two soldiers come forward to seize* ANDERSON.]

Anderson [*thrusting a paper under* SWINDON'S *nose*].   There's my safe-conduct, sir.
Swindon [*taken aback*].   Safe-conduct! Are you—!
Anderson [*emphatically*].   I am. [*The two soldiers take him by the elbows*] Tell these men to take their hands off me.
Swindon [*to the men*].   Let him go.
Sergeant.   Fall back.

[*The two men return to their places. The townsfolk raise a cheer and begin to exchange exultant looks, with a presentiment of triumph as they see their Pastor speaking with their enemies in the gate.*]

Anderson [*exhaling a deep breath of relief and dabbing his perspiring brow with his handkerchief*].   Thank God, I was in time!
Burgoyne [*calm as ever, and still watch in hand*].   Ample time, sir. Plenty of time. I should never dream of hanging any gentleman by an American clock. [*He puts up his watch.*]
Anderson.   Yes, we are some minutes ahead of you already, General. Now tell them to take the rope from the neck of that American citizen.

Burgoyne [*to the executioner in the cart—very politely*]. Kindly undo Mr. Dudgeon.

[*The executioner takes the rope from* RICHARD'S *neck, unties his hands, and helps him on with his coat.*]

Judith [*stealing timidly to* ANDERSON]. Tony.

Anderson [*putting his arm round her shoulders and bantering her affectionately*]. Well, what do you think of your husband now, eh?—eh? ?—eh? ? ?

Judith. I am ashamed— [*She hides her face against his breast.*]

Burgoyne [*to* SWINDON]. You look disappointed, Major Swindon.

Swindon. You look defeated, General Burgoyne.

Burgoyne. I am, sir; and I am humane enough to be glad of it. [RICHARD *jumps down from the cart,* BRUDENELL *offering his hand to help him, and runs to* ANDERSON, *whose left hand he shakes heartily, the right being occupied by* JUDITH] By the way, Mr. Anderson, I do not quite understand. The safe-conduct was for a commander of the militia. I understand you are a—[*He looks as pointedly as his good manners permit at the riding boots, the pistols, and* RICHARD'S *coat, and adds*]—a clergyman.

Anderson [*between* JUDITH *and* RICHARD]. Sir, it is in the hour of trial that a man finds his true profession. This foolish young man [*placing his hand on* RICHARD'S *shoulder*] boasted himself the Devil's Disciple; but when the hour of trial came to him, he found that it was his destiny to suffer and be faithful to the death. I thought myself a decent minister of the gospel of peace; but when the hour of trial came to me, I found that it was my destiny to be a man of action and that my place was amid the thunder of the captains and the shouting. So I am starting life at fifty as Captain Anthony Anderson of the Springtown militia; and the Devil's Disciple here will start presently as the Reverend Richard Dudgeon, and wag his pow[1] in my old pulpit, and give good advice to this silly sentimental little wife of mine [*putting his other hand on her shoulder. She steals a glance at* RICHARD *to see how the prospect pleases him*]. Your mother told me, Richard, that I should never have chosen Judith if I'd been born for the ministry. I am afraid she was right; so, by your leave, you may keep my coat and I'll keep yours.

Richard. Minister—I should say Captain. I have behaved like a fool.

Judith. Like a hero.

Richard. Much the same thing, perhaps. [*With some bitterness towards himself*] But no; if I had been any good, I should have done for you what you did for me, instead of making a vain sacrifice.

Anderson. Not vain, my boy. It takes all sorts to make a world—saints as well as soldiers. [*Turning to* BURGOYNE] And now, General, time presses; and America is in a hurry. Have you realized that though you may occupy towns and win battles, you cannot conquer a nation?

Burgoyne. My good sir, without a Conquest you cannot have an aristocracy. Come and settle the matter at my quarters.

Anderson. At your service, sir. [*To* RICHARD] See Judith home for me, will you,

---

1 Head (Scotch colloquialism).

my boy. [*He hands her over to him*] Now, General. [*He goes busily up the market place towards the Town Hall, leaving* JUDITH *and* RICHARD *together.* BURGOYNE *follows him a step or two, then checks himself and turns to* RICHARD.]

Burgoyne.   Oh, by the way, Mr. Dudgeon, I shall be glad to see you at lunch at half-past one. [*He pauses a moment and adds, with politely veiled slyness*] Bring Mrs. Anderson, if she will be so good. [*To* SWINDON, *who is fuming*] Take it quietly, Major Swindon; your friend the British soldier can stand up to anything except the British War Office. [*He follows* ANDERSON.]

Sergeant [*to* SWINDON].   What orders, sir?

SWINDON [*savagely*].   Orders! What use are orders now! There's no army. Back to quarters; and be d— [*He turns on his heel and goes.*]

Sergeant [*pugnacious and patriotic, repudiating the idea of defeat*].   'Tention. Now then: cock up your chins, and show 'em you don't care a damn for 'em. Slope arms! Fours! Wheel! Quick march!

[*The drums mark time with a tremendous bang; the band strikes up British Grenadiers; and the* SERGEANT, BRUDENELL, *and the English troops march off defiantly to their quarters. The townsfolk press in behind and follow them up the market, jeering at them; and the town band, a very primitive affair, brings up the rear, playing Yankee Doodle.* ESSIE, *who comes in with them, runs to* RICHARD.]

Essie.   Oh, Dick!

Richard [*good-humoredly, but wilfully*].   Now, now; come, come! I don't mind being hanged; but I will not be cried over.

Essie.   No, I promise. I'll be good. [*She tries to restrain her tears, but cannot*] I—I want to see where the soldiers are going to. [*She goes a little way up the market, pretending to look after the crowd.*]

Judith.   Promise me you will never tell him.

Richard.   Don't be afraid.

[*They shake hands on it.*]

Essie [*calling to them*].   They're coming back. They want you.

[*Jubilation in the market. The townsfolk surge back again in wild enthusiasm with their band and hoist* RICHARD *on their shoulders, cheering him.*]

[*The Curtain Falls.*]

Strindberg: A DREAM PLAY

A Dream Play, written in 1902, was first performed in 1907 when August Strindberg was in his late fifties. Although this tormented Swedish artist wrote numerous plays that have been associated with the movement of naturalism, even his work dramatizing the destiny of men beset by uncontrollable forces of an indifferent universe emphasizes the powers of the psyche rather than of society and its institutions as the chief determinant of human suffering.

Strindberg fought a lifelong battle with mental illness that gave him the searingly insightful sort of super-sanity that sometimes lies on the far side of madness. Convinced that inner experience is more revealing than external existence and that the subjective world of a sensitive man's perceptions has claim to a truthful reality every bit as meaningful to him as that which the scientist discerns in objective fact, Strindberg developed a form of dramatic composition in which he, more than any playwright before him, gave a stage life to states of human consciousness. Not long after his death, this technique became known as expressionism. Such plays attempt to delineate what goes on inside a man's heart and head by viewing the external world through his subjectively distorted vision rather than that of a detached observer. They externalize a frame of mind and dramatize a *response* to reality rather than the *stimuli* that evoke it; they give objective form on the stage not to what some hypothetical onlooker sees, but to what an involved perceiver experiences. In seeing such a play, an audience will share the nightmares, hallucinations, and distortions of the central sensibility around whom the action revolves. That sensibility may be either the dramatist himself or the play's protagonist. An expressionistic play is unencumbered by the logic demanded of a drama that undertakes a faithful representation of experience. Rather it is fragmentary and episodic, and it partakes of that inexorable logic that a dream has to its dreamer. And, as in a dream, it tends to formulate its vision of reality in symbols rather than in concrete facts. Unlike the naturalist, the expressionist frees himself from the imitation of nature and concentrates on the artist's perception of it.

The expressionistic technique of organizing experience has, since the days of Strindberg, spilled over onto the common ground of playwriting. The dramatization of the interior vision, usually employed more sparingly than in *A Dream Play*, can be seen in the German theatre of the 1920's, in the work of O'Neill and Miller, and in the use of dream sequences in even frivolous plays. Maybe it has been used most effectively in recent years in motion pictures wherein the camera sees with the eye of a participant in the dramatic action of the film.

Strindberg felt that the large, opulent theatres, so popular in the late nineteenth century, were unsuitable for the intensely personal rapport he hoped to establish between play and audience. Such huge playhouses compelled performers to overact, to play directly to the audience rather than to each other, to be subjected to excessive and garish makeup, and to be bathed in the sort of artificial lighting patterns that made them look like the handiwork of an undertaker. In the year that *A Dream Play* was first produced, Strindberg established his Intimate Theatre in Stockholm. It was not long before theatrical managers throughout Europe realized the need for small playhouses that afforded production options not possible in the large theatres. August Strindberg's influence on stagecraft and theatre architecture was a considerable part of his impact on modern dramaturgy.

A DREAM PLAY

Translated by Elizabeth Sprigge

The Characters[1]

(The voice of) Father Indra
Indra's Daughter
The Glazier
The Officer
The Father
The Mother
Lina
The Doorkeeper
The Billsticker
The Prompter
The Policeman
The Lawyer
The Dean of Philosophy
The Dean of Theology
The Dean of Medicine
The Dean of Law
The Chancellor
Kristin
The Quarantine Master
The Elderly Fop
The Coquette
The Friend
The Poet
He
She (doubles with Victoria's voice)
The Pensioner
Ugly Edith
Edith's Mother
The Naval Officer
Alice
The Schoolmaster
Nils
The Husband
The Wife
The Blind Man
1st Coal Heaver
2nd Coal Heaver

[1] There is no list of characters in the original (translator's note).

The Gentleman
The Lady
Singers and Dancers (Members of the Opera Company)
Clerks, Graduates, Maids, Schoolboys,
Children, Crew, Righteous People.

AUTHOR'S NOTE

In this dream play, as in his former dream play TO DAMASCUS, the Author has sought to reproduce the disconnected but apparently logical form of a dream. Anything can happen; everything is possible and probable. Time and space do not exist; on a slight groundwork of reality, imagination spins and weaves new patterns made up of memories, experiences, unfettered fancies, absurdities and improvisations.

The characters are split, double and multiply; they evaporate, crystallize, scatter and converge. But a single consciousness holds sway over them all—that of the dreamer. For him there are no secrets, no incongruities, no scruples and no law. He neither condemns nor acquits, but only relates, and since on the whole, there is more pain than pleasure in the dream, a tone of melancholy, and of compassion for all living things, runs through the swaying narrative. Sleep, the liberator, often appears as a torturer, but when the pain is at its worst, the sufferer awakes—and is thus reconciled with reality. For however agonising real life may be, at this moment, compared with the tormenting dream, it is a joy.

Prologue

An impression of clouds, crumbling cliffs, ruins of castles and fortresses.
The constellations Leo, Virgo and Libra are seen, with the planet Jupiter shining brightly among them.
On the highest cloud-peak stands THE DAUGHTER OF INDRA.[1] INDRA'S VOICE is heard from above.

Indra's Voice.   Where art thou, Daughter?
Daughter.   Here, Father, here!
Indra's Voice.   Thou hast strayed, my child.
  Take heed, thou sinkest.
  How cam'st thou here?
Daughter.   Borne on a cloud, I followed the lightning's
  blazing trail from the ethereal heights.
  But the cloud sank, and still is falling.
  Tell me, great Father Indra, to what region
  am I come? The air's so dense, so hard to breathe.

---

[1]   Hindu god of the heavens, rain, and thunder. In the early stages of the Hindu religion, he was the chief god, but he was later viewed as subordinate to Brahma, the god of creation. No mention is made in Hindu mythology of a daughter of Indra.

Indra's Voice.   *Leaving the second world thou camest to the third.*
   From Cucra, Star of the Morning,
   Far art thou come and enterest
   Earth's atmosphere. Mark there
   The Sun's Seventh House that's called the Scales.
   The Morning Star is at the autumn weighing,
   When day and night are equal.
Daughter.   *Thou speak'st of Earth. Is that the dark*
   and heavy world the moon lights up?
Indra's Voice.   *It is the darkest and the heaviest*
   of all the spheres that swing in space.
Daughter.   *Does not the sun shine there?*
Indra's Voice.   *It shines, but not unceasingly.*
Daughter.   *Now the clouds part, and I can see . . .*
Indra's Voice.   *What see'st thou, child?*
Daughter.   *I see . . . that Earth is fair . . . It has green woods,*
   blue waters, white mountains, yellow fields.
Indra's Voice.   *Yes, it is fair, as all that Brahma shaped,*
   yet in the dawn of time
   was fairer still. Then came a change,
   a shifting of the orbit, maybe of more.
   Revolt followed by crime which had to be suppressed.
Daughter.   *Now I hear sounds arising . . .*
   What kind of creatures dwell down there?
Indra's Voice.   *Go down and see. The Creator's children I would not decry,*
   but it's their language that thou hearest.
Daughter.   *It sounds as if . . . it has no cheerful ring.*
Indra's Voice.   *So I believe. Their mother-tongue*
   is called Complaint. Truly a discontented,
   thankless race is this of Earth.
Daughter.   *Ah, say not so! Now I hear shouts of joy,*
   and blare and boom. I see the lightning flash.
   Now bells are pealing and the fires are lit.
   A thousand thousand voices rise,
   singing their praise and thanks to heaven.
   Pause.
   Thy judgment is too hard on them, my Father.
Indra.   *Descend and see, and hear, then come again*
   and tell me if their lamentations
   and complaint are justified.
Daughter.   *So be it. I descend. Come with me, Father!*
Indra.   *No. I cannot breathe their air.*
Daughter.   *Now the cloud sinks. It's growing dense. I suffocate!*
   This is not air, but smoke and water that I breathe,
   so heavy that it drags me down and down.
   And now I clearly feel its reeling!
   This third is surely not the highest world.
Indra.   *Neither the highest, truly, nor the lowest.*

It is called Dust, and whirls with all the rest,
And so at times its people, struck with dizziness,
live on the borderline of folly and insanity . . .
Courage, my child, for this is but a test!
Daughter, *on her knees as the cloud descends.*
I am sinking!

[*The curtain rises on* THE GROWING CASTLE.]

[*The background shows a forest of giant hollyhocks in bloom: white, pink,*
crimson, sulphur-yellow and violet. Above this rises the gilded roof of a castle
with a flowerbud crowning its summit. Under the walls of the castle lie heaps of
straw and stable-muck.
On each side of the stage are stylised representations of interiors, architecture
and landscape which remain unchanged throughout the play.
The GLAZIER *and the* DAUGHTER *enter together.*]

Daughter. The castle keeps on growing up out of the earth. Do you see how it
has grown since last year?
Glazier [*to himself*]. I've never seen that castle before—and I've never heard of
a castle growing . . . but . . . [*to the* DAUGHTER *with conviction*] Yes, it's
grown six feet, but that's because they've manured it. And if you look carefully,
you'll see it's put out a wing on the sunny side.
Daughter. Ought it not to blossom soon? We are already halfway through the
summer.
Glazier. Don't you see the flower up there?
Daughter [*joyfully*]. Yes, I see it. Father, tell me something. Why do flowers
grow out of dirt?
Glazier. They don't like the dirt, so they shoot up as fast as they can into the
light—to blossom and to die.
Daughter. Do you know who lives in the castle?
Glazier. I used to know, but I've forgotten.
Daughter. I believe there is a prisoner inside, waiting for me to set him free.
Glazier. What will you get if you do?
Daughter. Ones does not bargain about what one has to do. Let us go into the
castle.
Glazier. Very well, we will.

[*They go towards the background which slowly vanishes to the sides, disclosing*
a simple bare room with a table and a few chairs. A screen cuts the stage in two
(*the other half unlighted*). A YOUNG OFFICER *in an unconventional modern*
uniform sits rocking his chair and striking the table with his sword.]

[*The* DAUGHTER *and the* GLAZIER *enter.*]

[*She goes up to the* OFFICER *and gently takes the sword from his hands.*]

Daughter. No, no, you mustn't do that.
Officer. Please, Agnes, let me keep my sword.
Daughter. But you are cutting the table to pieces. [*To the* GLAZIER] Father,

you go down to the harness room and put in that window pane, and we will
meet later.

[*Exit* GLAZIER.]

Daughter.   You are a prisoner in your own room. I have come to set you free.

Officer.   I have been waiting for this, but I wasn't sure you would want to.

Daughter.   The castle is strong—it has seven walls—but it shall be done. Do you
want to be set free—or not?

Officer.   To tell the truth, I don't know. Either way I'll suffer. Every joy has to be
paid for twice over with sorrow. It's wretched here, but I'd have to endure three
times the agony for the joys of freedom . . . Agnes, I'll bear it, if only I may
see you.

Daughter.   What do you see in me?

Officer.   The beautiful, which is the harmony of the universe. There are lines in
your form which I have only found in the movement of the stars, in the melody
of strings, in the vibrations of light. You are a child of heaven.

Daughter.   So are you.

Officer.   Then why do I have to groom horses, clean stables and have the muck
removed?

Daughter.   So that you may long to get away.

Officer.   I do. But it's so hard to pull oneself out of it all.

Daughter.   It is one's duty to seek freedom in the light.

Officer.   Duty? Life has not done its duty by me.

Daughter.   You feel wronged by life?

Officer.   Yes. It has been unjust. . . .

[*Voices are now heard from behind the dividing screen, which is drawn aside
(as the lights go up on the other set: a homely living-room). The* OFFICER *and
the* DAUGHTER *stand watching, gestures and expression held. The* MOTHER, *an
invalid, sits at a table. In front of her is a lighted candle, which from time to
time she trims with snuffers. On the table are piles of new underclothing, which
she is marking with a quill pen. Beyond is a brown cupboard.*]

[*The* FATHER *brings her a silk shawl.*]

Father [*gently*].   I have brought you this.

Mother.   What use is a silk shawl to me, my dear, when I am going to die so
soon?

Father.   You believe what the doctor says?

Mother.   What he says too, but most of all I believe the voice that speaks within
me.

Father [*sorrowfully*].   Then it really is grave . . . And you are thinking of your
children, first and last.

Mother.   They were my life, my justification, my happiness, and my sorrow.

Father.   Kristina, forgive me . . . for everything.

Mother.   For what? Ah, my dear, forgive *me*! We have both hurt each other.
Why, we don't know. We could not do otherwise . . . However, here is the
children's new linen. See that they change twice a week—on Wednesdays and
Sundays, and that Louisa washes them—all over . . . Are you going out?

Father. I have to go to the school at eleven.

Mother. Before you go ask Alfred to come.

Father [pointing to the OFFICER*].* But, dear heart, he is here.

Mother. My sight must be going too . . . Yes, it's getting so dark. [*Snuffs candle*] Alfred, come!

[*The* FATHER *goes out through the middle of the wall, nodding goodbye. The* OFFICER *moves forward to the* MOTHER.]

Mother. Who is that girl?

Officer [whispering]. That's Agnes.

Mother. Oh, is it Agnes? Do you know what they are saying? That she is the daughter of the God Indra, who begged to come down to Earth so as to know what it is really like for human beings. But don't say anything.

Officer. She *is* a child of the Gods.

Mother [raising her voice]. Alfred, my son, I shall soon be leaving you and your brothers and sisters. I want to say one thing—for you to remember all your life.

Officer [sadly]. What is it, Mother?

Mother. Only one thing: never quarrel with God.

Officer. What do you mean, Mother?

Mother. You must not go on feeling you have been wronged by life.

Officer. But I've been treated so unjustly.

Mother. You're still harping on the time you were unjustly punished for taking that money which was afterwards found.

Officer. Yes. That piece of injustice gave a twist to the whole of my life.

Mother. I see. Well now, you just go over to that cupboard . . .

Officer [ashamed]. So you know about that. The . . .

Mother. "The Swiss Family Robinson" which . . .

Officer. Don't say any more . . .

Mother. Which your brother was punished for . . . when it was *you* who had torn it to pieces and hidden it.

Officer. Think of that cupboard still being there after twenty years. We have moved so many times—and my mother died ten years ago.

Mother. Yes. What of it? You are always questioning everything, and so spoiling the best of life for yourself . . . Ah, here's Lina!

[*Enter* LINA.]

Lina. Thank you very much all the same, Ma'am, but I can't go to the christening.

Mother. Why not, child?

Lina. I've got nothing to wear.

Mother. You can borrow this shawl of mine.

Lina. Oh no, Ma'am, you're very kind, but that would never do.

Mother. I can't see why not. I shan't be going to any more parties.

Officer. What will Father say? After all, it's a present from him.

Mother. What small minds!

Father [putting his head in]. Are you going to lend my present to the maid?

Mother. Don't talk like that! Remember I was in service once myself. Why should you hurt an innocent girl?

Father. Why should you hurt me, your husband?

Mother. Ah, this life! If you do something good, someone else is sure to think it bad; if you are kind to one person, you're sure to harm another. Ah, this life!

[*She snuffs the candle so that it goes out. The room grows dark and the screen is drawn forward again.*]

Daughter. Human beings are to be pitied.

Officer. Do you think so?

Daughter. Yes, life is hard. But love conquers everything. Come and see.

[*They withdraw and the background disappears. The* OFFICER *vanishes and the* DAUGHTER *comes forward alone.*]

[*The new scene shows an old derelict wall. In the middle of the wall a gate opens on an alley leading to a green plot where a giant blue monkshood[1] is growing. To the left of the gate is the door-window of the Stage Doorkeeper's lodge. The Stage Doorkeeper is sitting with a grey shawl over her head and shoulders, crocheting a star-patterned coverlet. On the right is an announcement board which the* BILLSTICKER *is washing. Near him is a fishnet with a green handle and a green fish box. Further right the cupboard (from the previous set) has become a door with an air-hole shaped like a four-leafed clover. To the left is a small lime tree with a coal-black stem and a few pale green leaves.*]

[*The* DAUGHTER *goes up to the* DOORKEEPER.]

Daughter. Isn't the star coverlet finished yet?

Doorkeeper. No, my dear. Twenty-six years is nothing for such a piece of work.

Daughter. And your sweetheart never came back?

Doorkeeper. No, but it wasn't his fault. He *had* to take himself off, poor fellow. That was thirty years ago.

Daughter [*to* BILLSTICKER]. She was in the ballet, wasn't she? Here—at the Opera.

Billsticker. She was the prima ballerina, but when *he* went away, it seems he took her dancing with him . . . so she never got any more parts.

Daughter. All complain—with their eyes, and with their voices too.

Billsticker. I haven't much to complain of—not now I've got my net and a green fish box.

Daughter. Does that make you happy?

Billsticker. Yes, very happy. That was my dream when I was little, and now it's come true. I'm all of fifty now, you know.

Daughter. Fifty years for a fishnet and a box!

Billsticker. A *green* box, a *green* one . . .

Daughter [*to* DOORKEEPER]. Let me have that shawl now, and I'll sit here and watch the children of men. But you must stand behind and tell me about them.

---

[1] A poisonous plant, also known as aconite.

[*The* DAUGHTER *puts on the shawl and sits down by the gate.*]

Doorkeeper. This is the last day of the Opera season. They hear now if they've been engaged for the next.

Daughter. And those who have not?

Doorkeeper. Lord Jesus, what a scene! I always pull my shawl over my head.

Daughter. Poor things!

Doorkeeper. Look, here's one coming. She's not been engaged. See how she's crying!

[*The* SINGER *rushes in from the right and goes through the gate with her handkerchief to her eyes. She pauses a moment in the alley beyond and leans her head against the wall, then goes quickly out.*]

Daughter. Human beings are to be pitied.

Doorkeeper. But here comes one who seems happy enough.

[*The* OFFICER *comes down the alley, wearing a frock-coat and top hat. He carries a bouquet of roses and looks radiantly happy.*]

Doorkeeper. He's going to marry Miss Victoria.

Officer [*downstage, looks up and sings*]. Victoria!

Doorkeeper. The young lady will be down in a minute.

Woman's Voice [*from above, sings*]. I am here!

Officer [*pacing*]. Well, I am waiting.

Daughter. Don't you know me?

Officer. No, I know only one woman—Victoria! Seven years I have come here to wait for her—at noon when the sun reaches the chimneys, and in the evening as darkness falls. Look at the paving. See? Worn by the steps of the faithful lover? Hurrah! She is mine. [*Sings*] Victoria! [*No answer*] Well, she's dressing now. [*To the* BILLSTICKER] Ah, a fishnet I see! Everyone here at the Opera is crazy about fishnets—or rather about fish. Dumb fish—because they cannot sing . . . What does a thing like that cost?

Billsticker. It's rather dear.

Officer [*sings*]. Victoria! . . . [*Shakes the lime tree*] Look, it's budding again! For the eighth time. [*Sings*] Victoria! . . . Now she's doing her hair . . . [*To* DAUGHTER] Madam, kindly allow me to go up and fetch my bride.

Doorkeeper. Nobody's to go on the stage.

Officer. Seven years I've walked up and down here. Seven times three hundred and sixty-five I make two thousand five hundred and fifty-five. [*Stops and pokes the door with the clover-shaped hole*] Then this door I've seen two thousand five hundred and fifty-five times and I still don't know where it leads to. And this clover leaf to let in the light. Who does it let the light in for? Is anyone inside? Does anybody live there?

Doorkeeper. I don't know. I've never seen it open.

Officer. It looks like a larder door I saw when I was four years old, when I went out one Sunday afternoon with the maid—to see another family and other maids. But I only got as far as the kitchen, where I sat between the water barrel and the salt tub. I've seen so many kitchens in my time, and the larders are always in the passage, with round holes and a clover leaf in the door. But the

Opera can't have a larder as it hasn't got a kitchen. [*Sings*] Victoria! [*To* DAUGHTER] Excuse me, Madam, she can't leave by any other way, can she?

Doorkeeper. No, there is no other way.

Officer. Good. Then I'm bound to meet her.

[*Members of the Opera Company swarm out of the building, scrutinised by the* OFFICER. *They go out by the gate.*]

She's sure to come. [*To* DAUGHTER] Madam, that blue monkshood out there— I saw it when I was a child. Is it the same one? I remember it in a rectory garden when I was seven—with two doves, blue doves, under the hood. Then a bee came and went into the hood, and I thought: "Now I've got you," so I grabbed the flower, but the bee stung through it, and I burst into tears. However, the rector's wife came and put moist earth on it—and then we had wild strawberries and milk for supper . . . I believe it's growing dark already. Where are you off to, Billsticker?

Billsticker. Home to my supper.

[*Exit with fishnet and box.*]

Officer [*rubbing his eyes*]. Supper? At this time of day? . . . [*To* DAUGHTER] Excuse me, may I just step inside a moment and telephone to the Growing Castle?

Daughter. What do you want to say to them?

Officer. I want to tell the glazier to put in the double windows. It will be winter soon and I'm so dreadfully cold.

[*The* OFFICER *goes into the* DOORKEEPER'S *Lodge.*]

Daughter. Who is Miss Victoria?

Doorkeeper. She is his love.

Daughter. A true answer. What she is to us or others doesn't matter to him. Only what she is to *him*, that's what she *is*.

[*It grows dark suddenly.*]

Doorkeeper [*lighting the lantern*]. Dusk falls quickly today.

Daughter. To the gods a year is as a minute.

Doorkeeper. While to human beings a minute may be as long as a year.

[*The* OFFICER *comes out again. He looks shabbier, and the roses are withered.*]

Officer. Hasn't she come yet?

Doorkeeper. No.

Officer. She's sure to come. She'll come. [*Paces up and down*] But all the same . . . perhaps it would be wiser to cancel that luncheon . . . as it's now evening. Yes, that's what I'll do. [*Goes in and telephones.*]

Doorkeeper [*To* DAUGHTER]. May I have my shawl now?

Daughter. No, my friend. You rest and I'll take your place, because I want to know about human beings and life—to find out if it really is as hard as they say.

Doorkeeper. But you don't get any sleep on this job. Never any sleep, night or day.

Daughter. No sleep at night?

Doorkeeper. Well, if you can get any with the bell wire on your arm, because the night watchmen go up on the stage and are changed every three hours . . .

Daughter. That must be torture.

Doorkeeper. So you think, but we others are glad enough to get such a job. If you knew how much I'm envied.

Daughter. Envied? Does one envy the tortured?

Doorkeeper. Yes. But I'll tell you what's worse than nightwatching and drudgery and draughts and cold and damp. That's having to listen, as I do, to all their tales of woe. They all come to me. Why? Perhaps they read in my wrinkles the runes of suffering, and that makes them talk. In that shawl, my dear, thirty years of torment's hidden—my own and others.

Daughter. That's why it is so heavy and stings like nettles.

Doorkeeper. Wear it if you like. When it gets too heavy, call me and I'll come and relieve you of it.

Daughter. Goodbye. What you can bear, surely I can.

Doorkeeper. We shall see. But be kind to my young friends and put up with their complaining.

[*The* DOORKEEPER *disappears down the alley. The stage is blacked out. When light returns, the lime tree is bare, the blue monkshood withered, and the green plot at the end of the alley has turned brown.*]

[*The* OFFICER *enters. His hair is grey and he has a grey beard. His clothes are ragged; his collar soiled and limp. He still carries the bouquet of roses, but the petals have dropped.*]

Officer [*wandering round*]. By all the signs, summer is over and autumn at hand. I can tell that by the lime tree—and the monkshood. [*Pacing*] But autumn is *my* spring, for then the theatre opens again. And then she is bound to come. [*To* DAUGHTER] Dear lady, may I sit on this chair for a while?

Daughter. Do, my friend. I can stand.

Officer [*sitting*]. If only I could sleep a little it would be better.

[*He falls asleep for a moment, then starts up and begins walking again. He stops by the clover-leaf door and pokes it.*]

Officer. This door—it gives me no peace. What is there behind it? Something must be. [*Soft ballet music is heard from above*] Ah, the rehearsals have begun! [*The lights come and go like a lighthouse beam*] What's this? [*Speaking in time with the flashes*] Light and darkness; light and darkness.

Daughter [*with the same timing*]. Day and night; day and night. A merciful providence wants to shorten your waiting. And so the days fly, chasing the nights.

[*The light is now constant. The* BILLSTICKER *enters with his net and his implements.*]

Officer.   Here's the Billsticker with his net. How was the fishing?

Billsticker.   Not too bad. The summer was hot and a bit long . . . the net was all right, but not quite what I had in mind.

Officer.   "Not quite what I had in mind." Excellently put. Nothing ever is as one imagined it—because one's mind goes further than the act, goes beyond the object. [*He walks up and down striking the bouquet against the walls until the last leaves fall.*]

Billsticker.   Hasn't she come down yet?

Officer.   No, not yet, but she'll come soon. Do you know what's behind that door, Billsticker?

Billsticker.   No, I've never seen it open.

Officer.   I'm going to telephone to a locksmith to come and open it. [*Goes into the Lodge. The* BILLSTICKER *pastes up a poster and moves away.*]

Daughter.   What was wrong with the fishnet?

Billsticker.   Wrong? Well, there wasn't anything wrong exactly. But it wasn't what I'd had in mind, and so I didn't enjoy it *quite* as much . . .

Daughter.   How did you imagine the net?

Billsticker.   How? I can't quite tell you . . .

Daughter.   Let me tell you. In your imagination it was different—green but not *that* green.

Billsticker.   You understand, Madam. You understand everything. That's why they all come to you with their troubles. Now if you'd only listen to me, just this once . . .

Daughter.   But I will, gladly. Come in here and pour out your heart. [*She goes into the Lodge. The* BILLSTICKER *stays outside and talks to her through the window.*]

[*The stage is blacked out again, then gradually the lights go up. The lime tree is in leaf; the monkshood in bloom; the sun shines on the greenery at the end of the alley. The* BILLSTICKER *is still at the window and the* DAUGHTER *can be seen inside.*]

[*The* OFFICER *enters from the Lodge. He is old and white-haired; his clothes and shoes are in rags. He carries the stems of the bouquet. He totters backwards and forwards slowly like a very old man, and reads the poster.*]

[A BALLET GIRL *comes out of the Theatre.*]

Officer.   Has Miss Victoria gone?

Ballet Girl.   No, she hasn't.

Officer.   Then I'll wait. Will she come soon?

Ballet Girl [*gravely*].   Yes, she's sure to.

Officer.   Don't go—then you'll be able to see what's behind that door. I've sent for the locksmith.

Ballet Girl.   That will be really interesting to see this door opened. The door and the Growing Castle. Do you know the Growing Castle?

Officer.   Do I? Wasn't I imprisoned there?

Ballet Girl.   Really, was that you? But why did they have so many horses there?

Officer.   It was a stable castle, you see.

Ballet girl [*distressed*].   How silly of me not to have thought of that.

[*Moves towards the Lodge. A* chorus girl *comes out of the Theatre.*]

Officer.   Has Miss Victoria gone?
Chorus Girl [*gravely*].   No, she hasn't gone. She never goes.
Officer.   That's because she loves me. No, you mustn't go before the locksmith comes. He's going to open this door.
Chorus Girl.   Oh, is the door going to be opened? Really? What fun! I just want to ask the Doorkeeper something.

[*She joins the* billsticker *at the window. The* prompter *comes out of the Theatre.*]

Officer.   Has Miss Victoria gone?
Prompter.   Not so far as I know.
Officer.   There you are! Didn't I say she was waiting for me? No, don't go. The door's going to be opened.
Prompter.   Which door?
Officer.   Is there more than one door?
Prompter.   Oh, I see—the one with the clover-leaf! Of course I'll stay. I just want to have a few words with the Doorkeeper.

[*He joins the group at the window. They all speak in turn to the* daughter. *The* glazier *comes through the gate.*]

Officer.   Are you the locksmith?
Glazier.   No, the locksmith had company. But a glazier's just as good.
Officer.   Yes, indeed . . . indeed. But . . . er . . . have you brought your diamond with you?
Glazier.   Of course. A glazier without a diamond—what good would that be?
Officer.   None. Let's get to work then. [*He claps his hands. All group themselves in a circle round the door.* male chorus *in costumes of Die Meistersinger, and* girl dancers *from Aïda come out of the theatre and join them*] Locksmith— or Glazier—do your duty! [*The* glazier *goes towards the door holding out his diamond*] A moment such as this does not recur often in a lifetime. Therefore, my good friends, I beg you to reflect seriously upon . . .

[*During the last words the* policeman *has entered by the gate.*]

Policeman.   In the name of the law I forbid the opening of this door.
Officer.   Oh God, what a fuss there is whenever one wants to do anything new and great! Well—we shall take proceedings . . . To the lawyer then, and we will see if the law holds good. To the lawyer!

[*Without any lowering of the curtain the scene changes to the* lawyer's *office. The gate has now become the gate in an office railing stretching across the stage. The* doorkeeper's *Lodge is a recess for the* lawyer's *desk, the lime tree, leafless, a coat-and-hat stand. The announcement-board is covered with proclamations and Court decrees and the clover-door is a document cupboard.*
The lawyer *in frock coat and white tie is sitting on the left inside the railing of the gate, at this high desk covered with papers. His appearance bears witness to unspeakable suffering. His face is chalk-white, furrowed and purple-shadowed.*

He is hideous; his face mirrors all the crime and vice with which, through his profession, he has been involved.
Of his two clerks one has only one arm; the other a single eye.
The people, who had gathered to witness the opening of the door, are now clients waiting to see the LAWYER, *and look as if they have always been there.*
The DAUGHTER, *wearing the shawl, and the* OFFICER *are in front. The* OFFICER *looks curiously at the cupboard door and from time to time pokes it.*]

[*The* LAWYER *goes up to the* DAUGHTER.]

Lawyer.   If you let me have that shawl, my dear, I'll hang it here until the stove is lighted and then I'll burn it with all its griefs and miseries.

Daughter.   Not yet, my friend. I must let it get quite full first, and I want above all to gather *your* sufferings up in it, the crimes you have absorbed from others, the vices, swindles, slanders, libel . . .

Lawyer.   My child, your shawl would not be big enough. Look at these walls! Isn't the wall-paper stained as if by every kind of sin? Look at these documents in which I write records of evil! Look at me! . . . Nobody who comes here ever smiles. Nothing but vile looks, bared teeth, clenched fists, and all of them squirt their malice, their envy, their suspicions over me. Look, my hands are black and can never be clean! See how cracked they are and bleeding! I can never wear my clothes for more than a few days because they stink of other people's crimes. Sometimes I have the place fumigated with sulphur, but that doesn't help. I sleep in the next room and dream of nothing but crime. I have a murder case in Court now—that's bad enough—but do you know what's worst of all? Separating husbands and wives. Then earth and heaven seem to cry aloud, to cry treason against primal power, the source of good, against love! And then, do you know, after reams of paper have been filled with mutual accusations, if some kindly person takes one or other of the couple aside and asks them in a friendly sort of way the simple question—"What have you really got against your husband—or your wife?"—then he, or she, stands speechless. They don't know. Oh, once it was something to do with a salad, another time about some word. Usually it's about nothing at all. But the suffering, the agony! All this I have to bear. Look at me! Do you think, marked as I am by crime, I can ever win a woman's love? Or that anyone wants to be the friend of a man who has to enforce payment of all the debts of the town? It's misery to be human.

Daughter.   Human life is pitiable!

Lawyer.   It is indeed. And what people live on is a mystery to me. They marry with an income of two thousand crowns when they need four. They borrow, to be sure, they all borrow, and so scrape along somehow by the skin of their teeth until they die. Then the estate is always insolvent. Who has to pay up in the end? Tell me that.

Daughter.   He who feeds the birds.

Lawyer.   Well, if He who feeds the birds would come down to earth and see the plight of the unfortunate children of men, perhaps He would have some compassion . . .

Daughter.   Human life is pitiful.

Lawyer.   Yes, that's the truth. [*To the* OFFICER] What do you want?

Officer.   I only want to ask if Miss Victoria has gone.

Lawyer. No, she hasn't. You can rest assured of that. Why do you keep poking my cupboard?

Officer. I thought the door was so very like . . .

Lawyer. Oh, no, no, no!

[*Church bells ring.*]

Officer. Is there a funeral in the town?

Lawyer. No, it's Graduation—the conferring of Doctors' degrees. I myself am about to receive the degree of Doctor of Law. Perhaps you would like to graduate and receive a laurel wreath?

Officer. Why not? It would be a little distraction.

Lawyer. Then perhaps we should proceed at once to the solemn rites. But you must go and change.

[*Exit* OFFICER.]

[*The stage is blacked out and changes to the interior of the Church.*
The barrier now serves as the chancel rail. The announcement-board shows the numbers of the hymns. The lime-tree hatstand has become a candelabra, the LAWYER'S *desk is the* CHANCELLOR'S *lectern, and the clover-door leads to the vestry. The Chorus from Die Meistersinger are ushers with wands. The dancers carry the laurel wreaths. The rest of the people are the congregation.*
The new background shows only a gigantic organ, with a mirror over the keyboard.
Music is heard. At the sides stand the four Deans of the Faculties—Philosophy, Theology, Medicine and Law. For a moment there is no movement, then:
The USHERS *come forward from the right.*[1]
The DANCERS *follow, holding laurel wreaths in their outstretched hands.*
Three GRADUATES *come in from the left, are crowned in turn by the* DANCERS *and go out to the right.*
The LAWYER *advances to receive his wreath.*
The DANCERS *turn away, refusing to crown him, and go out.*
The LAWYER, *greatly agitated, leans against a pillar.*
Everyone disappears. The LAWYER *is alone.*]

[*The* DAUGHTER *enters with a white shawl over her head and shoulders.*]

Daughter. Look, I have washed the shawl. But what are you doing here? Didn't you get your laurels?

Lawyer. No. I was discredited.

Daughter. Why? Because you have defended the poor, said a good word for the sinner, eased the burden of the guilty, obtained reprieve for the condemned? Woe to mankind! Men are not angels, but pitiable creatures.

Lawyer. Do not judge men harshly. It is my business to plead for them.

---

[1] This scene follows exactly the normal ceremony in a Swedish university when Doctors' degrees are conferred. As each Graduate has the wreath put on his head, a gun outside is fired. The Chancellor and the Faculties bow. Then the new doctor bows to them.

One of the Graduates should be the Officer and another the Schoolmaster of the later scene (translator's note).

Daughter [*leaning against the organ*].   Why do they strike their friends in the face?

Lawyer.   They know no better.

Daughter.   Let us enlighten them—you and I together. Will you?

Lawyer.   There can be no enlightenment for them. Oh that the gods in heaven might hear our woe!

Daughter.   It shall reach the throne. [*Sits at the organ*] Do you know what I see in this mirror? The world as it should be. For as it is it's wrong way up.

Lawyer.   How did it come to be wrong way up?

Daughter.   When the copy was made.

Lawyer.   Ah! You yourself have said it—the copy! I always felt this must be a poor copy, and when I began to remember its origin nothing satisfied me. Then they said I was cynical and had a jaundiced eye, and so forth.

Daughter.   It is a mad world. Consider these four Faculties. Organized society subsidizes all four: Theology, the doctrine of Divinity, continually attacked and ridiculed by Philosophy claiming wisdom for itself; and Medicine always giving the lie to Philosophy and discounting Theology as one of the sciences, calling it superstition. And there they sit together on the Council, whose function is to teach young men respect for the University. Yes, it's a madhouse. And woe to him who first recovers his senses!

Lawyer.   The first to discover it are the theologians. For their preliminary studies they take Philosophy, which teaches them that Theology is nonsense, and then they learn from Theology that Philosophy is nonsense. Madness.

Daughter.   Then there's Law, serving all but its servants.

Lawyer.   Justice, to the just unjust. Right so often wrong.

Daughter.   Thus you have made it, O Children of Men! Child, come! You shall have a wreath from me . . . one more fitting. [*She puts a crown of thorns on his head*] Now I will play to you. [*She sits at the organ and plays a Kyrie, but instead of the organ, voices are heard singing. The last note of each phrase is sustained.*]

Children's Voices.   Lord! Lord!

Women's Voices.   Be merciful!

Men's Voices [*Tenor*].   Deliver us for Thy mercy's sake.

Men's Voices [*Bass*].   Save Thy children, O Lord, and be not wrathful against us.

All.   Be merciful! Hear us! Have compassion for mortals. Are we so far from Thee? Out of the depths we call. Grace, Lord! Let not the burden be too heavy for Thy children. Hear us! Hear us!

[*The stage darkens as the* DAUGHTER *rises and approaches the* LAWYER.]

[*By means of lighting the organ is changed to the wall of a grotto. The sea seeps in between basalt pillars with a harmony of waves and wind.*]

Lawyer.   Where are we?

Daughter.   What do you hear?

Lawyer.   I hear drops falling.

Daughter.   Those are the tears of mankind weeping. What more do you hear?

Lawyer.   A sighing . . . a moaning . . . a wailing.

Daughter. The lamentation of mortals has reached so far, no further. But why this endless lamentation? Is there no joy in life?

Lawyer. Yes. The sweetest which is also the bitterest—love! Marriage and a home. The highest and the lowest.

Daughter. Let me put it to the test.

Lawyer. With me?

Daughter. With you. You know the rocks, the stumbling stones. Let us avoid them.

Lawyer. I am poor.

Daughter. Does that matter if we love one another? And a little beauty costs nothing.

Lawyer. My antipathies may be your sympathies.

Daughter. They can be balanced.

Lawyer. Supposing we tire?

Daughter. Children will come, bringing ever new interests.

Lawyer. You? You will take me, poor, ugly, despised, discredited?

Daughter. Yes. Let us join our destinies.

Lawyer. So be it.

[*The scene changes to a very simple room adjoining the* LAWYER's *office. On the right is a large curtained double bed, close to it a window with double panes; on the left a stove and kitchen utensils.*]

[*At the back an open door leads to the office, where a number of poor people can be seen awaiting admission.* KRISTIN, *the maid, is pasting strips of paper along the edges of the inner window.*]

[*The* DAUGHTER, *pale and worn, is at the stove.*]

Kristin. I paste, I paste.

Daughter. You are shutting out the air. I am suffocating.

Kristin. Now there's only one small crack left.

Daughter. Air, air! I cannot breathe.

Kristin. I paste, I paste.

Lawyer [*from the office*]. That's right, Kristin. Warmth is precious.

[KRISTIN *pastes the last crack.*]

Daughter. Oh, it's as if you are glueing up my mouth!

Lawyer [*coming to the doorway with a document in his hand*]. Is the child asleep?

Daughter. Yes, at last.

Lawyer [*mildly*]. That screaming frightens away my clients.

Daughter [*gently*]. What can be done about it?

Lawyer. Nothing.

Daughter. We must take a bigger flat.

Lawyer. We have no money.

Daughter. May I open the window, please? This bad air is choking me.

Lawyer. Then the warmth would escape, and we should freeze.

Daughter. It's horrible! Can't we at least scrub the place?

Lawyer.   You can't scrub—neither can I, and Kristin must go on pasting. She must paste up the whole house, every crack in floor and walls and ceiling.

[*Exit* KRISTIN, *delighted.*]

Daughter.   I was prepared for poverty, not dirt.
Lawyer.   Poverty is always rather dirty.
Daughter.   This is worse than I dreamt.
Lawyer.   We haven't had the worst. There's still food in the pot.
Daughter.   But what food!
Lawyer.   Cabbage is cheap, nourishing and good.
Daughter.   For those who like cabbage. To me it's repulsive.
Lawyer.   Why didn't you say so?
Daughter.   Because I loved you. I wanted to sacrifice my taste.
Lawyer.   Now I must sacrifice my taste for cabbage. Sacrifices must be mutual.
Daughter.   Then what shall we eat? Fish? But you hate fish.
Lawyer.   And it's dear.
Daughter.   This is harder than I believed.
Lawyer [*gently*].   You see how hard it is. And the child which should be our bond and blessing is our undoing.
Daughter.   Dearest! I am dying in this air, in this room with its backyard view, with babies screaming through endless sleepless hours, and those people out there wailing and quarrelling and accusing . . . Here I can only die.
Lawyer.   Poor little flower, without light, without air.
Daughter.   And you say there are others worse off.
Lawyer.   I am one of the envied of the neighbourhood.
Daughter.   None of it would matter, if only I could have some beauty in our home.
Lawyer.   I know what you're thinking of—a plant, a heliotrope to be exact; but that costs as much as six quarts of milk or half a bushel of potatoes.
Daughter.   I would gladly go without food to have my flower.
Lawyer.   There is one kind of beauty that costs nothing. Not to have it in his home is sheer torture for a man with any sense of beauty.
Daughter.   What is that?
Lawyer.   If I tell you, you will lose your temper.
Daughter.   We agreed never to lose our tempers.
Lawyer.   We agreed. Yes. All will be well, Agnes, if we can avoid those sharp hard tones. You know them—no, not yet.
Daughter.   We shall never hear those.
Lawyer.   Never, if it depends on me.
Daughter.   Now tell me.
Lawyer.   Well, when I come into a house, first I look to see how the curtains are hung. [*Goes to the window and adjusts the curtain*] If they hang like a bit of string or rag, I soon leave. Then I glance at the chairs. If they are in their places, I stay. [*Puts a chair straight against the wall*] Next I look at the candlesticks. If the candles are crooked, then the whole house is askew. [*Straightens a candle on the bureau*] That you see, my dear, is the beauty which costs nothing.
Daughter [*bowing her head*].   Not that sharp tone, Axel!

Lawyer.   It wasn't sharp.

Daughter.   Yes it was.

Lawyer.   The devil take it!

Daughter.   What kind of language is that?

Lawyer.   Forgive me, Agnes. But I have suffered as much from your untidiness as you do from the dirt. And I haven't dared straighten things myself, because you would have been offended and thought I was reproaching you. Oh, shall we stop this?

Daughter.   It is terribly hard to be married, harder than anything. I think one has to be an angel.

Lawyer.   I think one has.

Daughter.   I am beginning to hate you after all this.

Lawyer.   Alas for us then! But let us prevent hatred. I promise never to mention untidiness again, although it is torture to me.

Daughter.   And I will eat cabbage, although that is torment to me.

Lawyer.   And so—life together is a torment. One's pleasure is the other's pain.

Daughter.   Human beings are pitiful.

Lawyer.   You see that now?

Daughter.   Yes. But in God's name let us avoid the rocks, now that we know them so well.

Lawyer.   Let us do that. We are tolerant, enlightened people. Of course we can make allowances and forgive.

Daughter.   Of course we can smile at trifles.

Lawyer.   We, only we can do it. Do you know, I read in the paper this morning . . . By the way, where is the paper?

Daughter [embarrassed].   Which paper?

Lawyer [harshly].   Do I take more than one newspaper?

Daughter.   Smile—and don't speak harshly! I lit the fire with your newspaper.

Lawyer [violently].   The devil you did!

Daughter.   Please smile. I burnt it because it mocked what to me is holy.

Lawyer.   What to me is unholy! Huh! [*Striking his hands together, beside himself*] I'll smile, I'll smile till my back teeth show. I'll be tolerant and swallow my opinions and say yes to everything and cant and cringe. So you've burnt my paper, have you? [*Pulls the bed curtains*] Very well. Now I'm going to tidy up until you lose your temper . . . Agnes, this is quite impossible!

Daughter.   Indeed it is.

Lawyer.   Yet we must stay together. Not for our vows' sake, but for the child's.

Daughter.   That's true—for the child's sake. Yes, yes, we must go on.

Lawyer.   And now I must attend to my clients. Listen to them muttering. They can't wait to tear one another to pieces, to get each other fined and imprisoned. Benighted souls!

[*Enter* KRISTEN *with pasting materials.*]

Daughter.   Wretched, wretched beings! And all this pasting! [*She bows her head in dumb despair.*]

Kristin.   I paste, I paste!

[*The* LAWYER *standing by the door, nervously fingers the handle.*]

Daughter. Oh how that handle squeaks! It is as if you were twisting my heart-strings.
Lawyer. I twist, I twist!
Daughter. Don't!
Lawyer. I twist . . .
Daughter. No!
Lawyer. I . . .

[*The* OFFICER (*now middle-aged*) *takes hold of the handle from inside the office.*]

Officer. May I?
Lawyer [*letting go of the handle*]. Certainly. As you have got your degree.
Officer [*entering*]. The whole of life is now mine. All paths are open to me. I have set foot on Parnassus, the laurels are won. Immortality, fame, all are mine!
Lawyer. What are you going to live on?
Officer. Live on?
Lawyer. You'll need a roof surely, and clothes and food?
Officer. Those are always to be had, as long as there's someone who cares for you.
Lawyer. Fancy that now, fancy that! Paste, Kristin, paste! Until they cannot breathe. [*Goes out backwards, nodding.*]
Kristin. I paste, I paste! Until they cannot breathe.
Officer. Will you come now?
Daughter. Oh quickly! But where to?
Officer. To Fairhaven, where it is summer and the sun is shining. Youth is there, children and flowers, singing and dancing, feasting and merrymaking.

[*Exit* KRISTIN.]

Daughter. I would like to go there.
Officer. Come!
Lawyer [*entering*]. Now I shall return to my first hell. This one was the second—and worst. The sweetest hell is the worst. Look, she's left hairpins all over the floor again! [*Picks one up.*]
Officer. So he has discovered the hairpins too.
Lawyer. Too? Look at this one. There are two prongs but one pin. Two and yet one. If I straighten it out, it becomes one single piece. If I bend it, it is two, without ceasing to be one. In other words the two are one. But if I break it—like this—[*breaks it in half*]—then the two are two. [*He throws away the pieces.*]
Officer. So much he has seen. But before one can break it, the prongs must diverge. If they converge, it holds.
Lawyer. And if they are parallel, they never meet. Then it neither holds nor breaks.
Officer. The hairpin is the most perfect of all created things. A straight line which is yet two parallel lines.
Lawyer. A lock that closes when open.
Officer. Closes open—a plait of hair loosed while bound.

Lawyer. Like this door. When I close it, I open the way out, for you, Agnes.

[*Goes out, closing the door.*]

Daughter. And now?

[*The scene changes. The bed with its hangings is transformed into a tent, the stove remaining. The new background shows a beautiful wooded shore, with beflagged landing stages and white boats, some with sails set. Among the trees are little Italianesque villas, pavilions, kiosks and marble statues.*
In the middle distance is a strait.
The foreground presents a sharp contrast with the background. Burnt hillsides, black and white tree stumps as after a forest fire, red heather, red pigsties and outhouses. On the right is an open-air establishment for remedial exercise, where people are being treated on machines resembling instruments of torture.
On the left is part of the Quarantine Station; open sheds with furnaces, boilers and pipes.]

[*The* DAUGHTER *and the* OFFICER *are standing as at the end of the previous scene.*]

[*The* QUARANTINE MASTER, *dressed as a blackamoor, comes along the shore.*]

Officer [*going up and shaking hands with the* QUARANTINE MASTER]. What? You here, old Gasbags?[1]
Q. Master. Yes, I'm here.
Officer. Is this place Fairhaven?
Q. Master. No, that's over there. [*Points across the strait*] This is Foulstrand.
Officer. Then we've come wrong.
Q. Master. We! Aren't you going to introduce me?
Officer. It wouldn't do. [*Low*] That is the Daughter of Indra.
Q. Master. Of Indra? I thought it must be Varuna[2] himself. Well, aren't you surprised to find me black in the face?
Officer. My dear fellow, I am over fifty, at which age one ceases to be surprised. I assumed at once that you were going to a fancy dress ball this afternoon.
Q. Master. Quite correct. I hope you'll come with me.
Officer. Certainly, for there doesn't seem to be any attraction in this place. What kind of people live here?
Q. Master. The sick live here, and the healthy over there.
Officer. But surely only the poor here?
Q. Master. No, my boy, here you have the rich. [*Indicates the gymnasium*] Look at that man on the rack. He's eaten too much pâté-de-foie-gras with truffles, and drunk so much Burgundy that his feet are knotted.
Officer. Knotted?

1 Original "Ordström," meaning "Stream of Words" (translator's note).
2 In early Hindu mythology, Varuna seems to be a sky god or a sea god. The name means "coverer" (*cf.* Uranus). The reference here seems to be his later position in Hindu lore, that of a judge and punisher who oversees the order of both cosmos and morality. In the Hindu hierarchy, he is below Brahma but above Indra.

Q. Master. He's got knotted feet, and that one lying on the guillotine has drunk so much brandy that his backbone's got to be mangled.

Officer. That's not very pleasant either.

Q. Master. What's more here on this side live all those who have some misery to hide. Look at this one coming now, for instance.

[*An elderly fop is wheeled on to the stage in a bath chair, accompanied by a gaunt and hideous coquette of sixty, dressed in the latest fashion and attended by the "Friend," a man of forty.*]

Officer. It's the Major! Our schoolfellow.

Q. Master. Don Juan! You see, he's still in love with the spectre at his side. He doesn't see that she has grown old, that she is ugly, faithless, cruel.

Officer. There's true love for you. I never would have thought that flighty fellow had it in him to love so deeply and ardently.

Q. Master. That's a nice way of looking at it.

Officer. I've been in love myself—with Victoria. As a matter of fact I still pace up and down the alley, waiting for her.

Q. Master. So you're the fellow who waits in the alley?

Officer. I am he.

Q. Master. Well, have you got that door open yet?

Officer. No, we're still fighting the case. The Billsticker is out with his fishnet, you see, which delays the taking of evidence. Meanwhile, the Glazier has put in windowpanes at the castle, which has grown half a story. It has been an unusually good year this year—warm and damp.

Q. Master [*pointing to the sheds*]. But you've certainly had nothing like the heat of my place there.

Officer. What's the temperature of your furnaces then?

Q. Master. When we're disinfecting cholera suspects, we keep them at sixty degrees.

Officer. But is there cholera about again?

Q. Master. Didn't you know?

Officer. Of course I know. But I so often forget what I know.

Q. Master. And I so often wish I could forget—especially myself. That's why I go in for masquerades, fancy dress, theatricals.

Officer. Why. What's the matter with you?

Q. Master. If I talk, they say I'm bragging. If I hold my tongue they call me a hypocrite.

Officer. Is that why you blacked your face?

Q. Master. Yes. A shade blacker than I am.

Officer. Who's this coming?

Q. Master. Oh, he's a poet! He's going to have his mud bath.

[*The* POET *enters, looking at the sky and carrying a pail of mud.*]

Officer. But good heavens, he ought to bathe in light and air!

Q. Master. No, he lives so much in the higher spheres that he gets homesick for the mud. It hardens his skin to wallow in the mire, just as it does with pigs. After his bath he doesn't feel the gadflies stinging.

Officer. What a strange world of contradictions!

Poet [*ecstatically*]. Out of clay the god Ptah[1] fashioned man on a potter's wheel, a lathe, [*mockingly*] or some other damned thing . . . [*Ecstatically*] Out of clay the sculptor fashions his more or less immortal masterpieces, [*mockingly*] which are usually only rubbish. [*Ecstatically*] Out of clay are formed those objects, so domestically essential bearing the generic name of pots and pans. [*Mockingly*] Not that it matters in the least to me what they're called. [*Ecstatically*] Such is clay! When clay is fluid, it is called mud. *C'est mon affaire!* [*Calls*] Lina!

[*Enter* LINA *with a bucket.*]

Poet. Lina, show yourself to Miss Agnes! She knew you ten years ago when you were a young, happy, and, let me add, pretty girl. [*To* DAUGHTER] Look at her now! Five children, drudgery, squalling, hunger, blows. See how beauty has perished, how joy has vanished in the fulfilment of duties which should give that inner contentment which shows in the harmonious lines of a face, in the tranquil shining of the eyes . . .

Q. Master [*putting a hand to the* POET's *lips*]. Shut up! Shut up!

Poet. That's what they all say. But if you are silent, they tell you to talk. How inconsistent people are!

[*Distant dance music is heard.*]

Daughter [*going up to* LINA]. Tell me your troubles.

Lina. No, I daren't. I'd catch it all the worse if I did.

Daughter. Who is so cruel?

Lina. I daren't talk about it. I'll be beaten.

Poet. May be, but I shall talk about it even if the Blackamoor knocks my teeth out. I shall talk about all the injustice there is here. Agnes, Daughter of the Gods, do you hear that music up on the hill? Well, that's a dance for Lina's sister, who has come home from town—where she went astray, you understand. Now they are killing the fatted calf, while Lina, who stayed at home, has to carry the swill pail and feed the pigs.

Daughter. There is rejoicing in that home because the wanderer has forsaken the path of evil, not only because she has come home. Remember that.

Poet. Then give a ball and a supper every evening for this blameless servant who has never gone astray. Do that for her—they never do. On the contrary, when Lina is free, she has to go to prayer meetings where she's reprimanded for not being perfect. Is that justice?

Daughter. Your questions are difficult to answer, because there are so many unknown factors.

Poet. The Caliph, Harun the Just,[2] was of the same opinion. Sitting quietly on his exalted throne he could never see how those below were faring. Presently complaints reached his lofty ear, so one fine day he stopped down in disguise and walked unobserved among the crowd to watch the workings of justice.

---

1 The creator of gods and men in the religion of ancient Egypt.

2 Harun-al-Raschid, Caliph of Bagdad (786–809). Romantic tales of how he travelled among his people incognito are told in the *Arabian Nights*.

Daughter.   You do not think I am Harun the Just, do you?
Officer.   Let's change the subject. Here are newcomers.

[*A white boat, shaped like a dragon, glides into the Strait. It has a light blue silken sail on a gilded yard, and a golden mast with a rose-red pennon. At the helm, with their arms round each other's waists, sit* HE *and* SHE.]

There you see perfect happiness, utter bliss, the ecstasy of young love.

[*The light grows stronger.* HE *stands up in the boat and sings.*]

> Hail fairest bay!
> Where I passed youth's spring tide,
> where I dreamed its first roses,
> I come now again,
> no longer alone.
> Forests and havens,
> heaven and sea,
> greet her!
> My love, my bride,
> my sun, my life!

[*The flags on Fairhaven dip in salute. White handkerchiefs wave from villas and shores. The music of harps and violins sound over the strait.*]

Poet.   See how light streams from them! And sound rings across the water! Eros![1]
Officer.   It is Victoria.
Q. Master.   Well, if it is . . .
Officer.   It is his Victoria. I have my own, and mine no one will ever see. Now hoist the quarantine flag while I haul in the catch.

[*The* QUARANTINE MASTER *waves a yellow flag. The* OFFICER *pulls on a line which causes the boat to turn in towards Foulstrand.*]

Hold hard there!

[HE *and* SHE *become aware of the dreadful landscape and show their horror.*]

Q. Master.   Yes, yes, it's hard lines, but everyone has to land here, everyone coming from infectious areas.
Poet.   Think of being able to speak like that—to behave like that when you see two human beings joined in love. Do not touch them! Do not lay hands on love—that is high treason. Alas, alas! All that is most lovely will now be dragged down, down into the mud.

[HE *and* SHE *come ashore, shamed and sad.*]

He.   What is it? What have we done?
Q. Master.   You don't have to do anything in order to meet with life's little discomforts.
She.   How brief are joy and happiness!
He.   How long must we stay here?

---

[1]   Greek god of love.

Q. Master.   Forty days and forty nights.

She.   We would rather throw ourselves into the sea.

He.   Live here—among burnt hills and pigsties?

Poet.   Love can overcome everything, even sulphur fumes and carbolic acid.[1]

[*The* QUARANTINE MASTER *goes into a shed. Blue sulphurous vapour pours out.*]

Q. Master [*coming out*].   I'm burning the sulphur. Will you kindly step inside.

She.   Oh, my blue dress will lose its colour!

Q. Masster.   And turn white. Your red roses will turn white too.

He.   So will your cheeks, in forty days.

She [*to the* OFFICER].   That will please you.

Officer.   No, it won't. True, your happiness was the source of my misery, but
. . . that's no matter. [HE *and* SHE *go into the shed*] [*To* DAUGHTER] I've got
my degree now, and a job as tutor over there. [*Indicates Fairhaven*] Heigho!
And in the fall I'll get a post in a school, teaching the boys the same lessons I
learnt myself, all through my childhood, all through my youth. Teach them the
same lessons I learnt all through my manhood and finally all through my old
age. The same lessons! What is twice two? How many times does two go into
four without remainder? Until I get a pension and have nothing to do but wait
for meals and the newspapers, until in the end I'm carried out to the crema-
torium and burnt to ashes.

[*To* QUARANTINE MASTER *as he comes out of the shed.*]

Have you no pensioners here? To be a pensioner is the worst fate after the twice
two is four, going to school again when one's taken one's degree, asking the
same questions until one dies . . .

[*An elderly man walks past with his hands behind his back.*]

Look, there goes a pensioner waiting for his life to ebb. A Captain, probably,
who failed to become a Major, or a Clerk to the Court who was never promoted. Many are called, but few are chosen. He's just walking about, waiting
for breakfast.

Pensioner.   No, for the paper, the morning paper!

Officer.   And he is only fifty-four. He may go on for another twenty-five years,
waiting for meals and the newspaper. Isn't that dreadful?

Pensioner.   What is not dreadful? Tell me that. Tell me that.

Officer.   Yes. Let him tell who can.

[*Exit* PENSIONER.]

Now I shall teach boys twice two is four. How many times does two go into four
without remainder? [*He clutches his head in despair.*]

[*Enter* HE *and* SHE *from the shed. Her dress and roses are white, her face pale.
His clothes are also bleached.*]

---

1   The Poet does not speak again and is not mentioned until the end of the later quayside
scene, so perhaps here he goes out (translator's note).

And Victoria whom I loved, for whom I desired the greatest happiness on earth, she has her happiness now, the greatest happiness she can know, while I suffer, suffer, suffer!

She. Do you think I can be happy, seeing your suffering? How can you believe that? Perhaps it comforts you to know that I shall be a prisoner here for forty days and forty nights. Tell me, does it comfort you?

Officer. Yes and no. I cannot have pleasure while you have pain. Oh!

He. And do you think my happiness can be built on your agony?

Officer. We are all to be pitied—all of us.

[*All lift their hands to heaven. A discordant cry of anguish breaks from their lips.*]

All. Oh!

Daughter. O God, hear them! Life is evil! Mankind is to be pitied.

All [*as before*]. Oh!

[*The stage is blacked out and the scene changes.*
The whole landscape is in winter dress with snow on the ground and on the leafless trees. Foulstrand is in the background, in shadow.
The strait is still in the middle distance. On the near side is a landing stage with white boats and flags flying from flagstaffs. In the strait a white warship, a brig with gunports, is anchored.
The foreground presents Fairhaven, in full light.
On the right is a corner of the Assembly Rooms with open windows through which are seen couples dancing. On a box outside stand three MAIDS, *their arms round each other's waists, watching the dancing.*
On the steps is a bench on which UGLY EDITH *is sitting, bareheaded and sorrowful, with long dishevelled hair, before an open piano.*
On the left is a yellow wooden house outside which two children in summer dresses are playing ball.]

[*The* DAUGHTER *and* OFFICER *enter.*]

Daughter. Here is peace and happiness. Holiday time. Work over, every day a festival, everyone in holiday attire. Music and dancing even in the morning. [*To the* MAIDS] Why don't you go in and dance, my dears?

Servants. Us?

Officer. But they are servants.

Daughter. True. But why is Edith sitting there instead of dancing?

[EDITH *buries her face in her hands.*]

Officer. Don't ask her! She has been sitting there for three hours without being invited to dance. [*He goes into the yellow house.*]

Daughter. What cruel pleasure!

[*The* MOTHER, *in a décolleté dress, comes out of the Assembly Rooms and goes up to* EDITH.]

Mother. Why don't you go in as I told you?

Edith. Because . . . because I can't be my own partner. I know I'm ugly and no one wants to dance with me, but I can avoid being reminded of it. [*She begins to play Bach's Toccata con Fuga, No. 10.*]

[*The waltz at the ball is heard too, first faintly, then growing louder as if in competition with the Toccata. Gradually* EDITH *overcomes it and reduces it to silence. Dance couples appear in the doorway, and everyone stands reverently listening.*]

[*A* NAVAL OFFICER *seizes* ALICE, *one of the guests, by the waist.*]

N. *Officer.*   Come, quick! [*He leads her down to the landing stage.* EDITH *breaks off, rises and watches them in despair. She remains standing as if turned to stone.*]

[*The front wall of the yellow house vanishes. Boys are sitting on forms, among them the* OFFICER *looking uncomfortable and worried. In front of them stands the* SCHOOLMASTER, *wearing spectacles and holding chalk and a cane.*]

Schoolmaster [*to the* OFFICER].   Now, my boy, can you tell me what twice two is?

[*The* OFFICER *remains seated, painfully searching his memory without finding an answer.*]

You must stand up when you are asked a question.

Officer [*rising anxiously*].   Twice two . . . let me see . . . That makes two twos.

S. *Master.*   Aha! So you have not prepared your lesson.

Officer [*embarrassed*].   Yes, I have, but . . . I know what it is, but I can't say it.

S. *Master.*   You're quibbling. You know the answer, do you? But you can't say it. Perhaps I can assist you. [*Pulls the* OFFICER's *hair.*]

Officer.   Oh, this is dreadful, really dreadful!

S. *Master.*   Yes, it is dreadful that such a big boy should have no ambition.

Officer [*agonised*].   A *big* boy. Yes. I certainly am big, much bigger than these others. I am grown up, I have left school . . . [*As if waking*] I have even graduated. Why am I sitting here then? Haven't I got my degree?

S. *Master.*   Certainly. But you have got to stay here and mature. Do you see? You must mature. Isn't that so?

Officer [*clasping his head*].   Yes, that's so, one must mature . . . Twice two—is two, and this I will demonstrate by analogy, the highest form of proof. Listen! Once one is one, therefore twice two is two. For that which applies to the one must also apply to the other.

S. *Master.*   The proof is perfectly in accord with the laws of logic, but the answer is wrong.

Officer.   What is in accord with the laws of logic cannot be wrong. Let us put it to the test. One into one goes once, therefore two into two goes twice.

S. *Master.*   Quite correct according to analogy. But what then is once three?

Officer.   It is three.

S. *Master.*   Consequently twice three is also three.

Officer [*pondering*].   No, that can't be right . . . It can't be, for if so . . . [*Sits down in despair*] No, I am not mature yet . . .

S. *Master.*   No, you are not mature by a long way.

Officer.   Then how long shall I have to stay here?

S. Master.   How long? Here? You believe that time and space exist? Assuming time does exist, you ought to be able to say what time is. What is time?

Officer.   Time . . . [*Considers*] I can't say, although I know what it is. Ergo, I may know what twice two is without being able to say it. Can you yourself say what time is?

S. Master.   Certainly I can.

All the Boys.   Tell us then!

S. Master.   Time? . . . Let me see. [*Stands motionless with his finger to his nose*] While we speak, time flies. Consequently time is something which flies while I am speaking.

Boy [*rising*].   You're speaking now, sir, and while you're speaking, I fly. Consequently I am time. [*Flies.*]

S. Master.   That is quite correct according to the laws of logic.

Officer.   Then the laws of logic are absurd, for Nils, though he did fly, can't be time.

S. Master.   That is also quite correct according to the laws of logic, although it is absurd.

Officer.   Then logic is absurd.

S. Master.   It really looks like it. But if logic is absurd, then the whole world is absurd . . . and I'll be damned if I stay here and teach you absurdities! If anyone will stand us a drink, we'll go and bathe.

Officer.   That's a *posterus prius*, a world back to front, for it's customary to bathe first and have one's drink afterwards. You old fossil!

S. Master.   Don't be so conceited, Doctor.

Officer.   Captain, if you please. I am an officer, and I don't understand why I should sit here among a lot of schoolboys and be insulted.

S. Master [*wagging his finger*].   We must mature!

[*Enter* QUARANTINE MASTER.]

Q. Master.   The quarantine period has begun.

Officer.   So there you are. Fancy this fellow making me sit here on a form, when I've taken my degree.

Q. Master.   Well, why don't you go away?

Officer.   Go away? That's easier said than done.

S. Master.   So I should think. Try!

Officer [*to* QUARANTINE MASTER].   Save me! Save me from his eyes!

Q. Master.   Come on then! Come and help us dance. We must dance before the plague breaks out. We must.

Officer.   Will the ship sail then?

Q. Master.   The ship will sail first. A lot of tears will be shed of course.

Officer.   Always tears; when she comes in and when she sails. Let's go.

[*They go out. The* SCHOOLMASTER *continues to give his lesson in mime.*]

[*The* MAIDS, *who were standing at the window of the ballroom, walk sadly down to the quay.* EDITH, *until then motionless beside the piano, follows them.*]

Daughter [*to* OFFICER].   Isn't there one happy person in this paradise?

Officer.   Yes, here comes a newly wed couple. Listen to them.

[*The* NEWLY WED COUPLE *enter.*]

Husband [*to* WIFE].   My happiness is so complete that I wish to die.
Wife.   But why to die?
Husband.   In the midst of happiness grows a seed of unhappiness. Happiness consumes itself like a flame. It cannot burn for ever, it must go out, and the presentiment of its end destroys it at its very peak.
Wife.   Let us die together, now at once.
Husband.   Die! Yes, let us die. For I fear happiness, the deceiver.

[*They go towards the sea and disappear.*]

Daughter [*to the* OFFICER].   Life is evil. Human beings are to be pitied!
Officer.   Look who's coming now. This is the most envied mortal in the place [*The* BLIND MAN *is led in*] He is the owner of these hundreds of Italian villas. He owns all these bays and creeks and shores and woods, the fish in the water, the birds in the air and the game in the woods. These thousands of people are his tenants, and the sun rises over his sea and sets over his lands.
Daughter.   And does he complain too?
Officer.   Yes, with good cause, as he cannot see.
Q. Master.   He is blind.
Daughter.   The most envied of all!
Officer.   Now he's going to see the ship sail with his son aboard.
Blind Man.   I do not see, but I hear. I hear the fluke of the anchor tearing the clay bed, just as when the hook is dragged out of a fish and the heart comes up too through the gullet. My son, my only child, is going to journey to strange lands across the great sea. Only my thoughts can go with him . . . Now I hear the chain clanking . . . and there's something flapping and lashing like washing on a clothes line . . . Wet handkerchiefs perhaps . . . And I hear a sound of sighing . . . or sobbing . . . like people crying . . . Maybe the plash of small waves against the hull, or maybe the girls on the quay, the abandoned, the inconsolable. I once asked a child why the sea was salt, and the child, whose father was on a long voyage, replied at once: "The sea is salt because sailors cry so much." "But why do sailors cry so much?" "Well," he said, "because they keep going away . . . And so they're always drying their handkerchiefs up on the masts." "And why do people cry when they're sad?" I asked. "Oh," said he, "that's because the eye window must be washed sometimes, so we can see better."

[*The brig has set sail and glided away. The girls on the quay alternately wave their handkerchiefs and dry their eyes. Now on the topmast is hoisted the signal* "YES," *a red ball on a white ground.* ALICE *waves a triumphant reply.*

Daughter [*to* OFFICER].   What does that flag mean?
Officer.   It means "yes." It is the lieutenant's "yes" in red, red as heart's blood, written on the blue cloth of the sky.
Daughter.   Then what is "no" like?
Officer.   Blue as tainted blood in blue veins. Look how elated Alice is.
Daughter.   And how Edith is weeping.

Blind Man.   Meeting and parting, parting and meeting. That's life. I met his
mother, then she went away. My son was left; now he has gone.
Daughter.   But he will come back.
Blind Man.   Who is speaking to me? I have heard that voice before. In my
dreams, in boyhood when summer holidays began, in early married life when my
child was born. Whenever life smiled, I heard that voice, like the whisper of the
South wind, like the sounds of a heavenly harp, like the angels' greeting, as I
imagine it, on Christmas Eve.

[*The* LAWYER *enters, goes up to the* BLIND MAN *and whispers.*]

Really?
Lawyer.   Yes, it's a fact. [*Goes across to the* DAUGHTER] You have seen most
things now, but you have not yet experienced the worst thing of all.
Daughter.   What can that be?
Lawyer.   Repetitions, reiterations. Going back. Doing one's lessons again . . .
Come!
Daughter.   Where to?
Lawyer.   To your duties.
Daughter.   What are they?
Lawyer.   Everything you abominate. Everything you least want to do, and yet
must. They are to abstain and renounce, to go without, to leave behind. They
are everything that is disagreeable, repulsive, painful.
Daughter.   Are there no pleasant duties?
Lawyer.   They become pleasant when they are done.
Daughter.   When they no longer exist. So duty is altogether unpleasant. What
then can one enjoy?
Lawyer.   What one enjoys is sin.
Daughter.   Sin?
Lawyer.   Which is punished. Yes. If I enjoy myself one day, one evening, the
next day I have a bad conscience and go through the torments of hell.
Daughter.   How strange!
Lawyer.   I wake in the morning with a headache, and then the repetition begins,
but it is a distorted repetition, so that everything which was charming and witty
and beautiful the night before appears in memory ugly, stupid, repulsive.
Pleasure stinks, and enjoyment falls to pieces. What people call success is always
a step towards the next failure. The successes in my life have been my downfall.
Men have an instinctive dread of another's good fortune. They feel it's unjust
that fate should favour any one man, so try to restore the balance by rolling
boulders across his path. To have talent is to be in danger of one's life—one
may so easily starve to death. However, you must go back to your duties, or I
shall take proceedings against you, and we shall go through all three Courts,
first, second, third.
Daughter.   Go back? To the stove and the cabbage and the baby clothes?
Lawyer.   Yes. And it's washing day—the big wash when all the handkerchiefs
have to be done.
Daughter.   Oh, must I do that again?
Lawyer.   The whole of life is only repetition. Look at the schoolmaster there.
Yesterday he took his doctor's degree, was crowned with laurels, scaled Parnas-

sus, was embraced by the monarch. Today he is back at school, asking what twice two is . . . and that's what he will go on doing until he dies. But come now, back to your home.

Daughter. I would rather die.

Lawyer. Die? One can't do that. To begin with taking one's own life is so dishonourable that even one's corpse is dishonoured. And to add to that one is damned, for it is a mortal sin.

Daughter. It is not easy to be human.

All. Hear, hear!

Daughter. I will not go back with you to humiliation and dirt. I shall return to the place from which I came. But first the door must be opened, so that I may know the secret. I wish the door to be opened.

[*Enter the* POET.]

Lawyer. Then you must retrace your steps, go back the way you came, and put up with all the horrors of a lawsuit; the repetitions, the redraftings, the re-iterations.

Daughter. So be it. But first I shall seek solitude in the wilderness to find myself. We shall meet again. [*To the* POET.] Come with me.

[*A distant cry of lamentation rises.*]

Voices. Oh! oh! oh!

Daughter. What was that?

Lawyer. The doomed at Foulstrand.

Daughter. Why do they wail so today?

Lawyer. Because here the sun is shining, here is music and dance and youth. This makes them suffer more.

Daughter. We must set them free.

Lawyer. Try! Once a deliverer came, but he was hanged upon a cross.

Daughter. By whom?

Lawyer. By all the righteous.

Daughter. Who are they?

Lawyer. Don't you know the righteous? Well, you will.

Daughter. Was it they who refused you your degree?

Lawyer. Yes.

Daughter. Then I do know them.

[*The scene changes to a Mediterranean resort. In the background are villas, a Casino with a terrace, and a blue strip of sea. In the foreground is a white wall over which hang branches of orange trees in fruit. Below this to one side a huge heap of coal and two wheelbarrows.*

The DAUGHTER *and the* LAWYER *come on to the terrace.*]

Daughter. This is paradise.

1st. Coal Heaver. This is hell.

2nd. Coal Heaver. A hundred and twenty in the shade.

1st. Coal Heaver. Shall we get into the sea?

2nd. Coal Heaver. Then the police'd come: "You mustn't bathe here!"

1st. Coal Heaver.   Can't we have a bit of fruit off that tree?

2nd. Coal Heaver.   No. The police would come.

1st. Coal Heaver.   One can't work in this heat. I'm going to chuck it.

2nd. Coal Heaver.   Then the police will come and take you up. [*Pause.*] Besides, you'll have nothing to eat.

1st. Coal Heaver.   Nothing to eat! We, who do the most work, get the least food. And the rich, who do nothing, get it all. Might one not, without taking liberties with the truth, call this unjust? What has the Daughter of the Gods up there to say about it?

Daughter.   I have no answer. But, tell me, what have you done to get so black and have so hard a lot?

1st. Coal Heaver.   What have we done? Got ourselves born of poor and pretty bad parents. Been sentenced a couple of times maybe.

Daughter.   Sentenced?

1st. Coal Heaver.   Yes. The ones that don't get caught sit up there in the Casino eating eight course dinners with wine.

Daughter [*to* LAWYER].   Can this be true?

Lawyer.   More or less, yes.

Daughter.   Do you mean that everyone at some time or other deserves imprisonment?

Lawyer.   Yes.

Daughter.   Even you?

Lawyer.   Yes.

Daughter.   Is it true those poor men aren't allowed to bathe in that sea?

Lawyer.   No, not even with their clothes on. Only those who try to drown themselves avoid paying. And they are more than likely to get beaten up at the police station.

Daughter.   Can't they go and bathe outside the town—in the country?

Lawyer.   There is no country. It's all fenced in.

Daughter.   I mean where it is open and free.

Lawyer.   Nothing is free. Everything is owned.

Daughter.   Even the sea, the vast, wide . . .?

Lawyer.   Everything. You can't go out in a boat, nor can you land, without it all being booked and paid for. It's marvellous.

Daughter.   This is not paradise.

Lawyer.   I promise you that.

Daughter.   Why don't people do anything to improve conditions?

Lawyer.   They certainly do. But all reformers end in prison or the madhouse.

Daughter.   Who puts them in prison?

Lawyer.   All the righteous, all the respectable.

Daughter.   Who puts them in the madhouse?

Lawyer.   Their own despair when they see the hopelessness of the struggle.

Daughter.   Has it occurred to anyone that there may be unknown reasons for this state of things?

Lawyer.   Yes, the well-off always think that is so.

Daughter.   That there is nothing wrong with things as they are?

1st. Coal Heaver.   And yet we are the foundation of society. If there's no coal, the kitchen stove goes out and the fire on the hearth too. The machines in the factory stop working; the lights in streets and shops and homes all go out. Darkness and cold descend on you. That's why we sweat like hell carrying filthy coal. What do you give us in return?

Lawyer [*to* DAUGHTER].   Help them. [*Pause*.] I know things can't be exactly the same for everybody, but why should there be such inequality?

[*The* GENTLEMAN *and the* LADY *cross the terrace*.]

Lady.   Are you coming to play cards?

Gentleman.   No, I must go for a little walk to get an appetite for dinner.

[*Exeunt*.]

1st. Coal Heaver.   To get an appetite!

2nd. Coal Heaver.   To get . . . !

[*Children enter. When they catch sight of the black workers they scream with terror and run off*.]

1st. Coal Heaver.   They scream when they see us. They scream!

2nd Coal Heaver.   Curse it! We'd better get out the scaffolds soon and execute this rotten body.

1st. Coal Heaver.   Curse it, I say too!

Lawyer [*to* DAUGHTER].   It's all wrong. It's not the people who are so bad, but . . .

Daughter.   But?

Lawyer.   The system.

Daughter [*hiding her face in her hands*].   This is not paradise.

1st. Coal Heaver.   No. This is hell, pure hell.

[*The scene changes to* (*the earlier set of*) *Fingal's Cave*.[1] *Long green billows roll gently into the cave. A red bellbuoy rocks upon the waves, but gives no sound until later. Music of the winds. Music of the waves. The* DAUGHTER *is with the* POET.]

Poet.   Where have you brought me?

Daughter.   Far from the murmur and wailing of the children of men. To this grotto at the ends of the oceans to which we give the name *Indra's Ear*, for here, it is said, the King of Heaven listens to the lamentations of mortals.

Poet.   Why here?

Daughter.   Do you not see that this cave is shaped like a shell? Yes, you see it. Do you not know that your ear is shaped like a shell? You know, but you have given it no thought. [*She picks up a shell*.] As a child, did you never hold a shell to your ear and listen to the whisper of your heart's blood, to the humming of thoughts in your brain, to the parting of a thousand little worn-out tissues in the fabric of your body? All this you can hear in a small shell. Think then what may be heard in this great one.

---

[1]   A grotto on Staffa Island, one of the Inner Hebrides off the coast of Scotland. Fingal, a hero of Irish legend, was a defender of the downtrodden.

Poet [*listening*].   I hear nothing but the sighing of the wind.
Daughter.   Then I will be its interpreter. Listen to the lamentation of the winds.

[*She speaks to soft music.*]

> Born under heaven's clouds,
> chased were we by Indra's fires
> down to the crust of earth.
> The mould of acres soiled our feet,
> we had to bear
> the dust of roads and city smoke,
> the kitchen's reek and fumes of wine.
> Out to these spacious seas we blew,
> to air our lungs,
> to shake our wings
> and bathe our feet.
> Indra, Lord of Heaven,
> hear us!
> Listen to our sighing!
> Earth is not clean,
> life is not just,
> men are not evil
> nor are they good.
> They live as best they may
> from one day to another,
> Sons of dust in dust they walk,
> born of the dust,
> dust they become.
> Feet they have to trudge,
> no wings.
> Dust-soiled they grow.
> Is the fault theirs
> or Thine?

Poet.   So I heard once . . .
Daughter.   Hush! The winds are still singing.

[*Continues to soft music.*]

> We, the winds, the sons of air,
> bear man's lamentation.
> Thou hast heard us
> on autumn eves in the chimney stack,
> in the stove-pipe's vent,
> in the window cracks,
> as the rain wept on the tiles.
> Or on winter nights,
> mid the pine-wood's snows,
> or on the stormy ocean,
> hast heard the moaning and the whine,
> of rope and sail.
> That is us, the winds,
> the sons of air,

> who from human breasts
> we pierced ourselves,
> these sounds of suffering learnt.
> In sickroom, on the battlefield,
> and most where the newborn lie,
> screaming, complaining,
> of the pain of being alive.
> It is we, we, the winds
> who whine and whistle,
> woe! woe! woe!

Poet. It seems to me that once before . . .
Daughter. Hush! The waves are singing.

[*Speaks to soft music.*]

> It is we, we the waves,
> that rock the winds
> to rest.
> Green cradling waves,
> wet are we and salt.
> Like flames of fire,
> wet flames we are.
> Quenching, burning,
> cleansing, bathing,
> generating, multiplying.
> We, we the waves,
> that rock the winds
> to rest.

False waves and faithless. Everything on earth that is not burned is drowned by those waves. Look there! [*She points to the wreckage.*] Look what the sea has stolen and destroyed! All that remains of those sunken ships is their figure-heads . . . and the names—Justice, Friendship, Golden Peace, and Hope. That's all that's left of hope, treacherous hope. Spars, rowlocks, bailers. And see! The lifebuoy which saved itself, letting those in need perish.

Poet [*searching the wreckage*]. Here is the name of the ship Justice. This is the ship which sailed from Fairhaven with the Blind Man's son on board. So she sank. And Alice's sweetheart was in her too, Edith's hopeless love.

Daughter. The blind man? Fairhaven? Surely that I dreamt. Alice's sweetheart, ugly Edith, Foulstrand and the quarantine, the sulphur and carbolic, graduation in the church, the lawyer's office, the alley and Victoria, The Growing Castle and the Officer . . . These things I dreamt.

Poet. Of these things I once made poetry.

Daughter. You know then what poetry is?

Poet. I know what dreams are. What is poetry?

Daughter. Not reality, but more than reality. Not dreams, but waking dreams.

Poet. Yet the children of men believe that poets merely play—invent and fabricate.

Daughter. It is just as well, my friend, or else the world would be laid waste from lack of endeavour. All men would lie upon their backs, gazing at the heavens; no hand would be lifted to plough or spade, or plane or axe.

Poet.   Do you speak thus, Daughter of Indra? You, who are half of heaven?

Daughter.   You are right to reproach me. I have lived too long down here, and like you have bathed in mud. My thoughts can no longer fly. Clay is on their wings and soil about their feet. And I myself [*she raises her arms*] I am sinking, sinking! Help me, Father, God of Heaven! [*Silence.*] No longer can I hear His answer. The ether no longer carries the sound of His lips to the shell of my ear . . . the silver thread has snapped. Alas, I am earth-bound!

Poet.   Do you mean then soon—to go?

Daughter.   As soon as I have burnt this earthly matter, for the waters of the ocean cannot cleanse me. Why do you ask?

Poet.   I have a prayer—a petition.

Daughter.   A petition?

Poet.   A petition from mankind to the ruler of the universe, drawn up by a dreamer.

Daughter.   Who is to present it?

Poet.   Indra's Daughter.

Daughter.   Can you speak the words?

Poet.   I can.

Daughter.   Speak them then.

Poet.   It is better that you should.

Daughter.   Where shall I read them?

Poet.   In my thoughts—or here. [*He gives her a scroll.*]

Daughter.   So be it. I will speak them. [*She takes the scroll but does not read.*]

> "Why with anguish are you born?
> Why do you hurt your mother so,
> Child of man, when bringing her
> the joy of motherhood,
> joy beyond all other joys?
> Why wake to life,
> why greet the light
> with a cry of fury and of pain,
> Child of man, when to be glad
> should be the gift of life?
> Why are we born like animals?
> We who stem from God and man,
> whose souls are longing to be clothed
> in other than this blood and filth.
> Must God's own image cut its teeth?"

[*Speaking her own thoughts.*]

Silence! No more! The work may not condemn the master. Life's riddle still remains unsolved.

[*Continuing the* POET's *bitter words.*]

> "And then the journey's course begins,
> over thistles, thorns and stones.
> If it should touch a beaten track,
> comes at once the cry: 'Keep off!'

Pluck a flower, straight you'll find
the bloom you picked to be another's.
If cornfields lie across your path
and you must pursue your way,
trampling on another's crops,
others then will trample yours
that your loss may equal theirs.
Every pleasure you enjoy
brings to all your fellows sorrow,
yet your sorrow gives no gladness.
So sorrow, sorrow upon sorrow
on your way—until you're dead
and then, alas, give others bread.

[Her own thought.]

Poet.

Is it thus, O son of dust,
You seek to win the ear of God?
How may son of dust find words,
so pure, so light, so luminous,
that they can rise up from the earth?
Child of the Gods, translate for me,
this lamentation into speech
fit for Immortal ears.

Daughter. I will.

Poet [pointing]. What is floating there—a buoy?

Daughter. Yes.

Poet. It is like a lung with a windpipe.

Daughter. It is the watchman of the sea. When danger is abroad, it sings.

Poet. It seems to me that the sea is rising, and the waves beginning to . . .

Daughter. You are not mistaken.

Poet. Alas, what do I see? A ship—on the rocks.

Daughter. What ship can it be?

Poet. I believe it is the ghost-ship.

Daughter. What is that?

Poet. The Flying Dutchman.[1]

Daughter. He? Why is he punished so cruelly, and why does he not come ashore?

Poet. Because he had seven unfaithful wives.

Daughter. Shall he be punished for that?

Poet. Yes. All righteous men condemned him.

Daughter. Incomprehensible world! How can he be freed from this curse?

Poet. Freed? One would beware of freeing him.

Daughter. Why?

Poet. Because . . . No, that is not the Dutchman. It is an ordinary ship in distress. Then why does the buoy not sound? Look how the sea is rising! The waves are towering, and soon we shall be imprisoned in this cave. Now the

---

[1] Several legends surround this spectre ship and its captain, condemned to sail forever without making port.

ship's bell is ringing. Soon there will be another figurehead in here. Cry out buoy! Watchman, do your duty!

[*The buoy sounds a four-part chord in fifths and sixths, like foghorns.*]

The crew is waving to us . . . but we ourselves perish.
Daughter. Do you not want to be set free?
Poet. Yes, yes I do! But not now . . . and not by water!
The Crew [*singing four-part*]. Christ Kyrie!
Poet. They are calling and the sea is calling. But no one hears.
Crew [*singing as before*]. Christ Kyrie!
Daughter. Who is it coming there?
Poet. Walking upon the water! Only One walks upon the water. It is not Peter, the rock, for he sank like a stone.

[*A white light appears over the sea.*]

Crew [*as before*]. Christ Kyrie!
Daughter. Is it He?
Poet. It is He, the crucified.
Daughter. Why, tell me why He was crucified.
Poet. Because He wished to set men free.
Daughter. Who—I have forgotten—who crucified Him?

[*The cave grows darker.*]

Poet. All righteous men.
Daughter. This incomprehensible world!
Poet. The sea is rising. Darkness is falling on us. The storm is growing wilder.

[*The* CREW *shriek.*]

The crew are screaming with horror because they have seen their Saviour . . . and now . . . they are throwing themselves overboard in terror of the Redeemer.

[*The* CREW *shriek again.*]

Now they are screaming because they are going to die. They were born screaming and they die screaming.

[*The mounting waves threaten to drown them in the cave. The light begins to change.*]

Daughter. If I were sure it was a ship . . .
Poet. Indeed, I do not think it is a ship. It's a two storied house, with trees round it . . . and a telephone tower—a tower reaching to the skies. It's the modern Tower of Babel, sending up its wires to communicate with those above.
Daughter. Child, man's thought needs no wires for its flight. The prayers of the devout penetrate all worlds. That is surely no Tower of Babel. If you wish to storm the heavens, storm them with your prayers.
Poet. No, it's not a house . . . not a telephone tower. Do you see?
Daughter. What do you see?

[*During the following speech, the scene changes to the alley of the Opera House.*]

Poet. I see a snow-covered heath . . . a parade ground. The winter sun is shining behind a church on the hill, so that the tower casts its long shadow on the snow. Now a troop of soldiers comes marching over the heath. They march on the tower and up the spire . . . Now they are on the cross, and I seem to know that the first to tread on the weathercock must die . . . They are drawing near it. It's the Corporal at their head who . . . Ah! A cloud is sailing over the heath, across the sun . . . Now everything has gone. The moisture of the cloud has put out the fire of the sun. The sunlight created a shadowy image of the tower, but the shadow of the cloud smothered the image of the tower.

[*It is springtime. The tree and the monkshood are in bud. The* STAGE DOOR-KEEPER *sits in her old place. The* DAUGHTER *enters, followed by the* POET.]

Daughter [*to* DOORKEEPER]. Has the Chancellor arrived yet?
Doorkeeper. No.
Daughter. Nor the Deans?
Doorkeeper. No.
Daughter. You must send for them at once. The door is going to be opened.
Doorkeeper. Is it so urgent?
Daughter. Yes. It's thought that the answer to the riddle of the universe is locked up in there. So send for the Chancellor and the Deans of the four Faculties. [*The* DOORKEEPER *blows a whistle.*] And don't forget the Glazier and his diamond, or nothing can be done.

[*The personnel of the Opera pour from the building as in the earlier scene. The* OFFICER (*young again*), *in morning coat and top hat, comes through the gate, carrying a bouquet of roses and looking radiantly happy.*]

Officer [*singing*]. Victoria!
Doorkeeper. The young lady will be down in a minute.
Officer. Good. The carriage is waiting, the table is laid, the champagne is on the ice . . . Let me embrace you, Madam. [*Embraces the* DOORKEEPER]. Victoria!
Woman's Voice [*from above, singing*]. I am here.
Officer [*pacing*]. Well, I am waiting.
Poet. I seem to have lived through all this before.
Daughter. I too.
Poet. Perhaps I dreamt it.
Daughter. Or made a poem of it.
Poet. Or made a poem.
Daughter. You know then what poetry is.
Poet. I know what dreaming is.
Daughter. I feel that once before, somewhere else, we said these words.
Poet. Then soon you will know what reality is.
Daughter. Or dreaming.
Poet. Or poetry.

[*Enter the* CHANCELLOR *and the* DEANS OF THEOLOGY, PHILOSOPHY, MEDICINE *and* LAW, *followed by the* GLAZIER *and a group of* RIGHTEOUS PEOPLE].

Chancellor. It's all a question of the door, you understand. What does the Dean of Theology think about it?

Dean of Theology. I don't think—I believe. Credo.

Dean of Philosophy. I think.

Dean of Medicine. I know.

Dean of Law. I doubt—until I have heard the evidence and witnesses.

Chancellor. Now they will quarrel again. Well then, first what does Theology believe?

Theology. I believe that this door ought not to be opened, as it conceals dangerous truths.

Philosophy. The truth is never dangerous.

Medicine. What is truth?

Law. Whatever can be proved by two witnesses.

Theology. Anything can be proved by two false witnesses—if you're a pettifogger.

Philosophy. Truth is wisdom, and wisdom and knowledge are philosophy itself. Philosophy is the science of sciences, the knowledge of knowledge. All other sciences are its servants.

Medicine. The only science is natural science. Philosophy is not science. It is mere empty speculation.

Theology. Bravo!

Philosophy [*to* DEAN OF THEOLOGY]. You say bravo. And what, may I ask, are you? The arch enemy of knowledge, the antithesis of science. You are ignorance and darkness.

Medicine. Bravo!

Theology [*to* DEAN OF MEDICINE]. And you say bravo—you who can't see further than the end of your own nose in a magnifying glass. You who believe in nothing but your deceptive senses—in your eyes, for instance, which may be long-sighted, short-sighted, blind, purblind, squinting, one-eyed, colour-blind, red-blind, green-blind . . .

Medicine. Blockhead!

Theology. Ass!

[*They fight.*]

Chancellor. Enough! Birds of a feather shouldn't peck each other's eyes out.

Philosophy. Had I to choose between these two, Theology and Medicine, I should choose—neither.

Law. And if I had to sit in judgment over you three, I should condemn—every one of you . . . You can't agree upon a single point, and never have been able to. Let's get back to the matter in hand. What's your opinion, Chancellor, of this door and the opening of it?

Chancellor. Opinion? I don't have opinions. I am merely appointed by the Government to see you don't break each other's arms and legs in the Senate in the course of educating the young. Opinions? No, I take good care not to have any. I had a few once, but they were soon exploded. Opinions always are exploded—by opponents, of course. Perhaps we had better have the door opened now, even at the risk of it concealing dangerous truths.

Law. What is truth? What is the truth?

Theology. I am the Truth and the Life . . .

Philosophy. I am the knowledge of knowledge.

Medicine. I am exact knowledge . . .

Law. I doubt.

[*They fight.*]

Daughter. Shame on you, teachers of youth!

Law. Chancellor, as delegate of the Government and head of the teaching staff, denounce this woman. She has cried "shame on you" which is contumely, and she has ironically referred to you as "teachers of youth," which is slander.

Daughter. Poor youth!

Law. She pities youth, and that's tantamount to accusing us. Chancellor, denounce her!

Daughter. Yes, I accuse you—all of you—of sowing the seeds of doubt and dissension in the minds of the young.

Law. Listen to her! She herself is raising doubts in the young as to our authority, yet she is accusing us of raising doubts. I appeal to all righteous men. Is this not a criminal offence?

All the Righteous. Yes, it is criminal.

Law. The righteous have condemned you. Go in peace with your gains. Otherwise . . .

Daughter. My gains? Otherwise what?

Law. Otherwise you will be stoned.

Poet. Or crucified.

Daughter [*to the* POET]. I am going. Come with me and learn the answer to the riddle.

Poet. Which riddle?

Daughter. What does he mean by my "gains"?

Poet. Probably nothing at all. That's what we call idle chatter. He was just chattering.

Daughter. But that hurt me more than anything else.

Poet. That's why he said it. Human beings are like that.

[*The* GLAZIER *opens the door and looks inside.*]

All the Righteous. Hurrah! The door is open.

[*The* DEANS *look inside.*]

Chancellor. What was concealed behind that door?

Glazier. I can't see anything.

Chancellor. He can't see anything. Well, I'm not surprised. Deans! What was concealed behind that door?

Theology. Nothing. That is the solution of the riddle of the universe. Out of nothing in the beginning God created heaven and earth.

Philosophy. Out of nothing comes nothing.

Medicine.   Bosh! That is nothing.

Law.   I doubt everything. And there's some swindle here. I appeal to all righteous men.

Daughter [to POET].   Who are these righteous?

Poet.   Let him tell you who can. All the righteous are often just one person. Today they are me and mine, tomorrow you and yours. One is nominated for the post, or rather, one nominates oneself.

All the Righteous.   We have been swindled.

Chancellor.   Who has swindled you?

All the Righteous.   The Daughter!

Chancellor.   Will the Daughter kindly inform us what her idea was in having the door opened.

Daughter.   No, my friends. If I told you, you would not believe it.

Medicine.   But there's nothing there.

Daughter.   What you say is correct. But you have not understood it.

Medicine.   What she says is bosh.

All.   Bosh!

Daughter [to POET].   They are to be pitied.

Poet.   Do you mean that seriously?

Daughter.   Very seriously.

Poet.   Do you think the righteous are to be pitied too?

Daughter.   They most of all perhaps.

Poet.   And the four Faculties?

Daughter.   They too, and not least. Four heads and four minds with a single body. Who created such a monster?

All.   She does not answer.

Chancellor.   Then stone her!

Daughter.   This is the answer.

Chancellor.   Listen! She is answering.

All.   Stone her! She is answering.

[*Enter* LAWYER.]

Daughter.   If she answers, or if she does not answer, stone her! [*To* POET.] Come, you Seer, and I will answer the riddle, but far from here, out in the wilderness, where none can hear us, none can see us. For . . .

[*The* LAWYER *interrupts by taking hold of her arm.*]

Lawyer.   Have you forgotten your duties?

Daughter.   God knows I have not. But I have higher duties.

Lawyer.   But your child?

Daughter.   My child? Yes?

Lawyer.   Your child is calling you.

Daughter.   My child! Alas, I am earthbound! And this anguish in my breast, this agony, what is it?

Lawyer.   Don't you know?

Daughter.   No.

Lawyer.   It is the pangs of conscience.

Daughter. The pangs of conscience?

Lawyer. Yes. They come after every neglected duty, after every pleasure, however innocent—if there is such a thing as an innocent pleasure, which is doubtful. And they also come every time one causes pain to one's neighbour.

Daughter. Is there no remedy?

Lawyer. Yes, but only one. To do one's duty instantly.

Daughter. You look like a devil when you say the word "duty." But when one has, as I, two duties?

Lawyer. Fulfil first one and then the other.

Daughter. The higher first. Therefore, you look after my child, and I will do my duty.

Lawyer. Your child is unhappy without you. Can you let another suffer on your account?

Daughter. There is conflict in my soul. It is pulled this way and that until it is torn in two.

Lawyer. These, you see, are life's little trials.

Daughter. Oh, how they tear one!

Poet. You would have nothing to do with me, if you knew what misery I have caused through following my vocation—yes, my vocation, which is the highest duty of all.

Daughter. What do you mean?

Poet. I had a father, whose hopes were centred in me, his only son. I was to have carried on his business, but I ran away from the Commercial College. Worry brought my father to his grave. My mother wanted me to be religious. I couldn't be religious. She disowned me. I had a friend who helped me when I was desperate, but that friend turned out to be a tyrant to the very people whose cause I upheld. So to save my soul I had to strike down my friend and bene-factor. Since that time I have had no peace. I am considered base, contemptible, the scum of the earth. Nor do I get any comfort from my conscience when it tells me I did right, for the next moment it assures me I did wrong. That is the way of life.

Daughter. Come with me, out into the wilderness.

Lawyer. Your child!

Daughter [*indicating all present*]. These are my children. Each one of them is good, but as soon as they are together they fight and turn into devils. Farewell!

[*Blackout. When the lights go up the scene has changed to: Outside the Castle.*

The set is the same as the earlier one, except that now the ground is covered with blue monkshood, aconite and other flowers. The chrysanthemum bud at the top of the tower is on the point of bursting. The Castle windows are lit with candles. In the foreground is a fire.]

Daughter. The hour is at hand when with the aid of fire I shall ascend again into the ether. This is what you call death and approach with so much fear.

Poet. Fear of the unknown.

Daughter. Which yet you know.

Poet. Who knows it?

Daughter. Mankind. Why do you not believe your prophets?

Poet. Prophets have never been believed. Why is that? If they truly speak with the voice of God, why then do men not believe? His power to convince should be irresistible.

Daughter. Have you always doubted?

Poet. No, I have had faith many times, but after a while it drifted away, like a dream when one awakens.

Daughter. To be mortal is not easy.

Poet. You understand this now?

Daughter. Yes.

Poet. Tell me, did not Indra once send his son down to earth to hear man's complaint?

Daughter. He did. And how was he received?

Poet. How did he fulfil his mission?—to answer with a question.

Daughter. To answer with another—was not the state of mankind bettered by his visit to the earth? Answer truly.

Poet. Bettered? Yes, a little, a very little. Now, instead of further questions, will you tell me the answer to the riddle?

Daughter. What purpose would that serve? You would not believe me.

Poet. I shall believe you, for I know who you are.

Daughter. Then I will tell you. In the dawn of time, before your sun gave light, Brahma, the divine primal force let himself be seduced by Maya, the World Mother, that he might propagate. This mingling of the divine element with the earthly was the Fall from heaven. This world, its life and its inhabitants are therefore only a mirage, a reflection, a dream image.

Poet. My dream!

Daughter. A true dream. But, in order to be freed from the earthly element, the descendants of Brahma sought renunciation and suffering. And so you have suffering as the deliverer. But this yearning for suffering comes into conflict with the longing for joy, for love. Now you understand what love is; supreme joy in the greatest suffering, the sweetest is the most bitter. Do you understand now what woman is? Woman, through whom sin and death entered into life.

Poet. I understand. And the outcome?

Daughter. What you yourself know. Conflict between the pain of joy and the joy of pain, between the anguish of the penitent and the pleasure of the sensual.

Poet. And the conflict?

Daughter. The conflict of opposites generates power, as fire and water create the force of steam.

Poet. But peace? Rest?

Daughter. Hush! You must ask no more, nor may I answer. The altar is decked for the sacrifice, the flowers keep vigil, the candles are lighted, the white sheet hangs in the window, the threshold is strewn with pine.[1]

Poet. How calmly you speak! As if suffering did not exist for you.

Daughter. Not exist? I suffered all your sufferings a hundred fold because my sensibilities were finer.

[1] Signs of mourning in Sweden (translator's note).

Poet. Tell me your sorrows.

Daughter. Poet, could you tell your own with utter truth? Could your words ever once convey your thoughts?

Poet. You are right. No. To myself I have always seemed a deaf mute, and while the crowd was acclaiming my song, to me it seemed a jangle. And so, you see, I was always ashamed when men paid me homage.

Daughter. And yet you wish me to speak? Look into my eyes.

Poet. I cannot endure your gaze.

Daughter. How then will you endure my words, if I speak in my own language?

Poet. Even so, before you go, tell me from what you suffered most down here.

Daughter. From living. From feeling my vision dimmed by having eyes, my hearing dulled by having ears, and my thought, my airy, luminous thought, bound down in a labyrinth of fat. You have seen a brain. What twisting channels, what creeping ways!

Poet. Yes, and that is why the minds of the righteous are twisted.

Daughter. Cruel, always cruel, each one of you.

Poet. How can we be otherwise?

Daughter. Now first I shake the dust from my feet, the earth, the clay. [*She takes off her shoes and puts them in the fire.*]

[*One after another the following characters come in, put their contributions on the fire, cross the stage and go out, while the* POET *and the* DAUGHTER *stand watching.*]

Doorkeeper. Perhaps I may burn my shawl too?

Officer. And I my roses, of which only the thorns are left.

Billsticker. The posters can go, but my fishnet never.

Glazier. Farewell to the diamond that opened the door.

Lawyer. The report of the proceedings in the High Court touching the Pope's beard or the diminishing water supply in the sources of the Ganges.

Quarantine Master. A small contribution in the shape of the black mask which turned me into a blackamoor against my will.

Victoria [*She*]. My beauty—my sorrow.

Edith. My ugliness—my sorrow.

Blindman [*putting his hand in the fire*]. I give my hand which is my sight.

[DON JUAN *is pushed in in the bathchair (accompanied by the* COQUETTE *and the* FRIEND)].

Don Juan. Make haste, make haste! Life is short.

Poet. I have read that when a life is nearing its end, everything and everyone pass by in a single stream. Is this the end?

Daughter. For me, yes. Farewell!

Poet. Say a parting word!

Daughter. No, I cannot. Do you think your language can express our thoughts?

[*Enter the* DEAN OF THEOLOGY, *raging.*]

Theology. I am disowned by God; I am persecuted by men; I am abandoned by the Government, and scorned by my colleagues. How can I have faith when no

one else has faith? How can I defend a God who does not defend His own
people? It's all bosh!

[*He throws a book on the fire and goes out. The* POET *snatches the book from
the flames.*]

Poet.   Do you know what this is? A Book of Martyrs, a calendar with a martyr for
each day of the year.
Daughter.   A martyr?
Poet.   Yes, one who was tortured and put to death for his faith. Tell me why. Do
you believe all who are tortured suffer, all who are put to death feel pain? Surely
suffering is redemption and death deliverance.

[KRISTIN *enters with her paste and strips of paper.*]

Kristin.   I paste, I paste, till there is nothing left to paste.
Poet.   If heaven itself cracked open, you would try to paste it up. Go away!
Kristin.   Are there no inner windows in the Castle?
Poet.   No, none there.
Kristin.   I'll go then, I'll go.

[*Exit.*]

[*As the* DAUGHTER *speaks her last lines the flames rise until the Castle is on
fire.*]

Daughter.   The parting time has come; the end draws near.
                     Farewell, you child of man, dreamer,
                     poet, who knows best the way to live.
                     Above the earth on wings you hover,
                     plunging at times to graze the dust,
                     but not to be submerged.
                     Now I am going, now the hour has come
                     to leave both friend and place,
                     how sharp the loss of all I loved,
                     how deep regret for all destroyed!
                     Ah, now I know the whole of living's pain!
                     This then it is to be a human being—
                     ever to miss the thing one never prized
                     and feel remorse for what one never did,
                     to yearn to go, yet long to stay.
                     And so the human heart is split in two,
                     emotions by wild horses torn—
                     conflict, discord and uncertainty.
                     Farewell! Tell all on earth I shall remember them.
                     Where I am going, and in your name
                     carry their lamentations to the throne.
                     Farewell!

[*She goes into the Castle. Music is heard. The background is lighted up by the
burning Castle, and now shows a wall of human faces, questioning, mourning,
despairing. While the Castle is burning, the flower-bud on the roof bursts into a
giant chrysanthemum.*]

Chekhov: THE CHERRY ORCHARD

A character in a Hollywood film of the 1950's casually drops this line: "Any idiot can face a crisis; it's this day-to-day living that wears you out." The screenplay was by Clifford Odets, America's chief inheritor of the dramatic tradition of Anton Chekhov, and in that one line, he epitomized the lesson of his master.

Chekhov was born one year before the emancipation of the Russian serfs and died in the year preceding the unsuccessful revolution of 1905. His lifetime spanned two worlds: a dead one that Chekhov was glad to bury yet able to mourn, and an unborn one that he considered inevitable and necessary but not worthy of admiration. It is the cultural setting of this interim world that Chekhov inhabited that provides the milieu of his plays: a useless intelligentsia, an indolent as well as a profligate aristocracy, an impoverished and ignorant commonfolk, all living a provincial existence even when in the cities. Sad souls mechanically going through the motions of dreary lives—sad and yet funny; ridiculous and yet pathetic—and Chekhov loved them all, because they were human beings and therefore entitled to some dignity and some fulfillment, for no matter how silly he may seem to outsiders, every man is the hero of his own life. Everyone, not just Arthur Miller's salesman, has got to dream.

Anton Chekhov's training as a physician may well have given him both the objectivity and the compassion to present life as it is, and to imply that this was not the way it should be. He was mindful of the needs of men learning to live with the irreconcilable paradox that life is both meaningful and meaningless. To understand the sensitivity of Anton Chekhov, one need only read his letters.

The heart of Chekhovian drama is the power of trifles in human life, that day-to-day living that wears you out. As one season silently slips into another in Chekhov's plays, so his characters, beset by an inexplicable sense of loss and an overwhelming sense of boredom, wonder, "Where did it all go?" Life is uneventful, tedious, empty, aimless, and yet we suffer and exult, we laugh and we cry, we desperately try to get through to each other and still we are ultimately engulfed by the horror of loneliness. Families live together for generations only to find that they are a house of strangers. In such a view of the human condition, the old dramatic labels become meaningless, for it denies the clear separation of the comic from the tragic. The laughter bubbles through the tears, and the sadness underscores the merriment. Unsentimental but totally sympathetic toward the people in his plays, Chekhov was able to laugh with compassion and to cry with good humor. He respected the individuality and the dignity of even the most foolish of men, and it was his fondest wish never to humiliate any human being.

The mood, the details, and the people are the core of a play by Anton Chekhov. The plot, the idiot in crisis, is secondary, for the inner truth as Chekhov saw it was that the little things are most revealing and insightful. So much happens when nothing happens, the unspoken often says more than the word, and life's little climaxes always fizz out into foolishness. It was the peculiar gift of this kindest of men to dramatize what at first glance seems to defy dramatic treatment: tedium. Chekhov paid little attention to the rules of a bygone day. One of the conventions of the theatre since its inception was that when a character speaks, others listen and respond. In Chekhov, people often pay no attention to what anyone else is saying, whether it be of love or tea and roasted nuts. Those who insist that "realism" and "art" are mutually exclusive terms will be eternally confronted and refuted by Anton Chekhov.

The Moscow Art Theatre, founded in 1898 by Vladimir Nemirovich-Danchenko and Konstantin Stanislavski, was dedicated to establishing a form of dramatic playing that did away with the strutting, posing, mechanical acting of the era of the great bombastic stars who concentrated only on the externals of their craft. Stanislavski, father of modern realistic acting, insisted that an actor must familiarize himself with the most minute details of the character he was playing and of the world in which he lived. To get to "the inner truth," the psychological complexity to be found in all human beings, an actor must play with a conviction he can achieve only by finding his own experiences equivalent to those of the character he portrays. The Moscow Art Theatre worked for a unity of theatrical mood, attention to detail, and ensemble playing in order to perform "life as it is." The company needed plays suited to its new mode of presentation; Chekhov needed a theatre sympathetic to his new conception of playwriting. It was a happy union, and its prolific offspring dwell on many stages of the twentieth century theatre.

Stanislavski refused to the end to bow to Chekhov's wish to emphasize the comic in the plays. This engendered a tradition that has cursed many productions ever since, and it has become the mark of a consummate theatrical company to be able to achieve the elusive synthesis of the comic and the tragic in Chekhov.

The Cherry Orchard was first performed by the Moscow Art Theatre on January 17, 1904. It was Anton Chekhov's 44th and last birthday.

THE CHERRY ORCHARD

Translated by Avrahm Yarmolinsky

The Characters

Lubov Andreyevna Ranevskaya, a landowner
Anya, her seventeen-year-old daughter
Varya, her adopted daughter, twenty-two years old
Leonid Andreyevich Gayev, Mme. Ranevskaya's brother
Yermolay Alexeyevich Lopahin, a merchant
Pyotr Sergeyevich Trofimov, a student
Simeonov-Pishchik, a landowner
Charlotta Ivanovna, a governess
Semyon Yepihodov, a clerk
Dunyasha, a maid
Firs (pronounced "fierce"), a man-servant, aged eighty-seven
Yasha, a young valet
A Tramp
Stationmaster, Post Office Clerk, Guests, Servants

The action takes place on MME. RANEVSKAYA'S *estate.*[1]

Act I

[*A room that is still called the nursery. One of the doors leads into* ANYA'S *room. Dawn, the sun will soon rise. It is May, the cherry trees are in blossom, but it is cold in the orchard; there is a morning frost. The windows are shut. Enter* DUNYASHA *with a candle, and* LOPAHIN *with a book in his hand.*]

Lopahin. The train is in, thank God. What time is it?
Dunyasha. Nearly two. [*Puts out the candle.*] It's light already.
Lopahin. How late is the train, anyway? Two hours at least. [*Yawns and stretches.*] I'm a fine one! What a fool I've made of myself! I came here on purpose to meet them at the station, and then I went and overslept. I fell asleep in my chair. How annoying! You might have waked me. . . .
Dunyasha. I thought you'd left. [*Listens.*] I think they're coming!
Lopahin [*listens*]. No, they've got to get the luggage, and one thing and another. . . . [*Pause.*] Lubov Andreyevna spent five years abroad, I don't know what she's like now. . . . She's a fine person—lighthearted, simple. I remember when I was a boy of fifteen, my poor father—he had a shop here in the village then—punched me in the face with his fist and made my nose bleed. We'd come into the yard, I don't know what for, and he'd had a drop too much. Lubov Andreyevna, I remember her as if it were yesterday—she was still

---

[1] The time of the action was the present for Chekhov: the opening years of the twentieth century. It had been forty years since the end of Russian feudalism and the emancipation of the serfs (1861). There was an unsuccessful revolution in Russia in 1905.

young and so slim—led me to the wash-basin, in this very room . . . in the
nursery. "Don't cry, little peasant," she said, "it'll heal in time for your wedding . . ." [*Pause.*] Little peasant . . . my father was a peasant, it's true, and
here I am in a white waistcoat and yellow shoes. A pig in a pastry shop, you
might say. It's true I'm rich, I've got a lot of money. . . . But when you look
at it closely, I'm a peasant through and through. [*Pages the book.*] Here I've
been reading this book and I didn't understand a word of it. . . . I was reading
it and fell asleep. . . . [*Pause.*]

Dunyasha. And the dogs were awake all night; they feel that their masters are
coming.

Lopahin. Dunyasha, why are you so—

Dunyasha. My hands are trembling. I'm going to faint.

Lopahin. You're too soft, Dunyasha. You dress like a lady, and look at the way
you do your hair. That's not right. One should remember one's place. [*Enter*
YEPIHODOV *with a bouquet; he wears a jacket and highly polished boots that
squeak badly. He drops the bouquet as he comes in.*]

Yepihodov [*picking up the bouquet*]. Here, the gardener sent these, said you're
to put them in the dining room. [*Hands the bouquet to* DUNYASHA.]

Lopahin. And bring me some kvass.[1]

Dunyasha. Yes, sir. [*Exits.*]

Yepihodov. There's a frost this morning—three degrees below—and yet the
cherries are all in blossom. I cannot approve of our climate. [*Sighs.*] I cannot.
Our climate does not activate properly. And, Yermolay Alexeyevich, allow me to
make a further remark. The other day I bought myself a pair of boots, and I
make bold to assure you, they squeak so that it is really intolerable. What
should I grease them with?

Lopahin. Oh, get out! I'm fed up with you.

Yepihodov. Every day I meet with misfortune. And I don't complain, I've got
used to it, I even smile.

[DUNYASHA *enters, hands* LOPAHIN *the kvass.*]

Yepihodov. I am leaving. [*Stumbles against a chair, which falls over.*] There!
[*Triumphantly, as it were.*] There again, you see what sort of circumstance,
pardon the expression. . . . It is absolutely phenomenal! [*Exits.*]

Dunyasha. You know, Yermolay Alexeyevich, I must tell you, Yepihodov has
proposed to me.

Lopahin. Ah!

Dunyasha. I simply don't know . . . he's a quiet man, but sometimes when he
starts talking, you can't make out what he means. He speaks nicely—and it's
touching—but you can't understand it. I sort of like him though, and he is
crazy about me. He's an unlucky man . . . every day something happens to
him. They tease him about it here . . . they call him Two-and-Twenty
Troubles.

Lopahin [*listening*]. There! I think they're coming.

Dunyasha. They *are* coming! What's the matter with me? I feel cold all over.

---

1 Fermented drink resembling sour beer.

Lopahin. They really are coming. Let's go and meet them. Will she recognize me? We haven't seen each other for five years.

Dunyasha [in a flutter]. I'm going to faint this minute. . . . Oh, I'm going to faint!

[*Two carriages are heard driving up to the house.* LOPAHIN *and* DUNYASHA *go out quickly. The stage is left empty. There is a noise in the adjoining rooms.* FIRS, *who had driven to the station to meet* LUBOV ANDREYEVNA RANEVSKAYA, *crosses the stage hurriedly, leaning on a stick. He is wearing an old-fashioned livery and a tall hat. He mutters to himself indistinctly. The hubbub off-stage increases.* A VOICE: "Come, let's go this way." *Enter* LUBOV ANDREYEVNA, ANYA *and* CHARLOTTA IVANOVNA, *with a pet dog on a leash, all in traveling dresses;* VARYA, *wearing a coat and kerchief;* GAYEV, SIMEONOV-PISHCHIK, LOPAHIN, DUNYASHA *with a bag and an umbrella, servants with luggage. All walk across the room.*]

Anya. Let's go this way. Do you remember what room this is, mamma?

Mme. Ranevskaya [joyfully, through her tears]. The nursery!

Varya. How cold it is! My hands are numb. [*To* MME. RANEVSKAYA.] Your rooms are just the same as they were, mamma, the white one and the violet.

Mme. Ranevskaya. The nursery! My darling, lovely room! I slept here when I was a child. . . . [*Cries.*] And here I am, like a child again! [*Kisses her brother and* VARYA, *and then her brother again.*] Varya's just the same as ever, like a nun. And I recognized Dunyasha. [*Kisses* DUNYASHA.]

Gayev. The train was two hours late. What do you think of that? What a way to manage things!

Charlotta [to PISHCHIK].* My dog eats nuts, too.

Pishchik [in amazement]. You don't say so!

[*All go out, except* ANYA *and* DUNYASHA.]

Dunyasha. We've been waiting for you for hours. [*Takes* ANYA's *hat and coat.*]

Anya. I didn't sleep on the train for four nights and now I'm frozen. . . .

Dunyasha. It was Lent when you left; there was snow and frost, and now . . . My darling! [*Laughs and kisses her.*] I have been waiting for you, my sweet, my darling! But I must tell you something. . . . I can't put it off another minute. . . .

Anya [listlessly]. What now?

Dunyasha. The clerk, Yepihodov, proposed to me, just after Easter.

Anya. There you are, at it again. . . . [*Straightening her hair.*] I've lost all my hairpins. . . . [*She is staggering with exhaustion.*]

Dunyasha. Really, I don't know what to think. He loves me—he loves me so!

Anya [looking towards the door of her room, tenderly]. My own room, my windows, just as though I'd never been away. I'm home! Tomorrow morning I'll get up and run into the orchard. Oh, if I could only get some sleep. I didn't close my eyes during the whole journey—I was so anxious.

Dunyasha. Pyotr Sergeyevich came the day before yesterday.

Anya [joyfully]. Petya!

Dunyasha. He's asleep in the bath-house. He has settled there. He said he was afraid of being in the way. [*Looks at her watch.*] I should wake him, but Miss Varya told me not to. "Don't you wake him," she said.

[*Enter* VARYA *with a bunch of keys at her belt.*]

Varya. Dunyasha, coffee, and be quick. . . . Mamma's asking for coffee.
Dunyasha. In a minute. [*Exits.*]
Varya. Well, thank God, you've come. You're home again. [*Fondling* ANYA.] My darling is here again. My pretty one is back.
Anya. Oh, what I've been through!
Varya. I can imagine.
Anya. When we left, it was Holy Week, it was cold then, and all the way Charlotta chattered and did her tricks. Why did you have to saddle me with Charlotta?
Varya. You couldn't have traveled all alone, darling—at seventeen!
Anya. We got to Paris, it was cold there, snowing. My French is dreadful. Mamma lived on the fifth floor; I went up there, and found all kinds of Frenchmen, ladies, an old priest with a book. The place was full of tobacco smoke, and so bleak. Suddenly I felt sorry for mamma, so sorry, I took her head in my arms and hugged her and couldn't let go of her. Afterwards mamma kept fondling me and crying. . . .
Varya [*through tears*]. Don't speak of it . . . don't.
Anya. She had already sold her villa at Mentone, she had nothing left, nothing. I hadn't a kopeck[1] left either, we had only just enough to get home. And mamma wouldn't understand! When we had dinner at the stations, she always ordered the most expensive dishes, and tipped the waiters a whole ruble. Charlotta, too. And Yasha kept ordering, too—it was simply awful. You know Yasha's mamma's footman now, we brought him here with us.
Varya. Yes, I've seen the blackguard.
Anya. Well, tell me—have you paid the interest?
Varya. How could we?
Anya. Good heavens, good heavens!
Varya. In August the estate will be put up for sale.
Anya. My God!

[LOPAHIN *peeps in at the door and bleats.*]

Lopahin. Meh-h-h. [*Disappears.*]
Varya [*through tears*]. What I couldn't do to him! [*Shakes her fist threateningly.*]
Anya [*embracing* VARYA, *gently*]. Varya, has he proposed to you? [VARYA *shakes her head.*] But he loves you. Why don't you come to an understanding? What are you waiting for?
Varya. Oh, I don't think anything will ever come of it. He's too busy, he has no time for me . . . pays no attention to me. I've washed my hands of him—I can't bear the sight of him. They all talk about our getting married, they all

---

[1] One hundredth of a ruble, the smallest denomination of Russian coin.

congratulate me—and all the time there's really nothing to it—it's all like a dream. [*In another tone.*] You have a new brooch—like a bee.

Anya [*sadly*].   Mamma bought it. [*She goes into her own room and speaks gaily like a child.*] And you know, in Paris I went up in a balloon.

Varya.   My darling's home, my pretty one is back! [DUNYASHA *returns with the coffee-pot and prepares coffee.* VARYA *stands at the door of* ANYA's *room.*] All day long, darling, as I go about the house, I keep dreaming. If only we could marry you off to a rich man, I should feel at ease. Then I would go into a convent, and afterwards to Kiev, to Moscow. . . . I would spend my life going from one holy place to another. . . . I'd go on and on. . . . What a blessing that would be!

Anya.   The birds are singing in the orchard. What time is it?

Varya.   It must be after two. Time you were asleep, darling. [*Goes into* ANYA's *room.*] What a blessing that would be!

[YASHA *enters with a plaid and a traveling bag, crosses the stage.*]

Yasha [*finically*].   May I pass this way, please?

Dunyasha.   A person could hardly recognize you, Yasha. Your stay abroad has certainly done wonders for you.

Yasha.   Hm-m . . . and who are you?

Dunyasha.   When you went away I was that high—[*indicating with her hand.*] I'm Dunyasha—Fyodor Kozoyedev's daughter. Don't you remember?

Yasha.   Hm! What a peach! [*He looks round and embraces her. She cries out and drops a saucer.* YASHA *leaves quickly.*]

Varya [*in the doorway, in a tone of annoyance*].   What's going on here?

Dunyasha [*through tears*].   I've broken a saucer.

Varya.   Well, that's good luck.

Anya [*coming out of her room*].   We ought to warn mamma that Petya's here.

Varya.   I left orders not to wake him.

Anya [*musingly*].   Six years ago father died. A month later brother Grisha was drowned in the river. . . . Such a pretty little boy he was—only seven. It was more than mamma could bear, so she went away, went away without looking back. . . . [*Shudders.*] How well I understand her, if she only knew! [*Pauses.*] And Petya Trofimov was Grisha's tutor, he may remind her of it all. . . .

[*Enter* FIRS, *wearing a jacket and a white waistcoat. He goes up to the coffee-pot.*]

Firs [*anxiously*].   The mistress will have her coffee here. [*Puts on white gloves.*] Is the coffee ready? [*Sternly, to* DUNYASHA.] Here, you! And where's the cream?

Dunyasha.   Oh, my God! [*Exits quickly.*]

Firs [*fussing over the coffee-pot*].   Hah! the addlehead! [*Mutters to himself.*] Home from Paris. And the old master used to go to Paris too . . . by carriage. [*Laughs.*]

Varya.   What is it, Firs?

Firs.   What is your pleasure, Miss? [*Joyfully.*] My mistress has come home, and I've seen her at last! Now I can die. [*Weeps with joy.*]

[*Enter* MME. RANEVSKAYA, GAYEV, *and* SIMEONOV-PISHCHIK. *The latter is wearing a tight-waisted, pleated coat of fine cloth, and full trousers.* GAYEV, *as he comes in, goes through the motions of a billiard player with his arms and body.*]

Mme. Ranevskaya.   Let's see, how does it go? Yellow ball in the corner! Bank shot in the side pocket!

Gayev.   I'll tip it in the corner! There was a time, sister, when you and I used to sleep in this very room, and now I'm fifty-one, strange as it may seem.

Lopahin.   Yes, time flies.

Gayev.   Who?

Lopahin.   I say, time flies.

Gayev.   It smells of patchouli[1] here.

Anya.   I'm going to bed. Good night, mamma. [*Kisses her mother.*]

Mme. Ranevskaya.   My darling child! [*Kisses her hands.*] Are you happy to be home? I can't come to my senses.

Anya.   Good night, uncle.

Gayev [*kissing her face and hands*].   God bless you, how like your mother you are! [*To his sister.*] At her age, Luba, you were just like her. [ANYA *shakes hands with* LOPAHIN *and* PISHCHIK, *then goes out, shutting the door behind her.*]

Mme. Ranevskaya.   She's very tired.

Pishchik.   Well, it was a long journey.

Varya [*to* LOPAHIN *and* PISHCHIK].   How about it, gentlemen? It's past two o'clock—isn't it time for you to go?

Mme. Ranevskaya [*laughs*].   You're just the same as ever, Varya. [*Draws her close and kisses her.*] I'll have my coffee and then we'll all go. [FIRS *puts a small cushion under her feet.*] Thank you, my dear. I've got used to coffee. I drink it day and night. Thanks, my dear old man. [*Kisses him.*]

Varya.   I'd better see if all the luggage has been brought in. [*Exits.*]

Mme. Ranevskaya.   Can it really be I sitting here? [*Laughs.*] I feel like dancing, waving my arms about. [*Covers her face with her hands.*] But maybe I am dreaming! God knows I love my country, I love it tenderly; I couldn't look out of the window in the train, I kept crying so. [*Through tears.*] But I must have my coffee. Thank you, Firs, thank you, dear old man. I'm so happy that you're still alive.

Firs.   Day before yesterday.

Gayev.   He's hard of hearing.

Lopahin.   I must go soon, I'm leaving for Kharkov about five o'clock. How annoying! I'd like to have a good look at you, talk to you. . . . You're just as splendid as ever.

Pishchik [*breathing heavily*].   She's even better-looking. . . . Dressed in the latest Paris fashion. . . . Perish my carriage and all its four wheels. . . .

Lopahin.   Your brother, Leonid Andreyevich, says I'm a vulgarian and an exploiter. But it's all the same to me—let him talk. I only want you to trust me as you used to. I want you to look at me with your touching, wonderful eyes as you used to. Dear God! My father was a serf of your father's and grandfather's,

---

[1] Strong perfume derived from an East Indian herb. Lopahin seems to have doused himself with a substantial application.

but you, you yourself, did so much for me once . . . so much . . . that I've forgotten all about that; I love you as though you were my sister—even more.

Mme. Ranevskaya. I can't sit still, I simply can't. [*Jumps up and walks about in violent agitation.*] This joy is too much for me. . . . Laugh at me, I'm silly! My own darling bookcase! My darling table! [*Kisses it.*]

Gayev. While you were away, nurse died.

Mme. Ranevskaya [*sits down and takes her coffee*]. Yes, God rest her soul; they wrote me about it.

Gayev. And Anastasy is dead. Petrushka Kossoy has left me and has gone into town to work for the police inspector. [*Takes a box of sweets out of his pocket and begins to suck one.*]

Pishchik. My daughter Dashenka sends her regards.

Lopahin. I'd like to tell you something very pleasant—cheering. [*Glancing at his watch.*] I am leaving directly. There isn't much time to talk. But I will put it in a few words. As you know, your cherry orchard is to be sold to pay your debts. The sale is to be on the twenty-second of August; but don't you worry, my dear, you may sleep in peace; there is a way out. Here is my plan. Give me your attention! Your estate is only fifteen miles from the town; the railway runs close by it; and if the cherry orchard and the land along the river bank were cut up into lots and these leased for summer cottages, you would have an income of at least 25,000 rubles a year out of it.

Gayev. Excuse me. . . . What nonsense.

Mme. Ranevskaya. I don't quite understand you, Yermolay Alexeyevich.

Lopahin. You will get an annual rent of at least ten rubles per acre, and if you advertise at once, I'll give you any guarantee you like that you won't have a square foot of ground left by autumn, all the lots will be snapped up. In short, congratulations, you're saved. The location is splendid—by that deep river. . . . Only, of course, the ground must be cleared . . . all the old buildings, for instance, must be torn down, and this house, too, which is useless, and, of course, the old cherry orchard must be cut down.

Mme. Ranevskaya. Cut down? My dear, forgive me, but you don't know what you're talking about. If there's one thing that's interesting—indeed, remarkable—in the whole province, it's precisely our cherry orchard.

Lopahin. The only remarkable thing about this orchard is that it's a very large one. There's a crop of cherries every other year, and you can't do anything with them; no one buys them.

Gayev. This orchard is even mentioned in the Encyclopedia.

Lopahin [*glancing at his watch*]. If we can't think of a way out, if we don't come to a decision, on the twenty-second of August the cherry orchard and the whole estate will be sold at auction. Make up your minds! There's no other way out—I swear. None, none.

Firs. In the old days, forty or fifty years ago, the cherries were dried, soaked, pickled, and made into jam, and we used to—

Gayev. Keep still, Firs.

Firs. And the dried cherries would be shipped by the cartload. It meant a lot of money! And in those days the dried cherries were soft and juicy, sweet, fragrant. . . . They knew the way to do it, then.

Mme. Ranevskaya. And why don't they do it that way now?

Firs. They've forgotten. Nobody remembers it.

Pishchik [*to* MME. RANEVSKAYA]. What's doing in Paris? Eh? Did you eat frogs there?

Mme. Ranevskaya. I ate crocodiles.

Pishchik. Just imagine!

Lopahin. There used to be only landowners and peasants in the country, but now these summer people have appeared on the scene. . . . All the towns, even the small ones, are surrounded by these summer cottages; and in another twenty years, no doubt, the summer population will have grown enormously. Now the summer resident only drinks tea on his porch, but maybe he'll take to working his acre, too, and then your cherry orchard will be a rich, happy, luxuriant place.

Gayev [*indignantly*]. Poppycock!

[*Enter* VARYA *and* YASHA.]

Varya. There are two telegrams for you, mamma dear. [*Picks a key from the bunch at her belt and noisily opens an old-fashioned bookcase.*] Here they are.

Mme. Ranevskaya. They're from Paris. [*Tears them up without reading them.*] I'm through with Paris.

Gayev. Do you know, Luba, how old this bookcase is? Last week I pulled out the bottom drawer and there I found the date burnt in it. It was made exactly a hundred years ago. Think of that! We could celebrate its centenary. True, it's an inanimate object, but nevertheless, a bookcase. . . .

Pishchik [*amazed*]. A hundred years! Just imagine!

Gayev. Yes. [*Tapping it.*] That's something. . . . Dear, honored bookcase, hail to you who for more than a century have served the glorious ideals of goodness and justice! Your silent summons to fruitful toil has never weakened in all those hundred years [*through tears*], sustaining, through successive generations of our family, courage and faith in a better future, and fostering in us ideals of goodness and social consciousness. . . . [*Pauses.*]

Lopahin. Yes. . . .

Mme. Ranevskaya. You haven't changed a bit, Leonid.

Gayev [*somewhat embarrassed*]. I'll play it off the red in the corner! Tip it in the side pocket!

Lopahin [*looking at his watch*]. Well, it's time for me to go. . . .

Yasha [*handing a pill box to* MME. RANEVSKAYA]. Perhaps you'll take your pills now.

Pishchik. One shouldn't take medicines, dearest lady; they do neither harm nor good. . . . Give them here, my valued friend. [*Takes the pill box, pours the pills into his palm, blows on them, puts them in his mouth, and washes them down with some kvass.*] There!

Mme. Ranevskaya [*frightened*]. You must be mad!

Pishchik. I've taken all the pills.

Lopahin. What a glutton!

[*All laugh.*]

Firs. The gentleman visited us in Easter week, ate half a bucket of pickles, he did. . . . [*Mumbles.*]

Mme. Ranevskaya. What's he saying?

Varya. He's been mumbling like that for the last three years—we're used to it.

Yasha. His declining years!

[CHARLOTTA IVANOVNA *very thin, tightly laced, dressed in white, a lorgnette at her waist, crosses the stage.*]

Lopahin. Forgive me, Charlotta Ivanovna, I've not had time to greet you. [*Tries to kiss her hand.*]

Charlotta [*pulling away her hand*]. If I let you kiss my hand, you'll be wanting to kiss my elbow next, and then my shoulder.

Lopahin. I've no luck today. [*All laugh.*] Charlotta Ivanovna, show us a trick.

Mme. Ranevskaya. Yes, Charlotta, do a trick for us.

Charlotta. I don't see the need. I want to sleep. [*Exits.*]

Lopahin. In three weeks we'll meet again. [*Kisses* MME. RANEVSKAYA'S *hand.*] Good-by till then. Time's up. [*To* GAYEV.] Bye-bye. [*Kisses* PISHCHIK.] Bye-bye. [*Shakes hands with* VARYA, *then with* FIRS *and* YASHA] I hate to leave. [*To* MME. RANEVSKAYA.] If you make up your mind about the cottages, let me know; I'll get you a loan of 50,000 rubles. Think it over seriously.

Varya [*crossly*]. Will you never go!

Lopahin. I'm going, I'm going. [*Exits.*]

Gayev. The vulgarian. But, excuse me . . . Varya's going to marry him, he's Varya's fiancé.

Varya. You talk too much, uncle dear.

Mme. Ranevskaya. Well, Varya, it would make me happy. He's a good man.

Pishchik. Yes, one must admit, he's a most estimable man. And my Dashenka . . . She too says that . . . she says . . . lots of things. [*Snores; but wakes up at once.*] All the same, my valued friend, could you oblige me . . . with a loan of 240 rubles? I must pay the interest on the mortgage tomorrow.

Varya [*alarmed*]. We can't, we can't!

Mme. Ranevskaya. I really haven't any money.

Pishchik. It'll turn up. [*Laughs.*] I never lose hope, I thought everything was lost, that I was done for, when lo and behold, the railway ran through my land . . . and I was paid for it. . . . And something else will turn up again, if not today, then tomorrow. . . . Dashenka will win two hundred thousand . . . she's got a lottery ticket.

Mme. Ranevskaya. I've had my coffee, now let's go to bed.

Firs [*brushes off* GAYEV; *admonishingly*]. You've got the wrong trousers on again. What am I to do with you?

Varya [*softly*]. Anya's asleep. [*Gently opens the window.*] The sun's up now, it's not a bit cold. Look, mamma dear, what wonderful trees. And heavens, what air! The starlings are singing!

Gayev [*opens the other window*]. The orchard is all white. You've not forgotten it, Luba? That's the long alley that runs straight, straight as an arrow; how it shines on moonlight nights, do you remember? You've not forgotten?

Mme. Ranevskaya [*looking out of the window into the orchard*]. Oh, my childhood, my innocent childhood. I used to sleep in this nursery—I used to look out into the orchard, happiness waked with me every morning, the orchard was just the same then . . . nothing has changed. [*Laughs with joy.*] All, all white! Oh, my orchard! After the dark, rainy autumn and the cold winter, you are young again, and full of happiness, the heavenly angels have not left you. . . . If I could free my chest and my shoulders from this rock that weighs on me, if I could only forget the past!

Gayev. Yes, and the orchard will be sold to pay our debts, strange as it may seem. . . .

Mme. Ranevskaya. Look! There is our poor mother walking in the orchard . . . all in white. . . . [*Laughs with joy.*] It is she!

Gayev. Where?

Varya. What are you saying, mamma dear!

Mme. Ranevskaya. There's no one there, I just imagined it. To the right, where the path turns towards the arbor, there's a little white tree, leaning over, that looks like a woman. . . .

[TROFIMOV *enters, wearing a shabby student's uniform and spectacles.*]

Mme. Ranevskaya. What an amazing orchard! White masses of blossom, the blue sky. . . .

Trofimov. Lubov Andreyevna! [*She looks round at him.*] I just want to pay my respects to you, then I'll leave at once. [*Kisses her hand ardently.*] I was told to wait until morning, but I hadn't the patience. . . . [MME. RANEVSKAYA *looks at him, perplexed.*]

Varya [*through tears*]. This is Petya Trofimov.

Trofimov. Petya Trofimov, formerly your Grisha's tutor. . . . Can I have changed so much? [MME. RANEVSKAYA *embraces him and weeps quietly.*]

Gayev [*embarrassed*]. Don't, don't, Luba.

Varya [*crying*]. I told you, Petya, to wait until tomorrow.

Mme. Ranevskaya. My Grisha . . . my little boy . . . Grisha . . . my son.

Varya. What can one do, mamma dear, it's God's will.

Trofimov [*softly, through tears*]. There . . . there.

Mme. Ranevskaya [*weeping quietly*]. My little boy was lost . . . drowned. Why? Why, my friend? [*More quietly.*] Anya's sleep in there, and here I am talking so loudly . . . making all this noise. . . . But tell me, Petya, why do you look so badly? Why have you aged so?

Trofimov. A mangy master, a peasant woman in the train called me.

Mme. Ranevskaya. You were just a boy then, a dear little student, and now your hair's thin—and you're wearing glasses! Is it possible you're still a student? [*Goes towards the door.*]

Trofimov. I suppose I'm a perpetual student.

Mme. Ranevskaya [*kisses her brother, then* VARYA]. Now, go to bed . . . You have aged, too, Leonid.

Pishchik [*follows her*]. So now we turn in. Oh, my gout! I'm staying the night here. . . . Lubov Andreyevna, my angel, tomorrow morning. . . . I do need 240 rubles.

Gayev. He keeps at it.

Pishchik.   I'll pay it back, dear . . . it's a trifling sum.

Mme. Ranevskaya.   All right, Leonid will give it to you. Give it to him, Leonid.

Gayev.   Me give it to him! That's a good one!

Mme. Ranevskaya.   It can't be helped. Give it to him! He needs it. He'll pay it back.

[MME. RANEVSKAYA, TROFIMOV, PISHCHIK, *and* FIRS *go out;* GAYEV, VARYA, *and* YASHA *remain.*]

Gayev.   Sister hasn't got out of the habit of throwing money around. [*To* YASHA.] Go away, my good fellow, you smell of the barnyard.

Yasha [*with a grin*].   And you, Leonid Andreyevich, are just the same as ever.

Gayev.   Who? [*To* VARYA.] What did he say?

Varya [*to* YASHA].   Your mother's come from the village; she's been sitting in the servants' room since yesterday, waiting to see you.

Yasha.   Botheration!

Varya.   You should be ashamed of yourself!

Yasha.   She's all I needed! She could have come tomorrow. [*Exits.*]

Varya.   Mamma is just the same as ever; she hasn't changed a bit. If she had her own way, she'd keep nothing for herself.

Gayev.   Yes . . . [*Pauses.*] If a great many remedies are offered for some disease, it means it is incurable; I keep thinking and racking my brains; I have many remedies, ever so many, and that really means none. It would be fine if we came in for a legacy; it would be fine if we married off our Anya to a very rich man; or we might go to Yaroslavl and try our luck with our aunt, the Countess. She's very, very rich, you know. . . .

Varya [*weeping*].   If only God would help us!

Gayev.   Stop bawling. Aunt's very rich, but she doesn't like us. In the first place, sister married a lawyer who was no nobleman. . . . [ANYA *appears in the doorway.*] She married beneath her, and it can't be said that her behavior has been very exemplary. She's good, kind, sweet, and I love her, but no matter what extenuating circumstances you may adduce, there's no denying that she has no morals. You sense it in her least gesture.

Varya [*in a whisper*].   Anya's in the doorway.

Gayev.   Who? [*Pauses.*] It's queer, something got into my right eye—my eyes are going back on me. . . . And on Thursday, when I was in the circuit court—

[*Enter* ANYA.]

Varya.   Why aren't you asleep, Anya?

Anya.   I can't get to sleep, I just can't.

Gayev.   My little pet! [*Kisses* ANYA's *face and hands.*] My child! [*Weeps.*] You are not my niece, you're my angel! You're everything to me. Believe me, believe—

Anya.   I believe you, uncle. Everyone loves you and respects you . . . but, uncle dear, you must keep still. . . . You must. What were you saying just now about my mother? Your own sister? What made you say that?

Gayev. Yes, yes. . . . [*Covers his face with her hand.*] Really, that was awful! Good God! Heaven help me! Just now I made a speech to the bookcase . . . so stupid! And only after I was through, I saw how stupid it was.

Varya. It's true, uncle dear, you ought to keep still. Just don't talk, that's all.

Anya. If you could only keep still, it would make things easier for you too.

Gayev. I'll keep still. [*Kisses* ANYA's *and* VARYA's *hands.*] I will. But now about business. On Thursday I was in court; well, there were a number of us there, and we began talking of one thing and another, and this and that, and do you know, I believe it will be possible to raise a loan on a promissory note, to pay the interest at the bank.

Varya. If only God would help us!

Gayev. On Tuesday I'll go and see about it again. [*To* VARYA.] Stop bawling. [*To* ANYA.] Your mamma will talk to Lopahin, and he, of course, will not refuse her . . . and as soon as you're rested, you'll go to Yaroslavl to the Countess, your great-aunt. So we'll be working in three directions at once, and the thing is in the bag. We'll pay the interest—I'm sure of it. [*Puts a candy in his mouth.*] I swear on my honor, I swear by anything you like, the estate shan't be sold. [*Excitedly.*] I swear by my own happiness! Here's my hand on it, you can call me a swindler and a scoundrel if I let it come to an auction! I swear by my whole being.

Anya [*relieved and quite happy again*]. How good you are, uncle, and how clever! [*Embraces him.*] Now I'm at peace, quite at peace, I'm happy.

[*Enter* FIRS.]

Firs [*reproachfully*]. Leonid Andreyevich, have you no fear of God? When are you going to bed?

Gayev. Directly, directly. Go away, Firs, I'll . . . yes, I will undress myself. Now, children, 'nightie-'nightie. We'll consider details tomorrow, but now go to sleep. [*Kisses* ANYA *and* VARYA.] I am a man of the 'Eighties; they have nothing good to say of that period nowadays. Nevertheless, in the course of my life I have suffered not a little for my convictions. It's not for nothing that the peasant loves me; one should know the peasant; one should know from which—

Anya. There you go again, uncle.

Varya. Uncle dear, be quiet.

Firs [*angrily*]. Leonid Andreyevich!

Gayev. I'm coming, I'm coming! Go to bed! Double bank shot in the side pocket! Here goes a clean shot. . . .

[*Exits,* FIRS *hobbling after him.*]

Anya. I am at peace now. I don't want to go to Yaroslavl—I don't like my great-aunt, but still, I am at peace, thanks to uncle. [*Sits down.*]

Varya. We must get some sleep. I'm going now. While you were away something unpleasant happened. In the old servants' quarters there are only the old people, as you know; Yefim, Polya, Yevstigney, and Karp, too. They began letting all sorts of rascals in to spend the night. . . . I didn't say anything. Then I heard they'd been spreading a report that I gave them nothing but dried peas to eat—out of stinginess, you know . . . and it was all Yevstigney's

doing. . . . All right, I thought, if that's how it is, I thought, just wait. I sent
for Yevstigney. . . . [*Yawns.*] He comes. . . . "How's this, Yevstigney?" I
say, "You fool. . . ." [*Looking at* AYNA.] Anichka! [*Pauses.*] She's asleep.
[*Puts her arm around* ANYA.] Come to your little bed. . . . Come. . . .
[*Leads her.*] My darling has fallen asleep. . . . Come.

[*They go out. Far away beyond the orchard a shepherd is piping.* TROFIMOV
crosses the stage and, seeing VARYA *and* ANYA, *stands still.*]

Varya.   Sh! She's asleep . . . asleep . . . Come, darling.
Anya [*softly, half-asleep*].   I'm so tired. Those bells . . . uncle . . . dear. . . .
   Mamma and uncle. . . .
Varya.   Come, my precious, come along. [*They go into* ANYA's *room.*]
Trofimov [*with emotion*].   My sunshine, my spring!

   [*The Curtain Falls.*]

Act II

[*A meadow. An old, long-abandoned, lopsided little chapel; near it, a well, large
slabs, which had apparently once served as tombstones, and an old bench. In
the background, the road to the Gayev estate. To one side poplars loom darkly,
where the cherry orchard begins. In the distance a row of telegraph poles, and
far off, on the horizon, the faint outline of a large city which is seen only in fine,
clear weather. The sun will soon be setting.* CHARLOTTA, YASHA, *and* DUNYASHA
are seated on the bench. YEPIHODOV *stands near and plays a guitar. All are
pensive.* CHRLOTTA *wears an old peaked cap. She has taken a gun from her
shoulder and is straightening the buckle on the strap.*]

Charlotta [*musingly*].   I haven't a real passport, I don't know how old I am, and
   I always feel that I am very young. When I was a little girl, my father and
   mother used to go from fair to fair and give performances, very good ones. And
   I used to do the *salto mortale*,[1] and all sorts of other tricks. And when papa and
   mamma died, a German lady adopted me and began to educate me. Very good.
   I grew up and became a governess. But where I come from and who I am, I
   don't know. . . . Who were my parents? Perhaps they weren't even married.
   . . . I don't know. . . . [*Takes a cucumber out of her pocket and eats it.*] I
   don't know a thing. [*Pause.*] One wants so much to talk, and there isn't anyone
   to talk to. . . . I haven't anybody.
Yepihodov [*plays the guitar and sings*].   "What care I for the jarring world?
   What's friend or foe to me? . . ." How agreeable it is to play the mandolin.
Dunyasha.   That's a guitar, not a mandolin. [*Looks in a hand mirror and
   powders her face.*]
Yepihodov.   To a madman in love it's a mandolin. [*Sings.*] "Would that the
   heart were warmed by the fire of mutual love!" [YASHA *joins in.*]
Charlotta.   How abominably these people sing. Pfui! Like jackals!

---

1   Italian for "death defying leap."

Dunyasha [*to* YASHA]. How wonderful it must be though to have stayed abroad!

Yasha. Ah, yes, of course, I cannot but agree with you there. [*Yawns and lights a cigar.*]

Yepihodov. Naturally. Abroad, everything has long since achieved full perplexion.

Yasha. That goes without saying.

Yepihodov. I'm a cultivated man, I read all kinds of remarkable books. And yet I can never make out what direction I should take, what is it that I want, properly speaking. Should I live, or should I shoot myself, properly speaking? Nevertheless, I always carry a revolver about me. . . . Here it is. . . . [*Shows revolver.*]

Charlotta. I've finished. I'm going. [*Puts the gun over her shoulder.*] You are a very clever man, Yepihodov, and a very terrible one; women must be crazy about you. Br-r-r! [*Starts to go.*] These clever men are all so stupid; there's no one for me to talk to . . . always alone, alone, I haven't a soul . . . and who I am, and why I am, nobody knows. [*Exits unhurriedly.*]

Yepihodov. Properly speaking and letting other subjects alone, I must say regarding myself, among other things, that fate treats me mercilessly, like a storm treats a small boat. If I am mistaken, let us say, why then do I wake up this morning, and there on my chest is a spider of enormous dimensions . . . like this . . . [*indicates with both hands*]. Again, I take up a pitcher of kvass to have a drink, and in it there is something unseemly to the highest degree, something like a cockroach. [*Pause.*] Have you read Buckle?[1] [*Pause.*] I wish to have a word with you, Avdotya Fyodorovna, if I may trouble you.

Dunyasha. Well, go ahead.

Yepihodov. I wish to speak with you alone. [*Sighs.*]

Dunyasha [*embarrassed*]. Very well. Only first bring me my little cape. You'll find it near the wardrobe. It's rather damp here.

Yepihodov. Certainly, ma'am; I will fetch it, ma'am. Now I know what to do with my revolver. [*Takes the guitar and goes off playing it.*]

Yasha. Two-and-Twenty Troubles! An awful fool, between you and me. [*Yawns.*]

Dunyasha. I hope to God he doesn't shoot himself! [*Pause.*] I've become so nervous, I'm always fretting. I was still a little girl when I was taken into the big house, I am quite unused to the simple life now, and my hands are white, as white as a lady's. I've become so soft, so delicate, so refined, I'm afraid of everything. It's so terrifying; and if you deceive me, Yasha, I don't know what will happen to my nerves. [YASHA *kisses her.*]

Yasha. You're a peach! Of course, a girl should never forget herself; and what I dislike more than anything is when a girl don't behave properly.

Dunyasha. I've fallen passionately in love with you; you're educated—you have something to say about everything. [*Pause.*]

Yasha [*yawns*]. Yes, ma'am. Now the way I look at it, if a girl loves someone, it means she is immoral. [*Pause.*] It's agreeable smoking a cigar in the fresh air. [*Listens.*] Someone's coming this way. . . . It's our madam and the others. [DUNYASHA *embraces him impulsively.*] You go home, as though you'd been to

---

1 Henry Buckle (1821–1862), an Englishman who studied the influence of natural conditions such as climate, soil, and topography upon the history of nations.

the river to bathe; go by the little path, or else they'll run into you and suspect me of having arranged to meet you here. I can't stand that sort of thing.

Dunyasha [*coughing softly*]. Your cigar's made my head ache. [*Exits.* YASHA *remains standing near the chapel. Enter* MME. RANEVSKAYA, GAYEV, *and* LOPAHIN.]

Lopahin. You must make up your mind once and for all—there's no time to lose. It's quite a simple question, you know. Do you agree to lease your land for summer cottages or not? Answer in one word, yes or no; only one word!

Mme. Ranevskaya. Who's been smoking such abominable cigars here? [*Sits down.*]

Gayev. Now that the railway line is so near, it's made things very convenient. [*Sits down.*] Here we've been able to have lunch in town. Yellow ball in the side pocket! I feel like going into the house and playing just one game.

Mme. Ranevskaya. You can do that later.

Lopahin. Only one word! [*Imploringly.*] Do give me an answer!

Gayev [*yawning*]. Who?

Mme. Ranevakaya [*looks into her purse*]. Yesterday I had a lot of money and now my purse is almost empty. My poor Varya tries to economize by feeding us just milk soup; in the kitchen the old people get nothing but dried peas to eat, while I squander money thoughtlessly. [*Drops the purse, scattering gold pieces.*] You see there they go. . . . [*Shows vexation.*]

Yasha. Allow me—I'll pick them up. [*Picks up the money.*]

Mme. Ranevskaya. Be so kind, Yasha. And why did I go to lunch in town? That nasty restaurant, with its music and the tablecloth smelling of soap . . . Why drink so much, Leonid? Why eat so much? Why talk so much? Today again you talked a lot, and all so inappropriately about the 'Seventies, about the decadents. And to whom? Talking to waiters about decadents!

Lopahin. Yes.

Gayev [*waving his hand*]. I'm incorrigible; that's obvious. [*Irritably, to* YASHA.] Why do you keep dancing about in front of me?

Yasha [*laughs*]. I can't hear your voice without laughing—

Gayev. Either he or I—

Mme. Ranevskaya. Go away, Yasha; run along.

Yasha [*handing* MME. RANEVSKAYA *her purse*]. I'm going, at once. [*Hardly able to suppress his laughter.*] This minute. [*Exits.*]

Lopahin. That rich man, Deriganov, wants to buy your estate. They say he's coming to the auction himself.

Mme. Ranevskaya. Where did you hear that?

Lopahin. That's what they are saying in town.

Gayev. Our aunt in Yaroslavl has promised to help; but when she will send the money, and how much, no one knows.

Lopahin. How much will she send? A hundred thousand? Two hundred?

Mme. Ranevskaya. Oh, well, ten or fifteen thousand; and we'll have to be grateful for that.

Lopahin. Forgive me, but such frivolous people as you are, so queer and unbusinesslike—I never met in my life. One tells you in plain language that your estate is up for sale, and you don't seem to take it in.

Mme. Ranevskaya. What are we to do? Tell us what to do.

Lopahin. I do tell you, every day; every day I say the same thing! You must lease the cherry orchard and the land for summer cottages, you must do it and as soon as possible—right away. The auction is close at hand. Please understand! Once you've decided to have the cottages, you can raise as much money as you like, and you're saved.

Mme. Ranevskaya. Cottages—summer people—forgive me, but it's all so vulgar.

Gayev. I agree with you absolutely.

Lopahin. I shall either burst into tears or scream or faint! I can't stand it! You've worn me out! [*To* GAYEV.] You're an old woman!

Gayev. Who?

Lopahin. An old woman! [*Gets up to go.*]

Mme. Ranevskaya [*alarmed*]. No, don't go! Please stay, I beg you, my dear. Perhaps we shall think of something.

Lopahin. What is there to think of?

Mme. Ranevskaya. Don't go, I beg you. With you here it's more cheerful anyway. [*Pause.*] I keep expecting something to happen; it's as though the house were going to crash about our ears.

Gayev [*in deep thought*]. Bank shot in the corner. . . . Three cushions in the side pocket. . . .

Mme. Ranevskaya. We have been great sinners. . . .

Lopahin. What sins could you have committed?

Gayev [*putting a candy in his mouth*]. They say I've eaten up my fortune in candy! [*Laughs.*]

Mme. Ranevskaya. Oh, my sins! I've squandered money away recklessly, like a lunatic, and I married a man who made nothing but debts. My husband drank himself to death on champagne, he was a terrific drinker. And then, to my sorrow, I fell in love with another man, and I lived with him. And just then— that was my first punishment—a blow on the head: my little boy was drowned here in the river. And I went abroad, went away forever . . . never to come back, never to see this river again. . . . I closed my eyes and ran, out of my mind. . . . But he followed me, pitiless, brutal. I bought a villa near Mentone, because he fell ill there; and for three years, day and night, I knew no peace, no rest. The sick man wore me out, he sucked my soul dry. Then last year, when the villa was sold to pay my debts, I went to Paris, and there he robbed me, abandoned me, took up with another woman; I tried to poison myself—it was stupid, so shameful—and then suddenly I felt drawn back to Russia, back to my own country, to my little girl. [*Wipes her tears away.*] Lord, Lord! Be merciful, forgive me my sins—don't punish me any more! [*Takes a telegram out of her pocket.*] This came today from Paris—he begs me to forgive him, implores me to go back. . . . [*Tears up the telegram.*] Do I hear music? [*Listens.*]

Gayev. That's our famous Jewish band, you remember? Four violins, a flute, and a double bass.

Mme. Ranevskaya. Does it still exist? We ought to send for them some evening and have a party.

Lopahin [*listens*]. I don't hear anything. [*Hums softly.*] "The Germans for a fee will Frenchify a Russian." [*Laughs.*] I saw a play at the theater yesterday— awfully funny.

Mme. Ranevskaya. There was probably nothing funny about it. You shouldn't go to see plays, you should look at yourselves more often. How drab your lives are—how full of unnecessary talk.

Lopahin. That's true; come to think of it, we do live like fools. [*Pause.*] My pop was a peasant, an idiot; he understood nothing, never taught me anything, all he did was beat me when he was drunk, and always with a stick. Fundamentally, I'm just the same kind of blockhead and idiot. I was never taught anything—I have a terrible handwriting; I write so that I feel ashamed before people, like a pig.

Mme. Ranevskaya. You should get married, my friend.

Lopahin. Yes . . . that's true.

Mme. Ranevskaya. To our Varya, she's a good girl.

Lopahin. Yes.

Mme. Ranevskaya. She's a girl who comes of simple people, she works all day long; and above all, she loves you. Besides, you've liked her for a long time now.

Lopahin. Well, I've nothing against it. She's a good girl. [*Pause.*]

Gayev. I've been offered a place in the bank—6,000 a year. Have you heard?

Mme. Ranevskaya. You're not up to it. Stay where you are.

[FIRS *enters, carrying an overcoat.*]

Firs [*to* GAYEV]. Please put this on, sir, it's damp.

Gayev [*putting it on*]. I'm fed up with you, brother.

Firs. Never mind. This morning you drove off without saying a word. [*Looks him over.*]

Mme. Ranevskaya. How you've aged, Firs.

Firs. I beg your pardon?

Lopahin. The lady says you've aged.

Firs. I've lived a long time; they were arranging my wedding and your papa wasn't born yet. [*Laughs.*] When freedom came I was already head footman. I wouldn't consent to be set free then; I stayed on with the master. . . . [*Pause.*] I remember they were all very happy, but why they were happy, they didn't know themselves.

Lopahin. It was fine in the old days! At least there was flogging!

Firs [*not hearing*]. Of course. The peasants kept to the masters, the masters kept to the peasants; but now they've all gone their own ways, and there's no making out anything.

Gayev. Be quiet, Firs. I must go to town tomorrow. They've promised to introduce me to a general who might let us have a loan.

Lopahin. Nothing will come of that. You won't even be able to pay the interest, you can be certain of that.

Mme. Ranevskaya. He's raving, there isn't any general. [*Enter* TROFIMOV, ANYA, *and* VARYA.]

Gayev. Here come our young people.

Anya. There's mamma, on the bench.

Mme. Ranevskaya [*tenderly*]. Come here, come along, my darlings. [*Embraces* ANYA *and* VARYA.] If you only knew how I love you both! Sit beside me—there, like that. [*All sit down.*]

Lopahin. Our perpetual student is always with the young ladies.

Trofimov. That's not any of your business.

Lopahin. He'll soon be fifty, and he's still a student!

Trofimov. Stop your silly jokes.

Lopahin. What are you so cross about, you queer bird?

Trofimov. Oh, leave me alone.

Lopahin [*laughs*]. Allow me to ask you, what do you think of me?

Trofimov. What I think of you, Yermolay Alexeyevich, is this: you are a rich man who will soon be a millionaire. Well, just as a beast of prey, which devours everything that comes in its way, is necessary for the process of metabolism to go on, so you too are necessary. [*All laugh.*]

Varya. Better tell us something about the planets, Petya.

Mme. Ranevskaya. No, let's go on with yesterday's conversation.

Trofimov. What was it about?

Gayev. About man's pride.

Trofimov. Yesterday we talked a long time, but we came to no conclusion. There is something mystical about man's pride in your sense of the word. Perhaps you're right, from your own point of view. But if you reason simply, without going into subtleties, then what call is there for pride? Is there any sense in it, if man is so poor a thing physiologically, and if, in the great majority of cases, he is coarse, stupid, and profoundly unhappy? We should stop admiring ourselves. We should work, and that's all.

Gayev. You die, anyway.

Trofimov. Who knows? And what does it mean—to die? Perhaps man has a hundred senses, and at his death only the five we know perish, while the other ninety-five remain alive.

Mme. Ranevskaya. How clever you are, Petya!

Lopahin [*ironically*]. Awfully clever!

Trofimov. Mankind goes forward, developing its powers. Everything that is now unattainable for it will one day come within man's reach and be clear to him; only we must work, helping with all our might those who seek the truth. Here among us in Russia only the very few work as yet. The great majority of the intelligentsia, as far as I can see, seek nothing, do nothing, are totally unfit for work of any kind. They call themselves the intelligentsia, yet they are uncivil to their servants, treat the peasants like animals, are poor students, never read anything serious, do absolutely nothing at all, only talk about science, and have little appreciation of the arts. They are all solemn, have grim faces, they all philosophize and talk of weighty matters. And meanwhile the vast majority of us, ninety-nine out of a hundred, live like savages. At the least provocation—a punch in the jaw, and curses. They eat disgustingly, sleep in filth and stuffiness, bedbugs everywhere, stench and damp and moral slovenliness. And obviously, the only purpose of all our fine talk is to hoodwink ourselves and others. Show me where the public nurseries are that we've heard so much about, and the libraries. We read about them in novels, but in reality they don't exist; there is nothing but dirt, vulgarity, and Asiatic backwardness. I don't like very solemn faces, I'm afraid of them, I'm afraid of serious conversations. We'd do better to keep quiet for a while.

Lopahin. Do you know, I get up at five o'clock in the morning, and I work from morning till night; and I'm always handling money, my own and other people's, and I see what people around me are really like. You've only to start doing anything to see how few honest, decent people there are. Sometimes when I lie awake at night, I think: "Oh, Lord, thou hast given us immense forests, boundless fields, the widest horizons, and living in their midst, we ourselves ought really to be giants."

Mme. Ranevskaya. Now you want giants! They're only good in fairy tales; otherwise they're frightening.

[YEPIHODOV *crosses the stage at the rear, playing the guitar.*]

Mme. Ranevskaya [*pensively*].   There goes Yepihodov.
Anya [*pensively*].   There goes Yepihodov.
Gayev.   Ladies and gentlemen, the sun has set.
Trofimov.   Yes.
Gayev [*in a low voice, declaiming as it were*].   Oh, Nature, wondrous Nature, you shine with eternal radiance, beautiful and indifferent! You, whom we call our mother, unite within yourself life and death! You animate and destroy!
Varya [*pleadingly*].   Uncle dear!
Anya.   Uncle, again!
Trofimov.   You'd better bank the yellow ball in the side pocket.
Gayev.   I'm silent, I'm silent. . . .

[*All sit plunged in thought. Stillness reigns. Only* FIRS's *muttering is audible. Suddenly a distant sound is heard, coming from the sky as it were, the sound of a snapping string, mournfully dying away.*]

Mme. Ranevskaya.   What was that?
Lopahin.   I don't know. Somewhere far away, in the pits, a bucket's broken loose; but somewhere very far away.
Gayev.   Or it might be some sort of bird, perhaps a heron.
Trofimov.   Or an owl. . . .
Mme. Ranevskaya [*shudders*].   It's weird, somehow. [*Pause.*]
Firs.   Before the calamity the same thing happened—the owl screeched, and the samovar hummed all the time.
Gayev.   Before what calamity?
Firs.   Before the Freedom.[*Pause.*]
Mme. Ranevskaya.   Come, my friends, let's be going. It's getting dark. [*To* ANYA.] You have tears in your eyes. What is it, my little one? [*Embraces her.*]
Anya.   I don't know, mamma; it's nothing.
Trofimov.   Somebody's coming.

[*A* TRAMP *appears, wearing a shabby white cap and an overcoat. He is slightly drunk.*]

Tramp.   Allow me to inquire, will this short-cut take me to the station?
Gayev.   It will. Just follow that road.
Tramp.   My heartfelt thanks. [*Coughing.*] The weather is glorious. [*Recites.*] "My brother, my suffering brother . . . Go down to the Volga! Whose groans . . . ?" [*To* VARYA.] Mademoiselle, won't you spare 30 kopecks for a hungry Russian?

[VARYA, *frightened, cries out.*]

Lopahin [*angrily*].   Even panhandling has its proprieties.

Mme. Ranevskaya [*scared*].   Here, take this. [*Fumbles in her purse.*] I haven't any silver . . . never mind, here's a gold piece.

Tramp.   My heartfelt thanks. [*Exits. Laughter.*]

Varya [*frightened*].   I'm leaving, I'm leaving . . . Oh, mamma dear, at home the servants have nothing to eat, and you gave him a gold piece!

Mme. Ranevskaya.   What are you going to do with me? I'm such a fool. When we get home, I'll give you everything I have. Yermolay Alexeyevich, you'll lend me some more. . . .

Lopahin.   Yes, ma'am.

Mme. Ranevskaya.   Come, ladies and gentlemen, it's time to be going. Oh! Varya, we've settled all about your marriage. Congratulations!

Varya [*through tears*].   Really mamma, that's not a joking matter.

Lopahin.   "Aurelia, get thee to a nunnery, go . . ."

Gayev.   And do you know, my hands are trembling: I haven't played billiards in a long time.

Lopahin.   "Aurelia, nymph, in your orisons, remember me!"

Mme. Ranevskaya.   Let's go, it's almost suppertime.

Varya.   He frightened me! My heart's pounding.

Lopahin.   Let me remind you, ladies and gentlemen, on the 22nd of August the cherry orchard will be up for sale. Think about that! Think!

[*All except* TROFIMOV *and* ANYA *go out.*]

Anya [*laughs*].   I'm grateful to that tramp; he frightened Varya and so we're alone.

Trofimov.   Varya's afraid we'll fall in love with each other all of a sudden. She hasn't left us alone for days. Her narrow mind can't grasp that we're above love. To avoid the petty and illusory, everything that prevents us from being free and happy—that is the goal and meaning of our life. Forward! Do not fall behind, friends!

Anya [*strikes her hands together*].   How well you speak! [*Pause.*] It's wonderful here today.

Trofimov.   Yes, the weather's glorious.

Anya.   What have you done to me, Petya? Why don't I love the cherry orchard as I used to? I loved it so tenderly. It seemed to me there was no spot on earth lovelier than our orchard.

Trofimov.   All Russia is our orchard. Our land is vast and beautiful, there are many wonderful places in it. [*Pause.*] Think of it, Anya, your grandfather, your great-grandfather and all your ancestors were serf-owners, owners of living souls, and aren't human beings looking at you from every tree in the orchard, from every leaf, from every trunk? Don't you hear voices? Oh, it's terrifying! Your orchard is a fearful place, and when you pass through it in the evening or at night, the old bark on the trees gleams faintly, and the cherry trees seem to be dreaming of things that happened a hundred, two hundred years ago and to be tormented by painful visions. What is there to say? We're at least two hundred years behind, we've really achieved nothing yet, we have no definite attitude to the past, we only philosophize, complain of the blues, or drink vodka. It's all so clear: in order to live in the present, we should first redeem our past, finish with it, and we can expiate it only by suffering, only by extraordinary, unceasing labor. Realize that, Anya.

Anya. The house in which we live has long ceased to be our own, and I will leave it, I give you my word.

Trofimov. If you have the keys, fling them into the well and go away. Be free as the wind.

Anya [*in ecstasy*]. How well you put that!

Trofimov. Believe me, Anya, believe me! I'm not yet thirty, I'm young, I'm still a student—but I've already suffered so much. In winter I'm hungry, sick, harassed, poor as a beggar, and where hasn't Fate driven me? Where haven't I been? And yet always, every moment of the day and night, my soul is filled with inexplicable premonitions. . . . I have a premonition of happiness, Anya. . . . I see it already!

Anya [*pensively*]. The moon is rising.

[YEPIHODOV *is heard playing the same mournful tune on the guitar. The moon rises. Somewhere near the poplars* VARYA *is looking for* ANYA *and calling* "Anya, where are you?"]

Trofimov. Yes, the moon is rising. [*Pause.*] There it is, happiness, it's approaching, it's coming nearer and nearer, I can already hear its footsteps. And if we don't see it, if we don't know it, what does it matter? Others will!

Varya's voice. "Anya! Where are you?"

Trofimov. That Varya again! [*Angrily.*] It's revolting!

Anya. Never mind, let's go down to the river. It's lovely there.

Trofimov. Come on. [*They go.*]

Varya's voice. "Anya! Anya!"

[*The Curtain Falls.*]

Act III

[A *drawing-room separated by an arch from a ballroom. Evening. Chandelier burning. The Jewish band is heard playing in the anteroom. In the ballroom they are dancing the* Grand Rond. PISHCHIK *is heard calling,* "Promenade à une paire." PISHCHIK *and* CHARLOTTA, TROFIMOV *and* MME. RANEVSKAYA, ANYA *and the* POST OFFICE CLERK, VARYA *and the* STATIONMASTER, *and others, enter the drawing-room in couples.* DUNYASHA *is in the last couple.* VARYA *weeps quietly, wiping her tears as she dances. All parade through drawing-room.* PISHCHIK *calling* "Grand rond, balancez!" *and* "Les cavaliers à genoux et remerciez vos dames!" FIRS, *wearing a dress-coat, brings in soda-water on a tray.* PISHCHIK *and* TROFIMOV *enter the drawing-room.*]

Pishchik. I'm a full-blooded man; I've already had two strokes. Dancing's hard work for me; but as they say, "If you run with the pack, you can bark or not, but at least wag your tail." Still, I'm as strong as a horse. My late lamented father, who would have his joke, God rest his soul, used to say, talking about our origin, that the ancient line of the Simeonov-Pishchiks was descended from the very horse that Caligula had made a senator. [*Sits down.*] But the trouble is, I have no money. A hungry dog believes in nothing but meat. [*Snores and wakes up at once.*] It's the same with me—I can think of nothing but money.

Trofimov. You know, there *is* something equine about your figure.

Pishchik. Well, a horse is a fine animal—one can sell a horse.

[*Sound of billiards being played in an adjoining room.* VARYA *appears in the archway.*]

Trofimov [*teasing her*]. Madam Lopahina! Madam Lopahina!

Varya [*angrily*]. Mangy master!

Trofimov. Yes, I am a mangy master and I'm proud of it.

Varya [*reflecting bitterly*]. Here we've hired musicians, and what shall we pay them with? [*Exits.*]

Trofimov [*to* PISHCHIK]. If the energy you have spent during your lifetime looking for money to pay interest had gone into something else, in the end you could have turned the world upside down.

Pishchik. Nietzsche, the philosopher, the greatest, most famous of men, that colossal intellect, says in his works, that it is permissible to forge banknotes.

Trofimov. Have you read Nietzsche?

Pishchik. Well . . . Dashenka told me . . . And now I've got to the point where forging banknotes is about the only way out for me. . . . The day after tomorrow I have to pay 310 rubles—I already have 130. . . . [*Feels in his pockets. In alarm*] The money's gone! I've lost my money! [*Through tears.*] Where's my money? [*Joyfully.*] Here it is! Inside the lining. . . . I'm all in a sweat. . . .

[*Enter* MME. RANEVSKAYA *and* CHARLOTTA.]

Mme. Ranevskaya [*hums the "Lezginka"*[1]]. Why isn't Leonid back yet? What is he doing in town? [*To* DUNYASHA.] Dunyasha, offer the musicians tea.

Trofimov. The auction hasn't taken place, most likely.

Mme. Ranevskaya. It's the wrong time to have the band, and the wrong time to give a dance. Well, never mind. [*Sits down and hums softly.*]

Charlotta [*hands* PISHCHIK *a pack of cards*]. Here is a pack of cards. Think of any card you like.

Pishchik. I've thought of one.

Charlotta. Shuffle the pack now. That's right. Give it here, my dear Mr. Pishchik. *Ein, zwei, drei!* Now look for it—it's in your side pocket.

Pishchik [*taking the card out of his pocket*]. The eight of spades! Perfectly right! Just imagine!

Charlotta [*holding pack of cards in her hands. To* TROFIMOV]. Quickly, name the top card.

Trofimov. Well, let's see—the queen of spades.

Charlotta. Right! [*To* PISHCHIK.] Now name the top card.

Pishchik. The ace of hearts.

---

[1] Vigorous folk dance from the Caucasus.

Charlotta. Right! [*Claps her hands and the pack of cards disappears.*] Ah, what lovely weather it is today! [*A mysterious feminine voice which seems to come from under the floor, answers her*] "Oh, yes, it's magnificent weather, madam."

Charlotta. You are my best ideal.

Voice. "And I find you pleasing too, madam."

Stationmaster [*applauding*]. The lady ventriloquist, bravo!

Pishchik [*amazed*]. Just imagine! Enchanting Charlotta Ivanovna, I'm simply in love with you.

Charlotta. In love? [*Shrugs her shoulders.*] Are you capable of love? *Guter Mensch, aber schlechter Musikant!*[1]

Trofimov [*claps* PISHCHIK *on the shoulder*]. You old horse, you!

Charlotta. Attention please! One more trick! [*Takes a plaid from a chair.*] Here is a very good plaid; I want to sell it. [*Shaking it out.*] Does anyone want to buy it?

Pishchik [*in amazement*]. Just imagine!

Charlotta. Ein, zwei, drei! [*Raises the plaid quickly; behind it stands* ANYA. *She curtsies, runs to her mother, embraces her, and runs back into the ballroom, amidst general enthusiasm.*]

Mme. Ranevskaya [*applauds*]. Bravo! Bravo!

Charlotta. Now again! Ein, zwei, drei! [*Lifts the plaid; behind it stands* VARYA *bowing.*]

Pishchik [*running after her*]. The rascal! What a woman, what a woman! [*Exits.*]

Mme. Ranevskaya. And Leonid still isn't here. What is he doing in town so long? I don't understand. It must be all over by now. Either the estate has been sold, or the auction hasn't taken place. Why keep us in suspense so long?

Varya [*trying to console her*]. Uncle's bought it, I feel sure of that.

Trofimov [*mockingly*]. Oh, yes!

Varya. Great-aunt sent him an authorization to buy it in her name, and to transfer the debt. She's doing it for Anya's sake. And I'm sure that God will help us, and uncle will buy it.

Mme. Ranevskaya. Great-aunt sent fifteen thousand to buy the estate in her name; she doesn't trust us, but that's not even enough to pay the interest. [*Covers her face with her hands.*] Today my fate will be decided, my fate—

Trofimov [*teasing* VARYA]. Madam Lopahina!

Varya [*angrily*]. Perpetual student! Twice already you've been expelled from the university.

Mme. Ranevskaya. Why are you so cross, Varya? He's teasing you about Lopahin. Well, what of it? If you want to marry Lopahin, go ahead. He's a good man, and interesting; if you don't want to, don't. Nobody's compelling you, my pet!

Varya. Frankly, mamma dear, I take this thing seriously; he's a good man and I like him.

Mme. Ranevskaya. All right then, marry him. I don't know what you're waiting for.

Varya. But, mamma, I can't propose to him myself. For the last two years

[1] German for "Good man, but a bad musician."

everyone's been talking to me about him—talking. But he either keeps silent, or else cracks jokes. I understand; he's growing rich, he's absorbed in business—he has no time for me. If I had money, even a little, say, 100 rubles, I'd throw everything up and go far away—I'd go into a nunnery.

Trofimov. What a blessing. . . .

Varya. A student ought to be intelligent. [*Softly, with tears in her voice.*] How homely you've grown, Petya! How old you look! [*To* MME. RANEVSKAYA, *with dry eyes.*] But I can't live without work, mamma dear; I must keep busy every minute.

[*Enter* YASHA.]

Yasha [*hardly restraining his laughter*]. Yepihodov has broken a billiard cue!

[*Exits.*]

Varya. Why is Yepihodov here? Who allowed him to play billiards? I don't understand these people! [*Exits.*]

Mme. Ranevskaya. Don't tease her, Petya. She's unhappy enough without that.

Trofimov. She bustles so—and meddles in other people's business. All summer long she's given Anya and me no peace. She's afraid of a love-affair between us. What business is it of hers? Besides, I've given no grounds for it, and I'm far from such vulgarity. We are above love.

Mme. Ranevskaya. And I suppose I'm beneath love? [*Anxiously.*] What can be keeping Leonid? If I only knew whether the estate has been sold or not. Such a calamity seems so incredible to me that I don't know what to think—I feel lost. . . . I could scream. . . . I could do something stupid. . . . Save me, Petya, tell me something, talk to me!

Trofimov. Whether the estate is sold today or not, isn't it all one? That's all done with long ago—there's no turning back, the path is overgrown. Calm yourself, my dear. You mustn't deceive yourself. For once in your life you must face the truth.

Mme. Ranevskaya. What truth? You can see the truth, you can tell it from falsehood, but I seem to have lost my eyesight, I see nothing. You settle every great problem so boldly, but tell me, my dear boy, isn't it because you're young, because you don't yet know what one of your problems means in terms of suffering? You look ahead fearlessly, but isn't it because you don't see and don't expect anything dreadful, because life is still hidden from your young eyes? You're bolder, more honest, more profound than we are, but think hard, show just a bit of magnanimity, spare me. After all, I was born here, my father and mother lived here, and my grandfather; I love this house. Without the cherry orchard, my life has no meaning for me, and if it really must be sold, then sell me with the orchard. [*Embraces* TROFIMOV, *kisses him on the forehead.*] My son was drowned here. [*Weeps.*] Pity me, you good, kind fellow!

Trofimov. You know, I feel for you with all my heart.

Mme. Ranevskaya. But that should have been said differently, so differently! [*Takes out her handkerchief—a telegram falls on the floor.*] My heart is so heavy today—you can't imagine! The noise here upsets me—my inmost being trembles at every sound—I'm shaking all over. But I can't go into my own room; I'm afraid to be alone. Don't condemn me, Petya. . . . I love you as though you were one of us, I would gladly let you marry Anya—I swear I would—only, my dear boy, you must study—you must take your degree—you do nothing, you let yourself be tossed by Fate from place to place—it's so strange. It's true, isn't it? And you should do something about your beard, to make it grow somehow! [*Laughs*] You're so funny!

Trofimov [*picks up the telegram*]. I've no wish to be a dandy.

Mme. Ranevskaya. That's a telegram from Paris. I get one every day. One yesterday and one today. That savage is ill again—he's in trouble again. He begs forgiveness, implores me to go to him, and really I ought to go to Paris to be near him. Your face is stern, Petya; but what is there to do, my dear boy? What am I to do? He's ill, he's alone and unhappy, and who is to look after him, who is to keep him from doing the wrong thing, who is to give him his medicine on time? And why hide it or keep still about it—I love him! That's clear. I love him, love him! He's a millstone round my neck, he'll drag me to the bottom, but I love that stone, I can't live without it. [*Presses* TROFIMOV's *hand.*] Don't think badly of me, Petya, and don't say anything, don't say. . . .

Trofimov [*through tears*]. Forgive me my frankness in heaven's name; but you know, he robbed you!

Mme. Ranevskaya. No, no, no, you mustn't say such things! [*Covers her ears.*]

Trofimov. But he's a scoundrel! You're the only one who doesn't know it. He's a petty scoundrel—a nonentity!

Mme. Ranevskaya [*controlling her anger*]. You are twenty-six or twenty-seven years old, but you're still a schoolboy.

Trofimov. That may be.

Mme. Ranevskaya. You should be a man at your age. You should understand people who love—and ought to be in love yourself. You ought to fall in love! [*Angrily.*] Yes, yes! And it's not purity in you, it's prudishness, you're simply a queer fish, a comical freak!

Trofimov [*horrified*]. What is she saying?

Mme. Ranevskaya. "I am above love!" You're not above love, but simply, as our Firs says, you're an addlehead. At your age not to have a mistress!

Trofimov [*horrified*]. This is frightful! What is she saying! [*Goes rapidly into the ballroom, clutching his head.*] It's frightful—I can't stand it, I won't stay! [*Exits, but returns at once.*] All is over between us! [*Exits into anteroom.*]

Mme. Ranevskaya [*shouts after him*]. Petya! Wait! You absurd fellow, I was joking. Petya!

[*Sound of somebody running quickly downstairs and suddenly falling down with a crash.* ANYA *and* VARYA *scream. Sound of laughter a moment later.*]

Mme. Ranevskaya. What's happened?

[ANYA *runs in.*]

Anya [*laughing*]. Petya's fallen downstairs! [*Runs out.*]

Mme. Ranevskaya. What a queer bird that Petya is!

[STATIONMASTER, *standing in the middle of the ballroom, recites Alexey Tolstoy's "Magdalene," to which all listen, but after a few lines, the sound of a*

waltz is heard from the anteroom and the reading breaks off. All dance. TRO-
FIMOV, ANYA, VARYA, *and* MME. RANEVSKAYA *enter from the anteroom.*]

Mme. Ranevskaya.   Petya, you pure soul, please forgive me. . . . Let's dance.

[*Dances with* PETYA. ANYA *and* VARYA *dance.* FIRS *enters, puts his stick down by
the side door.* YASHA *enters from the drawing-room and watches the dancers.*]

Yasha.   Well, grandfather?
Firs.   I'm not feeling well. In the old days it was generals, barons, and admirals
that were dancing at our balls, and now we have to send for the Post Office
clerk and the Stationmaster, and even they aren't too glad to come. I feel kind
of shaky. The old master that's gone, their grandfather, dosed everyone with
sealing-wax, whatever ailed 'em. I've been taking sealing-wax every day for
twenty years or more. Perhaps that's what's kept me alive.
Yasha.   I'm fed up with you, grandpop. [*Yawns.*] It's time you croaked.
Firs.   Oh, you addlehead! [*Mumbles.*]

[TROFIMOV *and* MME. RANEVSKAYA *dance from the ballroom into the drawing-
room.*]

Mme. Ranevskaya.   Merci. I'll sit down a while. [*Sits down.*] I'm tired.

[*Enter* ANYA.]

Anya [*excitedly*].   There was a man in the kitchen just now who said the cherry
orchard was sold today.
Mme. Ranevskaya.   Sold to whom?
Anya.   He didn't say. He's gone. [*Dances off with* TROFIMOV.]
Yasha.   It was some old man gabbing, a stranger.
Firs.   And Leonid Andreyevich isn't back yet; he hasn't come. And he's wearing
his lightweight between-season overcoat; like enough, he'll catch cold. Ah, when
they're young they're green.
Mme. Ranevskaya.   This is killing me. Go, Yasha, find out to whom it has been
sold.
Yasha.   But the old man left long ago. [*Laughs.*]
Mme. Ranevskaya.   What are you laughing at? What are you pleased about?
Yasha.   That Yepihodov is such a funny one. A funny fellow, Two-and-Twenty
Troubles!
Mme. Ranevskaya.   Firs, if the estate is sold, where will you go?
Firs.   I'll go where you tell me.
Mme. Ranevskaya.   Why do you look like that? Are you ill? You ought to go to
bed.
Firs.   Yes! [*With a snigger.*] Me go to bed, and who's to hand things round?
Who's to see to things? I'm the only one in the whole house.
Yasha [*to* MME. RANEVSKAYA].   Lubov Andreyevna, allow me to ask a favor of
you, be so kind! If you go back to Paris, take me with you, I beg you. It's
positively impossible for me to stay here. [*Looking around; sotto voce*] What's
the use of talking? You see for yourself, it's an uncivilized country, the people
have no morals, and then the boredom! The food in the kitchen's revolting, and

besides there's this Firs wanders about mumbling all sorts of inappropriate words. Take me with you, be so kind!

[*Enter* PISHCHIK.]

Pishchik.   May I have the pleasure of a waltz with you, charming lady? [MME. RANEVSKAYA *accepts*] All the same, enchanting lady, you must let me have 180 rubles. . . . You must let me have [*dancing*] just one hundred and eighty rubles. [*They pass into the ballroom.*]

Yasha [*hums softly*].   "Oh, wilt thou understand the tumult in my soul?" [*In the ballroom a figure in a gray top hat and checked trousers is jumping about and waving its arms; shouts:* "Bravo, Charlotta Ivanovna!"]

Dunyasha [*stopping to powder her face; to* FIRS].   The young miss has ordered me to dance. There are so many gentlemen and not enough ladies. But dancing makes me dizzy, my heart begins to beat fast, Firs Nikolayevich. The Post Office clerk said something to me just now that quite took my breath away. [*Music stops.*]

Firs.   What did he say?

Dunyasha.   "You're like a flower," he said.

Yasha [*yawns*].   What ignorance. [*Exits.*]

Dunyasha.   "Like a flower!" I'm such a delicate girl. I simply adore pretty speeches.

Firs.   You'll come to a bad end.

[*Enter* YEPIHODOV.]

Yepihodov [*to* DUNYASHA].   You have no wish to see me, Avdotya Fyodorovna . . . as though I was some sort of insect. [*Sighs*] Ah, life!

Dunyasha.   What is it you want?

Yepihodov.   Indubitably you may be right. [*Sighs.*] But of course, if one looks at it from the point of view, if I may be allowed to say so, and apologizing for my frankness, you have completely reduced me to a state of mind. I know my fate. Every day some calamity befalls me, and I grew used to it long ago, so that I look upon my fate with a smile. You gave me your word, and though I—

Dunyasha.   Let's talk about it later, please. But just now leave me alone, I am daydreaming. [*Plays with a fan.*]

Yepihodov.   A misfortune befalls me every day; and if I may be allowed to say so, I merely smile, I even laugh.

[*Enter* VARYA.]

Varya [*to* YEPIHODOV].   Are you still here? What an impertinent fellow you are really! Run along, Dunyasha. [*To* YEPIHODOV.] Either you're playing billiards and breaking a cue, or you're wandering about the drawing-room as though you were a guest.

Yepihodov.   You cannot, permit me to remark, penalize me.

Varya.   I'm not penalizing you; I'm just telling you. You merely wander from place to place, and don't do your work. We keep you as a clerk, but Heaven knows what for.

Yepihodov [*offended*].   Whether I work or whether I walk, whether I eat or whether I play billiards, is a matter to be discussed only by persons of under-standing and of mature years.

Varya [*enraged*].   You dare say that to me—you dare? You mean to say I've no understanding? Get out of here at once! This minute!

Yepihodov [*scared*].   I beg you to express yourself delicately.

Varya [*beside herself*].   Clear out this minute! Out with you!

[YEPIHODOV *goes towards the door,* VARYA *following.*]

Varya.   Two-and-Twenty Troubles! Get out—don't let me set eyes on you!

[*Exit* YEPIHODOV. *His voice is heard behind the door:* "I shall lodge a complaint against you!"]

Varya.   Oh, you're coming back? [*She seizes the stick left near door by* FIRS.] Well, come then . . . come . . . I'll show you . . . Ah, you're coming? You're coming? . . . Come. . . . [*Swings the stick just as* LOPAHIN *enters.*]

Lopahin.   Thank you kindly.

Varya [*angrily and mockingly*].   I'm sorry.

Lopahin.   It's nothing. Thank you kindly for your charming reception.

Varya.   Don't mention it. [*Walks away, looks back and asks softly.*] I didn't hurt you, did I?

Lopahin.   Oh, no, not at all. I shall have a large bump, though.

[*Voices from the ballroom:* "Lopahin is here! Lopahin!" *Enter* PISHCHIK.]

Pishchik.   My eyes do see, my ears do hear! [*Kisses* LOPAHIN.]

Lopahin.   You smell of cognac, my dear friends. And we've been celebrating here, too.

[*Enter* MME. RANEVSKAYA.]

Mme. Ranevskaya.   Is that you, Yermolay Alexeyevich? What kept you so long? Where's Leonid?

Lopahin.   Leonid Andreyevich arrived with me. He's coming.

Mme. Ranevskaya.   Well, what happened? Did the sale take place? Speak!

Lopahin [*embarrassed, fearful of revealing his joy*].   The sale was over at four o'clock. We missed the train—had to wait till half past nine. [*Sighing heavily.*] Ugh. I'm a little dizzy.

[*Enter* GAYEV. *In his right hand he holds parcels, with his left he is wiping away his tears.*]

Mme. Ranevskaya.   Well, Leonid? What news? [*Impatiently, through tears.*] Be quick, for God's sake!

Gayev [*not answering, simply waves his hand. Weeping, to* FIRS].   Here, take these; anchovies, Kerch herrings. . . . I haven't eaten all day. What I've been through! [*The click of billiard balls comes through the open door of the billiard room and* YASHA's *voice is heard:* "Seven and eighteen!" GAYEV's *expression changes, he no longer weeps.*] I'm terribly tired. Firs, help me change. [*Exits, followed by* FIRS.]

Pishchik.   How about the sale? Tell us what happened.

Mme. Ranevskaya.   Is the cherry orchard sold?
Lopahin.   Sold.
Mme. Ranevskaya.   Who bought it?
Lopahin.   I bought it.

[*Pause.* MME. RANEVSKAYA *is overcome. She would fall to the floor, were it not for the chair and table near which she stands.* VARYA *takes the keys from her belt, flings them on the floor in the middle of the drawing-room and goes out.*]

Lopahin.   I bought it. Wait a bit, ladies and gentlemen, please, my head is swimming, I can't talk. [*Laughs.*] We got to the auction and Deriganov was there already. Leonid Andreyevich had only 15,000 and straight off Deriganov bid 30,000 over and above the mortgage. I saw how the land lay, got into the fight, bid 40,000. He bid 45,000. I bid fifty-five. He kept adding five thousands, I ten. Well . . . it came to an end. I bid ninety above the mortgage and the estate was knocked down to me. Now the cherry orchard's mine! Mine! [*Laughs uproariously.*] Lord! God in Heaven! The cherry orchard's mine! Tell me that I'm drunk—out of my mind—that it's all a dream. [*Stamps his feet.*] Don't laugh at me! If my father and my grandfather could rise from their graves and see all that has happened—how their Yermolay, who used to be flogged, their half-literate Yermolay, who used to run about barefoot in winter, how that very Yermolay has bought the most magnificent estate in the world. I bought the estate where my father and grandfather were slaves, where they weren't even allowed to enter the kitchen. I'm asleep—it's only a dream—I only imagine it. . . . It's the fruit of your imagination, wrapped in the darkness of the unknown! [*Picks up the keys, smiling genially.*] She threw down the keys, wants to show she's no longer mistress here. [*Jingles keys.*] Well, no matter. [*The band is heard tuning up.*] Hey, musicians! Strike up! I want to hear you! Come, everybody, and see how Yermolay Lopahin will lay the ax to the cherry orchard and how the trees will fall to the ground. We will build summer cottages there, and our grandsons and great-grandsons will see a new life here. Music! Strike up!

[*The band starts to play.* MME. RANEVSKAYA *has sunk into a chair and is weeping bitterly.*]

Lopahin [*reproachfully*].   Why, why didn't you listen to me? My dear friend, my poor friend, you can't bring it back now. [*Tearfully.*] Oh, if only this were over quickly! Oh, if only our wretched, disordered life were changed!
Pishchik [*takes him by the arm; sotto voce*].   She's crying. Let's go into the ballroom. Let her be alone. Come. [*Takes his arm and leads him into the ballroom.*]
Lopahin.   What's the matter? Musicians, play so I can hear you! Let me have things the way I want them. [*Ironically.*] Here comes the new master, the owner of the cherry orchard. [*Accidentally he trips over a little table, almost upsetting the candelabra.*] I can pay for everything. [*Exits with* PISHCHIK. MME. RANEVSKAYA, *alone, sits huddled up, weeping bitterly. Music plays softly. Enter* ANYA *and* TROFIMOV *quickly.* ANYA *goes to her mother and falls on her knees before her.* TROFIMOV *stands in the doorway.*]

Anya.   Mamma, mamma, you're crying! Dear, kind, good mamma, my precious, I love you, I bless you! The cherry orchard is sold, it's gone, that's true, quite true. But don't cry, mamma, life is still before you, you still have your kind, pure heart. Let us go, let us go away from here, darling. We will plant a new orchard, even more luxuriant than this one. You will see it, you will understand, and like the sun at evening, joy—deep, tranquil joy—will sink into your soul, and you will smile, mamma. Come, darling, let us go.

[*The Curtain Falls.*]

Act IV

[*Scene as in Act One. No window curtains or pictures, only a little furniture, piled up in a corner, as if for sale. A sense of emptiness. Near the outer door and at the back, suitcases, bundles, etc., are piled up. A door open on the left and the voices of* VARYA *and* ANYA *are heard.* LOPAHIN *stands waiting.* YASHA *holds a tray with glasses full of champagne.* YEPIHODOV *in the anteroom is tying up a box. Behind the scene a hum of voices: peasants have come to say good-by. Voice of* GAYEV: "*Thanks, brothers, thank you.*"]

Yasha.   The country folk have come to say good-by. In my opinion, Yermolay Alexeyevich, they are kindly souls, but there's nothing in their heads.

[*The hum dies away. Enter* MME. RANEVSKAYA *and* GAYEV. *She is not crying, but is pale, her face twitches and she cannot speak.*]

Gayev.   You gave them your purse, Luba. That won't do! That won't do!
Mme. Ranevskaya.   I couldn't help it! I couldn't! [*They go out.*]
Lopahin [*calls after them*].   Please, I beg you, have a glass at parting. I didn't think of bringing any champagne from town and at the station I could find only one bottle. Please, won't you? [*Pause.*] What's the matter, ladies and gentlemen, don't you want any? [*Moves away from the door.*] If I'd known, I wouldn't have bought it. Well, then I won't drink any, either. [YASHA *carefully sets the tray down on a chair.*] At least you have a glass, Yasha.
Yasha.   Here's to the travelers! And good luck to those that stay! [*Drinks.*] This champagne isn't the real stuff, I can assure you.
Lopahin.   Eight rubles a bottle. [*Pause.*] It's devilishly cold here.
Yasha.   They didn't light the stoves today—it wasn't worth it, since we're leaving. [*Laughs.*]
Lopahin.   Why are you laughing?
Yasha.   It's just that I'm pleased.
Lopahin.   It's October, yet it's as still and sunny as though it were summer. Good weather for building. [*Looks at his watch, and speaks off.*] Bear in mind, ladies and gentlemen, the train goes in forty-seven minutes, so you ought to start for the station in twenty minutes. Better hurry up!

[*Enter* TROFIMOV *wearing an overcoat.*]

Trofimov. I think it's time to start. The carriages are at the door. The devil only knows what's become of my rubbers; they've disappeared. [*Calling off.*] Anya! My rubbers are gone. I can't find them.

Lopahin. I've got to go to Kharkov. I'll take the same train you do. I'll spend the winter in Kharkov. I've been hanging round here with you, till I'm worn out with loafing. I can't live without work—I don't know what to do with my hands, they dangle as if they didn't belong to me.

Trofimov. Well, we'll soon be gone; then you can go on with your useful labors again.

Lopahin. Have a glass.

Trofimov. No, I won't.

Lopahin. So you're going to Moscow now?

Trofimov. Yes. I'll see them into town, and tomorrow I'll go on to Moscow.

Lopahin. Well, I'll wager the professors aren't giving any lectures; they're waiting for you to come.

Trofimov. That's none of your business.

Lopahin. Just how many years have you been at the university?

Trofimov. Can't you think of something new? Your joke's stale and flat. [*Looking for his rubbers.*] We'll probably never see each other again, so allow me to give you a piece of advice at parting: don't wave your hands about! Get out of the habit. And another thing: building bungalows, figuring that summer residents will eventually become small farmers, figuring like that is just another form of waving your hands about. . . . Never mind, I love you anyway; you have fine, delicate fingers, like an artist; you have a fine, delicate soul.

Lopahin [*embracing him*]. Good-by, my dear fellow. Thank you for everything. Let me give you some money for the journey, if you need it.

Trofimov. What for? I don't need it.

Lopahin. But you haven't any.

Trofimov. Yes, I have, thank you. I got some money for a translation—here it is in my pocket. [*Anxiously.*] But where are my rubbers?

Varya [*from the next room*]. Here! Take the nasty things. [*Flings a pair of rubbers onto the stage.*]

Trofimov. What are you so cross about, Varya? Hm . . . and these are not my rubbers.

Lopahin. I sowed three thousand acres of poppies in the spring, and now I've made 40,000 on them, clear profit; and when my poppies were in bloom, what a picture it was! So, as I say, I made 40,000; and I am offering you a loan because I can afford it. Why turn up your nose at it? I'm a peasant—I speak bluntly.

Trofimov. Your father was a peasant, mine was a druggist—that proves absolutely nothing whatever. [LOPAHIN *takes out his wallet.*] Don't, put that away! If you were to offer me two hundred thousand I wouldn't take it. I'm a free man. And everything that all of you, rich and poor alike, value so highly and hold so dear, hasn't the slightest power over me. It's like so much fluff floating in the air. I can get on without you, I can pass you by, I'm strong and proud. Mankind is moving towards the highest truth, towards the highest happiness possible on earth, and I am in the front ranks.

Lopahin. Will you get there?

Trofimov. I will. [*Pause.*] I will get there, or I will show others the way to get there.

[*The sound of axes chopping down trees is heard in the distance.*]

Lopahin. Well, good-by, my dear fellow. It's time to leave. We turn up our noses at one another, but life goes on just the same. When I'm working hard, without resting, my mind is easier, and it seems to me that I too know why I exist. But how many people are there in Russia, brother, who exist nobody knows why? Well, it doesn't matter. That's not what makes the wheels go round. They say Leonid Andreyevich has taken a position in the bank, 6,000 rubles a year. Only, of course, he won't stick to it, he's too lazy. . . .

Anya [*in the doorway*]. Mamma begs you not to start cutting down the cherry trees until she's gone.

Trofimov. Really, you should have more tact! [*Exits.*]

Lopahin. Right away—right away! Those men. . . . [*Exits.*]

Anya. Has Firs been taken to the hospital?

Yasha. I told them this morning. They must have taken him.

Anya [*to* YEPIHODOV, *who crosses the room*]. Yepihodov, please find out if Firs has been taken to the hospital.

Yasha [*offended*]. I told Yegor this morning. Why ask a dozen times?

Yepihodov. The aged Firs, in my definitive opinion, is beyond mending. It's time he was gathered to his fathers. And I can only envy him. [*Puts a suitcase down on a hat-box and crushes it.*] There now, of course. I knew it! [*Exits.*]

Yasha [*mockingly*]. Two-and-Twenty Troubles!

Varya [*through the door*]. Has Firs been taken to the hospital?

Anya. Yes.

Varya. Then why wasn't the note for the doctor taken too?

Anya. Oh! Then someone must take it to him. [*Exits.*]

Varya [*from adjoining room*]. Where's Yasha? Tell him his mother's come and wants to say good-by.

Yasha [*waves his hand*]. She tries my patience.

[DUNYASHA *has been occupied with the luggage. Seeing* YASHA *alone, she goes up to him.*]

Dunyasha. You might just give me one little look, Yasha. You're going away. . . . You're leaving me. . . . [*Weeps and throws herself on his neck.*]

Yasha. What's there to cry about? [*Drinks champagne.*] In six days I shall be in Paris again. Tomorrow we get into an express train and off we go, that's the last you'll see of us. . . . I can scarcely believe it. *Vive la France!* It don't suit me here, I just can't live here. That's all there is to it. I'm fed up with the ignorance here, I've had enough of it. [*Drinks champagne.*] What's there to cry about? Behave yourself properly, and you'll have no cause to cry.

Dunyasha [*powders her face, looking in pocket mirror*]. Do send me a letter from Paris. You know I loved you, Yasha, how I loved you! I'm a delicate creature, Yasha.

Yasha. Somebody's coming! [*Busies himself with the luggage; hums softly.*]

[*Enter* MME. RANEVSKAYA, GAYEV, ANYA, *and* CHARLOTTA.]

Gayev. We ought to be leaving. We haven't much time. [*Looks at* YASHA.] Who smells of herring?

Mme. Ranevskaya. In about ten minutes we should be getting into the carriages. [*Looks around the room.*] Good-by, dear old home, good-by, grandfather. Winter will pass, spring will come, you will no longer be here, they will have torn you down. How much these walls have seen! [*Kisses* ANYA *warmly.*] My treasure, how radiant you look! Your eyes are sparkling like diamonds. Are you glad? Very?

Anya [*gaily*]. Very glad. A new life is beginning, mamma.

Gayev. Well, really, everything is all right now. Before the cherry orchard was sold, we all fretted and suffered; but afterwards, when the question was settled finally and irrevocably, we all calmed down, and even felt quite cheerful. I'm a bank employee now, a financier. The yellow ball in the side pocket! And anyhow, you are looking better, Luba; there's no doubt of that.

Mme. Ranevskaya. Yes, my nerves are better, that's true. [*She is handed her hat and coat.*] I sleep well. Carry out my things, Yasha. It's time. [*To* ANYA.] We shall soon see each other again, my little girl. I'm going to Paris, I'll live there on the money your great-aunt sent us to buy the estate with—long live Auntie! But that money won't last long.

Anya. You'll come back soon, soon, mamma, won't you? Meanwhile I'll study, I'll pass my high school examination, and then I'll go to work and help you. We'll read all kinds of books together, mamma, won't we? [*Kisses her mother's hands.*] We'll read in the autumn evenings, we'll read lots of books, and a new wonderful world will open up before us. [*Falls into a revery.*] Mamma, do come back.

Mme. Ranevskaya. I will come back, my precious. [*Embraces her daughter. Enter* LOPAHIN *and* CHARLOTTA, *who is humming softly.*]

Gayev. Charlotta's happy: she's singing.

Charlotta [*picks up a bundle and holds it like a baby in swaddling-clothes*]. Bye, baby, bye. [*A baby is heard crying* "Wah! Wah!"] Hush, hush, my pet, my little one. "Wah! Wah!" I'm so sorry for you! [*Throws the bundle down.*] You will find me a position, won't you? I can't go on like this.

Lopahin. We'll find one for you, Charlotta Ivanovna, don't worry.

Gayev. Everyone's leaving us. Varya's going away. We've suddenly become of no use.

Charlotta. There's no place for me to live in town; I must go away. [*Hums.*]

[*Enter* PISHCHIK.]

Lopahin. There's nature's masterpiece!

Pishchik [*gasping*]. Oh . . . let me get my breath . . . I'm in agony. . . . Esteemed friends . . . Give me a drink of water. . . .

Gayev. Wants some money, I suppose. No, thank you . . . I'll keep out of harm's way. [*Exits.*]

Pishchik. It's a long while since I've been to see you, most charming lady. [*To* LOPAHIN.] So you are here . . . glad to see you, you intellectual giant . . . There. . . . [*Gives* LOPAHIN *money.*] Here's 400 rubles, and I still owe you 840.

Lopahin [*shrugging his shoulders in bewilderment*]. I must be dreaming. . . . Where did you get it?

Pishchik. Wait a minute. . . . It's hot. . . . A most extraordinary event! Some Englishmen came to my place and found some sort of white clay on my land. . . . [*To* MME. RANEVSKAYA.] And 400 for you . . . most lovely . . . most wonderful. . . . [*Hands her the money.*] The rest later. [*Drinks water.*] A young man in the train was telling me just now that a great philosopher recommends jumping off roofs. "Jump!" says he; "that's the long and the short of it!" [*In amazement.*] Just imagine! Some more water!

Lopahin. What Englishmen?

Pishchik. I leased them the tract with the clay on it for twenty-four years. . . . And now, forgive me, I can't stay. . . . I must be dashing on. . . . I'm going over to Znoikov . . . to Kardamanov. . . . I owe them all money. . . . [*Drinks water.*] Good-by, everybody. . . . I'll look in on Thursday. . . .

Mme. Ranevskaya. We're just moving into town; and tomorrow I go abroad.

Pishchik [*upset*]. What? Why into town? That's why the furniture is like that . . . and the suitcases. . . . Well, never mind! [*Through tears.*] Never mind. . . . Men of colossal intellect, these Englishmen. . . . Never mind. . . . Be happy. God will come to your help. . . . Never mind. . . . Every thing in this world comes to an end. [*Kisses* MME. RANEVSKAYA's *hand.*] If the rumor reaches you that it's all up with me, remember this old . . . horse, and say: Once there lived a certain . . . Simeonov-Pishchik . . . the kingdom of Heaven be his . . . Glorious weather! . . . Yes. . . . [*Exits, in great confusion, but at once returns and says in the doorway.*] My daughter Dashenka sends her regards. [*Exit.*]

Mme. Ranevskaya. Now we can go. I leave with two cares weighing on me. The first is poor old Firs. [*Glancing at her watch.*] We still have about five minutes.

Anya. Mamma, Firs has already been taken to the hospital. Yasha sent him there this morning.

Mme. Ranevskaya. My other worry is Varya. She's used to getting up early and working; and now, with no work to do, she is like a fish out of water. She has grown thin and pale, and keeps crying, poor soul. [*Pause.*] You know this very well, Yermolay Alexeyevich; I dreamed of seeing her married to you, and it looked as though that's how it would be. [*Whispers to* ANYA, *who nods to* CHARLOTTA, *and both go out.*] She loves you. You find her attractive. I don't know, I don't know why it is you seem to avoid each other; I can't understand it.

Lopahin. To tell you the truth, I don't understand it myself. It's all a puzzle. If there's still time, I'm ready now, at once. Let's settle it straight off, and have done with it! Without you, I feel I'll never be able to propose.

Mme. Ranevskaya. That's splendid. After all, it will only take a minute. I'll call her at once. . . .

Lopahin. And luckily, here's champagne too. [*Looks at the glasses.*] Empty! Somebody's drunk it all. [YASHA *coughs.*] That's what you might call guzzling. . . .

Mme. Ranevskaya [*animatedly*]. Excellent! We'll go and leave you alone. Yasha, *allez!* I'll call her. [*At the door.*] Varya, leave everything and come here. Come! [*Exits with* YASHA.]

Lopahin [*looking at his watch*]. Yes. . . . [*Pause behind the door, smothered laughter and whispering; at last, enter* VARYA.]

Varya [*looking over the luggage in leisurely fashion*]. Strange, I can't find it. . . .

Lopahin. What are you looking for?

Varya. Packed it myself, and I don't remember. . . . [*Pause.*]

Lopahin. Where are you going now, Varya?

Varya. I? To the Ragulins'. I've arranged to take charge there—as housekeeper, if you like.

Lopahin. At Yashnevo? About fifty miles from here. [*Pause.*] Well, life in this house is ended!

Varya [*examining luggage*]. Where is it? Perhaps I put it in the chest. Yes, life in this house is ended. . . . There will be no more of it.

Lopahin. And I'm just off to Kharkov—by this next train. I've a lot to do there. I'm leaving Yepihodov here. . . . I've taken him on.

Varya. Oh!

Lopahin. Last year at this time it was snowing, if you remember, but now it's sunny and there's no wind. It's cold, though. . . . It must be three below.

Varya. I didn't look. [*Pause.*] And besides, our thermometer's broken. [*Pause. Voice from the yard:* "Yermolay Alexeyevich!"]

Lopahin [*as if he had been waiting for the call*]. This minute! [*Exit quickly.* VARYA *sits on the floor and sobs quietly, her head on a bundle of clothes. Enter* MME. RANEVSKAYA *cautiously.*]

Mme. Ranevskaya. Well? [*Pause.*] We must be going.

Varya [*wiping her eyes*]. Yes, it's time, mamma dear. I'll be able to get to the Ragulins' today, if only we don't miss the train.

Mme. Ranevskaya [*at the door*]. Anya, put your things on. [*Enter* ANYA, GAYEV, CHARLOTTA. GAYEV *wears a heavy overcoat with a hood. Enter servants and coachmen.* YEPIHODOV *bustles about the luggage.*]

Mme. Ranevskaya. Now we can start on our journey.

Anya [*joyfully*]. On our journey!

Gayev. My friends, my dear, cherished friends, leaving this house forever, can I be silent? Can I at leave-taking refrain from giving utterance to those emotions that now fill my being?

Anya [*imploringly*]. Uncle!

Varya. Uncle, uncle dear, don't.

Gayev [*forlornly*]. I'll bank the yellow in the side pocket. . . . I'll be silent. . . .

[*Enter* TROFIMOV, *then* LOPAHIN.]

Trofimov. Well, ladies and gentlemen, it's time to leave.

Lopahin. Yepihodov, my coat.

Mme. Ranevskaya. I'll sit down just a minute. It seems as though I'd never before seen what the walls of this house were like, the ceilings, and now I look at them hungrily, with such tender affection.

Gayev. I remember when I was six years old sitting on that window sill on Whitsunday, watching my father going to church.

Mme. Ranevskaya.   Has everything been taken?

Lopahin.   I think so. [*Putting on his overcoat.*] Yepihodov, see that everything's in order.

Yepihodov [*in a husky voice*].   You needn't worry, Yermolay Alexeyevich.

Lopahin.   What's the matter with your voice?

Yepihodov.   I just had a drink of water. I must have swallowed something.

Yasha [*contemptuously*].   What ignorance!

Mme. Ranevskaya.   When we're gone, not a soul will be left here.

Lopahin.   Until the spring.

[VARYA *pulls an umbrella out of a bundle, as though about to hit someone with it.* LOPAHIN *pretends to be frightened.*]

Varya.   Come, come, I had no such idea!

Trofimov.   Ladies and gentlemen, let's get into the carriages—it's time. The train will be in directly.

Varya.   Petya, there they are, your rubbers, by that trunk. [*Tearfully.*] And what dirty old things they are!

Trofimov [*puts on rubbers*].   Let's go, ladies and gentlemen.

Gayev [*greatly upset, afraid of breaking down*].   The train . . . the station. . . . Three cushions in the side pocket, I'll bank this one in the corner. . . .

Mme. Ranevskaya.   Let's go.

Lopahin.   Are we all here? No one in there? [*Locks the side door on the left.*] There are some things stored here, better lock up. Let us go!

Anya.   Good-by, old house! Good-by, old life!

Trofimov.   Hail to you, new life!

[*Exit with* ANYA. VARYA *looks round the room and goes out slowly.* YASHA *and* CHARLOTTA *with her dog go out.*]

Lopahin.   And so, until the spring. Go along, friends. . . . 'Bye-'bye! [*Exits.*]

[MME. RANEVSKAYA *and* GAYEV *remain alone. As though they had been waiting for this, they throw themselves on each other's necks, and break into subdued, restrained sobs, afraid of being overheard.*]

Gayev [*in despair*].   My sister! My sister!

Mme. Ranevskaya.   Oh, my orchard—my dear, sweet, beautiful orchard! My life, my youth, my happiness—good-by! Good-by! [*Voice of* ANYA, *gay and summoning:* "Mamma!" *Voice of* TROFIMOV, *gay and excited:* "Halloo!"]

Mme. Ranevskaya.   One last look at the walls, at the windows. . . . Our poor mother loved to walk about this room. . . .

Gayev.   My sister, my sister! [*Voice of* ANYA: "Mamma!" *Voice of* TROFIMOV: "Halloo!"]

Mme. Ranevskaya.   We're coming.

[*They go out. The stage is empty. The sound of doors being locked, of carriages driving away. Then silence. In the stillness is heard the muffled sound of the ax striking a tree, a mournful, lonely sound.*

Footsteps are heard. FIRS *appears in the doorway on the right. He is dressed as usual in a jacket and white waistcoat and wears slippers. He is ill.*]

Firs [*goes to the door, tries the handle*]. Locked! They've gone. . . . [*Sits down on the sofa.*] They've forgotten me. . . . Never mind. . . . I'll sit here a bit. . . . I'll wager Leonid Andreyevich hasn't put his fur coat on; he's gone off in his light overcoat. . . . [*Sighs anxiously.*] I didn't keep an eye on him. . . . Ah, when they're young, they're green. . . . [*Mumbles something indistinguishable.*] Life has gone by as if I had never lived. [*Lies down.*] I'll lie down a while. . . . There's no strength left in you, old fellow; nothing is left, nothing. Ah, you addlehead! [*Lies motionless. A distant sound is heard coming from the sky as it were, the sound of a snapping string mournfully dying away. All is still again, and nothing is heard but the strokes of the ax against a tree far away in the orchard.*]

[*The Curtain Falls.*]

Brecht: THE CAUCASIAN CHALK CIRCLE

Bertolt Brecht (1898–1956) learned to hate war while serving as a field hospital medic in World War I, even as he had learned to despise the bourgeois morality in his boyhood home in Augsburg. After the war, he abandoned his medical career, supported himself by performing his witty, bawdy, and satirical ballads (to his own crude guitar strumming) in the cabarets of revolution-torn Germany, and then turned to playwriting.

Brecht's early plays, chiefly nihilistic, owed a good deal to the expressionist movement, but he soon came under the influence of Erwin Piscator, who shared Brecht's politico-economic views and also saw the theatre as a social force. Both men envisioned a new stage-craft that combined drama, narration, recordings, films, slides, cartoons, and intrusive cabaret-like songs. Piscator coined the term "epic theatre," always associated with Brecht, who even then was beginning to write plays that were didactic, poetic, and richly comic in their fusion of traditional and revolutionary themes and techniques.

When Brecht wrote, he always had a theatre and a viewer in mind; never a script or a reader. Epic drama is not nearly as complex a concept as he often pretended. It is the development of a dramatic action in a series of self-contained units rather than in a line of rising action to be resolved in climax and denouement. The responsibility of the performers is to demonstrate the characters to the audience rather than to create the illusion of impersonation, to *tell* a story rather than to make it seem to happen for the first time. Epic theatre does not strive for an empathic response. Brecht's objection to conventional drama, particularly tragedy, was that it involved its audience by creating a bond of identification that brought about catharsis and release. The viewer leaves the theatre feeling cleansed; Brecht wanted his audience to feel dirty. His purpose was to evoke an intellectual response, to impel his viewer to make a moral decision rather than to indulge his feelings. "I want a wide-awake theatre," he said, not a "culinary" one—a cerebrally engaged audience, not emotional consumers.

To gain the effect of detachment necessary for such a response, Brecht developed a method of dramaturgy that created aesthetic distance. He used the stage as stage and made no effort to conceal his apparatus, thereby making the audience constantly aware that it was not watching an imitation of life but a comment upon it in a theatre. This technique has been called "theatricalism" or "anti-illusionism" by many; Brecht called it the Verfrem-dungseffekt—the emotional alienation of the audience so that it could concentrate on the intellectual heart of the play. Despite his avowed ambition to keep his characterizations inhuman, Brecht happily failed to do so with some regularity.

Brecht thought his style of composition ideally suited to Marxist purposes, but he is not really dialectical, for he does not reconcile antitheses; he analyzes and reveals them in paradox and irony, in poetic and colloquial diction, in song and in uninhibited imagination. What political preachments his plays make are really quite subordinate to his overriding sympathy for the poor, the exploited, and the oppressed. Brecht's humane and humanistic variety of German communism was a very personal code, and always at odds with the party. It pervades all of his work, but with few exceptions his art far transcends politics. His richly textured plays examine in depth the moral crises of this and any age. Brecht thought the destiny of society to be of greater importance than the fate of individuals, but he knew that society is made up of individual human beings.

The range and power of Bertolt Brecht cannot be appreciated from a reading of just one of his plays. Indeed, Brecht demands seeing rather than reading, and his drama is really incomplete without the music. He was a poet of the first rank (usually defying translation) and a uniquely gifted lyricist as well as a pioneer of dramatic form. It is virtually impossible to see an important play written since 1955 that has not in some way been influenced by the spirit of Bertolt Brecht.

Brecht fled Nazi Germany the day after the Reichstag fire. *The Caucasian Chalk Circle* was completed in 1945 during his American sojourn, and had its premiere in English at Carleton College in Minnesota in 1948. The first performance in German was by the Berliner Ensemble in 1954. Brecht's sources were a Chinese play of the Yuan Dynasty (1259–1368), a nineteenth century French adaptation of it, and a 1924 reworking of the chalk circle legend by the German dramatist Klabund. Brecht's conception of the legend is completely original, but illustrates how his is a voice both traditional and experimental, both contemporary and timeless. The twentieth century has not produced a more significant playwright.

THE CAUCASIAN CHALK CIRCLE

Translated by Eric Bentley

The Characters

Old Man, on the right
Peasant Woman, on the right
Young Peasant
A Very Young Worker
Old Man, on the left
Peasant Woman, on the left
Agriculturist Kato
Girl Tractorist
Wounded Soldier
The Delegate, from the capital
The Singer
Georgi Abashwili, the Governor
Natella, the Governor's wife
Michael, their son
Shalva, an adjutant
Arsen Kazbeki, a fat prince
Messenger, from the capital
Niko Mikadze and
Mika Loladze, doctors
Simon Shashava, a soldier
Grusha Vashnadze, a kitchen maid
Old Peasant, with the milk
Corporal and Private
Peasant and His Wife
Lavrenti Vashnadze, Grusha's brother
Aniko, his wife
Peasant Woman, for a while Grusha's mother-in-law
Jussup, her son
Monk
Azdak, village recorder
Shauwa, a policeman
Grand Duke
Doctor
Invalid
Limping Man
Blackmailer
Ludovica
Innkeeper, her father-in-law

Stableboy
Poor Old Peasant Woman
Irakli, her brother-in-law, a bandit
Three Wealthy Farmers
Illo Shuboladze and
Sandro Oboladze, lawyers
Old Married Couple
Soldiers, Servants, Peasants,
Beggars, Musicians, Merchants,
Nobles, and Architects

Prologue

[Among the ruins of a war-ravaged Caucasian village the MEMBERS of two Kolkhoz[1] villages, mostly women and older men, are sitting in a circle, smoking and drinking wine. With them is a DELEGATE of the State Reconstruction Commission from Nuka, the capital.]

Peasant Woman [left, pointing].   In those hills over there we stopped three Nazi tanks, but the apple orchard was already destroyed.
Old Man [right].   Our beautiful dairy farm; a ruin.
Girl Tractorist.   I laid the fire, Comrade.

[Pause.]

Delegate.   Now listen to the report. Delegates from the goat-breeding Kolkhoz "Rosa Luxemburg" have been to Nuka. When Hitler's armies approached, the Kolkhoz had moved its goat herds further east on orders from the authorities. They are now thinking of returning. Their delegates have investigated the village and the land and found a lot of it destroyed. [DELEGATES on right nod.] The neighboring fruit-culture Kolkhoz [to the left] "Galinsk" is proposing to use the former grazing land of Kolkhoz "Rosa Luxemburg," a valley in which grass doesn't grow very well, for orchards and vineyards. As a delegate of the Reconstruction Commission, I request that the two Kolkhoz villages decide between themselves whether Kolkhoz "Rosa Luxemburg" shall return here or not.
Old Man [right].   First of all, I want to protest against the time limit on discussion. We of Kolkhoz "Rosa Luxemburg" have spent three days and three nights getting here. And now discussion is limited to half a day.
Wounded Soldier [left].   Comrade, we haven't as many villages as we used to have. We haven't as many hands. We haven't as much time.
Girl Tractorist.   All pleasures have to be rationed. Tobacco is rationed, and wine. Discussion should be rationed.
Old Man [right, sighing].   Death to the fascists! But I will come to the point and explain why we want our valley back. There are a great many reasons, but I'll begin with one of the simplest. Makinä Abakidze, unpack the goat cheese.

---

[1]   Collective farm in U.S.S.R.

[PEASANT WOMAN *on the right takes from a basket an enormous cheese wrapped in a cloth. Applause and laughter.*] Help yourselves, Comrades, start in!

Old Man [*left, suspiciously*].   Is this a way of influencing us?

Old Man [*right, amid laughter*].   How could it be a way of influencing you, Surab, you valley-thief? Everyone knows you'll take the cheese and the valley, too. [*Laughter.*] All I expect from you is an honest answer. Do you like the cheese?

Old Man [*left*].   The answer is: yes.

Old Man, [*right*].   Really. [*bitterly*] I ought to have known you know nothing about cheese.

Old Man [*left*].   Why not? When I tell you I like it?

Old Man [*right*].   Because you can't like it. Because it's not what it was in the old days. And why not? Because our goats don't like the new grass as they did the old. Cheese is not cheese because grass is not grass, that's the thing. Please put that in your report.

Old Man [*left*].   But your cheese is excellent.

Old Man [*right*].   It isn't excellent. It's just passable. The new grazing land is no good, whatever the young people may say. One can't live there. It doesn't even smell of morning in the morning. [*Several people laugh.*]

Delegate.   Don't mind their laughing: they understand you. Comrades, why does one love one's country? Because the bread tastes better there, the air smells better, voices sound stronger, the sky is higher, the ground is easier to walk on. Isn't that so?

Old Man [*right*].   The valley has belonged to us from all eternity.

Soldier [*left*].   What does *that* mean—from all eternity? Nothing belongs to anyone from all eternity. When you were young you didn't even belong to yourself. You belonged to the Kazbeki princes.

Old Man [*right*].   Doesn't it make a difference, though, what kind of trees stand next to the house you are born in? Or what kind of neighbors you have? Doesn't that make a difference? We want to go back just to have you as our neighbors, valley-thieves! Now you can all laugh again.

Old Man [*left, laughing*].   Then why don't you listen to what your neighbor, Kato Wachtang, our agriculturist, has to say about the valley?

Peasant Woman [*right*].   We've not said all there is to be said about our valley. By no means. Not all the houses are destroyed. As for the dairy farm, at least the foundation wall is still standing.

Delegate.   You can claim State support—here and there—you know that. I have suggestions here in my pocket.

Peasant Woman [*right*].   Comrade Specialist, we haven't come here to bargain. I can't take your cap and hand you another, and say "This one's better." The other one might *be* better, but you *like* yours better.

Girl Tractorist.   A piece of land is not a cap—not in our country, Comrade.

Delegate.   Don't get mad. It's true we have to consider a piece of land as a tool to produce something useful, but it's also true that we must recognize love for a particular piece of land. As far as I'm concerned, I'd like to find out more exactly what you [*to those on the left*] want to do with the valley.

Others.   Yes, let Kato speak.

Delegate.   Comrade Agriculturist!

Kato [*rising; she's in military uniform*]. Comrades, last winter, while we were fighting in these hills here as Partisans, we discussed how, once the Germans were expelled, we could build up our fruit culture to ten times its original size. I've prepared a plan for an irrigation project. By means of a cofferdam on our mountain lake, 300 hectares of unfertile land can be irrigated. Our Kolkhoz could not only cultivate more fruit, but also have vineyards. The project, however, would pay only if the disputed valley of Kolkhoz "Galinsk" were also included. Here are the calculations. [*She hands* DELEGATE *a briefcase*.]

Old Man [*right*]. Write into a report that our Kolkhoz plans to start a new stud farm.

Girl Tractorist. Comrades, the project was conceived during days and nights when we had to take cover in the mountains. We were often without ammunition for our half-dozen rifles. Even finding a pencil was difficult. [*Applause from both sides.*]

Old Man [*right*]. Our thanks to the Comrades of Kolkhoz "Galinsk" and all those who've defended our country! [*They shake hands and embrace.*]

Peasant Woman [*left*]. In doing this our thought was that our soldiers—both your men and our men—should return to a still more productive homeland.

Girl Tractorist. As the poet Mayakovsky said: "The home of the Soviet people shall also be the home of Reason"!

[*The* DELEGATES *including the* OLD MAN *have got up, and with the* DELEGATE *specified proceed to study the Agriculturist's drawings. Exclamations such as:* "Why is the altitude of all 22 meters?"—"This rock must be blown up"— "Actually, all they need is cement and dynamite"—"They force the water to come down here, that's clever!"]

A Very Young Worker [*right, to* OLD MAN, *right*]. They're going to irrigate all the fields between the hills, look at that, Aleko!

Old Man [*right*]. I'm not going to look. I knew the project would be good. I won't have a pistol pointed at me!

Delegate. But they only want to point a pencil at you! [*Laughter.*]

Old Man [*right, gets up gloomily, and walks over to look at the drawings*]. These valley-thieves know only too well that we in this country are suckers for machines and projects.

Peasant Woman [*right*]. Aleko Bereshwili, you have a weakness for new projects. That's well known.

Delegate. What about my report? May I write that you will all support the cession of your old valley in the interests of this project when you get back to your Kolkhoz?

Peasant Woman [*right*]. I will. What about you, Aleko?

Old Man [*right, bent over drawings*]. I suggest that you give us copies of the drawings to take along.

Peasant Woman [*right*]. Then we can sit down and eat. Once he has the drawings and he's ready to discuss them, the matter is settled. I know him. And it will be the same with the rest of us.

[DELEGATES *laughingly embrace again.*]

Old Man [*left*].   Long live the Kolkhoz "Rosa Luxemburg" and much luck to your horse-breeding project!

Peasant Woman [*left*].   In honor of the visit of the delegates from Kolkhoz "Rosa Luxemburg" and of the Specialist, the plan is that we all hear a presentation of the Singer Arkadi Tscheidse.

[*Applause.* GIRL TRACTORIST *has gone off to bring the* SINGER.]

Peasant Woman [*right*].   Comrades, your entertainment had better be good. It's going to cost us a valley.

Peasant Woman [*left*].   Arkadi Tscheidse knows about our discussion. He's promised to perform something that has a bearing on the problem.

Kato.   We wired to Tiflis[1] three times. The whole thing nearly fell through at the last minute because his driver had a cold.

Peasant Woman [*left*].   Arkadi Tscheidse knows 21,000 lines of verse.

Old Man [*left*].   He's hard to get. You and the Planning Commission should persuade him to come north more often, Comrade.

Delegate.   We are more interested in economics, I'm afraid.

Old Man [*left, smiling*].   You arrange the redistribution of vines and tractors, why not songs?

[*Enter the* SINGER *Arkadi Tscheidse, led by* GIRL TRACTORIST. *He is a well-built man of simple manners, accompanied by* FOUR MUSICIANS *with their instruments. The artists are greeted with applause.*]

Girl Tractorist.   This is the Comrade Specialist, Arkadi.

[*The* SINGER *greets them all.*]

Delegate.   Honored to make your acquaintance. I heard about your songs when I was a boy at school. Will it be one of the old legends?

The Singer.   A very old one. It's called "The Chalk Circle" and comes from the Chinese. But we'll do it, of course, in a changed version. Comrades, it's an honor for me to entertain you after a difficult debate. We hope you will find that the voice of the old poet also sounds well in the shadow of Soviet tractors. It may be a mistake to mix different wines, but old and new wisdom mix admirably. Now I hope we'll get something to eat before the performance begins—it would certainly help.

Voices.   Surely. Everyone into the Club House!

[*While everyone begins to move,* DELEGATE *turns to* GIRL TRACTORIST.]

Delegate.   I hope it won't take long. I've got to get back tonight.

Girl Tractorist.   How long will it last, Arkadi? The Comrade Specialist must get back to Tiflis tonight.

The Singer [*casually*].   It's actually two stories. An hour or two.

Girl Tractorist [*confidentially*].   Couldn't you make it shorter?

The Singer.   No.

---

[1]   Capital of the Republic of Georgia, U.S.S.R.

Voice. Arkadi Tscheidse's performance will take place here in the square after the meal.

[*They all go happily to eat.*]

The Noble Child

[*As the lights go up, the* SINGER *is seen sitting on the floor, a black sheepskin cloak round his shoulders, and a little, well-thumbed notebook in his hand. A small group of listeners—the* CHORUS—*sits with him. The manner of his recitation makes it clear that he has told his story over and over again. He mechanically fingers the pages, seldom looking at them. With appropriate gestures, he gives the signal for each scene to begin.*]

The Singer.

In olden times, in a bloody time,
There ruled in a Caucasian city—
Men called it City of the Damned—
A Governor.
His name was Georgi Abashwili.
He was rich as Croesus
He had a beautiful wife
He had a healthy baby.
No other governor in Grusinia
Had so many horses in his stable
So many beggars on his doorstep
So many soldiers in his service
So many petitioners in his courtyard.
Georgi Abashwili—how shall I describe him to you?
He enjoyed his life.
On the morning of Easter Sunday
The Governor and his family went to church.

[*At the left a large doorway, at the right an even larger gateway.* BEGGARS *and* PETITIONERS *pour from the gateway, holding up thin* CHILDREN, *crutches, and petitions. They are followed by* IRONSHIRTS, *and then, expensively dressed, the* GOVERNOR'S FAMILY.]

Beggars and Petitioners. Mercy! Mercy, Your Grace! The taxes are too high.
—I lost my leg in the Persian War, where can I get . . .
—My brother is innocent, Your Grace, a misunderstanding . . .
—The child is starving in my arms!
—Our petition is for our son's discharge from the army, our last remaining son!
—Please, Your Grace, the water inspector takes bribes.

[ONE SERVANT *collects the petitions.* ANOTHER *distributes coins from a purse.* SOLDIERS *push the crowd back, lashing at them with thick leather whips.*]

The Soldier. Get back! Clear the church door!

[*Behind the* GOVERNOR, *his* WIFE, *and the* ADJUTANT, *the* GOVERNOR'S CHILD *is brought through the gateway in an ornate carriage.*]

The crowd.   The baby!
—I can't see it, don't shove so hard!
—God bless the child, Your Grace!

The Singer [*while the crowd is driven back with whips*].
For the first time on that Easter Sunday, the people saw the Governor's heir.
Two doctors never moved from the noble child, apple of the Governor's eye.
Even the mighty Prince Kazbeki bows before him at the church door.

[A FAT PRINCE *steps forward and greets the* FAMILY.]

The Fat Prince.   Happy Easter, Natella Abashwili! What a day! When it was raining last night, I thought to myself, gloomy holidays! But this morning the sky was gay. I love a gay sky, a simple heart, Natella Abashwili. And little Michael is a governor from head to foot! Tititi! [*He tickles the* CHILD.]

The Governor's Wife.   What do you think, Arsen, at last Georgi has decided to start building the east wing. All those wretched slums are to be torn down to make room for the garden.

The Fat Prince.   Good news after so much bad! What's the latest on the war, Brother Georgi? [*The* GOVERNOR *indicates a lack of interest.*] Strategical retreat, I hear. Well, minor reverses are to be expected. Sometimes things go well, sometimes not. Such is war. Doesn't mean a thing, does it?

The Governor's Wife.   He's coughing. Georgi, did you hear? [*She speaks sharply to the* DOCTORS, *two dignified men standing close to the little carriage.*] He's coughing!

The First Doctor [*to the* SECOND]. May I remind you, Niko Mikadze, that I was against the lukewarm bath? [*to the* GOVERNOR'S WIFE] There's been a little error over warming the bath water, Your Grace.

The Second Doctor [*equally polite*]. Mika Loladze, I'm afraid I can't agree with you. The temperature of the bath water was exactly what our great, beloved Mishiko Oboladze prescribed. More likely a slight draft during the night, Your Grace.

The Governor's Wife.   But do pay more attention to him. He looks feverish, Georgi.

The First Doctor [*bending over the* CHILD]. No cause for alarm, Your Grace. The bath water will be warmer. It won't occur again.

The Second Doctor [*with a venomous glance at the* FIRST]. I won't forget that, my dear Mika Loladze. No cause for concern, Your Grace.

The Fat Prince.   Well, well, well! I always say: "A pain in my liver? Then the doctor gets fifty strokes on the soles of his feet." We live in a decadent age. In the old days one said: "Off with his head!"

The Governor's Wife.   Let's go into church. Very likely it's the draft here.

[*The procession of* FAMILY *and* SERVANTS *turns into the doorway. The* FAT PRINCE *follows, but the* GOVERNOR *is kept back by the* ADJUTANT, *a handsome young man. When the crowd of* PETITIONERS *has been driven off, a young dust-stained* RIDER, *his arm in a sling, remains behind.*]

The Adjutant [pointing at the RIDER, *who steps forward]*. Won't you hear the messenger from the capital, Your Excellency? He arrived this morning. With confidential papers.

The Governor. Not before Service, Shalva. But did you hear Brother Kazbeki wish me a happy Easter? Which is all very well, but I don't believe it did rain last night.

The Adjutant [nodding]. We must investigate.

The Governor. Yes, at once, Tomorrow.

[*They pass through the doorway. The* RIDER, *who has waited in vain for an audience, turns sharply round and, muttering a curse, goes off. Only one of the palace guards—*SIMON SHASHAVA—*remains at the door.*]

The Singer.

> The city is still.
> Pigeons strut in the church square.
> A Soldier of the Palace Guard
> Is joking with a kitchen maid
> As she comes up from the river with a bundle.

[*A girl—*GRUSHA VASHADZE—*comes through the gateway with a bundle made of large green leaves under her arm.*]

Simon. What, the young lady is not in church? Shirking?

Grusha. I was dressed to go. But they needed another goose for the banquet. And they asked me to get it. I know about geese.

Simon. A goose? [*He feigns suspicion.*] I'd like to see that goose. [GRUSHA *does not understand.*] One must be on one's guard with women. "I only went for a fish," they tell you, but it turns out to be something else.

Grusha [walking resolutely toward him and showing him the goose]. There! If it isn't a fifteen-pound goose stuffed full of corn, I'll eat the feathers.

Simon. A queen of a goose! The Governor himself will eat it. So the young lady has been down to the river again?

Grusha. Yes, at the poultry farm.

Simon. Really? At the poultry farm, down by the river . . . not higher up maybe? Near those willows?

Grusha. I only go to the willows to wash the linen.

Simon [insinuatingly]. Exactly.

Grusha. Exactly what?

Simon [winking]. Exactly that.

Grusha. Why shouldn't I wash the linen by the willows?

Simon [with exaggerated laughter]. "Why shouldn't I wash the linen by the willows!" That's good, really good!

Grusha. I don't understand the soldier. What's so good about it?

Simon [slyly]. "If something I know someone learns, she'll grow hot and cold by turns!"

Grusha. I don't know what I could learn about those willows.

Simon. Not even if there was a bush opposite? That one could see everything from? Everything that goes on there when a certain person is—"washing linen"?

Grusha.   What does go on? Won't the soldier say what he means and have
   done?
Simon.   Something goes on. Something can be seen.
Grusha.   Could the soldier mean I dip my toes in the water when it's hot?
   There's nothing else.
Simon.   There's more. Your toes. And more.
Grusha.   More what? At most my foot?
Simon.   Your foot. And a little more. [*He laughs heartily.*]
Grusha [*angrily*].   Simon Shashava, you ought to be ashamed of yourself! To sit
   in a bush on a hot day and wait till a girl comes and dips her legs in the river!
   And I bet you bring a friend along too!

[*She runs off.*]

Simon [*shouting after her*].   I didn't bring any friend along!

[*As the* SINGER *resumes his tale, the* SOLDIER *steps into the doorway as though
to listen to the service.*]

The Singer.

> The city lies still
> But why are there armed men?
> The Governor's palace is at peace
> But why is it a fortress?
> And the Governor returned to his palace
> And the fortress was a trap
> And the goose was plucked and roasted
> But the goose was not eaten this time
> And noon was no longer the hour to eat:
> Noon was the hour to die.

[*From the doorway at the left the* FAT PRINCE *quickly appears, stands still, looks
around. Before the gateway at the right* TWO IRONSHIRTS *are squatting and
playing dice. The* FAT PRINCE *sees them, walks slowly past, making a sign to
them. They rise: one goes through the gateway, the other goes off at the right.
Muffled voices are heard from various directions in the rear: "To your posts!"
The palace is surrounded. The* FAT PRINCE *quickly goes off. Church bells in the
distance. Enter, through the doorway, the* GOVERNOR'S FAMILY *and procession,
returning from church.*]

The Governor's Wife [*passing the* ADJUTANT].   It's impossible to live in such a
   slum. But Georgi, of course, will only build for his little Michael. Never for me!
   Michael is all! All for Michael!

[*The procession turns into the gateway. Again the* ADJUTANT *lingers behind. He
waits. Enter the wounded* RIDER *from the doorway.* TWO IRONSHIRTS *of the
Palace Guard have taken up positions by the gateway.*]

The Adjutant [*to the* RIDER].   The Governor does not wish to receive military
   news before dinner—especially if it's depressing, as I assume. In the afternoon
   His Excellency will confer with prominent architects. They're coming to dinner

too. And here they are! [*Enter* THREE GENTLEMEN *through the doorway.*] Go
to the kitchen and eat, my friend. [*As the* RIDER *goes, the* ADJUTANT *greets the*
ARCHITECTS.] Gentlemen, His Excellency expects you at dinner. He will devote
all his time to you and your great new plans. Come!

One of the Architects. We marvel that His Excellency intends to build. There
are disquieting rumors that the war in Persia has taken a turn for the worse.

The Adjutant. All the more reason to build! There's nothing to those rumors
anyway. Persia is a long way off, and the garrison here would let itself be hacked
to bits for its Governor. [*Noise from the palace. The shrill scream of a woman.
Someone is shouting orders. Dumbfounded, the* ADJUTANT *moves toward the
gateway. An* IRONSHIRT *steps out, points his lance at him.*] What's this? Put
down that lance, you dog.

One of the Architects. It's the Princes! Don't you know the Princes met last
night in the capital? And they're against the Grand Duke and his Governors?
Gentlemen, we'd better make ourselves scarce.

[*They rush off. The* ADJUTANT *remains helplessly behind.*]

The adjutant [*furiously to the Palace Guard*]. Down with those lances! Don't
you see the Governor's life is threatened?

[*The* IRONSHIRTS *of the Palace Guard refuse to obey. They stare coldly and
indifferently at the* ADJUTANT *and follow the next events without interest.*]

The Singer.

> O blindness of the great!
> They go their way like gods,
> Great over bent backs,
> Sure of hired fists,
> Trusting in the power
> Which has lasted so long.
> But long is not forever.
> O change from age to age!
> Thou hope of the people!

[*Enter the* GOVERNOR, *through the gateway, between* TWO SOLDIERS *armed to
the teeth. He is in chains. His face is gray.*]

> Up, great sir, deign to walk upright!
> From your palace the eyes of many foes follow you!
> And now you don't need an architect, a carpenter will do.
> You won't be moving into a new palace
> But into a little hole in the ground.
> Look about you once more, blind man!

[*The* ARRESTED MAN *looks round.*]

> Does all you had please you?
> Between the Easter Mass and the Easter meal
> You are walking to a place whence no one returns.

[*The* GOVERNOR *is led off. A horn sounds an alarm. Noise behind the gateway.*]

When the house of a great one collapses
Many little ones are slain.
Those who had no share in the *good* fortunes of the mighty
Often have a share in their *mis*fortunes.
The plunging wagon
Drags the sweating oxen down with it
Into the abyss.

[*The* SERVANTS *come rushing through the gateway in panic.*]

The Servants [*among themselves*].   The baskets!
   —Take them all into the third courtyard! Food for five days!
   —The mistress has fainted! Someone must carry her down.
   —She must get away.
   —What about us? We'll be slaughtered like chickens, as always.
   —Goodness, what'll happen? There's bloodshed already in the city, they
say.
   —Nonsense, the Governor has just been asked to appear at a Princes'
meeting. All very correct. Everything'll be ironed out. I heard this on the best
authority . . .

[*The* TWO DOCTORS *rush into the courtyard.*]

The First Doctor [*trying to restrain the other*].   Niko Mikadze, it is your duty as
   a doctor to attend Natella Abashwili.
The Second Doctor.   My duty! It's yours!
The First Doctor.   Whose turn is it to look after the child today, Niko Mikadze,
   yours or mine?
The Second Doctor.   Do you really think, Mika Loladze, I'm going to stay a
   minute longer in this accursed house on that little brat's account? [*They start
   fighting. All one hears is:* "You neglect your duty!" *and* "Duty, my foot!" *Then
   the* SECOND DOCTOR *knocks the* FIRST *down.*] Go to hell!

[*Exit.*]

[*Enter the soldier,* SIMON SHASHAVA. *He searches in the crowd for* GRUSHA.]

Simon.   Grusha! There you are at last! What are you going to do?
Grusha.   Nothing. If worst comes to worst, I've a brother in the mountains. How
   about you?
Simon.   Forget about me. [*formally again*] Gruusha Vashnadze, your wish to
   know my plans fills me with satisfaction. I've been ordered to accompany
   Madam Natella Abashwili as her guard.
Grusha.   But hasn't the Palace Guard mutinied?
Simon [*seriously*].   That's a fact.
Grusha.   Isn't it dangerous to go with her?
Simon.   In Tiflis, they say: Isn't the stabbing dangerous for the knife?
Grusha.   You're not a knife, you're a man, Simon Shashava, what has that
   woman to do with you?
Simon.   That woman has nothing to do with me. I have my orders, and I go.

Grusha. The soldier is pigheaded: he is running into danger for nothing—nothing at all. I must get into the third courtyard, I'm in a hurry.

Simon. Since we're both in a hurry we shouldn't quarrel. You need time for a good quarrel. May I ask if the young lady still has parents?

Grusha. No, just a brother.

Simon. As time is short—my second question is this: Is the young lady as healthy as a fish in water?

Grusha. I may have a pain in the right shoulder once in a while. Otherwise I'm strong enough for my job. No one has complained. So far.

Simon. That's well known. When it's Easter Sunday, and the question arises who'll run for the goose all the same, she'll be the one. My third question is this: Is the young lady impatient? Does she want apples in winter?

Grusha. Impatient? No. But if a man goes to war without any reason and then no message comes—that's bad.

Simon. A message will come. And now my final question . .

Grusha. Simon Shashava, I must get to the third courtyard at once. My answer is yes.

Simon [very embarrassed]. Haste, they say, is the wind that blows down the scaffolding. But they also say: The rich don't know what haste is. I'm from . . .

Grusha. Kutsk.

Simon. The young lady has been inquiring about me? I'm healthy, I have no dependents, I make ten piasters a month, as paymaster twenty piasters, and I'm asking—very sincerely—for your hand.

Grusha. Simon Shashava, it suits me well.

Simon [taking from his neck a thin chain with a little cross on it]. My mother gave me this cross, Grusha Vashnadze. The chain is silver. Please wear it.

Grusha. Many thanks, Simon.

Simon [hangs it round her neck]. It would be better to go to the third courtyard now. Or there'll be difficulties. Anyway, I must harness the horses. The young lady will understand?

Grusha. Yes, Simon.

[*They stand undecided.*]

Simon. I'll just take the mistress to the troops that have stayed loyal. When the war's over, I'll be back. In two weeks. Or three. I hope my intended won't get tired, awaiting my return.

Grusha.

> Simon Shashava, I shall wait for you.
> Go calmly into battle, soldier,
> The bloody battle, the bitter battle
> From which not everyone returns:
> When you return I shall be there.
> I shall be waiting for you under the green elm
> I shall be waiting for you under the bare elm
> I shall wait until the last soldier has returned
> And longer.

When you come back from the battle
No boots will stand at my door
The pillow beside mine will be empty
And my mouth will be unkissed.
When you return, when you return
You will be able to say: It is just as it was.

Simon.   I thank you, Grusha Vashnadze. And good-bye!

[*He bows low before her. She does the same before him. Then she runs quickly off without looking round. Enter the* ADJUTANT *from the gateway.*]

The Adjutant [*harshly*].   Harness the horses to the carriage! Don't stand there doing nothing, louse!

[SIMON SHASHAVA *stands to attention and goes off.* TWO SERVANTS *crowd from the gateway, bent low under huge trunks. Behind them, supported by her* WOMEN, *stumbles* NATELLA ABASHWILI. *She is followed by a* WOMAN *carrying the* CHILD.]

The Governor's Wife.   I hardly know if my head's still on. Where's Michael? Don't hold him so clumsily. Pile the trunks onto the carriage. No news from the city, Shalva?

The Adjutant.   None. All's quiet so far, but there's not a minute to lose. No room for all these trunks in the carriage. Pick out what you need.

[*Exit quickly.*]

The Governor's Wife.   Only essentials! Quick, open the trunks! I'll tell you what I need. [*The trunks are lowered and opened. She points at some brocade dresses.*] The green one! And, of course, the one with the fur trimming. Where are Niko Mikadze and Mika Loladze? I've suddenly got the most terrible migraine again. It always starts in the temples. [*Enter* GRUSHA.] Taking your time, eh? Go and get the hot water bottles this minute! [GRUSHA *runs off, returns later with hot water bottles; the* GOVERNOR'S WIFE *orders her about by signs.*] Don't tear the sleeves.

A Young Woman.   Pardon, madam, no harm has come to the dress.

The Governor's Wife.   Because I stopped you. I've been watching you for a long time. Nothing in your head but making eyes at Shalva Tzereteli. I'll kill you, you bitch! [*She beats the* YOUNG WOMAN.]

The Adjutant [*appearing in the gateway*].   Please make haste, Natella Abashwili. Firing has broken out in the city.

[*Exit.*]

The Governor's Wife [*letting go of the* YOUNG WOMAN].   Oh dear, do you think they'll lay hands on us? Why should they? Why? [*She herself begins to rummage in the trunks.*] How's Michael? Asleep?

The Woman with the Child.   Yes, madam.

The Governor's Wife.   Then put him down a moment and get my little saffron-colored boots from the bedroom. I need them for the green dress. [*The* WOMAN *puts down the* CHILD *and goes off.*] Just look how these things have been packed! No love! No understanding! If you don't give them every order yourself . . . At such moments you realize what kind of servants you have! They gorge themselves at your expense, and never a word of gratitude! I'll remember this.

The Adjutant [entering, very excited]. Natella, you must leave at once!

The Governor's Wife. Why? I've got to take this silver dress—it cost a thousand piasters. And that one there, and where's the wine-colored one?

The Adjutant [trying to pull her away]. Riots have broken out! We must leave at once. Where's the baby?

The Governor's Wife [calling to the YOUNG WOMAN *who was holding the baby].* Maro, get the baby ready! Where on earth are you?

The Adjutant [leaving]. We'll probably have to leave the carriage behind and go ahead on horseback.

[*The* GOVERNOR'S WIFE *rummages again among her dresses, throws some onto the heap of chosen clothes, then takes them off again. Noises, drums are heard. The* YOUNG WOMAN *who was beaten creeps away. The sky begins to grow red.*]

The Governor's Wife [rummaging desperately]. I simply cannot find the wine-colored dress. Take the whole pile to the carriage. Where's Asja? And why hasn't Maro come back? Have you all gone crazy?

The Adjutant [returning]. Quick! Quick!

The Governor's Wife [to the FIRST WOMAN*].* Run! Just throw them into the carriage!

The Adjutant. We're not taking the carriage. And if you don't come now, I'll ride off on my own.

The Governor's Wife [as the FIRST WOMAN *can't carry everything.*] Where's that bitch Asja? [*The* ADJUTANT *pulls her away.*] Maro, bring the baby! [*To the* FIRST WOMAN] Go and look for Masha. No, first take the dresses to the carriage. Such nonsense! I wouldn't dream of going on horseback! [*Turning round, she sees the red sky, and starts back rigid. The fire burns. She is pulled out by the* ADJUTANT. *Shaking, the* FIRST WOMAN *follows with the dresses.*]

Maro [*from the doorway with the boots*]. Madam! [*She sees the trunks and dresses and runs toward the* BABY, *picks it up, and holds it a moment.*] They left it behind, the beasts. [*She hands it to* GRUSHA.] Hold it a moment. [*She runs off, following the* GOVERNOR'S WIFE.]

[*Enter* SERVANTS *from the gateway.*]

The Cook. Well, so they've actually gone. Without the food wagons, and not a minute too early. It's time for us to clear out.

A Groom. This'll be an unhealthy neighborhood for quite a while. [*To* ONE OF WOMEN] Suliko, take a few blankets and wait for me in the foal stables.

Grusha. What have they done with the Governor?

The Groom [gesturing throat cutting]. Ffffft.

A Fat Woman [seeing the gesture and becoming hysterical]. Oh dear, oh dear, oh dear, oh dear! Our master Georgi Abashwili! A picture of health he was, at the morning Mass—and now! Oh, take me away, we're all lost, we must die in sin like our master, Georgi Abashwili!

The Other Woman [*soothing her*]. Calm down, Nina! You'll be taken to safety. You've never hurt a fly.

The Fat Woman [*being led out*]. Oh dear, oh dear, oh dear! Quick! Let's all get out before they come, before they come!

A Young Woman. Nina takes it more to heart than the mistress, that's a fact. They even have to have their weeping done for them.

The Cook. We'd better get out, all of us.

Another Woman [*glancing back*]. That must be the East Gate burning.

The Young Woman [*seeing the* CHILD *in* GRUSHA'S *arms*]. The baby! What are you doing with it?

Grusha. It got left behind.

The Young Woman. She simply left it there. Michael, who was kept out of all the drafts!

[*The* SERVANTS *gather round the* CHILD.]

Grusha. He's waking up.

The Groom. Better put him down, I tell you. I'd rather not think what'd happen to anybody who was found with that baby.

The Cook. That's right. Once they get started, they'll kill each other off, whole families at a time. Let's go.

[*Exeunt all but* GRUSHA, *with the* CHILD *on her arm, and* TWO WOMEN.]

The Two Women. Didn't you hear? Better put him down.

Grusha. The nurse asked me to hold him a moment.

The Older Woman. She's not coming back, you simpleton.

The Younger Woman. Keep your hands off it.

The Older Woman [*amiably*]. Grusha, you're a good soul, but you're not very bright, and you know it. I tell you, if he had the plague he couldn't be more dangerous.

Grusha [*stubbornly*]. He hasn't got the plague. He looks at me! He's human!

The Older Woman. Don't look at *him*. You're a fool—the kind that always gets put upon. A person need only say, "Run for the salad, you have the longest legs," and you run. My husband has an ox cart—you can come with us if you hurry! Lord, by now the whole neighborhood must be in flames.

[BOTH WOMEN *leave, sighing. After some hesitation,* GRUSHA *puts the sleeping* CHILD *down, looks at it for a moment, then takes a brocade blanket from the heap of clothes and covers it. Then* BOTH WOMEN *return, dragging bundles.* GRUSHA *starts guiltily away from the* CHILD *and walks a few steps to one side.*]

The Younger Woman. Haven't you packed anything yet? There isn't much time, you know. The Ironshirts will be here from the barracks.

Grusha. Coming!

[*She runs through the doorway.* BOTH WOMEN *go to the gateway and wait. The sound of horses is heard. They flee, screaming. Enter the* FAT PRINCE *with drunken* IRONSHIRTS. *One of them carries the Governor's head on a lance.*]

The Fat Prince. Here! In the middle! [ONE SOLDIER *climbs onto the* OTHER'S *back, takes the head, holds it tentatively over the door.*] That's not the middle. Farther to the right. That's it. What I do, my friends, I do well. [*While, with hammer and nail, the* SOLDIER *fastens the head to the wall by its hair*] This morning at the church door I said to Georgi Abashwili: "I love a clear sky." Actually, I prefer the lightning that comes out of a clear sky. Yes, indeed. It's a pity they took the brat along, though, I need him, urgently.

[*Exit with* IRONSHIRTS *through the gateway. Trampling of horses again. Enter* GRUSHA *through the doorway looking cautiously about her. Clearly she has waited for the* IRONSHIRTS *to go. Carrying a bundle, she walks toward the gateway. At the last moment, she turns to see if the* CHILD *is still there. Catching sight of the head over the doorway, she screams. Horrified, she picks up her bundle again, and is about to leave when the* SINGER *starts to speak. She stands rooted to the spot.*]

The Singer.

> As she was standing between courtyard and gate,
> She heard or she thought she heard a low voice calling.
> The child called to her,
> Not whining, but calling quite sensibly,
> Or so it seemed to her.
> "Woman," it said, "help me."
> And it went on, not whining, but saying quite sensibly:
> "Know, woman, he who hears not a cry for help
> But passes by with troubled ears will never hear
> The gentle call of a lover nor the blackbird at dawn
> Nor the happy sigh of the tired grape-picker as the Angelus rings."

[*She walks a few steps toward the* CHILD *and bends over it.*]

> Hearing this she went back for one more look at the child:
> Only to sit with him for a moment or two,
> Only till someone should come,
> His mother, or anyone.

[*Leaning on a trunk, she sits facing the* CHILD.]

> Only till she would have to leave, for the danger was too great,
> The city was full of flame and crying.

[*The light grows dimmer, as though evening and night were coming on.*]

> Fearful is the seductive power of goodness!

[GRUSHA *now settles down to watch over the* CHILD *through the night. Once, she lights a small lamp to look at it. Once, she tucks it in with a coat. From time to time she listens and looks to see whether someone is coming.*]

> And she sat with the child a long time,
> Till evening came, till night came, till dawn came.
> She sat too long, too long she saw
> The soft breathing, the small clenched fists,

Till toward morning the seduction was complete
And she rose, and bent down and, sighing, took the child
And carried it away.

[*She does what the* SINGER *says as he describes it.*]

As if it was stolen goods she picked it up.
As if she was a thief she crept away.

The Flight into the Northern Mountains

The Singer.

When Grusha Vashnadze left the city
On the Grusinian highway
On the way to the Northern Mountains
She sang a song, she bought some milk.

The Chorus.

How will this human child escape
The bloodhounds, the trap-setters?
Into the deserted mountains she journeyed
Along the Grusinian highway she journeyed
She sang a song, she bought some milk.

[GRUSHA VASHNADZE *walks on. On her back she carries the* CHILD *in a sack, in one hand is a large stick, in the other a bundle. She sings.*]

The Song of the Four Generals

Four generals
Set out for Iran.
With the first one, war did not agree.
The second never won a victory.
For the third the weather never was right.
For the fourth the men would never fight.
Four generals
And not a single man!
Sosso Robakidse
Went marching to Iran
With him the war did so agree
He soon had won a victory.
For him the weather was always right.
For him the men would always fight.
Sosso Robakidse,
He is our man!

[*A peasant's cottage appears.*]

Grusha [*to the* CHILD].   Noontime is meal time. Now we'll sit hopefully in the grass, while the good Grusha goes and buys a little pitcher of milk. [*She lays the*

CHILD *down and knocks at the cottage door. An* OLD MAN *opens it.*] Grandfather, could I have a little pitcher of milk? And a corn cake, maybe?

The Old Man. Milk? We have no milk. The soldiers from the city have our goats. Go to the soldiers if you want milk.

Grusha. But grandfather, you must have a little pitcher of milk for a baby?

The Old Man. And for a God-bless-you, eh?

Grusha. Who said anything about a God-bless-you? [*She shows her purse.*] We'll pay like princes. "Head in the clouds, backside in the water." [*The* PEASANT *goes off, grumbling, for milk.*] How much for the milk?

The Old Man. Three piasters. Milk has gone up.

Grusha. Three piasters for this little drop? [*Without a word the* OLD MAN *shuts the door in her face.*] Michael, did you hear that? Three piasters! We can't afford it! [*She goes back, sits down again, and gives the* CHILD *her breast.*] Suck. Think of the three piasters. There's nothing there, but you *think* you're drinking, and that's something. [*Shaking her head, she sees that the* CHILD *isn't sucking any more. She gets up, walks back to the door, and knocks again.*] Open, grandfather, we'll pay. [*Softly*] May lightning strike you! [*When the* OLD MAN *appears*] I thought it would be half a piaster. But the baby must be fed. How about one piaster for that little drop?

The Old Man. Two.

Grusha. Don't shut the door again. [*She fishes a long time in her bag.*] Here are two piasters. The milk better be good. I still have two days' journey ahead of me. It's a murderous business you have here—and sinful, too.

The Old Man. Kill the soldiers if you want milk.

Grusha [*giving the* CHILD *some milk*]. This is an expensive joke. Take a sip, Michael, it's a week's pay. Around here they think we earned our money just sitting around. Oh, Michael, Michael, you're a nice little load for a girl to take on! [*Uneasy, she gets up, puts the* CHILD *on her back, and walks on. The* OLD MAN, *grumbling, picks up the pitcher and looks after her unmoved.*]

The Singer.

> As Grusha Vashnadze went northward
> The Princes' Ironshirts went after her.

The Chorus.

> How will the barefoot girl escape the Ironshirts,
> The bloodhounds, the trap-setters?
> They hunt even by night.
> Pursuers never tire.
> Butchers sleep little.

[TWO IRONSHIRTS *are trudging along the highway.*]

The Corporal. You'll never amount to anything, blockhead, your heart's not in it. Your senior officer sees this in little things. Yesterday, when I made the fat gal, yes, you grabbed her husband as I commanded, and you did kick him in the stomach, at my request, but did not *enjoy* it, like a loyal Private, or were you just doing your duty? I've kept an eye on you blockhead, you're a hollow reed

and a tinkling cymbal, you won't get promoted. [*They walk a while in silence.*]
Don't think I've forgotten how insubordinate you are, either. Stop limping! I
forbid you to limp! You limp because I sold the horses, and I sold the horses
because I'd never have got that price again. You limp to show me you don't like
marching. I know you. It won't help. You wait. Sing!

The Two Ironshirts [*singing*].

> Sadly to war I went my way
> Leaving my loved one at her door.
> My friends will keep her honor safe
> Till from the war I'm back once more.

The Corporal.   Louder!
The Two Ironshirts [*singing*].

> When 'neath a headstone I shall be
> My love a little earth will bring:
> "Here rest the feet that oft would run to me
> And here the arms that oft to me would cling."

[*They begin to walk again in silence.*]

The Corporal.   A good soldier has his heart and soul in it. When he receives an
order, he gets a hard on, and when he drives his lance into the enemy's guts, he
comes. [*He shouts for joy.*] He lets himself be torn to bits for his superior
officer, and as he lies dying he takes note that his corporal is nodding approval,
and that is reward enough, it's his dearest wish. *You* won't get any nod of
approval, but you'll croak all right. Christ, how'm I to get my hands on the
Governor's bastard with the help of a fool like you! [*They stay on stage behind.*]

The Singer.

> When Grusha Vashnadze came to the River Sirra
> Flight grew too much for her, the helpless child too heavy.
> In the cornfields the rosy dawn
> Is cold to the sleepless one, only cold.
> The gay clatter of the milk cans in the farmyard where the smoke rises
> Is only a threat to the fugitive.
> She who carries the child feels its weight and little more.

[GRUSHA *stops in front of a farm. A fat* PEASANT WOMAN *is carrying a milk can
through the door.* GRUSHA *waits until she has gone in, then approaches the
house cautiously.*]

Grusha [*to the child*].   Now you've wet yourself again, and you know I've no
linen. Michael, this is where we part company. It's far enough from the city.
They wouldn't want you *so* much that they'd follow you all *this* way, little good-
for-nothing. The peasant woman is kind, and can't you just smell the milk?
[*She bends down to lay the* CHILD *on the threshold.*] So farewell, Michael, I'll
forget how you kicked me in the back all night to make me walk faster. And you
can forget the meager fare—it was meant well. I'd like to have kept you—your

nose is so tiny—but it can't be. I'd have shown you your first rabbit, I'd have trained you to keep dry, but now I must turn around. My sweetheart the soldier might be back soon, and suppose he didn't find me? You can't ask that, can you?

[*She creeps up to the door and lays the* CHILD *on the threshold. Then, hiding behind a tree, she waits until the* PEASANT WOMAN *opens the door and sees the bundle.*]

The Peasant Woman.   Good heavens, what's this? Husband!

The Peasant.   What is it? Let me finish my soup.

The Peasant Woman [*to the* CHILD].   Where's your mother then? Haven't you got one? It's a boy. Fine linen. He's from a good family, you can see that. And they just leave him on our doorstep. Oh, these are times!

The Peasant.   If they think we're going to feed it, they're wrong. You can take it to the priest in the village. That's the best we can do.

The Peasant Woman.   What'll the priest do with him? He needs a mother. There, he's waking up. Don't you think we could keep him, though?

The Peasant [*shouting*].   No!

The Peasant Woman.   I could lay him in the corner by the armchair. All I need is a crib. I can take him into the fields with me. See him laughing? Husband, we have a roof over our heads. We can do it. Not another word out of you!

[*She carries the* CHILD *into the house. The* PEASANT *follows protesting.* GRUSHA *steps out from behind the tree, laughs, and hurries off in the opposite direction.*]

The Singer.

> Why so cheerful, making for home?

The Chorus.

> Because the child has won new parents with a laugh,
> Because I'm rid of the little one, I'm cheerful.

The Singer.

> And why so sad?

The Chorus.

> Because I'm single and free, I'm sad
> Like someone who's been robbed
> Someone who's newly poor.

[*She walks for a short while, then meets the* TWO IRONSHIRTS *who point their lances at her.*]

The Corporal.   Lady, you are running straight into the arms of the Armed Forces. Where are you coming from? And when? Are you having illicit relations with the enemy? Where is he hiding? What movements is he making in your rear? How about the hills? How about the valleys? How are your stockings held in position? [GRUSHA *stands there frightened.*] Don't be scared, we always stage a retreat, if necessary . . . what, blockhead? I always stage retreats. In that respect at least, I can be relied on. Why are you staring like that at my lance? In the field no soldier drops his lance, that's a rule. Learn it by heart, blockhead. Now, lady, where are you headed?

Grusha. To meet my intended, one Simon Shashava, of the Palace Guard in Nuka.

The Corporal. Simon Shashava? Sure, I know him. He gave me the key so I could look you up once in a while. Blockhead, we are getting to be unpopular. We must make her realize we have honorable intentions. Lady, behind apparent frivolity I conceal a serious nature, so let me tell you officially: I want a child from you. [GRUSHA *utters a little scream.*] Blockhead, she understood me. Uh-huh, isn't it a sweet shock? "Then first I must take the noodles out of the oven, Officer. Then first I must change my torn shirt, Colonel." But away with jokes, away with my lance! We are looking for a baby. A baby from a good family. Have you heard of such a baby, from the city, dressed in fine linen, and suddenly turning up here?

Grusha. No, I haven't heard a thing. [*Suddenly she turns round and runs back, panic-stricken. The* IRONSHIRTS *glance at each other, then follow her, cursing.*]

The Singer.

> Run, kind girl! The killers are coming!
> Help the helpless babe, helpless girl!
> And so she runs!

The Chorus.

> In the bloodiest times
> There are kind people.

[*As* GRUSHA *rushes into the cottage, the* PEASANT WOMAN *is bending over the* CHILD's *crib.*]

Grusha. Hide him. Quick! The Ironshirts are coming! I laid him on your doorstep. But he isn't mine. He's from a good family.

The Peasant Woman. Who's coming? What Ironshirts?

Grusha. Don't ask questions. The Ironshirts that are looking for it.

The Peasant Woman. They've no business in my house But I must have a little talk with you, it seems.

Grusha. Take off the fine linen. It'll give us away.

The Peasant Woman. Linen, my foot! In this house I make the decisions! "You can't vomit in *my* room!" Why did you abandon it? It's a sin.

Grusha [*looking out of the window*]. Look, they're coming out from behind those trees! I shouldn't have run away, it made them angry. Oh, what shall I do?

The Peasant Woman [*looking out of the window and suddenly starting with fear*]. Gracious! Ironshirts!

Grusha. They're after the baby.

The Peasant Woman. Suppose they come in!

Grusha. You mustn't give him to them. Say he's yours.

The Peasant Woman. Yes.

Grusha. They'll run him through if you hand him over.

The Peasant Woman. But suppose they ask for it? The silver for the harvest is in the house.

Grusha. If you let them have him, they'll run him through, right here in this room! You've got to say he's yours!

The Peasant Woman. Yes. But what if they don't believe me?

Grusha. You must be firm.

The Peasant Woman. They'll burn the roof over our heads.

Grusha. That's why you must say he's yours. His name's Michael. But I shouldn't have told you. [*The* PEASANT WOMAN *nods.*] Don't nod like that. And don't tremble—they'll notice.

The Peasant Woman. Yes.

Grusha. And stop saying yes, I can't stand it. [*She shakes the* WOMAN.] Don't you have any children?

The Peasant Woman [*muttering*]. He's in the war.

Grusha. Then maybe *he's* an Ironshirt? Do you want *him* to run children through with a lance? You'd bawl him out. "No fooling with lances in my house!" you'd shout, "is that what I've reared you for? Wash your neck before you speak to your mother!"

The Peasant Woman. That's true, he couldn't get away with anything around here!

Grusha. So you'll say he's yours?

The Peasant Woman. Yes.

Grusha. Look! They're coming!

[*There is a knocking at the door. The* WOMEN *don't answer. Enter* IRONSHIRTS. *The* PEASANT WOMAN *bows low.*]

The Corporal. Well, here she is. What did I tell you? What a nose I have! I *smelt* her. Lady, I have a question for you. Why did you run away? What did you think I would do to you? I'll bet it was something dirty. Confess!

Grusha [*while the* PEASANT WOMAN *bows again and again*]. I'd left some milk on the stove, and I suddenly remembered it.

The Corporal. Or maybe you imagined I looked at you in a dirty way? Like there could be something between us? A lewd sort of look, know what I mean?

Grusha. I didn't see it.

The Corporal. But it's possible, huh? You admit that much. After all, I might be a pig. I'll be frank with you: I could think of all sorts of things if we were alone. [*To the* PEASANT WOMAN.] Shouldn't you be busy in the yard? Feeding the hens?

The Peasant Woman [*falling suddenly to her knees*]. Soldier, I didn't know a thing about it. Please don't burn the roof over our heads.

The Corporal. What are you talking about?

The Peasant Woman. I had nothing to do with it. She left it on my doorstep, I swear it!

The Corporal [*suddenly seeing the* CHILD *and whistling*]. Ah, so there's a little something in the crib! Blockhead, I smell a thousand piasters. Take the old girl outside and hold on to her. It looks like I have a little cross-examining to do.

[*The* PEASANT WOMAN *lets herself be led out by the* PRIVATE, *without a word.*]
So, you've got the child I wanted from you! [*He walks toward the crib.*]

Grusha.   Officer, he's mine. He's not the one you're after.

The Corporal.   I'll just take a look. [*He bends over the crib.* GRUSHA *looks round in despair.*]

Grusha.   He's mine! He's mine!

The Corporal.   Fine linen!

[GRUSHA *dashes at him to pull him away. He throws her off and again bends over the crib. Again looking round in despair, she sees a log of wood, seizes it, and hits the* CORPORAL *over the head from behind. The* CORPORAL *collapses. She quickly picks up the* CHILD *and rushes off.*]

The Singer.

> And in her flight from the Ironshirts
> After twenty-two days of journeying
> At the foot of the Janga-Tu Glacier
> Grusha Vashnadze decided to adopt the child.

The Chorus.

> The helpless girl adopted the helpless child.

[GRUSHA *squats over a half-frozen stream to get the* CHILD *water in the hollow of her hand.*]

Grusha.

> Since no one else will take you, son,
> I must take you.
> Since no one else will take you, son,
> You must take me.
> O black day in a lean, lean year,
> The trip was long, the milk was dear,
> My legs are tired, my feet are sore:
> But I wouldn't be without you any more.
> I'll throw your silken shirt away
> And dress you in rags and tatters.
> I'll wash you, son, and christen you in glacier water.
> We'll see it through together.

[*She has taken off the child's fine linen and wrapped it in a rag.*]

The Singer.

> When Grusha Vashnadze
> Pursued by the Ironshirts
> Came to the bridge on the glacier
> Leading to the villages of the Eastern Slope
> She sang the Song of the Rotten Bridge
> And risked two lives.

[*A wind has risen. The bridge on the glacier is visible in the dark. One rope is broken and half the bridge is hanging down the abyss.* MERCHANTS, *two men*

and a woman, stand undecided before the bridge as GRUSHA *and the* CHILD
arrive. ONE MAN *is trying to catch the hanging rope with a stick.*]

The First Man. Take your time, young woman. You won't get across here
anyway.

Grusha. But I *have* to get the baby to the east side. To my brother's place.

The Merchant Woman. Have to? How d'you mean, "have to"? I have to get
there, too—because I have to buy carpets in Atum—carpets a woman had to sell
because her husband had to die. But can *I* do what I have to? Can she? Andrei's
been fishing for that rope for hours. And I ask you, how are we going to fasten
it, even if he gets it up?

The First Man [*listening*].   Hush, I think I hear something.

Grusha. The bridge isn't quite rotted through. I think I'll try it.

The Merchant Woman. I wouldn't—if the devil himself were after me. It's
suicide.

The First Man [*shouting*].   Hi!

Grusha. Don't shout! [*To the* MERCHANT WOMAN] Tell him not to shout.

The First Man. But there's someone down there calling. Maybe they've lost their
way.

The Merchant Woman. Why shouldn't he shout? Is there something funny
about you? Are they after you?

Grusha. All right, I'll tell. The Ironshirts are after me. I knocked one down.

The Second Man. Hide our merchandise! [*The* WOMAN *hides a sack behind a
rock.*]

The First Man. Why didn't you say so right away? [*To the others.*] If they
catch her they'll make mincemeat out of her!

Grusha. Get out of my way. I've got to cross that bridge.

The Second Man. You can't. The precipice is two thousand feet deep.

The First Man. Even with the rope it'd be no use. We could hold it up with our
hands. But then we'd have to do the same for the Ironshirts.

Grusha. Go away.

[*There are calls from the distance:* "Hi, up there!"]

The Merchant Woman. They're getting near. But you can't take the child on
that bridge. It's sure to break. And look!

[GRUSHA *looks down into the abyss. The* IRONSHIRTS *are heard calling again
from below.*]

The Second Man. Two thousand feet!

Grusha. But those men are worse.

The First Man. You can't do it. Think of the baby. Risk your life but not a
child's.

The Second Man. With the child she's that much heavier!

The Merchant Woman. Maybe she's *really* got to get across. Give *me* the baby.
I'll hide it. Cross the bridge alone!

Grusha. I won't. We belong together. [*To the* CHILD.] "Live together, die
together." [*She sings.*]

The Song of the Rotten Bridge

> Deep is the abyss, son,
> I see the weak bridge sway;
> But it's not for us, son,
> To choose the way.
> The way I know
> Is the one you must tread,
> And all you will eat
> Is my bit of bread.
> Of every four pieces
> You shall have three.
> Would that I knew
> How big they will be!

Get out of my way, I'll try it without the rope.
The Merchant Woman.   You are tempting God!

[*There are shouts from below.*]

Grusha.   Please, throw that stick away, or they'll get the rope and follow me.
[*Pressing the* CHILD *to her, she steps onto the swaying bridge. The* MERCHANT
WOMAN *screams when it looks as though the bridge is about to collapse. But*
GRUSHA *walks on and reaches the far side.*]
The First Man.   She made it!
The Merchant Woman [*Who has fallen on her knees and begun to pray,
angrily.*]   I still think it was a sin.

[*The* IRONSHIRTS *appear; the* CORPORAL'S *head is bandaged.*]

The Corporal.   Seen a woman with a child?
The First Man [*while the* SECOND MAN *throws the stick into the abyss*].   Yes,
there! But the bridge won't carry you!
The Corporal.   You'll pay for this, blockhead!

[GRUSHA, *from the far bank, laughs and shows the* CHILD *to the* IRONSHIRTS. *She
walks on. The wind blows.*]

Grusha [*turning to the* CHILD].   You mustn't be afraid of the wind. He's a poor
thing too. He has to push the clouds along and he gets quite cold doing it.
[*Snow starts falling.*] And the snow isn't so bad, either, Michael. It covers the
little fir trees so they won't die in winter. Let me sing you a little song. [*She
sings.*]

The Song of the Child

> Your father is a bandit
> A harlot the mother who bore you.
> Yet honorable men
> Shall kneel down before you.
> Food to the baby horses

> The tiger's son will take.
> The mothers will get milk
> From the son of the snake.

In the Northern Mountains

The Singer.

> Seven days the sister, Grusha Vashnadze,
> Journeyed across the glacier
> And down the slopes she journeyed.
> "When I enter my brother's house," she thought,
> "He will rise and embrace me."
> "Is that you, sister?" he will say,
> "I have long expected you.
> This is my dear wife,
> And this is my farm, come to me by marriage,
> With eleven horses and thirty-one cows. Sit down.
> Sit down with your child at our table and eat."
> The brother's house was in a lovely valley.
> When the sister came to the brother,
> She was ill from walking.
> The brother rose from the table.

[*A* FAT PEASANT COUPLE *rise from the table.* LAVRENTI VASHNADZE *still has a napkin round his neck, as* GRUSHA, *pale and supported by a* SERVANT, *enters with the* CHILD.]

Lavrenti. Where've *you* come from, Grusha?
Grusha [*feebly*]. Across the Janga-Tu Pass, Lavrenti.
The Servant. I found her in front of the hay barn. She has a baby with her.
The Sister-in-Law. Go and groom the mare.

[*Exit the* SERVANT.]

Lavrenti. This is my wife Aniko.
The Sister-in-Law. I thought you were in service in Nuka.
Grusha [*barely able to stand*]. Yes, I was.
The Sister-in-law. Wasn't it a good job? We were told it was.
Grusha. The Governor got killed.
Lavrenti. Yes, we heard there were riots. Your aunt told us. Remember, Aniko?
The Sister-in-Law. Here with us, it's very quiet. City people always want something going on. [*She walks toward the door, calling.*] Sosso, Sosso, don't take the cake out of the oven yet, d'you hear? Where on earth are you?

[*Exit, calling.*]

Lavrenti [*quietly, quickly*]. Is there a father? [*As she shakes her head.*] I thought not. We must think up something. She's religious.
The Sister-in-Law [*returning*]. Those servants! [*To* GRUSHA.] You have a child.
Grusha. It's mine. [*She collapses.* LAVRENTI *rushes to her assistance.*]

The Sister-in-Law. Heavens, she's ill—what are we going to do?

Lavrenti [*escorting her to a bench near the stove*]. Sit down, sit. I think it's just weakness, Aniko.

The Sister-in-Law. As long as it's not scarlet fever!

Lavrenti. She'd have spots if it was. It's only weakness. Don't worry, Aniko. [*To* GRUSHA.] Better, sitting down?

The Sister-in-Law. Is the child hers?

Grusha. Yes, mine.

Lavrenti. She's on her way to her husband.

The Sister-in-Law. I see. Your meat's getting cold. [LAVRENTI *sits down and begins to eat.*] Cold food's not good for you, the fat mustn't get cold, you know your stomach's your weak spot. [*To* GRUSHA.] If your husband's not in the city, where is he?

Lavrenti. She got married on the other side of the mountain, she says.

The Sister-in-Law. On the other side of the mountain. I see. [*She also sits down to eat.*]

Grusha. I think I should lie down somewhere, Lavrenti.

The Sister-in-Law. If it's consumption we'll all get it. [*She goes on cross-examining her.*] Has your husband got a farm?

Grusha. He's a soldier.

Lavrenti. But he's coming into a farm—a small one—from his father.

The Sister-in-Law. Isn't he in the war? Why not?

Grusha [*with effort*]. Yes, he's in the war.

The Sister-in-Law. Then why d'you want to go to the farm?

Lavrenti. When he comes back from the war, he'll return to his farm.

The Sister-in-Law. But you're going there now?

Lavrenti. Yes, to wait for him.

The Sister-in-Law [*calling shrilly*]. Sosso, the cake!

Grusha [*murmuring feverishly*]. A farm—a soldier—waiting—sit down, eat.

The Sister-in-Law. It's scarlet fever.

Grusha [*starting up*]. Yes, he's got a farm!

Lavrenti. I think it's just weakness, Aniko. Would you look after the cake yourself, dear?

The Sister-in-Law. But when will he come back if war's broken out again as people say? [*She waddles off, shouting.*] Sosso! Where on earth are you? Sosso!

Lavrenti [*getting up quickly and going to* GRUSHA]. You'll get a bed in a minute. She has a good heart. But wait till after supper.

Grusha [*holding out the* CHILD *to him*]. Take him.

Lavrenti [*taking it and looking around*]. But you can't stay here long with the child. She's religious, you see. [GRUSHA *collapses.* LAVRENTI *catches her.*]

The Singer.

> The sister was so ill,
> The cowardly brother had to give her shelter.
> Summer departed, winter came.
> The winter was long, the winter was short,
> People mustn't know anything,
> Rats mustn't bite,
> Spring mustn't come.

[GRUSHA *sits over the weaving loom in a workroom. She and the* CHILD, *who is squatting on the floor, are wrapped in blankets. She sings.*]

The Song of the Center

> And the lover started to leave
> And his betrothed ran pleading after him
> Pleading and weeping, weeping and teaching:
> "Dearest mine, dearest mine
> When you go to war as now you do
> When you fight the foe as soon you will
> Don't lead with the front line
> And don't push with the rear line
> At the front is red fire
> In the rear is red smoke
> Stay in the war's center
> Stay near the standard bearer
> The first always die
> The last are also hit
> Those in the center come home."

Michael, we must be clever. If we make ourselves as small as cockroaches, the sister-in-law will forget we're in the house, and then we can stay till the snow melts.

[*Enter* LAVRENTI. *He sits down beside his* SISTER.]

Lavrenti. Why are you sitting there muffled up like coachmen, you two? Is it too cold in the room?

Grusha [*hastily removing one shawl*]. It's not too cold, Lavrenti.

Lavrenti. If it's too cold, you shouldn't be sitting here with the child. Aniko would never forgive herself! [*Pause.*] I hope our priest didn't question you about the child?

Grusha. He did, but I didn't tell him anything.

Lavrenti. That's good. I wanted to speak to you about Aniko. She has a good heart but she's very, very sensitive. People need only mention our farm and she's worried. She takes everything hard, you see. One time our milkmaid went to church with a hole in her stocking. Ever since, Aniko has worn two pairs of stockings in church. It's the old family in her. [*He listens.*] Are you sure there are no rats around? If there are rats, you couldn't live here. [*There are sounds as of dripping from the roof.*] What's that, dripping?

Grusha. It must be a barrel leaking.

Lavrenti. Yes, it must be a barrel. You've been here six months, haven't you? Was I talking about Aniko? [*They listen again to the snow melting.*] You can't imagine how worried she gets about your soldier-husband. "Suppose he comes back and can't find her!" she says and lies awake. "He can't come before the spring," I tell her. The dear woman! [*The drops begin to fall faster.*] When d'you think he'll come? What do *you* think? [GRUSHA *is silent.*] Not before the spring, you agree? [GRUSHA *is silent.*] You don't believe he'll come at all? [GRUSHA *is silent.*] But when the spring comes and the snow melts here and on the passes, you can't stay on. They may come and look for you. There's already talk of an illegitimate child. [*The "glockenspiel" of the falling drops has grown faster and steadier.*] Grusha, the snow is melting on the roof. Spring is here.

Grusha.   Yes.

Lavrenti [*eagerly*].   I'll tell you what we'll do. You need a place to go, and because of the child [*he sighs*], you have to have a husband, so people won't talk. Now I've made cautious inquiries to see if we can find you a husband. Grusha, I *have* one. I talked to a peasant woman who has a son. Just the other side of the mountain. A small farm. And she's willing.

Grusha.   But I *can't* marry! I must wait for Simon Shashava.

Lavrenti.   Of course. That's all been taken care of. You don't need a man in bed—you need a man on paper. And I've found you one. The son of this peasant woman is going to die. Isn't that wonderful? He's at his last gasp. And all in line with our story—a husband from the other side of the mountain! And when you met him he was at the last gasp. So you're a widow. What do you say?

Grusha.   It's true I could use a document with stamps on it for Michael.

Lavrenti.   Stamps make all the difference. Without something in writing the Shah couldn't prove he's a Shah. And you'll have a place to live.

Grusha.   How much does the peasant woman want?

Lavrenti.   Four hundred piasters.

Grusha.   Where will you find it?

Lavrenti [*guiltily*].   Aniko's milk money.

Grusha.   No one would know us there. I'll do it.

Lavrenti [*getting up*].   I'll let the peasant woman know.

   [*Quick exit.*]

Grusha.   Michael, you cause a lot of fuss. I came to you as the pear tree comes to the sparrows. And because a Christian bends down and picks up a crust of bread so nothing will go to waste. Michael, it would have been better had I walked quickly away on that Easter Sunday in Nuka in the second courtyard. Now I *am* a fool.

The Singer.

> The bridegroom was on his deathbed when the bride arrived.
> The bridegroom's mother was waiting at the door, telling her to hurry.
> The bride brought a child along.
> The witness hid it during the wedding.

[*On one side the bed. Under the mosquito net lies a very sick* MAN. GRUSHA *is pulled in at a run by her future* MOTHER-IN-LAW. *They are followed by* LAVRENTI *and the* CHILD.]

The Mother-in-Law.   Quick! Quick! Or he'll die on us before the wedding. [*To* LAVRENTI] I was never told she had a child already.

Lavrenti.   What difference does it make? [*Pointing toward the* DYING MAN.] It can't matter to him—in his condition.

The Mother-in-Law.   To him? But I'll never survive the shame! We are honest people. [*She begins to weep.*] My Jussup doesn't have to marry a girl with a child!

Lavrenti. All right, make it another two hundred piasters. You'll have it in writing that the farm will go to you: but she'll have the right to live here for two years.

The Mother-in-Law [*drying her tears*]. It'll hardly cover the funeral expenses. I hope she'll really lend a hand with the work. And what's happened to the monk? He must have slipped out through the kitchen window. We'll have the whole village on our necks when they hear Jussup's end is come! Oh dear! I'll go get the monk. But he mustn't see the child!

Lavrenti. I'll take care he doesn't. But why only a monk? Why not a priest?

The Mother-in-Law. Oh, he's just as good. I only made one mistake: I paid half his fee in advance. Enough to send him to the tavern. I only hope . . .

[*She runs off.*]

Lavrenti. She saved on the priest, the wretch! Hired a cheap monk.

Grusha. You *will* send Simon Shashava to see me if he turns up after all?

Lavrenti. Yes. [*Pointing at the* SICK MAN.] Won't you take a look at him? [GRUSHA, *taking* MICHAEL *to her, shakes her head.*] He's not moving an eyelid. I hope we aren't too late.

[*They listen. On the opposite side enter* NEIGHBORS *who look around and take up positions against the walls, thus forming another wall near the bed, yet leaving an opening so that the bed can be seen. They start murmuring prayers. Enter the* MOTHER-IN-LAW *with a* MONK. *Showing some annoyance and surprise, she bows to the* GUESTS.]

The Mother-in-Law. I hope you won't mind waiting a few moments? My son's bride has just arrived from the city. An emergency wedding is about to be celebrated. [*To the* MONK *in the bedroom*] I might have known you couldn't keep your trap shut. [*To* GRUSHA] The wedding can take place at once. Here's the license. Me and the bride's brother [LAVRENTI *tries to hide in the background, after having quietly taken* MICHAEL *back from* GRUSHA. *The* MOTHER-IN-LAW *waves him away*] are the witnesses.

[GRUSHA *has bowed to the* MONK. *They go to the bed. The* MOTHER-IN-LAW *lifts the mosquito net. The* MONK *starts reeling off the marriage ceremony in Latin. Meanwhile, the* MOTHER-IN-LAW *beckons to* LAVRENTI *to get rid of the* CHILD, *but fearing that it will cry he draws its attention to the ceremony.* GRUSHA *glances once at the* CHILD, *and* LAVRENTI *waves the* CHILD's *hand in a greeting.*]

The Monk. Are you prepared to be a faithful, obedient, and good wife to his man, and to cleave to him until death you do part?

Grusha [*looking at the* CHILD]. I am.

The Monk [*to the* SICK PEASANT]. Are you prepared to be a good and loving husband to your wife until death you do part? [*As the* SICK PEASANT *does not answer, the* MONK *looks inquiringly around.*]

The Mother-in-Law. Of course he is! Didn't you hear him say yes?

The Monk. All right. We declare the marriage contracted! How about extreme unction?

The Mother-in-Law. Nothing doing! The wedding cost quite enough. Now I must take care of the mourners. [*To* LAVRENTI.] Did we say seven hundred?

Lavrenti. Six hundred. [*He pays.*] Now I don't want to sit with the guests and get to know people. So farewell, Grusha, and if my widowed sister comes to visit me, she'll get a welcome from my wife, or I'll show my teeth. [*Nods, gives the* CHILD *to* GRUSHA, *and leaves. The* MOURNERS *glance after him without interest.*]

The Monk. May one ask where this child comes from?

The Mother-in-Law. Is there a child? I don't see a child. And you don't see a child either—you understand? Or it may turn out I saw all sorts of things in the tavern! Now come on. [*After* GRUSHA *has put the* CHILD *down and told him to be quiet, they move over left;* GRUSHA *is introduced to the* NEIGHBORS.] This is my daughter-in-law. She arrived just in time to find dear Jussup still alive.

One Woman. He's been ill now a whole year, hasn't he? When our Vassili was drafted he was there to say good-bye.

Another Woman. Such things are terrible for a farm. The corn all ripe and the farmer in bed! It'll really be a blessing if he doesn't suffer too long, I say.

The First Woman [*confidentially*]. You know why we thought he'd taken to his bed? Because of the draft! And now his end is come!

The Mother-in-Law. Sit yourselves down, please! And have some cakes!

[*She beckons to* GRUSHA *and* BOTH WOMEN *go into the bedroom, where they pick up the cake pans off the floor. The* GUESTS, *among them the* MONK, *sit on the floor and begin conversing in subdued voices.*]

One Peasant [*to whom the* MONK *has handed the bottle which he has taken from his soutane*]. There's a child, you say! How can that have happened to Jussup?

A Woman. She was certainly lucky to get herself hitched, with him so sick!

The Mother-in-Law. They're gossiping already. And wolfing down the funeral cakes at the same time! If he doesn't die today, I'll have to bake some more tomorrow!

Grusha. I'll bake them for you.

The Mother-in-Law. Yesterday some horsemen rode by, and I went out to see who it was. When I came in again he was lying there like a corpse! So I sent for you. It can't take much longer. [*She listens.*]

The Monk. Dear wedding and funeral guests! Deeply touched, we stand before a bed of death and marriage. The bride gets a veil; the groom, a shroud: how varied, my children, are the fates of men! Alas! One man dies and has a roof over his head, and the other is married and the flesh turns to dust from which it was made. Amen.

The Mother-in-Law. He's getting his own back. I shouldn't have hired such a cheap one. It's what you'd expect. A more expensive monk would behave himself. In Sura there's one with a real air of sanctity about him, but of course he charges a fortune. A fifty-piaster monk like that has no dignity, and as for piety, just fifty piasters' worth and no more! When I came to get him in the tavern he'd just made a speech, and he was shouting: "The war is over, beware of the peace!" We must go in.

Grusha [*giving* MICHAEL *a cake*]. Eat this cake, and keep nice and still, Michael.

[*The* TWO WOMEN *offer cakes to the* GUESTS. *The* DYING MAN *sits up in bed. He puts his head out from under the mosquito net, stares at the* TWO WOMEN, *then sinks back again. The* MONK *takes two bottles from his soutane and offers them to the* PEASANT *beside him. Enter* THREE MUSICIANS *who are greeted with a sly wink by the* MONK.]

The Mother-in-Law [*to the* MUSICIANS]. What are you doing here? With instruments?

One Musician. Brother Anastasius here [*pointing at the* MONK] told us there was a wedding on.

The Mother-in-Law. What? You brought them? Three more on my neck! Don't you know there's a dying man in the next room?

The Monk. A very tempting assignment for a musician: something that could be either a subdued Wedding March or a spirited Funeral Dance.

The Mother-in-Law. Well, you might as well play. Nobody can stop you eating in any case.

[*The* MUSICIANS *play a potpourri. The* WOMEN *serve cakes.*]

The Monk. The trumpet sounds like a whining baby. And you, little drum, what have you got to tell the world?

The Drunken Peasant [*beside the* MONK, *sings*].

> Miss Roundass took the old old man
> And said that marriage was the thing
> To everyone who met 'er.
> She later withdrew from the contract because
> Candles are better.

[*The* MOTHER-IN-LAW *throws the* DRUNKEN PEASANT *out. The music stops. The* GUESTS *are embarrassed.*]

The Guests [*loudly*]. Have you heard? The Grand Duke is back! But the Princes are against him.

—They say the Shah of Persia has lent him a great army to restore order in Grusinia.

—But how is that possible? The Shah of Persia is the enemy . . .

—The enemy of Grusinia, you donkey, not the enemy of the Grand Duke!

—In any case, the war's over, so our soldiers are coming back.

[GRUSHA *drops a cake pan.* GUESTS *help her pick up the cake.*]

An Old Woman [*to* GRUSHA]. Are you feeling bad? It's just excitement about dear Jussup. Sit down and rest a while, my dear. [GRUSHA *staggers.*]

The Guests. Now everything'll be the way it was. Only the taxes'll go up because now we'll have to pay for the war.

Grusha [*weakly*]. Did someone say the soldiers are back?

A Man. I did.

Grusha. It can't be true.

The First Man [*to a* WOMAN]. Show her the shawl. We bought it from a soldier. It's from Persia.

Grusha [*looking at the shawl*]. They are here. [*She gets up, takes a step, kneels down in prayer, takes the silver cross and chain out of her blouse, and kisses it.*]

The Mother-in-Law [*while the* GUESTS *silently watch* GRUSHA]. What's the matter with you? Aren't you going to look after our guests? What's all this city nonsense got to do with us?

The Guests [*resuming conversation while* GRUSHA *remains in prayer*]. You can buy Persian saddles from the soldiers too. Though many want crutches in exchange for them.

    —The big shots on one side can win a war, the soldiers on both sides lose it.

    —Anyway, the war's over. It's something they can't draft you any more.

[*The* DYING MAN *sits bolt upright in bed. He listens.*]

    —What we need is two weeks of good weather.

    —Our pear trees are hardly bearing a thing this year.

The Mother-in-Law [*offering cakes*]. Have some more cakes and welcome! There are more!

[*The* MOTHER-IN-LAW *goes to the bedroom with the empty cake pans. Unaware of the* DYING MAN, *she is bending down to pick up another tray when he begins to talk in a hoarse voice.*]

The Peasant. How many more cakes are you going to stuff down their throats? D'you think I can shit money?

[*The* MOTHER-IN-LAW *starts, stares at him aghast, while he climbs out from behind the mosquito net.*]

The First Woman [*talking kindly to* GRUSHA *in the next room*]. Has the young wife got someone at the front?

A Man. It's good news that they're on their way home, huh?

The Peasant. Don't stare at me like that! Where's this wife you've saddled me with?

[*Receiving no answer, he climbs out of bed and in his nightshirt staggers into the other room. Trembling, she follows him with the cake pan.*]

The Guests [*seeing him and shrieking*]. Good God! Jussup!

[*Everyone leaps up in alarm. The* WOMEN *rush to the door.* GRUSHA, *still on her knees, turns round and stares at the* MAN.]

The Peasant. A funeral supper! You'd enjoy that, wouldn't you? Get out before I throw you out! [*As the* GUESTS *stampede from the house, gloomily to* GRUSHA] I've upset the apple cart, huh? [*Receiving no answer, he turns round and takes a cake from the pan which his mother is holding.*]

The Singer.

        O confusion! The wife discovers she has a husband.
        By day there's the child, by night there's the husband.
        The lover is on his way both day and night.
        Husband and wife look at each other.
        The bedroom is small.

[*Near the bed the* PEASANT *is sitting in a high wooden bathtub, naked, the* MOTHER-IN-LAW *is pouring water from a pitcher. Opposite* GRUSHA *cowers with* MICHAEL, *who is playing at mending straw mats.*]

The Peasant [*to his* MOTHER]. That's her work, not yours. Where's she hiding out now?

The Mother-in-Law [*calling*]. Grusha! The peasant wants you!

Grusha [*to* MICHAEL]. There are still two holes to mend.

The Peasant [*when* GRUSHA *approaches*]. Scrub my back!

Grusha. Can't the peasant do it himself?

The Peasant. "Can't the peasant do it himself?" Get the brush! To hell with you! Are you the wife here? Or are you a visitor? [*To the* MOTHER-IN-LAW] It's too cold!

The Mother-in-Law. I'll run for hot water.

Grusha. Let me go.

The Peasant. You stay here. [*The* MOTHER-IN-LAW *exits.*] Rub harder. And no shirking. You've seen a naked fellow before. That child didn't come out of thin air.

Grusha. The child was not conceived in joy, if that's what the peasant means.

The Peasant [*turning and grinning*]. You don't look the type. [GRUSHA *stops scrubbing him, starts back. Enter the* MOTHER-IN-LAW.]

The Peasant. A nice thing you've saddled me with! A simpleton for a wife!

The Mother-in-Law. She just isn't cooperative.

The Peasant. Pour—but go easy! Ow! Go easy, I said. [*To* GRUSHA] Maybe you did something wrong in the city . . . I wouldn't be surprised. Why else should you be here? But I won't talk about that. I've not said a word about the illegitimate object you brought into my house either. But my patience has limits! It's against nature. [*To the* MOTHER-IN-LAW] More! [*To* GRUSHA] And even if your soldier does come back, you're married.

Grusha. Yes.

The Peasant. But your soldier won't come back. Don't you believe it.

Grusha. No.

The Peasant. You're cheating me. You're my wife and you're not my wife. Where you lie, nothing lies, and yet no other woman can lie there. When I go to work in the morning I'm tired—when I lie down at night I'm awake as the devil. God has given you sex—and what d'you do? I don't have ten piasters to buy myself a woman in the city. Besides, it's a long way. Woman weeds the fields and opens up her legs, that's what our calendar says. D'you hear?

Grusha [*quietly*]. Yes. I didn't mean to cheat you out of it.

The Peasant. She didn't mean to cheat me out of it! Pour some more water! [*The* MOTHER-IN-LAW *pours.*] Ow!

The Singer.

> As she sat by the stream to wash the linen
> She saw his image in the water
> And his face grew dimmer with the passing moons.
> As she raised herself to wring the linen
> She heard his voice from the murmuring maple
> And his voice grew fainter with the passing moons.
> Evasions and sighs grew more numerous,
> Tears and sweat flowed.
> With the passing moons the child grew up.

[GRUSHA *sits by a stream, dipping linen into the water. In the rear, a few* CHILDREN *are standing.*]

Grusha [*to* MICHAEL]. You can play with them, Michael, but don't let them boss you around just because you're the littlest. [MICHAEL *nods and joins the* CHILDREN. *They start playing.*]

The Biggest Boy. Today it's the Heads-Off Game. [*To a* FAT BOY] You're the Prince and you laugh. [*To* MICHAEL] You're the Governor. [*To a* GIRL] You're the Governor's wife and you cry when his head's cut off. And I do the cutting. [*He shows his wooden sword*] With this. First, they lead the Governor into the yard. The Prince walks in front. The Governor's wife comes last.

[*They form a procession. The* FAT BOY *is first and laughs. Then comes* MICHAEL, *then the* BIGGEST BOY, *and then the* GIRL, *who weeps.*]

Michael [*standing still*]. Me cut off head!
The Biggest Boy. That's my job. You're the littlest. The Governor's the easy part. All you do is kneel down and get your head cut off—simple.
Michael. Me want sword!
The Biggest Boy. It's mine! [*He gives him a kick.*]
The Girl [*shouting to* GRUSHA]. He won't play his part!
Grusha [*laughing*]. Even the little duck is a swimmer, they say.
The Biggest Boy. You can be the Prince if you can laugh. [MICHAEL *shakes his head.*]
The Fat Boy. I laugh best. Let him cut off the head just once. Then you do it, then me.

[*Reluctantly, the* BIGGEST BOY *hands* MICHAEL *the wooden sword and kneels down. The* FAT BOY *sits down, slaps his thigh, and laughs with all his might. The* GIRL *weeps loudly.* MICHAEL *swings the big sword and "cuts off" the head. In doing so, he topples over.*]

The Biggest Boy. Hey! I'll show you how to cut heads off!

[MICHAEL *runs away. The* CHILDREN *run after him.* GRUSHA *laughs, following them with her eyes. On looking back, she sees* SIMON SHASHAVA *standing on the opposite bank. He wears a shabby uniform.*]

Grusha. Simon!
Simon. Is that Grusha Vashnadze?
Grusha. Simon!
Simon [*formally*]. A good morning to the young lady. I hope she is well.
Grusha [*getting up gaily and bowing low*]. A good morning to the soldier. God be thanked he has returned in good health.
Simon. They found better fish, so they didn't eat me, said the haddock.
Grusha. Courage, said the kitchen boy. Good luck, said the hero.
Simon. How are things here? Was the winter bearable? The neighbor considerate?
Grusha. The winter was a trifle rough, the neighbor as usual, Simon.
Simon. May one ask if a certain person still dips her toes in the water when rinsing the linen?

Grusha.   The answer is no. Because of the eyes in the bushes.

Simon.   The young lady is speaking of soldiers. Here stands a paymaster.

Grusha.   A job worth twenty piasters?

Simon.   And lodgings.

Grusha [*with tears in her eyes*].   Behind the barracks under the date trees.

Simon.   Yes, there. A certain person has kept her eyes open.

Grusha.   She has, Simon.

Simon.   And has not forgotten? [GRUSHA *shakes her head.*] So the door is still on its hinges as they say? [GRUSHA *looks at him in silence and shakes her head again.*] What's this? Is anything not as it should be?

Grusha.   Simon Shashava, I can never return to Nuka. Something has happened.

Simon.   What can have happened?

Grusha.   For one thing, I knocked an Ironshirt down.

Simon.   Grusha Vashnadze must have had her reasons for that.

Grusha.   Simon Shashava, I am no longer called what I used to be called.

Simon [*after a pause*].   I do not understand.

Grusha.   When do women change their names, Simon? Let me explain. Nothing stands between us. Everything is just as it was. You must believe that.

Simon.   Nothing stands between us and yet there's something?

Grusha.   How can I explain it so fast and with the stream between us? Couldn't you cross the bridge there?

Simon.   Maybe it's no longer necessary.

Grusha.   It is very necessary. Come over on this side, Simon. Quick!

Simon.   Does the young lady wish to say someone has come too late?

[GRUSHA *looks up at him in despair, her face streaming with tears.* SIMON *stares before him. He picks up a piece of wood and starts cutting it.*]

The Singer.

> So many words are said, so many left unsaid.
> The soldier has come.
> Where he comes from, he does not say.
> Hear what he thought and did not say:
> "The battle began, gray at dawn, grew bloody at noon.
> The first man fell in front of me, the second behind me, the third at my side.
> I trod on the first, left the second behind, the third was run through by the captain.
> One of my brothers died by steel, the other by smoke.
> My neck caught fire, my hands froze in my gloves, my toes in my socks.
> I fed on aspen buds, I drank maple juice, I slept on stone, in water."

Simon.   I see a cap in the grass. Is there a little one already?

Grusha.   There is, Simon. There's no keeping *that* from you. But please don't worry, it is not mine.

Simon.   When the wind once starts to blow, they say, it blows through every cranny. The wife need say no more. [GRUSHA *looks into her lap and is silent.*]

The Singer.

> There was yearning but there was no waiting.
> The oath is broken. Neither could say why.

> Hear what she thought but did not say:
> "While you fought in the battle, soldier,
> The bloody battle, the bitter battle
> I found a helpless infant
> I had not the heart to destroy him
> I had to care for a creature that was lost
> I had to stoop for breadcrumbs on the floor
> I had to break myself for that which was not mine
> That which was other people's.
> Someone must help!
> For the little tree needs water
> The lamb loses its way when the shepherd is asleep
> And its cry is unheard!"

Simon.   Give me back the cross I gave you. Better still, throw it in the stream. [*He turns to go.*]

Grusha [*getting up*].   Simon Shashava, don't go away! He isn't mine! He isn't mine! [*She hears the* CHILDREN *calling.*] What's the matter, children?

Voices.   Soldiers! And they're taking Michael away!

[GRUSHA *stands aghast as* TWO IRONSHIRTS, *with* MICHAEL *between them, come toward her.*]

One of the Ironshirts.   Are you Grusha? [*She nods.*] Is this your child?

Grusha.   Yes. [SIMON *goes.*] Simon!

The Ironshirt.   We have orders, in the name of the law, to take this child, found in your custody, back to the city. It is suspected that the child is Michael Abashwili, son and heir of the late Governor Georgi Abashwili, and his wife, Natella Abashwili. Here is the document and the seal. [*They lead the* CHILD *away.*]

Grusha [*running after them, shouting*].   Leave him here. Please! He's mine!

The Singer.

> The Ironshirts took the child, the beloved child.
> The unhappy girl followed them to the city, the dreaded city.
> She who had borne him demanded the child.
> She who had raised him faced trial.
> Who will decide the case?
> To whom will the child be assigned?
> Who will the judge be? A good judge? A bad?
> The city was in flames.
> In the judge's seat sat Azdak.[1]

The Story of the Judge

The Singer.

> Hear the story of the judge
> How he turned judge, how he passed judgment, what kind of judge he was.
> On that Easter Sunday of the great revolt, when the Grand Duke was overthrown

---

[1]   The accent is on the second syllable.

And his Governor Abashwili, father of our child, lost his head
The Village Scrivener Azdak found a fugitive in the woods and hid him in his hut.

[AZDAK, *in rags and slightly drunk, is helping an* OLD BEGGAR *into his cottage.*]

Azdak.   Stop snorting, you're not a horse. And it won't do you any good with the police to run like a snotty nose in April. Stand still, I say. [*He catches the* OLD MAN, *who has marched into the cottage as if he'd like to go through the walls.*] Sit down. Feed. Here's a hunk of cheese. [*From under some rags, in a chest, he fishes out some cheese, and the* OLD MAN *greedily begins to eat.*] Haven't eaten in a long time, huh? [*The* OLD MAN *growls.*] Why were you running like that, asshole? The cop wouldn't even have seen you.
The Old Man.   Had to! Had to!
Azdak.   Blue funk? [*The* OLD MAN *stares, uncomprehending.*] Cold feet? Panic? Don't lick your chops like a Grand Duke. Or an old sow. I can't stand it. We have to accept respectable stinkers as God made them, but not you! I once heard of a senior judge who farted at a public dinner to show an independent spirit! Watching you eat like that gives me the most awful ideas. Why don't you say something? [*Sharply.*] Show me your hand. Can't you hear? [*The* OLD MAN *slowly puts out his hand.*] White! So you're not a beggar at all! A fraud, a walking swindle! And I'm hiding you from the cops like you were an honest man! Why were you running like that if you're a landowner? For that's what you are. Don't deny it! I see it in your guilty face! [*He gets up.*] Get out! [*The* OLD MAN *looks at him uncertainly.*] What are you waiting for, peasant-flogger?
The Old Man.   Pursued. Need undivided attention. Make proposition . . .
Azdak.   Make what? A proposition? Well, if that isn't the height of insolence. He's making me a proposition! The bitten man scratches his fingers bloody, and the leech that's biting him makes him a proposition! Get out, I tell you!
The Old Man.   Understand point of view! Persuasion! Pay hundred thousand piasters one night! Yes?
Azdak.   What, you think you can buy me? For a hundred thousand piasters? Let's say a hundred and fifty thousand. Where are they?
The Old Man.   Have not them here. Of course. Will be sent. Hope do not doubt.
Azdak.   Doubt very much. Get out!

[*The* OLD MAN *gets up, waddles to the door. A* VOICE *is heard off-stage.*]

A Voice.   Azdak!

[*The* OLD MAN *turns, waddles to the opposite corner, stands still.*]

Azdak [*calling out*].   I'm not in! [*He walks to door.*] So you're sniffing around here again, Shauwa?
Policeman Shauwa [*reproachfully*].   You caught another rabbit, Azdak. And you'd promised me it wouldn't happen again!
Azdak [*severely*].   Shauwa, don't talk about things you don't understand. The rabbit is a dangerous and destructive beast. It feeds on plants, especially on the species of plants known as weeds. It must therefore be exterminated.
Shauwa.   Azdak, don't be so hard on me. I'll lose my job if I don't arrest you. I know you have a good heart.

Azdak. I do not have a good heart! How often must I tell you I'm a man of intellect?

Shauwa [slyly]. I know, Azdak. You're a superior person. You say so yourself. I'm just a Christian and an ignoramus. So I ask you: When one of the Prince's rabbits is stolen, and I'm a policeman, what should I do with the offending party?

Azdak. Shauwa, Shauwa, shame on you. You stand and ask me a question, than which nothing could be more seductive. It's like you were a woman—let's say that bad girl Nunowna, and you showed me your thigh—Nunowna's thigh, that would be—and asked me: "What shall I do with my thigh, it itches?" Is she as innocent as she pretends? Of course not. I catch a rabbit, but you catch a man. Man is made in God's image. Not so a rabbit, you know that. I'm a rabbit-eater, but you're a man-eater, Shauwa. And God will pass judgment on you. Shauwa, go home and repent. No, stop, there's something . . . [*He looks at the* OLD MAN *who stands trembling in the corner.*] No, it's nothing. Go home and repent. [*He slams the door behind* SHAUWA.] Now you're surprised, huh? Surprised I didn't hand you over? I couldn't hand over a bedbug to that animal. It goes against the grain. Now don't tremble because of a cop! So old and still so scared? Finish your cheese, but eat it like a poor man, or else they'll still catch you. Must I even explain how a poor man behaves? [*He pushes him down, and then gives him back the cheese.*] That box is the table. Lay your elbows on the table. Now, encircle the cheese on the plate like it might be snatched from you at any moment—what right have you to be safe, huh?—now, hold your knife like an undersized sickle, and give your cheese a troubled look because, like all beautiful things, it's already fading away. [AZDAK *watches him.*] They're after you, which speaks in your favor, but how can we be sure they're not mistaken about you? In Tiflis one time they hanged a landowner, a Turk, who could prove he quartered his peasants instead of merely cutting them in half, as is the custom, and he squeezed twice the usual amount of taxes out of them, his zeal was above suspicion. And yet they hanged him like a common criminal—because he was a Turk—a thing he couldn't do much about. What injustice! He got onto the gallows by a sheer fluke. In short, I don't trust you.

The Singer.

> Thus Azdak gave the old beggar a bed,
> And learned that old beggar was the old butcher, the Grand Duke himself,
> And was ashamed.
> He denounced himself and ordered the policeman to take him to Nuka,
>   to court, to be judged.

[*In the court of justice* THREE IRONSHIRTS *sit drinking. From a beam hangs a man in judge's robes. Enter* AZDAK, *in chains, dragging* SHAUWA *behind him.*]

Azdak [shouting]. I've helped the Grand Duke, the Grand Thief, the Grand Butcher, to escape! In the name of justice I ask to be severely judged in public trial!

The First Ironshirt. Who's this queer bird?

Shauwa. That's our Village Scrivener, Azdak.

Azdak. I am contemptible! I am a traitor! A branded criminal! Tell them, flatfoot, how I insisted on being tied up and brought to the capital. Because I sheltered the Grand Duke, the Grand Swindler, by mistake. And how I found out afterwards. See the marked man denounce himself! Tell them how I forced you to walk half the night with me to clear the whole thing up.

Shauwa. And all by threats. That wasn't nice of you, Azdak.

Azdak. Shut your mouth, Shauwa. You don't understand. A new age is upon us! It'll go thundering over you. You're finished. The police will be wiped out— poof! Everything will be gone into, everything will be brought into the open. The guilty will give themselves up. Why? They couldn't escape the people in any case. [*To* SHAUWA] Tell them how I shouted all along Shoemaker Street [*with big gestures, looking at the* IRONSHIRTS]: "In my ignorance I let the Grand Swindler escape! So tear me to pieces, brothers!" I wanted to get it in first.

The First Ironshirt. And what did your brothers answer?

Shauwa. They comforted him in Butcher Street, and they laughed themselves sick in Shoemaker Street. That's all.

Azdak. But with you it's different. I can see you're men of iron. Brothers, where's the judge? I must be tried.

The First Ironshirt [*pointing at the hanged man*]. There's the judge. And please stop "brothering" us. It's rather a sore spot this evening.

Azdak. "There's the judge." An answer never heard in Grusinia before. Towns-man, where's His Excellency the Governor? [*Pointing to the ground*] There's His Excellency, stranger. Where's the Chief Tax Collector? Where's the official Recruiting Officer? The Patriarch? The Chief of Police? There, there, there—all there. Brother, I expected no less of you.

The Second Ironshirt. What? *What* was it you expected, funny man?

Azdak. What happened in Persia, brother, what happened in Persia?

The Second Ironshirt. What did happen in Persia?

Azdak. Everybody was hanged. Viziers, tax collectors. Everybody. Forty years ago now. My grandfather, a remarkable man by the way, saw it all. For three whole days. Everywhere.

The Second Ironshirt. And who ruled when the Vizier was hanged?

Azdak. A peasant ruled when the Vizier was hanged.

The Second Ironshirt. And who commanded the army?

Azdak. A soldier, a soldier.

The Second Ironshirt. And who paid the wages?

Azdak. A dyer. A dyer paid the wages.

The Second Ironshirt. Wasn't it a weaver, maybe?

The First Ironshirt. And why did all this happen, Persian?

Azdak. Why did all this happen? Must there be a special reason? Why do you scratch yourself, brother? War! Too long a war! And no justice! My grandfather brought back a song that tells how it was. I will sing it for you. With my friend the policeman. [*To* SHAUWA] And hold the rope tight. It's very suitable. [*He sings, with* SHAUWA *holding the rope tight around him.*]

The Song of Injustice in Persia

Why don't our sons bleed any more? Why don't our daughters weep?
Why do only the slaughterhouse cattle have blood in their veins?
Why do only the willows shed tears on Lake Urmi?

The king must have a new province, the peasant must give up his savings.
That the roof of the world might be conquered, the roof of the cottage is torn down.
Our men are carried to the ends of the earth, so that great ones can eat at home.
The soldiers kill each other, the marshals salute each other.
They bite the widow's tax money to see if it's good, their swords break.
The battle was lost, the helmets were paid for.
Refrain: Is it so? Is it so?
Shauwa [*refrain*].   Yes, yes, yes, yes, yes it's so.
Azdak.   Want to hear the rest of it? [*The* FIRST IRONSHIRT *nods.*]
The Second Ironshirt [*to* SHAUWA].   Did he teach you that song?
Shauwa.   Yes, only my voice isn't very good.
The Second Ironshirt.   No. [*To* AZDAK] Go on singing.
Azdak.   The second verse is about the peace. [*He sings.*]

> The offices are packed, the streets overflow with officials.
> The rivers jump their banks and ravage the fields.
> Those who cannot let down their own trousers rule countries.
> They can't count up to four, but they devour eight courses.
> The corn farmers, looking round for buyers, see only the starving.
> The weavers go home from their looms in rags.
> *Refrain:* Is it so? Is it so?

Shauwa [*refrain*].   Yes, yes, yes, yes, yes it's so.
Azdak.

> That's why our sons don't bleed any more, that's why our daughters don't weep
> That's why only the slaughterhouse cattle have blood in their veins,
> And only the willows shed tears by Lake Urmi toward morning

The First Ironshirt.   Are you going to sing that song here in town?
Azdak.   Sure. What's wrong with it?
The First Ironshirt.   Have you noticed that the sky's getting red? [*Turning round,* AZDAK *sees the sky red with fire.*] It's the people's quarters on the outskirts of town. The carpet weavers have caught the "Persian Sickness," too. And they've been asking if Prince Kazbeki isn't eating too many courses. This morning they strung up the city judge. As for us we beat them to pulp. We were paid one hundred piasters per man, you understand?
Azdak [*after a pause*].   I understand. [*He glances shyly round and, creeping away, sits down in a corner, his head in his hands.*]
The Ironshirts [*to each other*].   If there ever was a troublemaker it's him.
—He must've come to the capital to fish in the troubled waters.
Shauwa.   Oh, I don't think he's a really bad character, gentlemen. Steals a few chickens here and there. And maybe a rabbit.
The Second Ironshirt [*approaching* AZDAK].   Came to fish in the troubled waters, huh?
Azdak [*looking up*].   I don't know why I came.
The Second Ironshirt.   Are you in with the carpet weavers maybe? [AZDAK *shakes his head.*] How about that song?
Azdak.   From my grandfather. A silly and ignorant man.
The Second Ironshirt.   Right. And how about the dyer who paid the wages?
Azdak [*muttering*].   That was in Persia.

The First Ironshirt. And this denouncing of yourself? Because you didn't hang the Grand Duke with your own hands?
Azdak. Didn't I tell you I let him run? [*He creeps farther away and sits on the floor.*]
Shauwa. I can swear to that: he let him run.

[*The* IRONSHIRTS *burst out laughing and slap* SHAUWA *on the back.* AZDAK *laughs loudest. They slap* AZDAK *too, and unchain him. They all start drinking as the* FAT PRINCE *enters with a* YOUNG MAN.]

The First Ironshirt [*to* AZDAK, *pointing at the* FAT PRINCE]. There's your "new age" for you! [*More laughter.*]
The Fat Prince. Well, my friends, what is there to laugh about? Permit me a serious word. Yesterday morning the Princes of Grusinia overthrew the war-mongering government of the Grand Duke and did away with his Governors. Unfortunately the Grand Duke himself escaped. In this fateful hour our carpet weavers, those eternal troublemakers, had the effrontery to stir up a rebellion and hang the universally loved city judge, our dear Illo Orbeliani. Ts— ts— ts. My friends, we need peace, peace, peace in Grusinia! And justice! So I've brought along my dear nephew Bizergan Kazbeki. He'll be the new judge, hm? A very gifted fellow. What do you say? I want your opinion. Let the people decide!
The Second Ironshirt. Does this mean *we* elect the judge?
The Fat Prince. Precisely. Let the people propose some very gifted fellow! Confer among yourselves, my friends. [*The* IRONSHIRTS *confer.*] Don't worry, my little fox. The job's yours. And when we catch the Grand Duke we won't have to kiss this rabble's ass any longer.
The Ironshirts [*among themselves*]. Very funny: they're wetting their pants because they haven't caught the Grand Duke.
—When the outlook isn't so bright, they say: "My friends!" and "Let the people decide!"
—Now he even wants justice for Grusinia! But fun is fun as long as it lasts! (*Pointing at* AZDAK.] He knows all about justice. Hey, rascal, would you like this nephew fellow to be the judge?
Azdak. Are you asking me? You're not asking *me?!*
The First Ironshirt. Why not? Anything for a laugh!
Azdak. You'd like to test him to the marrow, correct? Have you a criminal on hand? An experienced one? So the candidate can show what he knows?
The Second Ironshirt. Let's see. We do have a couple of doctors downstairs. Let's use them.
Azdak. Oh, no, that's no good, we can't take real criminals till we're sure the judge will be appointed. He may be dumb, but he must be appointed, or the law is violated. And the law is a sensitive organ. It's like the spleen, you mustn't hit it—that would be fatal. Of course you can hang those two without violating the law, because there was no judge in the vicinity. But judgment, whe pronounced, must be pronounced with absolute gravity—it's all such nonsense. Suppose, for instance, a judge jails a woman—let's say she's stolen a corn cake to feed her child—and this judge isn't wearing his robes—or maybe he's scratch-

ing himself while passing sentence and half his body is uncovered—a man's thigh *will* itch once in a while—the sentence this judge passes is a disgrace and the law is violated. In short it would be easier for a judge's robe and a judge's hat to pass judgment than for a man with no robe and no hat. If you don't treat it with respect, the law just disappears on you. Now you don't try out a bottle of wine by offering it to a dog; you'd only lose your wine.

The First Ironshirt. Then what do you suggest, hairsplitter?

Azdak. I'll be the defendant.

The First Ironshirt. You? [*He bursts out laughing.*]

The Fat Prince. What have you decided?

The First Ironshirt. We've decided to stage a rehearsal. Our friend here will be the defendant. Let the candidate be the judge and sit there.

The Fat Prince. It isn't customary, but why not? [*To the* NEPHEW.] A mere formality, my little fox. What have I taught you? Who got there first—the slow runner or the fast?

The Nephew. The silent runner, Uncle Arsen.

[*The* NEPHEW *takes the chair. The* IRONSHIRTS *and the* FAT PRINCE *sit on the steps, Enter* AZDAK, *mimicking the gait of the Grand Duke.*]

Azdak [*in the Grand Duke's accent*]. Is any here knows me? Am Grand Duke.

The Ironshirts. What is he?

—The Grand Duke. He knows him, too.

—Fine. So get on with the trial.

Azdak. Listen! Am accused instigating war? Ridiculous! Am saying ridiculous! That enough? If not, have brought lawyers. Believe five hundred. [*He points behind him, pretending to be surrounded by lawyers.*] Requisition all available seats for lawyers! [*The* IRONSHIRTS *laugh; the* FAT PRINCE *joins in.*]

The Nephew [*to the* IRONSHIRTS]. You really wish me to try this case? I find it rather unusual. From the taste angle, I mean.

The First Ironshirt. Let's go!

The Fat Prince [*smiling*]. Let him have it, my little fox!

The Nephew. All right. People of Grusinia versus Grand Duke. Defendant, what have you got to say for yourself?

Azdak. Plenty. Naturally, have read war lost. Only started on the advice of patriots. Like Uncle Arsen Kazbeki. Call Uncle Arsen as witness.

The Fat Prince [*to the* IRONSHIRTS, *delightedly*]. What a screwball!

The Nephew. Motion rejected. One cannot be arraigned for declaring a war, which every ruler has to do once in a while, but only for running a war badly.

Azdak. Rubbish! Did not run it at all! Had it run! Had it run by Princes! Naturally, they messed it up.

The Nephew. Do you by any chance deny having been commander-in-chief?

Azdak. Not at all! Always *was* commander-in-chief. At birth shouted at wet nurse. Was trained drop turds in toilet, grew accustomed to command. Always commanded officials rob my cash box. Officers flog soldiers only on command. Landowners sleep with peasants' wives only on strictest command. Uncle Arsen here grew his belly at *my* command!

The Ironshirts [*clapping*]. He's good! Long live the Grand Duke!

The Fat Prince. Answer him, my little fox. I'm with you.

The Nephew. I shall answer him according to the dignity of the law. Defendant, preserve the dignity of the law!

Azdak. Agreed. Command you proceed with trial!

The Nephew. It is not your place to command me. You claim that the Princes forced you to declare war. How can you claim then, that they—er—"messed it up"?

Azdak. Did not send enough people. Embezzled funds. Sent sick horses. During attack, drinking in whorehouse. Call Uncle Arsen as witness.

The Nephew. Are you making the outrageous suggestion that the Princes of this country did not fight?

Azdak. No. Princes fought. Fought for war contracts.

The Fat Prince [*jumping up*]. That's too much! This man talks like a . carpet weaver!

Azdak. Really? Told nothing but truth.

The Fat Prince. Hang him! Hang him!

The First Ironshirt [*pulling the* PRINCE *down*]. Keep quiet! Go on, Excellency!

The Nephew. Quiet! I now render a verdict: You must be hanged! By the neck! Having lost war!

Azdak. Young man, seriously advise not fall publicly into jerky clipped speech. Cannot be watchdog if howl like wolf. Got it? If people realize Princes speak same language as Grand Duke, may hang Grand Duke *and Princes,* huh? By the way, must overrule verdict. Reason? War lost, but not for Princes. Princes won their war. Got 3,863,000 piasters for horses not delivered, 8,240,000 piasters for food supplies not produced. Are therefore victors. War lost only for Grusinia, which is not present in this court.

The Fat Prince. I think that will do, my friends. [*To* AZDAK] You can withdraw, funny man. [*To the* IRONSHIRTS] You may now ratify the new judge's appointment, my friends.

The First Ironshirt. Yes, we can. Take down the judge's gown. [ONE IRONSHIRT *climbs on the back of the* OTHER, *pulls the gown off the hanged man.*] [*To the* NEPHEW] Now you run away so the right ass can get on the right chair. [*To* AZDAK.] Step forward! Go to the judge's seat! Now sit in it! [AZDAK *steps up, bows, and sits down.*] The judge was always a rascal! Now the rascal shall be a judge! [*The judge's gown is placed round his shoulders, the hat on his head.*] And what a judge!

The Singer.

> And there was civil war in the land.
> The mighty were not safe.
> And Azdak was made a judge by the Ironshirts.
> And Azdak remained a judge for two years.

The Singer and Chorus.

> When the towns were set afire
> And rivers of blood rose higher and higher,
> Cockroaches crawled out of every crack.
> And the court was full of schemers
> And the church of foul blasphemers.

> In the judge's cassock sat Azdak.

[AZDAK *sits in the judge's chair, peeling an apple.* SHAUWA *is sweeping out the hall. On one side an* INVALID *in a wheelchair. Opposite, a* YOUNG MAN *accused of blackmail. An* IRONSHIRT *stands guard, holding the Ironshirts banner.*]

Azdak.   In consideration of the large number of cases, the Court today will hear two cases at a time. Before I open the proceedings, a short announcement—I accept. [*He stretches out his hand. The* BLACKMAILER *is the only one to produce any money. He hands it to* AZDAK.] I reserve the right to punish one of the parties for contempt of court. [*He glances at the* INVALID.] You [*to the* DOCTOR] are a doctor, and you [*to the* INVALID] are bringing a complaint against him. Is the doctor responsible for your condition?

The Invalid.   Yes. I had a stroke on his account.

Azdak.   That would be professional negligence.

The Invalid.   Worse than negligence. I gave this man money for his studies. So far, he hasn't paid me back a cent. It was when I heard he was treating a patient free that I had my stroke.

Azdak.   Rightly. [*To a* LIMPING MAN.] And what are *you* doing here?

The Limping Man.   I'm the patient, Your Honor.

Azdak.   He treated your leg for nothing?

The Limping Man.   The wrong leg! My rheumatism was in the left leg, he operated on the right. That's why I limp.

Azdak.   And you were treated free?

The Invalid.   A five-hundred-piaster operation free! For nothing! For a God-bless-you! And I paid for this man's studies! [*To the* DOCTOR.] Did they teach you to operate free?

The Doctor.   Your Honor, it is the custom to demand the fee before the operation, as the patient is more willing to pay before an operation than after. Which is only human. In the case in question I was convinced, when I started the operation, that my servant had already received the fee. In this I was mistaken.

The Invalid.   He was mistaken! A good doctor doesn't make mistakes! He examines before he operates!

Azdak.   That's right. [*To* SHAUWA.] Public Prosecutor, what's the other case about?

Shauwa [*busily sweeping*].   Blackmail.

The Blackmailer.   High Court of Justice, I'm innocent. I only wanted to find out from the landowner concerned if he really *had* raped his niece. He informed me very politely that this was not the case, and gave me the money only so I could pay for my uncle's studies.

Azdak.   Hm. [*To the* DOCTOR.] You, on the other hand, can cite no extenuating circumstances for your offense, huh?

The Doctor.   Except that to err is human.

Azdak.   And you are aware that in money matters a good doctor is a highly responsible person? I once heard of a doctor who got a thousand piasters for a sprained finger by remarking that sprains have something to do with blood circulation, which after all a less good doctor might have overlooked, and who on another occasion made a real gold mine out of a somewhat disordered gallbladder, he treated it with such loving care. You have no excuse, Doctor. The corn merchant Uxu had his son study medicine to get some knowledge of trade, our medical schools are so good. [*To the* BLACKMAILER.] What's the landowner's name?

Shauwa. He doesn't want it mentioned.

Azdak. In that case I will pass judgment. The Court considers the blackmail proved. And you [*to the* INVALID] are sentenced to a fine of one thousand piasters. If you have a second stroke, the doctor will have to treat you free. Even if he has to amputate. [*To the* LIMPING MAN.] As compensation, you will receive a bottle of rubbing alcohol. [*To the* BLACKMAILER.] You are sentenced to hand over half the proceeds of your deal to the Public Prosecutor to keep the landowner's name secret. You are advised, moreover, to study medicine—you seem well suited to that calling. [*To the* DOCTOR.] You have perpetrated an unpardonable error in the practice of your profession: you are acquitted. Next cases!

The Singer and Chorus.

> Men won't do much for a shilling.
> For a pound they may be willing.
> For twenty pounds the verdict's in the sack.
> As for the many, all too many,
> Those who've only got a penny—
> They've one single, sole recourse: Azdak.

[*Enter* AZDAK *from the caravansary on the highroad, followed by an old bearded* INNKEEPER. *The judge's chair is carried by a* STABLEMAN *and* SHAUWA. *An* IRONSHIRT, *with a banner, takes up his position.*]

Azdak. Put me down. Then we'll get some air, maybe even a good stiff breeze from the lemon grove there. It does justice good to be done in the open: the wind blows her skirts up and you can see what she's got. Shauwa, we've been eating too much. These official journeys are exhausting. [*To the* INNKEEPER.] It's a question of your daughter-in-law?

The Innkeeper. Your Worship, it's a question of the family honor. I wish to bring an action on behalf of my son, who's away on business on the other side of the mountain. This is the offending stableman, and here's my daughter-in-law.

[*Enter the* DAUGHTER-IN-LAW, *a voluptuous wench. She is veiled.*]

Azdak [*sitting down*]. I accept. [*Sighing, the* INNKEEPER *hands him some money.*] Good. Now the formalities are disposed of. This is a case of rape?

The Innkeeper. Your Honor, I caught the fellow in the act. Ludovica was in the straw on the stable floor.

Azdak. Quite right, the stable. Lovely horses! I specially liked the little roan.

The Innkeeper. The first thing I did, of course, was to question Ludovica. On my son's behalf.

Azdak [*seriously*]. I said I specially liked the little roan.

The Innkeeper [*coldly*]. Really? Ludovica confessed the stableman took her against her will.

Azdak. Take your veil off, Ludovica. [*She does so.*] Ludovica, you please the Court. Tell us how it happened.

Ludovica [*well schooled*]. When I entered the stable to see the new foal the stableman said to me on his own accord: "It's hot today!" and laid his hand on my left breast. I said to him: "Don't do that!" But he continued to handle me indecently, which provoked my anger. Before I realized his sinful intentions, he got much closer. It was all over when my father-in-law entered and accidentally trod on me.

The Innkeeper [*explaining*].   On my son's behalf.

Azdak [*to the* STABLEMAN].   You admit you started it?

The Stableman.   Yes.

Azdak.   Ludovica, you like to eat sweet things?

Ludovica.   Yes, sunflower seeds!

Azdak.   You like to lie a long time in the bathtub?

Ludovica.   Half an hour or so.

Azdak.   Public Prosecutor, drop your knife—there—on the ground. [SHAUWA *does so.*] Ludovica, pick up that knife. [LUDOVICA, *swaying her hips, does so.*] See that? [*He points at her.*] The way it moves? The rape is now proven. By eating too much—sweet things, especially—by lying too long in warm water, by laziness and too soft a skin, you have raped that unfortunate man. Think you can run around with a behind like that and get away with it in court? This is a case of intentional assault with a dangerous weapon! You are sentenced to hand over to the Court the little roan which your father liked to ride "on his son's behalf." And now, come with me to the stables, so the Court can inspect the scene of the crime, Ludovica.

The Singer and Chorus.

> When the sharks the sharks devour
> Little fishes have their hour.
> For a while the load is off their back.
> On Grusinia's highways faring
> Fixed-up scales of justice bearing
> Strode the poor man's magistrate: Azdak.
> And he gave to the forsaken
> All that from the rich he'd taken.
> And a bodyguard of roughnecks was Azdak's.
> And our good and evil man, he
> Smiled upon Grusinia's Granny.
> His emblem was a tear in sealing wax.
> All mankind should love each other
> But when visiting your brother
> Take an ax along and hold it fast.
> Not in theory but in practice
> Miracles are wrought with axes
> And the age of miracles is not past.

[AZDAK's *judge's chair is in a tavern.* THREE RICH FARMERS *stand before* AZDAK. SHAUWA *brings him wine. In a corner stands an* OLD PEASANT WOMAN. *In the open doorway, and outside, stand* VILLAGERS *looking on. An* IRONSHIRT *stands guard with a banner.*]

Azdak.   The Public Prosecutor has the floor.

Shauwa.   It concerns a cow. For five weeks the defendant has had a cow in her stable, the property of the farmer Suru. She was also found to be in possession of a stolen ham, and a number of cows belonging to Shutoff were killed after he asked the defendant to pay the rent on a piece of land.

The Farmers.   It's a matter of my ham, Your Honor.

—It's a matter of my cow, Your Honor.

—It's a matter of my land, Your Honor.

Azdak.   Well, Granny, what have *you* got to say to all this?

The Old Woman.   Your Honor, one night toward morning, five weeks ago, there was a knock at my door, and outside stood a bearded man with a cow. "My dear woman," he said, "I am the miracle-working Saint Banditus and because your son has been killed in the war, I bring you this cow as a souvenir. Take good care of it."

The Farmers.   The robber, Irakli, Your Honor!

—Her brother-in-law, Your Honor!

—The cow-thief!

—The incendiary!

—He must be beheaded!

[*Outside, a woman screams. The* CROWD *grows restless, retreats.*]

[*Enter the* BANDIT *Irakli with a huge ax.*]

The Bandit.   A very good evening, dear friends! A glass of vodka!

The Farmers [*crossing themselves*].   Irakli!

Azdak.   Public Prosecutor, a glass of vodka for our guest. And who are you?

The Bandit.   I'm a wandering hermit, Your Honor. Thanks for the gracious gift. [*He empties the glass which* SHAUWA *has brought.*] Another!

Azdak.   I am Azdak. [*He gets up and bows. The* BANDIT *also bows.*] The Court welcomes the foreign hermit. Go on with your story, Granny.

The Old Woman.   Your Honor, that first night I didn't yet know Saint Banditus could work miracles, it was only the cow. But one night, a few days later, the farmer's servants came to take the cow away again. Then they turned round in front of my door and went off without the cow. And bumps as big as a fist sprouted on their heads. So I knew that Saint Banditus had changed their hearts and turned them into friendly people.

[*The* BANDIT *roars with laughter.*]

The First Farmer.   I know what changed them.

Azdak.   That's fine. You can tell us later. Continue.

The Old Woman.   Your Honor, the next one to become a good man was the farmer Shutoff—a devil, as everyone knows. But Saint Banditus arranged it so he let me off the rent on the little piece of land.

The Second Farmer.   Because my cows were killed in the field.

[*The* BANDIT *laughs.*]

The Old Woman [*answering* AZDAK's *sign to continue*].   Then one morning the ham came flying in at my window. It hit me in the small of the back. I'm still lame, Your Honor, look. [*She limps a few steps. The* BANDIT *laughs.*] Your Honor, was there ever a time when a poor old woman could get a ham *without* a miracle?

[*The* BANDIT *starts sobbing.*]

Azdak [*rising from his chair*].   Granny, that's a question that strikes straight at the Court's heart. Be so kind as to sit here. [*The* OLD WOMAN, *hesitating, sits in the judge's chair.*]
Azdak [*sits on the floor, glass in hand, reciting*].

> Granny
> We could almost call you Granny Grusinia
> The Woebegone
> The Bereaved Mother
> Whose sons have gone to war
> Receiving the present of a cow
> She bursts out crying.
> When she is beaten
> She remains hopeful.
> When she's not beaten
> She's surprised.
> On us
> Who are already damned
> May you render a merciful verdict
> Granny Grusinia!

[*Bellowing at the* FARMERS] Admit you don't believe in miracles, you atheists! Each of you is sentenced to pay five hundred piasters! For godlessness! Get out! [*The* FARMERS *slink out.*] And you Granny, and you [*to the* BANDIT] pious man, empty a pitcher of wine with the Public Prosecutor and Azdak!

The Singer and Chorus.

> And he broke the rules to save them.
> Broken law like bread he gave them,
> Brought them to shore upon his crooked back.
> At long last the poor and lowly
> Had someone who was not too holy
> To be bribed by empty hands: Azdak.
> For two years it was his pleasure
> To give the beasts of prey short measure:
> He became a wolf to fight the pack.
> From All Hallows to All Hallows
> On his chair beside the gallows
> Dispensing justice in his fashion sat Azdak.

The Singer.

> But the era of disorder came to an end.
> The Grand Duke returned.
> The Governor's wife returned.
> A trial was held.
> Many died.

The people's quarters burned anew.
And fear seized Azdak.

[AZDAK'S *judge's chair stands again in the court of justice.* AZDAK *sits on the floor, shaving and talking to* SHAUWA. *Noises outside. In the rear the* FAT PRINCE'S *head is carried by on a lance.*]

Azdak. Shauwa, the days of your slavery are numbered, maybe even the minutes. For a long time now I have held you in the iron curb of reason, and it has torn your mouth till it bleeds. I have lashed you with reasonable arguments, I have manhandled you with logic. You are by nature a weak man, and if one slyly throws an argument in your path, you *have* to snap it up, you can't resist. It is your nature to lick the hand of some superior being. But superior beings can be of very different kinds. And now, with your liberation, you will soon be able to follow your natural inclinations, which are low. You will be able to follow your infallible instinct, which teaches you to plant your fat heel on the faces of men. Gone is the era of confusion and disorder, which I find described in the Song of Chaos. Let us now sing that song together in memory of those terrible days. Sit down and don't do violence to the music. Don't be afraid. It sounds all right. And it has a fine refrain. [*He sings.*]

The Song of Chaos

Sister, hide your face! Brother, take your knife!
The times are out of joint!
Big men are full of complaint
And small men full of joy.
The city says:
"Let us drive the strong ones from our midst!"
Offices are raided. Lists of serfs are destroyed.
They have set Master's nose to the grindstone.
They who lived in the dark have seen the light.
The ebony poor box is broken.
Sesnem wood is sawed up for beds.
Who had no bread have barns full.
Who begged for alms of corn now mete it out.

Shauwa [*refrain*].   Oh, oh, oh, oh.
Azdak [*refrain*].

Where are you, General, where are you?
Please, please, please, restore order!

The nobleman's son can no longer be recognzied;
The lady's child becomes the son of her slave.
The councilors meet in a shed.
Once, this man was barely allowed to sleep on the wall;
Now, he stretches his limbs in a bed.
Once, this man rowed a boat, now, he owns ships.
Their owner looks for them, but they're his no longer.

Five men are sent on a journey by their master.
"Go yourself," they say, "we have arrived."

Shauwa [*refrain*].   Oh, oh, oh, oh.
Azdak [*refrain*].

Where are you, General, where are you?
Please, please, please, restore order!

Yes, so it might have been, had order been neglected much longer. But now the Grand Duke has returned to the capital, and the Persians have lent him an army to restore order with. The suburbs are already aflame. Go and get me the big book I always sit on. [SHAUWA *brings the big book from the judge's chair.* AZDAK *opens it.*] This is the Statute Book and I've always used it, as you can testify. Now I'd better look in this book and see what they can do to me. I've let the down-and-outs get away with murder, and I'll have to pay for it. I helped poverty onto its skinny legs, so they'll hang me for drunkenness. I peeped into the rich man's pocket, which is bad taste. And I can't hide anywhere—everybody knows me because I've helped everybody.
Shauwa.   Someone's coming!
Azdak [*in panic, he walks trembling to the chair*].   It's the end. And now they'd enjoy seeing what a Great Man I am. I'll deprive them of that pleasure. I'll beg on my knees for mercy. Spittle will slobber down my chin. The fear of death is in me.

[*Enter Natella Abashwili, the* GOVERNOR'S WIFE, *followed by the* ADJUTANT *and an* IRONSHIRT.]

The Governor's Wife.   What sort of a creature is that, Shalva?
Azdak.   A willing one, Your Highness, a man ready to oblige.
The Adjutant.   Natella Abashwili, wife of the late Governor, has just returned. She is looking for her two-year-old son, Michael. She has been informed that the child was carried off to the mountains by a former servant.
Azdak.   The child will be brought back, Your Highness, at your service.
The Adjutant.   They say that the person in question is passing it off as her own.
Azdak.   She will be beheaded, Your Highness, at your service.
The Adjutant.   That is all.
The Governor's Wife [*leaving*].   I don't like that man.
Azdak [*following her to door, bowing*].   At your service, Your Highness, it will all be arranged.

The Chalk Circle

The Singer.

Hear now the story of the trial
Concerning Governor Abashwili's child
And the establishing of the true mother
By the famous test of the Chalk Circle.

[*Law court in Nuka.* IRONSHIRTS *lead* MICHAEL *across stage and out at the back.* IRONSHIRTS *hold* GRUSHA *back with their lances under the gateway until the child has been led through. Then she is admitted. She is accompanied by the former Governor's* COOK. *Distant noises and a fire-red sky.*]

Grusha [*trying to hide*].   He's brave, he can wash himself now.

The Cook.   You're lucky. It's not a real judge. It's Azdak, a drunk who doesn't know what he's doing. The biggest thieves have got by through him. Because he gets everything mixed up and the rich never offer him big enough bribes, the likes of us sometimes do pretty well.

Grusha.   I *need* luck right now.

The Cook.   Touch wood. [*She crosses herself.*] I'd better offer up another prayer that the judge may be drunk. [*She prays with motionless lips, while* GRUSHA *looks around, in vain, for the child.*] Why must you hold on to it at any price if it isn't yours? In days like these?

Grusha.   He's mine. I brought him up.

The Cook.   Have you never thought what'd happen when she came back?

Grusha.   At first I thought I'd give him to her. Then I thought she wouldn't come back.

The Cook.   And even a borrowed coat keeps a man warm, hm? [GRUSHA *nods.*] I'll swear to anything for you. You're a decent girl. [*She sees the soldier* SIMON SHASHAVA *approaching.*] You've done wrong by Simon, though. I've been talking with him. He just can't understand.

Grusha [*unaware of* SIMON'S *presence*].   Right now I can't be bothered whether he understands or not!

The Cook.   He knows the child isn't yours, but you—married and not free "till death you do part"—he can't understand *that*.

[GRUSHA *sees* SIMON *and greets him.*]

Simon [*gloomily*].   I wish the lady to know I will swear I am the father of the child.

Grusha [*low*].   Thank you, Simon.

Simon.   At the same time I wish the lady to know my hands are not tied—nor are hers.

The Cook.   You needn't have said that. You know she's married.

Simon.   And it needs no rubbing in.

[*Enter an* IRONSHIRT.]

The Ironshirt.   Where's the judge? Has anyone seen the judge?

Another Ironshirt [*stepping forward*].   The judge isn't here yet. Nothing but a bed and a pitcher in the whole house!

[*Exeunt* IRONSHIRTS.]

The Cook.   I hope nothing has happened to him. With any other judge you'd have as much chance as a chicken has teeth.

Grusha [*who has turned away and covered her face*].   Stand in front of me. I shouldn't have come to Nuka. If I run into the Ironshirt, the one I hit over the head . . .

[*She screams. An* IRONSHIRT *had stopped and, turning his back, had been listening to her. He now wheels around. It is the* CORPORAL, *and he has a huge scar across his face.*]

The Ironshirt [*in the gateway*].   What's the matter, Shotta? Do you know her?
The Corporal [*after staring for some time*].   No.
The Ironshirt.   She's the one who stole the Abashwili child, or so they say. If you know anything about it you can make some money, Shotta.

[*Exit the* CORPORAL, *cursing.*]

The Cook.   Was it him? [GRUSHA *nods.*] I think he'll keep his mouth shut, or he'd be admitting he was after the child.
Grusha.   I'd almost forgotten him.

[*Enter the* GOVERNOR'S WIFE, *followed by the* ADJUTANT *and* TWO LAWYERS.]

The Governor's Wife.   At least there are no common people here, thank God. I can't stand their smell. It always give me migraine.
The First Lawyer.   Madam, I must ask you to be careful what you say until we have another judge.
The Governor's Wife.   But I didn't say anything, Illo Shuboladze. I love the people with their simple straightforward minds. It's only that their smell brings on my migraine.
The Second Lawyer.   There won't be many spectators. The whole population is sitting at home behind locked doors because of the riots on the outskirts of town.
The Governor's Wife [*looking at* GRUSHA].   Is that the creature?
The First Lawyer.   Please, most gracious Natella Abashwili, abstain from invective until it is certain the Grand Duke has appointed a new judge and we're rid of the present one, who's about the lowest fellow ever seen in a judge's gown. Things are all set to move, you see.

[*Enter* IRONSHIRTS *from the courtyard.*]

The Cook.   Her Grace would pull your hair out on the spot if she didn't know Azdak is for the poor. He goes by the face.

[IRONSHIRTS *begin fastening a rope to a beam.* AZDAK, *in chains, is led in, followed by* SHAUWA, *also in chains. The* THREE FARMERS *bring up the rear.*]

An Ironshirt.   Trying to run away, were you? [*He strikes* AZDAK.]
One Farmer.   Off with his judge's gown before we string him up!

[IRONSHIRTS *and* FARMERS *tear off* AZDAK'S *gown. His torn underwear is visible. Then someone kicks him.*]

An Ironshirt [*pushing him into someone else*].   Want a load of justice? Here it is!

[*Accompanied by shouts of "You take it!" and "Let me have him, Brother!" they throw* AZDAK *back and forth until he collapses. Then he is lifted up and dragged under the noose.*]

The Governor's Wife [*who, during this "ballgame," has clapped her hands hysterically*]. I disliked that man from the moment I first saw him.

Azdak [*covered with blood, panting*]. I can't see. Give me a rag.

An Ironshirt. What is it you want to see?

Azdak. You, you dogs! [*He wipes the blood out of his eyes with his shirt.*] Good morning, dogs! How goes it, dogs! How's the dog world? Does it smell good? Got another boot for me to lick? Are you back at each other's throats, dogs?

[*Accompanied by a* CORPORAL, *a dust-covered* RIDER *enters. He takes some documents from a leather case, looks at them, then interrupts.*]

The Rider. Stop! I bring a dispatch from the Grand Duke, containing the latest appointments.

The Corporal [*bellowing*]. Atten—shun!

The Rider. Of the new judge it says: "We appoint a man whom we have to thank for saving a life indispensable to the country's welfare—a certain Azdak of Nuka." Which is he?

Shauwa [*pointing*]. That's him, Your Excellency.

The Corporal [*bellowing*]. What's going on here?

An Ironshirt. I beg to report that His Honor Azdak was already His Honor Azdak, but on these farmers' denunciation was pronounced the Grand Duke's enemy.

The Corporal [*pointing at the* FARMERS]. March them off! [*They are marched off. They bow all the time.*] See to it that His Honor Azdak is exposed to no more violence.

[*Exeunt* RIDER *and* CORPORAL.]

The Cook [*to* SHAUWA]. She clapped her hands! I hope he saw it!

The First Lawyer. It's a catastrophe.

[AZDAK *has fainted. Coming to, he is dressed again in judge's robes. He walks, swaying, toward the* IRONSHIRTS.]

An Ironshirt. What does Your Honor desire?

Azdak. Nothing, fellow dogs, or just an occasional boot to lick. [*To* SHAUWA.] I pardon you. [*He is unchained.*] Get me some red wine, the sweet kind. [SHAUWA *stumbles off.*] Get out of here, I've got to judge a case. [*Exeunt* IRONSHIRTS. SHAUWA *returns with a pitcher of wine.* AZDAK *gulps it down.*] Something for my backside. [SHAUWA *brings the Statute Book, puts it on the judge's chair.* AZDAK *sits on it.*] I accept.

[*The* PROSECUTORS, *among whom a worried council has been held, smile with relief. They whisper.*]

The Cook. Oh dear!

Simon. A well can't be filled with dew, they say.

The Lawyers [*approaching* AZDAK, *who stands up, expectantly*]. A quite ridiculous case, Your Honor. The accused has abducted a child and refuses to hand it over.

Azdak [*stretching out his hand, glancing at* GRUSHA]. A most attractive person. [*He fingers the money, then sits down, satisfied.*] I declare the proceeds open and demand the whole truth. [*To* GRUSHA] Especially from you.

The First Lawyer. High Court of Justice! Blood, as the popular saying goes, is thicker than water. This old adage . . .

Azdak [*interrupting*]. The Court wants to know the lawyers' fee.

The First Lawyer [*surprised*]. I beg your pardon? [AZDAK, *smiling, rubs his thumb and index finger.*] Oh, I see. Five hundred piasters, Your Honor, to answer the Court's somewhat unusual question.

Azdak. Did you hear? The question is unusual. I ask it because I listen in quite a different way when I know you're good.

The First Lawyer [*bowing*]. Thank you, Your Honor. High Court of Justice, of all ties the ties of blood are strongest. Mother and child—is there a more intimate relationship? Can one tear a child from its mother? High Court of Justice, she has conceived it in the holy ecstasies of love. She has carried it in her womb. She has fed it with her blood. She has borne it with pain. High Court of Justice, it has been observed that even the wild tigress, robbed of her young, roams restless through the mountains, shrunk to a shadow. Nature herself . . .

Azdak [*interrupting, to* GRUSHA]. What's your answer to all this and anything else that lawyer might have to say?

Grusha. He's mine.

Azdak. Is that all? I hope you can prove it. Why should I assign the child to you in any case?

Grusha. I brought him up like the priest says "according to my best knowledge and conscience." I always found him something to eat. Most of the time he had a roof over his head. And I went to such trouble for him. I had expenses too. I didn't look out for my own comfort. I brought the child up to be friendly with everyone, and from the beginning taught him to work. As well as he could, that is. He's still very little.

The First Lawyer. Your Honor, it is significant that the girl herself doesn't claim any tie of blood between her and the child.

Azdak. The Court takes note of that.

The First Lawyer. Thank you, Your Honor. And now permit a woman bowed in sorrow—who has already lost her husband and now has also to fear the loss of her child—to address a few words to you. The gracious Natella Abashwili is . . .

The Governor's Wife [*quietly*]. A most cruel fate, sir, forces me to describe to you the tortures of a bereaved mother's soul, the anxiety, the sleepless nights, the . . .

The Second Lawyer [*bursting out*]. It's outrageous the way this woman is being treated! Her husband's palace is closed to her! The revenue of her estates is blocked, and she is cold-bloodedly told that it's tied to the heir. She can't do a thing without that child. She can't even pay her lawyers!! [*To the* FIRST LAWYER, *who, desperate about this outburst, makes frantic gestures to keep him from speaking*] Dear Illo Shuboladze, surely it can be divulged now that the Abashwili estates are at stake?

The First Lawyer. Please, Honored Sandro Oboladze! We agreed . . . [*To* AZDAK] Of course it is correct that the trial will also decide if our noble client can dispose of the Abashwili estates, which are rather extensive. I say "also" advisedly, for in the foreground stands the human tragedy of a mother, as Natella Abashwili very properly explained in the first words of her moving statement. Even if Michael Abashwili were not heir to the estates, he would still be the dearly beloved child of my client.

Azdak. Stop! The Court is touched by the mention of estates. It's a proof of human feeling.

The Second Lawyer. Thanks, Your Honor. Dear Illo Shuboladze, we can prove in any case that the woman who took the child is not the child's mother. Permit me to lay before the Court the bare facts. High Court of Justice, by an unfortunate chain of circumstances, Michael Abashwili was left behind on that Easter Sunday while his mother was making her escape. Grusha, a palace kitchen maid, was seen with the baby . . .

The Cook. All her mistress was thinking of was what dresses she'd take along!

The Second Lawyer [*unmoved*]. Nearly a year later Grusha turned up in a mountain village with a baby and there entered into the state of matrimony with . . .

Azdak. How'd you get to that mountain village?

Grusha. On foot, Your Honor. And he was mine.

Simon. I'm the father, Your Honor.

The Cook. I used to look after it for them, Your Honor. For five piasters.

The Second Lawyer. This man is engaged to Grusha, High Court of Justice: his testimony is suspect.

Azdak. Are you the man she married in the mountain village?

Simon. No, Your Honor, She married a peasant.

Azdak [*to* GRUSHA]. Why? [*Pointing at* SIMON] Is he no good in bed? Tell the truth.

Grusha. We didn't get that far. I married because of the baby. So he'd have a roof over his head. [*Pointing at* SIMON] He was in the war, Your Honor.

Azdak. And now he wants you back again, huh?

Simon. I wish to state in evidence . . .

Grusha [*angrily*]. I am no longer free, Your Honor.

Azdak. And the child, you claim, comes from whoring? [GRUSHA *doesn't answer.*] I'm going to ask you a question: What kind of child is he? A ragged little bastard? Or from a good family?

Grusha [*angrily*]. He's an ordinary child.

Azdak. I mean—did he have refined features from the beginning?

Grusha. He had a nose on his face.

Azdak. A very significant comment! It has been said of me that I went out one time and sniffed at a rosebush before rendering a verdict—tricks like that are needed nowadays. Well, I'll make it short, and not listen to any more lies. [*To* GRUSHA] Especially not yours. [*To all the accused*] I can imagine what you've cooked up to cheat me! I know you people. You're swindlers.

Grusha [*suddenly*]. I can understand your wanting to cut it short, now I've seen what you accepted!

Azdak. Shut up! Did I accept anything from you?

Grusha [*while the* COOK *tries to restrain her*]. I haven't got anything.

Azdak. True. Quite true. From starvelings, I never get a thing. I might just as well starve, myself. You want justice, but do you want to pay for it, hm? When you go to a butcher you know you have to pay, but you people go to a judge as if you were off to a funeral supper.

Simon [*loudly*].   When the horse was shod, the horsefly held out its leg, as the saying is.

Azdak [*eagerly accepting the challenge*].   Better a treasure in manure than a stone in a mountain stream.

Simon.   A fine day. Let's go fishing, said the angler to the worm.

Azdak.   I'm my own master, said the servant, and cut off his foot.

Simon.   I love you as a father, said the Czar to the peasants, and had the Czarevitch's head chopped off.

Azdak.   A fool's worst enemy is himself.

Simon.   However, a fart has no nose.

Azdak.   Fined ten piasters for indecent language in court! That'll teach you what justice is.

Grusha [*furiously*].   A fine kind of justice! You play fast and loose with us because we don't talk as refined as that crowd with their lawyers!

Azdak.   That's true. You people are too dumb. It's only right you should get it in the neck.

Grusha.   You want to hand the child over to her, and she wouldn't even know how to keep it dry, she's so "refined"! You know about as much about justice as I do!

Azdak.   There's something in that. I'm an ignorant man. Haven't even a decent pair of pants on under this gown. Look! With me, everything goes for food and drink—I was educated in a convent. Incidentally, I'll fine you ten piasters for contempt of court. And you're a very silly girl, to turn me against you, instead of making eyes at me and wiggling your backside a little to keep me in a good temper. Twenty piasters!

Grusha.   Even if it was thirty, I'd tell you what I think of your justice, you drunken onion! [*Incoherently*] How dare you talk to me like the cracked Isaiah on the church window? As if you were somebody? For you weren't born to this. You weren't born to rap your own mother on the knuckles if she swipes a little bowl of salt someplace. Aren't you ashamed of yourself when you see how I tremble before you? You've made yourself their servant so no one will take their houses from them—houses they had stolen! Since when have houses belonged to the bedbugs? But you're on the watch, or they couldn't drag our men into their wars! You bribetaker! [AZDAK *half gets up, starts beaming. With his little hammer he halfheartedly knocks on the table as if to get silence. As* GRUSHA'S *scolding continues, he only beats time with his hammer.*] I've no respect for you. No more than for a thief or a bandit with a knife! You can do what you want. You can take the child away from me, a hundred against one, but I tell you one thing: only extortioners should be chosen for a profession like yours, and men who rape children! As punishment! Yes, let *them* sit in judgment on their fellow creatures. It is worse than to hang from the gallows.

Azdak [*sitting down*].   Now it'll be thirty! And I won't go on squabbling with you—we're not in a tavern. What'd happen to my dignity as a judge? Anyway, I've lost interest in your case. Where's the couple who wanted a divorce? [*To* SHAUWA] Bring 'em in. This case is adjourned for fifteen minutes.

The First Lawyer [*to the* GOVERNOR'S WIFE]. Even without using the rest of the evidence, Madam, we have the verdict in the bag.

The Cook [*to* GRUSHA]. You've gone and spoiled your chances with him. You won't get the child now.

The Governor's Wife. Shalva, my smelling salts!

[*Enter a* VERY OLD COUPLE.]

Azdak. I accept. [*The* OLD COUPLE *don't understand.*] I hear you want to be divorced. How long have you been together?

The Old Man. Forty years, Your Honor.

Azdak. And why do you want a divorce?

The Old Man. We don't like each other, Your Honor.

Azdak. Since when?

The Old Woman. Oh, from the very beginning, Your Honor.

Azdak. I'll think about your request and render my verdict when I'm through with the other case. [SHAUWA *leads them back.*] I need the child. [*He beckons* GRUSHA *to him and bends not unkindly toward her.*] I've noticed you have a soft spot for justice. I don't believe he's your child, but if he *were* yours, woman, wouldn't you want him to be rich? You'd only have to say he wasn't yours, and he'd have a palace and many horses in his stable and many beggars on his doorstep and many soldiers in his service and many petitioners in his courtyard, wouldn't he? What do you say—don't you want him to be rich? [GRUSHA *is silent.*]

The Singer.

> Hear now what the angry girl thought but did not say:
> Had he golden shoes to wear
> He'd be cruel as a bear.
> Evil would his life disgrace.
> He'd laugh in my face.
> Carrying a heart of flint
> Is too troublesome a stint.
> Being powerful and bad
> Is hard on a lad.
> Then let hunger be his foe!
> Hungry men and women, no.
> Let him fear the darksome night
> But not daylight!

Azdak. I think I understand you, woman.

Grusha [*suddenly and loudly*]. I won't give him up. I've raised him, and he knows me.

[*Enter* SHAUWA *with the* CHILD.]

The Governor's Wife. He's in rags!

Grusha. That's not true. But I wasn't given time to put his good shirt on.

The Governor's Wife. He must have been in a pigsty.

Grusha [*furiously*]. I'm not a pig, but there are some who are! Where did you leave your baby?

The Governor's Wife. I'll show you, you vulgar creature! [*She is about to throw herself on* GRUSHA, *but is restrained by her* LAWYERS.] She's a criminal, she must be whipped. Immediately!

The Second Lawyer [*holding his hand over her mouth*]. Natella Abashwili, you promised . . . Your Honor, the plaintiff's nerves . . .

Azdak. Plaintiff and defendant! The Court has listened to your case, and has come to no decision as to who the real mother is; therefore, I, the judge, am obliged to *choose* a mother for the child. I'll make a test. Shauwa, get a piece of chalk and draw a circle on the floor. [SHAUWA *does so.*] Now place the child in the center. [SHAUWA *puts* MICHAEL, *who smiles at* GRUSHA, *in the center of the circle.*] Stand near the circle, both of you. [*The* GOVERNOR'S WIFE *and* GRUSHA *step up to the circle.*] Now each of you take the child by one hand. [*They do so.*] The true mother is she who can pull the child out of the circle.

The Second Lawyer [*quickly*]. High Court of Justice, I object! The fate of the great Abashwili estates, which are tied to the child, as the heir, should not be made dependent on such a doubtful duel. In addition, my client does not command the strength of this person, who is accustomed to physical work.

Azdak. She looks pretty well fed to me. Pull! [*The* GOVERNOR'S WIFE *pulls the* CHILD *out of the circle on her side;* GRUSHA *has let go and stands aghast.*] What's the matter with you? You didn't pull!

Grusha. I didn't hold on to him.

The First Lawyer [*congratulating the* GOVERNOR'S WIFE]. What did I say! The ties of blood!

Grusha [*running to* AZDAK]. Your Honor, I take back everything I said against you. I ask your forgiveness. But could I keep him till he can speak all the words? He knows a few.

Azdak. Don't influence the Court. I bet you only know about twenty words yourself. All right, I'll make the test once more, just to be certain. [*The* TWO WOMEN *take up their positions again.*] Pull! [*Again* GRUSHA *lets go of the* CHILD.]

Grusha [*in despair*]. I brought him up! Shall I also tear him to bits? I can't!

Azdak [*rising*]. And in this manner the Court has established the true mother. [*To* GRUSHA] Take your child and be off. I advise you not to stay in the city with him. [*To the* GOVERNOR'S WIFE] And you disappear before I fine you for fraud. Your estates fall to the city. They'll be converted into a playground for the children. They need one, and I've decided it'll be called after me: Azdak's Garden. [*The* GOVERNOR'S WIFE *has fainted and is carried out by the* LAWYERS *and the* ADJUTANT. GRUSHA *stands motionless.* SHAUWA *leads the* CHILD *toward her.*] Now I'll take off this judge's gown—it's got too hot for me. I'm not cut out for a hero. In token of farewell I invite you all to a little dance in the meadow outside. Oh, I'd almost forgotten something in my excitement . . . to sign the divorce decree. [*Using the judge's chair as a table, he writes something on a piece of paper, and prepares to leave. Dance music has started.*]

Shauwa [*having read what is on the paper*]. But that's not right. You've not divorced the old people. You've divorced Grusha!

Azdak. Divorced the wrong couple? What a pity! And I never retract! If I did, how could we keep order in the land? [*To the* OLD COUPLE] I'll invite you to my party instead. You don't mind dancing with each other, do you? [*To* GRUSHA *and* SIMON] I've got forty piasters coming from you.

Simon [*pulling out his purse*]. Cheap at the price, Your Honor. And many
thanks.

Azdak [*pocketing the cash*]. I'll be needing this.

Grusha [to MICHAEL]. So we'd better leave the city tonight, Michael? [*To*
SIMON] You like him?

Simon. With my respects, I like him.

Grusha. Now I can tell you: I took him because on that Easter Sunday I got
engaged to you. So he's a child of love. Michael, let's dance.

[*She dances with* MICHAEL, SIMON *dances with the* COOK, *the* OLD COUPLE *with
each other.* AZDAK *stands lost in thought. The dancers soon hide him from view.
Occasionally he is seen, but less and less as* MORE COUPLES *join the dance.*]

The Singer.

> And after that evening Azdak vanished and was never seen again.
> The people of Grusinia did not forget him but long remembered
> The period of his judging as a brief golden age,
> Almost an age of justice.

[*All the couples dance off.* AZDAK *has disappeared.*]

> But you, you who have listened to the Story of the Chalk Circle,
> Take note what men of old concluded:
> That what there is shall go to those who are good for it,
> Children to the motherly, that they prosper,
> Carts to good drivers, that they be driven well,
> The valley to the waterers, that it yield fruit.

Miller: THE CRUCIBLE

No problem in the modern drama has elicited as much learned and pedantic disputation as has the question of whether or not tragedy is still possible, given the ethical, social, aesthetic, political, theological, and psychological standards of the twentieth century. Whether or not we believe in its possibility, one thing is clear: if the notion of tragedy is still a meaningful view of life rather than a historical curiosity or a classroom exercise divorced from real human conduct, we must realize that modern drama has broken the strictures imposed in ages past on both the form of tragedy and the nature of its heroes. When viewing modern attempts at creating the tragic mode, we should remember that it was always the plays that came first; then the rules. The fifth century B.C. Athenian had to respond to Sophocles without benefit of Aristotle. The rules described what men had observed in plays that evoked the tragic response. The labels of dramatic criticism are useful, but it is imperative to realize that the terminology of that criticism provides us with only a language for discussion; it can never be an end unto itself.

There are plays that, though they may not conform to the rigid rules, ask the questions that have intrigued dramatists since the days of Periclean Athens: How much does a man mold his own destiny? Are there any stable values by which he may measure his conduct? Do his moral choices have any meaning? The old fate and gods may be gone, but not so man's quest for the dignity of his name and his defiance of a world out of joint. The questions of tragedy have always been those that the courageous must ask and only the presumptuous answer. A man may not, after all, be the complete victim of the universe, but only a fool will subscribe to a naive reading of the idea of individual will. The closing sentiment of Henley's "Invictus"—"I am the master of my fate;/ I am the captain of my soul" —is a bizarre joke to the modern sensibility.

It is an axiom of the tragic spirit in drama that man is tied to a limited world because of his mortality, and that both his glory and his obligatory defeat result from his dignified desire and effort to transcend that mortality. He must try to do more than other men could do under the same circumstances, and he must court catastrophe rather than abrogate his personal sense of dignity, responsibility, or identity. Tragedy tests the norms of a world whose norms are desperately in need of testing, even if it means that the tester must hazard his own destruction. However, the tragic hero's vision goes beyond mortality; mere physical defeat does not destroy him. He makes us reaffirm our belief not in the limitations of human flesh but in the capabilities of the human spirit. If, as some practical men maintain, politics is the art of the possible, tragedy must surely be the art of the admirably and tantalizingly impossible. We experience the tragic evocation in a play in which we see the waste of a man who has dared to expand the realm of the possible, and who has redefined our concept of human potential by setting our sights a little higher. Such a man has learned to risk commitment where to be uncommitted is the safe way. If that man retains his integrity and discovers his identity, that is his victory in a world where lesser men would call it defeat. We, the audience to his passion, will weep at his fall while we marvel at his stature.

Arthur Miller, more than any other contemporary dramatist, has given serious consideration to the concept of tragedy in modern life. His major plays are all attempts to make tragedy meaningful in the twentieth century—not an age of kings or blank verse, but an age that asks its own important questions.

The Crucible was first performed in January, 1953, in New York. At that time, it suffered from a weak production and from guilt by association with the latter-day witchhunts of Senator Joseph McCarthy. That the play was, in part, a comment on those distressing activities of hysteria and malice is assuredly a fact and a cogent piece of its frame of reference. Today, however, The Crucible can be seen in its entire moral, philosophical, and artistic perspective. It has lost none of its intensity, but it has grown in stature.

THE CRUCIBLE

The Characters

Reverend Parris
Betty Parris
Tituba
Abigail Williams
Susanna Walcott
Mrs. Ann Putnam
Thomas Putnam
Mercy Lewis
Mary Warren
John Proctor
Rebecca Nurse
Giles Corey
Reverend John Hale
Elizabeth Proctor
Francis Nurse
Ezekiel Cheever
Marshal Herrick
Judge Hathorne
Deputy Governor Danforth
Sarah Good
Hopkins

A Note on the Historical Accuracy of This Play

This play is not history in the sense in which the word is used by the academic historian. Dramatic purposes have sometimes required many characters to be fused into one; the number of girls involved in the "crying-out" has been reduced; Abigail's age has been raised; while there were several judges of almost equal authority, I have symbolized them all in Hathorne and Danforth. However, I believe that the reader will discover here the essential nature of one of the strangest and most awful chapters in human history. The fate of each character is exactly that of his historical model, and there is no one in the drama who did not play a similar—and in some cases exactly the same—role in history.

As for the characters of the persons, little is known about most of them excepting what may be surmised from a few letters, the trial record, certain broadsides written at the time, and references to their conduct in sources of varying reliability. They may therefore be taken as creations of my own, drawn to the best of my ability in conformity with their known behavior, except as indicated in the commentary I have written for this text.

Act I

(An Overture)

A small upper bedroom in the home of Reverend Samuel Parris, Salem, Massachusetts, in the spring of the year 1692.

[There is a narrow window at the left. Through its leaded panes the morning sunlight streams. A candle still burns near the bed, which is at the right. A chest, a chair, and a small table are the other furnishings. At the back a door opens on the landing of the stairway to the ground floor. The room gives off an air of clean spareness. The roof rafters are exposed, and the wood colors are raw and unmellowed.]

[As the curtain rises, REVEREND PARRIS is discovered kneeling beside the bed, evidently in prayer. His daughter, BETTY PARRIS, aged ten, is lying on the bed, inert.]

At the time of these events Parris was in his middle forties. In history he cut a villainous path, and there is very little good to be said for him. He believed he was being persecuted wherever he went, despite his best efforts to win people and God to his side. In meeting, he felt insulted if someone rose to shut the door without first asking his permission. He was a widower with no interest in children, or talent with them. He regarded them as young adults, and until this strange crisis he, like the rest of Salem, never conceived that the children were anything but thankful for being permitted to walk straight, eyes slightly lowered, arms at the sides, and mouths shut until bidden to speak.

His house stood in the "town"—but we today would hardly call it a village. The meeting house was nearby, and from this point outward—toward the bay or inland—there were a few small-windowed, dark houses snuggling against the raw Massachusetts winter. Salem had been established hardly forty years before. To the European world the whole province was a barbaric frontier inhabited by a sect of fanatics who, nevertheless, were shipping out products of slowly increasing quantity and value.

No one can really know what their lives were like. They had no novelists—and would not have permitted anyone to read a novel if one were handy. Their creed forbade anything resembling a theater or "vain enjoyment." They did not celebrate Christmas, and a holiday from work meant only that they must concentrate even more upon prayer.

Which is not to say that nothing broke into this strict and somber way of life. When a new farmhouse was built, friends assembled to "raise the roof," and there would be special foods cooked and probably some potent cider passed around. There was a good supply of ne'er-do-wells in Salem, who dallied at the shovelboard in Bridget Bishop's tavern. Probably more than the creed, hard work kept the morals of the place from spoiling, for the people were forced to fight the land like heroes for every grain of corn, and no man had very much time for fooling around.

That there were some jokers, however, is indicated by the practice of appointing a two-man patrol whose duty was to "walk forth in the time of God's worship to take notice of such as either lye about the meeting house, without attending to the word and ordinances, or that lye at home or in the fields without giving good account thereof, and to take the names of such persons, and to present them to the magistrates, whereby they may be accordingly proceeded against." This predilection for minding other people's business was time-honored among the people of Salem, and it undoubtedly created many of the suspicions which were to feed the coming madness. It was also, in my opinion, one of the things that a John Proctor would rebel against, for the time of the armed camp had almost passed, and since the country was reasonably—although not wholly—safe, the old disciplines were beginning to rankle. But, as in all such matters, the issue was not clearcut, for danger was still a possibility, and in unity still lay the best promise of safety.

The edge of the wilderness was close by. The American continent stretched endlessly west, and it was full of mystery for them. It stood, dark and threatening, over their shoulders night and day, for out of it Indian tribes marauded from time to time, and Reverend Parris had parishioners who had lost relatives to these heathen.

The parochial snobbery of these people was partly responsible for their failure to convert the Indians. Probably they also preferred to take land from heathens rather than from fellow Christians. At any rate, very few Indians were converted, and the Salem folk believed that the virgin forest was the Devil's last preserve, his home base and the citadel of his final stand. To the best of their knowledge the American forest was the last place on earth that was not paying homage to God.

For these reasons, among others, they carried about an air of innate resistance, even of persecution. Their fathers had, of course, been persecuted in England. So now they and their church found it necessary to deny any other sect its freedom, lest their New Jerusalem be defiled and corrupted by wrong ways and deceitful ideas.

They believed, in short, that they held in their steady hands the candle that would light the world. We have inherited this belief, and it has helped and hurt us. It helped them with the discipline it gave them. They were a dedicated folk, by and large, and they had to be to survive the life they had chosen or been born into in this country.

The proof of their belief's value to them may be taken from the opposite character of the first Jamestown settlement, farther south, in Virginia. The Englishmen who landed there were motivated mainly by a hunt for profit. They had thought to pick off the wealth of the new country and then return rich to England. They were a band of individualists, and a much more ingratiating group than the Massachusetts men. But Virginia destroyed them. Massachusetts tried to kill off the Puritans, but they combined; they set up a communal society which, in the beginning, was little more than an armed camp with an autocratic and very devoted leadership. It was, however, an autocracy by consent, for they were united from top to bottom by a commonly held ideology whose perpetuation was the reason and justification for all their sufferings. So their self-denial, their purposefulness, their suspicion of all vain pursuits, their hard-handed justice, were altogether perfect instruments for the conquest of this space so antagonistic to man.

But the people of Salem in 1692 were not quite the dedicated folk that arrived on the *Mayflower*. A vast differentiation had taken place, and in their own time a revolution had unseated the royal government and substituted a junta which was at this moment in power. The times, to their eyes, must have been out of joint, and to the common folk must have seemed as insoluble and complicated as do ours today. It is not hard to see how easily many could have been led to believe that the time of confusion had been brought upon them by deep and darkling forces. No hint of such speculation appears on the court record, but social disorder in any age breeds such mystical suspicions, and when, as in Salem, wonders are brought forth from below the social surface, it is too much to expect people to hold back very long from laying on the victims with all the force of their frustrations.

The Salem tragedy, which is about to begin in these pages, developed from a paradox. It is a paradox in whose grip we still live, and there is no prospect yet that we will discover its resolution. Simply, it was this: for good purposes, even high purposes, the people of Salem developed a theocracy, a combine of state and religious power whose function was to keep the community together, and to prevent any kind of disunity that might open it to destruction by material or ideological enemies. It was forged for a necessary purpose and accomplished that purpose. But all organization is and must be grounded on the idea of exclusion and prohibition, just as two objects cannot occupy the same space. Evidently the time came in New England when the repressions of order were heavier than seemed warranted by the dangers against which the order was organized. The witch-hunt was a perverse manifestation of the panic which set in among all classes when the balance began to turn toward greater individual freedom.

When one rises above the individual villainy displayed, one can only pity them all, just as we shall be pitied someday. It is still impossible for man to organize his social life without repressions, and the balance has yet to be struck between order and freedom.

The witch-hunt was not, however, a mere repression. It was also, and as importantly, a long overdue opportunity for everyone so inclined to express publicly his guilt and sins, under the cover of accusations against the victims. It suddenly became possible—and patriotic and holy—for a man to say that Martha Corey had come into his bedroom at night, and that, while his wife was sleeping at his side, Martha laid herself down on his chest and "nearly suffocated him." Of course it was her spirit only, but his satisfaction at confessing himself was no lighter than if it had been Martha herself. One could not ordinarily speak such things in public.

Long-held hatreds of neighbors could now be openly expressed, and vengeance taken, despite the Bible's charitable injunctions. Land-lust which had been expressed before by constant bickering over boundaries and deeds, could now be elevated to the arena of morality; one could cry witch against one's neighbor and feel perfectly justified in the bargain. Old scores could be settled on a plane of heavenly combat between Lucifer and the Lord; suspicions and the envy of the miserable toward the happy could and did burst out in the general revenge.

[REVEREND PARRIS *is praying now, and, though we cannot hear his words, a sense of his confusion hangs about him. He mumbles, then seems about to*

weep; then he weeps, then prays again; but his daughter does not stir on the
bed.]

[*The door opens, and his Negro slave enters.* TITUBA *is in her forties.* PARRIS
*brought her with him from Barbados, where he spent some years as a merchant
before entering the ministry. She enters as one does who can no longer bear to
be barred from the sight of her beloved, but she is also very frightened because
her slave sense has warned her that, as always, trouble in this house eventually
lands on her back.*]

Tituba [*already taking a step backward*].   My Betty be hearty soon?
Parris.   Out of here!
Tituba [*backing to the door*].   My Betty not goin' die . . .
Parris [*scrambling to his feet in a fury*].   Out of my sight! [*She is gone.*] Out of
my— [*He is overcome with sobs. He clamps his teeth against them and closes
the door and leans against it, exhausted.*] Oh, my God! God help me! [*Quaking with fear, mumbling to himself through his sobs, he goes to the bed and
gently takes* BETTY's *hand.*] Betty. Child. Dear child. Will you wake, will you
open up your eyes! Betty, little one . . .

[*He is bending to kneel again when his niece,* ABIGAIL WILLIAMS, *seventeen,
enters—a strikingly beautiful girl, an orphan, with an endless capacity for
dissembling. Now she is all worry and apprehension and propriety.*]

Abigail.   Uncle? [*He looks to her.*] Susanna Walcott's here from Doctor Griggs.
Parris.   Oh? Let her come, let her come.
Abigail [*leaning out the door to call to* SUSANNA, *who is down the hall a few steps*].
Come in, Susanna.

[SUSANNA WALCOTT, *a little younger than* ABIGAIL, *a nervous, hurried girl,
enters.*]

Parris [*eagerly*].   What does the doctor say, child?
Susanna [*craning around* PARRIS *to get a look at* BETTY].   He bid me come and
tell you, reverend sir, that he cannot discover no medicine for it in his books.
Parris.   Then he must search on.
Susanna.   Aye, sir, he have been searchin' his books since he left you, sir. But he
bid me tell you, that you might look to unnatural things for the cause of it.
Parris [*his eyes going wide*].   No—no. There be no unnatural cause here. Tell
him I have sent for Reverend Hale of Beverly, and Mr. Hale will surely confirm
that. Let him look to medicine and put out all thought of unnatural causes here.
There be none.
Susanna.   Aye, sir. He bid me tell you. [*She turns to go.*]
Abigail.   Speak nothin' of it in the village, Susanna.
Parris.   Go directly home and speak nothing of unnatural causes.
Susanna.   Aye, sir. I pray for her. [*She goes out.*]
Abigail.   Uncle, the rumor of witchcraft is all about; I think you'd best go down
and deny it yourself. The parlor's packed with people, sir. I'll sit with her.
Parris [*pressed, turns on her*].   And what shall I say to them? That my daughter
and my niece I discovered dancing like heathen in the forest?

Abigail. Uncle, we did dance; let you tell them I confessed it—and I'll be whipped if I must be. But they're speakin' of witchcraft. Betty's not witched.

Parris. Abigail, I cannot go before the congregation when I know you have not opened with me. What did you do with her in the forest?

Abigail. We did dance, uncle, and when you leaped out of the bush so suddenly, Betty was frightened and then she fainted. And there's the whole of it.

Parris. Child. Sit you down.

Abigail [*quavering, as she sits*]. I would never hurt Betty. I love her dearly.

Parris. Now look you, child, your punishment will come in its time. But if you trafficked with spirits in the forest I must know it now, for surely my enemies will, and they will ruin me with it.

Abigail. But we never conjured spirits.

Parris. Then why can she not move herself since midnight? This child is desperate! [ABIGAIL *lowers her eyes.*] It must come out—my enemies will bring it out. Let me know what you done there. Abigail, do you understand that I have many enemies?

Abigail. I have heard of it, uncle.

Parris. There is a faction that is sworn to drive me from my pulpit. Do you understand that?

Abigail. I think so, sir.

Parris. Now then, in the midst of such disruption, my own household is discovered to be the very center of some obscene practice. Abominations are done in the forest—

Abigail. It were sport, uncle!

Parris [*pointing at* BETTY]. You call this sport? [*She lowers her eyes. He pleads.*] Abigail, if you know something that may help the doctor, for God's sake tell it to me. [*She is silent.*] I saw Tituba waving her arms over the fire when I came on you. Why was she doing that? And I heard a screeching and gibberish coming from her mouth. She were swaying like a dumb beast over that fire!

Abigail. She always sings her Barbados songs, and we dance.

Parris. I cannot blink what I saw, Abigail, for my enemies will not blink it. I saw a dress lying on the grass.

Abigail [*innocently*]. A dress?

Parris [*it is very hard to say*]. Aye, a dress. And I thought I saw—someone naked running through the trees!

Abigail [*in terror*]. No one was naked! You mistake yourself, uncle!

Parris [*with anger*]. I saw it! [*He moves from her. Then, resolved.*] Now tell me true, Abigail. And I pray you feel the weight of truth upon you, for now my ministry's at stake, my ministry and perhaps your cousin's life. Whatever abomination you have done, give me all of it now, for I dare not be taken unaware when I go before them down there.

Abigail. There is nothin' more. I swear it, uncle.

Parris [*studies her, then nods, half convinced*]. Abigail, I have fought here three long years to bend these stiff-necked people to me, and now, just now when some good respect is rising for me in the parish, you compromise my very character. I have given you a home, child, I have put clothes upon your back—now give me upright answer. Your name in the town—it is entirely white, is it not?

Abigail [*with an edge of resentment*]. Why, I am sure it is, sir. There be no blush about my name.

Parris [*to the point*]. Abigail, is there any other cause than you have told me, for your being discharged from Goody Proctor's service? I have heard it said, and I tell you as I heard it, that she comes so rarely to the church this year for she will not sit so close to something soiled. What signified that remark?

Abigail. She hates me, uncle, she must, for I would not be her slave. It's a bitter woman, a lying, cold, sniveling woman, and I will not work for such a woman!

Parris. She may be. And yet it has troubled me that you are now seven month out of their house, and in all this time no other family has ever called for your service.

Abigail. They want slaves, not such as I. Let them send to Barbados for that. I will not black my face for any of them! [*With ill-concealed resentment at him.*] Do you begrudge my bed, uncle?

Parris. No—no.

Abigail [*in a temper*]. My name is good in the village! I will not have it said my name is soiled! Goody Proctor is a gossiping liar!

[*Enter* MRS. ANN PUTNAM. *She is a twisted soul of forty-five, a death-ridden woman, haunted by dreams.*]

Parris [*as soon as the door begins to open*]. No—no, I cannot have anyone. [*He sees her, and a certain deference springs into him, although his worry remains.*] Why, Goody Putnam, come in.

Mrs. Putnam [*full of breath, shiny-eyed*]. It is a marvel. It is surely a stroke of hell upon you.

Parris. No, Goody Putnam, it is—

Mrs. Putnam [*glancing at* BETTY]. How high did she fly, how high?

Parris. No, no, she never flew—

Mrs. Putnam [*very pleased with it*]. Why, it's sure she did. Mr. Collins saw her goin' over Ingersoll's barn, and come down light as bird, he says!

Parris. Now, look you, Goody Putnam, she never— [*Enter* THOMAS PUTNAM, *a well-to-do, hard-handed landowner, near fifty.*] Oh, good morning, Mr. Putnam.

Putnam. It is a providence the thing is out now! It is a providence. [*He goes directly to the bed.*]

Parris. What's out, sir, what's—?

[MRS. PUTNAM *goes to the bed.*]

Putnam [*looking down at* BETTY]. Why, *her* eyes is closed! Look you, Ann.

Mrs. Putnam. Why, that's strange. [*To* PARRIS.] Ours is open.

Parris [*shocked*]. Your Ruth is sick?

Mrs. Putnam [*with vicious certainty*]. I'd not call it sick; the Devil's touch is heavier than sick. It's death, y'know, it's death drivin' into them, forked and hoofed.

Parris. Oh, pray not! Why, how does Ruth ail?

Mrs. Putnam. She ails as she must—she never waked this morning, but her eyes open and she walks, and hears naught, sees naught, and cannot eat. Her soul is taken, surely.

[PARRIS *is struck.*]

Putnam [*as though for further details*].   They say you've sent for Reverend Hale of Beverly?

Parris [*with dwindling conviction now*].   A precaution only. He has much experience in all demonic arts, and I—

Mrs. Putnam.   He has indeed; and found a witch in Beverly last year, and let you remember that.

Parris.   Now, Goody Ann, they only thought that were a witch, and I am certain there be no element of witchcraft here.

Putnam.   No witchcraft! Now look you, Mr. Parris—

Parris.   Thomas, Thomas, I pray you, leap not to witchcraft. I know that you— you least of all, Thomas, would ever wish so disastrous a charge laid upon me. We cannot leap to witchcraft. They will howl me out of Salem for such corruption in my house.

A word about Thomas Putnam. He was a man with many grievances, at least one of which appears justified. Some time before, his wife's brother-in-law, James Bayley, had been turned down as minister at Salem. Bayley had all the qualifications, and a two-thirds vote into the bargain, but a faction stopped his acceptance, for reasons that are not clear.

Thomas Putnam was the eldest son of the richest man in the village. He had fought the Indians at Narragansett, and was deeply interested in parish affairs. He undoubtedly felt it poor payment that the village should so blatantly disregard his candidate for one of its more important offices, especially since he regarded himself as the intellectual superior of most of the people around him.

His vindictive nature was demonstrated long before the witchcraft began. Another former Salem minister, George Burroughs, had had to borrow money to pay for his wife's funeral, and, since the parish was remiss in his salary, he was soon bankrupt. Thomas and his brother John had Burroughs jailed for debts the man did not owe. The incident is important only in that Burroughs succeeded in becoming minister where Bayley, Thomas Putnam's brother-in-law, had been rejected; the motif of resentment is clear here. Thomas Putnam felt that his own name and the honor of his family had been smirched by the village, and he meant to right matters however he could.

Another reason to believe him a deeply embittered man was his attempt to break his father's will, which left a disproportionate amount to a stepbrother. As with every other public cause in which he tried to force his way, he failed in this.

So it is not surprising to find that so many accusations against people are in the handwriting of Thomas Putnam, or that his name is so often found as a witness corroborating the supernatural testimony, or that his daughter led the crying-out at the most opportune junctures of the trials, especially when—But we'll speak of that when we come to it.

Putnam [*—at the moment he is intent upon getting Parris, for whom he has only contempt, to move toward the abyss*].   Mr. Parris, I have taken your part in all contention here, and I would continue; but I cannot if you hold back in this. There are hurtful, vengeful spirits layin' hands on these children.

Parris.   But, Thomas, you cannot—

Putnam.   Ann! Tell Mr. Paris what you have done.

Mrs. Putnam.   Reverend Parris, I have laid seven babies unbaptized in the earth. Believe me, sir, you never saw more hearty babies born. And yet, each would wither in my arms the very night of their birth. I have spoke nothin', but my heart has clamored intimations. And now, this year, my Ruth, my only— I see her turning strange. A secret child she has become this year, and shrivels like a sucking mouth were pullin' on her life too. And so I thought to send her to your Tituba—

Parris.   To Tituba! What may Tituba—?

Mrs. Putnam.   Tituba knows how to speak to the dead, Mr. Parris.

Parris.   Goody Ann, it is a formidable sin to conjure up the dead!

Mrs. Putnam.   I take it on my soul, but who else may surely tell us what person murdered my babies?

Parris [*horrified*].   Woman!

Mrs. Putnam.   They were murdered, Mr. Parris! And mark this proof! Mark it! Last night my Ruth were ever so close to their little spirits; I know it, sir. For how else is she struck dumb now except some power of darkness would stop her mouth? It is a marvelous sign, Mr. Parris!

Putnam.   Don't you understand it, sir? There is a murdering witch among us, bound to keep herself in the dark. [PARIS *turns to* BETTY, *a frantic terror rising in him.*] Let your names make of it what they will, you cannot blink it more.

Parris [*to* ABIGAIL].   Then you were conjuring spirits last night.

Abigail [*whispering*].   Not I, sir—Tituba and Ruth.

Parris [*turns now, with new fear, and goes to* BETTY, *looks down at her, and then, gazing off*].   Oh, Abigail, what proper payment for my charity! Now I am undone.

Putnam.   You are not undone! Let you take hold here. Wait for no one to charge you—declare it yourself. You have discovered witchcraft—

Parris.   In my house? In my house, Thomas? They will topple me with this! They will make of it a—

[*Enter* MERCY LEWIS, *the* PUTNAMS' *servant, a fat, sly, merciless girl of eighteen.*]

Mercy.   Your pardons. I only thought to see how Betty is.

Putnam.   Why aren't you home? Who's with Ruth?

Mercy.   Her grandma come. She's improved a little, I think—she give a powerful sneeze before.

Mrs. Putnam.   Ah, there's a sign of life!

Mercy.   I'd fear no more, Goody Putnam. It were a grand sneeze; another like it will shake her wits together, I'm sure. [*She goes to the bed to look.*]

Parris.   Will you leave me now, Thomas? I would pray a while alone.

Abigail.   Uncle, you've prayed since midnight. Why do you not go down and—

Parris. No—no. [*To* PUTNAM.] I have no answer for that crowd. I'll wait till
Mr. Hale arrives. [*To get* MRS. PUTNAM *to leave.*] If you will, Goody Ann . . .
Putnam. Now look you, sir. Let you strike out against the Devil, and the
village will bless you for it! Come down, speak to them—pray with them.
They're thirsting for your word, Mister! Surely you'll pray with them.
Parris [*swayed*]. I'll lead them in a psalm, but let you say nothing of witch-
craft yet. I will not discuss it. The cause is yet unknown. I have had enough
contention since I came; I want no more.
Mrs. Putnam. Mercy, you go home to Ruth, d'y'hear?
Mercy. Aye, mum.

[MRS. PUTNAM *goes out.*]

Parris [*to* ABIGAIL]. If she starts for the window, cry for me at once.
Abigail. I will, uncle.
Parris [*to* PUTNAM]. There is a terrible power in her arms today. [*He goes
out with* PUTNAM.]
Abigail [*with hushed trepidation*]. How is Ruth sick?
Mercy. It's weirdish, I know not—she seems to walk like a dead one since
last night.
Abigail [*turns at once and goes to* BETTY, *and now, with fear in her voice*].
Betty? [BETTY *doesn't move. She shakes her.*] Now stop this! Betty! Sit up
now!

[BETTY *doesn't stir.* MERCY *comes over.*]

Mercy. Have you tried beatin' her? I gave Ruth a good one and it waked
her for a minute. Here, let me have her.
Abigail [*holding* MERCY *back*]. No, he'll be comin' up. Listen, now; if they
be questioning us, tell them we danced—I told him as much already.
Mercy. Aye. And what more?
Abigail. He knows Tituba conjured Ruth's sisters to come out of the grave.
Mercy. And what more?
Abigail. He saw you naked.
Mercy [*clapping her hands together with a frightened laugh*]. Oh, Jesus!

[*Enter* MARY WARREN, *breathless. She is seventeen, a subservient, naïve,
lonely girl.*]

Mary Warren. What'll we do? The village is out! I just come from the farm;
the whole country's talkin' witchcraft! They'll be callin' us witches, Abby!
Mercy [*pointing and looking at* MARY WARREN]. She means to tell, I know it.
Mary Warren. Abby, we've got to tell. Witchery's a hangin' error, a hangin'
like they done in Boston two year ago! We must tell the truth, Abby! You'll
only be whipped for dancin', and the other things!
Abigail. Oh, *we'll* be whipped!
Mary Warren. I never done none of it, Abby. I only looked!
Mercy [*moving menacingly toward* MARY]. Oh, you're a great one for lookin',
aren't you, Mary Warren? What a grand peeping courage you have!

[BETTY, *on the bed, whimpers. Abigail turns to her at once.*]

Abigail. Betty? [*She goes to* BETTY.] Now, Betty, dear, wake up now. It's Abigail. [*She sits* BETTY *up and furiously shakes her.*] I'll beat you, Betty! [BETTY *whimpers.*] My, you seem improving. I talked to your papa and I told him everything. So there's nothing to—

Betty [*darts off the bed, frightened of* ABIGAIL, *and flattens herself against the wall*]. I want my mama!

Abigail [*with alarm, as she cautiously approaches* BETTY]. What ails you, Betty? Your mama's dead and buried.

Betty. I'll fly to Mama. Let me fly! [*She raises her arms as though to fly, and streaks for the window, gets one leg out.*]

Abigail [*pulling her away from the window*]. I told him everything; he knows now, he knows everything we—

Betty. You drank blood, Abby! You didn't tell him that!

Abigail. Betty, you never say that again! You will never—

Betty. You did, you did! You drank a charm to kill John Proctor's wife! You drank a charm to kill Goody Proctor!

Abigail [*smashes her across the face*]. Shut it! Now shut it!

Betty [*collapsing on the bed*]. Mama, Mama! [*She dissolves into sobs.*]

Abigail. Now look you. All of you. We danced. And Tituba conjured Ruth Putnam's dead sisters. And that is all. And mark this. Let either of you breathe a word, or the edge of a word, about the other things, and I will come to you in the black of some terrible night and I will bring a pointy reckoning that will shudder you. And you know I can do it; I saw Indians smash my dear parents' heads on the pillow next to mine, and I have seen some reddish work done at night, and I can make you wish you had never seen the sun go down! [*She goes to* BETTY *and roughly sits her up.*] Now, you—sit up and stop this!

[*But* BETTY *collapses in her hands and lies inert on the bed.*]

Mary Warren [*with hysterical fright*]. What's got her? [ABIGAIL *stares in fright at* BETTY.] Abby, she's going to die! It's a sin to conjure, and we—

Abigail [*starting for* MARY]. I say shut it, Mary Warren!

[*Enter* JOHN PROCTOR. *On seeing him,* MARY WARREN *leaps in fright.*]

Proctor was a farmer in his middle thirties. He need not have been a partisan of any faction in the town, but there is evidence to suggest that he had a sharp and biting way with hypocrites. He was the kind of man— powerful of body, even-tempered, and not easily led—who cannot refuse support to partisans without drawing their deepest resentment. In Proctor's presence a fool felt his foolishness instantly—and a Proctor is always marked for calumny therefore.

But as we shall see, the steady manner he displays does not spring from an untroubled soul. He is a sinner, a sinner not only against the moral fashion of the time, but against his own vision of decent conduct. These people had no ritual for the washing away of sins. It is another trait we inherited from them, and it has helped to discipline us as well as to breed hypocrisy among us. Proctor, respected and even feared in Salem, has come to regard himself as a kind of fraud. But no hint of this has yet appeared on the surface, and as he enters from the crowded parlor below it is a man in his prime we see, with a quiet confidence and an unexpressed, hidden force. Mary Warren, his servant, can barely speak for embarrassment and fear.

Mary Warren.   Oh! I'm just going home, Mr. Proctor.
Proctor.   Be you foolish, Mary Warren? Be you deaf? I forbid you leave the house, did I not? Why shall I pay you? I am looking for you more often than my cows!
Mary Warren.   I only come to see the great doings in the world.
Proctor.   I'll show you a great doin' on your arse one of these days. Now get you home; my wife is waitin' with your work! [*Trying to retain a shred of dignity, she goes slowly out.*]
Mercy Lewis [*both afraid of him and strangely titillated*].   I'd best be off. I have my Ruth to watch. Good morning, Mr. Proctor.

[MERCY *sidles out. Since* PROCTOR'S *entrance,* ABIGAIL *has stood as though on tiptoe, absorbing his presence, wide-eyed. He glances at her then goes to* BETTY *on the bed.*]

Abigail.   Gad. I'd almost forgot how strong you are, John Proctor!
Proctor [*looking at* ABIGAIL *now, the faintest suggestion of a knowing smile on his face*].   What's this mischief here?
Abigail [*with a nervous laugh*].   Oh, she's only gone silly somehow.
Proctor.   The road past my house is a pilgrimage to Salem all morning. The town's mumbling witchcraft.
Abigail.   Oh, posh! [*Winningly she comes a little closer, with a confidential, wicked air.*] We were dancin' in the woods last night, and my uncle leaped in on us. She took fright, is all.
Proctor [*his smile widening*].   Ah, you're wicked yet, aren't y'! [*A trill of expectant laughter escapes her, and she dares come closer, feverishly looking into his eyes.*] You'll be clapped in the stocks before you're twenty.

[*He takes a step to go, and she springs into his path.*]

Abigail.   Give me a word, John. A soft word. [*Her concentrated desire destroys his smile.*]
Proctor.   No, no, Abby. That's done with.
Abigail [*tauntingly*].   You come five mile to see a silly girl fly? I know you better.
Proctor [*setting her firmly out of his path*].   I come to see what mischief your uncle's brewin' now. [*With final emphasis.*] Put it out of mind, Abby.
Abigail [*grasping his hand before he can release her*].   John—I am waitin' for you every night.
Proctor.   Abby, I never give you hope to wait for me.
Abigail [*now beginning to anger—she can't believe it*].   I have something better than hope, I think!
Proctor.   Abby, you'll put it out of mind. I'll not be comin' for you more.
Abigail.   You're surely sportin' with me.

Proctor. You know me better.

Abigail. I know how you clutched my back behind your house and sweated like a stallion whenever I come near! Or did I dream that? It's she put me out, you cannot pretend it were you. I saw your face when she put me out, and you loved me then and you do now!

Proctor. Abby, that's a wild thing to say—

Abigail. A wild thing may say wild things. But not so wild, I think. I have seen you since she put me out; I have seen you nights.

Proctor. I have hardly stepped off my farm this seven-month.

Abigail. I have a sense for heat, John, and yours has drawn me to my window, and I have seen you looking up, burning in your loneliness. Do you tell me you've never looked up at my window?

Proctor. I may have looked up.

Abigail [*now softening*]. And you must. You are no wintry man. I know you, John. I *know* you. [*She is weeping.*] I cannot sleep for dreamin'; I cannot dream but I wake and walk about the house as though I'd find you comin' through some door. [*She clutches him desperately.*]

Proctor [*gently pressing her from him, with great sympathy but firmly*]. Child—

Abigail [*with a flash of anger*]. How do you call me child!

Proctor. Abby, I may think of you softly from time to time. But I will cut off my hand before I'll ever reach for you again. Wipe it out of mind. We never touched, Abby.

Abigail. Aye, but we did.

Proctor. Aye, but we did not.

Abigail [*with a bitter anger*]. Oh, I marvel how such a strong man may let such a sickly wife be—

Proctor [*angered—at himself as well*]. You'll speak nothin' of Elizabeth!

Abigail. She is blackening my name in the village! She is telling lies about me! She is a cold, sniveling woman, and you bend to her! Let her turn you like a—

Proctor [*shaking her*]. Do you look for whippin'?

[*A psalm is heard being sung below.*]

Abigail [*in tears*]. I look for John Proctor that took me from my sleep and put knowledge in my heart! I never knew what pretense Salem was, I never knew the lying lessons I was taught by all these Christian women and their covenanted men! And now you bid me tear the light out of my eyes? I will not, I cannot! You loved me, John Proctor, and whatever sin it is, you love me yet! [*He turns abruptly to go out. She rushes to him.*] John, pity me, pity me!

[*The words "going up to Jesus" are heard in the psalm, and* BETTY *claps her ears suddenly and whines loudly.*]

Abigail. Betty? [*She hurries to* BETTY, *who is now sitting up and screaming.* PROCTOR *goes to* BETTY *as* ABIGAIL *is trying to pull her hands down, calling* "BETTY!"]

Proctor [*growing unnerved*]. What's she doing? Girl, what ails you? Stop that wailing!

[*The singing has stopped in the midst of this, and now* PARRIS *rushes in.*]

Parris. What happened? What are you doing to her? Betty! [*He rushes to the bed, crying, "Betty, Betty!"* MRS. PUTNAM *enters, feverish with curiosity, and with her* THOMAS PUTNAM *and* MERCY LEWIS. PARRIS, *at the bed, keeps lightly slapping* BETTY's *face, while she moans and tries to get up.*]
Abigail. She heard you singin' and suddenly she's up and screamin'.
Mrs. Putnam. The psalm! The psalm! She cannot bear to hear the Lord's name!
Parris. No, God forbid. Mercy, run to the doctor! Tell him what's happened here! [MERCY LEWIS *rushes out.*]
Mrs. Putnam. Mark it for a sign, mark it!

[REBECCA NURSE, *seventy-two, enters. She is white-haired, leaning upon her walking-stick.*]

Putnam [*pointing at the whimpering* BETTY]. That is a notorious sign of witchcraft afoot, Goody Nurse, a prodigious sign!
Mrs. Putnam. My mother told me that! When they cannot bear to hear the name of—
Parris [*trembling*]. Rebecca, Rebecca, go to her, we're lost. She suddenly cannot bear to hear the Lord's—

[GILES COREY, *eighty-three, enters. He is knotted with muscle, canny, inquisitive, and still powerful.*]

Rebecca. There is hard sickness here, Giles Corey, so please to keep the quiet.
Giles. I've not said a word. No one here can testify I've said a word. Is she going to fly again? I hear she flies.
Putnam. Man, be quiet now!

[*Everything is quiet.* REBECCA *walks across the room to the bed. Gentleness exudes from her.* BETTY *is quietly whimpering, eyes shut.* REBECCA *simply stands over the child, who gradually quiets.*]

And while they are so absorbed, we may put a word in for Rebecca. Rebecca was the wife of Francis Nurse, who, from all accounts, was one of those men for whom both sides of the argument had to have respect. He was called upon to arbitrate disputes as though he were an unofficial judge, and Rebecca also enjoyed the high opinion most people had for him. By the time of the delusion, they had three hundred acres, and their children were settled in separate homesteads within the same estate. However, Francis had originally rented the land, and one theory has it that, as he gradually paid for it and raised his social status, there were those who resented his rise.

Another suggestion to explain the systematic campaign against Rebecca, and inferentially against Francis, is the land war he fought with his neighbors, one of whom was a Putnam. This squabble grew to the proportions of a battle in the woods between partisans of both sides, and it is said to have lasted for two days. As for Rebecca herself, the general opinion of her character was so high that to explain how anyone dared cry her out for a witch—and more, how adults could bring themselves to lay hands on her—we must look to the fields and boundaries of that time.

As we have seen, Thomas Putnam's man for the Salem ministry was Bayley. The Nurse clan had been in the faction that prevented Bayley's taking office. In addition, certain families allied to the Nurses by blood or friendship, and whose farms were contiguous with the Nurse farm or close to it, combined to break away from the Salem town authority and set up Topsfield, a new and independent entity whose existence was resented by old Salemites.

That the guiding hand behind the outcry was Putnam's is indicated by the fact that, as soon as it began, this Topsfield-Nurse faction absented themselves from church in protest and disbelief. It was Edward and Jonathan Putnam who signed the first complaint against Rebecca; and Thomas Putnam's little daughter was the one who fell into a fit at the hearing and pointed to Rebecca as her attacker. To top it all, Mrs. Putnam—who is now staring at the bewitched child on the bed—soon accused Rebecca's spirit of "tempting her to iniquity," a charge that had more truth in it than Mrs. Putnam could know.

Mrs. Putnam [*astonished*].   What have you done?

[REBECCA, *in thought, now leaves the bedside and sits.*]

Parris [*wondrous and relieved*].   What do you make of it, Rebecca?
Putnam [*eagerly*].   Goody Nurse, will you go to my Ruth and see if you can wake her?
Rebecca [*sitting*].   I think she'll wake in time. Pray calm yourselves. I have eleven children, and I am twenty-six times a grandma, and I have seen them all through their silly seasons, and when it come on them they will run the Devil bowlegged keeping up with their mischief. I think she'll wake when she tires of it. A child's spirit is like a child, you can never catch it by running after it; you must stand still, and, for love, it will soon itself come back.
Proctor.   Aye, that's the truth of it, Rebecca.
Mrs. Putnam.   This is no silly season, Rebecca. My Ruth is bewildered, Rebecca; she cannot eat.
Rebecca.   Perhaps she is not hungered yet. [*To* PARRIS.] I hope you are not decided to go in search of loose spirits, Mr. Parris. I've heard promise of that outside.
Parris.   A wide opinion's running in the parish that the Devil may be among us, and I would satisfy them that they are wrong.
Proctor.   Then let you come out and call them wrong. Did you consult the wardens before you called this minister to look for devils?
Parris.   He is not coming to look for devils!
Proctor.   Then what's he coming for?
Putnam.   There be children dyin' in the village, Mister!

Proctor. I seen none dyin'. This society will not be a bag to swing around your head, Mr. Putnam. [*To* PARRIS.] Did you call a meeting before you—?

Putnam. I am sick of meetings; cannot the man turn his head without he have a meeting?

Proctor. He may turn his head, but not to Hell!

Rebecca. Pray, John, be calm. [*Pause. He defers to her.*] Mr. Parris, I think you'd best send Reverend Hale back as soon as he come. This will set us all to arguin' again in the society, and we thought to have peace this year. I think we ought rely on the doctor now, and good prayer.

Mrs. Putnam. Rebecca, the doctor's baffled!

Rebecca. If so he is, then let us go to God for the cause of it. There is prodigious danger in the seeking of loose spirits. I fear it, I fear it. Let us rather blame ourselves and—

Putnam. How may we blame ourselves? I am one of nine sons; the Putnam seed have peopled this province. And yet I have but one child left of eight—and now she shrivels!

Rebecca. I cannot fathom that.

Mrs. Putnam [*with a growing edge of sarcasm*]. But I must! You think it God's work you should never lose a child, nor grandchild either, and I bury all but one? There are wheels within wheels in this village, and fires within fires!

Putnam [*to* PARRIS]. When Reverend Hale comes, you will proceed to look for signs of witchcraft here.

Proctor [*to* PUTNAM]. You cannot command Mr. Parris. We vote by name in this society, not by acreage.

Putnam. I never heard you worried so on this society, Mr. Proctor. I do not think I saw you at Sabbath meeting since snow flew.

Proctor. I have trouble enough without I come five mile to hear him preach only hellfire and bloody damnation. Take it to heart, Mr. Parris. There are many others who stay away from church these days because you hardly ever mention God any more.

Parris [*now aroused*]. Why, that's a drastic charge!

Rebecca. It's somewhat true; there are many that quail to bring their children—

Parris. I do not preach for children, Rebecca. It is not the children who are unmindful of their obligations toward this ministry.

Rebecca. Are there really those unmindful?

Parris. I should say the better half of Salem village—

Putnam. And more than that!

Parris. Where is my wood? My contract provides I be supplied with all my firewood. I am waiting since November for a stick, and even in November I had to show my frostbitten hands like some London beggar!

Giles. You are allowed six pound a year to buy your wood, Mr. Parris.

Parris. I regard that six pound as part of my salary. I am paid little enough without I spend six pound on firewood.

Proctor. Sixty, plus six for firewood—

Parris. The salary is sixty-six pound, Mr. Proctor! I am not some preaching farmer with a book under my arm; I am a graduate of Harvard College.

Giles. Aye, and well instructed in arithmetic!

Parris. Mr. Corey, you will look far for a man of my kind at sixty pound a year! I am not used to this poverty; I left a thrifty business in the Barbados to serve the Lord. I do not fathom it, why am I persecuted here? I cannot offer one proposition but there be a howling riot of argument. I have often wondered if the Devil be in it somewhere; I cannot understand you people otherwise.

Proctor. Mr. Parris, you are the first minister ever did demand the deed to this house—

Parris. Man! Don't a minister deserve a house to live in?

Proctor. To live in, yes. But to ask ownership is like you shall own the meeting house itself; the last meeting I were at you spoke so long on deeds and mortgages I thought it were an auction.

Parris. I want a mark of confidence, is all! I am your third preacher in seven years. I do not wish to be put out like the cat whenever some majority feels the whim. You people seem not to comprehend that a minister is the Lord's man in the parish; a minister is not to be so lightly crossed and contradicted—

Putnam. Aye!

Parris. There is either obedience or the church will burn like Hell is burning!

Proctor. Can you speak one minute without we land in Hell again? I am sick of Hell!

Parris. It is not for you to say what is good for you to hear!

Proctor. I may speak my heart, I think!

Parris [*in a fury*]. What, are we Quakers? We are not Quakers here yet, Mr. Proctor. And you may tell that to your followers!

Proctor. My followers!

Parris [*now he's out with it*]. There is a party in this church. I am not blind; there is a faction and a party.

Proctor. Against you?

Putnam. Against him and all authority!

Proctor. Why, then I must find it and join it.

[*There is shock among the others.*]

Rebecca. He does not mean that.

Putnam. He confessed it now!

Proctor. I mean it solemnly, Rebecca; I like not the smell of this "authority."

Rebecca. No, you cannot break charity with your minister. You are another kind, John. Clasp his hand, make your peace.

Proctor. I have a crop to sow and lumber to drag home. [*He goes angrily to the door and turns to* corey *with a smile.*] What say you, Giles, let's find the party. He says there's a party.

Giles. I've changed my opinion of this man, John. Mr. Parris, I beg your pardon. I never thought you had so much iron in you.

Parris [*surprised*]. Why, thank you, Giles!

Giles. It suggests to the mind what the trouble be among us all these years. [*To all.*] Think on it. Wherefore is everybody suing everybody else? Think on it now, it's a deep thing, and dark as a pit. I have been six time in court this year—

Proctor [*familiarly, with warmth, although he knows he is approaching the edge of* GILES' *tolerance with this*].   Is it the Devil's fault that a man cannot say you good morning without you clap him for defamation? You're old, Giles, and you're not hearin' so well as you did.

Giles [*he cannot be crossed*].   John Proctor, I have only last month collected four pound damages for you publicly sayin' I burned the roof off your house, and I—

Proctor [*laughing*].   I never said no such thing, but I've paid you for it, so I hope I can call you deaf without charge. Now come along, Giles, and help me drag my lumber home.

Putnam.   A moment, Mr. Proctor. What lumber is that you're draggin', if I may ask you?

Proctor.   My lumber. From out my forest by the riverside.

Putnam.   Why, we are surely gone wild this year. What anarchy is this? That tract is in my bounds, it's in my bounds, Mr. Proctor.

Proctor.   In your bounds! [*Indicating* REBECCA.] I bought that tract from Goody Nurse's husband five months ago.

Putnam.   He had no right to sell it. It stands clear in my grandfather's will that all the land between the river and—

Proctor.   Your grandfather had a habit of willing land that never belonged to him, if I may say it plain.

Giles.   That's God's truth; he nearly willed away my north pasture but he knew I'd break his fingers before he'd set his name to it. Let's get your lumber home, John. I feel a sudden will to work coming on.

Putnam.   You load one oak of mine and you'll fight to drag it home!

Giles.   Aye, and we'll win too, Putnam—this fool and I. Come on! [*He turns to* PROCTOR *and starts out.*]

Putnam.   I'll have my men on you, Corey! I'll clap a writ on you!

[*Enter* REVEREND JOHN HALE *of Beverly.*]

Mr. Hale is nearing forty, a tight-skinned, eager-eyed intellectual. This is a beloved errand for him; on being called here to ascertain witchcraft he felt the pride of the specialist whose unique knowledge has at last been publicly called for. Like almost all men of learning, he spent a good deal of his time pondering the invisible world, especially since he had himself encountered a witch in his parish not long before. That woman, however, turned into a mere pest under his searching scrutiny, and the child she had allegedly been afflicting recovered her normal behavior after Hale had given her his kindness and a few days of rest in his own house. However, that experience never raised a doubt in his mind as to the reality of the underworld or the existence of Lucifer's many-faced lieutenants. And his belief is not to his discredit. Better minds than Hale's were—and still are—convinced that there is a society of spirits beyond our ken. One cannot help noting that one of his lines has never yet raised a laugh in any audience that has seen this play; it is his assurance that "We cannot look to superstition in this. The Devil is precise." Evidently we are not quite certain even now whether diabolism is holy and not to be scoffed at. And it is no accident that we should be so bemused.

Like Reverend Hale and the others on this stage, we conceive the Devil as a necessary part of a respectable view of cosmology. Ours is a divided empire in which certain ideas and emotions and actions are of God, and their opposites are of Lucifer. It is as impossible for most men to conceive of a morality without sin as of an earth without "sky." Since 1692 a great but superficial change has wiped out God's beard and the Devil's horns, but the world is still gripped between two diametrically opposed absolutes. The concept of unity, in which positive and negative are attributes of the same force, in which good and evil are relative, ever-changing, and always joined to the same phenomenon—such a concept is still reserved to the physical sciences and to the few who have grasped the history of ideas. When it is recalled that until the Christian era the underworld was never regarded as a hostile area, that all gods were useful and essentially friendly to man despite occasional lapses; when we see the steady and methodical inculcation into humanity of the idea of man's worthlessness—until redeemed—the necessity of the Devil may become evident as a weapon, a weapon designed and used time and time again in every age to whip men into a surrender to a particular church or church-state.

Our difficulty in believing the—for want of a better word—political inspiration of the Devil is due in great part to the fact that he is called up and damned not only by our social antagonists but by our own side, whatever it may be. The Catholic Church, through its Inquisition, is famous for cultivating Lucifer as the arch-fiend, but the Church's enemies relied no less upon the Old Boy to keep the human mind enthralled. Luther was himself accused of alliance with Hell, and he in turn accused his enemies. To complicate matters further, he believed that he had had contact with the Devil and had argued theology with him. I am not surprised at this, for at my own university a professor of history—a Lutheran, by the way—used to assemble his graduate students, draw the shades, and commune in the classroom with Erasmus. He was never, to my knowledge, officially scoffed at for this, the reason being that the university officials, like most of us, are the children of a history which still sucks at the Devil's teats. At this writing, only England has held back before the temptations of contemporary diabolism. In the countries of the Communist ideology, all resistance of any import is linked to the totally malign capitalist succubi, and in America any man who is not reactionary in his views is open to the charge of alliance with the Red hell. Political opposition, thereby, is given an inhumane overlay which then justifies the abrogation of all normally applied customs of civilized intercourse. A political policy is equated with moral right, and opposition to it with diabolical malevolence. Once such an equation is effectively made, society becomes a congerie of plots and counterplots, and the main role of government changes from that of the arbiter to that of the scourge of God.

The results of this process are no different now from what they ever were, except sometimes in the degree of cruelty inflicted, and not always even in that department. Normally the actions and deeds of a man were all that society felt comfortable in judging. The secret intent of an action was left to the ministers, priests, and rabbis to deal with. When diabolism rises, however, actions are the least important manifests of the true nature of a man. The Devil, as Reverend Hale said, is a wily one, and until an hour before he fell, even God thought him beautiful in Heaven.

The analogy, however, seems to falter when one considers that, while there were no witches then, there are Communists and capitalists now, and in each camp there is certain proof that spies of each side are at work undermining the other. But this is a snobbish objection and not at all warranted by the facts. I have no doubt that people *were* communing with, and even worshiping, the Devil in Salem, and if the whole truth could be known in this case, as it is in others, we should discover a regular and conventionalized propitiation of the dark spirit. One certain evidence of this is the confession of Tituba, the slave of Reverend Parris, and another is the behavior of the children who were known to have indulged in sorceries with her.

There are accounts of similar *klatches* in Europe, where the daughters of the towns would assemble at night and, sometimes with fetishes, sometimes with a selected young man, give themselves to love, with some bastardly results. The Church, sharp-eyed as it must be when gods long dead are brought to life, condemned these orgies as witchcraft and interpreted them, rightly, as a resurgence of the Dionysiac forces it had crushed long before. Sex, sin, and the Devil were early linked, and so they continued to be in Salem, and are today. From all accounts there are no more puritanical mores in the world than those enforced by the Communists in Russia, where women's fashions, for instance, are as prudent and all-covering as any American Baptist would desire. The divorce laws lay a tremendous responsibility on the father for the care of his children. Even the laxity of divorce regulations in the early years of the revolution was undoubtedly a revulsion from the nineteenth-century Victorian immobility of marriage and the consequent hypocrisy that developed from it. If for no other reasons, a state so powerful, so jealous of the uniformity of its citizens, cannot long tolerate the atomization of the family. And yet, in American eyes at least, there remains the conviction that the Russian attitude toward women is lascivious. It is the Devil working again, just as he is working within the Slav who is shocked at the very idea of a woman's disrobing herself in a burlesque show. Our opposites are always robed in sexual sin, and it is from this unconscious conviction that demonology gains both its attractive sensuality and its capacity to infuriate and frighten.

Coming into Salem now, Reverend Hale conceives of himself much as a young doctor on his first call. His painfully acquired armory of symptoms, catchwords, and diagnostic procedures are now to be put to use at last. The road from Beverly is unusually busy this morning, and he has passed a hundred rumors that make him smile at the ignorance of the yeomanry in this most precise science. He feels himself allied with the best minds of Europe—kings, philosophers, scientists, and ecclesiasts of all churches. His goal is light, goodness and its preservation, and he knows the exaltation of the blessed whose intelligence, sharpened by minute examinations of enormous tracts, is finally called upon to face what may be a bloody fight with the Fiend himself.

[*He appears loaded down with half a dozen heavy books.*]

Hale. Pray you, someone take these!

Parris [*delighted*]. Mr. Hale! Oh! it's good to see you again! [*Taking some books.*] My, they're heavy!

Hale [*setting down his books*]. They must be; they are weighted with authority.

Parris [*a little scared*]. Well, you do come prepared!

Hale. We shall need hard study if it comes to tracking down the Old Boy. [*Noticing* REBECCA.] You cannot be Rebecca Nurse?

Rebecca. I am, sir. Do you know me?

Hale. It's strange how I knew you, but I suppose you look as such a good soul should. We have all heard of your great charities in Beverly.

Parris. Do you know this gentleman? Mr. Thomas Putnam. And his good wife Ann.

Hale. Putnam! I had not expected such distinguished company, sir.

Putnam [*pleased*]. It does not seem to help us today, Mr. Hale. We look to you to come to our house and save our child.

Hale. Your child ails too?

Mrs. Putnam. Her soul, her soul seems flown away. She sleeps and yet she walks . . .

Putnam. She cannot eat.

Hale. Cannot eat! [*Thinks on it. Then, to* PROCTOR *and* GILES COREY.] Do you men have afflicted children?

Parris. No, no, these are farmers. John Proctor—

Giles Corey. He don't believe in witches.

Proctor [*to* HALE]. I never spoke on witches one way or the other. Will you come, Giles?

Giles. No—no, John, I think not. I have some few queer questions of my own to ask this fellow.

Proctor. I've heard you to be a sensible man, Mr. Hale. I hope you'll leave some of it in Salem.

[PROCTOR *goes.* HALE *stands embarrassed for an instant.*]

Parris [*quickly*]. Will you look at my daughter, sir? [*Leads* HALE *to the bed.*] She has tried to leap out the window; we discovered her this morning on the highroad, waving her arms as though she'd fly.

Hale [*narrowing his eyes*]. Tries to fly.

Putnam. She cannot bear to hear the Lord's name, Mr. Hale; that's a sure sign of witchcraft afloat.

Hale [*holding up his hands*]. No, no. Now let me instruct you. We cannot look to superstition in this. The Devil is precise; the marks of his presence are definite as stone, and I must tell you all that I shall not proceed unless you are prepared to believe me if I should find no bruise of hell upon her.

Parris. It is agreed, sir—it is agreed—we will abide by your judgment.

Hale. Good then. [*He goes to the bed, looks down at* BETTY. *To* PARRIS.] Now, sir, what were your first warning of this strangeness?

Parris. Why, sir—I discovered her [*indicating* ABIGAIL] and my niece and ten or twelve of the other girls, dancing in the forest last night.

Hale [*surprised*]. You permit dancing?

Parris. No, no, it were secret—

Mrs. Putnam [*unable to wait*]. Mr. Parris's slave has knowledge of conjurin', sir.

Parris [*to* MRS. PUTNAM]. We cannot be sure of that, Goody Ann—

Mrs. Putnam [*frightened, very softly*]. I know it, sir. I sent my child—she should learn from Tituba who murdered her sisters.

Rebecca [*horrified*]. Goody Ann! You sent a child to conjure up the dead?

Mrs. Putnam. Let God blame me, not you, not you, Rebecca! I'll not have you judging me any more! [*To* HALE.] Is it a natural work to lose seven children before they live a day?

Parris. Sssh!

[REBECCA, *with a great pain, turns her face away. There is a pause.*]

Hale. Seven dead in childbirth.

Mrs. Putnam [*softly*]. Aye. [*Her voice breaks; she looks up at him. Silence.* HALE *is impressed.* PARRIS *looks to him. He goes to his books, opens one, turns pages, then reads. All wait, avidly.*]

Parris [*hushed*]. What book is that?

Mrs. Putnam. What's there, sir?

Hale [*with a tasty love of intellectual pursuit*]. Here is all the invisible world, caught, defined, and calculated. In these books the Devil stands stripped of all his brute disguises. Here are all your familiar spirits—your incubi and succubi; your witches that go by land, by air, and by sea; your wizards of the night and of the day. Have no fear now—we shall find him out if he has come among us, and I mean to crush him utterly if he has shown his face! [*He starts for the bed.*]

Rebecca. Will it hurt the child, sir?

Hale. I cannot tell. If she is truly in the Devil's grip we may have to rip and tear to get her free.

Rebecca. I think I'll go, then. I am too old for this. [*She rises.*]

Parris [*striving for conviction*]. Why, Rebecca, we may open up the boil of all our troubles today!

Rebecca. Let us hope for that. I go to God for you, sir.

Parris [*with trepidation—and resentment*]. I hope you do not mean to go to Satan here! [*Slight pause.*]

Rebecca. I wish I knew. [*She goes out; they feel resentful of her note of moral superiority.*]

Putnam [*abruptly*]. Come, Mr. Hale, let's get on. Sit you here.

Giles. Mr. Hale, I have always wanted to ask a learned man—what signifies the readin' of strange books?

Hale. What books?

Giles. I cannot tell; she hides them.

Hale. Who does this?

Giles. Martha, my wife. I have waked at night many a time and found her in a corner, readin' of a book. Now what do you make of that?

Hale. Why, that's not necessarily—

Giles. It discomfits me! Last night—and mark this—I tried and tried and could not say my prayers. And then she close her book and walks out of the house, and suddenly—mark this—I could pray again!

Old Giles must be spoken for, if only because his fate was to be so remarkable and so different from that of all the others. He was in his early eighties at this time, and was the most comical hero in the history. No man has ever been blamed for so much. If a cow was missed, the first thought was to look for her around Corey's house; a fire blazing up at night brought suspicion of arson to his door. He didn't give a hoot for public opinion, and only in his last years— after he had married Martha—did he bother much with the church. That she stopped his prayer is very probable, but he forgot to say that he'd only recently learned any prayers and it didn't take much to make him stumble over them. He was a crank and a nuisance, but withal a deeply innocent and brave man. In court, once, he was asked if it were true that he had been frightened by the strange behavior of a hog and had then said he knew it to be the Devil in an animal's shape. "What frighted you?" he was asked. He forgot everything but the word "frighted," and instantly replied, "I do not know that I ever spoke that word in my life."

Hale. Ah! The stoppage of prayer—that is strange. I'll speak further on that with you.

Giles. I'm not sayin' she's touched the Devil, now, but I'd admire to know what books she reads and why she hides them. She'll not answer me, y' see.

Hale. Aye, we'll discuss it. [*To all.*]. Now mark me, if the Devil is in her you will witness some frightful wonders in this room, so please to keep your wits about you. Mr. Putnam, stand close in case she flies. Now, Betty, dear, will you sit up? [PUTNAM *comes in closer, ready-handed.* HALE *sits* BETTY *up, but she hangs limp in his hands.*] Hmmm. [*He observes her carefully. The others watch breathlessly.*] Can you hear me? I am John Hale, minister of Beverly. I have come to help you, dear. Do you remember my two little girls in Beverly? [*She does not stir in his hands.*]

Parris [*in fright*]. How can it be the Devil? Why would he choose my house to strike? We have all manner of licentious people in the village!

Hale. What victory would the Devil have to win a soul already bad? It is the best the Devil wants, and who is better than the minister?

Giles. That's deep, Mr. Parris, deep, deep!

Parris [*with resolution now*]. Betty! Answer Mr. Hale! Betty!

Hale. Does someone afflict you, child? It need not be a woman, mind you, or a man. Perhaps some bird invisible to others comes to you—perhaps a pig, a mouse, or any beast at all. Is there some figure bids you fly? [*The child remains limp in his hands. In silence he lays her back on the pillow. Now, holding out his hands toward her, he intones.*] In nomine Domini Sabaoth sui filiique ite ad infernos. [*She does not stir. He turns to* ABIGAIL, *his eyes narrowing.*] Abigail, what sort of dancing were you doing with her in the forest?

Abigail. Why—common dancing is all.

Parris. I think I ought to say that I—I saw a kettle in the grass where they were dancing.

Abigail. That were only soup.

Hale. What sort of soup were in this kettle, Abigail?

Abigail. Why, it were beans—and lentils, I think, and—

Hale. Mr. Parris, you did not notice, did you, any living thing in the kettle? A mouse, perhaps, a spider, a frog—?

Parris [*fearfully*]. I—do believe there were some movement—in the soup.

Abigail. That jumped in, we never put it in!

Hale [*quickly*]. What jumped in?

Abigail. Why, a very little frog jumped—

Parris. A frog, Abby!

Hale [*grasping* ABIGAIL]. Abigail, it may be your cousin is dying. Did you call the Devil last night?

Abigail. I never called him! Tituba, Tituba . . .

Parris [*blanched*]. She called the Devil?

Hale. I should like to speak with Tituba.

Parris. Goody Ann, will you bring her up? [MRS. PUTNAM *exits.*]

Hale. How did she call him?

Abigail. I know not—she spoke Barbados.

Hale. Did you feel any strangeness when she called him? A sudden cold wind, perhaps? A trembling below the ground?

Abigail. I didn't see no Devil! [*Shaking* BETTY.] Betty, wake up. Betty! Betty!

Hale. You cannot evade me, Abigail. Did your cousin drink any of the brew in that kettle?

Abigail. She never drank it!

Hale. Did you drink it?

Abigail. No, sir!

Hale. Did Tituba ask you to drink it?

Abigail. She tried, but I refused.

Hale. Why are you concealing? Have you sold yourself to Lucifer?

Abigail. I never sold myself! I'm a good girl! I'm a proper girl!

[MRS. PUTNAM *enters with* TITUBA, *and instantly* ABIGAIL *points at* TITUBA.]

Abigail. She made me do it! She made Betty do it!

Tituba [*shocked and angry*]. Abby!

Abigail. She makes me drink blood!

Parris. Blood!!

Mrs. Putnam. My baby's blood?

Tituba. No, no, chicken blood. I give she chicken blood!

Hale. Woman, have you enlisted these children for the Devil?

Tituba. No, no sir, I don't truck with no Devil!

Hale. Why can she not wake? Are you silencing this child?

Tituba. I love me Betty!

Hale. You have sent your spirit out upon this child, have you not? Are you gathering souls for the Devil?

Abigail. She sends her spirit on me in church; she makes me laugh at prayer!

Parris. She have often laughed at prayer!

Abigail. She comes to me every night to go and drink blood!

Tituba. You beg *me* to conjure! She beg *me* make charm—

Abigail. Don't lie! [*To* HALE.] She comes to me while I sleep; she's always making me dream corruptions!

Tituba. Why you say that, Abby?

Abigail. Sometimes I wake and find myself standing in the open doorway and not a stitch on my body! I always hear her laughing in my sleep. I hear her singing her Barbados songs and tempting me with—

Tituba. Mister Reverend, I never—

Hale [*resolved now*]. Tituba, I want you to wake this child.

Tituba. I have no power on this child, sir.

Hale. You most certainly do, and you will free her from it now! When did you compact with the Devil?

Tituba. I don't compact with no Devil!

Parris. You will confess yourself or I will take you out and whip you to your death, Tituba!

Putnam. This woman must be hanged! She must be taken and hanged!

Tituba [*terrified, falls to her knees*]. No, no, don't hang Tituba! I tell him I don't desire to work for him, sir.

Parris. The Devil?

Hale. Then you saw him! [TITUBA *weeps.*] Now Tituba, I know that when we bind ourselves to Hell it is very hard to break with it. We are going to help you tear yourself free—

Tituba [*frightened by the coming process*]. Mister Reverend, I do believe somebody else be witchin' these children.

Hale. Who?

Tituba. I don't know, sir, but the Devil got him numerous witches.

Hale. Does he! [*It is a clue.*] Tituba, look into my eyes. Come, look into me. [*She raises her eyes to his fearfully.*] You would be a good Christian woman, would you not, Tituba?

Tituba. Aye, sir, a good Christian woman.

Hale. And you love these little children?

Tituba. Oh, yes, sir, I don't desire to hurt little children.

Hale. And you love God, Tituba?

Tituba. I love God with all my bein'.

Hale. Now, in God's holy name—

Tituba. Bless Him. Bless Him. [*She is rocking on her knees, sobbing in terror.*]

Hale. And to His glory—

Tituba. Eternal glory. Bless Him—bless God . . .

Hale. Open yourself, Tituba—open yourself and let God's holy light shine on you.

Tituba. Oh, bless the Lord.

Hale. When the Devil comes to you does he ever come—with another person? [*She stares up into his face.*] Perhaps another person in the village? Someone you know.

Parris. Who came with him?

Putnam.   Sarah Good? Did you ever see Sarah Good with him? Or Osburn?
Parris.   Was it man or woman came with him?
Tituba.   Man or woman. Was—was woman.
Parris.   What woman? A woman, you said. What woman?
Tituba.   It was black dark, and I—
Parris.   You could see him, why could you not see her?
Tituba.   Well, they was always talking; they was always runnin' round and carryin' on—
Parris.   You mean out of Salem? Salem witches?
Tituba.   I believe so, yes, sir.

[Now HALE *takes her hand. She is surprised.*]

Hale.   Tituba. You must have no fear to tell us who they are, do you understand? We will protect you. The Devil can never overcome a minister. You know that, do you not?
Tituba [*kisses* HALE's *hand*].   Aye, sir, oh, I do.
Hale.   You have confessed yourself to witchcraft, and that speaks a wish to come to Heaven's side. And we will bless you, Tituba.
Tituba [*deeply relieved*].   Oh, God bless you, Mr. Hale!
Hale [*with rising exaltation*].   You are God's instrument put in our hands to discover the Devil's agent among us. You are selected, Tituba, you are chosen to help us cleanse our village. So speak utterly, Tituba, turn your back on him and face God—face God, Tituba, and God will protect you.
Tituba [*joining with him*].   Oh, God, protect Tituba!
Hale [*kindly*].   Who came to you with the Devil? Two? Three? Four? How many?

[TITUBA *pants, and begins rocking back and forth again, staring ahead.*]

Tituba.   There was four. There was four.
Parris [*pressing in on her*].   Who? Who? Their names, their names!
Tituba [*suddenly bursting out*].   Oh, how many times he bid me kill you, Mr. Parris!
Parris.   Kill me!
Tituba [*in a fury*].   He say Mr. Parris must be kill! Mr. Parris no goodly man, Mr. Parris mean man and no gentle man, and he bid me rise out of my bed and cut your throat! [*They gasp.*] But I tell him "No! I don't hate that man. I don't want kill that man." But he say, "You work for me, Tituba, and I make you free! I give you pretty dress to wear, and put you way high up in the air, and you gone fly back to Barbados!" And I say, "You lie, Devil, you lie!" And then he come one stormy night to me, and he say, "Look! I have *white* people belong to me." And I look—and there was Goody Good.
Parris.   Sarah Good!
Tituba [*rocking and weeping*].   Aye, sir, and Goody Osburn.
Mrs. Putnam.   I knew it! Goody Osburn were midwife to me three times. I begged you, Thomas, did I not? I begged him not to call Osburn because I feared her. My babies always shriveled in her hands!

Hale. Take courage, you must give us all their names. How can you bear to see this child suffering? Look at her, Tituba. [*He is indicating* BETTY *on the bed.*] Look at her God-given innocence; her soul is so tender; we must protect her, Tituba; the Devil is out and preying on her like a beast upon the flesh of the pure lamb. God will bless you for your help.

[ABIGAIL *rises, staring as though inspired, and cries out.*]

Abigail. I want to open myself! [*They turn to her, startled. She is enraptured, as though in a pearly light.*] I want the light of God, I want the sweet love of Jesus! I danced for the Devil; I saw him; I wrote in his book; I go back to Jesus; I kiss His hand. I saw Sarah Good with the Devil! I saw Goody Osburn with the Devil! I saw Bridget Bishop with the Devil!

[*As she is speaking,* BETTY *is rising from the bed, a fever in her eyes, and picks up the chant.*]

Betty [*staring too*]. I saw George Jacobs with the Devil! I saw Goody Howe with the Devil!
Parris. She speaks! [*He rushes to embrace* BETTY.] She speaks!
Hale. Glory to God! It is broken, they are free!
Betty [*calling out hysterically and with great relief*]. I saw Martha Bellows with the Devil!
Abigail. I saw Goody Sibber with the Devil! [*It is rising to a great glee.*]
Putnam. The marshal, I'll call the marshal!

[PARRIS *is shouting a prayer of thanksgiving.*]

Betty. I saw Alice Barrow with the Devil!

[*The curtain begins to fall.*]

Hale [*as* PUTNAM *goes out*]. Let the marshal bring irons!
Abigail. I saw Goody Hawkins with the Devil!
Betty. I saw Goody Bibber with the Devil!
Abigail. I saw Goody Booth with the Devil!

[*On their ecstatic cries*]

[*The Curtain Falls*]

Act II

The common room of Proctor's house, eight days later.

[*At the right is a door opening on the fields outside. A fireplace is at the left, and behind it a stairway leading upstairs. It is the low, dark, and rather long living room of the time. As the curtain rises, the room is empty. From above,* ELIZABETH *is heard softly singing to* THE CHILDREN. *Presently the door opens and* JOHN PROCTOR *enters, carrying his gun. He glances about the room as he comes toward the fireplace, then halts for an instant as he hears her singing. He continues on to the fireplace, leans the gun against the wall as he swings a pot out of the fire and smells it. Then he lifts out the ladle and tastes. He is not quite pleased. He reaches to a cupboard, takes a pinch of salt, and drops it into the pot. As he is tasting again, her footsteps are heard on the stair. He swings the pot into the fireplace and goes to a basin and washes his hands and face.* ELIZABETH *enters.*]

Elizabeth.   What keeps you so late? It's almost dark.
Proctor.   I were planting far out to the forest edge.
Elizabeth.   Oh, you're done then.
Proctor.   Aye, the farm is seeded. The boys asleep?
Elizabeth.   They will be soon. [*And she goes to the fireplace, proceeds to ladle up stew in a dish.*]
Proctor.   Pray now for a fair summer.
Elizabeth.   Aye.
Proctor.   Are you well today?
Elizabeth.   I am. [*She brings the plate to the table, and, indicating the food.*] It is a rabbit.
Proctor [*going to the table*].   Oh, is it! In Jonathan's trap?
Elizabeth.   No, she walked into the house this afternoon; I found her sittin' in the corner like she come to visit.
Proctor.   Oh, that's a good sign walkin' in.
Elizabeth.   Pray God. It hurt my heart to strip her, poor rabbit. [*She sits and watches him taste it.*]
Proctor.   It's well seasoned.
Elizabeth [*blushing with pleasure*].   I took great care. She's tender?
Proctor.   Aye. [*He eats. She watches him.*] I think we'll see green fields soon. It's warm as blood beneath the clods.
Elizabeth.   That's well.

[PROCTOR *eats, then looks up.*]

Proctor.   If the crop is good I'll buy George Jacobs' heifer. How would that please you?
Elizabeth.   Aye, it would.
Proctor [*with a grin*].   I mean to please you, Elizabeth.
Elizabeth [*it is hard to say*].   I know it, John.

[*He gets up, goes to her, kisses her. She receives it. With a certain disappointment, he returns to the table.*]

Proctor [*as gently as he can*].   Cider?
Elizabeth [*with a sense of reprimanding herself for having forgot*].   Aye! [*She gets up and goes and pours a glass for him. He now arches his back.*]
Proctor.   This farm's a continent when you go foot by foot droppin' seeds in it.
Elizabeth [*coming with the cider*].   It must be.
Proctor [*drinks a long draught, then, putting the glass down*].   You ought to bring some flowers in the house.
Elizabeth.   Oh! I forgot! I will tomorrow.

Proctor. It's winter in here yet. On Sunday let you come with me, and we'll walk the farm together; I never see such a load of flowers on the earth. [*With good feeling he goes out and looks up at the sky through the open doorway.*] Lilacs have a purple smell. Lilac is the smell of nightfall, I think. Massachusetts is a beauty in the spring!

Elizabeth. Aye, it is.

[*There is a pause. She is watching him from the table as he stands there absorbing the night. It is as though she would speak but cannot. Instead, now, she takes up his plate and glass and fork and goes with them to the basin. Her back is turned to him. He turns to her and watches her. A sense of their separation rises.*]

Proctor. I think you're sad again. Are you?

Elizabeth [*she doesn't want friction, and yet she must*]. You come so late I thought you'd gone to Salem this afternoon.

Proctor. Why? I have no business in Salem.

Elizabeth. You did speak of going, earlier this week.

Proctor [*he knows what she means*]. I thought better of it since.

Elizabeth. Mary Warren's there today.

Proctor. Why'd you let her? You heard me forbid her go to Salem any more!

Elizabeth. I couldn't stop her.

Proctor [*holding back a full condemnation of her*]. It is a fault, it is a fault, Elizabeth—you're the mistress here, not Mary Warren.

Elizabeth. She frightened all my strength away.

Proctor. How may that mouse frighten you, Elizabeth? You—

Elizabeth. It is a mouse no more. I forbid her go, and she raises up her chin like the daughter of a prince and says to me, "I must go to Salem, Goody Proctor; I am an official of the court!"

Proctor. Court! What court?

Elizabeth. Aye, it is a proper court they have now. They've sent four judges out of Boston, she says, weighty magistrates of the General Court, and at the head sits the Deputy Governor of the Province.

Proctor [*astonished*]. Why, she's mad.

Elizabeth. I would to God she were. There be fourteen people in the jail now, she says. [PROCTOR *simply looks at her, unable to grasp it.*] And they'll be tried, and the court have power to hang them too, she says.

Proctor [*scoffing, but without conviction*]. Ah, they'd never hang—

Elizabeth. The Deputy Governor promise hangin' if they'll not confess, John. The town's gone wild, I think. She speak of Abigail, and I thought she were a saint, to hear her. Abigail brings the other girls into the court, and where she walks the crowd will part like the sea for Israel. And folks are brought before them, and if they scream and howl and fall to the floor—the person's clapped in the jail for bewitchin' them.

Proctor [*wide-eyed*]. Oh, it is a black mischief.

Elizabeth. I think you must go to Salem, John. [*He turns to her.*] I think so. You must tell them it is a fraud.

Proctor [*thinking beyond this*]. Aye, it is, it is surely.

Elizabeth. Let you go to Ezekiel Cheever—he knows you well. And tell him what she said to you last week in her uncle's house. She said it had naught to do with witchcraft, did she not?

Proctor [*in thought*]. Aye, she did, she did. [*Now, a pause.*]

Elizabeth [*quietly, fearing to anger him by prodding*]. God forbid you keep that from the court, John. I think they must be told.

Proctor [*quietly, struggling with his thought*]. Aye, they must, they must. It is a wonder they do believe her.

Elizabeth. I would go to Salem now, John—let you go tonight.

Proctor. I'll think on it.

Elizabeth [*with her courage now*]. You cannot keep it, John.

Proctor [*angering*]. I know I cannot keep it. I say I will think on it!

Elizabeth [*hurt, and very coldly*]. Good, then, let you think on it. [*She stands and starts to walk out of the room.*]

Proctor. I am only wondering how I may prove what she told me, Elizabeth. If the girl's a saint now, I think it is not easy to prove she's fraud, and the town gone so silly. She told it to me in a room alone—I have no proof for it.

Elizabeth. You were alone with her?

Proctor [*stubbornly*]. For a moment alone, aye.

Elizabeth. Why, then, it is not as you told me.

Proctor [*his anger rising*]. For a moment, I say. The others come in soon after.

Elizabeth [*quietly—she has suddenly lost all faith in him*]. Do as you wish, then. [*She starts to turn.*]

Proctor. Woman. [*She turns to him.*] I'll not have your suspicion any more.

Elizabeth [*a little loftily*]. I have no—

Proctor. I'll not have it!

Elizabeth. Then let you not earn it.

Proctor [*with a violent undertone*]. You doubt me yet?

Elizabeth [*with a smile, to keep her dignity*]. John, if it were not Abigail that you must go to hurt, would you falter now? I think not.

Proctor. Now look you—

Elizabeth. I see what I see, John.

Proctor [*with solemn warning*]. You will not judge me more, Elizabeth. I have good reason to think before I charge fraud on Abigail, and I will think on it. Let you look to your own improvement before you go to judge your husband any more. I have forgot Abigail, and—

Elizabeth. And I.

Proctor. Spare me! You forget nothin' and forgive nothin'. Learn charity, woman. I have gone tiptoe in this house all seven month since she is gone. I have not moved from there to there without I think to please you, and still an everlasting funeral marches round your heart. I cannot speak but I am doubted, every moment judged for lies, as though I come into a court when I come into this house!

Elizabeth. John, you are not open with me. You saw her with a crowd, you said. Now you—

Proctor. I'll plead my honesty no more, Elizabeth.

Elizabeth [*now she would justify herself*]. John, I am only—

Proctor. No more! I should have roared you down when first you told me your suspicion. But I wilted, and, like a Christian, I confessed. Confessed! Some dream I had must have mistaken you for God that day. But you're not, you're not, and let you remember it! Let you look sometimes for the goodness in me, and judge me not.

Elizabeth. I do not judge you. The magistrate sits in your heart that judges you. I never thought you but a good man, John—[*with a smile*]—only somewhat bewildered.

Proctor [*laughing bitterly*]. Oh, Elizabeth, your justice would freeze beer! [*He turns suddenly toward a sound outside. He starts for the door as Mary Warren enters. As soon as he sees her, he goes directly to her and grabs her by the cloak, furious.*] How do you go to Salem when I forbid it? Do you mock me? [*Shaking her.*] I'll whip you if you dare leave this house again!

[*Strangely, she doesn't resist him, but hangs limply by his grip.*]

Mary Warren. I am sick, I am sick, Mr. Proctor. Pray, pray, hurt me not. [*Her strangeness throws him off, and her evident pallor and weakness. He frees her.*] My insides are all shuddery; I am in the proceedings all day, sir.

Proctor [*with draining anger—his curiosity is draining it*]. And what of these proceedings here? When will you proceed to keep this house, as you are paid nine pound a year to do—and my wife not wholly well?

[*As though to compensate,* MARY WARREN *goes to* ELIZABETH *with a small rag doll.*]

Mary Warren. I made a gift for you today, Goody Proctor. I had to sit long hours in a chair, and passed the time with sewing.

Elizabeth [*perplexed, looking at the doll*]. Why, thank you, it's a fair poppet.

Mary Warren [*with a trembling, decayed voice*]. We must all love each other now, Goody Proctor.

Elizabeth [*amazed at her strangeness*]. Aye, indeed we must.

Mary Warren [*glancing at the room*]. I'll get up early in the morning and clean the house. I must sleep now. [*She turns and starts off.*]

Proctor. Mary. [*She halts.*] Is it true? There be fourteen women arrested?

Mary Warren. No, sir. There be thirty-nine now— [*She suddenly breaks off and sobs and sits down, exhausted.*]

Elizabeth. Why, she's weepin'! What ails you, child?

Mary Warren. Goody Osburn—will hang!

[*There is a shocked pause, while she sobs.*]

Proctor. Hang! [*He calls into her face.*] Hang, y'say?

Mary Warren [*through her weeping*]. Aye.

Proctor. The Deputy Governor will permit it?

Mary Warren. He sentenced her. He must. [*To ameliorate it.*] But not Sarah Good. For Sarah Good confessed, y'see.

Proctor. Confessed! To what?

Mary Warren. That she [*in horror at the memory*] she sometimes made a compact with Lucifer, and wrote her name in his black book—with her blood—

and bound herself to torment Christians till God's thrown down—and we all must worship Hell forevermore.

[*Pause.*]

Proctor. But—surely you know what a jabberer she is. Did you tell them that?

Mary Warren. Mr. Proctor, in open court she near to choked us all to death.

Proctor. How, choked you?

Mary Warren. She sent her spirit out.

Elizabeth. Oh, Mary, Mary, surely you—

Mary Warren [*with an indignant edge*]. She tried to kill me many times, Goody Proctor!

Elizabeth. Why, I never heard you mention that before.

Mary Warren. I never knew it before. I never knew anything before. When she come into the court I say to myself, I must not accuse this woman, for she sleep in ditches, and so very old and poor. But then—then she sit there, denying and denying, and I feel a misty coldness climbin' up my back, and the skin on my skull begin to creep, and I feel a clamp around my neck and I cannot breathe air; and then [*entranced*] I hear a voice, a screamin' voice, and it were my voice—and all at once I remembered everything she done to me!

Proctor. Why? What did she do to you?

Mary Warren [*like one awakened to a marvelous secret insight*]. So many time, Mr. Proctor, she come to this very door, beggin' bread and a cup of cider—and mark this: whenever I turned her away empty, she *mumbled*.

Elizabeth. Mumbled! She may mumble if she's hungry.

Mary Warren. But *what* does she mumble? You must remember, Goody Proctor. Last month—a Monday, I think—she walked away, and I thought my guts would burst for two days after. Do you remember it?

Elizabeth. Why—I do, I think, but—

Mary Warren. And so I told that to Judge Hathorne, and he asks her so. "Goody Osburn," says he, "what curse do you mumble that this girl must fall sick after turning you away?" And then she replies [*mimicking an old crone*] "Why, your excellence, no curse at all. I only say my commandments; I hope I may say my commandments," says she!

Elizabeth. And that's an upright answer.

Mary Warren. Aye, but then Judge Hathorne say, "Recite for us your commandments!" [*leaning avidly toward them*] and of all the ten she could not say a single one. She never knew no commandments, and they had her in a flat lie!

Proctor. And so condemned her?

Mary Warren [*now a little strained, seeing his stubborn doubt*]. Why, they must when she condemned herself.

Proctor. But the proof, the proof!

Mary Warren [*with greater impatience with him*]. I told you the proof. It's hard proof, hard as rock, the judges said.

Proctor [*pauses an instant, then*]. You will not go to court again, Mary Warren.

Mary Warren. I must tell you, sir, I will be gone every day now. I am amazed you do not see what weighty work we do.

Proctor. What work you do! It's strange work for a Christian girl to hang old women!

Mary Warren. But, Mr. Proctor, they will not hang them if they confess. Sarah Good will only sit in jail some time [*recalling*] and here's a wonder for you; think on this. Goody Good is pregnant!

Elizabeth. Pregnant! Are they mad? The woman's near to sixty!

Mary Warren. They had Doctor Griggs examine her, and she's full to the brim. And smokin' a pipe all these years, and no husband either! But she's safe, thank God, for they'll not hurt the innocent child. But be that not a marvel? You must see it, sir, it's God's work we do. So I'll be gone every day for some time. I'm—I am an official of the court, they say, and I— [*She has been edging toward offstage.*]

Proctor. I'll official you! [*He strides to the mantel, takes down the whip hanging there.*]

Mary Warren [*terrified, but coming erect, striving for her authority*]. I'll not stand whipping any more!

Elizabeth [*hurriedly, as* PROCTOR *approaches*]. Mary, promise you'll stay at home—

Mary Warren [*backing from him, but keeping her erect posture, striving, striving for her way*]. The Devil's loose in Salem, Mr. Proctor; we must discover where he's hiding!

Proctor. I'll whip the Devil out of you! [*With whip raised he reaches out for her, and she streaks away and yells.*]

Mary Warren [*pointing at* ELIZABETH]. I saved her life today!

[*Silence. His whip comes down.*]

Elizabeth [*softly*]. I am accused?

Mary Warren [*quaking*]. Somewhat mentioned. But I said I never see no sign you ever sent your spirit out to hurt no one, and seeing I do live so closely with you, they dismissed it.

Elizabeth. Who accused me?

Mary Warren. I am bound by law, I cannot tell it. [*To* PROCTOR.] I only hope you'll not be so sarcastical no more. Four judges and the King's deputy sat to dinner with us but an hour ago. I—I would have you speak civilly to me, from this out.

Proctor [*in horror, muttering in disgust at her*]. Go to bed.

Mary Warren [*with a stamp of her foot*]. I'll not be ordered to bed no more, Mr. Proctor! I am eighteen and a woman, however single!

Proctor. Do you wish to sit up? Then sit up.

Mary Warren. I wish to go to bed!

Proctor [*in anger*]. Good night, then!

Mary Warren. Good night. [*Dissatisfied, uncertain of herself, she goes out. Wide-eyed, both,* PROCTOR *and* ELIZABETH *stand staring.*]

Elizabeth [*quietly*]. Oh, the noose, the noose is up!

Proctor. There'll be no noose.

Elizabeth. She wants me dead. I knew all week it would come to this!

Proctor [*without conviction*]. They dismissed it. You heard her say—

Elizabeth. And what of tomorrow? She will cry me out until they take me!

Proctor. Sit you down.

Elizabeth. She wants me dead, John, you know it!

Proctor. I say sit down! [*She sits, trembling. He speaks quickly, trying to keep his wits.*] Now we must be wise, Elizabeth.

Elizabeth [*with sarcasm, and a sense of being lost*]. Oh, indeed, indeed!

Proctor. Fear nothing. I'll find Ezekiel Cheever. I'll tell him she said it were all sport.

Elizabeth. John, with so many in the jail, more than Cheever's help is needed now, I think. Would you favor me with this? Go to Abigail.

Proctor [*his soul hardening as he senses . . .*]. What have I to say to Abigail?

Elizabeth [*delicately*]. John—grant me this. You have a faulty understanding of young girls. There is a promise made in any bed—

Proctor [*striving against his anger*]. What promise!

Elizabeth. Spoke or silent, a promise is surely made. And she may dote on it now—I am sure she does—and thinks to kill me, then to take my place.

[PROCTOR'S *anger is rising; he cannot speak.*]

Elizabeth. It is her dearest hope, John, I know it. There be a thousand names; why does she call mine? There be a certain danger in calling such a name—I am no Goody Good that sleeps in ditches, nor Osburn, drunk and half-witted. She'd dare not call out such a farmer's wife but there be monstrous profit in it. She thinks to take my place, John.

Proctor. She cannot think it! [*He knows it is true.*]

Elizabeth ["*reasonably*"]. John, have you ever shown her somewhat of contempt? She cannot pass you in the church but you will blush—

Proctor. I may blush for my sin.

Elizabeth. I think she sees another meaning in that blush.

Proctor. And what see you? What see you, Elizabeth?

Elizabeth ["*conceding*"]. I think you be somewhat ashamed, for I am there, and she so close.

Proctor. When will you know me, woman? Were I stone I would have cracked for shame this seven month!

Elizabeth. Then go and tell her she's a whore. Whatever promise she may sense—break it, John, break it.

Proctor [*between his teeth*]. Good, then. I'll go. [*He starts for his rifle.*]

Elizabeth [*trembling, fearfully*]. Oh, how unwillingly!

Proctor [*turning on her, rifle in hand*]. I will curse her hotter than the oldest cinder in hell. But pray, begrudge me not my anger!

Elizabeth. Your anger! I only ask you—

Proctor. Woman, am I so base? Do you truly think me base?

Elizabeth. I never called you base.

Proctor. Then how do you charge me with such a promise? The promise that a stallion gives a mare I gave that girl!

Elizabeth. Then why do you anger with me when I bid you break it?

Proctor. Because it speaks deceit, and I am honest! But I'll plead no more! I see now your spirit twists around the single error of my life, and I will never tear it free!

Elizabeth [crying out]. You'll tear it free—when you come to know that I will be your only wife, or no wife at all! She has an arrow in you yet, John Proctor, and you know it well!

[*Quite suddenly, as though from the air, a figure appears in the doorway. They start slightly. It is* MR. HALE. *He is different now—drawn a little, and there is a quality of deference, even of guilt, about his manner now.*]

Hale. Good evening.

Proctor [still in his shock]. Why, Mr. Hale! Good evening to you, sir. Come in, come in.

Hale [to Elizabeth]. I hope I do not startle you.

Elizabeth. No, no, it's only that I heard no horse—

Hale. You are Goodwife Proctor.

Proctor. Aye; Elizabeth.

Hale [nods, then]. I hope you're not off to bed yet.

Proctor [setting down his gun]. No, no. [HALE *comes further into the room. And* PROCTOR, *to explain his nervousness.*] We are not used to visitors after dark, but you're welcome here. Will you sit down, sir?

Hale. I will. [*He sits.*] Let you sit, Goodwife Proctor.

[*She does, never letting him out of her sight. There is a pause as* HALE *looks about the room.*]

Proctor [to break the silence]. Will you drink cider, Mr. Hale?

Hale. No, it rebels my stomach; I have some further traveling yet tonight. Sit you down, sir. [PROCTOR *sits.*] I will not keep you long, but I have some business with you.

Proctor. Business of the court?

Hale. No—no, I come of my own, without the court's authority. Hear me. [*He wets his lips.*] I know not if you are aware, but your wife's name is—mentioned in the court.

Proctor. We know it, sir. Our Mary Warren told us. We are entirely amazed.

Hale. I am a stranger here, as you know. And in my ignorance I find it hard to draw a clear opinion of them that come accused before the court. And so this afternoon, and now tonight, I go from house to house—I come now from Rebecca Nurse's house and—

Elizabeth [shocked]. Rebecca's charged!

Hale. God forbid such a one be charged. She is, however—mentioned somewhat.

Elizabeth [with an attempt at a laugh]. You will never believe, I hope, that Rebecca trafficked with the Devil.

Hale. Woman, it is possible.

Proctor [taken aback]. Surely you cannot think so.

Hale. This is a strange time, Mister. No man may longer doubt the powers of the dark are gathered in monstrous attack upon this village. There is too much evidence now to deny it. You will agree, sir?

Proctor [evading]. I—have no knowledge in that line. But it's hard to think so pious a woman be secretly a Devil's bitch after seventy year of such good prayer.

Hale. Aye. But the Devil is a wily one, you cannot deny it. However, she is far from accused, and I know she will not be. [*Pause.*] I thought, sir, to put some questions as to the Christian character of this house, if you'll permit me.

Proctor [*coldly, resentful*]. Why, we—have no fear of questions, sir.

Hale. Good, then. [*He makes himself more comfortable.*] In the book of record that Mr. Parris keeps, I note that you are rarely in the church on Sabbath Day.

Proctor. No, sir, you are mistaken.

Hale. Twenty-six time in seventeen month, sir. I must call that rare. Will you tell me why you are so absent?

Proctor. Mr. Hale, I never knew I must account to that man for I come to church or stay at home. My wife were sick this winter.

Hale. So I am told. But you, Mister, why could you not come alone?

Proctor. I surely did come when I could, and when I could not I prayed in this house.

Hale. Mr. Proctor, your house is not a church; your theology must tell you that.

Proctor. It does, sir, it does; and it tells me that a minister may pray to God without he have golden candlesticks upon the altar.

Hale. What golden candlesticks?

Proctor. Since we built the church there were pewter candlesticks upon the altar; Francis Nurse made them, y'know, and a sweeter hand never touched the metal. But Parris came, and for twenty week he preach nothin' but golden candlesticks until he had them. I labor the earth from dawn of day to blink of night, and I tell you true, when I look to heaven and see my money glaring at his elbows—it hurt my prayer, sir, it hurt my prayer. I think, sometimes, the man dreams cathedrals, not clapboard meetin' houses.

Hale [*thinks, then*]. And yet, Mister, a Christian on Sabbath Day must be in church. [*Pause.*] Tell me—you have three children?

Proctor. Aye. Boys.

Hale. How comes it that only two are baptized?

Proctor [*starts to speak, then stops, then, as though unable to restrain this*]. I like it not that Mr. Parris should lay his hand upon my baby. I see no light of God in that man. I'll not conceal it.

Hale. I must say it, Mr. Proctor; that is not for you to decide. The man's ordained, therefore the light of God is in him.

Proctor [*flushed with resentment but trying to smile*]. What's your suspicion, Mr. Hale?

Hale. No, no, I have no—

Proctor. I nailed the roof upon the church, I hung the door—

Hale. Oh, did you! That's a good sign, then.

Proctor. It may be I have been too quick to bring the man to book, but you cannot think we ever desired the destruction of religion. I think that's in your mind, is it not?

Hale [*not altogether giving way*]. I—have—there is a softness in your record, sir, a softness.

Elizabeth. I think, maybe, we have been too hard with Mr. Parris. I think so. But sure we never loved the Devil here.

Hale [*nods, deliberating this. Then, with the voice of one administering a secret test*]. Do you know your Commandments, Elizabeth?

Elizabeth [*without hesitation, even eagerly*]. I surely do. There be no mark of blame upon my life, Mr. Hale. I am a covenanted Christian woman.

Hale. And you, Mister?

Proctor [*a trifle unsteadily*]. I—am sure I do, sir.

Hale [*glances at her open face, then at* JOHN, *then*]. Let you repeat them, if you will.

Proctor. The Commandments.

Hale. Aye.

Proctor [*looking off, beginning to sweat*]. Thou shalt not kill.

Hale. Aye.

Proctor [*counting on his fingers*]. Thou shalt not steal. Thou shalt not covet thy neighbor's goods, nor make unto thee any graven image. Thou shalt not take the name of the Lord in vain; thou shalt have no other gods before me. [*With some hesitation.*] Thou shalt remember the Sabbath Day and keep it holy. [*Pause. Then.*] Thou shalt honor thy father and mother. Thou shalt not bear false witness. [*He is stuck. He counts back on his fingers, knowing one is missing.*] Thou shalt not make unto thee any graven image.

Hale. You have said that twice, sir.

Proctor [*lost*]. Aye. [*He is flailing for it.*]

Elizabeth [*delicately*]. Adultery, John.

Proctor [*as though a secret arrow had pained his heart*]. Aye. [*Trying to grin it away—to* HALE.] You see, sir, between the two of us we do know them all. [HALE *only looks at* PROCTOR, *deep in his attempt to define this man.* PROCTOR *grows more uneasy.*] I think it be a small fault.

Hale. Theology, sir, is a fortress; no crack in a fortress may be accounted small. [*He rises; he seems worried now. He paces a little, in deep thought.*]

Proctor. There be no love for Satan in this house, Mister.

Hale. I pray it, I pray it dearly. [*He looks to both of them, an attempt at a smile on his face, but his misgivings are clear.*] Well, then—I'll bid you good night.

Elizabeth [*unable to restrain herself*]. Mr. Hale. [*He turns.*] I do think you are suspecting me somewhat? Are you not?

Hale [*obviously disturbed—and evasive*]. Goody Proctor, I do not judge you. My duty is to add what I may to the godly wisdom of the court. I pray you both good health and good fortune. [*To* JOHN.] Good night, sir. [*He starts out.*]

Elizabeth [*with a note of desperation*]. I think you must tell him, John.

Hale. What's that?

Elizabeth [*restraining a call*]. Will you tell him?

[*Slight pause.* HALE *looks questioningly at* JOHN.]

Proctor [*with difficulty*]. I—I have no witness and cannot prove it, except my word be taken. But I know the children's sickness had naught to do with witchcraft.

Hale [*stopped, struck*]. Naught to do—?

Proctor. Mr. Parris discovered them sportin' in the woods. They were startled and took sick. ·

[*Pause.*]

Hale. Who told you this?
Proctor [*hesitates, then*]. Abigail Williams.
Hale. Abigail!
Proctor. Aye.
Hale [*his eyes wide*]. Abigail Williams told you it had naught to do with
  witchcraft!
Proctor. She told me the day you came, sir.
Hale [*suspiciously*]. Why—why did you keep this?
Proctor. I never knew until tonight that the world is gone daft with this
  nonsense.
Hale. Nonsense! Mister, I have myself examined Tituba, Sarah Good, and
  numerous others that have confessed to dealing with the Devil. They have
  confessed it.
Proctor. And why not, if they must hang for denyin' it? There are them that will
  swear to anything before they'll hang; have you never thought of that?
Hale. I have. I—I have indeed. [*It is his own suspicion, but he resists it. He
  glances at* ELIZABETH, *then at* JOHN.] And you—would you testify to this in
  court?
Proctor. I—had not reckoned with goin' into court. But if I must I will.
Hale. Do you falter here?
Proctor. I falter nothing, but I may wonder if my story will be credited in such a
  court. I do wonder on it, when such a steady-minded minister as you will
  suspicion such a woman that never lied, and cannot, and the world knows she
  cannot! I may falter somewhat, Mister; I am no fool.
Hale [*quietly—it has impressed him*]. Proctor, let you open with me now, for I
  have a rumor that troubles me. It's said you hold no belief that there may even
  be witches in the world. Is that true, sir?
Proctor [*he knows this is critical, and is striving against his disgust with* HALE *and
  with himself for even answering*]. I know not what I have said, I may have
  said it. I have wondered if there be witches in the world—although I cannot
  believe they come among us now.
Hale. Then you do not believe—
Proctor. I have no knowledge of it; the Bible speaks of witches, and I will not
  deny them.
Hale. And you, woman?
Elizabeth. I—I cannot believe it.
Hale [*shocked*]. You cannot!
Proctor. Elizabeth, you bewilder him!
Elizabeth [*to* HALE]. I cannot think the Devil may own a woman's soul, Mr.
  Hale, when she keeps an upright way, as I have. I am a good woman, I know it;
  and if you believe I may do only good work in the world, and yet be secretly
  bound to Satan, then I must tell you, sir, I do not believe it.
Hale. But, woman, you do believe there are witches in—
Elizabeth. If you think that I am one, then I say there are none.
Hale. You surely do not fly against the Gospel, the Gospel—

Proctor.   She believe in the Gospel, every word!

Elizabeth.   Question Abigail Williams about the Gospel, not myself!

[HALE *stares at her.*]

Proctor.   She do not mean to doubt the Gospel, sir, you cannot think it. This be a Christian house, sir, a Christian house.

Hale.   God keep you both; let the third child be quickly baptized, and go you without fail each Sunday in to Sabbath prayer; and keep a solemn, quiet way among you. I think—

[GILES COREY *appears in doorway.*]

Giles.   John!

Proctor.   Giles! What's the matter?

Giles.   They take my wife.

[FRANCIS NURSE *enters.*]

Giles.   And his Rebecca!

Proctor [*to Francis*].   Rebecca's in the *jail!*

Francis.   Aye, Cheever come and take her in his wagon. We've only now come from the jail, and they'll not even let us in to see them.

Elizabeth.   They've surely gone wild now, Mr. Hale!

Francis [*going to* HALE].   Reverend Hale! Can you not speak to the Deputy Governor? I'm sure he mistakes these people—

Hale.   Pray calm yourself, Mr. Nurse.

Francis.   My wife is the very brick and mortar of the church, Mr. Hale [*indicating* GILES] and Martha Corey, there cannot be a woman closer yet to God than Martha.

Hale.   How is Rebecca charged, Mr. Nurse?

Francis [*with a mocking, half-hearted laugh*].   For murder, she's charged! [*Mockingly quoting the warrant.*] "For the marvelous and supernatural murder of Goody Putnam's babies." What am I to do, Mr. Hale?

Hale [*turns from* FRANCIS, *deeply troubled, then*].   Believe me, Mr. Nurse, if Rebecca Nurse be tainted, then nothing's left to stop the whole green world from burning. Let you rest upon the justice of the court; the court will send her home, I know it.

Francis.   You cannot mean she will be tried in court!

Hale [*pleading*].   Nurse, though our hearts break, we cannot flinch; these are new times, sir. There is a misty plot afoot so subtle we should be criminal to cling to old respects and ancient friendships. I have seen too many frightful proofs in court—the Devil is alive in Salem, and we dare not quail to follow wherever the accusing finger points!

Proctor [*angered*].   How may such a woman murder children?

Hale [*in great pain*].   Man, remember, until an hour before the Devil fell, God thought him beautiful in Heaven.

Giles.   I never said my wife were a witch, Mr. Hale; I only said she were reading books!

Hale.   Mr. Corey, exactly what complaint were made on your wife?

Giles. That bloody mongrel Walcott charge her. Y'see, he buy a pig of my wife four or five year ago, and the pig died soon after. So he come dancin' in for his money back. So my Martha, she says to him, "Walcott, if you haven't the wit to feed a pig properly, you'll not live to own many," she says. Now he goes to court and claims that from that day to this he cannot keep a pig alive for more than four weeks because my Martha bewitch them with her books!

[*Enter* EZEKIEL CHEEVER. *A shocked silence.*]

Cheever. Good evening to you, Proctor.
Proctor. Why, Mr. Cheever. Good evening.
Cheever. Good evening, all. Good evening, Mr. Hale.
Proctor. I hope you come not on business of the court.
Cheever. I do, Proctor, aye. I am clerk of the court now, y'know.

[*Enter* MARSHAL HERRICK, *a man in his early thirties, who is somewhat shame-faced at the moment.*]

Giles. It's a pity, Ezekiel, that an honest tailor might have gone to Heaven must burn in Hell. You'll burn for this, do you know it?
Cheever. You know yourself I must do as I'm told. You surely know that, Giles. And I'd as lief you'd not be sending me to Hell. I like not the sound of it, I tell you; I like not the sound of it. [*He fears* PROCTOR, *but starts to reach inside his coat.*] Now believe me, Proctor, how heavy be the law, all its tonnage I do carry on my back tonight. [*He takes out a warrant.*] I have a warrant for your wife.
Proctor [*to* HALE]. You said she were not charged!
Hale. I know nothin' of it. [*To* CHEEVER.] When were she charged?
Cheever. I am given sixteen warrant tonight, sir, and she is one.
Proctor. Who charged her?
Cheeever. Why, Abigail Williams charge her.
Proctor. On what proof, what proof?
Cheever [*looking about the room*]. Mr. Proctor, I have little time. The court bid me search your house, but I like not to search a house. So will you hand me any poppets that your wife may keep here?
Proctor. Poppets?
Elizabeth. I never kept no poppets, not since I were a girl.
Cheever [*embarrassed, glancing toward the mantel where sits* MARY WARREN'S *poppet*]. I spy a poppet, Goody Proctor.
Elizabeth. Oh! [*Going for it.*] Why, this is Mary's.
Cheever [*shyly*]. Would you please to give it to me?
Elizabeth [*handing it to him, asks* HALE]. Has the court discovered a text in poppets now?
Cheever [*carefully holding the poppet*]. Do you keep any others in this house?
Proctor. No, nor this one either till tonight. What signifies a poppet?
Cheever. Why, a poppet [*he gingerly turns the poppet over*] a poppet may signify— Now, woman, will you please to come with me?
Proctor. She will not! [*To* ELIZABETH.] Fetch Mary here.
Cheever [*ineptly reaching toward* ELIZABETH]. No, no, I am forbid to leave her from my sight.

Proctor [*pushing his arm away*]. You'll leave her out of sight and out of mind, Mister. Fetch Mary, Elizabeth. [ELIZABETH *goes upstairs.*]

Hale. What signifies a poppet, Mr. Cheever?

Cheever [*turning the poppet over in his hands*]. Why, they say it may signify that she— [*he has lifted the poppet's skirt, and his eyes widen in astonished fear.*] Why, this, this—

Proctor [*reaching for the poppet*]. What's there?

Cheever. Why— [*He draws out a long needle from the poppet*] it is a needle! Herrick, Herrick, it is a needle!

[HERRICK *comes toward him.*]

Proctor [*angrily, bewildered*]. And what signifies a needle!

Cheever [*his hands shaking*]. Why, this go hard with her, Proctor, this—I had my doubts, Proctor, I had my doubts, but here's calamity. [*To* HALE, *showing the needle.*] You see it, sir, it is a needle!

Hale. Why? What meanin' has it?

Cheever [*wide-eyed, trembling*]. The girl, the Williams girl, Abigail Williams, sir. She sat to dinner in Reverend Parris's house tonight, and without word nor warnin' she falls to the floor. Like a struck beast, he says, and screamed a scream that a bull would weep to hear. And he goes to save her, and, stuck two inches in the flesh of her belly, he draw a needle out. And demandin' of her how she come to be so stabbed, she [*to* PROCTOR *now*] testify it were your wife's familiar spirit pushed it in.

Proctor. Why, she done it herself! [*To* HALE.] I hope you're not takin' this for proof, Mister!

[HALE, *struck by the proof, is silent.*]

Cheever. 'Tis hard proof! [*To* HALE.] I find here a poppet Goody Proctor keeps. I have found it, sir. And in the belly of the poppet a needle's stuck. I tell you true, Proctor, I never warranted to see such proof of Hell, and I bid you obstruct me not, for—

[*Enter* ELIZABETH *with* MARY WARREN. PROCTOR, *seeing* MARY WARREN, *draws her by the arm to* HALE.]

Proctor. Here now! Mary, how did this poppet come into my house?

Mary Warren [*frightened for herself, her voice very small*]. What poppet's that, sir?

Proctor [*impatiently, points at the doll in* CHEEVER's *hand*]. This poppet, this poppet.

Mary Warren [*evasively, looking at it*]. Why, I—I think it is mine.

Proctor. It is your poppet, is it not?

Mary Warren [*not understanding the direction of this*]. It—is, sir.

Proctor. And how did it come into this house?

Mary Warrren [*glancing about at the avid faces*]. Why—I made it in the court, sir, and—give it to Goody Proctor tonight.

Proctor [*to* HALE]. Now, sir—do you have it?

Hale. Mary Warren, a needle have been found inside this poppet.

Mary Warren [*bewildered*].   Why, I meant no harm by it, sir.

Proctor [*quickly*].   You stuck that needle in yourself?

Mary Warren.   I—I believe I did, sir, I—

Proctor [*to* HALE].   What say you now?

Hale [*watching* MARY WARREN *closely*].   Child, you are certain this be your
   natural memory? May it be, perhaps, that someone conjures you even now to
   say this?

Mary Warren.   Conjures me? Why, no, sir, I am entirely myself, I think. Let you
   ask Susanna Walcott—she saw me sewin' it in court. [*Or better still.*] Ask
   Abby, Abby sat beside me when I made it.

Proctor [*to* HALE, *of* CHEEVER].   Bid him begone. Your mind is surely settled
   now. Bid him out, Mr. Hale.

Elizabeth.   What signifies a needle?

Hale.   Mary—you charge a cold and cruel murder on Abigail.

Mary Warren.   Murder! I charge no—

Hale.   Abigail were stabbed tonight; a needle were found stuck into her belly—

Elizabeth.   And she charges me?

Hale.   Aye.

Elizabeth [*her breath knocked out*].   Why—! The girl is murder! She must be
   ripped out of the world!

Cheever [*pointing at* ELIZABETH].   You've heard that, sir! Ripped out of the
   world! Herrick, you heard it!

Proctor [*suddenly snatching the warrant out of* CEHEVER's *hands*].   Out with
   you.

Cheever.   Proctor, you dare not touch the warrant.

Proctor [*ripping the warrant*].   Out with you!

Cheever.   You've ripped the Deputy Governor's warrant, man!

Proctor.   Damn the Deputy Governor! Out of my house!

Hale.   Now, Proctor, Proctor!

Proctor.   Get y'gone with them! You are a broken minister.

Hale.   Proctor, if she is innocent, the court—

Proctor.   If *she* is innocent! Why do you never wonder if Parris be innocent, or
   Abigail? Is the accuser always holy now? Were they born this morning as clean
   as God's fingers? I'll tell you what's walking Salem—vengeance is walking
   Salem. We are what we always were in Salem, but now the little crazy children
   are jangling the keys of the kingdom, and common vengeance writes the law!
   This warrant's vengeance! I'll not give my wife to vengeance!

Elizabeth.   I'll go, John—

Proctor.   You will not go!

Herrick.   I have nine men outside. You cannot keep her. The law binds me, John,
   I cannot budge.

Proctor [*to* HALE, *ready to break him*].   Will you see her taken?

Hale.   Proctor, the court is just—

Proctor.   Pontius Pilate! God will not let you wash your hands of this!

Elizabeth.   John—I think I must go with them. [*He cannot bear to look at her.*]
   Mary, there is bread enough for the morning; you will bake, in the afternoon.
   Help Mr. Proctor as you were his daughter—you owe me that, and much more.
   [*She is fighting her weeping. To* PROCTOR.] When the children wake, speak
   nothing of witchcraft—it will frighten them. [*She cannot go on.*]

Proctor. I will bring you home. I will bring you soon.

Elizabeth. Oh, John, bring me soon!

Proctor. I will fall like an ocean on that court! Fear nothing, Elizabeth.

Elizabeth [*with great fear*]. I will fear nothing. [*She looks about the room, as though to fix it in her mind.*] Tell the children I have gone to visit someone sick.

[*She walks out the door,* HERRICK *and* CHEEVER *behind her. For a moment,* PROCTOR *watches from the doorway. The clank of chain is heard.*]

Proctor. Herrick! Herrick, don't chain her! [*He rushes out the door. From outside.*] Damn you, man, you will not chain her! Off with them! I'll not have it! I will not have her chained!

[*There are other men's voices against his.* HALE, *in a fever of guilt and uncertainty, turns from the door to avoid the sight;* MARY WARREN *bursts into tears and sits weeping.* GILES COREY *calls to* HALE.]

Giles. And yet silent, minister? It is fraud, you know it is fraud! What keeps you, man?

[PROCTOR *is half braced, half pushed into the room by two deputies and* HERRICK.]

Proctor. I'll pay you, Herrick, I will surely pay you!

Herrick [*panting*]. In God's name, John, I cannot help myself. I must chain them all. Now let you keep inside this house till I am gone! [*He goes out with his deputies.*]

[PROCTOR *stands there, gulping air. Horses and a wagon creaking are heard.*]

Hale [*in great uncertainty*]. Mr. Proctor—

Proctor. Out of my sight!

Hale. Charity, Proctor, charity. What I have heard in her favor, I will not fear to testify in court. God help me, I cannot judge her guilty or innocent—I know not. Only this consider: the world goes mad, and it profit nothing you should lay the cause to the vengeance of a little girl.

Proctor. You are a coward! Though you be ordained in God's own tears, you are a coward now!

Hale. Proctor, I cannot think God be provoked so grandly by such a petty cause. The jails are packed—our greatest judges sit in Salem now—and hangin's promised. Man, we must look to cause proportionate. Were there murder done, perhaps, and never brought to light? Abomination? Some secret blasphemy that stinks to Heaven? Think on cause, man, and let you help me to discover it. For there's your way, believe it, there is your only way, when such confusion strikes upon the world. [*He goes to* GILES *and* FRANCIS.] Let you counsel among yourselves; think on your village and what may have drawn from heaven such thundering wrath upon you all. I shall pray God open up our eyes.

[HALE *goes out.*]

Francis [*struck by* HALE'S *mood*]. I never heard no murder done in Salem.

Proctor [*he has been reached by* HALE'S *words*]. Leave me, Francis, leave me.

Giles [*shaken*].   John—tell me, are we lost?

Proctor.   Go home now, Giles. We'll speak on it tomorrow.

Giles.   Let you think on it. We'll come early, eh?

Proctor.   Aye. Go now, Giles.

Giles.   Good night, then.

[GILES COREY *goes out. After a moment.*]

Mary Warren [*in a fearful squeak of a voice*].   Mr. Proctor, very likely they'll let her come home once they're given proper evidence.

Proctor.   You're coming to the court with me, Mary. You will tell it in the court.

Mary Warren.   I cannot charge murder on Abigail.

Proctor [*moving menacingly toward her*].   You will tell the court how that poppet come here and who stuck the needle in.

Mary Warren.   She'll kill me for sayin' that! [PROCTOR *continues toward her.*] Abby'll charge lechery on you, Mr. Proctor!

Proctor [*halting*].   She's told you!

Mary Warren.   I have known it, sir. She'll ruin you with it, I know she will.

Proctor [*hesitating, and with deep hatred of himself*].   Good. Then her saintliness is done with. [MARY *backs from him.*] We will slide together into our pit; you will tell the court what you know.

Mary Warren [*in terror*].   I cannot, they'll turn on me—

[PROCTOR *strides and catches her, and she is repeating, "I cannot, I cannot!"*]

Proctor.   My wife will never die for me! I will bring your guts into your mouth but that goodness will not die for me!

Mary Warren [*struggling to escape him*].   I cannot do it, I cannot!

Proctor [*grasping her by the throat as though he would strangle her*].   Make your peace with it! Now Hell and Heaven grapple on our backs, and all our old pretense is ripped away—make your peace! [*He throws her to the floor, where she sobs, "I cannot, I cannot . . ." And now, half to himself, staring, and turning to the open door.*] Peace. It is a providence, and no great change; we are only what we always were, but naked now. [*He walks as though toward a great horror, facing the open sky.*] Aye, naked! And the wind, God's icy wind, will blow!

[*And she is over and over again sobbing, "I cannot, I cannot, I cannot," as*]

[*The Curtain Falls*]

Act III

The vestry room of the Salem meeting house, now serving as the anteroom of the General Court.

[*As the curtain rises, the room is empty, but for sunlight pouring through two high windows in the back wall. The room is solemn, even forbidding. Heavy beams jut out, boards of random widths make up the walls. At the right are two doors leading into the meeting house proper, where the court is being held. At the left another door leads outside.*

There is a plain bench at the left, and another at the right. In the center a rather long meeting table, with stools and a considerable armchair snugged up to it.

Through the partitioning wall at the right we hear a prosecutor's voice, JUDGE HATHORNE'S, *asking a question; then a woman's voice,* MARTHA COREY'S, *replying.*]

Hathorne's Voice.   Now, Martha Corey, there is abundant evidence in our hands to show that you have given yourself to the reading of fortunes. Do you deny it?

Martha Corey's Voice.   I am innocent to a witch. I know not what a witch is.

Hathorne's Voice.   How do you know, then, that you are not a witch?

Martha Corey's Voice.   If I were, I would know it.

Hathorne's Voice.   Why do you hurt these children?

Martha Corey's Voice.   I do not hurt them. I scorn it!

Giles' Voice [*roaring*].   I have evidence for the court!

[*Voices of townspeople rise in excitement.*]

Danforth's Voice.   You will keep your seat!

Giles' Voice.   Thomas Putnam is reaching out for land!

Danforth's Voice.   Remove that man, Marshal!

Giles' Voice.   You're hearing lies, lies!

[*A roaring goes up from the people.*]

Hathorne's Voice.   Arrest him, excellency!

Giles' Voice.   I have evidence. Why will you not hear my evidence?

[*The door opens and* GILES *is half carried into the vestry room by* HERRICK.]

Giles.   Hands off, damn you, let me go!

Herrick.   Giles, Giles!

Giles.   Out of my way, Herrick! I bring evidence—

Herrick.   You cannot go in there, Giles; it's a court!

[*Enter* HALE *from the court.*]

Hale.   Pray be calm a moment.

Giles.   You, Mr. Hale, go in there and demand I speak.

Hale.   A moment, sir, a moment.

Giles.   They'll be hangin' my wife!

[JUDGE HATHORNE *enters. He is in his sixties, a bitter, remorseless Salem judge.*]

Hathorne.   How do you dare come roarin' into this court! Are you gone daft, Corey?

Giles.   You're not a Boston judge, Hathorne. You'll not call me daft!

[*Enter* DEPUTY GOVERNOR DANFORTH *and, behind him,* EZEKIEL CHEEVER *and* PARRIS. *On his appearance, silence falls.* DANFORTH *is a grave man in his sixties, of some humor and sophistication that does not, however, interfere with an exact loyalty to his position and his cause. He comes down to* GILES, *who awaits his wrath.*]

Danforth [*looking directly at* GILES]. Who is this man?
Parris. Giles Corey, sir, and a more contentious—
Giles [*to* PARRIS]. I am asked the question, and I am old enough to answer it! [*To* DANFORTH, *who impresses him and to whom he smiles through his strain.*] My name is Corey, sir, Giles Corey. I have six hundred acres, and timber in addition. It is my wife you be condemning now. [*He indicates the courtroom.*]
Danforth. And how do you imagine to help her cause with such contemptuous riot? Now be gone. Your old age alone keeps you out of jail for this.
Giles [*beginning to plead*]. They be tellin' lies about my wife, sir, I—
Danforth. Do you take it upon yourself to determine what this court shall believe and what it shall set aside?
Giles. Your Excellency, we mean no disrespect for—
Danforth. Disrespect indeed! It is disruption, Mister. This is the highest court of the supreme government of this province, do you know it?
Giles [*beginning to weep*]. Your Excellency, I only said she were readin' books, sir, and they come and take her out of my house for—
Danforth [*mystified*]. Books! What books?
Giles [*through helpless sobs*]. It is my third wife, sir; I never had no wife that be so taken with books, and I thought to find the cause of it, d'y'see, but it were no witch I blamed her for. [*He is openly weeping.*] I have broke charity with the woman, I have broke charity with her. [*He covers his face, ashamed.* DANFORTH *is respectfully silent.*]
Hale. Excellency, he claims hard evidence for his wife's defense. I think that in all justice you must—
Danforth. Then let him submit his evidence in proper affidavit. You are certainly aware of our procedure here, Mr. Hale. [*To* HERRICK.] Clear this room.
Herrick. Come now, Giles. [*He gently pushes* COREY *out.*]
Francis. We are desperate, sir; we come here three days now and cannot be heard.
Danforth. Who is this man?
Francis. Francis Nurse, Your Excellency.
Hale. His wife's Rebecca that were condemned this morning.
Danforth. Indeed! I am amazed to find you in such uproar. I have only good report of your character, Mr. Nurse.
Hathorne. I think they must both be arrested in contempt, sir.
Danforth [*to* FRANCIS]. Let you write your plea, and in due time I will—
Francis. Excellency, we have proof for your eyes; God forbid you shut them to it. The girls, sir, the girls are frauds.
Danforth. What's that?
Francis. We have proof of it, sir. They are all deceiving you.

[DANFORTH *is shocked, but studying* FRANCIS.]

Hathorne. This is contempt, sir, contempt!
Danforth. Peace, Judge Hathorne. Do you know who I am, Mr. Nurse?

Francis. I surely do, sir, and I think you must be a wise judge to be what you are.

Danforth. And do you know that near to four hundred are in the jails from Marblehead to Lynn, and upon my signature?

Francis. I—

Danforth. And seventy-two condemned to hang by that signature?

Francis. Excellency, I never thought to say it to such a weighty judge, but you are deceived.

[*Enter* GILES COREY *from left. All turn to see as he beckons in* MARY WARREN *with* PROCTOR. MARY *is keeping her eyes to the ground;* PROCTOR *has her elbow as though she were near collapse.*]

Parris [*on seeing her, in shock*]. Mary Warren! [*He goes directly to bend close to her face.*] What are you about here?

Proctor [*pressing* PARRIS *away from her with a gentle but firm motion of protectiveness*]. She would speak with the Deputy Governor.

Danforth [*shocked by this, turns to* HERRICK]. Did you not tell me Mary Warren were sick in bed?

Herrick. She were, Your Honor. When I go to fetch her to the court last week, she said she were sick.

Giles. She has been strivin' with her soul all week, Your Honor; she comes now to tell the truth of this to you.

Danforth. Who is this?

Proctor. John Proctor, sir. Elizabeth Proctor is my wife.

Parris. Beware this man, Your Excellency, this man is mischief.

Hale [*excitedly*] I think you must hear the girl, sir, she—

Danforth [*who has become very interested in* MARY WARREN *and only raises a hand toward* HALE]. Peace. What would you tell us, Mary Warren?

[PROCTOR *looks at her, but she cannot speak.*]

Proctor. She never saw no spirits, sir.

Danforth [*with great alarm and surprise, to* MARY]. Never saw no spirits!

Giles [*eagerly*]. Never.

Proctor [*reaching into his jacket*]. She has signed a deposition, sir—

Danforth [*instantly*]. No, no, I accept no depositions. [*He is rapidly calculating this; he turns from her to* PROCTOR.] Tell me, Mr. Proctor, have you given out this story in the village?

Proctor. We have not.

Parris. They've come to overthrow the court, sir! This man is—

Danforth. I pray you, Mr. Parris. Do you know, Mr. Proctor, that the entire contention of the state in these trials is that the voice of Heaven is speaking through the children?

Proctor. I know that, sir.

Danforth [*thinks, staring at* PROCTOR, *then turns to* MARY WARREN]. And you, Mary Warren, how came you to cry out people for sending their spirits against you?

Mary Warren. It were pretense, sir.

Danforth. I cannot hear you.

Proctor. It were pretense, she says.

Danforth. Ah? And the other girls? Susanna Walcott, and—the others? They are also pretending?

Mary Warren. Aye, sir.

Danforth [*wide-eyed*]. Indeed. [*Pause. He is baffled by this. He turns to study* PROCTOR's *face.*]

Parris [*in a sweat*]. Excellency, you surely cannot think to let so vile a lie be spread in open court.

Danforth. Indeed not, but it strike hard upon me that she will dare come here with such a tale. Now, Mr. Proctor, before I decide whether I shall hear you or not, it is my duty to tell you this. We burn a hot fire here; it melts down all concealment.

Proctor. I know that, sir.

Danforth. Let me continue. I understand well, a husband's tenderness may drive him to extravagance in defense of a wife. Are you certain in your conscience, Mister, that your evidence is the truth?

Proctor. It is. And you will surely know it.

Danforth. And you thought to declare this revelation in the open court before the public?

Proctor. I thought I would, aye—with your permission.

Danforth [*his eyes narrowing*]. Now, sir, what is your purpose in so doing?

Proctor. Why, I—I would free my wife, sir.

Danforth. There lurks nowhere in your heart, nor hidden in your spirit, any desire to undermine this court?

Proctor [*with the faintest faltering*]. Why, no, sir.

Cheever [*clears his throat, awakening*]. I— Your Excellency.

Danforth. Mr. Cheever.

Cheever. I think it be my duty, sir— [*Kindly, to* PROCTOR] You'll not deny it, John. [*To* DANFORTH] When we come to take his wife, he damned the court and ripped your warrant.

Parris. Now you have it!

Danforth. He did that, Mr. Hale?

Hale [*takes a breath*]. Aye, he did.

Proctor. It were a temper, sir. I knew not what I did.

Danforth [*studying him*]. Mr. Proctor.

Proctor. Aye, sir.

Danforth [*straight into his eyes*]. Have you ever seen the Devil?

Proctor. No, sir.

Danforth. You are in all respects a Gospel Christian?

Proctor. I am, sir.

Parris. Such a Christian that will not come to church but once in a month!

Danforth [*restrained—he is curious*]. Not come to church?

Proctor. I—I have no love for Mr. Parris. It is no secret. But God I surely love.

Cheever. He plow on Sunday, sir.

Danforth. Plow on Sunday!

Cheever [*apologetically*]. I think it be evidence, John. I am an official of the court, I cannot keep it.

Proctor. I—I have once or twice plowed on Sunday. I have three children, sir, and until last year my land give little.

Giles. You'll find other Christians that do plow on Sunday if the truth be known.

Hale. Your Honor, I cannot think you may judge the man on such evidence.

Danforth. I judge nothing. [*Pause. He keeps watching* PROCTOR, *who tries to meet his gaze.*] I tell you straight, Mister—I have seen marvels in this court. I have seen people choked before my eyes by spirits; I have seen them stuck by pins and slashed by daggers. I have until this moment not the slightest reason to suspect that the children may be deceiving me. Do you understand my meaning?

Proctor. Excellency, does it not strike upon you that so many of these women have lived so long with such upright reputation, and—

Parris. Do you read the Gospel, Mr. Proctor?

Proctor. I read the Gospel.

Parris. I think not, or you should surely know that Cain were an upright man, and yet he did kill Abel.

Proctor. Aye, God tells us that. [*To* DANFORTH.] But who tells us Rebecca Nurse murdered seven babies by sending out her spirit on them? It is the children only, and this one will swear she lied to you.

[DANFORTH *considers, then beckons* HATHORNE *to him.* HATHORNE *leans in, and he speaks in his ear.* HATHORNE *nods.*]

Hathorne. Aye, she's the one.

Danforth. Mr. Proctor, this morning, your wife send me a claim in which she states that she is pregnant now.

Proctor. My wife pregnant!

Danforth. There be no sign of it—we have examined her body.

Proctor. But if she say she is pregnant, then she must be! That woman will never lie, Mr. Danforth.

Danforth. She will not?

Proctor. Never, sir, never.

Danforth. We have thought it too convenient to be credited. However, if I should tell you now that I will let her be kept another month; and if she begin to show her natural signs, you shall have her living yet another year until she is delivered—what say you to that? [JOHN PROCTOR *is struck silent.*] Come now. You say your only purpose is to save your wife. Good, then, she is saved at least this year, and a year is long. What say you, sir? It is done now. [*In conflict,* PROCTOR *glances at* FRANCIS *and* GILES.] Will you drop this charge?

Proctor. I—I think I cannot.

Danforth [*now an almost imperceptible hardness in his voice*]. Then your purpose is somewhat larger.

Parris. He's come to overthrow this court, Your Honor!

Proctor. These are my friends. Their wives are also accused—

Danforth [*with a sudden briskness of manner*]. I judge you not, sir. I am ready to hear your evidence.

Proctor. I come not to hurt the court; I only—

Danforth [*cutting him off*]. Marshal, go into the court and bid Judge Stoughton and Judge Sewall declare recess for one hour. And let them go to the tavern, if they will. All witnesses and prisoners are to be kept in the building.

Herrick. Aye, sir. [*Very deferentially.*] If I may say it, sir, I know this man all my life. It is a good man, sir.

Danforth [*it is the reflection on himself he resents*]. I am sure of it, Marshal. [HERRICK *nods, then goes out.*] Now, what deposition do you have for us, Mr. Proctor? And I beg you be clear, open as the sky, and honest.

Proctor [*as he takes out several papers*]. I am no lawyer, so I'll—

Danforth. The pure in heart need no lawyers. Proceed as you will.

Proctor [*handing* DANFORTH *a paper*]. Will you read this first, sir? It's a sort of testament. The people signing it declare their good opinion of Rebecca, and my wife, and Martha Corey. [DANFORTH *looks down at the paper.*]

Parris [*to enlist* DANFORTH'*s sarcasm*]. Their good opinion! [*But* DANFORTH *goes on reading, and* PROCTOR *is heartened.*]

Proctor. These are all landholding farmers, members of the church. [*Delicately, trying to point out a paragraph.*] If you'll notice, sir—they've known the women many years and never saw no sign they had dealings with the Devil.

[PARRIS *nervously moves over and reads over* DANFORTH'*s shoulder.*]

Danforth [*glancing down a long list*]. How many names are here?

Francis. Ninety-one, Your Excellency.

Parris [*sweating*]. These people should be summoned. [DANFORTH *looks up at him questioningly.*] For questioning.

Francis [*trembling with anger*]. Mr. Danforth, I gave them all my word no harm would come to them for signing this.

Parris. This is a clear attack upon the court!

Hale [*to* PARRIS, *trying to contain himself*]. Is every defense an attack upon the court? Can no one—?

Parris. All innocent and Christian people are happy for the courts in Salem! These people are gloomy for it. [*To* DANFORTH *directly.*] And I think you will want to know, from each and every one of them, what discontents them with you!

Hathorne. I think they ought to be examined, sir.

Danforth. It is not necessarily an attack, I think. Yet—

Francis. These are all covenanted Christians, sir.

Danforth. Then I am sure they may have nothing to fear. [*Hands* CHEEVER *the paper.*] Mr. Cheever, have warrants drawn for all of these—arrest for examination. [*To* PROCTOR.] Now, Mister, what other information do you have for us? [FRANCIS *is still standing, horrified.*] You may sit, Mr. Nurse.

Francis. I have brought trouble on these people; I have—

Danforth. No, old man, you have not hurt these people if they are of good conscience. But you must understand, sir, that a person is either with this court or he must be counted against it, there be no road between. This is a sharp time, now, a precise time—we live no longer in the dusky afternoon when evil mixed itself with good and befuddled the world. Now, by God's grace, the shining sun is up, and them that fear not light will surely praise it. I hope you will be one of those. [MARY WARREN *suddenly sobs.*] She's not hearty, I see.

Proctor. No, she's not, sir. [*To* MARY, *bending to her, holding her hand, quietly.*] Now remember what the angel Raphael said to the boy Tobias. Remember it.

Mary Warren [*hardly audible*]. Aye.

Proctor. "Do that which is good, and no harm shall come to thee."

Mary Warren. Aye.

Danforth. Come, man, we wait you.

[MARSHAL HERRICK *returns, and takes his post at the door.*]

Giles. John, my deposition, give him mine.

Proctor. Aye. [*He hands* DANFORTH *another paper.*] This is Mr. Corey's deposition.

Danforth. Oh? [*He looks down at it. Now* HATHORNE *comes behind him and reads with him.*]

Hathorne [*suspiciously*]. What lawyer drew this, Corey?

Giles. You know I never hired a lawyer in my life, Hathorne.

Danforth [*finishing the reading*]. It is very well phrased. My compliments. Mr. Parris, if Mr. Putnam is in the court, will you bring him in? [HATHORNE *takes the deposition, and walks to the window with it.* PARRIS *goes into the court.*] You have no legal training, Mr. Corey?

Giles [*very pleased*]. I have the best, sir—I am thirty-three time in court in my life. And always plaintiff, too.

Danforth. Oh, then you're much put-upon.

Giles. I am never put-upon; I know my rights, sir, and I will have them. You know, your father tried a case of mine—might be thirty-five year ago, I think.

Danforth. Indeed.

Giles. He never spoke to you of it?

Danforth. No, I cannot recall it.

Giles. That's strange, he give me nine pound damages. He were a fair judge, your father. Y'see, I had a white mare that time, and this fellow come to borrow the mare— [*Enter* PARRIS *with* THOMAS PUTNAM. *When he sees* PUTNAM, GILES' *ease goes; he is hard.*] Aye, there he is.

Danforth. Mr. Putnam, I have here an accusation by Mr. Corey against you. He states that you coldly prompted your daughter to cry witchery upon George Jacobs that is now in jail.

Putnam. It is a lie.

Danforth [*turning to* GILES]. Mr. Putnam states your charge is a lie. What say you to that?

Giles [*furious, his fists clenched*]. A fart on Thomas Putnam, that is what I say to that!

Danforth. What proof do you submit for your charge, sir?

Giles. My proof is there! [*Pointing to the paper.*] If Jacobs hangs for a witch he forfeit up his property—that's law! And there is none but Putnam with the coin to buy so great a peice. This man is killing his neighbors for their land!

Danforth. But proof, sir, proof.

Giles [*pointing at his deposition*]. The proof is there! I have it from an honest man who heard Putnam say it! The day his daughter cried out on Jacobs, he said she'd given him a fair gift of land.

Hathorne.   And the name of this man?

Giles [taken aback].   What name?

Hathorne.   The man that give you this information.

Giles [hesitates, then].   Why, I—I cannot give you his name.

Hathorne.   And why not?

Giles [hesitates, then bursts out].   You know well why not! He'll lay in jail if I give his name!

Hathorne.   This is contempt of the court, Mr. Danforth!

Danforth [to avoid that].   You will surely tell us the name.

Giles.   I will not give you no name. I mentioned my wife's name once and I'll burn in hell long enough for that. I stand mute.

Danforth.   In that case, I have no choice but to arrest you for contempt of this court, do you know that?

Giles.   This is a hearing; you cannot clap me for contempt of a hearing.

Danforth.   Oh, it is a proper lawyer! Do you wish me to declare the court in full session here? Or will you give me good reply?

Giles [faltering].   I cannot give you no name, sir, I cannot.

Danforth.   You are a foolish old man. Mr. Cheever, begin the record. The court is now in session. I ask you, Mr. Corey—

Proctor [breaking in].   Your Honor—he has the story in confidence, sir, and he—

Parris.   The Devil lives on such confidences! [To DANFORTH]. Without confidences there could be no conspiracy, Your Honor!

Hathorne.   I think it must be broken, sir.

Danforth [to GILES].   Old man, if your informant tells the truth let him come here openly like a decent man. But if he hide in anonymity I must know why. Now sir, the government and central church demand of you the name of him who reported Mr. Thomas Putnam a common murderer.

Hale.   Excellency—

Danforth.   Mr. Hale.

Hale.   We cannot blink it more. There is a prodigious fear of this court in the country—

Danforth.   Then there is a prodigious guilt in the country. Are *you* afraid to be questioned here?

Hale.   I may only fear the Lord, sir, but there is fear in the country nevertheless.

Danforth [angered now].   Reproach me not with the fear in the country; there is fear in the country because there is a moving plot to topple Christ in the country!

Hale.   But it does not follow that everyone accused is part of it.

Danforth.   No uncorrupted man may fear this court, Mr. Hale! None! [To GILES.] You are under arrest in contempt of this court. Now sit you down and take counsel with yourself, or you will be set in the jail until you decide to answer all questions.

[GILES COREY *makes a rush for* PUTNAM. PROCTOR *lunges and holds him.*]

Proctor.   No, Giles!

Giles [over PROCTOR'S *shoulder at* PUTNAM].*   I'll cut your throat, Putnam, I'll kill you yet!

Proctor [*forcing him into a chair*]. Peace, Giles, peace. [*Releasing him.*] We'll prove ourselves. Now we will. [*He starts to turn to* DANFORTH.]

Giles. Say nothin' more, John. [*Pointing at* DANFORTH.] He's only playin' you! He means to hang us all!

[MARY WARREN *bursts into sobs.*]

Danforth. This is a court of law, Mister. I'll have no effrontery here!

Proctor. Forgive him, sir, for his old age. Peace, Giles, we'll prove it all now. [*He lifts up* MARY's *chin.*] You cannot weep, Mary. Remember the angel, what he say to the boy. Hold to it, now; there is your rock. [MARY *quiets. He takes out a paper, and turns to* DANFORTH.] This is Mary Warren's deposition. I—I would ask you remember, sir, while you read it, that until two week ago she were no different than the other children are today. [*He is speaking reasonably restraining all his fears, his anger, his anxiety.*] You saw her scream, she howled, she swore familiar spirits choked her; she even testified that Satan, in the form of women now in jail, tried to win her soul away, and then when she refused—

Danforth. We know all this.

Proctor. Aye, sir. She swears now that she never saw Satan; nor any spirit, vague or clear, that Satan may have sent to hurt her. And she declares her friends are lying now.

[PROCTOR *starts to hand* DANFORTH *the deposition, and* HALE *comes up to* DANFORTH *in a trembling state.*]

Hale. Excellency, a moment. I think this goes to the heart of the matter.

Danforth [*with deep misgivings*]. It surely does.

Hale. I cannot say he is an honest man; I know him little. But in all justice, sir, a claim so weighty cannot be argued by a farmer. In God's name, sir, stop here; send him home and let him come again with a lawyer—

Danforth [*patiently*]. Now look you, Mr. Hale—

Hale. Excellency, I have signed seventy-two death warrants; I am a minister of the Lord, and I dare not take a life without there be a proof so immaculate no slightest qualm of conscience may doubt it.

Danforth. Mr. Hale, you surely do not doubt my justice.

Hale. I have this morning signed away the soul of Rebecca Nurse, Your Honor. I'll not conceal it, my hand shakes yet as with a wound! I pray you, sir, *this* argument let lawyers present to you.

Danforth. Mr. Hale, believe me; for a man of such terrible learning you are most bewildered—I hope you will forgive me. I have been thirty-two year at the bar, sir, and I should be confounded were I called upon to defend these people. Let you consider, now—[*To* PROCTOR *and the others.*] And I bid you all do likewise. In an ordinary crime, how does one defend the accused? One calls up witnesses to prove his innocence. But witchcraft is *ipso facto*, on its face and by its nature, an invisible crime, is it not? Therefore, who may possibly be witness to it? The witch and the victim. None other. Now we cannot hope the witch will accuse herself; granted? Therefore, we must rely upon her victims—and they do testify, the children certainly do testify. As for the witches, none will deny that we are most eager for all their confessions. Therefore, what is left for a lawyer to bring out? I think I have made my point. Have I not?

Hale. But this child claims the girls are not truthful, and if they are not—
Danforth. That is precisely what I am about to consider, sir. What more may you ask of me? Unless you doubt my probity?
Hale [*defeated*]. I surely do not, sir. Let you consider it, then.
Danforth. And let you put your heart to rest. Her deposition, Mr. Proctor.

[PROCTOR *hands it to him.* HATHORNE *rises, goes beside* DANFORTH, *and starts reading.* PARRIS *comes to his other side.* DANFORTH *looks at* JOHN PROCTOR, *then proceeds to read.* HALE *gets up, finds position near* THE JUDGE, *reads too.* PROCTOR *glances at* GILES. FRANCIS *prays silently, hands pressed together.* CHEEVER *waits placidly, the sublime official, dutiful.* MARY WARREN *sobs once.* JOHN PROCTOR *touches her head reassuringly.* Presently DANFORTH *lifts his eyes, stands up, takes out a kerchief and blows his nose. The others stand aside as he moves in thought toward the window.*]

Parris [*hardly able to contain his anger and fear*]. I should like to question—
Danforth [*—his first real outburst, in which his contempt for* PARRIS *is clear*]. Mr. Parris, I bid you be silent. [*He stands in silence, looking out the window. Now, having established that he will set the gait.*] Mr. Cheever, will you go into the court and bring the children here? [CHEEVER *gets up and goes out upstage.* DANFORTH *now turns to* MARY.] Mary Warren, how came you to this turn-about? Has Mr. Proctor threatened you for this deposition?
Mary Warren. No, sir.
Danforth. Has he ever threatened you?
Mary Warren [*weaker*]. No, sir.
Danforth [*sensing a weakening*]. Has he threatened you?
Mary Warren. No, sir.
Danforth. Then you tell me that you sat in my court, callously lying, when you knew that people would hang by your evidence? [*She does not answer.*] Answer me!
Mary Warren [*almost inaudibly*]. I did, sir.
Danforth. How were you instructed in your life? Do you not know that God damns all liars? [*She cannot speak.*] Or is it now that you lie?
Mary Warren. No, sir—I am with God now.
Danforth. You are with God now.
Mary Warren. Aye, sir.
Danforth [*containing himself*]. I will tell you this—you are either lying now, or you were lying in the court, and in either case you have committed perjury and you will go to jail for it. You cannot lightly say you lied, Mary. Do you know that?
Mary Warren. I cannot lie no more. I am with God, I am with God.

[*But she breaks into sobs at the thought of it, and the right door opens, and enter* SUSANNA WALCOTT, MERCY LEWIS, BETTY PARRIS, *and finally* ABIGAIL. CHEEVER *comes to* DANFORTH.]

Cheever. Ruth Putnam's not in the court, sir, nor the other children.
Danforth. These will be sufficient. Sit you down, children. [*Silently they sit.*] Your friend, Mary Warren, has given us a deposition. In which she swears that

she never saw familiar spirits, apparitions, nor any manifest of the Devil. She claims as well that none of you have seen these things either. [*Slight pause.*] Now, children, this is a court of law. The law, based upon the Bible, and the Bible, writ by Almighty God, forbid the practice of witchcraft, and describe death as the penalty thereof. But likewise, children, the law and Bible damn all bearers of false witness. [*Slight pause.*] Now then. It does not escape me that this deposition may be devised to blind us; it may well be that Mary Warren has been conquered by Satan, who sends her here to distract our sacred purpose. If so, her neck will break for it. But if she speak true, I bid you now drop your guile and confess your pretense, for a quick confession will go easier with you. [*Pause.*] Abigail Williams, rise. [ABIGAIL *slowly rises.*] Is there any truth in this?

Abigail. No, sir.

Danforth [*thinks, glances at* MARY, *then back to* ABIGAIL]. Children, a very augur bit will now be turned into your souls until your honesty is proved. Will either of you change your positions now, or do you force me to hard questioning?

Abigail. I have naught to change, sir. She lies.

Danforth [*to* MARY]. You would still go on with this?

Mary Warren [*faintly*]. Aye, sir.

Danforth [*turning to* ABIGAIL]. A poppet were discovered in Mr. Proctor's house, stabbed by a needle. Mary Warren claims that you sat beside her in the court when she made it, and that you saw her make it and witnessed how she herself stuck the needle into it for safe-keeping. What say you to that?

Abigail [*with a slight note of indignation*]. It is a lie, sir.

Danforth [*after a slight pause*]. While you worked for Mr. Proctor, did you see poppets in that house?

Abigail. Goody Proctor always kept poppets.

Proctor. Your Honor, my wife never kept no poppets. Mary Warren confesses it was her poppet.

Cheever. Your Excellency.

Danforth. Mr. Cheever.

Cheever. When I spoke with Goody Proctor in that house, she said she never kept no poppets. But she said she did keep poppets when she were a girl.

Proctor. She has not been a girl these fifteen years, Your Honor.

Hathorne. But a poppet will keep fifteen years, will it not?

Proctor. It will keep if it is kept, but Mary Warren swears she never saw no poppets in my house, nor anyone else.

Parris. Why could there not have been poppets hid where no one ever saw them?

Proctor [*furious*]. There might also be a dragon with five legs in my house, but no one has ever seen it.

Parris. We are here, Your Honor, precisely to discover what no one has ever seen.

Proctor. Mr. Danforth, what profit this girl to turn herself about? What may Mary Warren gain but hard questioning and worse?

Danforth. You are charging Abigail Williams with a marvelous cool plot to murder, do you understand that?

Proctor.   I do, sir. I believe she means to murder.

Danforth [*pointing at* ABIGAIL, *incredulously*].   This child would murder your wife?

Proctor.   It is not a child. Now hear me, sir. In the sight of the congregation she were twice this year put out of this meetin' house for laughter during prayer.

Danforth [*shocked, turning to* ABIGAIL].   What's this? Laughter during—!

Parris.   Excellency, she were under Tituba's power at that time, but she is solemn now.

Giles.   Aye, now she is solemn and goes to hang people!

Danforth.   Quiet, man.

Hathorne.   Surely it have no bearing on the question, sir. He charges contemplation of murder.

Danforth.   Aye. [*He studies* ABIGAIL *for a moment, then.*] Continue, Mr. Proctor.

Proctor.   Mary. Now tell the Governor how you danced in the woods.

Parris [*instantly*].   Excellency, since I come to Salem this man is blackening my name. He—

Danforth.   In a moment, sir. [*To* MARY WARREN, *sternly, and surprised.*] What is this dancing?

Mary Warren.   I—[*She glances at* ABIGAIL, *who is staring down at her remorselessly. Then, appealing to* PROCTOR.] Mr. Proctor—

Proctor [*taking it right up*].   Abigail leads the girls to the woods, Your Honor, and they have danced there naked—

Parris.   Your Honor, this—

Proctor [*at once*].   Mr. Parris discovered them himself in the dead of night! There's the "child" she is!

Danforth [*it is growing into a nightmare, and he turns, astonished, to* PARRIS].   Mr. Parris—

Parris.   I can only say, sir, that I never found any of them naked, and this man is—

Danforth.   But you discovered them dancing in the woods? [*Eyes on* PARRIS, *he points at* ABIGAIL.] Abigail?

Hale.   Excellency, when I first arrived from Beverly, Mr. Parris told me that.

Danforth.   Do you deny it, Mr. Parris?

Parris.   I do not, sir, but I never saw any of them naked.

Danforth.   But she have *danced?*

Parris [*unwillingly*].   Aye, sir.

[DANFORTH, *as though with new eyes, looks at* ABIGAIL.]

Hathorne.   Excellency, will you permit me? [*He points at* MARY WARREN.]

Danforth [*with great worry*].   Pray, proceed.

Hathorne.   You say you never saw no spirits, Mary, were never threatened or afflicted by any manifest of the Devil or the Devil's agents.

Mary Warren [*very faintly*].   No, sir.

Hathorne [*with a gleam of victory*].   And yet, when people accused of witchery confronted you in court, you would faint, saying their spirits came out of their bodies and choked you—

Mary Warren. That were pretense, sir.

Danforth. I cannot hear you.

Mary Warren. Pretense, sir.

Parris. But you did turn cold, did you not? I myself picked you up many times, and your skin were icy. Mr. Danforth, you—

Danforth. I saw that many times.

Proctor. She only pretended to faint, Your Excellency. They're all marvelous pretenders.

Hathorne. Then can she pretend to faint now?

Proctor. Now?

Parris. Why not? Now there are no spirits attacking her, for none in this room is accused of witchcraft. So let her turn herself cold now, let her pretend she is attacked now, let her faint. [*He turns to* mary warren.] Faint!

Mary Warren. Faint?

Parris. Aye, faint. Prove to us how you pretended in the court so many times.

Mary Warren [*looking to* proctor]. I—cannot faint now, sir.

Proctor [*alarmed, quietly*]. Can you not pretend it?

Mary Warren. I—[*She looks about as though searching for the passion to faint.*] I—have no *sense* of it now, I—

Danforth. Why? What is lacking now?

Mary Warren. I—cannot tell, sir, I—

Danforth. Might it be that here we have no afflicting spirit loose, but in the court there were some?

Mary Warren. I never saw no spirits.

Parris. Then see no spirits now, and prove to us that you can faint by your own will, as you claim.

Mary Warren [*stares, searching for the emotion of it, and then shakes her head*]. I—cannot do it.

Parris. Then you will confess, will you not? It were attacking spirits made you faint!

Mary Warren. No, sir, I—

Parris. Your Excellency, this is a trick to blind the court!

Mary Warren. It's not a trick! [*She stands.*] I—I used to faint because I—I thought I saw spirits.

Danforth. *Thought* you saw them!

Mary Warren. But I did not, Your Honor.

Hathorne. How could you think you saw them unless you saw them?

Mary Warren. I—I cannot tell how, but I did. I—I heard the other girls screaming, and you, Your Honor, you seemed to believe them, and I— It were only sport in the beginning, sir, but then the whole world cried spirits, spirits, and I—I promise you, Mr. Danforth, I only thought I saw them but I did not.

[danforth *peers at her.*]

Parris [*smiling, but nervous because* danforth *seems to be struck by* mary's *story*]. Surely Your Excellency is not taken by this simple lie.

Danforth [*turning worriedly to* abigail]. Abigail. I bid you now search your heart and tell me this—and beware of it, child, to God every soul is precious and His vengeance is terrible on them that take life without cause. Is it possible, child, that the spirits you have seen are illusion only, some deception that may cross your mind when—

Abigail. Why, this—this—is a base question, sir.

Danforth. Child, I would have you consider it—

Abigail. I have been hurt, Mr. Danforth; I have seen my blood runnin' out! I have been near to murdered every day because I done my duty pointing out the Devil's people—and this is my reward? To be mistrusted, denied, questioned like a—

Danforth [weakening]. Child, I do not mistrust you—

Abigail [in an open threat]. Let *you* beware, Mr. Danforth. Think you to be so mighty that the power of Hell may not turn *your* wits? Beware of it! There is—[*Suddenly, from an accusatory attitude, her face turns, looking into the air above—it is truly frightened.*]

Danforth [apprehensively]. What is it, child?

Abigail [looking about in the air, clasping her arms about her as though cold]. I—I know not. A wind, a cold wind, has come. [*Her eyes fall on* MARY WARREN.]

Mary Warren [terrified, pleading]. Abby!

Mercy Lewis [shivering]. Your Honor, I freeze!

Proctor. They're pretending!

Hathorne [touching ABIGAIL's *hand].* She is cold, Your Honor, touch her!

Mercy Lewis [through chattering teeth]. Mary, do you send this shadow on me?

Mary Warren. Lord, save me!

Susanna Walcott. I freeze, I freeze!

Abigail [shivering visibly]. It is a wind, a wind!

Mary Warren. Abby, don't do that!

Danforth [himself engaged and entered by ABIGAIL].* Mary Warren, do you witch her? I say to you, do you send your spirit out?

[*With a hysterical cry* MARY WARREN *starts to run.* PROCTOR *catches her.*]

Mary Warren [almost collapsing]. Let me go, Mr. Proctor, I cannot, I cannot—

Abigail [crying to Heaven]. Oh, Heavenly Father, take away this shadow!

[*Without warning or hesitation,* PROCTOR *leaps at* ABIGAIL *and, grabbing her by the hair, pulls her to her feet. She screams in pain.* DANFORTH, *astonished, cries,* "What are you about?" *and* HATHORNE *and* PARRIS *call,* "Take your hands off her!" *and out of it all comes* PROCTOR's *roaring voice.*]

Proctor. How do you call Heaven! Whore! Whore!

[HERRICK *breaks* PROCTOR *from her.*]

Herrick. John!

Danforth. Man! Man, what do you—

Proctor [breathless and in agony]. It is a whore!

Danforth [dumfounded]. You charge—?

Abigail. Mr. Danforth, he is lying!

Proctor. Mark her! Now she'll suck a scream to stab me with, but—

Danforth. You will prove this! This will not pass!

Proctor [*trembling, his life collapsing about him*]. I have known her, sir. I have known her.

Danforth. You—you are a lecher?

Francis [*horrified*]. John, you cannot say such a—

Proctor. Oh, Francis, I wish you had some evil in you that you might know me! [*To* DANFORTH.] A man will not cast away his good name. You surely know that.

Danforth [*dumfounded*]. In—in what time? In what place?

Proctor [*his voice about to break, and his shame great*]. In the proper place— where my beasts are bedded. On the last night of my joy, some eight months past. She used to serve me in my house, sir. [*He has to clamp his jaw to keep from weeping.*] A man may think God sleeps, but God sees everything. I know it now. I beg you, sir, I beg you—see her what she is. My wife, my dear good wife, took this girl soon after, sir, and put her out on the highroad. And being what she is, a lump of vanity, sir—[*He is being overcome.*] Excellency, forgive me, forgive me. [*Angrily against himself, he turns away from* THE GOVERNOR *for a moment. Then, as though to cry out is his only means of speech left.*] She thinks to dance with me on my wife's grave! And well she might, for I thought of her softly. God help me, I lusted, and there *is* a promise in such sweat. But it is a whore's vengeance, and you must see it; I set myself entirely in your hands. I know you must see it now.

Danforth [*blanched, in horror, turning to* ABIGAIL]. You deny every scrap and tittle of this?

Abigail. If I must answer that, I will leave and I will not come back again!

[DANFORTH *seems unsteady.*]

Proctor. I have made a bell of my honor! I have rung the doom of my good name—you will believe me, Mr. Danforth! My wife is innocent, except she knew a whore when she saw one!

Abigail [*stepping up to* DANFORTH]. What look do you give me? [DANFORTH *cannot speak.*] I'll not have such looks! [*She turns and starts for the door.*]

Danforth. You will remain where you are! [*Herrick steps into her path. She comes up short, fire in her eyes.*] Mr. Parris, go into the court and bring Goodwife Proctor out.

Parris [*objecting*]. Your Honor, this is all a—

Danforth [*sharply to* PARRIS]. Bring her out! And tell her not one word of what's been spoken here. And let you knock before you enter. [PARRIS *goes out.*] Now we shall touch the bottom of this swamp. [*To* PROCTOR.] Your wife, you say, is an honest woman.

Proctor. In her life, sir, she have never lied. There are them that cannot sing, and them that cannot weep—my wife cannot lie. I have paid much to learn it, sir.

Danforth. And when she put this girl out of your house, she put her out for a harlot?

Proctor. Aye, sir.

Danforth. And knew her for a harlot?

Proctor. Aye, sir, she knew her for a harlot.

Danforth. Good then. [*To* ABIGAIL.] And if she tell me, child, it were for harlotry, may God spread His mercy on you! [*There is a knock. He calls to the door.*] Hold! [*To* ABIGAIL.] Turn your back. Turn your back. [*To* PROCTOR.] Do likewise. [*Both turn their backs*—ABIGAIL *with indignant slowness.*] Now let neither of you turn to face Goody Proctor. No one in this room is to speak one word, or raise a gesture aye or nay. [*He turns toward the door, calls.*] Enter! [*The door opens.* ELIZABETH *enters with* PARRIS. PARRIS *leaves her. She stands alone, her eyes looking for* PROCTOR.] Mr. Cheever, report this testimony in all exactness. Are you ready?

Cheever. Ready, sir.

Danforth. Come here, woman. [ELIZABETH *comes to him, glancing at* PROCTOR'S *back.*] Look at me only, not at your husband. In my eyes only.

Elizabeth [*faintly*]. Good, sir.

Danforth. We are given to understand that at one time you dismissed your servant, Abigail Williams.

Elizabeth. That is true, sir.

Danforth. For what cause did you dismiss her? [*Slight pause. Then* ELIZABETH *tries to glance at* PROCTOR.] You will look in my eyes only and not at your husband. The answer is in your memory and you need no help to give it to me. Why did you dismiss Abigail Williams?

Elizabeth [*not knowing what to say, sensing a situation, wetting her lips to stall for time*]. She—dissatisfied me. [*Pause.*] And my husband.

Danforth. In what way dissatisfied you?

Elizabeth. She were—[*She glances at* PROCTOR *for a cue.*]

Danforth. Woman, look at me? [ELIZABETH *does.*] Were she slovenly? Lazy? What disturbance did she cause?

Elizabeth. Your Honor, I—in that time I were sick. And I—My husband is a good and righteous man. He is never drunk as some are, nor wastin' his time at the shovelboard, but always at his work. But in my sickness—you see, sir, I were a long time sick after my last baby, and I thought I saw my husband somewhat turning from me. And this girl—[*She turns to* ABIGAIL.]

Danforth. Look at me.

Elizabeth. Aye, sir. Abigail Williams—[*She breaks off.*]

Danforth. What of Abigail Williams?

Elizabeth. I came to think he fancied her. And so one night I lost my wits, I think, and put her out on the highroad.

Danforth. Your husband—did he indeed turn from you?

Elizabeth [*in agony*]. My husband—is a goodly man, sir.

Danforth. Then he did not turn from you.

Elizabeth [*starting to glance at* PROCTOR]. He—

Danforth [*reaches out and holds her face, then*]. Look at me! To your own knowledge, has John Porter ever committed the crime of lechery? [*In a crisis of indecision she cannot speak.*] Answer my question! Is your husband a lecher!

Elizabeth [*faintly*]. No, sir.

Danforth. Remove her, Marshal.

Proctor. Elizabeth, tell the truth!

Danforth. She has spoken. Remove her!

Proctor [*crying out*]. Elizabeth, I have confessed it!

Elizabeth. Oh, God! [*The door closes behind her.*]

Proctor. She only thought to save my name!

Hale. Excellency, it is a natural lie to tell; I beg you, stop now before another is condemned! I may shut my conscience to it no more—private vengeance is working through this testimony! From the beginning this man has struck me true. By my oath to Heaven, I believe him now, and I pray you call back his wife before we—

Danforth. She spoke nothing of lechery, and this man has lied!

Hale. I believe him! [*Pointing at* ABIGAIL.] This girl has always struck me false! She has—

[ABIGAIL, *with a weird, wild, chilling cry, screams up to the ceiling.*]

Abigail. You will not! Begone! Begone, I say!

Danforth. What is it, child? [*But* ABIGAIL, *pointing with fear, is now raising up her frightened eyes, her awed face, toward the ceiling—the girls are doing the same—and now* HATHORNE, HALE, PUTNAM, CHEEVER, HERRICK, *and* DANFORTH *do the same.*] What's there? [*He lowers his eyes from the ceiling, and now he is frightened; there is real tension in his voice.*] Child! [*She is transfixed—with all the girls, she is whimpering open-mouthed, agape at the ceiling.*] Girls! Why do you—?

Mercy Lewis [*pointing*]. It's on the beam! Behind the rafter!

Danforth [*looking up*]. Where!

Abigail. Why—? [*She gulps.*] Why do you come, yellow bird?

Proctor. Where's a bird? I see no bird!

Abigail [*to the ceiling*]. My face? My face?

Proctor. Mr. Hale—

Danforth. Be quiet!

Proctor [*to* HALE]. Do you see a bird?

Danforth. Be quiet!!

Abigail [*to the ceiling, in a genuine conversation with the "bird," as though trying to talk it out of attacking her*]. But God made my face; you cannot want to tear my face. Envy is a deadly sin, Mary.

Mary Warren [*on her feet with a spring, and horrified, pleading*]. Abby!

Abigail [*unperturbed, continuing to the "bird"*]. Oh, Mary, this is a black art to change your shape. No, I cannot, I cannot stop my mouth; it's God's work I do.

Mary Warren. Abby, I'm *here*!

Proctor [*frantically*]. They're pretending, Mr. Danforth!

Abigail [*now she takes a backward step, as though in fear the bird will swoop down momentarily*]. Oh, please, Mary! Don't come down.

Susanna Walcott. Her claws, she's stretching her claws!

Proctor. Lies, lies.

Abigail [*backing further, eyes still fixed above*]. Mary, please don't hurt me!

Mary Warren [*to* DANFORTH]. I'm not hurting her!

Danforth [*to* MARY WARREN]. Why does she see this vision?

Mary Warren. She sees nothin'!

Abigail [*now staring full front as though hypnotized, and mimicking the exact tone of* MARY WARREN'S *cry*].   She sees nothin'!

Mary Warren [*pleading*].   Abby, you mustn't!

Abigail and All the Girls [*all transfixed*].   Abby, you mustn't!

Mary Warren [*to all the girls*].   I'm here, I'm here!

Girls.   I'm here, I'm here!

Danforth [*horrified*].   Mary Warren! Draw back your spirit out of them!

Mary Warren.   Mr. Danforth!

Girls [*cutting her off*].   Mr. Danforth!

Danforth.   Have you compacted with the Devil? Have you?

Mary Warren.   Never, never!

Girls.   Never, never!

Danforth [*growing hysterical*].   Why can they only repeat you?

Proctor.   Give me a whip—I'll stop it!

Mary Warren.   They're sporting. They—!

Girls.   They're sporting!

Mary Warren [*turning on them all hysterically and stamping her feet*].   Abby, stop it!

Girls [*stamping their feet*].   Abby, stop it!

Mary Warren.   Stop it!

Girls.   Stop it!

Mary Warren [*screaming it out at the top of her lungs, and raising her fists*].   Stop it!!

Girls [*raising their fists*].   Stop it!!

[MARY WARREN, *utterly confounded, and becoming overwhelmed by* ABIGAIL'S —*and the* GIRLS'—*utter conviction, starts to whimper, hands half raised, powerless, and all the* GIRLS *begin whimpering exactly as she does.*]

Danforth.   A little while ago you were afflicted. Now it seems you afflict others; where did you find this power?

Mary Warren [*staring at* ABIGAIL].   I—have no power.

Girls.   I have no power.

Proctor.   They're gulling you, Mister!

Danforth.   Why did you turn about this past two weeks? You have seen the Devil, have you not?

Hale [*indicating* ABIGAIL *and the* GIRLS].   You cannot believe them!

Mary Warren.   I—

Proctor [*sensing her weakening*].   Mary, God damns all liars!

Danforth [*pounding it into her*].   You have seen the Devil, you have made compact with Lucifer, have you not?

Proctor.   God damns liars, Mary!

[MARY *utters something unintelligible, staring at* ABIGAIL, *who keeps watching the "bird" above.*]

Danforth.   I cannot hear you. What do you say? [MARY *utters again unintelligibly.*] You will confess yourself or you will hang! [*He turns her roughly to face him.*] Do you know who I am? I say you will hang if you do not open with me!

Proctor. Mary, remember the angel Raphael—do that which is good and—

Abigail [*pointing upward*]. The wings! Her wings are spreading! Mary, please, don't, don't—!

Hale. I see nothing, Your Honor!

Danforth. Do you confess this power! [*He is an inch from her face.*] Speak!

Abigail. She's going to come down! She's walking the beam!

Danforth. Will you speak!

Mary Warren [*staring in horror*]. I cannot!

Girls. I cannot!

Parris. Cast the Devil out! Look him in the face! Trample him! We'll save you, Mary, only stand fast against him and—

Abigail [*looking up*]. Look out! She's coming down!

[*She and all the* GIRLS *run to one wall, shielding their eyes. And now, as though cornered, they let out a gigantic scream, and* MARY, *as though infected, opens her mouth and screams with them. Gradually* ABIGAIL *and the* GIRLS *leave off, until only* MARY *is left there, staring up at the "bird," screaming madly. All watch her, horrified by this evident fit.* PROCTOR *strides to her.*]

Proctor. Mary, tell the Governor what they— [*He has hardly got a word out, when, seeing him coming for her, she rushes out of his reach, screaming in horror.*]

Mary Warren. Don't touch me—don't touch me! [*At which the* GIRLS *halt at the door.*]

Proctor [*astonished*]. Mary!

Mary Warren [*pointing at* PROCTOR]. You're the Devil's man!

[*He is stopped in his tracks.*]

Parris. Praise God!

Girls. Praise God!

Proctor [*numbed*]. Mary, how—?

Mary Warren. I'll not hang with you! I love God, I love God.

Danforth [*to* MARY]. He bid you do the Devil's work?

Mary Warren [*hysterically, indicating* PROCTOR]. He come at me by night and every day to sign, to sign, to—

Danforth. Sign what?

Parris. The Devil's book? He come with a book?

Mary Warren [*hysterically, pointing at* PROCTOR, *fearful of him*]. My name, he want my name. "I'll murder you," he says, "if my wife hangs! We must go and overthrow the court," he says!

[DANFORTH's *head jerks toward* PROCTOR, *shock and horror in his face.*]

Proctor [*turning, appealing to* HALE]. Mr. Hale!

Mary Warren [*her sobs beginning*]. He wake me every night, his eyes were like coals and his fingers claw my neck, and I sign, I sign . . .

Hale. Excellency, this child's gone wild!

Proctor [*as* DANFORTH'S *wide eyes pour on him*].   Mary, Mary!

Mary Warren [*screaming at him*].   No, I love God; I go your way no more. I love God, I bless God. [*Sobbing, she rushes to* ABIGAIL.] Abby, Abby, I'll never hurt you more! [*They all watch, as* ABIGAIL, *out of her infinite charity, reaches out and draws the sobbing* MARY *to her, and then looks up to* DANFORTH.]

Danforth [*to* PROCTOR].   What are you? [PROCTOR *is beyond speech in his anger.*] You are combined with anti-Christ, are you not? I have seen your power; you will not deny it! What say you, Mister?

Hale.   Excellency—

Danforth.   I will have nothing from you, Mr. Hale! [*To* PROCTOR.] Will you confess yourself befouled with Hell, or do you keep that black allegiance yet? What say you?

Proctor [*his mind wild, breathless*].   I say—I say—God is dead!

Parris.   Hear it, hear it!

Proctor [*laughs insanely, then*].   A fire, a fire is burning! I hear the boot of Lucifer, I see his filthy face! And it is my face, and yours, Danforth! For them that quail to bring men out of ignorance, as I have quailed, and as you quail now when you know in all your black hearts that this be fraud—God damns our kind especially, and we will burn, we will burn together.

Danforth.   Marshal! Take him and Corey with him to the jail!

Hale [*starting across to the door*].   I denounce these proceedings!

Proctor.   You are pulling Heaven down and raising up a whore!

Hale.   I denounce these proceedings, I quit this court! [*He slams the door to the outside behind him.*]

Danforth [*calling to him in a fury*].   Mr. Hale! Mr. Hale!

[*The curtain falls.*]

Act IV

A cell in Salem jail, that fall.

[*At the back is a high barred window; near it, a great, heavy door. Along the walls are two benches.*

The place is in darkness but for the moonlight seeping through the bars. It appears empty. Presently footsteps are heard coming down a corridor beyond the wall, keys rattle, and the door swings open. MARSHAL HERRICK *enters with a lantern.*

He is nearly drunk, and heavy-footed. He goes to a bench and nudges a bundle of rags lying on it.]

Herrick.   Sarah, wake up! Sarah Good! [*He then crosses to the other bench.*]

Sarah Good [*rising in her rags*].   Oh, Majesty! Comin', comin'! Tituba, he's here, His Majesty's come!

Herrick.   Go to the north cell; this place is wanted now. [*He hangs his lantern on the wall. Tituba sits up.*]

Tituba. That don't look to me like His Majesty; look to me like the marshal.

Herrick [*taking out a flask*]. Get along with you now, clear this place. [*He drinks, and* SARAH GOOD *comes and peers up into his face.*]

Sarah Good. Oh, is it you, Marshal! I thought sure you be the devil comin' for us. Could I have a sip of cider for me goin'-away?

Herrick [*handing her the flask*]. And where are you off to, Sarah?

Tituba [*as Sarah drinks*]. We goin' to Barbados, soon the Devil gits here with the feathers and the wings.

Herrick. Oh? A happy voyage to you.

Sarah Good. A pair of bluebirds wingin' southerly, the two of us! Oh, it be a grand transformation, Marshal! [*She raises the flask to drink again.*]

Herrick [*taking the flask from her lips*]. You'd best give me that or you'll never rise off the ground. Come along now.

Tituba. I'll speak to him for you, if you desires to come along, Marshal.

Herrick. I'd not refuse it, Tituba; it's the proper morning to fly into Hell.

Tituba. Oh, it be no Hell in Barbados. Devil, him be pleasureman in Barbados, him be singin' and dancin' in Barbados. It's you folks—you riles him up 'round here; it be too cold 'round here for that Old Boy. He freeze his soul in Massachusetts, but in Barbados he just as sweet and— [*A bellowing cow is heard, and* TITUBA *leaps up and calls to the window.*] Aye, sir! That's him, Sarah!

Sarah Good. I'm here, Majesty! [*They hurriedly pick up their rags as* HOPKINS, *a guard, enters.*]

Hopkins. The Deputy Governor's arrived.

Herrick [*grabbing* TITUBA]. Come along, come along.

Tituba [*resisting him*]. No, he comin' for me. I goin' home!

Herrick [*pulling her to the door*]. That's not Satan, just a poor old cow with a hatful of milk. Come along now, out with you!

Tituba [*calling to the window*]. Take me home, Devil! Take me home!

Sarah Good [*following the shouting* TITUBA *out*]. Tell him I'm goin', Tituba! Now you tell him Sarah Good is goin' too!

[*In the corridor outside* TITUBA *calls on—"Take me home, Devil; Devil take me home!" and* HOPKINS' *voice orders her to move on.* HERRICK *returns and begins to push old rags and straw into a corner. Hearing footsteps, he turns, and enter* DANFORTH *and* JUDGE HATHORNE. *They are in greatcoats and wear hats against the bitter cold. They are followed in by* CHEEVER, *who carries a dispatch case and a flat wooden box containing his writing materials.*]

Herrick. Good morning, Excellency.

Danforth. Where is Mr. Parris?

Herrick. I'll fetch him. [*He starts for the door.*]

Danforth. Marshal. [HERRICK *stops.*] When did Reverend Hale arrive?

Herrick. It were toward midnight, I think.

Danforth [*suspiciously*]. What is he about here?

Herrick. He goes among them that will hang, sir. And he prays with him. He sits with Goody Nurse now. And Mr. Parris with him.

Danforth. Indeed. That man have no authority to enter here, Marshal. Why have you let him in?

Herrick. Why, Mr. Parris command me, sir. I cannot deny him.

Danforth. Are you drunk, Marshal?

Herrick. No, sir; it is a bitter night, and I have no fire here.

Danforth [*containing his anger*]. Fetch Mr. Parris.

Herrick. Aye, sir.

Danforth. There is a prodigious stench in this place.

Herrick. I have only now cleared the people out for you.

Danforth. Beware hard drink, Marshal.

Herrick. Aye, sir. [*He waits an instant for further orders. But* DANFORTH, *in dissatisfaction, turns his back on him, and* HERRICK *goes out. There is a pause.* DANFORTH *stands in thought.*]

Hathorne. Let you question Hale, Excellency; I should not be surprised he have been preaching in Andover lately.

Danforth. We'll come to that; speak nothing of Andover. Parris prays with him. That's strange. [*He blows on his hands, moves toward the window, and looks out.*]

Hathorne. Excellency, I wonder if it be wise to let Mr. Parris so continuously with the prisoners. [DANFORTH *turns to him, interested.*] I think, sometimes, the man has a mad look these days.

Danforth. Mad?

Hathorne. I met him yesterday coming out of his house, and I bid him good morning—and he wept and went his way. I think it is not well the village sees him so unsteady.

Danforth. Perhaps he have some sorrow.

Cheever [*stamping his feet against the cold*]. I think it be the cows, sir.

Danforth. Cows?

Cheever. There be so many cows wanderin' the highroads, now their masters are in the jails, and much disagreement who they will belong to now. I know Mr. Parris be arguin' with farmers all yesterday—there is great contention, sir, about the cows. Contention make him weep, sir; it were always a man that weep for contention. [*He turns, as do* HATHORNE *and* DANFORTH, *hearing someone coming up the corridor.* DANFORTH *raises his head as* PARRIS *enters. He is gaunt, frightened, and sweating in his greatcoat.*]

Parris [*to* DANFORTH, *instantly*]. Oh, good morning, sir, thank you for coming. I beg your pardon wakin' you so early. Good morning, Judge Hathorne.

Danforth. Reverend Hale have no right to enter this—

Parris. Excellency, a moment. [*He hurries back and shuts the door.*]

Hathorne. Do you leave him alone with the prisoners?

Danforth. What's his business here?

Parris [*prayerfully holding up his hands*]. Excellency, hear me. It is a providence. Reverend Hale has returned to bring Rebecca Nurse to God.

Danforth [*surprised*]. He bids her confess?

Parris [*sitting*]. Hear me. Rebecca have not given me a word this three month since she came. Now she sits with him, and her sister and Martha Corey and two or three others, and he pleads with them, confess their crimes and save their lives.

Danforth. Why—this is indeed a providence. And they soften, they soften?

Parris. Not yet, not yet. But I thought to summon you, sir, that we might think on whether it be not wise, to— [*He dares not say it.*] I had thought to put a question, sir, and I hope you will not—

Danforth. Mr. Parris, be plain, what troubles you?

Parris. There is news, sir, that the court—the court must reckon with. My niece, sir, my niece—I believe she has vanished.

Danforth. Vanished!

Parris. I had thought to advise you of it earlier in the week, but—

Danforth. Why? How long is she gone?

Parris. This be the third night. You see, sir, she told me she would stay a night with Mercy Lewis. And next day, when she does not return, I send to Mr. Lewis to inquire. Mercy told him she would sleep in *my* house for a night.

Danforth. They are both gone?!

Parris [*in fear of him*]. They are, sir.

Danforth [*alarmed*]. I will send a party for them. Where may they be?

Parris. Excellency, I think they be aboard a ship. [DANFORTH *stands agape.*] My daughter tells me how she heard them speaking of ships last week, and tonight I discover my—my strongbox is broke into. [*He presses his fingers against his eyes to keep back tears.*]

Hathorne [*astonished*]. She have robbed you?

Parris. Thirty-one pound is gone. I am penniless. [*He covers his face and sobs.*]

Danforth. Mr. Parris, you are a brainless man! [*He walks in thought, deeply worried.*]

Parris. Excellency, it profit nothing you should blame me. I cannot think they would run off except they fear to keep in Salem any more. [*He is pleading.*] Mark it, sir, Abigail had close knowledge of the town, and since the news of Andover has broken here—

Danforth. Andover is remedied. The court returns there on Friday, and will resume examinations.

Parris. I am sure of it, sir. But the rumor here speaks rebellion in Andover, and it—

Danforth. There is no rebellion in Andover!

Parris. I tell you what is said here, sir. Andover have thrown out the court, they say, and will have no part of witchcraft. There be a faction here, feeding on that news, and I tell you true, sir, I fear there will be riot here.

Hathorne. Riot! Why at every execution I have seen naught but high satisfaction in the town.

Parris. Judge Hathorne—it were another sort that hanged till now. Rebecca Nurse is no Bridget that lived three year with Bishop before she married him. John Proctor is not Isaac Ward that drank his family to ruin. [TO DANFORTH.] I would to God it were not so, Excellency, but these people have great weight yet in the town. Let Rebecca stand upon the gibbet and send up some righteous prayer, and I fear she'll wake a vengeance on you.

Hathorne. Excellency, she is condemned a witch. The court have—

Danforth [*in deep concern, raising a hand to* HATHORNE]. Pray you. [TO PARRIS.] How do you propose, then?

Parris. Excellency, I would postpone these hangin's for a time.

Danforth. There will be no postponement.

Parris. Now Mr. Hale's returned, there is hope, I think—for if he bring even one of these to God, that confession surely damns the others in the public eye, and none may doubt more that they are all linked to Hell. This way, unconfessed and claiming innocence, doubts are multiplied, many honest people will weep for them, and our good purpose is lost in their tears.

Danforth [*after thinking a moment, then going to* CHEEVER]. Give me the list.

[CHEEVER *opens the dispatch case, searches.*]

Parris. It cannot be forgot, sir, that when I summoned the congregation for John Proctor's excommunication there were hardly thirty people come to hear it. That speak a discontent, I think, and—

Danforth [*studying the list*]. There will be no postponement.

Parris. Excellency—

Danforth. Now, sir—which of these in your opinion may be brought to God? I will myself strive with him till dawn. [*He hands the list to* PARRIS, *who merely glances at it.*]

Parris. There is not sufficient time till dawn.

Danforth. I shall do my utmost. Which of them do you have hope for?

Parris [*not even glancing at the list now, and in a quavering voice, quietly*]. Excellency—a dagger— [*He chokes up.*]

Danforth. What do you say?

Parris. Tonight, when I open my door to leave my house—a dagger clattered to the ground. [*Silence.* DANFORTH *absorbs this. Now* PARRIS *cries out.*] You cannot hang this sort. There is danger for me. I dare not step outside at night!

[REVEREND HALE *enters. They look at him for an instant in silence. He is steeped in sorrow, exhausted, and more direct than he ever was.*]

Danforth. Accept my congratulations, Reverend Hale; we are gladdened to see you returned to your good work.

Hale [*coming to* DANFORTH *now*]. You must pardon them. They will not budge.

[HERRICK *enters, waits.*]

Danforth [*conciliatory*]. You misunderstand, sir; I cannot pardon these when twelve are already hanged for the same crime. It is not just.

Parris [*with failing heart*]. Rebecca will not confess?

Hale. The sun will rise in a few minutes. Excellency, I must have more time.

Danforth. Now hear me, and beguile yourselves no more. I will not receive a single plea for pardon or postponement. Them that will not confess will hang. Twelve are already executed; the names of these seven are given out, and the village expects to see them die this morning. Postponement now speaks a floundering on my part; reprieve or pardon must cast doubt upon the guilt of them that died till now. While I speak God's law, I will not crack its voice with whimpering. If retaliation is your fear, know this—I should hang ten thousand that dared to rise against the law, and an ocean of salt tears could not melt the resolution of the statutes. Now draw yourselves up like men and help me, as you are bound by Heaven to do. Have you spoken with them all, Mr. Hale?

Hale. All but Proctor. He is in the dungeon.

Danforth [*to* HERRICK]. What's Proctor's way now?

Herrick. He sits like some great bird; you'd not know he lived except he will take food from time to time.

Danforth [*after thinking a moment*]. His wife—his wife must be well on with child now.

Herrick. She is, sir.

Danforth. What think you, Mr. Parris? You have closer knowledge of this man; might her presence soften him?

Parris. It is possible, sir. He have not laid eyes on her these three months. I should summon her.

Danforth [*to* HERRICK]. Is he yet adamant? Has he struck at you again?

Herrick. He cannot, sir, he is chained to the wall now.

Danforth [*after thinking on it*]. Fetch Goody Proctor to me. Then let you bring him up.

Herrick. Aye, sir. [HERRICK *goes. There is silence.*]

Hale. Excellency, if you postpone a week and publish to the town that you are striving for their confessions, that speak mercy on your part, not faltering.

Danforth. Mr. Hale, as God have not empowered me like Joshua to stop this sun from rising, so I cannot withhold from them the perfection of their punishment.

Hale [*harder now*]. If you think God wills you to raise rebellion, Mr. Danforth, you are mistaken!

Danforth [*instantly*]. You have heard rebellion spoken in the town?

Hale. Excellency, there are orphans wandering from house to house; abandoned cattle bellow on the highroads, the stink of rotting crops hangs everywhere, and no man knows when the harlots' cry will end his life—and you wonder yet if rebellion's spoke? Better you should marvel how they do not burn your province!

Danforth. Mr. Hale, have you preached in Andover this month?

Hale. Thank God they have no need of me in Andover.

Danforth. You baffle me, sir. Why have you returned here?

Hale. Why, it is all simple. I come to do the Devil's work. I come to counsel Christians they should belie themselves. [*His sarcasm collapses.*] There is blood on my head! Can you not see the blood on my head!!

Parris. Hush! [*For he has heard footsteps. They all face the door.* HERRICK *enters with* ELIZABETH. *Her wrists are linked by heavy chain, which* HERRICK *now removes. Her clothes are dirty; her face is pale and gaunt.* HERRICK *goes out.*]

Danforth [*very politely*]. Goody Proctor. [*She is silent.*] I hope you are hearty?

Elizabeth [*as a warning reminder*]. I am yet six months before my time.

Danforth. Pray be at your ease, we come not for your life. We—[*uncertain how to plead, for he is not accustomed to it.*] Mr. Hale, will you speak with the woman?

Hale. Goody Proctor, your husband is marked to hang this morning.

[*Pause.*]

Elizabeth [*quietly*]. I have heard it.

Hale. You know, do you not, that I have no connection with the court? [*She seems to doubt it.*] I come of my own, Goody Proctor. I would save your husband's life, for if he is taken I count myself his murderer. Do you understand me?

Elizabeth.   What do you want of me?

Hale.   Goody Proctor, I have gone this three month like our Lord into the wilderness. I have sought a Christian way, for damnation's doubled on a minister who counsels men to lie.

Hathorne.   It is no lie, you cannot speak of lies.

Hale.   It is a lie! They are innocent!

Danforth.   I'll hear no more of that!

Hale [*continuing to* ELIZABETH]. Let you not mistake your duty as I mistook my own. I came into this village like a bridegroom to his beloved, bearing gifts of high religion; the very crowns of holy law I brought, and what I touched with my bright confidence, it died; and where I turned the eye of my great faith, blood flowed up. Beware, Goody Proctor—cleave to no faith when faith brings blood. It is mistaken law that leads you to sacrifice. Life, woman, life is God's most precious gift; no principle, however glorious, may justify the taking of it. I beg you, woman, prevail upon your husband to confess. Let him give his lie. Quail not before God's judgment in this, for it may well be God damns a liar less than he that throws his life away for pride. Will you plead with him? I cannot think he will listen to another.

Elizabeth [*quietly*].   I think that be the Devil's argument.

Hale [*with a climactic desperation*].   Woman, before the laws of God we are as swine! We cannot read His will!

Elizabeth.   I cannot dispute with you, sir; I lack learning for it.

Danforth [*going to her*].   Goody Proctor, you are not summoned here for disputation. Be there no wifely tenderness within you? He will die with the sunrise. Your husband. Do you understand it? [*She only looks at him.*] What say you? Will you contend with him? [*She is silent.*] Are you stone? I tell you true, woman, had I no other proof of your unnatural life, your dry eyes now would be sufficient evidence that you delivered up your soul to Hell! A very ape would weep at such calamity! Have the devil dried up any tear of pity in you? [*She is silent.*] Take her out. It profit nothing she should speak to him!

Elizabeth [*quietly*].   Let me speak with him, Excellency.

Parris [*with hope*].   You'll strive with him? [*She hesitates.*]

Danforth.   Will you plead for his confession or will you not?

Elizabeth.   I promise nothing. Let me speak with him.

[*A sound—the sibilance of dragging feet on stone. They turn. A pause.* HERRICK *enters with* JOHN PROCTOR. *His wrists are chained. He is another man, bearded, filthy, his eyes misty as though webs had overgrown them. He halts inside the doorway, his eye caught by the sight of* ELIZABETH. *The emotion flowing between them prevents anyone from speaking for an instant. Now* HALE, *visibly affected, goes to* DANFORTH *and speaks quietly.*]

Hale.   Pray, leave them, Excellency.

Danforth [*pressing* HALE *impatiently aside*].   Mr. Proctor, you have been notified, have you not? [PROCTOR *is silent, staring at* ELIZABETH.] I see light in the sky, Mister; let you counsel with your wife, and may God help you turn your back on Hell. [PROCTOR *is silent, staring at* ELIZABETH.]

Hale [*quietly*].   Excellency, let—

[DANFORTH *brushes past* HALE *and walks out.* HALE *follows.* CHEEVER *stands and follows,* HATHORNE *behind.* HERRICK *goes.* PARRIS, *from a safe distance, offers.*]

Parris.   If you desire a cup of cider, Mr. Proctor, I am sure I— [PROCTOR *turns an icy stare at him, and he breaks off.* PARRIS *raises his palms toward* PROCTOR.] God lead you now. [PARRIS *goes out.*]

[*Alone.* PROCTOR *walks to her, halts. It is as though they stood in a spinning world. It is beyond sorrow, above it. He reaches out his hand as though toward an embodiment not quite real, and as he touches her, a strange soft sound, half laughter, half amazement, comes from his throat. He pats her hand. She covers his hand with hers. And then, weak, he sits. Then she sits, facing him.*]

Proctor.   The child?
Elizabeth.   It grows.
Proctor.   There is no word of the boys?
Elizabeth.   They're well. Rebecca's Samuel keeps them.
Proctor.   You have not seen them?
Elizabeth.   I have not. [*She catches a weakening in herself and downs it.*]
Proctor.   You are a—marvel, Elizabeth.
Elizabeth.   You—have been tortured?
Proctor.   Aye. [*Pause. She will not let herself be drowned in the sea that threatens her.*] They come for my life now.
Elizabeth.   I know it.

[*Pause.*]

Proctor.   None—have yet confessed?
Elizabeth.   There be many confessed.
Proctor.   Who are they?
Elizabeth.   There be a hundred or more, they say. Goody Ballard is one; Isaiah Goodkind is one. There be many.
Proctor.   Rebecca?
Elizabeth.   Not Rebecca. She is one foot in Heaven now; naught may hurt her more.
Proctor.   And Giles?
Elizabeth.   You have not heard of it?
Proctor.   I hear nothin', where I am kept.
Elizabeth.   Giles is dead.

[*He looks at her incredulously.*]

Proctor.   When were he hanged?
Elizabeth [*quietly, factually*].   He were not hanged. He would not answer aye or nay to his indictment; for if he denied the charge they'd hang him surely, and auction out his property. So he stand mute, and died Christian under the law. And so his sons will have his farm. It is the law, for he could not be condemned a wizard without he answer the indictment, aye or nay.
Proctor.   Then how does he die?
Elizabeth [*gently*].   They press him, John.

Proctor. Press?

Elizabeth. Great stones they lay upon his chest until he plead aye or nay. [*With a tender smile for the old man.*] They say he give them but two words. "More weight," he says. And died.

Proctor [*numbed—a thread to weave into his agony*]. "More weight."

Elizabeth. Aye. It were a fearsome man, Giles Corey.

[*Pause.*]

Proctor [*with great force of will, but not quite looking at her*]. I have been thinking I would confess to them, Elizabeth. [*She shows nothing.*] What say you? If I give them that?

Elizabeth. I cannot judge you, John.

[*Pause.*]

Proctor [*simply—a pure question*]. What would you have me do?

Elizabeth. As you will, I would have it. [*Slight pause.*] I want you living, John. That's sure.

Proctor [*pauses, then with a flailing of hope*]. Giles' wife? Have she confessed?

Elizabeth. She will not.

[*Pause.*]

Proctor. It is a pretense, Elizabeth.

Elizabeth. What is?

Proctor. I cannot mount the gibbet like a saint. It is a fraud. I am not that man. [*She is silent.*] My honesty is broke, Elizabeth; I am no good man. Nothing's spoiled by giving them this lie that were not rotten long before.

Elizabeth. And yet you've not confessed till now. That speak goodness in you.

Proctor. Spite only keeps me silent. It is hard to give a lie to dogs. [*Pause, for the first time he turns directly to her.*] I would have your forgiveness, Elizabeth.

Elizabeth. It is not for me to give, John, I am—

Proctor. I'd have you see some honesty in it. Let them that never lied die now to keep their souls. It is pretense for me, a vanity that will not blind God nor keep my children out of the wind. [*Pause.*] What say you?

Elizabeth [*upon a heaving sob that always threatens*]. John, it come to naught that I should forgive you, if you'll not forgive yourself. [*Now he turns away a little, in great agony.*] It is not my soul, John, it is yours. [*He stands, as though in physical pain, slowly rising to his feet with a great immortal longing to find his answer. It is difficult to say, and she is on the verge of tears.*] Only be sure of this, for I know it now: Whatever you will do, it is a good man does it. [*He turns his doubting, searching gaze upon her.*] I have read my heart this three month, John. [*Pause.*] I have sins of my own to count. It needs a cold wife to prompt lechery.

Proctor [*in great pain*]. Enough, enough—

Elizabeth [*now pouring out her heart*]. Better you should know me!

Proctor. I will not hear it! I know you!

Elizabeth. You take my sins upon you, John—

Proctor [*in agony*]. No, I take my own, my own!

Elizabeth. John, I counted myself so plain, so poorly made, no honest love could come to me! Suspicion kissed you when I did; I never knew how I should say my love. It were a cold house I kept! [*In fright, she swerves, as* HATHORNE *enters.*]

Hathorne. What say you, Proctor? The sun is soon up.

[PROCTOR, *his chest heaving, stares, turns to* ELIZABETH. *She comes to him as though to plead, her voice quaking.*]

Elizabeth. Do what you will. But let none be your judge. There be no higher judge under Heaven than Proctor is! Forgive me, forgive me, John—I never knew such goodness in the world! [*She covers her face, weeping.*]

[PROCTOR *turns from her to* HATHORNE; *he is off the earth, his voice hollow.*]

Proctor. I want my life.

Hathorne [*electrified, surprised.*]. You'll confess yourself?

Proctor. I will have my life.

Hathorne [*with a mystical tone*]. God be praised! It is a providence! [*He rushes out the door, and his voice is heard calling down the corridor.*] He will confess! Proctor will confess!

Proctor [*with a cry, as he strides to the door*]. Why do you cry it? [*In great pain he turns back to her.*] It is evil, is it not? It is evil.

Elizabeth [*in terror, weeping*]. I cannot judge you, John, I cannot!

Proctor. Then who will judge me? [*Suddenly clasping his hands.*] God in Heaven, what is John Proctor, what is John Proctor? [*He moves as an animal, and a fury is riding in him, a tantalized search.*] I think it is honest, I think so; I am no saint. [*As though she had denied this he calls angrily at her.*] Let Rebecca go like a saint; for me it is fraud!

[*Voices are heard in the hall, speaking together in suppressed excitement.*]

Elizabeth. I am not your judge, I cannot be. [*As though giving him release.*] Do as you will, do as you will!

Proctor. Would you give them such a lie? Say it. Would you ever give them this? [*She cannot answer.*] You would not; if tongs of fire were singeing you you would not! It is evil. Good, then—it is evil, and I do it!

[HATHORNE *enters with* DANFORTH, *and, with them,* CHEEVER, PARRIS, *and* HALE. *It is a businesslike, rapid entrance, as though the ice had been broken.*]

Danforth [*with great relief and gratitude*]. Praise to God, man, praise to God; you shall be blessed in Heaven for this. [CHEEVER *has hurried to the bench with pen, ink, and paper.* PROCTOR *watches him.*] Now then, let us have it. Are you ready, Mr. Cheever?

Proctor [*with a cold, cold horror at their efficiency*]. Why must it be written?

Danforth. Why, for the good instruction of the village, Mister; this we shall post upon the church door! [*To* PARRIS, *urgently.*] Where is the marshal?

Parris [*runs to the door and calls down the corridor*]. Marshal! Hurry!

Danforth. Now, then, Mister, will you speak slowly, and directly to the point, for Mr. Cheever's sake. [*He is on record now, and is really dictating to* CHEEVER, *who writes.*] Mr. Proctor, have you seen the Devil in your life? [PROCTOR's *jaws lock.*] Come, man, there is light in the sky; the town waits at the scaffold; I would give out this news. Did you see the Devil?

Proctor.   I did.

Parris.   Praise God!

Danforth.   And when he come to you, what were his demand? [PROCTOR *is silent.* DANFORTH *helps.*] Did he bid you to do his work upon the earth?

Proctor.   He did.

Danforth.   And you bound yourself to his service? [DANFORTH *turns, as* REBECCA NURSE *enters, with* HERRICK *helping to support her. She is barely able to walk.*] Come in, come in, woman!

Rebecca [*brightening as she sees* PROCTOR].   Ah, John! You are well, then, eh?

[PROCTOR *turns his face to the wall.*]

Danforth.   Courage, man, courage—let her witness your good example that she may come to God herself. Now hear it, Goody Nurse! Say on, Mr. Proctor. Did you bind yourself to the Devil's service?

Rebecca [*astonished*].   Why, John!

Proctor [*through his teeth, his face turned from* REBECCA].   I did.

Danforth.   Now, woman, you surely see it profit nothin' to keep this conspiracy any further. Will you confess yourself with him?

Rebecca.   Oh, John—God send his mercy on you!

Danforth.   I say, will you confess yourself, Goody Nurse?

Rebecca.   Why, it is a lie, it is a lie; how may I damn myself? I cannot, I cannot.

Danforth.   Mr. Proctor. When the Devil came to you did you see Rebecca Nurse in his company? [PROCTOR *is silent.*] Come, man, take courage—did you ever see her with the Devil?

Proctor [*almost inaudibly*].   No.

[DANFORTH, *now sensing trouble, glances at* JOHN *and goes to the table, and picks up a sheet—the list of condemned.*]

Danforth.   Did you ever see her sister, Mary Easty, with the Devil?

Proctor.   No, I did not.

Danforth [*his eyes narrow on* PROCTOR].   Did you ever see Martha Corey with the Devil?

Proctor.   I did not.

Danforth [*realizing, slowly putting the sheet down*].   Did you ever see anyone with the Devil?

Proctor.   I did not.

Danforth.   Proctor, you mistake me. I am not empowered to trade your life for a lie. You have most certainly seen some person with the Devil. [PROCTOR *is silent.*] Mr. Proctor, a score of people have already testified they saw this woman with the Devil.

Proctor.   Then it is proved. Why must I say it?

Danforth.   Why "must" you say it! Why, you should rejoice to say it if your soul is truly purged of any love for Hell!

Proctor.   They think to go like saints. I like not to spoil their names.

Danforth [*inquiring, incredulous*]. Mr. Proctor, do you think they go like saints?

Proctor [*evading*]. This woman never thought she done the Devil's work.

Danforth. Look you, sir. I think you mistake your duty here. It matters nothing what she thought—she is convicted of the unnatural murder of children, and you for sending your spirit out upon Mary Warren. Your soul alone is the issue here, Mister, and you will prove its whiteness or you cannot live in a Christian country. Will you tell me now what persons conspired with you in the Devil's company? [PROCTOR *is silent.*] To your knowledge was Rebecca Nurse ever—

Proctor. I speak my own sins; I cannot judge another. [*Crying out, with hatred.*] I have no tongue for it.

Hale [*quickly to* DANFORTH]. Excellency, it is enough he confess himself. Let him sign it, let him sign it.

Parris [*feverishly*]. It is a great service, sir. It is a weighty name; it will strike the village that Proctor confess. I beg you, let him sign it. The sun is up, Excellency!

Danforth [*considers; then with dissatisfaction*]. Come, then, sign your testimony. [*To* CHEEVER.] Give it to him. [CHEEVER *goes to* PROCTOR, *the confession and a pen in hand. Proctor does not look at it.*] Come, man, sign it.

Proctor [*after glancing at the confession*]. You have all witnessed it—it is enough.

Danforth. You will not sign it?

Proctor. You have all witnessed it; what more is neded?

Danforth. Do you sport with me? You will sign your name or it is no confession, Mister! [*His breast heaving with agonized breathing,* PROCTOR *now lays the paper down and signs his name.*]

Parris. Praise be to the Lord!

[PROCTOR *has just finished signing when* DANFORTH *reaches for the paper. But* PROCTOR *snatches it up, and now a wild terror is rising in him, and a boundless anger.*]

Danforth [*perplexed, but politely extending his hand*]. If you please, sir.

Proctor. No.

Danforth [*as though* PROCTOR *did not understand*]. Mr. Proctor, I must have—

Proctor. No, no. I have signed it. You have seen me. It is done! You have no need for this.

Parris. Proctor, the village must have proof that—

Proctor. Damn the village! I confess to God, and God has seen my name on this! It is enough!

Danforth. No, sir, it is—

Proctor. You came to save my soul, did you not? Here! I have confessed myself; it is enough!

Danforth. You have not con—

Proctor. I have confessed myself! Is there no good penitence but it be public? God does not need my name nailed upon the church! God sees my name; God knows how black my sins are! It is enough!

Danforth. Mr. Proctor—

Proctor. You will not use me! I am no Sarah Good or Tituba, I am John Proctor! You will not use me! It is no part of salvation that you should use me!

Danforth.   I do not wish to—

Proctor.   I have three children—how many I teach them to walk like men in the world, and I sold my friends?

Danforth.   You have not sold your friends—

Proctor.   Beguile me not! I blacken all of them when this is nailed to the church the very day they hang for silence!

Danforth.   Mr. Proctor, I must have good and legal proof that you—

Proctor.   You are the high court, your word is good enough! Tell them I confessed myself; say Proctor broke his knees and wept like a woman; say what you will, but my name cannot—

Danforth [*with suspicion*].   It is the same, is it not? If I report it or you sign to it?

Proctor [*he knows it is insane*].   No, it is not the same! What others say and what I sign to is not the same!

Danforth.   Why? Do you mean to deny this confession when you are free?

Proctor.   I mean to deny nothing!

Danforth.   Then explain to me, Mr. Proctor, why you will not let—

Proctor [*with a cry of his whole soul*].   Because it is my name! Because I cannot have another in my life! Because I lie and sign myself to lies! Because I am not worth the dust on the feet of them that hang! How may I live without my name? I have given you my soul; leave me my name!

Danforth [*pointing at the confession in* PROCTOR's *hand*].   Is that document a lie? If it is a lie I will not accept it! What say you? I will not deal in lies, Mister! [PROCTOR *is motionless.*] You will give me your honest confession in my hand, or I cannot keep you from the rope. [PROCTOR *does not reply.*] Which way do you go, Mister?

[*His breast heaving, his eyes staring,* PROCTOR *tears the paper and crumples it, and he is weeping in fury, but erect.*]

Danforth.   Marshal!

Parris [*hysterically, as though the tearing paper were his life*].   Proctor, Proctor!

Hale.   Man, you will hang! You cannot!

Proctor [*his eyes full of tears*].   I can. And there's your first marvel, that I can. You have made your magic now, for now I do think I see some shred of goodness in John Proctor. Not enough to weave a banner with, but white enough to keep it from such dogs. [ELIZABETH, *in a burst of terror, rushes to him and weeps against his hand.*] Give them no tear! Tears pleasure them! Show honor now, show a stony heart and sink them with it! [*He has lifted her, and kisses her now with great passion.*]

Rebecca.   Let you fear nothing! Another judgment waits us all!

Danforth.   Hang them high over the town! Who weeps for these, weeps for corruption! [*He sweeps out past them.* HERRICK *starts to lead* REBECCA, *who almost collapses, but* PROCTOR *catches her, and she glances up at him apologetically.*]

Rebecca.   I've had no breakfast.

Herrick.   Come, man.

[HERRICK *escorts them out,* HATHORNE *and* CHEEVER *behind them.* ELIZABETH *stands staring at the empty doorway.*]

Parris [in deadly fear, to ELIZABETH]. Go to him, Goody Proctor! There is yet time!

[*From outside a drumroll strikes the air.* PARRIS *is startled.* ELIZABETH *jerks about toward the window.*]

Parris. Go to him! [*He rushes out the door, as though to hold back his fate.*] Proctor! Proctor!

[*Again, a short burst of drums.*]

Hale. Woman, plead with him! [*He starts to rush out the door, and then goes back to her.*] Woman! It is pride, it is vanity. [*She avoids his eyes, and moves to the window. He drops to his knees.*] Be his helper!—What profit him to bleed? Shall the dust praise him? Shall the worms declare his truth? Go to him, take his shame away!

Elizabeth [supporting herself against collapse, grips the bars of the window, and with a cry]. He have his goodness now. God forbid I take it from him!

[*The final drumroll crashes, then heightens violently.* HALE *weeps in frantic prayer, and the new sun is pouring in upon her face, and the drums rattle like bones in the morning air.*]

[*The-Curtain Falls*]

ECHOES DOWN THE CORRIDOR

Not long after the fever died, Parris was voted from office, walked out on the highroad, and was never heard of again.

The legend has it that Abigail turned up later as a prostitute in Boston.

Twenty years after the last execution, the government awarded compensation to the victims still living, and to the families of the dead. However, it is evident that some people still were unwilling to admit their total guilt, and also that the factionalism was still alive, for some beneficiaries were actually not victims at all, but informers.

Elizabeth Proctor married again, four years after Proctor's death.

In solemn meeting, the congregation rescinded the excommunications—this in March 1712. But they did so upon orders of the government. The jury, however, wrote a statement praying forgiveness of all who had suffered.

Certain farms which had belonged to the victims were left to ruin, and for more than a century no one would buy them or live on them.

To all intents and purposes, the power of theocracy in Massachusetts was broken.

Dürrenmatt: THE VISIT

In his 1955 essay, "Problems of the Theatre," Friedrich Dürrenmatt says that in a world living under the threat of The Bomb, there can be no more tragedy. Tragedy is produced in an ordered world in which the polity has a sense of community, where there are criteria by which men can measure their stature, where there are heroes. Today, according to Dürrenmatt, we have only victims, incapable of meaningful action yet unable to escape from the horror of living out their days and ways. The central image in one of his short stories is of a man trapped in a tunnel without beginning or end. Tragedy, says Dürrenmatt, "Presupposes guilt, despair, moderation, lucidity, vision, a sense of responsibility. In the Punch-and-Judy show of our century . . . we are all collectively guilty. . . . Comedy alone is suitable for us. Our world has led to the grotesque . . ."; it calls not for a Sophocles but for a Swift. Dürrenmatt has therefore chosen to write tragicomedy with a scornful and fantastic view of a tragically irresponsible world that cannot bear the burden of its own tragedy.

To Dürrenmatt, the world stands as "something monstrous," but its chaos is an "enigmatic calamity" to which he refuses to surrender. He has said that if he felt that nothing had meaning or value, he would not bother to write. He holds that Existentialist belief that the universe is indifferent to man, but he believes that a man may, in fact must, make responsible decisions within it, no matter how futile the gesture. Although Dürrenmatt shares many of the tenets and techniques of the Theatre of the Absurd, he is much closer to the Sartrean notion that a man can find meaning, purpose, and direction only by ascribing them to his own life in a world where these three personal virtues do not exist externally.

No contemporary dramatist better illustrates the breakdown of all the old classifications and "isms" than does Friedrich Dürrenmatt. He transcends reality, yet employs techniques of realism within scenes. There is romance in his ironic fancy, expressionism in many of his symbolic sequences, epic theatre in his overall structure, social drama in his thematic material, and theatre of discussion in much of his dialogue. He is anti-illusionist, yet there is a haunting immediacy that involves our emotional responses in his plays. The modern drama has often been called eclectic, for desperate lack of a label by those who need one, and Dürrenmatt is perhaps the most eclectic of contemporary playwrights, making liberal use of established forms and traditions while emerging with a distinctly original style in his balance of old and new. There is something terrifyingly fascinating in this man's work that leaves you laughing all the way to the grave.

The macabre fable of *The Visit* was first performed in Zürich in 1956 when Dürrenmatt was 35 years old. He neither denies nor affirms that Mme. Zachanassian's name was suggested by Zacharoff, Onassis, and Gulbenkian, and he says that her resemblance to Sarah Bernhardt—the entourage, the young men, the coffin, the wooden leg, the panther—is accidental.

THE VISIT

Adapted by Maurice Valency

The Characters

Hofbauer, First Man
Helmesberger, Second Man
Wechsler, Third Man
Vogel, Fourth Man
Painter
Station Master
Burgomaster
Teacher
Pastor
Anton Schill
Claire Zachanassian
Conductor
Pedro Cabral
Bobby
Policeman
First Grandchild
Second Grandchild
Mike
Max
First Blind Man
Second Blind Man
Athlete
Frau Burgomaster
Frau Schill
Daughter
Son
Doctor Nüsslin
Frau Block, First Woman
Truck Driver
Reporter
Cameraman
Townsman
Townsman

[*The action of the play takes place in and around the little town of Güllen,*[1] *somewhere in Europe.*]

[*There are three acts.*]

---

[1] A Swiss localism that can be freely translated as "dungheap."

Act I

[*A railway-crossing bell starts ringing. Then is heard the distant sound of a locomotive whistle. The curtain rises.*]

[*The scene represents, in the simplest possible manner, a little town somewhere in Central Europe. The time is the present. The town is shabby and ruined, as if the plague had passed there. Its name, Güllen, is inscribed on the shabby signboard which adorns the façade of the railway station. This edifice is summarily indicated by a length of rusty iron paling, a platform parallel to the proscenium, beyond which one imagines the rails to be, and a baggage truck standing by a wall on which a torn timetable, marked "Fahrplan," is affixed by three nails. In the station wall is a door with a sign: "Eintritt Verboten."[1] This leads to the Station Master's office.*]

[*Left of the station is a little house of gray stucco, formerly white-washed. It has a tile roof, badly in need of repair. Some shreds of travel posters still adhere to the windowless walls. A shingle hanging over the entrance, left, reads: "Männer." On the other side the shingle reads: "Damen." Along the wall of the little house there is a wooden bench, blackless, on which four men are lounging cheerlessly, shabbily dressed, with cracked shoes. A fifth man is busied with paintpot and brush. He is kneeling on the ground, painting a strip of canvas with the words: "Welcome, Clara."*]

[*The warning signal rings uninterruptedly. The sound of the approaching train comes closer and closer. The Station Master issues from his office, advances to the center of the platform and salutes.*]

[*The train is heard thundering past in a direction parallel to the footlights, and is lost in the distance. The men on the bench follow its passing with a slow movement of their heads, from left to right.*]

First Man.   The "Emperor." Hamburg-Naples.
Second Man.   Then comes the "Diplomat."
Third Man.   Then the "Banker."
Fourth Man.   And at eleven twenty-seven the "Flying Dutchman." Venice-Stockholm.
First Man.   Our only pleasure—watching trains. [*The station bell rings again. The Station Master comes out of his office and salutes another train. The men follow its course, right to left.*]
Fourth Man.   Once upon a time the "Emperor" and the "Flying Dutchman" used to stop here in Güllen. So did the "Diplomat," the "Banker" and the "Silver Comet."
Second Man.   Now it's only the local from Kaffigen and the twelve-forty from Kalberstadt.
Third Man.   The fact is, we're ruined.
First Man.   What with the Wagonworks shut down . . .

[1]   "No admittance."

Second Man. The Foundry finished . . .

Fourth Man. The Golden Eagle Pencil Factory all washed up . . .

First Man. It's life on the dole.

Second Man. Did you say life?

Third Man. We're rotting.

First Man. Starving.

Second Man. Crumbling.

Fourth Man. The whole damn town. [*The station bell rings.*]

Third Man. Once we were a center of industry.

Painter. A cradle of culture.

Fourth Man. One of the best little towns in the country.

First Man. In the world.

Second Man. Here Goethe slept.

Fourth Man. Brahms composed a quartet.

Third Man. Here Berthold Schwarz invented gunpowder.

Painter. And I once got first prize at the Dresden Exhibition of Contemporary Art. What am I doing now? Painting signs. [*The station bell rings. The Station Master comes out. He throws away a cigarette butt. The men scramble for it.*]

First Man. Well, anyway, Madame Zachanassian will help us.

Fourth Man. If she comes . . .

Third Man. If she comes.

Second Man. Last week she was in France. She gave them a hospital.

First Man. In Rome she founded a free public nursery.

Third Man. In Leuthenau, a bird sanctuary.

Painter. They say she got Picasso to design her car.

First Man. Where does she get all that money?

Second Man. An oil company, a shipping line, three banks and five railways—

Fourth Man. And the biggest string of geisha houses in Japan.

[*From the direction of the town come the* BURGOMASTER, *the* PASTOR, *the* TEACHER *and* ANTON SCHILL. *The* BURGOMASTER, *the* TEACHER *and* SCHILL *are men in their fifties. The* PASTOR *is ten years younger. All four are dressed shabbily and are sad-looking. The* BURGOMASTER *looks official.* SCHILL *is tall and handsome, but graying and worn; nevertheless a man of considerable charm and presence. He walks directly to the little house and disappears into it.*]

Painter. Any news, Burgomaster? Is she coming?

All. Yes, is she coming?

Burgomaster. She's coming. The telegram has been confirmed. Our distinguished guest will arrive on the twelve-forty from Kalberstadt. Everyone must be ready.

Teacher. The mixed choir is ready. So is the children's chorus.

Burgomaster. And the church bell, Pastor?

Pastor. The church bell will ring. As soon as the new bell ropes are fitted. The man is working on them now.

Burgomaster. The town band will be drawn up in the market place and the Athletic Association will form a human pyramid in her honor—the top man will hold the wreath with her initials. Then lunch at the Golden Apostle. I shall say a few words.

Teacher. Of course.

Burgomaster. I had thought of illuminating the town hall and the cathedral, but we can't afford the lamps.

Painter. Burgomaster—what do you think of this? [*He shows the banner.*]

Burgomaster [*Calls*]. Schill! Schill!

Teacher. Schill! [*Schill comes out of the little house.*]

Schill. Yes, right away. Right away.

Burgomaster. This is more in your line. What do you think of this?

Schill [*Looks at the sign*]. No, no, no. That certainly won't do, Burgomaster. It's much too intimate. It shouldn't read: "Welcome, Clara." It should read: "Welcome, Madame . . ."

Teacher. Zachanassian.

Burgomaster. Zachanassian.

Schill. Zachanassian.

Painter. But she's Clara to us.

First Man. Clara Wäscher.

Second man. Born here.

Third Man. Her father was a carpenter. He built this. [*All turn and stare at the little house.*]

Schill. All the same . . .

Painter. If I . . .

Burgomaster. No, no, no. He's right. You'll have to change it.

Painter. Oh, well, I'll tell you what I'll do. I'll leave this and I'll put "Welcome, Madame Zachanassian" on the other side. Then if things go well, we can always turn it around.

Burgomaster. Good idea. [*To* SCHILL] Yes?

Schill. Well, anyway, it's safer. Everything depends on the first impression. [*The train bell is heard. Two clangs. The* PAINTER *turns the banner over and goes to work.*]

First Man. Hear that? The "Flying Dutchman" has just passed through Leuthenau.

Fourth Man. Eleven-twenty.

Burgomaster. Gentlemen, you know that the millionairess is our only hope.

Pastor. Under God.

Burgomaster. Under God. Naturally. Schill, we depend entirely on you.

Schill. Yes, I know. You keep telling me.

Burgomaster. After all, you're the only one who really knew her.

Schill. Yes, I knew her.

Pastor. You were really quite close to one another, I hear, in those days.

Schill. Close? Yes, we were close, there's no denying it. We were in love. I was young—good-looking, so they said—and Clara—you know, I can still see her in the great barn coming toward me—like a light out of the darkness. And in the Konradsweil Forest she'd come running to meet me—barefooted—her beautiful red hair streaming behind her. Like a witch. I was in love with her, all right. But you know how it is when you're twenty.

Pastor. What happened?

Schill [*Shrugs*]. Life came between us.

Burgomaster. You must give me some points about her for my speech. [*He takes out his notebook.*]

Schill. I think I can help you there.

Teacher. Well, I've gone through the school records. And the young lady's marks were, I'm afraid to say, absolutely dreadful. Even in deportment. The only subject in which she was even remotely passable was natural history.

Burgomaster. Good in natural history. That's fine. Give me a pencil. [*He makes a note.*]

Schill. She was an outdoor girl. Wild. Once, I remember, they arrested a tramp, and she threw stones at the policeman. She hated injustice passionately.

Burgomaster. Strong sense of justice. Excellent.

Schill. And generous . . .

All. Generous?

Schill. Generous to a fault. Whatever little she had, she shared—so good-hearted. I remember once she stole a bag of potatoes to give to a poor widow.

Burgomaster [*Writing in notebook*]. Wonderful generosity—

Teacher. Generosity.

Burgomaster. That, gentlemen, is something I must not fail to make a point of.

Schill. And such a sense of humor. I remember once when the oldest man in town fell and broke his leg, she said, "Oh, dear, now they'll have to shoot him."

Burgomaster. Well, I've got enough. The rest, my friend, is up to you. [*He puts the notebook away.*]

Schill. Yes, I know, but it's not so easy. After all, to part a woman like that from her millions—

Burgomaster. Exactly. Millions. We have to think in big terms here.

Teacher. If she's thinking of buying us off with a nursery school—

All. Nursery school!

Pastor. Don't accept.

Teacher. Hold out.

Schill. I'm not so sure that I can do it. You know, she may have forgotten me completely.

Burgomaster [*He exchanges a look with the* TEACHER *and the* PASTOR]. Schill, for many years you have been our most popular citizen. The most respected and the best loved.

Schill. Why, thank you . . .

Burgomaster. And therefore I must tell you—last week I sounded out the political opposition, and they agreed. In the spring you will be elected to succeed me as Burgomaster. By unanimous vote. [*The others clap their hands in approval.*]

Schill. But, my dear Burgomaster—!

Burgomaster. It's true.

Teacher. I'm a witness. I was at the meeting.

Schill. This is—naturally, I'm terribly flattered—It's a completely unexpected honor.

Burgomaster. You deserve it.

Schill. Burgomaster! Well, well—! [*Briskly*] Gentlemen, to business. The first chance I get, of course, I shall discuss our miserable position with Clara.

Teacher. But tactfully, tactfully—

Schill. What do you take me for? We must feel our way. Everything must be correct. Psychologically correct. For example, here at the railway station, a single blunder, one false note, could be disastrous.

Burgomaster. He's absolutely right. The first impression colors all the rest. Madame Zachanassian sets foot on her native soil for the first time in many years. She sees our love and she sees our misery. She remembers her youth, her friends. The tears well up into her eyes. Her childhood companions throng about her. I will naturally not present myself like this, but in my black coat with my top hat. Next to me, my wife. Before me, my two grandchildren all in white, with roses. My God, if it only comes off as I see it! If only it comes off. [*The station bell begins ringing.*] Oh, my God! Quick! We must get dressed.

First Man. It's not her train. It's only the "Flying Dutchman."

Pastor [*Calmly*]. We have still two hours before she arrives.

Schill. For God's sake, don't let's lose our heads. We still have a full two hours.

Burgomaster. Who's losing their heads? [*To* FIRST *and* SECOND MAN.] When her train comes, you two, Helmesberger and Vogel, will hold up the banner with "Welcome Madame Zachanassian." The rest will applaud.

Third Man. Bravo! [*He applauds.*]

Burgomaster. But, please, one thing—no wild cheering like last year with the government relief committee. It made no impression at all and we still haven't received any loan. What we need here is a feeling of genuine sincerity. That's how we greet with full hearts our beloved sister who has been away from us so long. Be sincerely moved, my friends, that's the secret; be sincere. Remember you're not dealing with a child. Next a few brief words from me. Then the church bell will start pealing—

Pastor. If he can fix the ropes in time. [*The station bell rings.*]

Burgomaster. —Then the mixed choir moves in. And then—

Teacher. We'll form a line down here.

Burgomaster. Then the rest of us will form in two lines leading from the station—[*He is interrupted by the thunder of the approaching train. The men crane their heads to see it pass. The Station Master advances to the platform and salutes. There is a sudden shriek of air brakes. The train screams to a stop. The four men jump up in consternation.*]

Painter. But the "Flying Dutchman" never stops!

First Man. It's stopping.

Second Man. In Güllen!

Third Man. In the poorest—

First Man. The dreariest—

Second Man. The lousiest—

Fourth Man. The most God-forsaken hole between Venice and Stockholm.

Station Master. It cannot stop! [*The train noises stop. There is only the panting of the engine.*]

Painter. It's stopped! [*The* STATION MASTER *runs out.*]

Offstage Voices. What's happened? Is there an accident? [*A hubbub of offstage voices, as if the passengers on the invisible train were alighting.*]

Claire [*Offstage*]. Is this Güllen?

Conductor [Offstage].   Here, here, what's going on?
Claire [Offstage].   Who the hell are you?
Conductor [Offstage].   But you pulled the emergency cord, madame!
Claire [Offstage].   I always pull the emergency cord.
Station Master [Offstage].   I must ask you what's going on here.
Claire [Offstage].   And who the hell are you?
Station Master [Offstage].   I'm the Station Master, madame, and I must ask
   you—
Claire [Enters].   No!

[*From the right* CLAIRE ZACHANASSIAN *appears. She is an extraordinary woman.
She is in her fifties, red-haired, remarkably dressed, with a face as impassive as
that of an ancient idol, beautiful still, and with a singular grace of movement
and manner. She is simple and unaffected, yet she has the haughtiness of a
world power. The entire effect is striking to the point of the unbelievable.
Behind her comes her fiancé,* PEDRO CABRAL, *tall, young, very handsome, and
completely equipped for fishing, with creel and net, and with a rod case in his
hand. An excited* CONDUCTOR *follows.*]

Conductor.   But, madame, I must insist! You have stopped "The Flying Dutch-
   man." I must have an explanation.
Claire.   Nonsense. Pedro.
Pedro.   Yes, my love?
Claire.   This is Güllen. Nothing has changed. I recognize it all. There's the
   forest of Konradsweil. There's a brook in it full of trout, where you can fish.
   And there's the roof of the great barn. Ha! God! What a miserable blot on the
   map.

[*She crosses the stage and goes off with* PEDRO.]

Schill.   My God! Clara!
Teacher.   Claire Zachanassian!
All.   Claire Zachanassian!
Burgomaster.   And the town band? The town band! Where is it?
Teacher.   The mixed choir! The mixed choir!
Pastor.   The church bell! The church bell!
Burgomaster [To the FIRST MAN].   Quick! My dress coat. My top hat. My
   grandchildren. Run! Run! [FIRST MAN *runs off. The* BURGOMASTER *shouts after
   him.*] And don't forget my wife! [*General panic. The* THIRD MAN *and* FOURTH
   MAN *hold up the banner, on which only part of the name has been painted:*
   "Welcome Mad—" *Claire and Pedro re-enter, right.*]
Conductor [Mastering himself with an effort].   Madame. The train is waiting.
   The entire international railway schedule has been disrupted. I await your
   explanation.
Claire.   You're a very foolish man. I wish to visit this town. Did you expect me to
   jump off a moving train?
Conductor [Stupefied].   You stopped the "Flying Dutchman" because you
   wished to visit the town?
Claire.   Naturally.

Conductor [*Inarticulate*].   Madame!

Station Master.   Madame, if you wished to visit the town, the twelve-forty from Kalberstadt was entirely at your service. Arrival in Güllen, one-seventeen.

Claire.   The local that stops at Loken, Beisenbach and Leuthenau? Do you expect me to waste three-quarters of an hour chugging dismally through this wilderness?

Conductor.   Madame, you shall pay for this!

Claire.   Bobby, give him a thousand marks. [*Bobby, her butler, a man in his seventies, wearing dark glasses, opens his wallet. The townspeople gasp.*]

Conductor [*Taking the money in amazement*].   But, madame!

Claire.   And three thousand for the Railway Widows' Relief Fund.

Conductor [*With the money in his hands*].   But we have no such fund, madame.

Claire.   Now you have. [*The* BURGOMASTER *pushes his way forward.*]

Burgomaster [*He whispers to the* CONDUCTOR *and* TEACHER].   The lady is Madame Claire Zachanassian.

Conductor.   Claire Zachanassian? Oh, my God! But that's naturally quite different. Needless to say, we would have stopped the train if we'd had the slightest idea. [*He hands the money back to* BOBBY.] Here, please. I couldn't dream of it. Four thousand. My God!

Claire.   Keep it. Don't fuss.

Conductor.   Would you like the train to wait, madame, while you visit the town? The administration will be delighted. The cathedral porch. The town hall—

Claire.   You may take the train away. I don't need it any more.

Station Master.   All aboard! [*He puts his whistle to his lips.* PEDRO *stops him.*]

Pedro.   But the press, my angel. They don't know anything about this. They're still in the dining car.

Claire.   Let them stay there. I don't want the press in Güllen at the moment. Later they will come by themselves. [*To* STATION MASTER] And now what are you waiting for?

Station Master.   All aboard! [*The* STATION MASTER *blows a long blast on his whistle. The train leaves. Meanwhile, the* FIRST MAN *has brought the* BURGO-MASTER's *dress coat and top hat. The* BURGOMASTER *puts on the coat, then advances slowly and solemnly.*]

Conductor.   I trust madame will not speak of this to the administration. It was a pure misunderstanding. [*He salutes and runs for the train as it starts moving.*]

Burgomaster [*Bows*].   Gracious lady, as Burgomaster of the town of Güllen, I have the honor—[*The rest of the speech is lost in the roar of the departing train. He continues speaking and gesturing, and at last bows amid applause as the train noises end.*]

Claire.   Thank you, Mr. Burgomaster. [*She glances at the beaming faces, and lastly at* SCHILL, *whom she does not recognize. She turns upstage.*]

Schill.   Clara!

Claire [*Turns and stares*].   Anton?

Schill.   Yes. It's good that you've come back.

Claire.   Yes. I've waited for this moment. All my life. Ever since I left Güllen.

Schill [*A little embarrassed*].   That is very kind of you to say, Clara.

Claire.   And have you thought about me?

Schill.   Naturally. Always. You know that.

Claire. Those were happy times we spent together.

Schill. Unforgettable. [*He smiles reassuringly at the* BURGOMASTER.]

Claire. Call me by the name you used to call me.

Schill [*Whispers*]. My kitten.

Claire. What?

Schill [*Louder*]. My kitten.

Claire. And what else?

Schill. Little witch.

Claire. I used to call you my black panther. You're gray now, and soft.

Schill. But you are still the same, little witch.

Claire. I am the same? [*She laughs.*] Oh, no, my black panther, I am not at all the same.

Schill [*Gallantly*]. In my eyes you are. I see no difference.

Claire. Would you like to meet my fiancé? Pedro Cabral. He owns an enormous plantation in Brazil.

Schill. A pleasure.

Claire. We're to be married soon.

Schill. Congratulations.

Claire. He will be my eighth husband. [PEDRO *stands by himself downstage, right.*] Pedro, come here and show your face. Come along, darling—come here! Don't sulk. Say hello.

Pedro. Hello.

Claire. A man of few words! Isn't he charming? A diplomat. He's interested only in fishing. Isn't he handsome, in his Latin way? You'd swear he was a Brazilian. But he's not—he's a Greek. His father was a White Russian. We were betrothed by a Bulgarian priest. We plan to be married in a few days here in the cathedral.

Burgomaster. Here in the cathedral? What an honor for us!

Claire. No. It was my dream, when I was seventeen, to be married in Güllen cathedral. The dreams of youth are sacred, don't you think so, Anton?

Schill. Yes, of course.

Claire. Yes, of course. I think so, too. Now I would like to look at the town.

[*The mixed choir arrives, breathless, wearing ordinary clothes with green sashes.*]

What's all this? Go away. [*She laughs.*] Ha! Ha! Ha!

Teacher. Dear Lady—[*He steps forward, having put on a sash also.*] Dear lady, as Rector of the high school and a devotee of that noble muse, Music, I take pleasure in presenting the Güllen mixed choir.

Claire. How do you do?

Teacher. Who will sing for you an ancient folk song of the region, with specially amended words—if you will deign to listen.

Claire. Very well. Fire away.

[*The* TEACHER *blows a pitch pipe. The mixed choir begins to sing the ancient folk song with the amended words. Just then the station bell starts ringing. The song is drowned in the roar of the passing express. The* STATION MASTER *salutes. When the train has passed, there is applause.*]

Burgomaster. The church bell! The church bell! Where's the church bell? [*The* PASTOR *shrugs helplessly.*]

Claire. Thank you, Professor. They sang beautifully. The little blond bass—no, not that one—the one with the big Adam's apple—was most impressive. [*The* TEACHER *bows. The* POLICEMAN *pushes his way professionally through the mixed choir and comes to attention in front of* CLAIRE ZACHANASSIAN.] Now, who are you?

Policeman [*Clicks heels*]. Police Chief Schultz. At your service.

Claire [*She looks him up and down*]. I have no need of you at the moment. But I think there will be work for you by and by. Tell me, do you know how to close an eye from time to time?

Policeman. How else could I get along in my profession?

Claire. You might practice closing both.

Schill [*Laughs*]. What a sense of humor, eh?

Burgomaster [*Puts on the top hat*]. Permit me to present my grandchildren, gracious lady. Hermine and Adolphine. There's only my wife still to come. [*He wipes the perspiration from his brow, and replaces the hat. The little girls present the roses with elaborate curtsies.*]

Claire. Thank you, my dears. Congratulations, Burgomaster. Extraordinary children. [*She plants the roses in* PEDRO'S *arms. The* BURGOMASTER *secretly passes his top hat to the* PASTOR, *who puts it on.*]

Burgomaster. Our pastor, madame. [*The* PASTOR *takes off the hat and bows.*]

Claire. Ah. The pastor. How do you do? Do you give consolation to the dying?

Pastor [*A bit puzzled*]. That is part of my ministry, yes.

Claire. And to those who are condemned to death?

Pastor. Capital punishment has been abolished in this country, madame.

Claire. I see. Well, it could be restored, I suppose. [*The* PASTOR *hands back the hat. He shrugs his shoulders in confusion.*]

Schill [*Laughs*]. What an original sense of humor! [*All laugh, a little blankly.*]

Claire. Well, I can't sit here all day—I should like to see the town. [*The* BURGOMASTER *offers his arm.*]

Burgomaster. May I have the honor, gracious lady?

Claire. Thank you, but these legs are not what they were. This one was broken in five places.

Schill [*Full of concern*]. My kitten!

Claire. When my airplane bumped into a mountain in Afghanistan. All the others were killed. Even the pilot. But as you see, I survived. I don't fly any more.

Schill. But you're as strong as ever now.

Claire. Stronger.

Burgomaster. Never fear, gracious lady. The town doctor has a car.

Claire. I never ride in motors.

Burgomaster. You never ride in motors?

Claire. Not since my Ferrari crashed in Hong Kong.

Schill. But how do you travel, then, little witch? On a broom?

Claire. Mike—Max! [*She claps her hands. Two huge bodyguards come in, left, carrying a sedan chair. She sits in it.*] I travel this way—a bit antiquated, of course. But perfectly safe. Ha! Ha! Aren't they magnificent? Mike and Max. I bought them in America. They were in jail, condemned to the chair. I had them pardoned. Now they're condemned to my chair. I paid fifty thousand dollars apiece for them. You couldn't get them now for twice the sum. The sedan chair comes from the Louvre. I fancied it so much that the President of France gave it to me. The French are so impulsive, don't you think so, Anton? Go! [*Mike and Max start to carry her off.*]

Burgomaster. You wish to visit the cathedral? And the old town hall?

Claire. No. The great barn. And the forest of Konradsweil. I wish to go with Anton and visit our old haunts once again.

The Pastor. Very touching.

Claire [*To the butler*]. Will you send my luggage and the coffin to the Golden Apostle?

Burgomaster. The coffin?

Claire. Yes. I brought one with me. Go!

Teacher. Hip-hip—

All. Hurrah! Hip-hip, hurrah! Hurrah! [*They bear her off in the direction of the town. The* TOWNSPEOPLE *burst into cheers. The church bell rings.*]

Burgomaster. Ah, thank God—the bell at last.

[*The* POLICEMAN *is about to follow the others, when the two* BLIND MEN *appear. They are not young, yet they seem childish—a strange effect. Though they are of different height and features, they are dressed exactly alike, and so create the effect of being twins. They walk slowly, feeling their way. Their voices, when they speak, are curiously high and flutelike, and they have a curious trick of repetition of phrases.*]

First Blind Man. We're in—

Both Blind Men. Güllen.

First Blind Man. We breathe—

Second Blind Man. We breathe—

Both Blind Men. We breathe the air, the air of Güllen.

Policeman [*Startled*]. Who are you?

First Blind Man. We belong to the lady.

Second Blind Man. We belong to the lady. She calls us—

First Blind Man. Kobby.

Second Blind Man. And Lobby.

Policeman. Madame Zachanassian is staying at the Golden Apostle.

First Blind Man. We're blind.

Second Blind Man. We're blind.

Policeman. Blind? Come along with me, then. I'll take you there.

First Blind Man. Thank you, Mr. Policeman.

Second Blind Man. Thanks very much.

Policeman. Hey! How do you know I'm a policeman, if you're blind?

Both Blind Men. By your voice. By your voice.

First Blind Man. All policemen sound the same.

Policeman. You've had a lot to do with the police, have you, little men?

First Blind Man. Men he calls us!

Both Blind Men. Men!

Policeman. What are you then?

Both Blind Men. You'll see. You'll see. [*The* POLICEMAN *claps his hands suddenly. The* BLIND MEN *turn sharply toward the sound. The* POLICEMAN *is convinced they are blind.*]

Policeman. What's your trade?

Both Blind Men. We have no trade.

Second Blind Man. We play music.

First Blind Man. We sing.

Second Blind Man. We amuse the lady.

First Blind Man. We look after the beast.

Second Blind Man. We feed it.

First Blind Man. We stroke it.

Second Blind Man. We take it for walks.

Policeman. What beast?

Both Blind Men. You'll see—you'll see.

Second Blind Man. We give it raw meat.

First Blind Man. And she gives us chicken and wine.

Second Blind Man. Every day—

Both Blind Men. Every day.

Policeman. Rich people have strange tastes.

Both Blind Men. Strange tastes—strange tastes. [*The* POLICEMAN *puts on his helmet.*]

Policeman. Come along, I'll take you to the lady. [*The two* BLIND MEN *turn and walk off.*]

Both Blind Men. We know the way—we know the way.

[*The station and the little house vanish. A sign representing the Golden Apostle descends. The scene dissolves into the interior of the inn. The Golden Apostle is seen to be in the last stages of decay. The walls are cracked and moldering, and the plaster is falling from the ancient lath. A table represents the café of the inn. The* BURGOMASTER *and the* TEACHER *sit at this table, drinking a glass together. A procession of* TOWNSPEOPLE, *carrying many pieces of luggage, passes. Then comes a coffin, and last, a large box covered with a canvas. They cross the stage from right to left.*]

Burgomaster. Trunks. Suitcases. Boxes. [*He looks up apprehensively at the ceiling.*] The floor will never bear the weight. [*As the large covered box is carried in, he peers under the canvas, then draws back.*] Good God!

Teacher. Why, what's in it?

Burgomaster. A live panther. [*They laugh. The* BURGOMASTER *lifts his glass solemnly.*] Your health, Professor. Let's hope she puts the Foundry back on its feet.

Teacher [*Lifts his glass*]. And the Wagonworks.

Burgomaster. And the Golden Eagle Pencil Factory. Once that starts moving, everything else will go. *Prosit.* [*They touch glasses and drink.*]

Teacher. What does she need a panther for?

Burgomaster. Don't ask me. The whole thing is too much for me. The Pastor had to go home and lie down.

Teacher [*Sets down his glass*]. If you want to know the truth, she frightens me.

Burgomaster [*Nods gravely*]. She's a strange one.

Teacher. You understand, Burgomaster, a man who for twenty-two years has been correcting the Latin compositions of the students of Güllen is not unaccustomed to surprises. I have seen things to make one's hair stand on end. But when this woman suddenly appeared on the platform, a shudder tore through me. It was as though out of the clear sky all at once a fury descended upon us, beating its black wings—

[*The* POLICEMAN *comes in. He mops his face.*]

Policeman. Ah! Now the old place is livening up a bit!

Burgomaster. Ah, Schultz, come and join us.

Policeman. Thank you. [*He calls.*] Beer!

Burgomaster. Well, what's the news from the front?

Policeman. I'm just back from Schiller's barn. My God! What a scene! She had us all tiptoeing around in the straw as if we were in church. Nobody dared to speak above a whisper. And the way she carried on! I was so embarrassed I let them go to the forest by themselves.

Burgomaster. Does the fiancé go with them?

Policeman. With his fishing rod and his landing net. In full marching order. [*He calls again.*] Beer!

Burgomaster. That will be her seventh husband.

Teacher. Her eighth.

Burgomaster. But what does she expect to find in the Konradsweil forest?

Policeman. The same thing she expected to find in the old barn, I suppose. The—the—

Teacher. The ashes of her youthful love.

Policeman. Exactly.

Teacher. It's poetry.

Policeman. Poetry.

Teacher. Sheer poetry! It makes one think of Shakespeare, of Wagner. Of Romeo and Juliet. [*The* SECOND MAN *comes in as a waiter. The* POLICEMAN *is served his beer.*]

Burgomaster. Yes, you're right. [*Solemnly*] Gentlemen, I would like to propose a toast. To our great and good friend, Anton Schill, who is even now working on our behalf.

Policeman. Yes! He's really working.

Burgomaster. Gentlemen, to the best-loved citizen of this town. My successor, Anton Schill!

[*They raise their glasses. At this point an unearthly scream is heard. It is the black panther howling offstage. The sign of the Golden Apostle rises out of sight. The lights go down. The inn vanishes. Only the wooden bench, on which the four men were lounging in the opening scene, is left on the stage, downstage right. The procession comes on upstage. The two bodyguards carry in* CLAIRE'S *sedan chair. Next to it walks* SCHILL. PEDRO *walks behind, with his fishing rod. Last come the two* BLIND MEN *and the* BUTLER. CLAIRE *alights.*]

Claire. Stop! Take my chair off somewhere else. I'm tired of looking at you [*The bodyguards and the sedan chair go off.*] Pedro darling, your brook is just a little

further along down that path. Listen. You can hear it from here. Bobby, take
him and show him where it is.
Both Blind Men.   We'll show him the way—we'll show him the way.

[*They go off, left.* PEDRO *follows.* BOBBY *walks off, right.*]

Claire.   Look, Anton. Our tree. There's the heart you carved in the bark long
ago.
Schill.   Yes. It's still there.
Claire.   How it has grown! The trunk is black and wrinkled. Why, its limbs are
twice what they were. Some of them have died.
Schill.   It's aged. But it's there.
Claire.   Like everything else. [*She crosses, examining other trees.*] Oh, how tall
they are. How long it is since I walked here, barefoot over the pine needles and
the damp leaves. Look, Anton. A fawn.
Schill.   Yes, a fawn. It's the season.
Claire.   I thought everything would be changed. But it's all just as we left it. This
is the seat we sat on years ago. Under these branches you kissed me. And over
there under the hawthorn, where the moss is soft and green, we would lie in
each other's arms. It is all as it used to be. Only we have changed.
Schill.   Not so much, little witch. I remember the first night we spent together,
you ran away and I chased you till I was quite breathless—
Claire.   Yes.
Schill.   Then I was angry and I was going home, when suddenly I heard you call
and I looked up, and there you were sitting in a tree, laughing down at me.
Claire.   No. It was in the great barn. I was in the hayloft.
Schill.   Were you?
Claire.   Yes. What else do you remember?
Schill.   I remember the morning we went swimming by the waterfall, and after-
wards we were lying together on the big rock in the sun, when suddenly we
heard footsteps and we just had time to snatch up 'our clothes and run behind
the bushes when the old pastor appeared and scolded you for not being in
school.
Claire.   No. It was the schoolmaster who found us. It was Sunday and I was
supposed to be in church.
Schill.   Really?
Claire.   Yes. Tell me more.
Schill.   I remember the time your father beat you, and you showed me the cuts
on your back, and I swore I'd kill him. And the next day I dropped a tile from a
roof top and split his head open.
Claire.   You missed him.
Schill.   No!
Claire.   You hit old Mr. Reiner.
Schill.   Did I?
Claire.   Yes. I was seventeen. And you were not yet twenty. You were so hand-
some. You were the best-looking boy in town. [*The two* BLIND MEN *begin
playing mandolin music offstage, very softly.*]
Schill.   And you were the prettiest girl.

Claire. We were made for each other.

Schill. So we were.

Claire. But you married Mathilde Blumhard and her store, and I married old Zachanassian and his oil wells. He found me in a whorehouse in Hamburg. It was my hair that entangled him, the old golden beetle.

Schill. Clara!

Claire. [*She claps her hands.*] Bobby! A cigar. [BOBBY *appears with a leather case. He selects a cigar, puts it in a holder, lights it, and presents it to* CLAIRE.]

Schill. My kitten smokes cigars!

Claire. Yes. I adore them. Would you care for one?

Schill. Yes, please. I've never smoked one of those.

Claire. It's a taste I acquired from old Zachanassian. Among other things. He was a real connoisseur.

Schill. We used to sit on this bench once, you and I, and smoke cigarettes. Do you remember?

Claire. Yes. I remember.

Schill. The cigarettes I bought from Mathilde.

Claire. No. She gave them to you for nothing.

Schill. Clara—don't be angry with me for marrying Mathilde.

Claire. She had money.

Schill. But what a lucky thing for you that I did!

Claire. Oh?

Schill. You were so young, so beautiful. You deserved a far better fate than to settle in this wretched town without any future.

Claire. Yes?

Schill. If you had stayed in Güllen and married me, your life would have been wasted, like mine.

Claire. Oh?

Schill. Look at me. A wretched shopkeeper in a bankrupt town!

Claire. But you have your family.

Schill. My family! Never for a moment do they let me forget my failure, my poverty.

Claire. Mathilde has not made you happy?

Schill [*Shrugs*]. What does it matter?

Claire. And the children?

Schill [*Shakes his head*]. They're so completely materialistic. You know, they have no interest whatever in higher things.

Claire. How sad for you. [*A moment's pause, during which only the faint tinkling of the music is heard.*]

Schill. Yes. You know, since you went away my life has passed by like a stupid dream. I've hardly once been out of this town. A trip to a lake years ago. It rained all the time. And once five days in Berlin. That's all.

Claire. The world is much the same everywhere.

Schill. At least you've seen it.

Claire. Yes. I've seen it.

Schill. You've lived in it.

Claire. I've lived in it. The world and I have been on very intimate terms.

Schill. Now that you've come back, perhaps things will change.

Claire.   Naturally, I certainly won't leave my native town in this condition.
Schill.   It will take millions to put us on our feet again.
Claire.   I have millions.
Schill.   One, two, three.
Claire.   Why not?
Schill.   You mean—you will help us?
Claire.   Yes. [*A woodpecker is heard in the distance.*]
Schill.   I knew it—I knew it. I told them you were generous. I told them you
were good. Oh, my kitten, my kitten. [*He takes her hand. She turns her head
away and listens.*]
Claire.   Listen! A woodpecker.
Schill.   It's all just the way it was in the days when we were young and full of
courage. The sun high above the pines. White clouds, piling up on one another.
And the cry of the cuckoo in the distance. And the wind rustling the leaves, like
the sound of surf on a beach. Just as it was years ago. If only we could roll back
time and be together always.
Claire.   Is that your wish?
Schill.   Yes. You left me, but you never left my heart. [*He raises her hand to his
lips.*] The same soft little hand.
Claire.   No, not quite the same. It was crushed in the plane accident. But they
mended it. They mend everything nowadays.
Schill.   Crushed? You wouldn't know it. See, another fawn.
Claire.   The old wood is alive with memories.

[PEDRO *appears, right, with a fish in his hand.*]

Pedro.   See what I've caught, darling. See? A pike. Over two kilos. [*The* BLIND
MEN *appear onstage.*]
Both BLIND MEN [*Clapping their hands*].   A pike! A pike! Hurrah! Hurrah!

[*As the* BLIND MEN *clap their hands,* CLAIRE *and* SCHILL *exit, and the scene
dissolves. The clapping of hands is taken up on all sides. The townspeople wheel
in the walls of the café. A brass band strikes up a march tune. The door of the
Golden Apostle descends. The townspeople bring in tables and set them with
ragged tablecloths, cracked china and glassware. There is a table in the center,
upstage, flanked by two tables perpendicular to it, right and left. The* PASTOR
and the BURGOMASTER *come in.* SCHILL *enters. Other townspeople filter in, left
and right. One, the* ATHLETE, *is in gymnastic costume. The applause continues.*]

Burgomaster.   She's coming! [CLAIRE *enters upstage, center, followed by* BOBBY.]
The applause is meant for you, gracious lady.
Claire.   The band deserves it more than I. They blow from the heart. And the
human pyramid was beautiful. You, show me your muscles. [*The* ATHLETE
kneels before her.] Superb. Wonderful arms, powerful hands. Have you ever
strangled a man with them?
Athlete.   Strangled?
Claire.   Yes. It's perfectly simple. A little pressure in the proper place, and the
rest goes by itself. As in politics.

[*The* BURGOMASTER'S WIFE *comes up, simpering.*]

Burgomaster [*Presents her*]. Permit me to present my wife, Madame Zachanassian.

Claire. Annette Dummermuth. The head of our class.

Burgomaster [*He presents another sour-looking woman*]. Frau Schill.

Claire. Mathilde Blumhard. I remember the way you used to follow Anton with
your eyes, from behind the shop door. You've grown a little thin and dry, my
poor Mathilde.

Schill. My daughter, Ottilie.

Claire. Your daughter . . .

Schill. My son, Karl.

Claire. Your son. Two of them!

[*The town* DOCTOR *comes in, right. He is a man of fifty, strong and stocky, with
bristly black hair, a mustache and a saber cut on his cheek. He is wearing an old
cutaway.*]

Doctor. Well, well, my old Mercedes got me here in time after all!

Burgomaster. Dr. Nüsslin, the town physician. Madame Zachanassian.

Doctor. Deeply honored, madame. [*He kisses her hand.* CLAIRE *studies him.*]

Claire. It is you who signs the death certificates?

Doctor. Death certificates?

Claire. When someone dies.

Doctor. Why certainly. That is one of my duties.

Claire. And when the heart dies, what do you put down? Heart failure?

Schill [*Laughing*]. What a golden sense of humor!

Doctor. Bit grim, wouldn't you say?

Schill [*Whispers*]. Not at all, not at all. She's promised us a million.

Burgomaster [*Turns his head*]. What?

Schill. A million!

All [*Whisper*]. A million! [CLAIRE *turns toward them.*]

Claire. Burgomaster.

Burgomaster. Yes?

Claire. I'm hungry. [*The girls and the waiter fill glasses and bring food. There is
a general stir. All take their places at the tables.*] Are you going to make a
speech? [*The* BURGOMASTER *bows.* CLAIRE *sits next to the* BURGOMASTER. *The*
BURGOMASTER *rises, tapping his knife on his glass. He is radiant with good will.*
ALL *applaud.*]

Burgomaster. Gracious lady and friends. Gracious lady, it is now many years
since you first left your native town of Güllen, which was founded by the
Elector Hasso and which nestles in the green slope between the forest of
Konradsweil and the beautiful valley of Pückenried. Much has taken place in
this time, much that is evil.

Teacher. That's true.

Burgomaster. The world is not what it was; it has become harsh and bitter, and
we too have had our share of harshness and bitterness. But in all this time, dear
lady, we have never forgotten our little Clara. [*Applause.*] Many years ago you
brightened the town with your pretty face as a child, and now once again you
brighten it with your presence. [*Polite applause.*] We haven't forgotten you,

and we haven't forgotten your family. Your mother, beautiful and robust even in her old age—[*He looks for his notes on the table.*]—although unfortunately taken from us in the bloom of her youth by an infirmity of the lungs. Your respected father, Siegfried Wäscher, the builder, an example of whose work next to our railway station is often visited—[SCHILL *covers his face.*]—that is to say, admired—a lasting monument of local design and local workmanship. And you, gracious lady, whom we remember as a golden-haired—[*He looks at her.*]— little red-headed sprite romping about our peaceful streets—on your way to school—which of us does not treasure your memory? [*He pokes nervously at his notebook.*] We well remember your scholarly attainments—

Teacher. Yes.

Burgomaster. Natural history . . . Extraordinary sense of justice . . . And, above all, your supreme generosity. [*Great applause.*] We shall never forget how you once spent the whole of your little savings to buy a sack of potatoes for a poor starving widow who was in need of food. Gracious lady, ladies and gentlemen, today our little Clara has become the world-famous Claire Zachanassian who has founded hospitals, soup kitchens, charitable institutes, art projects, libraries, nurseries and schools, and now that she has at last once more returned to the town of her birth, sadly fallen as it is, I say in the name of all her loving friends who have sorely missed her: Long live our Clara!

All. Long live our Clara! [*Cheers. Music. Fanfare. Applause.* CLAIRE *rises.*]

Claire. Mr. Burgomaster. Fellow townsmen. I am greatly moved by the nature of your welcome and the disinterested joy which you have manifested on the occasion of my visit to my native town. I was not quite the child the Burgomaster described in his gracious address . . .

Burgomaster. Too modest, madame.

Claire. In school I was beaten—

Teacher. Not by me.

Claire. And the sack of potatoes which I presented to Widow Boll, I stole with the help of Anton Schill, not to save the old trull from starvation, but so that for once I might sleep with Anton in a real bed instead of under the trees of the forest. [*The townspeople look grave, embarrassed.*] Nevertheless, I shall try to deserve your good opinion. In memory of the seventeen years I spent among you, I am prepared to hand over as a gift to the town of Güllen the sum of one billion marks. Five hundred million to the town, and five hundred million to be divided per capita among the citizens. [*There is a moment of dead silence.*]

Burgomaster. A billion marks?

Claire. On one condition. [*Suddenly a movement of uncontrollable joy breaks out. People jump on chairs, dance about, yell excitedly. The* ATHLETE *turns handsprings in front of the speaker's table.*]

Schill. Oh, Clara, you astonishing, incredible, magnificent woman! What a heart! What a gesture! Oh—my little witch! [*He kisses her hand.*]

Burgomaster [*Holds up his arms for order*]. Quiet! Quiet, please! On one condition, the gracious lady said. Now, madame, may we know what that condition is?

Claire. I will tell you. In exchange for my billion marks, I want justice. [*Silence.*]

Burgomaster. Justice, madame?

Claire. I wish to buy justice.

Burgomaster. But justice cannot be bought, madame.

Claire. Everything can be bought.

Burgomaster. I don't understand at all.

Claire. Bobby, step forward. [*The butler goes to the center of the stage. He takes off his dark glasses and turns his face with a solemn air.*]

Bobby. Does anyone here present recognize me?

Frau Schill. Hofer! Hofer!

All. Who? What's that?

Teacher. Not Chief Magistrate Hofer?

Bobby. Exactly. Chief Magistrate Hofer. When Madame Zachanassian was a girl, I was presiding judge at the criminal court of Güllen. I served there until twenty-five years ago, when Madame Zachanassian offered me the opportunity of entering her service as butler. I accepted. You may consider it a strange employment for a member of the magistracy, but the salary—[CLAIRE *bangs the mallet on the table.*]

Claire. Come to the point.

Bobby. You have heard Madame Zachanassian's offer. She will give you a billion marks—when you have undone the injustice that she suffered at your hands here in Güllen as a girl. [*All murmur.*]

Burgomaster. Injustice at our hands? Impossible!

Bobby. Anton Schill . . .

Schill. Yes?

Bobby. Kindly stand. [SCHILL *rises. He smiles, as if puzzled. He shrugs.*]

Schill. Yes?

Bobby. In those days, a bastardy case was tried before me. Madame Claire Zachanassian, at that time called Clara Wäscher, charged you with being the father of her illegitimate child. [*Silence.*] You denied the charge. And produced two witnesses in your support.

Schill. That's ancient history. An absurd business. We were children. Who remembers?

Claire. Where are the blind men?

Both Blind Men. Here we are. Here we are. [MIKE *and* MAX *push them forward.*]

Bobby. You recognize these men, Anton Schill?

Schill. I never saw them before in my life. What are they?

Both Blind Men. We've changed. We've changed.

Bobby. What were your names in your former life?

First Blind Man. I was Jacob Hueblein. Jacob Hueblein.

Second Blind Man. I was Ludwig Sparr. Ludwig Sparr.

Bobby [*To* SCHILL]. Well?

Schill. These names mean nothing to me.

Bobby. Jacob Hueblein and Ludwig Sparr, do you recognize the defendant?

First Blind Man. We're blind.

Second Blind Man. We're blind.

Schill. Ha-ha-ha!

Bobby. By his voice?

Both Blind Men. By his voice. By his voice.

Bobby. At that trial, I was the judge. And you?

Both Blind Men. We were the witnesses.

Bobby. And what did you testify on that occasion?

First Blind Man. That we had slept with Clara Wäscher.

Second Blind Man. Both us us. Many times.

Bobby. And was it true?

First Blind Man. No.

Second Blind Man. We swore falsely.

Bobby. And why did you swear falsely?

First Blind Man. Anton Schill bribed us.

Second Blind Man. He bribed us.

Bobby. With what?

Both Blind Men. With a bottle of schnapps.

Bobby. And now tell the people what happened to you. [*They hesitate and whimper.*] Speak!

First Blind Man [*In a low voice*]. She tracked us down.

Bobby. Madame Zachanassian tracked them down. Jacob Hueblein was found in Canada. Ludwig Sparr in Australia. And when she found you, what did she do to you?

Second Blind Man. She handed us over to Mike and Max.

Bobby. And what did Mike and Max do to you?

First Blind Man. They made us what you see. [*The* BLIND MEN *cover their faces.* MIKE *and* MAX *push them off.*]

Bobby. And there you have it. We are all present in Güllen once again. The plaintiff. The defendant. The two false witnesses. The judge. Many years have passed. Does the plaintiff have anything further to add?

Claire. There is nothing to add.

Bobby. And the defendant?

Schill. Why are you doing this? It was all dead and buried.

Bobby. What happened to the child that was born?

Claire [*In a low voice*]. It lived a year.

Bobby. And what happened to you?

Claire. I became a whore.

Bobby. Why?

Claire. The judgment of the court left me no alternative. No one would trust me. No one would give me work.

Bobby. So. And now, what is the nature of the reparation you demand?

Claire. I want the life of Anton Schill. [FRAU SCHILL *springs to* ANTON'S *side. She puts her arms around him. The children rush to him. He breaks away.*]

Frau Schill. Anton! No! No!

Schill. No— No— She's joking. That happened long ago. That's all forgotten.

Claire. Nothing is forgotten. Neither the mornings in the forest, nor the nights in the great barn, nor the bedroom in the cottage, nor your treachery at the end. You said this morning that you wished that time might be rolled back. Very well—I have rolled it back. And now it is I who will buy justice. You bought it with a bottle of schnapps. I am willing to pay one billion marks. [*The* BURGO-MASTER *stands up, very pale and dignified.*]

Burgomaster. Madame Zachanassian, we are not in the jungle. We are in Europe. We may be poor, but we are not heathens. In the name of the town of Güllen, I decline your offer. In the name of humanity. We shall never accept.

[*All applaud wildly. The applause turns into a sinister rhythmic beat. As* CLAIRE *rises, it dies away. She looks at the crowd, then at the* BURGOMASTER.]

Claire.   Thank you, Burgomaster. [*She stares at him a long moment.*] I can wait. [*She turns and walks off. Curtain.*]

Act II

[*The façade of the Golden Apostle, with a balcony on which chairs and a table are set out. To the right of the inn is a sign which reads: "Anton Schill, Handlung."*[1] *Under the sign the shop is represented by a broken counter. Behind the counter are some shelves with tobacco, cigarettes and liquor bottles. There are two milk cans. The shop door is imaginary, but each entrance is indicated by a doorbell with a tinny sound.*]

[*It is early morning.*]

[SCHILL *is sweeping the shop. The* SON *has a pan and brush and also sweeps. The* DAUGHTER *is dusting. They are singing "The Happy Wanderer."*]

Schill.   Karl—[KARL *crosses with a dustpan.* SCHILL *sweeps dust into the pan. The doorbell rings. The* THIRD MAN *appears, carrying a crate of eggs.*]

Third Man.   'Morning.

Schill.   Ah, good morning, Wechsler.

Third Man.   Twelve dozen eggs, medium brown. Right?

Schill.   Take them, Karl. [*The* SON *puts the crate in a corner.*] Did they deliver the milk yet?

Son.   Before you came down.

Third Man.   Eggs are going up again, Herr Schill. First of the month. [*He gives* SCHILL *a slip to sign.*]

Schill.   What? Again? And who's going to buy them?

Third Man.   Fifty pfennig a dozen.

Schill.   I'll have to cancel my order, that's all.

Third Man.   That's up to you, Herr Schill. [SCHILL *signs the slip.*]

Schill.   There's nothing else to do. [*He hands back the slip.*] And how's the family?

Third Man.   Oh, scraping along. Maybe now things will get better.

Schill.   Maybe.

Third Man [*Going*].   'Morning.

Schill.   Close the door. Don't let the flies in. [*The children resume their singing.*] Now, listen to me, children. I have a little piece of good news for you. I didn't mean to speak of it yet awhile, but well, why not? Who do you suppose is going to be the next Burgomaster? Eh? [*They look up at him.*] Yes, in spite of everything. It's settled. It's official. What an honor for the family, eh? Especially at a time like this. To say nothing of the salary and the rest of it.

Son.   Burgomaster!

---

1   "General Store."

Schill. Burgomaster. [*The* SON *shakes him warmly by the hand. The* DAUGHTER *kisses him.*] You see, you don't have to be entirely ashamed of your father. [*Silence.*] Is your mother coming down to breakfast soon?

Daughter. Mother's tired. She's going to stay upstairs.

Schill. You have a good mother, at least. There you are lucky. Oh, well, if she wants to rest, let her rest. We'll have breakfast together, the three of us. I'll fry some eggs and open a tin of the American ham. This morning we're going to breakfast like kings.

Son. I'd like to, only—I can't.

Schill. You've got to eat, you know.

Son. I've got to run down to the station. One of the laborers is sick. They said they could use me.

Schill. You want to work on the rails in all this heat? That's no work for a son of mine.

Son. Look, Father, we can use the money.

Schill. Well, if you feel you have to. [*The* SON *goes to the door. The* DAUGHTER *moves toward* SCHILL.]

Daughter. I'm sorry, Father. I have to go too.

Schill. You too? And where is the young lady going, if I may be so bold?

Daughter. There may be something for me at the employment agency.

Schill. Employment agency?

Daughter. It's important to get there early.

Schill. All right. I'll have something nice for you when you get home.

Son and Daughter [*Salute*]. Good day, Burgomaster.

[*The* SON *and* DAUGHTER *go out.*]

[*The* FIRST MAN *comes into* SCHILL'S *shop. Mandolin and guitar music are heard offstage.*]

Schill. Good morning, Hofbauer.

First Man. Cigarettes. [SCHILL *takes a pack from the shelf.*] Not those. I'll have the green today.

Schill. They cost more.

First Man. Put it in the book.

Schill. What?

First Man. Charge it.

Schill. Well, all right, I'll make an exception this time—seeing it's you, Hofbauer. [SCHILL *writes in his cash book.*]

First Man [*Opening the pack of cigarettes*]. Who's that playing out there?

Schill. The two blind men.

First Man. They play well.

Schill. To hell with them.

First Man. They make you nervous? [SCHILL *shrugs. The* FIRST MAN *lights a cigarette.*] She's getting ready for the wedding, I hear.

Schill. Yes. So they say.

[*Enter the* FIRST *and* SECOND WOMAN. *They cross to the counter.*]

First Woman.   Good morning, good morning.
Second Woman.   Good morning.
First Man.   Good morning.
Schill.   Good morning, ladies.
First Woman.   Good morning, Herr Schill.
Second Woman.   Good morning.
First Woman.   Milk please, Herr Schill.
Schill.   Milk.
Second Woman.   And milk for me too.
Schill.   A liter of milk each. Right away.
First Woman.   Whole milk, please, Herr Schill.
Schill.   Whole milk?
Second Woman.   Yes. Whole milk, please.
Schill.   Whole milk, I can only give you half a liter each of whole milk.
First Woman.   All right.
Schill.   Half a liter of whole milk here, and half a liter of whole milk here. There you are.
First Woman.   And butter please, a quarter kilo.
Schill.   Butter, I haven't any butter. I can give you some very nice lard?
First Woman.   No. Butter.
Schill.   Goose fat? [*The* FIRST WOMAN *shakes her head.*] Chicken fat?
First Woman.   Butter.
Shill.   Butter. Now, wait a minute, though. I have a tin of imported butter here somewhere. Ah. There you are. No, sorry, she asked first, but I can order some for you from Kalberstadt tomorrow.
Second Woman.   And white bread.
Schill.   White bread. [*He takes a loaf and a knife.*]
Second Woman.   The whole loaf.
Schill.   But a whole loaf would cost . . .
Second Woman.   Charge it.
Schill.   Charge it?
First Woman.   And a package of milk chocolate.
Schill.   Package of milk chocolate—right away.
Second Woman.   One for me, too, Herr Schill.
Schill.   And a package of milk chocolate for you, too.
First Woman.   We'll eat it here, if you don't mind.
Schill.   Yes, please do.
Second Woman.   It's so cool at the back of the shop.
Schill.   Charge it?
Women.   Of course.
Schill.   All for one, one for all.

[*The* SECOND MAN *enters.*]

Second Man.   Good morning.
The Two Women.   Good morning.
Schill.   Good morning, Helmesberger.
Second Man.   It's going to be a hot day.

Schill.   Phew!

Second Man.   How's business?

Schill.   Fabulous. For a while no one came, and now all of a sudden I'm running a luxury trade.

Second Man.   Good!

Schill.   Oh, I'll never forget the way you all stood by me at the Golden Apostle in spite of your need, in spite of everything. That was the finest hour of my life.

First Man.   We're not heathens, you know.

Second Man.   We're behind you, my boy; the whole town's behind you.

First Man.   As firm as a rock.

First Woman [*Munching her chocolate*].   As firm as a rock, Herr Schill.

Both Women.   As firm as a rock.

Second Man.   There's no denying it—you're the most popular man in town.

First Man.   The most important.

Second Man.   And in the spring, God willing, you will be our Burgomaster.

First Man.   Sure as a gun.

All.   Sure as a gun.

[*Enter* PEDRO *with fishing equipment and a fish in his landing net.*]

Pedro.   Would you please weigh my fish for me?

Schill [*Weighs it*].   Two kilos.

Pedro.   Is that all?

Schill.   Two kilos exactly.

Pedro.   Two kilos!

[*He gives* SCHILL *a tip and exits.*]

Second Woman.   The fiancé.

First Woman.   They're to be married this week. It will be a tremendous wedding.

Second Woman.   I saw his picture in the paper.

First Woman [*Sighs*].   Ah, what a man!

Second Man.   Give me a bottle of schnapps.

Schill.   The usual?

Second Man.   No, cognac.

Schill.   Cognac? But cognac costs twenty-two marks fifty.

Second Man.   We all have to splurge a little now and again—

Schill.   Here you are. Three Star.

Second Man.   And a package of pipe tobacco.

Schill.   Black or blond?

Second Man.   English.

Schill.   English! But that makes twenty-three marks eighty.

Second Man.   Chalk it up.

Schill.   Now, look. I'll make an exception this week. Only, you will have to pay me the moment your unemployment check comes in. I don't want to be kept waiting. [*Suddenly*] Helmesberger, are those new shoes you're wearing?

Second Man.   Yes, what about it?

Schill.   You too, Hofbauer. Yellow shoes! Brand new!

First Man.   So?

Schill [*To the women*]. And you. You all have new shoes! New shoes!

First Woman. A person can't walk around forever in the same old shoes.

Second Woman. Shoes wear out.

Schill. And the money. Where does the money come from?

First Woman. We got them on credit, Herr Schill.

Second Woman. On credit.

Schill. On credit? And where all of a sudden do you get credit?

Second Man. Everybody gives credit now.

First Woman. You gave us credit yourself.

Schill. And what are you going to pay with? Eh? [*They are all silent.* SCHILL *advances upon them threateningly.*] With what? Eh? With what? With what?

[*Suddenly he understands. He takes his apron off quickly, flings it on the counter, gets his jacket, and walks off with an air of determination. Now the shop sign vanishes. The shelves are pushed off. The lights go up on the balcony of the Golden Apostle, and the balcony unit itself moves forward into the optical center.* CLAIRE *and* BOBBY *step out on the balcony.* CLAIRE *sits down.* BOBBY *serves coffee.*]

Claire. A lovely autumn morning. A silver haze on the streets and a violet sky above. Count Holk would have liked this. Remember him, Bobby? My third husband?

Bobby. Yes, madame.

Claire. Horrible man!

Bobby. Yes, madame.

Claire. Where is Monsieur Pedro? Is he up yet?

Bobby. Yes, madame. He's fishing.

Claire. Already? What a singular passion!

[PEDRO *comes in with the fish.*]

Pedro. Good morning, my love.

Claire. Pedro! There you are.

Pedro. Look, my darling. Four kilos!

Claire. A jewel! I'll have it grilled for your lunch. Give it to Bobby.

Pedro. Ah—it is so wonderful here! I like your little town.

Claire. Oh, do you?

Pedro. Yes. These people, they are all so—what is the word?

Claire. Simple, honest, hard-working, decent.

Pedro. But, my angel, you are a mind reader. That's just what I was going to say—however did you guess?

Claire. I know them.

Pedro. Yet when we arrived it was all so dirty, so—what is the word?

Claire. Shabby.

Pedro. Exactly. But now everywhere you go, you see them busy as bees, cleaning their streets—

Claire. Repairing their houses, sweeping—dusting—hanging new curtains in the windows—singing as they work.

Pedro. But you astonishing, wonderful woman! You can't see all that from here.

Claire. I know them. And in their gardens—I am sure that in their gardens they are manuring the soil for the spring.

Pedro. My angel, you know everything. This morning on my way fishing I said to myself, look at them all manuring their gardens. It is extraordinary—and it's all because of you. Your return has given them a new—what is the word?

Claire. Lease on life?

Pedro. Precisely.

Claire. The town was dying, it's true. But a town doesn't have to die. I think they realize that now. People die, not towns. Bobby! [BOBBY *appears.*] A cigar.

[*The lights fade on the balcony, which moves back upstage. Somewhat to the right, a sign descends. It reads: "Polizei." The* POLICEMAN *pushes a desk under it. This, with the bench, becomes the police station. He places a bottle of beer and a glass on the desk, and goes to hang up his coat offstage. The telephone rings.*]

Policeman. Schultz speaking. Yes, we have a couple of rooms for the night. No, not for rent. This is not the hotel. This is the Güllen police station. [*He laughs and hangs up.* SCHILL *comes in. He is evidently nervous.*]

Schill. Schultz.

Policeman. Hello, Schill. Come in. Sit down. Beer?

Schill. Please. [*He drinks thirstily.*]

Policeman. What can I do for you?

Schill. I want you to arrest Madame Zachanassian.

Policeman. Eh?

Schill. I said I want you to arrest Madame Zachanassian.

Policeman. What the hell are you talking about?

Schill. I ask you to arrest this woman at once.

Policeman. What offense has the lady committed?

Schill. You know perfectly well. She offered a billion marks—

Policeman. And you want her arrested for that? [*He pours beer into his glass.*]

Schill. Schultz! It's your duty.

Schultz. Extraordinary! Extraordinary idea! [*He drinks his beer.*]

Schill. I'm speaking to you as your next Burgomaster.

Policeman. Schill, that's true. The lady offered us a billion marks. But that doesn't entitle us to take police action against her.

Schill. Why not?

Policeman. In order to be arrested, a person must first commit a crime.

Schill. Incitement to murder.

Policeman. Incitement to murder is a crime. I agree.

Schill. Well?

Policeman. And such a proposal—if serious—constitutes an assault.

Schill. That's what I mean.

Policeman. But her offer can't be serious.

Schill. Why?

Policeman. The price is too high. In a case like yours, one pays a thousand marks, at the most two thousand. But not a billion! That's ridiculous. And even if she meant it, that would only prove she was out of her mind. And that's not a matter for the police.

Schill. Whether she's out of her mind or not, the danger to me is the same. That's obvious.

Policeman. Look, Schill, you show us where anyone threatens your life in any way—say, for instance, a man points a gun at you—and we'll be there in a flash.

Schill [Gets up]. So I'm to wait till someone points a gun at me?

Policeman. Pull yourself together, Schill. We're all for you in this town.

Schill. I wish I could believe it.

Policeman. You don't believe it?

Schill. No. No, I don't. All of a sudden my customers are buying white bread, whole milk, butter, imported tobacco. What does it mean?

Policeman. It means business is picking up.

Schill. Helmesberger lives on the dole; he hasn't earned anything in five years. Today he bought French cognac.

Policeman. I'll have to try your cognac one of these days.

Schill. And shoes. They all have new shoes.

Policeman. And what have you got against new shoes? I'm wearing a new pair myself. [*He holds out his foot.*]

Schill. You too?

Policeman. Why not? [*He pours out the rest of his beer.*]

Schill. Is that Pilsen you're drinking now?

Policeman. It's the only thing.

Schill. You used to drink the local beer.

Policeman. Hogwash. [*Radio music is heard offstage.*]

Schill. Listen. You hear?

Policeman. "The Merry Widow." Yes.

Schill. No. It's a radio.

Policeman. That's Bergholzer's radio.

Schill. Bergholzer!

Policeman. You're right. He should close his window when he plays it. I'll make a note to speak to him. [*He makes a note in his notebook.*]

Schill. And how can Bergholzer pay for a radio?

Policeman. That's his business.

Schill. And you, Schultz, with your new shoes and your imported beer—how are you going to pay for them?

Policeman. That's my business. [*His telephone rings. He picks it up.*] Police Station, Güllen. What? What? Where? Where? How? Right, we'll deal with it. [*He hangs up.*]

Schill [He speaks during the POLICEMAN'S *telephone conversation*]. Schultz, listen. No. Schultz, please—listen to me. Don't you see they're all . . . Listen, please. Look, Schultz. They're all running up debts. And out of these debts comes this sudden prosperity. And out of this prosperity comes the absolute need to kill me.

Policeman [Putting on his jacket]. You're imagining things.

Schill. All she has to do is to sit on her balcony and wait.

Policeman. Don't be a child.

Schill.   You're all waiting.

Policeman [*Snaps a loaded clip into the magazine of a rifle*].   Look, Schill, you can relax. The police are here for your protection. They know their job. Let anyone, any time, make the slightest threat to your life, and all you have to do is let us know. We'll do the rest . . . Now, don't worry.

Schill.   No, I won't.

Policeman.   And don't upset yourself. All right?

Schill.   Yes. I won't. [*Then suddenly, in a low tone*] You have a new gold tooth in your mouth!

Policeman.   What are you talking about?

Schill [*Taking the* POLICEMAN'S *head in his hands, and forcing his lips open*].   A brand new, shining gold tooth.

Policeman [*Breaks away and involuntarily levels the gun at* SCHILL].   Are you crazy? Look, I've no time to waste. Madame Zachanassian's panther's broken loose.

Schill.   Panther?

Policeman.   Yes, it's at large. I've got to hunt it down.

Schill.   You're not hunting a panther and you know it. It's me you're hunting! [*The* POLICEMAN *clicks on the safety and lowers the gun.*]

Policeman.   Schill! Take my advice. Go home. Lock the door. Keep out of everyone's way. That way you'll be safe. Cheer up! Good times are just around the corner! [*The lights dim in this area and light up on the balcony.* PEDRO *is lounging in a chair.* CLAIRE *is smoking.*]

Pedro.   Oh, this little town oppresses me.

Claire.   Oh, does it? So you've changed your mind?

Pedro.   It is true, I find it charming, delightful—

Claire.   Picturesque.

Pedro.   Yes. After all, it's the place where you were born. But it is too quiet for me. Too provincial. Too much like all small towns everywhere. These people— look at them. They fear nothing, they desire nothing, they strive for nothing. They have everything they want. They are asleep.

Claire.   Perhaps one day they will come to life again.

Pedro.   My God—do I have to wait for that?

Claire.   Yes, you do. Why don't you go back to your fishing?

Pedro.   I think I will. [PEDRO *turns to go.*]

Claire.   Pedro.

Pedro.   Yes, my love?

Claire.   Telephone the president of Hambro's Bank. Ask him to transfer a billion marks to my current account.

Pedro.   A billion? Yes, my love.

[*He goes. The lights fade on the balcony. A sign is flown in. It reads:* "Rat- haus."[1] *The* THIRD MAN *crosses the stage, right to left, wheeling a new television set on a hand truck. The counter of* SCHILL'S *shop is transformed into the* BURGOMASTER'S *office. The* BURGOMASTER *comes in. He takes a revolver*

---

[1]   "City Hall."

from his pocket, examines it and sets it down on the desk. He sits down and starts writing. SCHILL *knocks.*]

Burgomaster. Come in.

Schill. I must have a word with you, Burgomaster.

Burgomaster. Ah, Schill. Sit down, my friend.

Schill. Man to man. As your successor.

Burgomaster. But of course. Naturally. [SCHILL *remains standing. He looks at the revolver.*]

Schill. Is that a gun?

Burgomaster. Madame Zachanassian's black panther's broken loose. It's been seen near the cathedral. It's as well to be prepared.

Schill. Oh, yes. Of course.

Burgomaster. I've sent out a call for all able-bodied men with firearms. The streets have been cleared. The children have been kept in school. We don't want any accidents.

Schill [*Suspiciously*]. You're making quite a thing of it.

Burgomaster [*Shrugs*]. Naturally. A panther is a dangerous beast. Well? What's on your mind? Speak out. We're old friends.

Schill. That's a good cigar you're smoking, Burgomaster.

Burgomaster. Yes. Havana.

Schill. You used to smoke something else.

Burgomaster. Fortuna.

Schill. Cheaper.

Burgomaster. Too strong.

Schill. A new tie? Silk?

Burgomaster. Yes. Do you like it?

Schill. And have you also bought new shoes?

Burgomaster [*Brings his feet out from under the desk*]. Why, yes. I ordered a new pair from Kalberstadt. Extraordinary! However did you guess?

Schill. That's why I'm here. [*The* THIRD MAN *knocks.*]

Burgomaster. Come in.

Third Man. The new typewriter, sir.

Burgomaster. Put it on the table. [*The* THIRD MAN *sets it down and goes.*] What's the matter with you? My dear fellow, aren't you well?

Schill. It's you who don't seem well, Burgomaster.

Burgomaster. What do you mean?

Schill. You look pale.

Burgomaster. I?

Schill. Your hands are trembling. [*The* BURGOMASTER *involuntarily hides his hands.*] Are you frightened?

Burgomaster. What have I to be afraid of?

Schill. Perhaps this sudden prosperity alarms you.

Burgomaster. Is prosperity a crime?

Schill. That depends on how you pay for it.

Burgomaster. You'll have to forgive me, Schill, but I really haven't the slightest idea what you're talking about. Am I supposed to feel like a criminal every time I order a new typewriter?

Schill. Do you?

Burgomaster. Well, I hope you haven't come here to talk about a new type-writer. Now, what was it you wanted?

Schill. I have come to claim the protection of the authorities.

Burgomaster. Ei! Against whom?

Schill. You know against whom.

Burgomaster. You don't trust us?

Schill. That woman has put a price on my head.

Burgomaster. If you don't feel safe, why don't you go to the police?

Schill. I have just come from the police.

Burgomaster. And?

Schill. The chief has a new gold tooth in his mouth.

Burgomaster. A new—? Oh, Schill, really! You're forgetting. This is Güllen, the town of humane traditions. Goethe slept here. Brahms composed a quartet. You must have faith in us. This is a law-abiding community.

Schill. Then arrest this woman who wants to have me killed.

Burgomaster. Look here, Schill. God knows the lady has every right to be angry with you. What you did there wasn't very pretty. You forced two decent lads to perjure themselves and had a young girl thrown out on the streets.

Schill. That young girl owns half the world. [*A moment's silence.*]

Burgomaster. Very well, then, we'll speak frankly.

Schill. That's why I'm here.

Burgomaster. Man to man, just as you said. [*He clears his throat.*] Now—after what you did, you have no moral right to say a word against this lady. And I advise you not to try. Also—I regret to have to tell you this—there is no longer any question of your being elected Burgomaster.

Schill. Is that official?

Burgomaster. Official.

Schill. I see.

Burgomaster. The man who is chosen to exercise the high post of Burgomaster must have, obviously, certain moral qualifications. Qualifications which, un-happily, you no longer possess. Naturally, you may count on the esteem and friendship of the town, just as before. That goes without saying. The best thing will be to spread the mantle of silence over the whole miserable business.

Schill. So I'm to remain silent while they arrange my murder? [*The* BURGO-MASTER *gets up.*]

Burgomaster [*Suddenly noble*]. Now, who is arranging your murder? Give me the names and I will investigate the case at once. Unrelentingly. Well? The names?

Schill. You.

Burgomaster. I resent this. Do you think we want to kill you for money?

Schill. No. You don't want to kill me. But you want to have me killed.

[*The lights go down. The stage is filled with men prowling about with rifles, as if they were stalking a quarry. In the interval the* POLICEMAN'S *bench and the* BURGOMASTER'S *desk are shifted somewhat, so that they will compose the setting for the sacristy. The stage empties. The lights come up on the balcony.*]

[CLAIRE *appears*]

Claire. Bobby, what's going on here? What are all these men doing with guns? Whom are they hunting?

Bobby. The black panther has escaped, madame.

Claire. Who let him out?

Bobby. Kobby and Lobby, madame.

Claire. How excited they are! There may be shooting?

Bobby. It is possible, madame.

[*The lights fade on the balcony. The sacristan comes in. He arranges the set, and puts the altar cloth on the altar. Then* SCHILL *comes on. He is looking for the* PASTOR. *The* PASTOR *enters, left. He is wearing his gown and carrying a rifle.*]

Schill. Sorry to disturb you, Pastor.

Pastor. God's house is open to all. [*He sees that* SCHILL *is staring at the gun.*] Oh, the gun? That's because of the panther. It's best to be prepared.

Schill. Pastor, help me.

Pastor. Of course. Sit down. [*He puts the rifle on the bench.*] What's the trouble?

Schill [*Sits on the bench*]. I'm frightened.

Pastor. Frightened? Of what?

Schill. Of everyone. They're hunting me down like a beast.

Pastor. Have no fear of man, Schill. Fear God. Fear not the death of the body. Fear the death of the soul. Zip up my gown behind, Sacristan.

Schill. I'm afraid, Pastor.

Pastor. Put your trust in heaven, my friend.

Schill. You see, I'm not well. I shake. I have such pains around the heart. I sweat.

Pastor. I know. You're passing through a profound psychic experience.

Schill. I'm going through hell.

Pastor. The hell you are going through exists only within yourself. Many years ago you betrayed a girl shamefully, for money. Now you think that we shall sell you just as you sold her. No, my friend, you are projecting your guilt upon others. It's quite natural. But remember, the root of our torment lies always within ourselves, in our hearts, in our sins. When you have understood this, you can conquer the fears that oppress you; you have weapons with which to destroy them.

Schill. Siemethofer has bought a new washing machine.

Pastor. Don't worry about the washing machine. Worry about your immortal soul.

Schill. Stockers has a television set.

Pastor. There is also great comfort in prayer. Sacristan, the bands. [SCHILL *crosses to the altar and kneels. The sacristan ties on the* PASTOR's *bands.*] Examine your conscience, Schill. Repent. Otherwise your fears will consume you. Believe me, this is the only way. We have no other. [*The church bell begins to peal.* SCHILL *seems relieved.*] Now I must leave you. I have a baptism. You may stay as long as you like. Sacristan, the Bible, Liturgy and Psalter. The child is beginning to cry. I can hear it from here. It is frightened. Let us make haste to give it the only security which this world affords.

Schill.   A new bell?

Pastor.   Yes. Its tone is marvelous, don't you think? Full. Sonorous.

Schill [*Steps back in horror*].   A new bell! You too, Pastor? You too? [*The* PASTOR *clasps his hands in horror. Then he takes* SCHILL *into his arms.*]

Pastor.   Oh, God, God forgive me. We are poor, weak things, all of us. Do not tempt us further into the hell in which you are burning. Go, Schill, my friend, go, my brother, go while there is time.

[*The* PASTOR *goes.*]

[SCHILL *picks up the rifle with a gesture of desperation. He goes out with it. As the lights fade, men appear with guns. Two shots are fired in the darkness. The lights come up on the balcony, which moves forward.*]

Claire.   Bobby! What was that shooting? Have they caught the panther?

Bobby.   He is dead, madame.

Claire.   There were two shots.

Bobby.   The panther is dead, madame.

Claire.   I loved him. [*Waves* BOBBY *away*] I shall miss him.

[*The* TEACHER *comes in with two little girls, singing. They stop under the balcony.*]

Teacher.   Gracious lady, be so good as to accept our heartfelt condolences. Your beautiful panther is no more. Believe me, we are deeply pained that so tragic an event should mar your visit here. But what could we do? The panther was savage, a beast. To him our human laws could not apply. There was no other way—[SCHILL *appears with the gun. He looks dangerous. The girls run off, frightened. The* TEACHER *follows the girls.*] Children—children—children!

Claire.   Anton, why are you frightening the children? [*He works the bolt, loading the chamber, and raises the gun slowly.*]

Schill.   Go away, Claire—I warn you. Go away.

Claire.   How strange it is, Anton! How clearly it comes back to me! The day we saw one another for the first time, do you remember? I was on a balcony then. It was a day like today, a day in autumn without a breath of wind, warm as it is now—only lately I am always cold. You stood down there and stared at me without moving. I was embarrassed. I didn't know what to do. I wanted to go back into the darkness of the room, where it was safe, but I couldn't. You stared up at me darkly, almost angrily, as if you wished to hurt me, but your eyes were full of passion. [SCHILL *begins to lower the rifle involuntarily.*] Then, I don't know why, I left the balcony and I came down and stood in the street beside you. You didn't greet me, you didn't say a word, but you took my hand and we walked together out of the town into the fields, and behind us came Kobby and Lobby, like two dogs, sniveling and giggling and snarling. Suddenly you picked up a stone and hurled it at them, and they ran yelping back into the town, and we were alone. [SCHILL *has lowered the rifle completely. He moves forward toward her, as close as he can come.*] That was the beginning, and everything else had to follow. There is no escape. [*She goes in and closes the shutters.*

SCHILL *stands immobile. The* TEACHER *tiptoes in. He stares at* SCHILL, *who doesn't see him. Then he beckons to the children.*]

Teacher. Come, children, sing. Sing. [*They begin singing. He creeps behind* SCHILL *and snatches away the rifle.* SCHILL *turns sharply. The* PASTOR *comes in.*]

Pastor. Go, Schill—go!

[SCHILL *goes out. The children continue singing, moving across the stage and off. The Golden Apostle vanishes. The crossing bell is heard. The scene dissolves into the railway-station setting, as in Act One. But there are certain changes. The timetable marked "Fahrplan" is now new, the frame freshly painted. There is a new travel poster on the station wall. It has a yellow sun and the words: "Reist in den Süden."[1] On the other side of the Fahrplan is another poster with the words: "Die Passionsspiele Oberammergau."[2] The sound of passing trains covers the scene change.* SCHILL *appears with an old valise in his hand, dressed in a shabby trench coat, his hat on his head. He looks about with a furtive air, walking slowly to the platform. Slowly, as if by chance, the townspeople enter, from all sides.* SCHILL *hesitates, stops.*]

Burgomaster [*From upstage, center*]. Good evening, Schill.
Schill. Good evening.
Policeman. Good evening.
Schill. Good evening.
Painter [*Enters*]. Good evening.
Schill. Good evening.
Doctor. Good evening.
Schill. Good evening
Burgomaster. So you're taking a little trip?
Schill. Yes. A little trip.
Policeman. May one ask where to?
Schill. I don't know.
Painter. Don't know?
Schill. To Kalberstadt.
Burgomaster [*With disbelief, pointing to the valise*]. Kalberstadt?
Schill. After that—somewhere else.
Painter. Ah. After that somewhere else.

[*The* FOURTH MAN *walks in.*]

Schill. I thought maybe Australia.
Burgomaster. Australia!
All. Australia!
Schill. I'll raise the money somehow.
Burgomaster. But why Australia?

---

[1] "Take a trip to the South!"

[2] "See the Oberammergau Passion Play." Oberammergau is a village in southern Germany which presents a day-long dramatization of the life and death of Jesus once every ten years. The players are all townsfolk. The Passion Play is a world-famous tourist attraction.

Policeman. What would you be doing in Australia?

Schill. One can't always live in the same town, year in, year out.

Painter. But Australia—

Doctor. It's a risky trip for a man of your age.

Burgomaster. One of the lady's little men ran off to Australia . . .

All. Yes.

Policeman. You'll be much safer here.

Painter. Much! [SCHILL *looks about him in anguish, like a beast at bay.*]

Schill [*Low voice*]. I wrote a letter to the administration at Kaffigen.

Burgomaster. Yes? And? [*They are all intent on the answer.*]

Schill. They didn't answer. [*All laugh.*]

Doctor. Do you mean to say you don't trust your old friends? That's not very flattering, you know.

Burgomaster. No one's going to do you any harm here.

Doctor. No harm here.

Schill. They didn't answer because our postmaster held up my letter.

Painter. Our postmaster? What an idea.

Burgomaster. The postmaster is a member of the town council.

Policeman. A man of the utmost integrity.

Doctor. He doesn't hold up letters. What an idea! [*The crossing bell starts ringing.*]

Station Master [*Announces*]. Local to Kalberstadt! [*The townspeople all cross down to see the train arrive. Then they turn, with their backs to the audience, in a line across the stage.* SCHILL *cannot get through to reach the train.*]

Schill [*In a low voice*]. What are you all doing here? What do you want of me?

Burgomaster. We don't like to see you go.

Doctor. We've come to see you off. [*The sound of the approaching train grows louder.*]

Schill. I didn't ask you to come.

Policeman. But we have come.

Doctor. As old friends.

All. As old friends. [*The* STATION MASTER *holds up his paddle. The train stops with a screech of brakes. We hear the engine panting offstage.*]

Voice [*Offstage*]. Güllen!

Burgomaster. A pleasant journey.

Doctor. And long life!

Painter. And good luck in Australia!

All. Yes, good luck in Australia. [*They press around him jovially. He stands motionless and pale.*]

Schill. Why are you crowding me?

Policeman. What's the matter now? [*The* STATION MASTER *blows a long blast on his whistle.*]

Schill. Give me room.

Doctor. But you have plenty of room. [*They all move away from him.*]

Policeman. Better get aboard, Schill.

Schill. I see. I see. One of you is going to push me under the wheels.

Policeman. Oh, nonsense. Go on, get aboard.

Schill. Get away from me, all of you.

Burgomaster. I don't know what you want. Just get on the train.

Schill. No. One of you will push me under.

Doctor. You're being ridiculous. Now, go on, get on the train.

Schill. Why are you all so near me?

Doctor. The man's gone mad.

Station Master. 'Board! [*He blows his whistle. The engine bell clangs. The train starts.*]

Burgomaster. Get aboard, man. Quick. [*The following speeches are spoken all together until the train noises fade away.*]

Doctor. The train's starting.

All. Get aboard, man. Get aboard. The train's starting.

Schill. If I try to get aboard, one of you will hold me back.

All. No, no.

Burgomaster. Get on the train.

Schill [*In terror, crouches against the wall of the* STATION MASTER'S *office*]. No—no—no. No. [*He falls on his knees. The others crowd around him. He cowers on the ground, abjectly. The train sounds fade away.*] Oh, no—no— don't push me, don't push me!

Policeman. There. It's gone off without you. [*Slowly they leave him. He raises himself up to a sitting position, still trembling. A* TRUCK DRIVER *enters with an empty can.*]

Truck Driver. Do you know where I can get some water? My truck's boiling over. [SCHILL *points to the station office.*] Thanks. [*He enters the office, gets the water and comes out. By this time,* SCHILL *is erect.*] Missed your train?

Schill. Yes.

Truck Driver. To Kalberstadt?

Schill. Yes.

Truck Driver. Well, come with me. I'm going that way.

Schill. This is my town. This is my home. [*With strange new dignity*] No, thank you. I've changed my mind. I'm staying.

Truck Driver [*Shrugs*]. All right.

[*He goes out.* SCHILL *picks up his bag, looks right and left, and slowly walks off. Curtain.*]

Act III

[*Music is heard. Then the curtain rises on the interior of the old barn, a dim, cavernous structure. Bars of light fall across the shadowy forms, shafts of sunlight from the holes and cracks in the walls and roof. Overhead hang old rags, decaying sacks, great cobwebs. Extreme left is a ladder leading to the loft. Near it, an old haycart. Left,* CLAIRE ZACHANASSIAN *is sitting in her gilded sedan chair, motionless, in her magnificent bridal gown and veil. Near the chair stands an old keg.*]

Bobby [*Comes in, treading carefully*]. The doctor and the teacher from the high school to see you, madame.

Claire [*Impassive*].   Show them in. [BOBBY *ushers them in as if they were entering a hall of state. The two grope their way through the litter. At last they find the lady, and bow. They are both well dressed in new clothes, but are very dusty.*]

Bobby.   Dr. Nüsslin and Professor Müller.

Doctor.   Madame.

Claire.   You look dusty, gentlemen.

Doctor [*Dusts himself off vigorously*].   Oh, forgive us. We had to climb over an old carriage.

Teacher.   Our respects.

Doctor.   A fabulous wedding.

Teacher.   Beautiful occasion.

Claire.   It's stifling here. But I love this old barn. The smell of hay and old straw and axle grease—it is the scent of my youth. Sit down. All this rubbish—the haycart, the old carriage, the cask, even the pitchfork—it was all here when I was a girl.

Teacher.   Remarkable place. [*He mops his brow.*]

Claire.   I thought the pastor's text was very appropriate. The lesson a trifle long.

Teacher.   I Corinthians 13.[1]

Claire.   Your choristers sang beautifully, Professor.

Teacher.   Bach. From the *St. Matthew Passion.*

Doctor.   Güllen has never seen such magnificence! The flowers! The jewels! And the people.

Teacher.   The theatrical world, the world of finance, the world of art, the world of science . . .

Claire.   All these worlds are now back in their Cadillacs, speeding toward the capital for the wedding reception. But I'm sure you didn't come here to talk about them.

Doctor.   Dear lady, we should not intrude on your valuable time. Your husband must be waiting impatiently.

Claire.   No, no, I've packed him off to Brazil.

Doctor.   To Brazil, madame?

Claire.   Yes. For his honeymoon.

Teacher and Doctor.   Oh! But your wedding guests?

Claire.   I've planned a delightful dinner for them. They'll never miss me. Now what was it you wished to talk about?

Teacher.   About Anton Schill, madame.

Claire.   Is he dead?

Teacher.   Madame, we may be poor. But we have our principles.

Claire.   I see. Then what do you want?

Teacher [*He mops his brow again*].   The fact is, madame, in anticipation of your well-known munificence, that is, feeling that you would give the town some sort of gift, we have all been buying things. Necessities . . .

Doctor.   With money we don't have. [*The* TEACHER *blows his nose.*]

---

[1]   I. *Corinthians* 13:13: "But now abideth faith, hope, love, these three; and the greatest of these is love."

Claire.   You've run into debt?

Doctor.   Up to here.

Claire.   In spite of your principles?

Teacher.   We're human, madame.

Claire.   I see.

Teacher.   We have been poor for a long time. A long, long time.

Doctor [He rises].   The question is, how are we going to pay?

Claire.   You already know.

Teacher [Courageously].   I beg you, Madame Zachanassian, put yourself in our position for a moment. For twenty-two years I've been cudgeling my brains to plant a few seeds of knowledge in this wilderness. And all this time, my gallant colleague, Dr. Nüsslin, has been rattling around in his ancient Mercedes, from patient to patient, trying to keep these wretches alive. Why? Why have we spent our lives in this miserable hole? For money? Hardly. The pay is ridiculous.

Doctor.   And yet, the professor here has declined an offer to head the high school in Kalberstadt.

Teacher.   And Dr. Nüsslin has refused an important post at the University of Erlangen. Madame, the simple fact is, we love our town. We were born here. It is our life.

Doctor.   That's true.

Teacher.   What has kept us going all these years is the hope that one day the community will prosper again as it did in the days when we were young.

Claire.   Good.

Teacher.   Madame, there is no reason for our poverty. We suffer here from a mysterious blight. We have factories. They stand idle. There is oil in the valley of Pückenried.

Doctor.   There is copper under the Konradsweil Forest. There is power in our streams, in our waterfalls.

Teacher.   We are not poor, madame. If we had credit, if we had confidence, the factories would open, orders and commissions would pour in. And our economy would bloom together with our cultural life. We would become once again like the towns around us, healthy and prosperous.

Doctor.   If the Wagonworks were put on its feet again—

Teacher.   The Foundry.

Doctor.   The Golden Eagle Pencil Factory.

Teacher.   Buy these plants, madame. Put them in operation once more, and I swear to you, Güllen will flourish and it will bless you. We don't need a billion marks. Ten million, properly invested, would give us back our life, and incidentally return to the investor an excellent dividend. Save us, madame. Save us, and we will not only bless you, we will make money for you.

Claire.   I don't need money.

Doctor.   Madame, we are not asking for charity. This is business.

Claire.   It's a good idea . . .

Doctor.   Dear lady! I knew you wouldn't let us down.

Claire.   But it's out of the question. I cannot buy the Wagonworks. I already own them.

Doctor.   The Wagonworks?

Teacher.   And the Foundry?

Claire.   And the Foundry.

Doctor.   And the Golden Eagle Pencil Factory?

Claire.   Everything. The valley of Pückenried with its oil, the forest of Konradsweil with its ore, the barn, the town, the streets, the houses, the shops, everything. I had my agents buy up this rubbish over the years, bit by bit, piece by
piece, until I had it all. Your hopes were an illusion, your vision empty, your self-
sacrifice a stupidity, your whole life completely senseless.

Teacher.   Then the mysterious blight—

Claire.   The mysterious blight was I.

Doctor.   But this is monstrous!

Claire.   Monstrous. I was seventeen when I left this town. It was winter. I was
dressed in a sailor suit and my red braids hung down my back. I was in my
seventh month. As I walked down the street to the station, the boys whistled
after me, and someone threw something. I sat freezing in my seat in the
Hamburg Express. But before the roof of the great barn was lost behind the
trees, I had made up my mind that one day I would come back . . .

Teacher.   But, madame—

Claire [She smiles].   And now I have. [*She claps her hands.*] Mike. Max. Take
me back to the Golden Apostle. I've been here long enough. [MIKE *and* MAX
start to pick up the sedan chair. The TEACHER *pushes* MIKE *away.*]

Teacher.   Madame. One moment. Please. I see it all now. I had thought of you as
an avenging fury, a Medea, a Clytemnestra—but I was wrong. You are a warm-
hearted woman who has suffered a terrible injustice, and now you have returned
and taught us an unforgettable lesson. You have stripped us bare. But now that
we stand before you naked, I know you will set aside these thoughts of vengeance. If we made you suffer, you too have put us through the fire. Have
mercy, madame.

Claire.   When I have had justice. Mike! [*She signals to* MIKE *and* MAX *to pick up
the sedan chair. They cross the stage. The* TEACHER *bars the way.*]

Teacher.   But, madame, one injustice cannot cure another. What good will it do
to force us into crime? Horror succeeds horror, shame is piled on shame. It
settles nothing.

Claire.   It settles everything. [*They move upstage toward the exit. The* TEACHER
follows.]

Teacher.   Madame, this lesson you have taught us will never be forgotten. We
will hand it down from father to son. It will be a monument more lasting than
any vengeance. Whatever we have been, in the future we shall be better because
of you. You have pushed us to the extreme. Now forgive us. Show us the way to
a better life. Have pity, madame—pity. That is the highest justice. [*The sedan
chair stops.*]

Claire.   The highest justice has no pity. It is bright and pure and clear. The world
made me into a whore; now I make the world into a brothel. Those who wish to
go down, may go down. Those who wish to dance with me, may dance with me.
[*To her porters.*] Go.

[*She is carried off.*]

[*The lights black out. Downstage, right, appears* SCHILL's *shop. It has a new
sign, a new counter. The doorbell, when it rings, has an impressive sound.* FRAU

SCHILL *stands behind the counter in a new dress. The* FIRST MAN *enters, left. He is dressed as a prosperous butcher, a few bloodstains on his snowy apron, a gold watch chain across his open vest.*]

First Man. What a wedding! I'll swear the whole town was there. Cigarettes.

Frau Schill. Clara is entitled to a little happiness after all. I'm happy for her. Green or white?

First Man. Turkish. The bridesmaids! Dancers and opera singers. And the dresses! Down to here.

Frau Schill. It's the fashion nowadays.

First Man. Reporters! Photographers! From all over the world! [*In a low voice.*] They will be here any minute.

Frau Schill. What have reporters to do with us? We are simple people, Herr Hofbauer. There is nothing for them here.

First Man. They're questioning everybody. They're asking everything. [*The* FIRST MAN *lights a cigarette. He looks up at the ceiling.*] Footsteps.

Frau Schill. He's pacing the room. Up and down. Day and night.

First Man. Haven't seen him all week.

Frau Schill. He never goes out.

First Man. It's his conscience. That was pretty mean, the way he treated poor Madame Zachanassian.

Frau Schill. That's true. I feel very badly about it myself.

First Man. To ruin a young girl like that—God doesn't forgive it. [FRAU SCHILL *nods solemnly with pursed lips. The butcher gives her a level glance.*] Look, I hope he'll have sense enough to keep his mouth shut in front of the reporters.

Frau Schill. I certainly hope so.

First Man. You know his character.

Frau Schill. Only too well, Herr Hofbauer.

First Man. If he tries to throw dirt at our Clara and tell a lot of lies, how she tried to get us to kill him, which anyway she never meant—

Frau Schill. Of course not.

First Man. —Then we'll really have to do something! And not because of the money—[*He spits.*] But out of ordinary human decency. God knows Madame Zachanassian has suffered enough through him already.

Frau Schill. She has indeed.

[*The* TEACHER *comes in. He is not quite sober.*]

Teacher [*Looks about the shop*]. Has the press been here yet?

First Man. No.

Teacher. It's not my custom, as you know, Frau Schill—but I wonder if I could have a strong alcoholic drink?

Frau Schill. It's an honor to serve you. Herr Professor. I have a good Steinhäger.[1] Would you like to try a glass?

Teacher. A very small glass. [FRAU SCHILL *serves bottle and glass. The* TEACHER *tosses off a glass.*]

Frau Schill. Your hand is shaking, Herr Professor.

---

[1] A strong drink in the gin-vodka family.

Teacher.   To tell the truth, I have been drinking a little already.

Frau Schill.   Have another glass. It will do you good. [*He accepts another glass.*]

Teacher.   Is that he up there, walking?

Frau Schill.   Up and down. Up and down.

First Man.   It's God punishing him.

[*The* PAINTER *comes in with the* SON *and the* DAUGHTER.]

Painter.   Careful! A reporter just asked us the way to this shop.

First Man.   I hope you didn't tell him.

Painter.   I told him we were strangers here. [*They all laugh. The door opens. The* SECOND MAN *darts into the shop.*]

Second Man.   Look out, everybody! The press! They are across the street in your shop, Hofbauer.

First Man.   My boy will know how to deal with them.

Second Man.   Make sure Schill doesn't come down, Hofbauer.

First Man.   Leave that to me. [*They group themselves about the shop.*]

Teacher.   Listen to me, all of you. When the reporters come I'm going to speak to them. I'm going to make a statement. A statement to the world on behalf of myself as Rector of Güllen High School and on behalf of you all, for all your sakes.

Painter.   What are you going to say?

Teacher.   I shall tell the truth about Claire Zachanassian.

Frau Schill.   You're drunk, Herr Professor; you should be ashamed of yourself.

Teacher.   I should be ashamed? You should all be ashamed!

Son.   Shut your trap. You're drunk.

Daughter.   Please, Professor—

Teacher.   Girl, you disappoint me. It is your place to speak. But you are silent and you force your old teacher to raise his voice. I am going to speak the truth. It is my duty and I am not afraid. The world may not wish to listen, but no one can silence me. I'm not going to wait—I'm going over to Hofbauer's shop now.

All.   No, you're not. Stop him. Stop him. [*They all spring at the* TEACHER. *He defends himself. At this moment,* SCHILL *appears through the door upstage. In contrast to the others, he is dressed shabbily in an old black jacket, his best.*]

Schill.   What's going on in my shop? [*The townsmen let go of the* TEACHER *and turn to stare at* SCHILL.] What's the trouble, Professor?

Teacher.   Schill, I am speaking out at last! I am going to tell the press everything.

Schill.   Be quiet, Professor.

Teacher.   What did you say?

Schill.   Be quiet.

Teacher.   You want me to be quiet?

Schill.   Please.

Teacher.   But, Schill, if I keep quiet, if you miss this opportunity—they're over in Hofbauer's shop now . . .

Schill.   Please.

Teacher.   As you wish. If you too are on their side, I have no more to say.

[*The doorbell jingles. A* REPORTER *comes in.*]

Reporter. Is Anton Schill here? [*Moves to* SCHILL.] Are you Herr Schill?
Schill. What?
Reporter. Herr Schill.
Schill. Er—no. Herr Schill's gone to Kalberstadt for the day.
Reporter. Oh, thank you. Good day.

[*He goes out.*]

Painter [*Mops his brow*]. Whew! Close shave.

[*He follows the* REPORTER *out.*]

Second Man [*Walking up to* SCHILL]. That was pretty smart of you to keep your mouth shut. You know what to expect if you don't.

[*He goes.*]

First Man. Give me a Havana. [SCHILL *serves him.*] Charge it. You bastard!

[*He goes.* SCHILL *opens his account book.*]

Frau Schill. Come along, children—

[FRAU SCHILL, *the* SON *and the* DAUGHTER *go off, upstage.*]

Teacher. They're going to kill you. I've known it all along, and you too, you must have known it. The need is too strong, the temptation too great. And now perhaps I too will join against you. I belong to them and, like them, I can feel myself hardening into something that is not human—not beautiful.
Schill. It can't be helped.
Teacher. Pull yourself together, man. Speak to the reporters; you've no time to lose. [SCHILL *looks up from his account book.*]
Schill. No. I'm not going to fight any more.
Teacher. Are you so frighted that you don't dare open your mouth?
Schill. I made Claire what she is, I made myself what I am. What should I do? Should I pretend that I'm innocent?
Teacher. No, you can't. You are as guilty as hell.
Schill. Yes.
Teacher. You are a bastard.
Schill. Yes.
Teacher. But that does not justify your murder. [SCHILL *looks at him.*] I wish I could believe that for what they're doing—for what they're going to do—they will suffer for the rest of their lives. But it's not true. In a little while they will have justified everything and forgotten everything.
Schill. Of course.
Teacher. Your name will never again be mentioned in this town. That's how it will be.
Schill. I don't hold it against you.
Teacher. But I do. I will hold it against myself all my life. That's why—[*The doorbell jingles. The* BURGOMASTER *comes in. The* TEACHER *stares at him, then goes out without another word.*]

Burgomaster. Good afternoon, Schill. Don't let me disturb you. I've just dropped in for a moment.

Schill. I'm just finishing my accounts for the week. [*A moment's pause.*]

Burgomaster. The town council meets tonight. At the Golden Apostle. In the auditorium.

Schill. I'll be there.

Burgomaster. The whole town will be there. Your case will be discussed and final action taken. You've put us in a pretty tight spot, you know.

Schill. Yes. I'm sorry.

Burgomaster. The lady's offer will be rejected.

Schill. Possibly.

Burgomaster. Of course, I may be wrong.

Schill. Of course.

Burgomaster. In that case—are you prepared to accept the judgment of the town? The meeting will be covered by the press, you know.

Schill. By the press?

Burgomaster. Yes, and the radio and the newsreel. It's a very ticklish situation. Not only for you—believe me, it's even worse for us. What with the wedding, and all the publicity, we've become famous. All of a sudden our ancient democratic institutions have become of interest to the world.

Schill. Are you going to make the lady's condition public?

Burgomaster. No, no, of course not. Not directly. We will have to put the matter to a vote—that is unavoidable. But only those involved will understand.

Schill. I see.

Burgomaster. As far as the press is concerned, you are simply the intermediary between us and Madame Zachanassian. I have whitewashed you completely.

Schill. That is very generous of you.

Burgomaster. Frankly, it's not for your sake, but for the sake of your family. They are honest and decent people.

Schill. Oh—

Burgomaster. So far we've all played fair. You've kept your mouth shut and so have we. Now can we continue to depend on you? Because if you have any idea of opening your mouth at tonight's meeting, there won't be any meeting.

Schill. I'm glad to hear an open threat at last.

Burgomaster. We are not threatening you. You are threatening us. If you speak, you force us to act—in advance.

Schill. That won't be necessary.

Burgomaster. So if the town decides against you?

Schill. I will accept their decision.

Burgomaster. Good. [*A moment's pause.*] I'm delighted to see there is still a spark of decency left in you. But—wouldn't it be better if we didn't have to call a meeting at all? [*He pauses. He takes a gun from his pocket and puts it on the counter.*] I've brought you this.

Schill. Thank you.

Burgomaster. It's loaded.

Schill. I don't need a gun.

Burgomaster [*He clears his throat.*] You see? We could tell the lady that we had condemned you in secret session and you had anticipated our decision. I've lost a lot of sleep getting to this point, believe me.

Schill. I believe you.

Burgomaster. Frankly, in your place, I myself would prefer to take the path of honor. Get it over with, once and for all. Don't you agree? For the sake of your friends! For the sake of our children, your own children—you have a daughter, a son—Schill, you know our need, our misery.

Schill. You've put me through hell, you and your town. You were my friends, you smiled and reassured me. But day by day I saw you change—your shoes, your ties, your suits—your hearts. If you had been honest with me then, perhaps I would feel differently toward you now. I might even use that gun you brought me. For the sake of my friends. But now I have conquered my fear. Alone. It was hard, but it's done. And now you will have to judge me. And I will accept your judgment. For me that will be justice. How it will be for you, I don't know. [*He turns away.*] You may kill me if you like. I won't complain, I won't protest, I won't defend myself. But I won't do your job for you either.

Burgomaster [*Takes up his gun*]. There it is. You've had your chance and you won't take it. Too bad. [*He takes out a cigarette.*] I suppose it's more than we can expect of a man like you. [SCHILL *lights the* BURGOMASTER'S *cigarette.*] Good day.

Schill. Good day. [*The* BURGOMASTER *goes.* FRAU SCHILL *comes in, dressed in a fur coat. The* DAUGHTER *is in a new red dress. The* SON *has a new sports jacket.*] What a beautiful coat, Mathilde!

Frau Schill. Real fur. You like it?

Schill. Should I? What a lovely dress, Ottilie!

Daughter. C'est très chic, n'est-ce-pas?

Schill. What?

Frau Schill. Ottilie is taking a course in French.

Schill. Very useful. Karl—whose automobile is that out there at the curb?

Son. Oh, it's only an Opel. They're not expensive.

Schill. You bought yourself a car?

Son. On credit. Easiest thing in the world.

Frau Schill. Everyone's buying on credit now, Anton. These fears of yours are ridiculous. You'll see. Clara has a good heart. She only means to teach you a lesson.

Daughter. She means to teach you a lesson, that's all.

Son. It's high time you got the point, Father.

Schill. I get the point. [*The church bells start ringing.*] Listen. The bells of Güllen. Do you hear?

Son. Yes, we have four bells now. It sounds quite good.

Daughter. Just like Gray's Elegy.

Schill. What?

Frau Schill. Ottilie is taking a course in English literature.

Schill. Congratulations! It's Sunday. I should very much like to take a ride in your car. Our car.

Son. You want to ride in the car?

Schill. Why not? I want to ride through the Konradsweil Forest. I want to see the town where I've lived all my life.

Frau Schill. I don't think that will look very nice for any of us.

Schill. No—perhaps not. Well, I'll go for a walk by myself.

Frau Schill. Then take us to Kalberstadt, Karl, and we'll go to a cinema.

Schill. A cinema? It's a good idea.

Frau Schill. See you soon, Anton.

Schill. Good-bye, Ottilie. Good-bye, Karl. Good-bye, Mathilde.

Family. Good-bye.

Schill. Good-bye. [*The shop sign flies off. The lights black out. They come up at once on the forest scene.*] Autumn. Even the forest has turned to gold. [SCHILL *wanders down to the bench in the forest. He sits.* CLAIRE's *voice is heard.*]

Claire [*Offstage*]. Stop. Wait here. [CLAIRE *comes in. She gazes slowly up at the trees, kicks at some leaves. Then she walks slowly down center. She stops before a tree, glances up at the trunk.*] Bark-borers. The old tree is dying. [*She catches sight of* SCHILL.]

Schill. Clara.

Claire. How pleasant to see you here. I was visiting my forest. May I sit by you?

Schill. Oh, yes. Please do. [*She sits next to him.*] I've just been saying good-bye to my family. They've gone to the cinema. Karl has bought himself a car.

Claire. How nice.

Schill. Ottilie is taking French lessons. And a course in English literature.

Claire. You see? They're beginning to take an interest in higher things.

Schill. Listen. A finch. You hear?

Claire. Yes. It's a finch. And a cuckoo in the distance. Would you like some music?

Schill. Oh, yes. That would be very nice.

Claire. Anything special?

Schill. "Deep in the Forest."

Claire. Your favorite song. They know it. [*She raises her hand. Offstage, the mandolin and guitar play the tune softly.*]

Schill. We had a child?

Claire. Yes.

Schill. Boy or girl?

Claire. Girl.

Schill. What name did you give her?

Claire. I called her Genevieve.

Schill. That's a very pretty name.

Claire. Yes.

Schill. What was she like?

Claire. I saw her only once. When she was born. Then they took her away from me.

Schill. Her eyes?

Claire. They weren't open yet.

Schill. And her hair?

Claire. Black, I think. It's usually black at first.

Schill. Yes, of course. Where did she die, Clara?

Claire. In some family. I've forgotten their name. Meningitis, they said. The officials wrote me a letter.

Schill. Oh, I'm so very sorry, Clara.

Claire. I've told you about our child. Now tell me about myself.

Schill. About yourself?

Claire.   Yes. How I was when I was seventeen in the days when you loved me.

Schill.   I remember one day you waited for me in the great barn. I had to look all over the place for you. At last I found you lying in the haycart with nothing on and a long straw between your lips . . .

Claire.   Yes. I was pretty in those days.

Schill.   You were beautiful, Clara.

Claire.   You were strong. The time you fought with those two railway men who were following me, I wiped the blood from your face with my red petticoat. [*The music ends.*] They've stopped.

Schill.   Tell them to play "Thoughts of Home."

Claire.   They know that too. [*The music plays.*]

Schill.   Here we are, Clara, sitting together in our forest for the last time. The town council meets tonight. They will condemn me to death, and one of them will kill me. I don't know who and I don't know where. Clara, I only know that in a little while a useless life will come to an end. [*He bows his head on her bosom. She takes him in her arms.*]

Claire [*Tenderly*].   I shall take you in your coffin to Capri. You will have your tomb in the park of my villa, where I can see you from my bedroom window. White marble and onyx in a grove of green cypress. With a beautiful view of the Mediterranean.

Schill.   I've always wanted to see it.

Claire.   Your love for me died years ago, Anton. But my love for you would not die. It turned into something strong, like the hidden roots of the forest; something evil, like white mushrooms that grow unseen in the darkness. And slowly it reached out for your life. Now I have you. You are mine. Alone. At last, and forever, a peaceful ghost in a silent house. [*The music ends.*]

Schill.   The song is over.

Claire.   Adieu, Anton. [CLAIRE *kisses* ANTON, *a long kiss. Then she rises.*]

Schill.   Adieu.

[*She goes.* SCHILL *remains sitting on the bench. A row of lamps descends from the flies. The townsmen come in from both sides, each bearing his chair. A table and chairs are set upstage, center. On both sides sit the townsmen. The* POLICEMAN, *in a new uniform, sits on the bench behind* SCHILL. *All the townsmen are in new Sunday clothes. Around them are technicians of all sorts, with lights, cameras and other equipment. The townswomen are absent. They do not vote. The* BURGOMASTER *takes his place at the table, center. The* DOCTOR *and the* PASTOR *sit at the same table, at his right, and the* TEACHER *in his academic gown, at his left.*]

Burgomaster [*At a sign from the radio technician, he pounds the floor with his wand of office*].   Fellow citizens of Güllen, I call this meeting to order. The agenda: there is only one matter before us. I have the honor to announce officially that Madame Claire Zachanassian, daughter of our beloved citizen, the famous architect Siegfried Wäscher, has decided to make a gift to the town of one billion marks. Five hundred million to the town, five hundred million to be divided per capita among the citizens. After certain necessary preliminaries, a vote will be taken, and you, as citizens of Güllen, will signify your will by a show of hands. Has anyone any objection to this mode of procedure? The pastor? [*Silence.*] The police? [*Silence.*] The town health official? [*Silence.*] The Rector of Güllen High School? [*Silence.*] The political opposition? [*Silence.*] I shall then proceed to the vote—[*The* TEACHER *rises. The* BURGO-MASTER *turns in surprise and irritation.*] You wish to speak?

Teacher. Yes.

Burgomaster. Very well. [*He takes his seat. The* TEACHER *advances. The movie camera starts running.*]

Teacher. Fellow townsmen. [*The photographer flashes a bulb in his face.*] Fellow townsmen. We all know that by means of this gift, Madame Claire Zachanassian intends to attain a certain object. What is this object? To enrich the town of her youth, yes. But more than that, she desires by means of this gift to re-establish justice among us. This desire expressed by our benefactress raises an all-important question. Is it true that our community harbors in its soul such a burden of guilt?

Burgomaster. Yes! True!

Second Man. Crimes are concealed among us.

Third Man [*He jumps up*]. Sins!

Fourth Man [*He jumps up also*]. Perjuries.

Painter. Justice!

Townsmen. Justice! Justice!

Teacher. Citizens of Güllen, this, then, is the simple fact of the case. We have participated in an injustice. I thoroughly recognize the material advantages which this gift opens to us—I do not overlook the fact that it is poverty which is the root of all this bitterness and evil. Nevertheless, there is no question here of money.

Townsmen. No! No!

Teacher. Here there is no question of our prosperity as a community, or our well-being as individuals—The question is—must be—whether or not we wish to live according to the principles of justice, those principles for which our forefathers lived and fought and for which they died, those principles which form the soul of our Western culture.

Townsmen. Hear! Hear! [*Applause.*]

Teacher [*Desperately, realizing that he is fighting a losing battle, and on the verge of hysteria*]. Wealth has meaning only when benevolence comes of it, but only he who hungers for grace will receive grace. Do you feel this hunger, my fellow citizens, this hunger of the spirit, or do you feel only that other profane hunger, the hunger of the body? That is the question which I, as Rector of your high school, now propound to you. Only if you can no longer tolerate the presence of evil among you, only if you can in no circumstances endure a world in which injustice exists, are you worthy to receive Madame Zachanassian's billion and fulfill the condition bound up with this gift. If not—[*Wild applause. He gestures desperately for silence.*] If not, then God have mercy on us!

[*The* TOWNSMEN *crowd around him, ambiguously, in a mood somewhat between threat and congratulation. He takes his seat, utterly crushed, exhausted by his effort. The* BURGOMASTER *advances and takes charge once again. Order is restored.*]

Burgomaster.   Anton Schill—[*The* POLICEMAN *gives* SCHILL *a shove.* SCHILL *gets up*.] Anton Schill, it is through you that this gift is offered to the town. Are you willing that this offer should be accepted? [SCHILL *mumbles something.*]

Radio Reporter [*Steps to his side*].   You'll have to speak up a little, Herr Schill.

Schill.   Yes.

Burgomaster.   Will you respect our decision in the matter before us?

Schill.   I will respect your decision.

Burgomaster.   Then I proceed to the vote. All those who are in accord with the terms on which this gift is offered will signify the same by raising their right hands. [*After a moment, the* POLICEMAN *raises his hand. Then one by one the others. Last of all, very slowly, the* TEACHER.] All against? The offer is accepted. I now solemnly call upon you, fellow townsmen, to declare in the face of all the world that you take this action, not out of love for worldly gain . . .

Townsmen [*In chorus*].   Not out of love for worldly gain . . .

Burgomaster.   But out of love for the right.

Townsmen.   But out of love for the right.

Burgomaster [*Holds up his hand, as if taking an oath*].   We join together, now, as brothers . . .

Townsmen [*Hold up their hands*].   We join together, now, as brothers . . .

Burgomaster.   To purify our town of guilt . . .

Townsmen.   To purify our town of guilt . . .

Burgomaster.   And to reaffirm our faith . . .

Townsmen.   And to reaffirm our faith . . .

Burgomaster.   In the eternal power of justice.

Townsmen.   In the eternal power of justice. [*The lights go off suddenly.*]

Schill [*A scream*].   Oh, God!

Voice.   I'm sorry, Herr Burgomaster. We seem to have blown a fuse. [*The lights go on.*] Ah—there we are. Would you mind doing that last bit again?

Burgomaster.   Again?

The Cameraman [*Walks forward*].   Yes, for the newsreel.

Burgomaster.   Oh, the newsreel. Certainly.

The Cameraman.   Ready now? Right.

Burgomaster.   And to reaffirm our faith . . .

Townsmen.   And to reaffirm our faith . . .

Burgomaster.   In the eternal power of justice.

Townsmen.   In the eternal power of justice.

The Cameraman [*To his assistant*].   It was better before, when he screamed "Oh, God." [*The assistant shrugs.*]

Burgomaster.   Fellow citizens of Güllen, I declare this meeting adjourned. The ladies and gentlemen of the press will find refreshments served downstairs, with the compliments of the town council. The exits lead directly to the restaurant.

The Cameraman.   Thank you. [*The newsmen go off with alacrity. The* TOWNSMEN *remain on the stage.* SCHILL *gets up.*]

Policeman [*Pushes* SCHILL *down*].   Sit down.

Schill.   Is it to be now?

Policeman.   Naturally, now.

Schill.   I thought it might be best to have it at my house.

Policeman.   It will be here.

Burgomaster.   Lower the lights. [*The lights dim.*] Are they all gone?
Voice.   All gone.
Burgomaster.   The gallery?
Second Voice.   Empty.
Burgomaster.   Lock the doors.
The Voice.   Locked here.
Second Voice.   Locked here.
Burgomaster.   Form a lane. [*The men form a lane. At the end stands the*
   ATHLETE *in elegant white slacks, a red scarf around his singlet.*] Pastor. Will
   you be so good? [*The* PASTOR *walks slowly to* SCHILL.]
Pastor.   Anton Schill, your heavy hour has come.
Schill.   May I have a cigarette?
Pastor.   Cigarette, Burgomaster.
Burgomaster.   Of course. With pleasure. And a good one. [*He gives his case to*
   the PASTOR, *who offers it to* SCHILL. *The* POLICEMAN *lights the cigarette. The*
   PASTOR *returns the case.*]
Pastor.   In the words of the prophet Amos—
Schill.   Please—[*He shakes his head.*]
Pastor.   You're no longer afraid?
Schill.   No. I'm not afraid.
Pastor.   I will pray for you.
Schill.   Pray for us all. [*The* PASTOR *bows his head.*]
Burgomaster.   Anton Schill, stand up! [SCHILL *hesitates.*]
Policeman.   Stand up, you swine!
Burgomaster.   Schultz, please.
Policeman.   I'm sorry. I was carried away. [SCHILL *gives the cigarette to the*
   POLICEMAN. *Then he walks slowly to the center of the stage and turns his back*
   on the audience.] Enter the lane.

[SCHILL *hesitates a moment. He goes slowly into the lane of silent men. The*
ATHLETE *stares at him from the opposite end.* SCHILL *looks in turn at the hard*
faces of those who surround him, and sinks slowly to his knees. The lane
contracts silently into a knot as the men close in and crouch over. Complete
silence. The knot of men pulls back slowly, coming downstage. Then it opens.
Only the DOCTOR *is left in the center of the stage, kneeling by the corpse, over*
which the TEACHER's *gown has been spread. The* DOCTOR *rises and takes off his*
stethoscope.]

Pastor.   Is it all over?
Doctor.   Heart failure.
Burgomaster.   Died of joy.
All.   Died of joy.

[*The* TOWNSMEN *turn their backs on the corpse and at once light cigarettes. A*
cloud of smoke rises over them. From the left comes CLAIRE ZACHANASSIAN,
dressed in black, followed by BOBBY. *She sees the corpse. Then she walks slowly*
to center stage and looks down at the body of SCHILL.]

Claire.   Uncover him. [BOBBY *uncovers* SCHILL's *face. She stares at it a long*
   moment. She sighs.] Cover his face.

[BOBBY *covers it.* CLAIRE *goes out, up center.* BOBBY *takes the check from his wallet, holds it out peremptorily to the* BURGOMASTER, *who walks over from the knot of silent men. He holds out his hand for the check. The lights fade. At once the warning bell is heard, and the scene dissolves into the setting of the railway station. The gradual transformation of the shabby town into a thing of elegance and beauty is now accomplished. The railway station glitters with neon lights and is surrounded with garlands, bright posters and flags. The townsfolk, men and women, now in brand new clothes, form themselves into a group in front of the station. The sound of the approaching train grows louder. The train stops.*]

Station Master.   Güllen-Rome Express. All aboard, please.

[*The church bells start pealing. Men appear with trunks and boxes, a procession which duplicates that of the lady's arrival, but in inverse order. Then come the* TWO BLIND MEN, *then* BOBBY, *and* MIKE *and* MAX *carrying the coffin. Lastly* CLAIRE. *She is dressed in modish black. Her head is high, her face as impassive as that of an ancient idol. The procession crosses the stage and goes off. The people bow in silence as the coffin passes. When* CLAIRE *and her retinue have boarded the train, the* STATION MASTER *blows a long blast.*]

'Bo—ard!

[*He holds up his paddle. The train starts and moves off slowly, picking up speed. The crowd turns slowly, gazing after the departing train in complete silence. The train sounds fade. The curtain falls slowly.*]

A NOTE ON THE VISIT

Mr. Valency's version of *Der Besuch der Alten Dame* is an adaptation made, with Dürrenmatt's approval, to accommodate what was believed to be American taste. It is interesting to consider some of the changes from the original German.

Anton Schill's name was Alfred Ill, changed to satisfy Alfred Lunt, who played the role, and to avoid the connotations of the surname. The character of Claire was appreciably mollified; the original is a dumpy, grotesque hag with more artificial parts than Valency's Mme. Zachanassian, thus making the love scenes far more grisly. The original text is much funnier, considered too risky a business on Broadway if a play is to be taken seriously. The trees in the forest scenes are played by citizens; too stylized for New York. In the Swiss play, Claire has a new husband in each act, all played by the same actor, not just one fiancé. Valency deletes a lot of bizarre hyperboles. Two scenes are cut: one in which Schill's son takes the family for a ride in his new car to show the glories of the reborn town to the man about to be sacrificed for them; another that is a pseudo-Greek epilogue in verse in which the townsfolk ask for divine grace for their new happiness and prosperity. In the original play, the Güllners are more horrifyingly unaware of their sell-out of Schill; it is a slower and more insidious development.

The adaptation loses much in irony, wit, language, texture, and Dürrenmatt's highly allusive condemnation of Western culture, but the larger frame of the play is untouched and its intentions do not suffer from tampering.